Michael Meyer is well known as a translator of Ibsen and Strindberg – his translations of Ibsen have been described by several authorities as definitive, and those of Strindberg won him the Gold Medal of the Swedish Academy in 1964. Mr Meyer is also the author of a novel, *The End of the Corridor*, two stage plays, *The Ortolan* and *Lunatic and Lover*, a biography of Strindberg and a volume of memoirs, *Not Prince Hamlet*, as well as several television and radio plays. His Ibsen biography won the Whitbread Biography Award in 1971.

Between 1947 and 1950 Michael Meyer was lecturer in English Literature at Uppsala University in Sweden. During 1957–8, as roving correspondent in the Far East for the Swedish newspaper *Svenska Dagbladet*, he travelled 5,000 miles through Red China alone and without a guide. He has been Visiting Professor of Drama at several American universities. Mr Meyer now lives in London. He has a daughter, Nora, born in 1968.

MICHAEL MEYER

Ibsen

Abridged by the author

caRDÍNaL

A CARDINAL BOOK

First published in Great Britain
by Rupert Hart-Davis 1967, 1971
Published in Pelican Books 1974
This edition published in Cardinal by Sphere Books Ltd, 1992

A CIP catalogue record for this book is available from the
British Library.

ISBN 0 7474 1026 7

Printed in England by Clays Ltd, St Ives plc

Sphere Books Ltd
A Division of Macdonald & Co (Publishers) Ltd
London & Sydney
165 Great Dover Street, London SE1 4YA
A member of Maxwell Macmillan Publishing Corporation

TO NORA

WITH LOVE

Contents

Note to this Edition

THE original edition of this biography ran to over 400,000 words, which could not manageably have been contained in a single paperback volume. For this edition, I have cut about a quarter of the text, principally: letters and reminiscences that reinforce already documented conclusions; minor incidents in Ibsen's life; quotations from his lesser prose works, such as his early essays and drama criticisms, and his account of his visit to Egypt; details and sometimes sub-plots concerning secondary figures; some of the contemporary Scandinavian reactions to his plays; some background details of the plays; and most reference footnotes. My principal sources are named in the Select Bibliography on p. 871.

MICHAEL MEYER

Introduction

OVER forty years have elapsed since the publication in 1928 of Halvdan Koht's monumental two-volume biography of Ibsen (though a revised and partly rewritten edition appeared in 1954). Koht was acquainted with Ibsen's work as few other men have been, and was able to tap the memories of the dramatist's family and acquaintances. He was, too, an historian of distinction, and his book must be the foundation stone for any new study of Ibsen.

But for all its many and admirable qualities, Koht's biography has long been regarded as not wholly satisfactory. It is written from a narrowly nationalistic standpoint; Koht himself grew up as a young man during the period of Norway's struggle for political independence, and this theme frequently occupies the centre of his biography, with Ibsen reduced to the status of a foreground, sometimes even of a background figure. (Ibsen's attitude towards his country's political problems was that of an independent observer rather than a committed patriot,) and Koht could not always forgive him for not, on certain occasions, having behaved and written like Bjørnson. Koht, too, was not a man of the theatre, and Ibsen interested him more as a writer for the printed page than as a dramatist who was exploring and revolutionizing the business of stagecraft. And Koht was born in 1873, only thirteen years after Chekhov, and his judgements are those of his generation. They are not necessarily the less correct for that, but a writer of Ibsen's stature means something different to every generation, and requires re-examination in every age.

Most importantly, however, Koht omits much vital and interesting factual information and leaves certain central questions unanswered. There is much that a student of

Ibsen needs to know and cannot find there, yet which is in fact available, widely scattered in memoirs, letters, theses and newspaper reports; for example, Ibsen's years as director of the ill-starred Norwegian Theatre in Christiania between 1857 and 1862; his life in Rome while he was writing *Brand* and *Peer Gynt*; those seemingly rather barren but (like so many seemingly barren periods in writers' lives) powerfully formative years in Dresden from 1868 to 1875; the truth of his relationship with Suzannah and with the young girls he loved, or became infatuated with, in his old age; and the reaction to his work of his great contemporaries such as Tolstoy, Strindberg, Freud, Chekhov, Zola, Hardy, Henry James, Yeats, Rilke and Joyce. Such questions the present biography seeks to answer, or at any rate to provide the information from which the reader may hazard his own answer.

At the same time, I have tried to reconsider Ibsen's development as a man and as a writer; to reassess his work, both intrinsically and historically; to portray the changing theatrical world of his time, and to show the impact of his achievements on various countries. For even when, as in *Brand* and *Peer Gynt*, he was writing not for the stage but for a private theatre of the imagination, Ibsen was restlessly testing and expanding his craft, as explosive an international force in his field as Darwin or Marx or Freud in theirs.

Of the many people who have helped me in my work, I must especially thank the poet's grandson, Mr Tancred Ibsen; Professor Francis Bull, whose knowledge of the subject is encyclopaedic; Mr Øyvind Anker, the librarian of Oslo University, and his ever-patient staff; and the staffs of Oslo Bymuseum, the University Library of Bergen, the University Library of Stockholm, the Royal Library of Stockholm, the Library of University College, London, the British Museum, the British Drama League, and the Victoria and Albert Museum, London. Professor Bull and Dr Elias Bredsdorff kindly read my first volume in typescript and made numerous valuable suggestions, and I must thank Dr Einar Østvedt, Mr Gordon Hølmebakk and Mr Rodney Blumer for their advice and encouragement.

This book rests heavily, not merely on Koht's biography, but on the great Centenary Edition of Ibsen's work edited by Koht, Professor Bull, and the late Professor Didrik Arup Seip, and published by Gyldendal of Oslo. Errors have been found in its twenty-one volumes, as in any work of such dimensions; they do not diminish it. My indebtedness to these three scholars' introductions to the plays and to the rest of Ibsen's work needs no underlining. I also pay respectful homage to Ibsen's earlier biographers: Paul Botten Hansen (1863), Henrik Jæger (1888), J. B. Halvorsen (1892), Edmund Gosse (1907), Gerhard Gran (1916–17), Halvdan Koht (1928) and A. E. Zucker (1929). My debt to other sources is acknowledged in the footnotes and bibliography.

My thanks are due to the following for permission to quote copyright material: Messrs Faber & Faber and the Society of Authors (various extracts from James Joyce's writings); Little, Brown & Co. (J. J. Robbins's translation of Konstantin Stanislavsky's *My Life in Art*); the Hogarth Press Ltd (John Linton's translation of Rainer Maria Rilke's *The Notebook of Malte Laurid's Brigge*); and Routledge & Kegan Paul Ltd (the extract from Sidney Keyes's poem, *Sour Land*).

I must also thank Mrs Reginald Orcutt for leave to quote from her father Basil King's articles, 'Ibsen and Emilie Bardach', published in the *Century Magazine* in October and November 1923, including his translations of Emilie's diary and Ibsen's letters to her. The late Richard Graves, Mr James Maxwell and Mrs Maria De Haan helped me with the translation of part of the German correspondence between Ibsen and Emilie Bardach and Helene Raff's diaries. All other translations of foreign passages, including Ibsen's letters, poems, speeches, and articles, are my own except where otherwise specified.

Finally, I owe, and gratefully admit, a debt of a different

kind to Mr Casper Wrede and Mr Michael Elliott, who between them taught me whatever theatrical insight into Ibsen's work I may have acquired. From them I learned to consider Ibsen as a man writing for the theatre rather than for the printed page, and it is primarily from that viewpoint that I have written this book.

London, 1970.

MICHAEL MEYER

Anyone who wishes to understand me fully must know Norway. The spectacular but severe landscape which people have around them in the north, and the lonely shut-off life – the houses often lie miles from each other – force them not to bother about other people, but only their own concerns, so that they become reflective and serious, they brood and doubt and often despair. In Norway every second man is a philosopher. And those dark winters, with the thick mists outside – ah, they long for the sun!

> Ibsen in conversation, quoted by Felix Philippi, 'Mein Verkehr mit Henrik Ibsen', in *Neue Freie Presse*, Vienna, 27 October 1902

We can see horribly clear in the works of such a man his whole life, as if we were God's spies.

John Keats, writing of Robert Burns to John Hamilton Reynolds

PART ONE

The Making of a Dramatist

Ancestry and Childhood
1828–43

HENRIK JOHAN IBSEN was born on 20 March 1828 in the small trading town of Skien on the east coast of Norway, a hundred miles south of the capital Christiania (now Oslo). He was the second child of a merchant, Knud Ibsen, and his wife Marichen, *née* Altenburg.

Ibsen is a Danish name (Ib is an old Danish form for Jacob), and in later years when he felt more than usually ill-disposed towards his native country, Henrik Ibsen was wont to assert that he had not a drop of Norwegian blood in his veins. In fact, thirteen of his sixteen great-great-grand-parents were Norwegian, and as far as can be calculated he was approximately two-thirds Norwegian, one-sixth Danish and a little less than one-sixth German, with a slight ad-mixture of Scottish. Apart from his father, his paternal an-cestors had for over two hundred years been sea-captains; and towards the end of his life Henrik Ibsen is said to have looked, and walked, more and more like a sea-captain him-self.

Henrich Petersen Ibsen, the dramatist's grandfather, was remembered as 'a witty, clear-minded man, with many lively and eager interests; of a sanguine temperament, always full of jests and pranks'. On 22 November 1797, when he was thirty-two, the vessel of which he was both owner and cap-tain went down with all hands off Hesnæs, near Grimstad, a tiny port a hundred miles south of Skien where, half a cen-tury later, his grandson was to write his first play. Only a few fragments of the wreck, including one bearing the name of the ship, drifted to land to tell the tale. Two years earlier he

had married the daughter of a local merchant, Johanne
Cathrine Plesner. She gave her husband two sons before he
died. Their first-born, Jacob von der Lippe Ibsen, died in
1805 as a child of nine; their second, born in 1797, they called
Knud Plesner Ibsen after his maternal grandfather.

The year after her husband's death, Johanne married
again, with a shipmaster named Ole Paus. She bore him
eight children, four boys and four girls. Two of her sisters
had married into rich merchant circles, so that she considerably raised the social standing of the Ibsens, and young
Knud grew up with his eight half-brothers and half-sisters
at a house in the parish of Gjerpen, just outside Skien, in an
atmosphere of greater pretension than any earlier Ibsen had
known.

On 1 December 1825, Knud Plesner Ibsen married Marichen Cornelia Martine Altenburg; he was twenty-eight, she
twenty-six. She was also of Danish and German as well as
Norwegian blood, and was an excellent match. Her father,
Johan Andreas Altenburg, who had died the previous year,
had been a wealthy shipmaster, and also, later, a merchant;
in 1804–5 he is known to have been worth twenty to thirty
thousand specie-dollars, or over five thousand pounds,[1] a
considerable fortune in the Norway of those days. They had
their first child, a boy, Johan Altenburg Ibsen, on 3 October
1826, but he died at the age of eighteen months on 14 April
1828. Three and a half weeks before this unhappy event, on
20 March, a second son was born whom they named Henrik
Johan, after his two grandfathers. They had four more children during the next seven years, all of whom survived into
adulthood: Johan Andreas Altenburg, Hedvig Cathrine,
Nicolai Alexander, and Ole Paus. Henrik Ibsen thus grew up
as the eldest of five.

The house in which he was born stood in the main square
of Skien and was named Stockmannsgaarden. It no longer
stands, having been destroyed, like most of the other houses

1. The specie-dollar may be reckoned as roughly 25 pence, the Norwegian crown as about 6 pence.

in the centre of the town, by the great fire of 1886. A contemporary water-colour portrays it as a pleasing wooden edifice of two storeys with tall windows divided into tiny panes. When Henrik was two, his father bought his widowed mother-in-law's house, Altenburggaarden, a larger and more opulent building with its own paddock, just around the corner in Prindsengade (now Henrik Ibsen's gate), and they moved there in the following year, 1831.

Ibsen's first full biographer, Henrik Jæger, writing in 1888, described the Skien of Ibsen's childhood as being 'a homely little timber town, containing scarcely three thousand inhabitants. But, small as it was, it was the scene of much busy life and a not unimportant centre of trade.' The town had made considerable economic progress since the turn of the century; many shipmasters and captains had earned useful fortunes during the Napoleonic Wars, and the export of timber to England had also proved rewarding. It possessed a flourishing timber trade, and in the eighteen-twenties boasted four spectacular weirs and some forty sawmills. Many years later, in 1895, Ibsen described it as 'the town of the storming, soughing, seething waters. Over the whole town there is, as it were, a song in the air from all the weirs. So at least I remember it ... It is not for nothing', he added, 'that I was born in the town of rushing waters.'[2]

The natives of Telemark, the province in which Skien lies, are, temperamentally, a race apart from their fellow-countrymen. Foreigners who know Norway only through Oslo, the west coast, and the northern and central ski resorts have written of Ibsen as an untypical Norwegian. He was by no means an untypical native of Telemark. 'They appear sanguine but are often melancholic,' a Norwegian historian has written. 'They analyse and pass judgement on themselves.' Another, speaking of the people of Skien in particular, observes:

They are proud and stiff, combative when anyone threatens their interest, dislike being told. They are reserved and cautious

2. Letter to Hildur Andersen, 29 July 1895.

towards strangers, do not easily accept their friendship, and are not very forthcoming even towards their own kin. Strangers who go to live there often feel isolated. The people of Skien are afraid openly to surrender to a mood, or let themselves be carried away; this apparent lack of spontaneity is what Ibsen calls the 'shyness of the soul'. They have an alert critical sense, but their criticism is not mercilessly direct and honest such as, for example, one finds in the people of Bergen. The citizens of Skien prefer to express theirs in quiet, ironical observations, in subtle satire, in mimicry. An unlucky and thoughtless utterance can easily be remembered so long that it becomes a proverb.

Apart from a few weeks in 1814, and we must remember this when considering Ibsen's early artistic and spiritual problems, Norway had not known true independence for nearly 450 years. This proudest of people had come under Danish rule in 1387, when the crown had passed to a member of the Danish royal house, and had remained thus, an Ireland to Denmark's England, until in 1814 the Treaty of Kiel at last freed her from this unwilling union. She at once tried to assert her independence by setting up a constitution, which still stands; but the Great Powers, led by England and Russia, promptly handed her over to Sweden as a reward for the latter country's support of their cause against Napoleon. The Norwegians took up arms in defence of their liberty, but the new king-elect of Sweden, Napoleon's long-nosed former marshal Bernadotte, shortly to become Carl XIV Johan,[3] defeated them in a brief campaign and forced them into yet another unwilling union, although he permitted them to keep their constitution and retained only a suspensive, not an absolute veto on the decisions of the Storthing, the Norwegian Parliament. Norway had thus merely exchanged the Danish yoke for a Swedish one. Politically, she was a province of Sweden; culturally, she remained a province of Denmark. Her citizens read Danish novels, or Danish translations from the English and French. Even the

3. The old king, Carl XIII, was childless, and the Swedish Parliament had chosen Bernadotte to succeed him.

written Norwegian language, *riksmaal*, was virtually indistinguishable from written Danish, though a movement was afoot to utilize the natural rhythms and idiomatic richness of the country dialects – a situation very similar, linguistically as politically, to that which was to exist in Ireland half a century later.

Unlike Ireland, however, Norway had virtually no literature to boast of: only one writer of international standing, the eighteenth-century dramatist Ludvig Holberg (1684–1754) – and he, though born in Norway, had done all his writing in Denmark for Danish readers – and in the nineteenth century two distinctive and interesting poets, Henrik Wergeland and J. S. Welhaven. Otherwise, there were only the old ballads and folk tales, which were now being reclaimed as, in the previous century, scholars such as Bishop Percy had reclaimed the Old English and Scottish ballads and, more recently, the brothers Grimm the folk tales of Germany. The Icelandic Sagas, written six centuries earlier by Norwegian emigrants to Iceland, were no more intelligible to nineteenth-century Norwegians than the Anglo-Saxon Chronicle is to modern Englishmen.

At the time of Ibsen's birth, Norway was still a very primitive country. Many of the houses in the remoter rural areas were windowless, as they had been in the Middle Ages, with only a hole in the roof to let out the smoke. Farming methods were extraordinarily antiquated; 'the cattle', we learn, 'wintered in stalls built without light or standing-room, so as to give the maximum of warmth, from which they were lifted out as living skeletons when spring came; the accumulated muck was then shovelled out on to the fields'. Fishermen still used the line instead of the costlier but far more effective net; and as late as the middle of the nineteenth century, leprosy was still to be found along the west coast, in some areas affecting as high a proportion as one per cent of the population. The towns were tiny. Even the capital Christiania (which had been Oslo until 1624, but was not to regain its old name until 1925) boasted less than

30,000 inhabitants. The country possessed no coal. Little of
her mountainous soil was cultivable (even today the figure is
less than 3 per cent), and a quarter was covered by forests.
Her people depended largely upon the sea for their livelihood and for their communications; Ibsen was a grown man
before the first railway was seen in Norway.

In 1881 Ibsen jotted down some childhood memories, the
only extended fragment of autobiography to which he ever
committed himself:

When a few years ago the streets in my birthplace of Skien
came to be named, or perhaps I should say re-named, I had the
honour to have one street called after me. Or so at any rate the
newspapers have reported, and I have also heard it from reliable
travellers.[4] They tell me that this street stretches from the main
square down towards the harbour.

But if this news is correct, I cannot think on what grounds the
street came to bear my name; for I was not born in it, and have
never lived in it. I was born in a house in the main square, Stockmannsgaarden, as it was then called. This house stood directly
opposite the front of the church, with its steep steps and lofty
tower. To the right of the church stood the town pillory, and to
the left the town hall, with its cell for delinquents and 'lunatic-
box'. The fourth side of the square was occupied by the Grammar School and Lower School. The church stands isolated in the
centre.

This prospect was accordingly the first sight of the world that
greeted my eyes. Only buildings; nothing green; no rural, open
landscape. But above this square of stone and timber the air was
filled all day long with the softly booming whisper of Langefoss
and Klosterfoss and the many other weirs; and through their
watery roar there penetrated, from morning to dusk, something
resembling the sharp cries of women, now shrieking, now moan-
ing. It was the hundreds of sawblades working out on the weirs.
When later I read of the guillotine, I always thought of those
sawblades.

The church was of course the town's most imposing building.

4. Ibsen had, at the time of writing, been resident in Italy and
Germany for seventeen years.

When on Christmas Eve towards the end of the last century, thanks to the carelessness of a servant-girl, Skien was burned down, the old church was burned too. The servant-girl was, not surprisingly, executed. But the town, which was rebuilt with broad and regular streets covering its hills and hollows, gained thereby a new church, of which the citizens used to claim with a certain pride that it was of yellow Dutch clinker, had been raised by a Copenhagen master builder, and exactly resembled the church at Konigsberg. These merits I understood at that time insufficiently to appreciate them; but what inscribed itself powerfully in my memory was a large, white, heavy-limbed angel which on weekdays hovered high up under the vaulting with a bowl in its hands, but on Sundays, when a child was to be baptized, descended softly among us.

Almost more than the white angel, however, another resident of the church excited my imagination; the black poodle, which dwelt at the top of the tower where the watchman called the hours at night. It had glowing eyes, but was not often seen; indeed, as far as I know it only showed itself once. It was a New Year's Eve, just as the watchman shouted 'One!' through the window in the front of the tower. Then the black poodle came up out of the staircase behind him, stood still, just looked at him with its glowing eyes, that was all; but the watchman fell through the window on to his head in the square, where they saw him lying dead, all the good people who walked that New Year's morning early to matins. Since that night, the watchman never shouts 'one' through *that* window in the church at Skien.

This business with the watchman and the poodle happened long before my time, and I have since heard tell that similar events occurred in olden times in several other Norwegian churches. But that same tower window held for me, when I was a child, an especial significance, in that it was there that I received the first conscious impression that has remained with me. My nursemaid carried me one day up into the tower and let me sit alone in the open window, safely held from behind, of course, by her faithful arms. I remember clearly how impressed I was at being able to see the crowns of people's hats; I looked down into our own rooms, saw the window frames, saw the curtains, saw my mother standing down there in one of the windows; yes, I could see over the rooftop and down into the courtyard, where our brown horse stood tied to the stable door swishing its tail. On the stable wall I remember there hung a pail. But then there was a hubbub, and a crowd of people, and a waving upwards from down there in the doorway, and the maid pulled me hurriedly away and ran down with me. I don't remember the rest; but afterwards they often told me how my mother had caught sight of me in the window of the tower, had shrieked, had fainted, as people did then, and later, having got me back, had wept and kissed and petted me. As a boy I never afterwards crossed the square without looking up at the window in the tower. I felt that that window belonged to me and the church poodle.

I have kept only one other memory from those earliest years. As a christening gift I had been given, among other things, a large silver coin with a man's head on it. The man had a high forehead, a big hooked nose and a protruding underlip; he was, moreover, bare-necked, which I found strange. The nursemaid taught me that the man on the coin was 'King Fredrik Rex', and once I tried to bowl it along the floor, with the unfortunate result that the coin rolled down into a crack. I think my parents interpreted this as an unlucky omen, it being a christening gift. The floor was taken up and they searched and dug around assiduously, but King Fredrik Rex never saw the light of day again. For a long time afterwards I could not help regarding myself as a wicked felon, and when I saw the town constable, Peter the German, emerge from the town hall and make his way towards our door, I ran as fast as I could into the nursery and hid myself beneath the bed.

As things turned out we did not live long in the house on the square. My father bought a bigger house, into which we moved when I must have been about four [*sic*] years old. This new home of mine was a corner house, sited a little higher up in the town, just at the foot of Hundevad Hill, so called after an old German-speaking doctor whose majestic wife drove around in something we called 'the glass coach', which in winter was used as a sleigh. This house had many large rooms, both downstairs and upstairs, and much entertaining went on. But we boys did not spend much time indoors. The main square, where the two biggest schools stood, was the natural meeting-place and battlefield for the youth of the town. The Grammar School was at that time ruled by the eminent and exceedingly lovable old Dr Ørn; while in

the Lower School the principal authority was, I believe, the jani-
tor Iver Flasrud, an equally impressive old man who also acted as
the town barber. Between the boys of these two schools many a
violent battle was waged around the church; but I, being a pupil
of neither, was for the most part merely an attendant spectator.
In any event I was as a child not, as a rule, combatively inclined.[5]
For me there resided a far more potent attraction in the aforementioned pillory and in the town hall with all its presumably
sinister secrets. The pillory was a reddish-brown post of about the
height of a man; above, it had a big round knob which had
originally been painted black. By now this knob looked like a
friendly and inviting human face, cocked slightly askew. On the
front of the post hung an iron chain and from this an open hoop,
which seemed to me like two small arms waiting gleefully to
fasten themselves around my throat. This had not been used for
many years; but I remember well that it stood there all the time I
was in Skien. Whether it still stands I do not know.

Then there was the town hall. Like the church, it had a steep
flight of steps. Beneath were the cells, with barred windows looking on to the square. Behind those bars. I have seen many pale
and sinister faces. One room deep down in the cellars was known
as the 'lunatic box' and must in fact, improbable as it now seems
to me, have been used in its time to confine lunatics. This room
had barred windows like the others, but behind the bars the
whole of the small window space was filled with a massive iron
screen, bored with innumerable tiny holes so that it resembled a
colander. This place was also said to have served as residence for
a famous criminal of the time known as Brandeis, because he
had been branded; and I believe it was, too, once occupied by an
escaped slave who had been recaptured and was flogged up in Li
Square. Of this last fellow eye-witnesses told how he had danced
as they led him to his place of punishment, but that when the
time came for him to return to prison he had to be carried in a
cart.

5. He was one of those children who seem old.
   Lacking the will to join his wild companions
   In their free play, he but looks quietly on,
   Sufficient to himself.
                    Epic version of *Brand*, 1865

Skien was, in the years of my childhood, an unusually gay and sociable town, very much the opposite of what it was later to become. Many highly cultivated, esteemed and prosperous families lived there then, either in the town itself or on the great estates outside. Most of these families were either closely or distantly related, and balls, dinner parties and musical gatherings followed each other in rapid succession, winter and summer. Many travellers also visited the town and, since there were then no proper hotels, they stayed with friends or relations. We almost always had people staying in our large and roomy house, which at Christmas and Fair-time would be full, an open table being kept from morning to night. Skien Fair was held in February, and was an especially happy occasion for all us boys; a full six months ahead we would begin to save our pennies so as to be able to watch the jugglers and the rope-dancers and the 'equine artists', and buy gingerbread in the market stalls. Whether this Fair greatly contributed to the commercial prosperity of the town I do not know; I remember it principally as a great popular feast which lasted for something like a whole week on end.

The 17th of May was not in those days an occasion of particular festivity in Skien. A few young people fired off popguns out on Bleaching Hill, or let off fireworks, but that was about all. I think this reserve in our otherwise ebullient town arose mainly from respect to a certain worthy gentleman whose ancestral home lay in the neighbourhood and whom for various reasons people were reluctant to offend.

But we made up for this on Midsummer Eve. This was not communally celebrated, but the boys and young men of the town would divide up into five or six groups, each devoted to gathering material for its own bonfire. As early as Whitsuntide we would start going around in packs to the shipyards and shops to 'beg' empty tar-barrels. One curious custom had survived from time immemorial. What was not freely given us we stole, without either the owner or the police ever considering laying a complaint against such outrageous behaviour. A group would thus gradually assemble a whole pile of empty tar-barrels. We enjoyed the same time-honoured right over old boats. Should we happen to come upon any of these drawn up on land, and succeed in dragging one or another of them away undetected and keeping our prize safely hidden, then our right of ownership was thereby conceded, or was anyway never challenged by anyone. Then, the day before Midsummer Eve, the boat would be carried in triumph through the streets to the place of our bonfire. Up in the boat would sit a fiddler. I have on several occasions witnessed a procession of this nature, and once myself took part in one.

Here Ibsen tantalizingly concludes his reminiscences. When he was seven, his childhood suddenly became clouded by misfortune and disgrace, and even in old age he evidently had no desire to commit his later memories to print.

Knud Ibsen ran a *bondehandel*, a general store which sold practically everything: groceries, dairy produce, glass, hardware, ice cream, wine and schnapps. This last commodity he distilled himself; indeed, his was the second largest distillery in town. He also acted as a general importer, and the customs records indicate the extent of his trade. From Bordeaux he imported wine, grape brandy and groceries; from Flensburg, dolls, pewter, ivory combs, glassware, hardware and catgut; from London, woollen and cotton goods; from Altona, aniseed, coriander and fennel seed, presumably for schnapps-making; from Hamburg, woollen goods; and from Newcastle, malt, mustard, stone goods and whetstones. He did well; in the year 1833-4, only sixteen private individuals in the district had a higher income, and around the middle of 1833, anxious no doubt to keep pace with his relatives and friends, he indulged in the luxury of buying a small country house with forty acres of land at Venstøp in the parish of Gjerpen, a couple of miles outside Skien, for 1,650 speciedollars (about £410).

No photograph or portrait of Knud Ibsen exists. He is remembered as having been 'under medium height, slight-limbed, oval-faced, with a rather long and slightly crooked nose and a small mouth; narrow between the eyes, with a somewhat sly expression; fair and rather long hair', and as 'a wag, a satirist, and very foxy'. Another witness who met him as an old man found him 'a trivial little fellow of

the most ordinary kind with no distinguishing characteristics, who, however much he talked, never said anything
of the faintest interest'; but that was when he was nearly
eighty and the years of failure, poverty and drink had taken
their toll. In his youth he seems to have been a good raconteur with a large stock of funny stories and a quickly inven-
tive tongue. He loved trotting and was a great hunter (there
were many wolves in the district then). In his last years he
'came every morning at eleven o'clock to a baker whose shop
stood next to the old school. In the back room of the bakery
was a little café, where Knud Ibsen would take a schnapps
and a glass of beer. As he sat there enjoying himself, the
boys from the school would often come and bang on the
window and shout abuse to annoy him. Then he would
become raging mad and rail at them furiously, but at the
same time so wittily that the words fairly crackled. It was
like a firework display.' His son was to paint three different
but equally recognizable portraits of him in his plays: as Jon
Gynt in *Peer Gynt*, Daniel Hejre in *The League of Youth*,
and Old Ekdal in *The Wild Duck*.

Knud Ibsen's wife Marichen (pronounced Marken) is said
to have been very beautiful. A silhouette of her as a young
girl (the only likeness we have) shows a pleasing profile with
a *retroussé* nose. As a young girl she was keen on drawing
and painting (some water-colours by her which have survived show a not negligible talent); and she was, then, merry
and gay, and worried her family by her passionate interest in
the theatre. Evening after evening she would slip away to
the performances that travelling Danish players gave in the
town. Her parents were also disturbed by her fondness, even
when she was a grown girl, for playing with dolls; an expression, it has been suggested, of her frustrated theatrical
passion. She played the piano and sang, was lively and spontaneous, small and dark-haired, with deep and sensitive
eyes.

Such were Henrik Ibsen's parents for the first seven years
of his life: a gay and prosperous couple, keeping open house.

But in 1834, when Henrik was six, his father's troubles began. On 10 June of that year the authorities closed his schnapps distillery, and he was distrained for thirteen thalers for tax arrears. This was less than a year after he had had the seventeenth largest private income in the town. During the latter half of 1834, most of 1835 and part of 1836 he was forced to mortgage or sell most of his possessions. His creditors did not, as has been supposed, bankrupt him, for his name remained on the list of citizens entitled to vote, from which bankrupts were excluded. They left him his small country house at Venstøp, and to this, probably early in June 1835, Knud and Marichen retired with their four children, and a fifth on the way.

Financial ruin has been known to alter a man's character for the better. It was not so with Knud Ibsen. He became combative, sarcastic and bitter towards those who were not his friends, and also very litigious. The legal archives of Skien are full of petty suits which he brought against this person and that, including even his servants. Marichen Ibsen, too, became a different person. The gay young woman with a passion for the theatre developed into a withdrawn and melancholy recluse. We are told that she hardly dared to speak to people after her husband's degradation, but hid herself away so as to attract as little notice as possible. 'Knud Ibsen scared the wits out of her,' an old lady recalled, 'so that in the end she became like a changeling'; and other witnesses confirmed that throughout the years at Venstøp she was silent and withdrawn. But she remained loyal to Knud Ibsen. Her daughter Hedvig, many years later, described her as 'a quiet, lovable woman, the soul of the house, everything for her husband and children. She always sacrificed herself; bitterness and fault-finding were unknown to her.'

To the disgrace of his father's financial ruin and social degradation was added another source of embarrassment which must profoundly have affected Henrik Ibsen's childhood. It was openly rumoured that Henrik was not Knud Ibsen's son, but that of an old admirer of his mother named

Tormod Knudsen. Marichen had met Knudsen in 1825, shortly before her marriage, when he had come to work as a clerk in the local sheriff's office, and although she was then already engaged, there is a strong tradition in Telemark that she and Knudsen were lovers. This tradition furthermore asserted that the affair continued after her marriage, and that Tormod not only was Henrik's father, but even claimed to be. Knudsen's legitimate son, Knut Knudsen, knew of this rumour years later, and believed it. And Ibsen's friend Christopher Due records that once at Grimstad, when Ibsen was in his late 'teens and drunk, he blurted out his suspicions to Due and to their friend Ole Schulerud. 'As he spoke,' writes Due, 'he gradually became very excited, said in plain words that there were irregularities connected with his birth and bluntly named Tormod Knudsen.' Due adds that he never liked to press Ibsen on the subject, and that Ibsen never mentioned it again.

Whether this rumour was true we shall never know. But one important piece of evidence is against it. Henrik Ibsen never remotely resembled Knudsen, whom photographs show as having a long face with a pointed jaw and a protruding underlip; but he very closely resembled Knud Ibsen. People in Skien used to say of Henrik Ibsen in his later years that 'it was like seeing old Ibsen [i.e. Knud] resurrected'. Knudsen's own claim to have been the father means little; men who covet another man's wife and are known or thought to have been intimate with her before marriage often claim to be the father of one of her children, especially if they are as vain as Tormod Kudsen is reputed to have been. But 'an unlucky and thoughtless utterance can be remembered so long that it becomes a proverb', and the rumour reached Henrik Ibsen's ears when he was a child, probably from other children who had heard it from their parents. He believed it, as would most children who heard rumours of their illegitimacy if, like Ibsen, they had no respect for their father, and it was something from which he was never to escape. Bankruptcy and illegitimacy recur spectre-like throughout his work. Hardly a play he wrote, from *The Pretenders* to *Rosmersholm*, but has its illegitimate or supposedly illegitimate child: Haakon and Peter in *The Pretenders*, the Ugly Brat in *Peer Gynt*, Regina in *Ghosts*, Hedvig in *The Wild Duck*, Rebecca West in *Rosmersholm*.

Such was the background against which Henrik Ibsen spent the next eight years of his childhood, from seven to fifteen. We know little about his early education. He began to read the Bible at the age of six or seven, and it was to remain his favourite book, though he was never a practising Christian. He may possibly have gone to a primary school in Skien before the move to Venstøp; after that, he may, as would seem logical, have been a pupil at a school near the Ibsen house which existed primarily for the benefit of employees at a local factory, but which other children were also permitted to attend. If so, he was fortunate. The headmaster was a young man of thirty-seven named Hans Isaksen who had travelled abroad, knew several languages and was celebrated for the beauty of his handwriting. Alternatively, he may have been educated by one Sexton Lund, who was a good friend of Knud Ibsen and had an excellent private school not far away, much patronized by children from Skien. Lund is known to have said of Ibsen as a child that he would become 'a great man', possibly from having known him in the classroom.[6]

The house at Venstøp had been somewhat ramshackle when Knud Ibsen bought it, having stood unoccupied for two years; the previous owner, a seaman's widow, had died in 1831. Her husband, a certain Niels Jørgen Hirscholm, had lived a romantic and dangerous life. Among other adven-

6. Sexton Lund's daughter, who was at school with Ibsen (either at her father's establishment or at Fossum) recalled three-quarters of a century later that Ibsen as a small boy sometimes used to go to school in a red woollen cap, and that when there was snow on the ground the top of his cap could be seen over the wall of a bridge he had to cross well before he himself, being small, came into sight.

tures, he had been a convict in England and a slave in the
Barbary States, and had acquired the nickname of 'The
Flying Dutchman'. He had died in 1828, the year of Henrik
Ibsen's birth. Many of his books remained in the large loft at
Venstøp and, although a lot were in English and therefore
unintelligible to him, the young Ibsen gained much of his
early knowledge from reading them. They included an old
illustrated edition of *Harrison's History of London*, that
book which was so to excite Hedvig Ekdal's imagination in
The Wild Duck.

There's a great big book called *Harryson's* [sic] *History of
London* – I should think it must be a hundred years old – and it's
got heaps and heaps of pictures in it. On the front there's a
picture of Death with an hour-glass, and a girl. That's horrid, I
think. But then there are lots of other pictures of churches and
castles and streets and great ships sailing on the sea . . . There
was an old sea captain who used to live here once and he brought
them home. They called him The Flying Dutchman. It's funny,
because he wasn't a Dutchman . . . In the end he got lost at sea
and left all these things behind.

Ibsen as a boy resembled his father, with the same short
build and strong nose, though he had his mother's dark
colouring. Apart from painting and reading, his chief
passion seems to have been clothes. Old Mr Lund, the father
of the aforementioned sexton, was something of a Beau
Brummell, and had a special uniform which he used to don
on festive occasions comprising velvet breeches, a waistcoat
of brown and yellow striped silk, a brown broadcloth coat, a
starched cravat and buckled shoes. Ibsen loved to be allowed
to watch while the old man put all this on. He liked also to
paint people in fine clothes and glue them on to bits of wood.
He amassed a collection of these, and would arrange them in
groups as though in conversation, as in a puppet theatre. No
one else was allowed to touch them. Sometimes, as he looked
at them, he would 'sit laughing silently to himself, so that he
shook'. He would also arrange living tableaux, a pastime in
vogue then, and enjoyed joining in when they went *på*

julebuk, going from house to house at Christmas to collect money like carol singers. Then he would 'dress up grandly, and cut the finest figure of them all'.

By the entrance to the kitchen at Venstøp (the house still stands, a spacious and agreeable wooden building of two storeys, with a fine view across the valley), one may still see the porch with the closet where Henrik Ibsen as a child used to lock himself in with his books, dolls and drawings. Soon he started his own puppet theatre. He also learned some skill as a conjuror: how to make a watch disappear from someone's pocket and replace it there unseen, or pound a watch in a mortar and restore it whole; and other tricks, including ventriloquism, with the aid of his young brother Nicolai concealed in a box. He made a little money by constructing small painted cardboard houses and so forth, which an old woman named Maren Mela sold at her fruit stall in the market square. Ibsen had inherited something of his father's satirical turn of mind; once, when he had been asked to paint a nice face on a doll for his sister, she found him working on it and laughing unpleasantly to himself. She ran to her mother, crying: 'Oh, now he's laughing again!' But when asked why, he replied that he was merely thinking of the face he *could* have painted. He loved to draw caricatures, and would occasionally harangue his brothers and sisters, standing on a barrel.

At the age of thirteen, Ibsen was enrolled at a small private school started that year (1841) by two young men with theological degrees, Johan Hansen and W. F. Stockfleth. Ibsen attended this school for two years. His favourite subjects were history, especially that of classical antiquity, and religion, when he would sit for hours looking up the passages in the Bible to which references were given. He also learned German, and had private lessons in Latin from Hansen, whom he later praised highly as a teacher, adding that he had 'a mild, amiable temper, like that of a child'. When Hansen died in 1865, Ibsen mourned him; he was practically the only person connected with his childhood, apart from his

sister, for whom he retained any affectionate sentiment. The
local sexton (not Lund), who helped with the lessons, recalled the young Ibsen as 'a quiet boy with a remarkable pair
of eyes, but with no particular cleverness apart from an unusual gift for drawing'. Ibsen took art lessons from a painter
named Mikkel Mandt and painted local scenes and romantic
subjects, including some based on illustrations in the Flying
Dutchman's books. If his father had continued on his earlier,
prosperous career, Henrik Ibsen might well have chosen to
become a painter. But fortunately for posterity, in those days
any Norwegian painter with serious intentions had to go
abroad for the necessary technical training, usually either to
Dresden, where the great Norwegian landscape artist J. C.
Dahl lived (and where he was to act as cicerone to Ibsen when
the latter visited the city in 1852 to study theatre), or to
Düsseldorf. So that career was closed to him.

He was not interested in any kind of sport, except fishing,
swimming and, perhaps surprisingly, dancing, though he
was physically tough and resilient. 'Withdrawn' is the word
used again and again to describe him at this time, as
throughout his life. His sister records that when she and
their four brothers were romping together out of doors, he
would retire into a little room by the kitchen entrance and
bolt himself in. 'He was never a sociable companion,' she
told Henrik Jæger, 'and we always tried our best to disturb
him by throwing stones or snowballs at the wall or door. We
wanted him to play with us, and when he couldn't stand our
taunts any longer, he would rush out and drive us away – but
since he had no talent for any kind of athletic exercise, and
violence was foreign to his character, nothing further ever
came of it. When he had chased us far enough, he would go
back into his room.'

His more boisterous companions found him self-important,
a judgement which, again, is confirmed by almost everyone who knew him at this period. He seems to have reacted
to the family's plunge into poverty, as so often happens in
such cases, by standing on his dignity; he was unwilling to

accept the country lads who were his neighbours as his social equals, and is even said to have given them money so that they would not accompany him to school. When he finally left for Grimstad, the local children shouted after him: 'Good riddance, ugly mug! (*Reis med dig styggen!*)' Several of these early traits – withdrawnness, social formality, obsessive interest in dress – he was to retain until his death.

With the other sex, in general, he got on better. Two old ladies interviewed in 1910 remembered him as 'nice, quiet, reticent, neat, not shy exactly, but unassuming and withdrawn. But you couldn't call him constrained; he was never at a loss for an answer. His fellows didn't care for him; they thought him pompous. But we girls liked him. He was nice looking and well set up. When he came and asked us to dance, we regarded it as a great honour. And he was a great ball-goer. He loved dancing and was good fun at parties. And once he had started dancing with a girl he would dance the rest of the evening with her, every single dance ... Occasionally he joined in the other boys' games, as when they went round the houses dressed up at Christmas, and then he cut the best figure of them all. He liked to dress up grand. And his father was very fond of Henrik and always gave him the best possible clothes.'

Knud Ibsen never succeeded in reinstating himself financially, and seems to have lived the last years of his life largely on the charity of his relatives. He applied repeatedly for a post in the customs, stressing that his financial troubles had occurred through no fault of his. Local worthies wrote in his support, praising his conscientiousness and meticulous attention to detail, characteristics which his dramatist son was to inherit to a marked degree. But all of his applications failed, and he was forced to take on a variety of minor odd jobs, still, apparently, keeping himself largely by borrowing. During the four years from 1848 to 1852, he had to appear no less than seventeen times before the commissioners to answer for unpaid debts. For a brief while he held a minor post at the Savings Bank; but before long he was categorized in the tax records of Skien as a 'pauper', from whom no tax was required, and for the last twenty years of his long life (he lived to be eighty) he appears to have had no regular work, doing the odd job, borrowing (mainly from his half-brothers, the Pauses) and sustaining himself with schnapps and day-dreams. As Oskar Mosfjeld, the chronicler of Ibsen's boy-hood, has observed: 'He had long since ceased to play the role of Jon Gynt, and was henceforth to alternate between the roles of Daniel Hejre, Old Ekdal and John Gabriel Borkman.'

Ibsen left school in the spring of 1843, shortly after his fifteenth birthday, and on 1 October of that year he was confirmed with several other boys in the church at Gjerpen. The order of the candidates was arranged strictly according to their social standing, and Ibsen was placed third. Knud Ibsen regarded this as a considerable social humiliation and groused about it for years; the only reason he could find was that the parents of the other two boys had given the pastor a fine joint of veal, while he had not been able to afford any such gift. The humiliations of life have a different effect on different people. They drove Knud Ibsen to drink and il-lusions, and turned his son into a dramatist.

That October, Knud and Marichen Ibsen moved from Venstøp to a house at Snipetorp, in the outskirts of Skien. Set on a slight hill away from the heart of the town, this building, two-storeyed like Stockmannsgaarden and likewise of wood, escaped the conflagration of 1886 and stands today. It was to be the family home for over twenty years, until 1865, but Henrik Ibsen was to live there for only a few weeks, during which time he decorated some of the door panels with large painted caricatures of his brothers and sister as animals; Johan as a monkey, Hedvig as a bear, Ole as a fox, and Nicolai as something that has never been satisfactorily identified.[7]

Now that Ibsen was nearly sixteen, it was time for him to

7. These paintings have survived, and may be seen in the Folk Museum at Skien.

seek a living; and he cannot have been sorry to go. There was a constant strife between his parents, his mother was withdrawing more and more into herself, and food was so short that the main meal of the day often consisted only of potatoes. Moreover, many people were emigrating across the Atlantic from the Telemark district, and the local newspapers of those years contain frequent letters from Norwegians who had made their homes in America, mostly in Wisconsin, Minnesota and Dakota, praising the conditions of freedom and opportunity which they had found in the New World. The windows of Snipetorp faced towards the harbour, and from his room the young Ibsen could watch the emigrants embark. In that unhappy house, he must surely have felt the longing to set out, like those hungry families, 'towards the new, towards the unknown, towards the strange shore and the saga that is to come'.[8] A friend of his father's, a travelling salesman, undertook to look out for a post for him, and found him one as assistant to an apothecary at Grimstad, a tiny huddle of houses around a harbour a hundred miles to the south.[9] Two days after Christmas, on 27 December 1843, he departed from Skien in a tiny sailing ship appropriately named *Lykkens Prøve*, the *Lucky Chance*.

Those eight years between the ages of seven and fifteen left a scar that was never wholly to be healed. In his last years, according to his niece Anna, he often spoke of returning to his birthplace, but could never bring himself to do so. He would, she records, shake his head slowly, and say: 'It is not easy to go to Skien.'

8. *The Pretenders*, Act Four.
9. Fru Mülertz, whose husband had bought half the Venstøp estate in 1837, owned an apothecary's shop in Skien called the Swan, and it has been suggested that Ibsen may have helped there after leaving school and so gained some knowledge of the work.

2

The Apothecary's Apprentice
1844–50

IBSEN arrived at Grimstad on 3 January 1844, two months short of his sixteenth birthday. He was to remain there for six and a quarter years.

Grimstad is a town that has been much maligned by Ibsen's biographers. Edmund Gosse dismissed it as 'a small, isolated, melancholy place, connected with nothing at all, visitable only by steamer. Featureless hills surround it, and it looks out into the east wind, over a dark bay dotted with naked rocks. No industry, no objects of interest in the vicinity, a perfect uniformity of little red houses where nobody seems to be doing anything.' Simple it certainly was, and is; but, visiting it on a sunny winter's day in 1965, I found it a pleasing cluster of wooden houses, many of them dating from Ibsen's time, attractively situated on its inlet. The surrounding landscape, less rugged than that around Skien, is of a gentle and unpretentious charm.

With its eight hundred inhabitants, Grimstad was no smaller than many a Norwegian coastal town then. At first sight, it appeared something of a backwater. Christopher Due, who came there eighteen months after Ibsen, and who well into the present century in extreme old age set down some of the most valuable reminiscences of the early Ibsen that we possess, recorded:

When I arrived one dark autumn evening in 1845, I at once received the impression of a primitive and impecunious place. There was no street lighting whatever. The feeble light from such windows [by no means few in number] as had no curtains, so that even in the so-called main street one could see families seated around tables illuminated by only a single tallow candle, merely served to make the street darker, and it was not undangerous to walk there because of the gutters down the middle.

Grimstad had no church of its own until December 1849, a few months before Ibsen's departure, and, more regrettably for posterity, no newspaper of its own until 1856 when *Grimstads Adressetidende* was founded. Nor does it seem to have had any good school, for the better families sent their children away to be educated.

But it was not a sleepy town. On the contrary, with its fine natural harbour and amply accessible timber it was, despite its smallness, a bustling and prosperous centre of shipbuilding.

In every inlet, and there are many inlets in or near the town, one saw a hull on the stocks and, as soon as this had been launched, the frame was erected for its successor ... Everyone who had any savings, or could manage to borrow some, bought shares in a ship. The priest, the doctor, the justice, not to speak of the seamen and tradespeople, the artisans and even the servant maids, were all, in greater or less degree, shipowners ... To own a share in a ship was reckoned as safe as, and much more profitable than, investing one's money in the Savings Bank. It not seldom happened that, freight rates being what they were then, a ship repaid the cost of its construction in two or three voyages. The greater part of the male population went to sea immediately after confirmation, and thereafter spent only the winter months at home ... The people were frugal, undemanding and, above all, peaceably inclined, living out their quiet and modest lives within their narrow circle.

For its period, Grimstad seems to have been a tolerant and friendly little place. The pietism that was to dominate it, like so many other Norwegian towns, later in the eighteen-fifties had not yet taken root: the local pastor, who bore the unChristian-sounding name of Pharo, was a worldly and eccentric figure. There was a billiards hall, where you could sit with a toddy; dances were held, sometimes masked; 'excursions with dance' were a popular diversion, and in the early forties at least there were amateur theatricals. Troupes of wandering players visited the town, as they did Skien, living from hand to mouth; and when the summer came and the citizens no longer wished to spend their evenings indoors (and the tallow candles which formed the only source of stage illumination could no longer fight the sunlight), they eked out their precarious existence as dancing and fencing masters until the autumn dusk began to close in. Ibsen was to recall these amateur groups and strolling players when, thirty years later, he wrote *The Pillars of Society*, a play that is full of Grimstad memories.

In a town that lived on its shipping, Ibsen must, through his work, have mixed a lot with sailors. There still lived in Grimstad several men who had been in prison in England during the Napoleonic Wars (in which Norway and Denmark sided with France), and others who had been prisoners in Gothenburg during the brief war against Sweden in 1814. Many foreign ships took refuge from storms in the harbour; the references to American sailors in *The Pillars of Society* make it clear that the inhabitants were well used to having such aliens in their midst.

Reimann, the apothecary to whom Ibsen was apprenticed, was an amiable but unpractical man of thirty-nine whose business was on the slide. His shop lay in a poor quarter of the town, occupying part of a small and exceedingly humbly furnished house, with small-paned windows in both of its two low storeys. The remainder of the house (i.e. that part not taken up by the shop) served as accommodation for the Reimanns, their numerous children, their two maids and their new apprentice. Everyone slept upstairs in three rooms. The inmost was occupied by the Reimanns and the smallest children, the second and central room by Ibsen and the three elder sons, and the third by the two maids. Only the last of these had direct access to the staircase, so that when, as happened frequently, anyone came with urgent re-

quirements in the night, Ibsen had to go through the maids'
room with his candle to answer the door.

The ground floor comprised the shop, a tiny waiting-room
and the kitchen. When Ibsen had to prepare anything that
required heating, he had to do it over the open fire in the
kitchen, often with one of the maids cooking a meal beside
him. 'When he came to the kitchen fire with his pots and
pans, and wanted all the room, we had words,' one of these
maids, Marie Thomsen, remembered sixty-five years later.
Christopher Due describes the background against which he
saw Ibsen for the first time:

As I passed [the shop] one day with a friend, the latter asked
me if I had seen the apothecary's apprentice, remarking that
there was something odd about him. I should explain that long
after his arrival there were many people who had not set eyes on
him unless they had had any business with the apothecary, since
Ibsen was never to be seen outside, at any rate in daytime.
Curious to inspect him I soon went into the shop. This comprised
a tiny room, so low that I could almost touch the ceiling with my
hand, and extremely shabby – undusted, dark and displeasing.
As an apothecary's it was primitively equipped in every respect
... There was no one to be seen, nor any sound to suggest that
anyone was present, so I had ample time to make these observations; but on banging upon the counter, I perceived some
movement behind the so-called prescription cabinet, and soon
afterwards there emerged somewhat abruptly a small young
man with an attractively vital face. I should here mention that
Ibsen in his youth wore a handsome full brown beard, unusually
well developed for one so young, which gave his face an energetic
and at the same time harmonious expression ... The total impression was that of a handsome young man with a good, shapely
figure.

Since Reimann, according to Marie Thomsen, 'spent most
of the time walking outside and did little work', Ibsen had to
see to practically everything. He was perpetually boiling and
compounding, breaking off only to serve a customer or to
deal with the town's post, for which Reimann was officially
responsible. He had desperately little free time ('You never

saw him in the streets of a weekday,' another inhabitant remembered), earned the most miserable of salaries, and did
not have enough to eat. Nevertheless, by stinting himself of
sleep, he managed to pack far more into each twenty-four
hours than most youths of his age. He painted a great deal,
drew caricatures of the local citizens, wrote lampoons about
them, and serious poetry as well. He also read much; he had
brought a whole box of books with him from Skien, and
among the authors he devoured were Dickens, Scott, Holberg, Voltaire (whom he especially admired), the contemporary Swedish novelist Fredrika Bremer and the
Danish novelist Fru Gyllembourg. Reimann was a member
of a reading circle, and allowed Ibsen to borrow books
through him.

Not content with such general reading, he studied at
night for his matriculation, in the hope that he might
eventually qualify to go to the University; and this, as we
shall see, was to provide him with the inspiration for his first
play. On the infrequent occasions on which he found himself free in the daytime, he took long solitary Wordsworth-
ian walks, often armed with a paintbox, and would
occasionally go for a row.

Jørgen Peder Eriksen, who had known Ibsen from the
time of the latter's arrival in Grimstad, recalled him as a
youth sixty-five years later. 'He was always wanting to do
handgrips and wrestle ... and we used to lift weights to see
who was the strongest. He looked strong, too; he was well
built, but small. He wasn't at all sullen; very talkative, and
mixed a lot with the other local youths. But he looked so old;
he had a coarse face, full of pimples.' Eriksen's sister,
Marthe, recalled that 'he used to lie on the hill and toboggan
with the young girls. With every one of them. There wasn't
such a difference between boys and girls then. They were
mostly the daughters of sailors and woodcutters.'[1] Jørgen
Eriksen also remembered that Ibsen was often to be seen

1. Another old lady who as a girl had known Ibsen in Grimstad
recalled how he liked to pull their plaits.

reading or painting on Vestre Varden, a high crag above the town.

Another portrait of Ibsen during his first two years at Grimstad comes from a schoolmaster, H. Terland, who in 1900 delivered a lecture to the Christiania Philological Society which was printed in the newspaper *Eidsvold*.

Quiet and withdrawn as he was, he made no effort to gain an acquaintance with the families of the town. Nor, certainly, could he be regarded as an acquisition to the social circles of Grimstad, being a mere boy and of a very unprepossessing exterior. Small and thin, but squarely built, of swarthy complexion, with a dark lock of hair hanging down over his forehead, and a shy glance which he continually averted – thus do old inhabitants of Grimstad depict the young Ibsen's appearance ... He was certainly no beauty, and when one recalls that he also had a curious introspective, old-mannish face, and an enclosed personality, it is not in the least surprising that people regarded the sixteen-or seventeen-year-old boy as a queer fish ... He was taciturn and withdrawn, didn't say much, but wrote short poems with extraordinary facility, always in rhyme ... One must remember that Ibsen was still in the hobbledehoy stage, and the need that boys have then to poke fun at the world and play-act found expression in him through this medium.

The apparent contradiction between Terland's account and that of the Eriksens and others need not trouble us. It is evident that Ibsen was one person when in the company of simple people, with whom he had no sense of social inferiority, and another when with ladies and gentlemen of 'good family'.

Ibsen does not appear to have made any close friends at Grimstad during his first couple of years there (he probably did not meet Due until some time in 1846). Then, two and a half years after his arrival, the thing that he could least afford happened.

One of the maids at the Reimanns was named Else Sofie Jensdatter. She was ten years older than Ibsen, having been born on 11 January 1818 in Børkedalen in Vestre Moland.

Else was not, as many commentators have taken for granted, a kitchen slut; her ancestors had been gentleman farmers, and the family had become impoverished in an honourable cause. Her grandfather, Christian Lofthuus, had led a rebellion of the Norwegian peasants against their Danish overlords in the previous century, as punishment for which his farm had been burned, his property declared forfeit, and he himself chained to a block in the fortress of Akershus, where, ten years later, he died.

Else was one of the two servant girls who slept in that outer room through which Ibsen had to pass on his way to answer the night bell. She was, moreover, his *husmor*, which means that it fell to her to see to his personal needs, such as mending. She attended to other needs too. On 9 October 1846, when she was twenty-eight and Ibsen was eighteen and a half, she bore him a son. The birth did not take place in Grimstad; she returned for the occasion to her parents in Børkedalen, so that the affair did not receive the full local publicity which would otherwise have been accorded it. But Ibsen had, out of his almost non-existent salary, to pay paternity costs towards the child's upbringing until he reached the age of fourteen.

Else named her son Hans Jacob Henriksen; and we may turn aside briefly from the story of Ibsen's own life to summarize the unhappy history of his illegitimate son and the latter's descendants. Hans Jacob lived with his mother at Børkedalen, east of Lillesand, until he was twenty-nine, eking out a hard living as a blacksmith. They were very poor; his mother seems to have been unable to do any kind of work, and there is an unconfirmed tradition that she went blind. When, finally, her parents' house was taken from them, Hans Jacob scrawled on a rock the grim word *Sultefjell* – Starvation Hill. Else moved to a 'small, grey hut' on a hillside at Tyttebærmœn, west of Lillesand, and died there, a pauper, on 5 June 1892, aged seventy-four. Hans Jacob became, according to one who remembered him late in his life, 'a very interesting man, who read a great deal, taking especial pleasure in history, geography and travel books. He was also a bit of a fiddler and fiddle-maker, in general a well appointed man; but unhappily he was a victim of drink.' In fact, he became an alcoholic and ne'er-do-well. He married three times and had seven children, but their fate, too, makes sad reading. Six died young; the fate of the seventh is unknown. We have no record of what happened to the eldest, Jens, born out of wedlock in 1876. Hans Jacob married the mother, Mathilde Andreasdotter, but she died five years later of tuberculosis. The following year, 1882, he married one Trine Marie Gunvaldsen; she bore him a daughter, Marie, two months afterwards, but the child lived only a fortnight and the mother died nine days later. In 1883 Hans Jacob made his third and final marriage, with Ida Gurine Olsdatter, who bore him five children. Ole (born 9 April 1884) died as a baby. Isak (born 9 March 1885) died on 7 April 1888, aged three. Inge (born 10 August 1888) was drowned off Rockall in the *Norge* on 28 June 1904, on her way to America, aged fifteen. Gunda (born 24 April 1892) died on 17 September 1896, aged four. The fifth and last child, Jenny, (born 8 March 1895) seemed likely to break this tragic sequence; she lived to the age of twenty-seven, working as a seamstress, but died on 22 September 1922 of tuberculosis shortly before she was due to be married. Hans Jacob himself lived on until 20 October 1916; he had no contact with his famous father until he saw him for the first time, briefly and dramatically, towards the end of the latter's life.

Shortly before the birth of Ibsen's illegitimate son, the unfortunate Reimann's debts at last caught up with him, and in August 1846, at the demand of a fellow-apothecary in Christiania to whom he owed nearly thirteen thousand crowns (about £650), his business was put up for auction and bought by one O. A. Haanshus. Early the next year Haanshus resold it to a former apprentice of Reimann named Lars Nielsen, the twenty-three-year-old bachelor son of a well-to-do local shipmaster. Nielsen transferred the shop from Storgaden 75 to a better locale at Østergade 13, a house owned by a stone-deaf and eccentric widow named Geelmuyden, who spent her whole day in a chair, occupied solely with her snuff-box.[2] Here, Nielsen leased two decent-sized rooms on the ground floor. The outer room, into which the front door opened, was the shop; the inner room, to the rear, served as a waiting-room, laboratory, parlour, dining-room and bedroom for the young apothecary and his 'qualified assistant' (*examinerade medhjelper*), for Nielsen raised Ibsen to this status from his previous one of apprentice and increased his salary. Reimann had given him an excellent reference, saying that he was unusually skilful at his work, conscientious and industrious. The building at Østergade 13 still stands, a pleasant wooden house of two storeys a stone's throw from the sea, and the two rooms are preserved much as they must have been in Ibsen's time, except that then the walls of the parlour were hung with Ibsen's own paintings, few of which have survived. In the shop itself perched a large stuffed owl, which had been shot in the tree outside Ibsen's window and which figures in one of his early poems.

A portrait of Ibsen at work as an apothecary comes to us from the other of the Reimanns' two maids, Marie Thomsen. She remembered him as 'very quiet; badly dressed; his clothes were as shiny as that stove; you could tell from them that he was hard at it all day'. There was an old man called Svend Fjeldmand (Svend the Hillman), who used to wash up and do odd jobs in the shop; he and Ibsen became friends and often took a walk together on Sundays to Fjære church-yard, half an hour away. Svend died shortly before Ibsen left Grimstad and Marie recalled that Ibsen painted a picture and put it on Svend's grave at Fjære 'with something he'd written'. He did a lot of painting; Marie and the Eriksens were agreed on this. At work he was perpetually boiling and

2. Fru Geelmuyden's maid Sofie Hoglund, who came to her in 1847 at the age of seventeen and stayed two years, remembered that Ibsen as a lodger was 'nice, a really nice person, never complained'.

mixing, breaking off only to attend a customer. He was neat at his packaging. Sometimes, in the kitchen, he would get bad-tempered and stump off into the shop. But

a moment later he'd come out again, and the mood would have left him. 'Feel better now?' I'd ask him. I could put him in the right humour, I could ... 'If you grow up and get married you'll plague the life out of your wife,' I told him. He was fun really. He liked playing jokes ... That Henrik was a terrible one for reading. He had a whole box bursting with books – but no clothes. He spent nearly the whole night writing and reading. Never in bed before two. Light? Yes, he had a tallow candle – I never heard them refuse him one. Sometimes I'd open the door and say: 'You go to bed now, lad. You'll get fuddle-headed with all this reading.' ... More than once he said: 'I'll never live to see the day when I get on the right shelf.' He never said what kind of a shelf that might be. We never knew what was going on in his mind, and didn't ask ... Most of his spare time he spent drawing and painting. The whole house was full of his pictures. Oh yes, they let him hang them up. No frames on them, though. He painted quick as lightning. Sometimes he'd paint in the shop, sometimes in the storehouse. I don't know whether he painted the shop sign outside [of a swan]. It was certainly done while he was there. He used pencils too. Drew us all – in our working clothes – as we stood washing ourselves and looking dreadful. Old Pharo, the father of the priest at Fjære, he did a drawing of him. He was the one who always went past the window with a finger through a hole in his coat. And he drew people who came to the shop. When he'd drawn anyone he'd come out to us in the kitchen and show it to us.

She confirmed that he liked climbing the hills around Grimstad, and rowing, and denied that he was miserable; the apothecary (Reimann), she said, made much of him.

If he'd been father to the boy he couldn't have been kinder to him. A fine man, the apothecary. Not at all bossy, nor was his wife really, only she was always so poorly. One Christmas they hadn't a bite to eat. My mother went down to Crawfurd's shop and got food from the English lady. The apothecary became angry when he heard this and wouldn't take it. 'Well, if you want your family to starve, that's your business,' I said. But in the end he let us keep it. Quite untrue that Ibsen starved – that's a lie. But he [Reimann] drank too much. Ibsen was quick in his movements, silent and quick as an owl.

With the children, he was not always so popular. J. Schulerud, whose brother Ole was to become one of Ibsen's few really close friends, relates: 'We small boys didn't like him, he was always so sour. When we went to the apothecary's to buy liquorice, he gave us miserably little for our halfpennies. Old Reimann gave us much more.' Schulerud added that he only once heard Ibsen laugh 'good and heartily, like other human beings'.

Nielsen, Ibsen's new employer, was a quiet and *soigné* young man, very different from Reimann. He ate all his meals at his parents' house a few minutes away, and at his suggestion Ibsen took lunch with them and had his breakfast and supper brought up to the shop. When they had visitors in the evening, they often invited Ibsen, leaving the maid Sofie to look after the shop and run down to fetch Ibsen if anyone should call. Old Nielsen, the apothecary's father, was a jovial man with a good stock of travellers' yarns. Among his ships was one named *The Palm Tree*, which was to figure, like so many other Grimstad memories, in *The Pillars of Society*.

No real friendship sprang up between Ibsen and his young employer. Ibsen used to refer disrespectfully to him in his absence as 'the animal', and when he borrowed Nielsen's galoshes called them 'the animal's hind footwear'; he was also heard to utter remarks about 'empty heads and full pockets'. Ibsen himself later wrote of Nielsen that he was 'good and clever, but entirely preoccupied with his work' (which included being cashier at the local Savings Bank, a task which took up more of his time than the shop). Like Reimann, he left the preparation of medicines and the reception of customers almost entirely to Ibsen. A thrifty man, he died in 1865 aged forty, leaving a sizeable fortune.

Among the people Ibsen met at the Nielsens was an old

Scottish lady named Georgiana Crawfurd. Her brother
Thomas, an engineer from Carron in Stirlingshire, had
settled in Grimstad in 1822, and she had joined him. She was
known in the town as *Tanten*, the old maid, but was a much
respected figure, and one of the few people in the town to
have a good private library. She took a liking to the abrupt
and awkward young newcomer with his radical views, and
her nephew, Jens, told sixty years later how, as a boy
of fourteen, 'I often took books from my old aunt to Ibsen.'
He remembered that she owned Kierkegaard's *Either-Or*,
published only a few years earlier in 1843, and she may well
have provided Ibsen with his first introduction to
Kierkegaard's work.[3]

It may also have been through Miss Crawfurd that Ibsen
first discovered the plays of Adam Oehlenschläger, the
great Danish poet then approaching the end of his career.
Oehlenschläger, as a dramatist, lay somewhere between
Corneille and Schiller, the latter being his idol; his plays,
like theirs, are written in distinguished, dignified and sometimes eloquent verse, but to a modern reader seem static and
declamatory, the kind of theatre that has been unkindly
described as grand opera without the music. But we must
remember that Ibsen, at this time, could read neither
English nor French, and German only with difficulty, and he
can have gained little from the poor Scandinavian translations then available of Shakespeare and other foreign
dramatists; nor, until he went to Copenhagen in 1852, did he
have the chance to see any great tragedy on the stage.
Oehlenschläger's poetic dramas, mostly set in Scandinavia
during the heroic age (*Earl Haakon the Mighty, The Vikings
in Byzantium*, and so forth), were Ibsen's first glimpse of
theatrical tragedy; and Oehlenschläger was to be his first
model, though he was quickly to discard him, as he was to
discard his other influences.

Jens Crawfurd also remembered that his aunt possessed
the poetical works of Henrik Wergeland, the Norwegian

3. On the possible influence of Kierkegaard on Ibsen, see pp. 186-8.

poet of freedom (1808–45), a great admirer of Shakespeare, who revered England as the home of the liberty that he was perpetually preaching. The earliest poems that we possess by Ibsen, dating from 1847 and 1848, are very much in the Wergeland manner; carrying titles such as 'Resignation', 'By the Sea', and 'Doubt and Hope', they are, in content, the usual adolescent mixture of eagerness and suicidal melancholy, and are interesting only for an unusual technical maturity, especially in the rhyming. Ibsen's extraordinary facility for writing verse, especially rhymed verse, in practically any metre was to dominate his early play-writing to its disadvantage. In his first ten plays, he is almost always at his best when subjecting himself to the tougher discipline of prose.

Ibsen gave some of his poems to old Miss Crawfurd as he wrote them, and on returning to her home after a Sunday at the Nielsens she would read them. She died in 1865 at the age of eighty-seven, late enough to learn of his success the previous year with *The Pretenders*, though unhappily just too early to hear of his greater triumph with *Brand*.

By the end of 1847, Ibsen was reading hard for his matriculation. The subjects in which he had to prepare himself included Latin and Greek; these, and other subjects, he read with two theological students who visited the shop. By now, much to his delight and profit, he was seeing more of Christopher Due, and a close bond sprang up between the two. Due writes:

I felt more and more strongly drawn to him. His intelligence and bubbling humour fascinated me all the more because these characteristics were lacking in my other acquaintances. Gradually I became a daily visitor to the shop, mostly in the evenings, when Ibsen would be sitting peacefully in his room. I used to look forward all day to these meetings. It was a new and entrancing experience to listen to his witty utterances, those independent and, to me, largely new views of life, somewhat audacious, to be sure, as they seemed to me, and full of paradoxes, but always interesting. And he found in me a grateful listener, enthusiastically following him in his occasionally somewhat wild flight from the prosaic material situation in which he lived and which, by this means, he, as it were, cast off, to our mutual advantage. As is usual among young persons, we discussed everything between heaven and earth, not least marriage. Among Ibsen's extravagant caprices I remember that he contended with a curious ardour that he and his wife, if he ever acquired one, would have to live on separate floors, see each other at meal-times, and not address each other as 'Du'. This was at that time his ideal of marriage ... Gradually people began to notice this intelligent and witty young man, and the waiting room of the apothecary's shop soon became, especially on Sundays and of an evening, a favourite meeting-place, to which new friends were continually introduced. It was always fun, with Ibsen as the centre-point of the grateful circle, for he bubbled with humour and, admittedly, with sarcasm too, and despite the poverty of his circumstances he was always in an excellent temper. One never got any feeling that he was depressed. He possessed to a high degree the elasticity of youth.

Due goes on to confirm that Ibsen often indulged his wit in the form of sharply satirical poems and caricatures. 'He had an astonishing talent for writing fluent verses, and was a very talented artist. His pencil swiftly and surely made its point.' Due quotes a kind of comic strip which Ibsen composed about a man and his horse, the horse eventually proving far more cunning than the man. He also wrote 'an excellent poem in rhyme' about a local youth, fitted to the melody of a popular Danish vaudeville of the time from which the youth in question was always singing extracts. Ibsen then got the subject of the poem to sing it to a gathering of friends, all of whom, except the singer, knew that it referred unflatteringly to the latter.

To see Ibsen's pleasure at the merriment which reigned among us when we persuaded the object of our banter to sing the verses of which he was himself the comic hero was indescribable. Ibsen's eyes glittered like fire ... In addition to such amusements, we occasionally held a card party of an evening in Ibsen's room. Only the more trustworthy among us were selected for these occasions, men who could keep silence about such enormities as that we drank punch from ointment pots which, should we be surprised by some suspicious intruder, were swiftly emptied and stuffed into our pockets. As midnight approached, one of the more thoughtful among us might suggest that Ibsen needed some peace, since we all knew that he used part of the night in studying for his examination, but he always assured us that there was still plenty of time left for both study and sleep.

Ibsen's capacity for work and physical resilience [*continues Due*] were phenomenal. Apart from a very few hours he literally worked throughout the day and night. Most of his day was of course taken up with the business of the shop. Since there was then only this one apothecary's business between Kristiansand and Arendal, a matter of some seventy kilometres, there was obviously a deal to do, and since the apothecary himself was much occupied with his duties as cashier and book-keeper at the local savings bank and was moreover in uncertain health, the result was that Ibsen did most of the work at the shop. This was, like the older shop [*i.e.* Reimann's], even by the humble standards of those days, very inadequately equipped. For example, there was no special room set aside as a laboratory. When any complicated potions had to be prepared, resort was made to the kitchen belonging to the lady who owned the house. She lived in one half of the ground floor of the little house while the apothecary's shop and waiting room occupied the other half. I have actually seen Ibsen in the kitchen over an open fireplace, without even a stove, busy preparing medicines next to Madame Geelmuyden's cooking pots. For smaller preparations a small spirit lamp in the shop served. In those days there was no such thing as a petroleum apparatus. With such primitive equipment the work of the shop was naturally extremely arduous and took a disproportionately long time, to Ibsen's chagrin, since it meant that he could spend less time on what most interested him . . .

It was quite incredible how much Ibsen got through in each twenty-four hours. Apart from his work in the shop, which as stated took up most of the daytime, he had his matriculation studies, which he had to pursue largely without assistance . . . These caused him considerable worry and trouble. Then, from a natural inner compulsion, he felt urged to spend part of the day or night writing, which more and more obsessed his thoughts.

And yet he also found time to employ his talent as an artist in many directions. Not only was his pencil continually active, he also painted landscapes . . . When one remembers that visits from his friends occupied part of each day too, it will be appreciated that there was little time left for sleep or rest. But I never heard Ibsen complain of being tired. His health was always exemplary. He must have been uncommonly tough physically. For example, his financial situation compelled him to exercise the strictest imaginable economy, to the point of having to manage without underpants and even, later, without socks. Since there was among the many female charmers of Grimstad a young lady towards whom he was inclined, I jestingly told him that he was acting *Love without Stockings*.[4] We had a good laugh over this. Ibsen was always ready to take a humorous view of his painful circumstances. These sartorial experiments of his succeeded even in winter, when he had, moreover, no overcoat, for I never knew him to catch cold, or suffer from any physical ailment.

One day Grimstad was surprised by the arrival of a young 'student' (i.e. someone who had passed the matriculation examination). 'A *student* was a rare sight in those parts,' comments Due. 'Among the natives of the town, for many years there had only been two. One looked up to an *akademiker* with a kind of involuntary respect.' This newcomer was Ole Carelius Schulerud, born 1827. Due, who knew Schulerud's father, quickly introduced him to Ibsen, and the three soon became firm friends.

Apart from our mutual sympathy and literary interests – in those days one eagerly studied Søren Kierkegaard's books *Either-Or, The Works of Love*, etc., and not least Oehlenschläger's tragedies, and *Clara Raphael's Letters*[5] – we were, all three, in contrast to our other comrades, 'as poor as church mice'. One of us had, for economic reasons, to do without lunch, the second could manage both board and lodging but seldom found

4. A parody of neo-classical French tragedy by J. H. Wessel (1742–85), set to music by Paolo Scalabrini.
5. One of the first calls for female emancipation.

the pocket money for a cigar, and the third, Ibsen, had from his pitiful salary to buy clothes and books, pay his matriculation tutor, and even, as 'apothecary's journeyman' (for thus, to his rage, he was described in the tax register), contribute to the town rates. Most of our fellows had, in varying degrees, shares in ships, and were therefore comfortably off. They could afford many things that we three had to deny ourselves. Their situation provided a marked contrast to that of the 'Triumvirate', with our humble get-togethers, and created, not least in Ibsen, a bitter resentment against 'empty brains with full wallets' ... There were a few families where a more intelligent life was carried on, but Ibsen never moved in their circles.

In so small and conservative a community as Grimstad, respectable citizens had begun to notice and shake their heads at the young radical, with his atheistic and republican views. For Ibsen was already a heretic in such matters as marriage, love, morality and religion. He had broken away from his early religious teaching, and was unwilling to believe in a God, except in generalized and agnostic terms. He had, as we know, studied Voltaire, and Due tells how 'he championed the latter's Deism and Pantheism ... He denied the existence of a personal God. In this he met strong opposition from one or two of us, and we tried our best to move him from his position of complete religious disbelief, but in vain.'

To so restless and questioning a soul, it was natural that the idea of republicanism should appeal, especially in a Norway which, for over thirty years, after the briefest period of independence from her old Danish yoke, had languished discontentedly under the suzerainty of a Swedish king and his appointed Norwegian cabinet. When therefore, in February 1848, the people of Paris rose against their king and, on the second day of the street fighting, 24 February, Louis Philippe abdicated and bolted to a villa in Surrey, and France proclaimed herself a republic, the effect on the young Ibsen, a fortnight short of his twentieth birthday, was explosive. According to Edmund Gosse, who once met and talked to Ibsen, this proclamation was 'the first political event that really interested him'. There was much more of the same kind to interest him in that tumultuous year. During the spring, revolution spread through Italy, touching Rome, Turin, Leghorn, Pisa, Florence and Milan. Even the mighty Austrian Empire was affected. On 13 March, a single day's rioting overthrew Metternich, a figure seemingly as impregnable as the Pope, if not more so, and gave Vienna to the people. At this news, even Venice bestirred herself and declared a republic. Later the same month there was rioting and bloodshed in Berlin as a result of Frederick William IV's delay in granting reform, and he was forced to permit the formation of a parliament. In May the Lombards rose and expelled their Austrian garrison. Nearer home, in response to the revolutionary feeling in Germany, the twin duchies of Schleswig and Holstein were up in arms.[6] To the young Ibsen, as to the young Wordsworth in 1789, it must have seemed that a new and glorious dawn was breaking for mankind.

Under the influence of these events, relates Due, Ibsen 'gradually became a full-blooded Republican. With him as inspiration social gatherings were arranged at which there was much jollification and speeches were made, with the ideals of republicanism as the leading theme. After the French pattern, we arranged a so-called "Reform Banquet", at which Ibsen made a fiery oration against all emperors and

6. Holstein was within, Schleswig without the confines of the German Confederation, but both had been governed by the King of Denmark continuously since 1490. The Danes were, in 1848, planning to incorporate Schleswig in their monarchy and sever its connection, long deemed indissoluble, with Holstein. German opinion was united in holding that the two Duchies must be subject to a single ruler. Confused and indeterminate fighting was ended by the intervention of the Powers only in 1852. King Frederik VII of Denmark had no male issue and by the Treaty of London that year it was decided that on his death Christian of Glucksburg should succeed him and rule in Denmark and the Duchies. This settled the matter until Frederik died in 1863, when the whole trouble flared up afresh.

kings, the vermin of society, and in defence of republicanism, the "only possible" form of government.'

It was in this exalted mood that Ibsen, during the summer of 1848, paid a short visit to his family in Skien – possibly his first since he had left them four and a half years before. We need not read any particular significance into his not visiting them during this period; he may well have had no holidays, and in any case probably could not afford the journey. We know nothing of what he found or felt on seeing his family again, nor how long he stayed. While he was there, however, the hopes that had been raised in him, as in so many others, by the revolutions of the spring began to be dashed one by one. In June there was civil war in the Paris streets, and Prince Windischgrätz turned his guns on Prague to crush the Bohemian rebellion. On 30 October, after Ibsen's return to Grimstad, the reactionary Jellačić defeated a Hungarian army marching to relieve Vienna against Windischgrätz on the plain of Schwechat. There was to be no more democracy in Vienna for nearly three-quarters of a century. In November, Frederick William IV dispersed the Berlin Parliament; in April of the following year he ruthlessly stamped out revolt in Saxony, Baden and Hanover; in June the French crushed Mazzini's Roman republic, despite a courageous defence by Garibaldi, recently returned from a nomadic existence in South America; and on 24 October, the Venetian republic also fell. Before long Louis Bonaparte was to stage a *coup d'état*, dissolve the Paris Chamber and make himself master of France.

Twenty-seven years later, Ibsen described his reaction to this volcanic upheaval in Europe.

It was a momentous era. The February revolution, the risings in Hungary and elsewhere, the Schleswig war – all this had a powerful and maturing effect on my development, long though it took for that process to unfold. I wrote resounding poems to the Magyars exhorting them in the name of freedom and humanity to continue steadfastly in the struggle against 'the tyrants'. I wrote a long sequence of sonnets to King Oscar [of Sweden and

Norway], mainly, as far as I can recall, entreating him to put aside all petty scruples and straightway, at the head of his army, to rally our brothers to defend the furthermost frontiers of Schleswig. Since I now, unlike then, doubt whether my winged appeals would markedly have assisted the cause either of the Magyars or of Scandinavia, it is probably fortunate that they remained in the semi-privacy of manuscript. But, my motives being so lofty, I could not refrain from expressing myself in a passionate manner, as befitted the mood of my poems, which, however, brought me but doubtful reward both from my friends and from those less amiably disposed towards me, being hailed by the former as demonstrating a bent for the unconsciously ridiculous, while the latter deemed it remarkable that a young person in my humble position should take it on himself to debate matters on which even they themselves did not presume to hold an opinion. I must in truth add that my conduct in more than one respect held out no great hope that society might count on any accession in me of civil virtues, the less so since I had, by reason of certain epigrams and caricatures, fallen out with individuals who deserved better of me and whose friendship I in fact valued. To sum up, while a great age thundered outside I found myself in a state of war with the little community within which, by the circumstances of my work, I sat imprisoned. Such was the situation when, preparing for my examination, I read Sallust's *Catiline*, and Cicero's speeches against the latter.[7]

The sonnets to King Oscar have, perhaps fortunately, disappeared, but two of Ibsen's exhortatory poems have survived: 'To Hungary', in which he comforts the Magyars with the assurance that, in years to come, their name will serve as a battle-cry for the new generation that will 'topple the pillars of tyranny', and 'Awake, Scandinavians!' a similarly unremarkable though lively piece, like inferior Kipling. Where, however, these contemporary rebels failed to inspire Ibsen to any uncommon literary achievement, the rebel who had died two millennia previously, and had been condemned by historians as an arrogant and misguided felon, succeeded. François Mauriac has written that a sinner is closer to a

7. Preface to the 1875 edition of *Catiline*.

saint than are the vast majority of harmless, middle-of-the-way mortals, because the requisite zeal and passion, and often even the selflessness, are there; it is simply that, perhaps through no fault of the individual, they are misdirected. The figure of the misguided reformer was one that was to fascinate Ibsen throughout his life, and the line of mighty, twisted figures that includes Brand, Julian the Apostate in *Emperor and Galilean*, Gregers Werle and John Gabriel Borkman began, in the ante-room of the apothecary's shop at Grimstad, with *Catiline*.

In his preface to the second edition published in 1875 Ibsen explained:

> My play was written at night. From my employer, a good and able man who, however, had no interests outside his work, I had virtually to steal free time in which to study, and from these purloined hours I thieved further moments in which to write. So I had little time left to me but the hours of night. I think this must be the unconscious reason why almost the whole action of the play takes place at night ... As may be seen, I did not share the two old Roman authors' opinion of Catiline's character and conduct, and I still incline to the view that there must have been something great, or at any rate noteworthy, about a man with whom so indefatigable and esteemed an advocate as Cicero did not dare to cross swords until events had taken such a turn that he could do so without fear of the consequences. It should also be remembered that there are few historical personages whose posthumous reputations have been more entirely dictated by their enemies than Catiline.

He wrote the play in the first three months of 1849, in blank verse, with occasional excursions into the rather unusual metre of rhymed trochees. Catiline, as portrayed by Ibsen, has a guilty secret; he once seduced a woman, who, in despair, drowned herself. Disillusioned with the corrupt rulers of Rome, he dreams of 'greatness, power and eternal fame'. His gentle wife, Aurelia, tries to dissuade him from mixing in politics, so that he can retire with her to a peaceful life in the country; but her influence is defeated by that of

Furia, the first of those domineering and destructive women whom Ibsen was to portray at intervals throughout his work: Margit in *The Feast at Solhaug*, Hjørdis in *The Vikings at Helgeland*, Rebecca West, Hedda Gabler, Hilde Wangel, Rita Allmers. She urges him to rebellion:

> I am your genius.
> I must lead you whithersoever you go.
> I am an image out of your own soul.

Furia then betrays his conspiracy, revealing herself to be the sister of the drowned woman. Finally, Catiline kills himself.

When in his later years Ibsen was asked what books he had read in his youth and which authors had influenced him, he tended to shy away from the question almost pathologically. Two of the few influences to whom he admitted were Ludvig Holberg and Oehlenschläger, and in 1880 he told Henrik Jæger that, as far as he could recall, they were the only two dramatists he had read when he wrote *Catiline*. Structurally, it is difficult to see what the play owes to either; it has nothing in common with the swift-moving, short-scene, colloquial comedies of Holberg, or with the static and ponderous tragedies of Oehlenschläger, though the latter may have served as a model poetically. The dramatist to whom the play seems to owe an obvious debt is one with whose work Ibsen can hardly have been totally unfamiliar even at that early stage in his career: Shakespeare. The character of Catiline himself has much in common with that of Brutus in *Julius Caesar*, and the scenes between Catiline and his fellow-conspirators, and that of his final suicide after his defeat in battle, seem plainly indebted to the same play. He could of course have learned Shakespeare's technique at second-hand, through the works of Schiller or, for that matter, through Oehlenschläger. But Miss Crawfurd, who guided Ibsen's reading so helpfully at this time, can surely not have omitted to draw Ibsen's attention to at least this fellow-countryman of hers; and although Ibsen's English, if it existed at all at this time, would certainly not have been good enough to read Shakespeare in the original, he would have had no difficulty in obtaining him in Danish translation.

Nevertheless, *Catiline* is far from being a mere pastiche. Apart from the considerable skill of the verse, a signpost to the flexible and muscular dramatic poetry that was to come in *Love's Comedy*, *Brand*, and *Peer Gynt*, the sharpness of the characterization, the continuous movement of the plot and, rarest of talents in a playwright, the ability to construct and develop not merely a character but a human relationship, are all evidence of uncommon maturity in a largely self-educated youth approaching his twenty-first birthday. Ibsen has rather touchingly described the emotions with which he re-read the play after a lapse of a quarter of a century.

I had almost forgotten the content, or anyway the details; but on reading it afresh, I found that it contained a good deal that I was still able to acknowledge, especially when one considers that it was my maiden play. Much that my later work has dealt with – the conflict between aspiration and capacity, between will and ability, the overlapping of tragedy and comedy, whether on a general or an individual scale – is already mistily indicated here.[8]

If, as has been argued, everything we write mirrors our internal conflict at the time we wrote it, it is possible to draw certain parallels between the content of *Catiline* and Ibsen's position at Grimstad during that winter of 1849. Like his hero, Ibsen must have been nagged by a sense of being insufficiently appreciated and an ambition for higher things; also, no doubt, by the consciousness of having shrugged off his responsibility towards a woman with whom he had had an affair. Perhaps, as some critics have suggested, the two women who contended for the possession of Catiline represented the conflict that takes place in every

8. loc. cit.

artist between settling for a peaceful life and the danger and uncertainty of an artist's career.

In this same preface to the second edition of *Catiline*, Ibsen recalled the enthusiasm with which Due and Schulerud received the news that he had written a play, and the efforts they made to launch it:

An occupation as incomprehensible to my associates as playwriting had of course to be kept dark; but a twenty-year-old poet cannot easily continue without confidants, and I therefore entrusted my guilty secret to two friends of my own age. We three built great hopes on *Catiline* once it was completed. First and most important, it had to be fair-copied so that, over a pseudonym, it might be submitted to the theatre in Christiania; after which it was to be offered to the public in print. One of my loyal disciples [Due] took it upon himself to produce a handsome and legible copy of my rough and uncorrected draft, a task which he performed so conscientiously that he did not omit a single one of the innumerable dashes which, in the heat of composition, I had employed whenever the appropriate expression had not immediately occurred to me. The other friend, whom I take leave to name since he is no longer among the living – Ole Schulerud, then a student, later a lawyer – went with this copy to Christiania. I still remember one of his letters, in which he tells me that *Catiline* has now been delivered to the theatre; that it will soon be performed, of that there can be no possible doubt, since the directorate of the theatre is composed of highly perceptive gentlemen; equally, it is beyond question that all the booksellers of the capital will compete for the honour of paying a good round honorarium for the first edition; the only problem, in his view, being to ascertain which will make the worthiest offer.

After a long and hopeful period of waiting, however, certain difficulties began to reveal themselves. The theatre returned the play to my friend with an exceedingly courteous but none the less conclusive letter of rejection. He then took the manuscript from bookshop to bookshop; but they, with one voice, all expressed the same opinion as the directors of the theatre. The best he could get was an offer to print the play for such and such a sum without any question of any money being paid to the author.

All this, however, far from dispelled my friend's confidence in ultimate victory. On the contrary, he wrote to me that what had happened was for the best; I would myself step forward into the limelight as publisher of my own drama; he would advance me the necessary money; the proceeds we would share, in anticipation of which he would take charge of all the business side – apart from the proof-reading, which he thought would be unnecessary, since the printer would have so beautiful and clear a manuscript to work from. In a later letter he declared that with such promising prospects in view he was thinking of giving up his studies entirely in order to devote himself wholly to the publication of my works; he thought I should have no difficulty in composing two or three plays a year, and by a sober reckoning the profit must in a short while enable us to make the journey we had so often agreed on, or at any rate discussed, across Europe to the Orient.

This was in October 1849. The previous month, an important and encouraging event had occurred for Ibsen; for the first time, a work of his appeared in print. It was a poem entitled 'In Autumn', and its publication was entirely thanks to Due who, on hearing Ibsen read the poem aloud, sent it to the *Christiania Post*, for which he acted as local correspondent. It was published as being by 'Brynjolf Bjarme', a pseudonym which Ibsen was to use for some time (*Catiline* was also to appear under it). When Due received the issue of 28 September containing the poem, he relates: 'I was very impatient for evening to come, when the shop would be quiet and I could show Ibsen the newspaper. Enthusiastically, and with a certain triumph at my friend's success, I displayed to him his first "poem in print". At first Ibsen turned quite pale with emotion, but soon a gush of joy streamed over his face.' In 1858 he was to recall the occasion in his poem 'Building Plans'.

Three letters which Ibsen wrote from Grimstad to Schulerud while the latter was trying to sell *Catiline* in Christiania have survived. The first, dated 15 October 1849, was evidently written as an apology for an impatient and suspicious earlier letter of the kind which Ibsen was often to pen in his maturer years, and which Schulerud, in obedience to Ibsen's expressed wish, must be presumed to have destroyed:

My dear friend!

Your last letter made me doubly happy, firstly because it promises a speedy outcome of our project, but even more because you have hereby proved yourself a true friend, by regarding my letter to you as a mere expression of impulse and over-enthusiasm. Such forbearance leads me to hope that you have imagined yourself in my position and realized how everything must have seemed to me. I am sure you will have guessed the frustration with which I have awaited every post-day, and how this put me in an unpleasant humour. Not being on the spot, I could not guess what was happening, and this uncertainty inevitably aroused a thousand doubts, all the more distressing because I could not in my heart believe that they could have any foundation.

Your letter has stilled every doubt I might have had concerning your conduct, and I should not be worthy of your friendship if I did not unreservedly withdraw anything I may have written which could cast doubt on the honesty of your intentions. I therefore beg you to forget the whole matter as something which can have no influence upon our future friendly relations, and I await an assurance of this in your next letter.

I have no time today to write more – Due asks me to thank you for the guitar, which he looks forward to receiving. I am equally grateful for the trousers – I had forgotten about them and thought they had slipped your memory too, but they are very welcome, as just now I have to save all I can. I have almost finished the first act of *Olaf Tr*. I think it will turn out really well, and hope this play will cause us less trouble than *C*.

> Best wishes,
> Your affectionate friend,
> Henr. Ibsen

P.S. Do me the favour of consigning my last letter to the flames. I hate to think of your having it.

Olaf Tr was probably to be about Olaf Tryggvason, a king of Norway (c. 995–1000) who was bred in Russia, became a Viking chieftain, led an invasion of England in 991 and, on the conclusion of peace, became a Christian and had the doubtful honour of being adopted as godson by King Ethelred II. He spread Christianity throughout Norway, by force where necessary, and even into Iceland and Greenland, before being killed in a battle against the Danes. He seems a promising subject for a play, and one would like to know what Ibsen would have made of him, especially in view of Ibsen's hostile attitude at this time towards state-established religions; but he never completed the work, and the fragment has not survived.

Twelve weeks later, on 5 January 1850, Ibsen again wrote to Schulerud:

My dear friend!

Your last letter contained news of *Catiline's* death sentence – it grieves me, but there is no use losing courage. You are perfectly right when you say that this apparent defeat must not be regarded as such. *C.* was only intended as a forerunner of the plans we agreed on in this field, and it may yet fulfil its purpose. I am absolutely of your opinion that it is wisest to sell the play, and I think its rejection, to judge from the theatre's reply, may turn out to our advantage rather than to our disadvantage, since it seems that it was not for any integral reason that it was not accepted. You must of course arrange the sale of the play at your own discretion; I would merely observe that it seems to me better to sell the publishing rights rather than have it printed at our own expense, since in the latter event we should have to pay a lot of money to cover the printing and, besides, would only gradually get any return from it, whereas in the former event we would receive an honorarium. However, you must do as circumstances suggest.

Now a little about my literary activity. As I think I told you, the first act of *Olaf T.* is almost ready; the little one-act play *The Norsemen*[9] has been revised, or rather will be – I am busy with it at the moment – and will in its new form deal with a broader theme than I had originally envisaged. I have used a few stories and descriptions from Telemark to write some short poems, adapted to fit well-known folk melodies, and have thus

9. Later adapted into *The Warrior's Barrow*.

had a shot at nationalistic writing. I have, too, half-completed a longish, perhaps rather over-dramatic poem entitled 'Memories of a Ball', which owed its existence to my supposed infatuation of last summer. But my most important work since you left has been a national-historical *nouvelle* which I have entitled *The Prisoner at Akershus*, and which treats of the sad fate of Christian Lofthuus. [A long paragraph follows telling Lofthuus's story].[10]

I think we should preface *Catiline* with some introductory remarks, and I therefore beg you to copy and insert the following:

FOREWORD

This play was originally intended for the stage, but the directorate of the theatre found it unsuitable for his purpose. Although the Author has grounds for supposing that the play's rejection does not stem from any integral defects, it is nevertheless not without a certain anxiety that he sets his essay before the public, from whom however he anticipates the forbearance for which a beginner may not unreasonably hope on his maiden appearance.

N.B. Please don't let any printing errors creep in. I should like to have the manuscript back, and should be grateful if you would let me have two copies of the play when it is ready . . .

Best wishes,

Your affectionate

Henr. Ibsen

The 'supposed infatuation of last summer' probably refers to a girl of nineteen named Clara Ebbell, to whom he had dedicated a poem that year entitled 'To the Star'. Neither it nor the longer 'Memories of a Ball' have much to recommend them beyond a technical facility; they are conventional adolescent poems of hopeless adoration, which rather suggest that Clara, a religious girl who disapproved of his free-thinking, did not reciprocate his feelings, at any rate with much passion. He remained in contact with her, how-

10. See p. 48.

ever, sending her poems from Christiania the following year, so that she cannot have rebuffed him completely.

Ibsen seems to have been somewhat timid as a suitor. 'He seldom expressed passion,' records Due. 'It was as though his spiritual life found expression exclusively, or at any rate essentially, through imagination and thought ... I got the impression that there was in his nature a deep-seated reluctance to lay bare his feelings. In particular, he had a notable talent for concealing his wants, so that they did not appear to bother him. Thus his acquaintances never found any cause to pity him, the less so since few of them fully comprehended his true circumstances. I, who was for a time his only confidant, sympathized with him deeply, and found it difficult to understand how, in his situation, he could be as merry and vital as he was.'

This timidity in relation to physical matters was to remain a feature of Ibsen's character. One of Reimann's sons who shared a room with him tells that he vividly remembered Ibsen going off in a sleigh 'at a spanking pace' to take some kind of apothecary's examination in Arendal. The man who gave him the lift could remember only one thing from the trip – 'the little chap was so scared, so dead scared, that he, the driver, had to laugh. They rode over some water. The ice boomed, as often happens in cold weather. But Ibsen got frightened and jumped out of the sleigh and ran for the shore. He wouldn't get back into the sleigh until it had crossed the ice.'

Occasionally Due seems to have succeeded in persuading Ibsen to indulge in the lighter side of life.

Now and then we arranged dance parties. Grimstad had no adequate locale for such entertainments, but we tackled the problem practically and shamelessly in the following manner. The moving spirits among us young people would approach in turn the good gentlemen who owned the largest houses and bluntly ask if we might hold a dance there. The kindly citizens of Grimstad usually granted permission, and with the assistance of two violins and a flute, home-mixed punch and negus, coffee or tea,

and cakes, our ball was ready. Several times I had exhorted Ibsen
to partake in these festivities, but important considerations had
compelled him to decline. The fact was that he had no evening
coat and, what was worse, had never danced and did not dare to
make his debut at a ball. The sartorial problem, however, was
solved by one of those with 'full wallets and empty heads' giving
him credit. This at first amazed Ibsen, but then he decided that
this confirmed his judgement of them, and when at the end of
the year he was presented with a bill for the garment, he merely
regarded this as providing further confirmation, saying in his
humorous way: 'First he is fool enough to give me credit, then
he's fool enough to expect me to pay the bill.' I can, though,
reveal that this debt of Ibsen's was fully honoured.

So now he was equipped to play the gallant, but the business of
inviting a partner and taking his place among the ranks of
dancers he found intimidating ... We sought, however, to instil
courage into Ibsen, and with the assistance of his lady and other
well-wishers succeeded in getting the couple launched into a
brisk gallop, not admittedly without its hazards in the early
stages, but with no sensational disasters; and soon it went
sweepingly, so that the situation was saved. Later he tried his
hand at other dances, with fair success.

It is interesting that Ibsen should have pretended that he
had never danced, since we know that, as a boy at Skien, he
had in fact been a keen dancer. Due adds: 'Ibsen was not
musical. When we had a sing-song, he would join in, but
incorrectly, since he had no ear.'

Of the projected *nouvelle*, *The Prisoner at Akershus*, referred to in Ibsen's last letter to Schulerud, a little over a
chapter has survived; this appears to have been all that he
wrote of it, although it is, in fact, the best thing he did at
Grimstad, matched only by perhaps a couple of scenes in
Catiline. But when a writer is twenty-one, poetry often seems
a more attractive medium than prose, and a fortnight after
he had mentioned *The Prisoner at Akershus* so excitedly to
Schulerud ('my most important work'), we find him turning
aside to compose an elegy in memory of his admired Adam
Oehlenschläger, who had just died at the age of seventy-one.

He sent this to Schulerud, explaining that he had composed it 'in melancholy ardour', and asking him to 'arrange to have it inserted in the *Christiania Post* as soon as possible'. It was printed there, rather belatedly, on 16 February.

The time had now come for Ibsen to make the final preparations for his matriculation examination, which would involve spending a term at a crammer's in Christiania. After six and a quarter years of boiling medicines and preparing plasters, he was to devote himself entirely to reading, painting and writing, and that exchange of ideas through discussion and debate which has always been the most valuable part of a university education. On 12 April 1850, at the request of a young lady named Sofie Holst, he wrote his last poem at Grimstad, 'Moonlight Wandering after a Ball'.

Hush! How still! No longer echo sounds of music and delight.
Now no voice, no violin breaks the soft silence of the night.

Westwards soon across the earth the moon her last still glance
    shall throw;
Earth that dreams in white oblivion 'neath the lilies of the
    snow.

Dance is ended; yet my eyes still see the dancers as they lead,
And are led in their sharp patterns swaying in a light sylphide.

Soon the moon will seek her valley, hands of sleep will close my
    eyes.
And my soul the sea of dreams will wander, winged with memories.

The same day, he wrote a farewell note in Christopher Due's album:

If friendship depended on constant companionship, ours would cease, but if it consists of mutual sympathy and the soaring of spirits in the same sphere, then our friendship can never die.

> Your affectionate friend,
> Henrik Ibsen

It was the custom for anyone leaving a job to burn his name and the date of his departure on some object. Such a branded inscription may be seen today on a cork drawer in the counter of the apothecary's at Grimstad (now the Ibsen Museum). It bears the statement like an epitaph: *Henr. J. Ibsen,* 15–4–50. The fifteenth was the day on which he officially terminated his employment; but it happened to be a Monday, and there is no record of any ship sailing eastwards from Grimstad that day. On Saturday 13 April, however, the *Prins Carl* left Grimstad early in the morning, and among the passengers whom it deposited at Brevik, not far from Skien, at 11.30 a.m. the same day, we find, in the list printed in the local newspaper *Adresse-Tidende for Brevik,* the name 'Ipsen'. He would have reached Skien by road the same afternoon or evening.

Ibsen had originally intended to proceed direct to Christiania from Grimstad without seeing his family, but before leaving he had received a letter from his sister Hedvig begging him to visit them en route. Ibsen at once agreed. 'He says', Hedvig explained in a letter to her cousin Hanna Stenersen, 'that he had always very much wanted to come here first, but didn't like to mention it because he didn't know if Father would approve.'[11] What lay behind these last seven words no one has ever been able to explain.

Ibsen stayed a fortnight with his family. They were one fewer than when he had left; Johan, the second son, had emigrated to California to seek his fortune in the goldfields. His letters home were to cease this year, and no more was ever heard from him; his family presumed him dead. Nicolai, the third son, had been dropped on the floor when a child, and the injury had affected him, making him abnormally shy and withdrawn. He, too, after failing in business, was to emigrate to, and die in, America. Ole, the youngest,

11. In her letters to Hanna around this time Hedvig refers thrice to letters from Ibsen, so he seems to have been corresponding with them at least fairly regularly up to the time of his departure from Grimstad. The break came later.

was not yet fifteen, and the only member of Ibsen's family with whom he could make any real contact was his sister Hedvig, three years his junior. During this stay, as she was to recall over half a century later, Ibsen took a long walk with her to Bratsberg and told her of his dreams. He wanted, he said, to achieve nothing less than complete fulfilment 'in greatness and in love'. 'And when you have done that?' she asked. 'Then,' he replied, 'I want to die.'

On 27 April he journeyed down to Brevik and sailed thence, with his schoolfriend Boye Ording, for Christiania, again in the *Prins Carl*. Not only did he never see his parents or any of his brothers again; he even ceased to write home. There has been much loose and unnecessary speculation as to the reason; Ibsen explained it clearly enough in a letter he wrote to his uncle Christian Paus in 1877 on Knud Ibsen's death.

> To uncomprehending eyes I know it looks as though I had voluntarily and deliberately cut myself off from my family, or at any rate permanently set a distance between myself and them; but I think I may say that impossible circumstances from a very early stage were the principal cause ... That I so seldom wrote home during those years of struggle was chiefly because I could not be of any assistance or support to my parents. I thought it vain to write when I could do nothing practical to help them; I stood in constant hope that my circumstances might improve, but that happened very late and not long ago ... I also felt a strong reluctance to come into close contact with certain spiritual trends then prevalent, with which I could feel no sympathy and a collision with which could easily have provoked unpleasantness, or at any rate an atmosphere of discord, which I wished to avoid.

The 'spiritual trends' were a reference to a priest named G. A. Lammers, who had become pastor at Skien in 1849. Lammers was a fervent evangelist who had become dissatisfied with the established state church, and by the following year he had decided to form a breakaway group. Ibsen's mother, sister and youngest brother, Ole, had all fallen under Lammers's spell and become strict pietists. To the free-thinking disciple of Voltaire such an atmosphere must have seemed peculiarly intolerable. His sister's defection appears particularly to have disturbed him. Nearly seventy years later, she wrote: 'When as a youngish girl I became gripped by the Lammers movement and became a dissenter, he greatly disapproved of this step. I think it was partly because of this that he never came back here.' Although she occasionally wrote to him over the next thirty years, it was only in old age that a close and warm friendship was renewed between them.

But no man can escape the roots of childhood. Skien remained strongly in Ibsen's mind. *Brand*, which he wrote in 1865, is full of memories of his birthplace; in 1869 he was to refer in a letter to Hedvig to 'the old home, to which I still cling fast by so many roots'; and when, in 1875, he sat down to write a preface to the second edition of *Catiline* and began to reminisce about Grimstad, Skien, too, came back to him and for the first time for over a quarter of a century he wrote a letter to his aged father. The letter is lost, but Knud Ibsen's reply has survived, with its pathetic expression of joy at hearing at last from his famous son: 'for I have not heard or seen anything of you, as you yourself say, for twenty-five years.' Unhappy memories have a more lasting influence than happy ones, and when Ibsen disembarked at Christiania from the *Prins Carl* on 28 April 1850 it must have been with a very firm resolve to renounce the past. He was not then to know, though it later became part of his philosophy, that whatever you turn your back on gets you in the end.

3

Ibsen at University
1850–51

THE Christiania which greeted Ibsen as a twenty-two-year-old student in 1850 was a small and, by any but the most humble standards, unimpressive town. Eighty years previously, at the time of the first official census in 1769, it had contained no more than seven and a half thousand inhabitants, and even now they numbered only thirty thousand. Few of the buildings stood higher than two storeys. There were no rail nor telegraphic communications, and no gas lighting in the streets, although pipes for the last-named amenity were just being laid. (London had known street gas-lighting for nearly forty years.) As late as 1855 a correspondent to *Morgenbladet* was to complain that the first sight to greet a visitor entering the city over the New Bridge was a vast dunghill, that the sewers were so inefficient that the filth in the streets reached to the edge of his galoshes, and that many gutters lay full, untouched and stinking throughout the summer. Between Piperviksstranden and Munkedamsveien lay a large swamp that, in warm weather, 'polluted the air with its foul water'.

The city contained few buildings of distinction. A handful remained from the eighteenth century, such as the military school, but these did not appeal to contemporary taste, which preferred the neo-classical, with pediments and pilasters – a style new to Norway, and exemplified in the new palace, started in 1823 and completed in 1848 on a hill a quarter of a mile outside the western limits of the city. Near the foot of this hill, the finishing touches were being applied to the university, the members of which were still in temporary housing on Prindsensgade. Fires had been so frequent that, by a recent ordinance, new buildings in the centre of the city had to be of brick; only in the outskirts could wooden houses be erected in the traditional style. But within the city limits, rebuilding was proceeding apace. Public edifices of varying degrees of hideousness were beginning to rise: St Olaf's Church, Holy Trinity Church (Trefoldighedskirken), Oskarshal pleasure palace, a fire station, a new prison and, ugliest of all, the eagerly awaited Parliament building, though this last was not to be completed until 1866. Constables had only recently replaced the old-fashioned watchmen, and foreign travellers were amazed to see iron-collared convicts from Akershus, where Christian Lofthuus had died, working in chain-gangs side by side with ordinary labourers.

On his arrival in the capital, Ibsen took lodgings with his friend Ole Schulerud in a house owned by an old lady called Mother Sæter at the corner of Vinkelgaden and Filosofgangen, and enlisted at a celebrated crammer's affectionately known as Heltberg's *studentfabrik*, or student factory, to prepare for his matriculation examination the following August. Many distinguished men passed through the doors of this remarkable establishment, to have the rough edges rubbed off their knowledge of logarithms and Latin grammar; and great was the variety of its occupants, 'a medley of human beings from all corners of the land and every stratum of society, from failed merchants and lamed cadets to middle-aged farmers and seamen whose love of adventure had driven them, first on long voyages to far-off lands, and then, when they did not find what they sought there, on a new long voyage to the golden shores of knowledge.' Heltberg himself, though by now crippled by gout and strangled by asthma, was a splendidly witty and original teacher in his dogskin breeches and fur boots; he is sympathetically remembered in many novels and books of reminiscences.

Of more immediate importance to Ibsen than his matriculation, however, was the fate of *Catiline*, which, after the various vicissitudes described above, had at length been published on 12 April, the day before Ibsen left Grimstad. This had been entirely due to the generosity of Schulerud who, having received a small legacy, had devoted it, with extraordinary faith, entirely to the publication of his friend's supposed masterpiece. *Catiline* was issued by a bookseller named P. F. Steensballe, on commission; and its appearance should have been something of an event in the Norwegian literary world, for, improbable as it may seem, it was the first Norwegian play to have been published since Henrik Wergeland's *The Venetians* seven years previously. The point underlines a state of affairs that was to dominate the next thirteen years of Ibsen's life, the fact that the Norwegian theatre was, at this time, totally dependent upon foreign plays, mainly Danish, French and German.

On the day after publication, a favourable notice of *Catiline* appeared in the handwritten student magazine *Samfundsbladet*. This review was written by the editor, a lively young man with few pretensions to original creative talent, but an unusually perceptive and widely read critic. His name was Paul Botten Hansen; he was three years older than Ibsen, and was to become a close friend – one of the few, apart from Due and Schulerud, that he was ever to know. Botten Hansen wrote that it was a pleasure to read a young poet who did not seek to pander to fashion. He discovered in the play 'a certain Shakespearean strength and earnestness', and especially praised the author for bringing about his hero's destruction as the result of inward spiritual conflict rather than of external circumstances.

A couple of weeks after Ibsen's arrival in Christiania, on 16 May, was printed the first, and indeed the only, review of *Catiline* to appear in any general newspaper: the *Christiania Post*, which had published the two poems 'In Autumn' and 'Elegy for Adam Oehlenschläger'. The reviewer, F. L. Vibe, was a classical philologist (a species with which the Scandinavian countries are heavily burdened), and he found much to criticize. The poet, he noted with regret, had departed from the historical facts and indulged in forced pathos, too often reminding one of *Love without Stockings*, that parody of neo-classical French tragedy by J. H. Wessel, reference to which recurs with such curious frequency in the articles and reminiscences of the time. However, he found the work not altogether lacking in merit. 'The author,' he concluded, 'has an unusual talent for raising himself to a tragic height and power, together with a rare gift for allowing the passions to emerge in full strength, and his language is of a purity such as we have seldom encountered.'

Not surprisingly, the book failed to attract the public. Of the edition of two hundred and fifty copies, only forty had been sold by the end of the year. Eventually, Ibsen and Schulerud resigned themselves to the book's failure. 'I remember,' wrote Ibsen in his preface to the second edition, 'that one evening, when our mutual household finances posed seemingly insuperable problems, we degraded this pile of print to the category of waste paper, and were fortunate enough to dispose of it to a pedlar. For the next few days we lacked none of the primary necessities of life.'

The failure of the play is not surprising. However much *Catiline* may have been in tune with the spirit of Europe in 1850, it was out of tune with the prevailing spirit in Norway. Ibsen's early biographer Gerhard Gran comments:

Norwegian spiritual life underwent an idyllic period during the eighteen-forties. Contemporary life was poor and lacking in impulse, all was peace, no danger threatened, people buried themselves in memories, and began for the first time to study their own history, their folk traditions, their national origins. Literature was a quiet lake, cut off from the oceans of the world, barely touched by the storms that raged outside ... *Catiline* is the only Norwegian work through whose pages there glows something of the tumultuous unrest and spirit of rebellion that gripped the world outside Norway in 1848.

Meanwhile Ibsen was, for the first time in his life, meeting people of his own age who knew more about literature than he did and who were, themselves, writers. One such was Paul

Botten Hansen. A gifted linguist with an immense range of reading, he was already beginning to acquire what was, during the next decade, to become one of the largest private libraries in the country. He had an extensive knowledge of European culture, and the following year was to write a long thesis on *The Young Germany*. What Coleridge was to Wordsworth, Botten Hansen was to Ibsen, opening up new horizons of thought and literature for him. Ibsen was to recall him affectionately as 'a man whose appreciation has always been precious and important to me, and to whom I hereby express my renewed gratitude'.

Another stimulating companion was a farmer's son from Telemark, whom he met at Heltberg's student factory Aasmund Vinje. Ten years older than Ibsen, and as heavily bearded, Vinje had a sharply satirical turn of mind and was a brilliant talker. At this early stage in his career, Vinje's powers were far from fully developed; he was inhibited by having to write in *riksmaal*, the formal language used for writing, which was based on Danish and was far removed from Norwegian conversational rhythms. *Landsmaal*, the language spoken by country people such as himself, was not yet accepted as a written form, though Vinje was to do much during the next few years to champion its use. This gap between the spoken and written tongues was a handicap to Norwegian writers which few foreigners can appreciate; to comprehend it, one must imagine a J. M. Synge or a Sean O'Casey forced to write in the language of Disraeli or Oscar Wilde.

Vinje was full of undigested knowledge, but he was a lively and exciting companion for Ibsen, whose radical opinions he shared to an even stronger degree. Another still more radical young man happened by chance to be living at Mother Sæter's, Theodor Abildgaard. Abildgaard was closely and vigorously associated with the workers' movement which Marcus Thrane had recently founded. Thrane, following a visit to Paris (where he had been imprisoned for two months as 'having no visible means of support') and to

the London of the Chartist manifesto, had been infected by
the English Christian Socialists' enthusiasm for the co-oper-
ative movement, and in eighteen months he had established
no fewer than 273 workers' associations in Norway, with
20,854 members, demanding among other things shorter
hours of labour, the abolition of trade monopolies and the
provision of small-holdings to reduce the competition for
employment. Abildgaard found a ready disciple in Ibsen,
and only a month after the latter's arrival in Christiania, on
29 May 1850, he and Vinje persuaded Ibsen to join them in a
political demonstration.

A German from Schleswig named Harro Harring, who
had fought for both the Greeks in their war of liberation
against the Turks, and the Poles in their rebellion against
the Russians, had come to Norway in 1849 to seek refuge in
his old age. There he founded and edited a radical paper,
The Voice of the People, and at the beginning of 1850 he had
published a play entitled *The American Testament* which
the authorities decided outstepped the limits of the freedom
of the press. An order was issued for his deportation, and on
the morning of 29 May the police entered his house and
escorted him on board a ship, where he was held prisoner
until it sailed. The news of this spread rapidly through the
town, and a protest was drawn up, signed by a hundred and
forty names, of which Ibsen's was one. This document
having been presented to the senior member of the cabinet,
the assembly made its way to the quay, where a deputation
went on board the steamer and addressed a few words to
Harring, who then appeared on deck and was hailed with
three times three cheers, followed by a cheer for Norway and
freedom. Ibsen, we are told, 'was from first to last an eager
participator in this affair'. It was the only political demonstration in which he was ever to take part.

In addition to Botten Hansen, Vinje, and Abildgaard,
there was a fourth student whom Ibsen met during these
first weeks in Christiania and who was, in the future, to have
a more important impact on his life than any of them.

Bjørnstjerne Bjørnson was younger than the others, only eighteen, the son of a country clergyman; but he attended Heltberg's only occasionally that spring, and it was some little time before he and Ibsen became closely acquainted (though he was among those who signed the Harring protest). In his poem 'Old Heltberg' (1873), Bjørnson remembered his young fellow-pupil:

> Thin and intense, with a face pale as gypsum
> Behind an immense coal-black beard, *Henrik Ibsen.*

During the Whitsun vacation Ibsen settled down to re-work the one-act play *The Norsemen* which he had begun at Grimstad. Botten Hansen, in his favourable review of *Catiline*, had expressed regret that Ibsen had not chosen a national-historical theme instead of setting his play in Ancient Rome. Ibsen himself appears to have had divided feelings at this time on the question of nationalistic literature. On the one hand, it was less than a year since he had written the passionate 'Sonnets to King Oscar' and 'Awake, Scandinavians!' But in his subsequent 'Elegy for Adam Oehlenschläger', while declaring that by the latter's death the Norse gods had lost their spokesman on earth, he at the same time expressed the hope that literature would now strike out on new roads, since poetry that sings of 'the enshrined past' could not answer the demands of the new age. None the less, *The Norsemen*, or, as he now re-entitled it, *The Warrior's Barrow*, turned out to be a dramatic poem very much in the mould of Oehlenschläger's historical tragedies. Set in Normandy during Viking times, it lacks any but the most meagre merits. Such virtues as it possesses are poetic rather than dramatic; like *Catiline*, it moves with considerable skill from rhymed to unrhymed verse, and contains several fine passages, notably those in which the hero proclaims his faith in the heathen gods.

It often happens, however, that a dramatist's inferior second play is accepted where his more original first effort has been rejected. Although patently less good than *Cat-*

iline, The Warrior's Barrow was more in tune with the current fashion of romantic nationalism, and the Christiania Theatre, which had turned down the earlier play, accepted this one for production that autumn. Ibsen had submitted it under the same pseudonym as before, Brynjolf Bjarme.

Encouraged by this, he started work almost immediately on a third play, in blank verse, again with a romantic-nationalistic theme, entitled *The Ptarmigan of Justedal*. In Andreas Faye's *Norwegian Tales* he must have read the story about a little girl who had been the only person in her valley to survive the Black Death; when, years later, people discovered her, she had become 'shy and wild as a bird', so that she came to be called the Ptarmigan of Justedal. In Ibsen's dramatization of the story, a young farmer's son, Bjørn, and an old hunter, Paal, are walking in the mountains. They begin to speak of the 'little people'; Paal tells how, recently, he took aim at a ptarmigan

> But in a trice the bird was gone
> And in its place a sprite crouched on the bough.

He asks Bjørn where he has been lately, and Bjørn replies that he has been exploring in Justedal. 'God forgive you!' cries Paal.

> No man has set foot there for many a year.
> It has lain desolate since the Black Death.
> Men say ghosts walk there, and the unburied dead
> Haunt its harsh hillsides.

Paal goes into the hut, and Bjørn, left alone, recalls sadly how

> She called me from her bough, winding her horn,
> Since when I have felt drawn towards that valley
> By some invisible power.

As he speaks, he hears the ptarmigan girl, Alfhild, singing.

Scene Two is in Bjørn's home. His father, a fierce old farmer named Bengt, has autocratically decided that Bjørn shall marry his foster-daughter, Mereta, though neither loves the other. To settle the matter he has summoned Mogens, a bibulous and pedantic priest, the forerunner of those other unsympathetic clerics whom Ibsen was to create: Pastor Strawman in *Love's Comedy*, the Provost in *Brand*, Pastor Manders in *Ghosts*, and the drunken Molvik in *The Wild Duck*. An old minstrel, Knud, appears, but Bengt drives him irritably away; when he tells Paal and Bjørn they are alarmed, for this Knud is a famous bard:

> He brings good luck to those who hearken to him.
> But if a man should drive him from his gate,
> His house is cursed.

Bjørn hears that his father plans to match him with Mereta, but will have none of it. He can only think of the ptarmigan who has bewitched him, and creeps secretly off to the unlucky valley of Justedal to find her.

In Act Two he meets her. Meanwhile, in Bengt's house, Mereta and a young friend of Bjørn's, Einar, pledge their love to each other. Old Bengt surprises them and warns Einar off.

At this point, half-way through the second act (the title page tells us that it was to consist of four), Ibsen abandoned the play, though he was to take it up again six years later and rewrite it as *Olaf Liljekrans*. *The Ptarmigan of Justedal* (like *Olaf Liljekrans*) has been over-readily dismissed by such few critics as have bothered to consider it; as far as it goes, in characterization and plot development, it was patently the best thing that Ibsen had yet done. The old people especially, Bengt the farmer, Paal the hunter, Mogens the priest, and Knud the minstrel, are splendidly drawn in brief, swift strokes, as is the atmosphere of sick enchantment. Why Ibsen stopped writing it we do not know; it may have been simply that, with his examination approaching, he felt he could no longer afford to spend time away from his studies.

Some time during the summer, Ibsen and Schulerud

moved from Mother Sæter's to a Fru Holt on Møllergaden. Living mainly on Schulerud's small allowance, they at first managed almost luxuriously, for it seems they were able to afford not merely dinners provided by their landlady, but even a servant. The latter, however, did not last long; and soon they had to drop the dinners too. Since it would have damaged their reputation, to say nothing of their credit, for it to be known that they could not afford a square meal, they made a habit of going out around dinner time and returning an hour or so later so that the other lodgers and the servants would imagine they were eating in town. They would then make do with coffee and sandwiches of cheese and sausage-meat. Botten Hansen tells that, although he saw Ibsen almost daily at this period, he had no inkling of the extreme poverty in which the latter lived; as at Grimstad, Ibsen's pride forbade him to reveal his circumstances to his friends. It was presumably during this summer or autumn that Ibsen and Schulerud took the desperate measure of selling their remaining copies of *Catiline* as waste paper.

Ole Schulerud's young brother Johan (the boy to whom Ibsen had, in Grimstad, been stingy with the liquorice) was staying with them now. The three inhabited a tiny room with space for only two beds, one of which the Scheluruds had to share. Johan remembered the three of them, Ole's tiny legacy having been exhausted on the publication of *Catiline*, as being 'permanently poor', and Ibsen as 'dark and unapproachable. I didn't like him, and I could see no evidence that he liked me. Small of stature, with an unattractive, square face.' Occasionally, Johan recalled, they would have parties with boston[1] and toddy, at which Botten Hansen and Abildgaard were frequent guests, and on these occasions Ibsen would be 'much more talkative and agreeable than at other times'.

However, a young man's first year at university is often spent in circumstances of comparative want, and that summer of 1850 must, in the main, have been a happy one

1. A kind of whist.

for Ibsen, rejoicing in his new friends, the liberating atmosphere of university life and the knowledge that a work of his
was to be presented at the country's leading theatre. Not
many youthful playwrights have been able to claim the
honour of seeing their first play printed and their second
accepted for production shortly after their twenty-second
birthday. Admittedly there came a slight setback in August;
Ibsen failed his matriculation. His tutor at the crammer's,
Thore J. Lie, wrote him a good reference, saying that he had
a 'right faithful and retentive memory, assisted by happy
natural gifts', but in no subject did he get the maximum
mark of 1, and in only one, German, did he even succeed in
achieving 2, or 'Very Good'. In most subjects, including Norwegian composition, he scored a moderate 3; on the three
Latin papers he got 3, 4, and 5 respectively; and in both
Greek and mathematics he failed with 6, so that his average
over the whole examination was no more than 3·67. But his
creative writing must already have seemed to him more
important than his university studies, for he never bothered
to attempt the Greek or mathematics papers again, although
in view of the papers which he had passed he was entitled to
style himself *Student* Ibsen. He continued to attend lectures,
but medicine, which he had originally intended to follow,
had apparently lost its interest for him; he now studied only
literature and aesthetics. He joined the student literary club
which had been founded the previous year, and made the
required inaugural speech, prefacing it with a recital of
seven of his own sonnets.

One would like to know what Ibsen was reading at this
time, but neither he nor his friends have left any record of
this. He may, as many have assumed, have continued to read
Kierkegaard, but it is by no means certain that he did. Such
evidence as there is of Kierkegaard's possible influence on
Ibsen's writing does not appear until over ten years later. It
has, similarly, been asserted that Ibsen probably studied
Hegel at this time, because Hegelian philosophy was now
sweeping Europe and the new professor of philosophy at the

university, M. J. Monrad, was a disciple of Hegel; but we have no evidence that Ibsen ever read a line of Hegel, and if he did, he may well, like Kierkegaard (cf. the latter's journal for 1843) have found Hegel 'merely comic' with his 'eternal hinting and deceiving'. One author who did make an impact on him, however, was the Danish poet, philosopher, critic and dramatist Johan Ludvig Heiberg (1791–1860), whom Ibsen was to meet in Copenhagen the following year and who was one of the very few writers from whom Ibsen, in later life, confessed to having learned something. Heiberg's influence was at its height in Scandinavia in 1850, and he was much discussed in the circles in which Ibsen moved; moreover, there is clear evidence in the drama criticisms which Ibsen was shortly to write that he was well acquainted with Heiberg's little book *On Vaudeville*. But, like so many young men who find themselves during their first year at university in stimulating company after years of forced reading, Ibsen may not have devoted overmuch time to books, and in any case he seems, in common with many dramatists and novelists, not greatly to have enjoyed or comprehended the abstractions of philosophy.

That summer and autumn he also wrote a number of poems. Twelve of these he copied neatly on to light blue paper in the scratchy, difficult, sharply slanted handwriting which we find in his early letters and manuscripts (and which contrasts so remarkably with the lucid bold copperplate of his maturity), and posted to Clara Ebbell at Grimstad. 'In sending you the enclosed writings,' he wrote stiffly in the short note which accompanied them, 'it is my hope that the mood which evoked these poems may serve as an excuse for the observations expressed therein, which might partly be misinterpreted by others and by you. I beg you to forgive me for not being able to refrain from adding these words, probably the last that I shall ever address to you.'[2]

2. In fact he wrote to her once more, the following February, enclosing a poem, 'To a Troubadour'. Shortly afterwards she married a wealthy man twice her age.

The poems included the sonnet sequence which Ibsen had read as a preface to his inaugural speech at the Students' Union, and three romantic trifles entitled 'In the Night' (which dates from Grimstad), 'Youthful Dreams' and 'Among the Ruins'. Of these, 'In the Night' and 'Among the Ruins' are conventional lyrics, and 'Youthful Dreams', although skilfully composed in rhymed stanzas, contains no original thought or idea. The sonnets, however, were much the best and most complex poems that Ibsen had written up to that time. On the lake of life, he says, there glide two ships, sailing in opposite directions. One, a merchantman laden to the waterline, rows slowly but safely in the lee of the shore; the other, all sails set, entrusts itself to the winds and tosses perilously upon the waves. Each of us must choose to which ship he will entrust his life. If we choose the second, the ideal instead of the material, our voyage will be hard and uncertain, and our reward will probably come late; but it is better to be like the swan, which discovers the joy of song only in its last moments, than to find those joys early and then lose our way, 'and wander lost across life's burning sands'. Over the next fifty years, Ibsen was to return again and again in his work to this theme, of the choice that faces man between idealism and compromise.

Of still greater interest are the two other poems which Ibsen sent to Clara Ebbell: 'The Miner' and 'The Bird and the Trapper'. They were the only two poems of this group which Ibsen retained for inclusion in the volume of collected verse that he published as his farewell to that medium in 1871. With the sonnets, they represent an important departure for Ibsen as a poet. Hitherto, his poems had been lyrical – except for the inferior, Kiplingesque exhortations inspired by the political events of 1848. But the sonnets, 'The Miner', and 'The Bird and the Trapper' are all dramatic poems, in the sense that the poet, instead of merely recording his emotions, dramatizes them, as one dramatizes an idea for a play; unlike his earlier, lyrical poems, they create strong visual images. The English poet whom Ibsen, in his shorter pieces, most closely resembles is Thomas Hardy (a writer with whom he had, of course, much in common when he turned to prose). Like Hardy, Ibsen was an accomplished lyricist but at his best as a poet when writing dramatic verse, whether in the form of dramatic monologues or of sharply told anecdotes. 'The Miner' is an example of the first category, 'The Bird and the Trapper' of the second.

Barely half a mile from Ibsen's childhood home at Venstøp was an iron mine, only just below ground surface. The noise from it must, when the wind was right, have been audible at the house, and as a child he must surely have gone and watched the men working there. The subject of the miner had attracted other poets: Oehlenschläger had written a poem on the theme, and so, in 1811, had the Swedish poet Erik Gustaf Geijer; but where Oehlenschläger had been attracted by the mystery of the darkness, and Geijer by the peace, Ibsen had been fascinated by the hard and remorseless toil. All of us who write poems, however badly, write at least one in adolescence or early manhood which foretells our future, and with Ibsen, that poem was 'The Miner':

> Groan and thunder, mountain wall,
> Before my heavy hammer blow.
> Downwards I must carve my way
> Till I hear the iron ore sing.
>
> Deep in the mountain's lonely night
> The rich treasure beckons me,
> Diamonds and precious stones
> Among the red branches of the gold.
>
> Here in the darkness there is peace,
> Peace and rest for eternity.
> Heavy hammer, break me the way
> To the heart-chamber of what lies hidden there . . .
>
> When I first entered here
> I thought in my innocence:
> 'The spirits of the dark will solve for me
> Life's obscure riddles.'

No spirit has yet taught me that strange answer.
No sun shines from the depths.

Was I wrong? Does this path
Not lead to the light?
But the light blinds my eyes
If I seek it in the mountains.

No, I must go down into the dark.
Eternal peace lies there.
Heavy hammer, break me the way
To the heart-chamber of what lies hidden there.

So blow follows blow
Till he sinks weak and tired.
No ray of morning shines.
No sun of hope rises.

'The Bird and the Trapper' anticipates, to English ears, the manner of a poet with whom, again, Ibsen had more in common than might at first appear – D. H. Lawrence:

Once when I was little
I was running in my father's garden.
The bird was singing its morning song
From its high branch and picket fence.

And I cut from the pine-branch
An ingenious bird-trap.
Before I can count ten
The bird sits there inside it!

And I carried with cruel delight,
Quickly, the trap into the house.
Frightened the bird with my angry
Glance, with my cries and threats.

When I had thus amused myself
And stated my cruelty,
I put the cage on the table;
Cautiously opened the door.

Oh, how it uses its wings!
It is offered life and freedom.
It would soar high to the light
But – crushes itself against the window pane.

You are revenged, cruelly revenged.
Now a power has trapped me
In a cage, where I can only flutter crazily.

And an eye stares at me
Coldly and scornfully through the bars.
This glance confuses my soul.
Fear makes my body shake.

And when I think I see
The path that leads to freedom,
I sink with broken wings
From my dreamed soaring.

Henrik Jæger tells that Ibsen planned during this first year in Christiania to publish a volume of verse, but gradually rejected poem after poem from his Grimstad days until there was hardly anything left. He no longer wanted to write poems of mood, but poems of ideas; and it was upon the latter kind, beginning with those quoted above, that he was to concentrate during the remainder of his time in Christiania.

On 26 September 1850 came the eagerly awaited production at the Christiania Theatre of *The Warrior's Barrow*. The heroine, Blanka, was performed by a young actress named Laura Svendsen; later, under her married name of Laura Gundersen, she was to become one of Norway's most famous actresses and was to create several of Ibsen's greatest roles, including Ellida in *The Lady from the Sea* and Gunhild Borkman. Ibsen, extremely nervous, hid himself, we are told, in the darkest corner of the theatre; but the play, surprisingly, was well received, and was repeated twice that autumn.

1850, then, had been a year of poetry. 1851 was to be primarily a year of journalism. Ibsen continued, naturally, to write poetry, as an undergraduate should; but he needed another medium as outlet for the combativeness which was so important a part of his character. An opportunity arose when, in the New Year, he found himself chosen by the Students' Union to become editor of their handwritten magazine, *Samfundsbladet*, in succession to Paul Botten Hansen, probably through the latter's influence.

Ibsen edited *Samfundsbladet* for nine months, but with decreasing assiduousness; in the first quarter of the year he produced three numbers, in the second quarter only one, and in the third quarter none at all. The reason for this was that his energies gradually became absorbed in a more exciting project which Botten Hansen and Vinje had just started, a new, independent literary and political weekly of their own. Their inspiration and model for this was the Danish magazine *The Corsair*, which Meïr Aron Goldschmidt had founded in Copenhagen; Vinje was a great admirer of that neurotic, battling controversialist who, like Vinje himself, despised all party ties and smote around at everyone and everything (among his targets had been such respected figures as Heiberg and Kierkegaard). An advertisement issued in Christiania on 5 March 1851 announced that the new magazine would contain, among other delights, 'Poems by Brynjolf Bjarme'; and since, following the production of *The Warrior's Barrow*, Ibsen was now allowed free tickets to the Christiania Theatre, he was also to write the drama criticisms. The magazine had no name. In place of a title, it carried on the front page of the first issue a picture of the main square of Christiania, Stortorvet, with a man in several grotesque postures, on foot and on horseback, eyeing the world satirically. Subsequently the same man was shown in the Storthing gallery alertly listening to the parliamentary debates and taking notes. As a result the magazine came to be known as *Manden*, 'The Man'.

For the next nine months, Ibsen busied himself with drama criticism and political and topical commentaries, as

well as with editorial and sub-editorial work and an occasional, and by no means unskilful, caricature. On 13 April
he published a review of a modern German play, Karl Gutzkow's *Zopf und Schwert*, which is interesting on two
grounds; it underlines how inadequate he found even at this
early stage in his career the trivia of Eugène Scribe, the most
popular and esteemed playright of the day (he calls Scribe's
plays 'dramatic candy-floss'),[3] and shows that he was
already aware of the possibilities of drama written to be read
rather than staged, the genre of which Alfred de Musset was
the contemporary master. Fifteen years later Ibsen, like de
Musset, was temporarily to abandon stageable drama for the
drama of the study and in so doing was to write what many
people regard as his two greatest and most theatrically exciting plays.

From May until August, Vinje was away on holiday, and
in his absence Ibsen took over the political commentary of
The Man, which the editors now decided to rename *Andhrimner*, after the cook who prepared the food for the gods
in Valhalla. On 18 May he reported a debate in the Storthing on the repeal of the usury law, which allowed money-
lenders to fix their own rates of interest for short-term loans
without security. Ibsen singled out for special scorn
A. B. Stabell, the member for Akershus and editor of the
then Liberal newspaper[4] *Morgenbladet*, who that year had
left the opposition party and joined the government, and
had delivered himself of the unfortunate remark that 'it
would be improper for educated men to listen to the clamour
of the rabble and allow themselves to be influenced by it'.

3. Ibsen told Henrik Jæger in 1887 that 'he of course saw much
Scribe in his youth, but that, dramatically, he then rated the elder
Dumas higher'. In an article printed on 4 May Ibsen dismissed
Scribe's *La Famille Riquebourg* and *Une Chaumière et son cœur* as
'two old plays that ought long ago to have been regarded as dead and
buried'.

4. It was to go Conservative in 1859, largely because of the foundation that year of a 'Reform Club' which it feared might be used for
revolutionary ends.

'These words,' commented Ibsen, 'were uttered in this year of grace 1851 by Herr Stabell, that same Stabell who for so many years has reiterated his faith in the infallibility of popular opinion ... Stabell's conduct reminds one of that resilient English priest who set his mind on dying, as he had lived, the guardian of his parishioners' souls, forswearing Catholicism under Henry VIII, re-embracing it under Mary, re-forswearing it under Elizabeth, re-embracing it yet again under James, and thus achieving his ambition.' Ibsen accompanied this article with an excellent caricature showing an unfortunate debtor being relieved of his clothes by two smiling usurers.

The next week, on 25 May, he contributed to *Andhrimner* a general theatrical article on a theme he had already touched upon in a review of Rossini's *William Tell*: the tendency to underrate the importance of libretti in opera. Ibsen never had much ear for or appreciation of music except in its simplest forms, such as folk song, and liked opera mainly for its dramatic quality, so that a bad libretto offended him more than it would musically minded spectators. The occasion of these observations was Bellini's opera *Norma*, about a Roman pro-consul, Severus, who, after seducing a priestess, Norma, and giving her two sons, deceives her with a temple maiden named Adalgisa. Ibsen saw it performed on 20 May, and within ten days wrote a parody, also entitled *Norma*, in which the characters were members of the Norwegian Storthing. Some ten pages long, it was published anonymously in *Andhrimner* in two instalments, on 1 and 8 June. A chorus of Druids (members of Parliament) is worshipping at the shrine of Freedom, which they have sworn to guard. Severus (Stabell) enters as they leave, and begins an eloquent speech in praise of Freedom; then he finds he is alone, and says he could have spared all that rubbish. Adalgisa, his present love (the Government), enters, and accuses him of still secretly loving Norma (the Opposition). Severus replies that she was merely a youthful passion, a foolish dream, of whom he is now well cured. Norma now enters

with her two children by Severus (votes of 'No confidence'[5]
in the Government); abandoned by their father, she
laments, they seem certain to die. Severus enters to her; she
upbraids him, and he begs the stage manager, for decency's
sake, to lower the curtain. When it rises again, the Druids
are asleep, although the day is well advanced, 'since, as is
well known' (the stage direction informs us), 'they are always
somewhat behind the time'. Norma raises her dagger to kill
Severus, but the Prime Minister 'appears in the form of an
angel and transforms Severus into a demi-god, or, as the
modern term is, a minister of the crown'. So all ends happily.

Norma was not intended to be performed, nor does it ever
appear to have been; yet it is not without significance in any
study of Ibsen's work. Written in brilliantly rhymed verse,
rather reminiscent, to an English reader, of the best of
R. H. Barham's *Ingoldsby Legends*, it was, if we except the
Grimstad lampoons, Ibsen's first essay at satirical verse, and
was a pointer to what was to come. Of his next ten plays, four
(*St John's Night, Love's Comedy, Peer Gynt,* and *The
League of Youth*) were conceived as satires, and a fifth,
Brand, was primarily regarded as such when it first appeared, although to modern readers (as with *Peer Gynt*) the
satire has dwindled and the tragedy remains.

On 8 June, in the issue that contained the final instalment
of *Norma*, Ibsen contributed two further parliamentary
commentaries, the second of which he illustrated with
another admirable caricature, of a man trying to push a pig
towards its trough while the pig resists, indignantly complaining: 'Leave me alone, I can find my own way!' These
commentaries, like his theatre articles, are uncommonly

5. Alarmed by the growing strength of the workers' movement
under Marcus Thrane, Stabell had, when in opposition, dropped the
vote of no confidence which he had been generally expected to move,
and which would almost certainly have been carried. Ibsen believed,
probably correctly, that Stabell was putting personal ambition before
political integrity.

lively and pungent pieces, and leave one to reflect how fortunate it was that no newspaper editor had the imagination to offer the young writer a position on his staff. The delights of journalism often seem more attractive to an undergraduate than those of creative writing, especially when he is near the starvation line, and, as we shall see, Ibsen was to snatch eagerly at the first salaried post that was offered to him. But *The Man* and its successor, *Andhrimner*, aroused an astonishing lack of interest among the students and citizens of Christiania (they never achieved even a hundred subscribers) so that it is quite possible that no newspaper editor in Christiania even read it; and subordinate journalists in a small town have their own mouths to think of without recommending lively young fellows who might jump ahead of them. In any event, journalism was poorly developed in Norway at this time; even the Christiania dailies such as *Morgenbladet* contained only four pages, including one of advertisements, and read like the more unprepossessing kind of provincial news-sheet.

All his articles and reviews had hitherto been unsigned; but before June was out, the name of Henrik Ibsen appeared in print for the first time, beneath two songs written for the gathering of students from the various Scandinavian countries which took place in Christiania that month. They are lively and agreeable lyrics of an undemanding kind, which stood up well to those composed for the occasion by established poets such as Welhaven, Munch and Jørgen Moe, and attracted favourable attention. The following month, July 1851, the pseudonym Brynjolf Bjarme was printed for the last time, over a long ballad (of a hundred and seventeen verses!) entitled 'Helge Hundingsbane', published in *Andhrimner*. From now on, Ibsen was to use his own name.

'Helge Hundingsbane' appeared in three parts, on 6, 13, and 20 July, and the day after the publication of the first instalment (though the events were unconnected) Ibsen found himself in trouble. In addition to his work for *The*

Man, *Andhrimner*, and *Samfundsbladet*, Ibsen had been
contributing to the radical newspaper *Arbejderforeningernes
Blad*, which had been edited since the beginning of the
year by his friend Theodor Abildgaard. Unfortunately we
do not know which of the articles in this newspaper were
written by Ibsen, since all contributions were unsigned
and no manuscripts have survived. He had also been helping Abildgaard with a local workers' Sunday school, presumably, since he was a free-thinker, in general rather
than religious subjects. On 7 July the police raided
the newspaper office, arrested Abildgaard and Marcus
Thrane, the workers' leader, and took away as many manuscript articles as they could lay hands on in order to identify
and act against the authors. Ibsen was saved only by the
quick thinking of the compositor, who crumpled up a
number of manuscripts and threw them on the floor, where
the police rather indolently took them to be waste paper.
These included all of Ibsen's unprinted contributions and,
whether for lack of evidence or because they were only
interested in the big fish, the authorities took no action
against him. Thrane and Abildgaard spent three years in
prison awaiting trial, and then served four-year sentences;
by the time they were released, in 1858, their movement lay
in ruins. Thrane's downfall bears a resemblance to that of
his predecessor among Norwegian champions of liberty,
Christian Lofthuus, and it is ironical that Ibsen, who was
himself to become a famous champion of liberty, should
have had such humiliating connections with them, fathering
an illegitimate child on to the granddaughter of the one
and, as it were, denying the other. A bolder spirit than Ibsen
might have declared himself and accompanied his friends to
prison; but Ibsen's courage, throughout his life, was limited
to the written word. He was, as the man who gave him the
lift from Grimstad across the ice had noticed, timid of physical danger.

The Sunday school closed, as a rather pathetic announce-
ment informed the pupils, 'since Stud. Ibsen does not feel

able to conduct it unassisted'. When it restarted in October, Ibsen was turning to other fields of activity, and Vinje took his place. Thus ended Ibsen's brief career as a Sunday school teacher.

During July and August the theatre was closed for the summer, and Ibsen, despite the fright he had been given, concentrated on political commentaries. But on 28 September 1851 *Andhrimner* folded, after thirty-nine issues. Despite the vigour and vitality of its contributions, it had steadily lost money, and eventually the publisher, Axelsen, decided that he could not afford to continue. Ibsen, who had a long memory, was to caricature him unkindly in *The League of Youth* in 1869, thinly disguised as Printer Aslaksen, a figure whom he also introduced into *An Enemy of the People* in 1881. The little magazine reads excellently, even at this distance of time, and it is a sad comment on the apathy of the Christiania students that it should never have succeeded in mustering even a hundred regular subscribers.

Ibsen now found himself at a period in life when three or four careers seemed to beckon to him, none of them very enticingly. He had given up his early ideas of becoming a doctor or a painter. He had completed two plays, but although one had been published and the other performed, neither had achieved any real success. The theatre as such does not appear particularly to have excited him. His dramatic reviews of 1851 hardly ever say anything interesting or constructive about the actual staging or performances, which usually receive only a short paragraph of conventional and uncritical praise. In the ordinary course of events he would probably have continued with his studies for another three, four, or even five years in the leisurely Scandinavian manner, or perhaps, if he could not make the necessary money on the side, have sought a job in journalism. He had written few poems during the nine months he had been working on *Samfundsbladet*, *The Man*, *Andhrimner*, and *Arbejderforeningernes Blad*; only half a dozen are known to have come from his hand during this time, most of those that appeared in print dating from the previous year. He had left *Olaf Tryggvason* and *The Ptarmigan of Justedal* both uncompleted. Play-writing can hardly have seemed to hold out any possibilities of a livelihood in a country where nearly all the actors were Danish, and where the capital itself was so small that even a successful serious play could scarcely hope to achieve more than half a dozen performances. It was chance, not inner compulsion, that at this particular juncture determined that Ibsen's career was to be in the theatre.

The man singled out by fate to be her instrument in this operation was a forty-one-year-old composer and violinist named Ole Bull. Born in Bergen in 1810, Bull had attended university at Christiania, ostensibly to study theology, but had devoted most of his time there to music and political agitation. Then, during a visit to Paris, he heard Paganini play, and immediately, with the impulsiveness which characterized his whole life, conceived the ambition of becoming a great violinist. He could afford little in the way of tuition, far less the expense of studying in a foreign conservatoire; nevertheless, despite being virtually self-taught, he developed a brilliant technique and, while still a young man, achieved international fame, not least through performances of his own works and arrangements. From 1843 to 1845 he spent two years in the United States, where his talents were particularly admired.

In the summer of 1849 Bull returned to his native Bergen and gave a series of concerts there. During this visit he learned that the citizens, infected by the widespread desire in Norway to develop a specifically national culture, were considering the project of founding a Norwegian National Theatre in their town; and they asked Bull, as their most famous living citizen, to lend his support. Bull, an erratic, attractive, ebullient character with a passion for idealistic causes (in 1848 he had waited on Alphonse Lamartine, with a Norwegian flag in his hand, to express the sympathy of the Norwegian people with the new Republic), at once agreed. The town already possessed a charming theatre, built in 1799 by the then flourishing local amateur dramatic society on a patch of raised ground overlooking the water, and capable of holding eight to nine hundred people. Bull, acting on behalf of his sponsors, leased it for the winter of 1849–50, and on 23 July 1849 he inserted an advertisement in the local newspaper *Bergenske Blade* inviting applications from anyone who wished to join as an actor, or to contribute in any other way. 'Those Ladies and Gentlemen,' the advertisement stated, 'who number among their accomplishments singing, instrumental music, acting, or national dancing, will be considered for engagement. Original dramatic and musical works are invited, and will be rewarded as circumstances permit.'

Lorentz Dietrichson, later to become a close friend, and also an enemy, of Ibsen, was a boy in Bergen at the time, and has described the response. 'From crofts and respectable villas, from factories and from the street itself, they came milling forth, labourers, kitchen-maids, errand-boys and crones ... Every scullery girl who could sing a note, every artisan who could recite a poem, sang, declaimed or acted, each convinced that he or she was destined to become a classical stage lover or a prima donna.' Even an old aunt of Dietrichson's applied, and was accepted, despite the fact that the absence of a front tooth rendered her speech somewhat indistinct; the theatre generously acquired a tooth for her and, when her engagement was terminated, less generously demanded the tooth back. Dietrichson recalled how he and his fellow schoolboys would wait for Bull outside the theatre and follow him cheering to his home where, never the man to miss an opportunity for a speech, he would address them from a first-floor window, promising 'to offer everything he possessed for the Norwegian Theatre, and vowing that as long as he had a farthing in his pocket and a drop of blood in his heart, he would consecrate them to the Theatre and to

Old Norway – speeches full of bombast and rant, but, at the time, most assuredly uttered from the heart. That a short while later he declared himself prepared to consecrate his last farthing and drop of blood to Oleana[6] on the other side of the globe did not abate our enthusiasm for him.'

From all these applicants Bull selected a company whose inexperience was matched only by their willingness to learn, and on 2 January 1850, the Norwegian Theatre held its first public performance. During the next five months, before the theatre closed for the summer on 2 June, twenty-seven performances were given, comprising sixteen different plays, eight of one act and eight of two or more acts. The enthusiasm in the town remained great; as early as 22 December 1849, before the season had even opened, Bull wrote to his wife that all seats had been taken for the twenty performances so far planned.

However, as was inevitable in so small a town (Bergen then contained only 25,000 inhabitants), no bill could be played for more than two or at the most three performances, and the income from the sale of seats proved insufficient to cover expenses. In September 1851, accordingly, Ole Bull went to Christiania to petition the Storthing to give the National Theatre in Bergen a monetary grant. His request was turned down. This refusal sparked off a violent debate throughout the country, and nowhere were the pros and cons of the matter more hotly argued than among the students of Christiania. When the University Literary Society debated the issue, a poet named Andreas Borchgrevink read a scornful paper on 'A Visit to the National Theatre at Bergen' in which he poked fun at the limitations and inexperience of Bull's company. After he had concluded, Ibsen rose and delivered an eloquent speech in Bull's defence. His words are unfortunately not recorded, but an eye-witness has stated that 'his countenance spoke the unmistakable language of anger'. It was almost certainly this speech that

6. A socialistic community which Bull unsuccessfully tried to found in Pennsylvania.

first brought the young Ibsen to Ole Bull's notice. The student supporters of the Norwegian Theatre promptly took further action. As a protest against the Storthing's decision, a motion was put before the Students' Union that a 'musical evening' be arranged to raise funds for the new enterprise. After a fiery debate the proposal was carried by a large majority.

On 15 October 1851, accordingly, a grand concert was held in Christiania. The house was full, over a thousand people somehow managing to fight their way in; many had to be turned away. Ole Bull, naturally, performed, and songs were sung by Emma Dahl, a famous operatic artiste of the day, and by the three choral societies of the capital, representing the students, the mercantile class and the manual workers respectively. Ibsen contributed two pieces, a prologue in nicely rhymed pentameters, read, according to *Morgenbladet*, 'with deep feeling and natural freshness' by Laura Svendsen, the young actress who had played Blanka in *The Warrior's Barrow*, and a choral piece, which the three choirs sang together to 'a powerful and impressive setting by Ole Bull'. Both of Ibsen's compositions were praised in the press, and down in Telemark the *Skien Correspondent* proudly reported the success of the local boy, not forgetting to add that 'Herr Ibsen is a son of Knud Ibsen, merchant of this town'.

The tickets were evidently very cheap, for the net takings amounted to no more than £75; but even that was an appreciable contribution to the Norwegian Theatre's resources. The occasion was, though, to have a much further-reaching effect. Bull met Ibsen, was impressed by him, and offered him a job. The salary was humble indeed: five pounds a month. But the prospect of being able to abandon Greek and mathematics (the two subjects which he still had to pass in order to matriculate), and of actually being paid to write, must have seemed irresistible. Barely a week after the concert, he said good-bye to Botten Hansen and Vinje, packed his few belongings and departed by steamer for Bergen. On

26 October *Bergenske Blade* listed, under the heading NEW ARRIVALS IN THE CITY, the name of 'Stud. H. Ibsen, c/o Sontum'. The minute book of the Bergen Theatre takes up the tale:

> On 6 November, Student Henrik Ibsen was engaged, having signified his willingness, to assist the Theatre as dramatic author, for which a monthly honorarium of twenty specie-dollars is to be paid him as from 1 October.

He was to spend six years there, years of poverty, bitterness, and failure, learning the alphabet of his craft.

[4]

The Unholy Trade
1851–4

'It is a most unholy trade'
– Henry James, on the theatre, to
William Heinemann.

BERGEN is, today, a much more attractive city than Oslo, and it must have been so then, perhaps to an even greater degree. Despite the great fire of 1830 it was, as contemporary photographs show, still essentially of the eighteenth century, with 'whitewashed wooden houses with pantiled red roofs, steep steps leading from the front doors to the street and, outside every house, the traditional water-butt and bench where the whole family would sit in the mild and humid summer evenings . . . receiving visits from friends and neighbours, the father in his dressing gown, nightcap and slippers, with a long pipe in his mouth, the mother with her knitting and her sons and daughters about her'. Thus Lorentz Dietrichson, who was a schoolboy when Ibsen arrived in Bergen, and other witnesses amplify the picture. 'The number of streets is very limited,' observed Professor Wittich from London University, 'and they are so narrow that there is hardly space sufficient to admit of the passage of two vehicles . . . The houses are huddled together, but they have about their exterior an air of cleanliness and comfort.' The harbour, he noted, 'very rarely freezes, although nearly half a degree nearer to the Pole than St Petersburg, whose harbour is closed up by ice for four months and longer every winter'; and the inhabitants struck him as being more cosmopolitan than those of other Norwegian towns.

The climate was (and is) very rainy. Every baby in Bergen was popularly supposed to be born with an umbrella; but the setting on the fjord, with its seven surrounding hills, was idyllic, even when, as was usually the case, the peaks of these were shrouded in cloud. 'Delectable, merry, earnest and peaceful,' Dietrichson apostrophized his birthplace, 'with all your strangeness, your rain and mist, your fresh beauty and your eternal youth.'

Fishing was the principal industry, and the principal topic of conversation; Bergen was not a place where the arts or any intellectual interest flourished. 'The habit of buying books,' Dietrichson tells us, 'had not yet become widespread, and only four or five houses boasted anything that could be called a library ... Apart from its theatre, the town possessed few sources of public entertainment.' These he enumerates. A Madame Davidsen challenged all comers, of whichever sex, to foot-races on Sunday afternoons; Rippo performed feats of strength, juggled, and walked a tightrope; there was a ventriloquist named Professor Bill, and a magician named Olivo who showed 'Cosmoramas'; and occasional visits were paid by a troupe of horseback artistes. Café life was virtually unknown, and a billiards saloon which had been opened in the late forties was regarded with suspicion. Two music societies existed, and an art society; and on Saturday afternoons in the summer one might see 'countless groups of both sexes, belonging to the lower middle class, singing their way into the countryside, with their baskets of food and drink ... always with a fiddler or a clarinettist at their head, the melody of whose instruments would last long into the bright summer night.' The citizens, Dietrichson concludes, were 'a curious mixture of calculation and idealism, provincialism and poetry'.

Ibsen was fortunate in his first landlady in Bergen – though landlady, to judge from the account of Thomas Forester, an English traveller who lodged with her a couple of years before Ibsen, is scarcely a dignified enough description.

There are besides the hotels several private establishments at Bergen where travellers are entertained with the advantages of more quiet and comfort than at the hotels. We considered ourselves fortunate in having been directed to that of Mrs Sontum. Well connected, and allied to persons of great consideration, circumstances having induced her to embark on her present undertaking, she is indefatigable in her endeavours to promote the comfort of her guests. Her house is the favourite resort of English travellers, and abundantly merits the preference given to it ... Nor must I omit the daughters of our hostess ... Two sorts of fish (trout and fried cod), besides lobsters and cutlets, with dishes of strawberries, wild and cultivated, were served for breakfast. The dinners were excellent. We had salmon, and more varieties of fish than I can name; and some national dishes which we thought admirable ... We had good Bordeaux wine at one and eightpence a bottle ... But the evening reunion was the most agreeable part of the day, when we assembled round the supper-table, spread with cold meat, lobsters, tarts and cakes, tea being served *à l'Anglaise*.

Nor was Fru Helene Sontum (as some might infer from the above account) a snob; on the contrary, all reports of her agree that she was a kindly lady who mothered her guests. Even if Ibsen did not get the full treatment accorded to Mr Forester, things must have seemed an extraordinary improvement on conditions at Mother Sæter's or Fru Holt's. Within five days of his arrival, he was writing an epithalamium for the wedding of Fru Sontum's son, Nicolai, a conventional but agreeable and deftly turned poem, which we must assume earned him, if he had not already received it, an invitation to the marriage feast.

During the six years he was to spend in Bergen, Ibsen performed practically every task associated with theatrical production except that of acting; he is one of the very few playwrights who seems never to have performed on any stage, not even as an amateur. But, in addition to writing plays and prologues to other people's plays, he directed, coached in movement and speech, designed sets and costumes, ran the business side and saw to the accounts. Evidence of all this activity is to be found in the archives of the theatre, now in Bergen University Library: the account books, most neatly kept (his experience at the apothecary's must have served him well here); and, an endless source of fascination, his prompt books, with his stage plots for various plays, the movements of the characters carefully traced in dotted lines, and his set and costume designs, extremely detailed (as one would expect, remembering his early interest in dress), and coloured with paint or crayon. His handwriting in these prompt books, as in his manuscripts and correspondence of this period, is small and crabbed; as he grew older and more famous his handwriting became, in contrast to the general rule, neater, not only in his correspondence but even, blessedly for his editors, in his rough drafts.

Ibsen's first official assignment at Bergen, appropriately enough, was to write a prologue for an entertainment which the theatre, in return for the support which the Christiania Students had given, performed on 17 November in aid of the Students' Union Building Fund. It was spoken by the most talented of the theatre's young actresses, Louise Brun; Ibsen's name, surprisingly considering that he was now a member of the company, is not mentioned in the programme. His next task was one which he must particularly have relished. The policy and performance of the Bergen Theatre had been attacked in one of the two town newspapers, *Bergenske Blade*, by a local worthy boasting the unfortunate name of Paul Stub, who, by coincidence, had acted as one of Ibsen's correspondence tutors when Ibsen was preparing in Grimstad for his matriculation. Stub had corrected Ibsen's Norwegian essays. Apparently the newspaper had received no free tickets since the opening performance, presumably because the entire season had been over-subscribed by the public, and this neglect seems to have influenced Stub's attitude, for he poked fun at the inexperienced actors in a pedantically spiteful and unnecessary way. Ibsen replied to Stub's remarks point by point in the rival paper, *Bergens*

Stiftstidende, on 30 November, attacking Stub particularly
for the negativeness of his criticisms. 'If a critic is to pose as
an actor's mentor,' suggested Ibsen, 'he must explain to him
how a role *should* be played, never mind how it should *not*' –
a remark that might profitably be pinned up above many a
critic's desk. He continued the assault on Stub in three
further articles, with a zest that makes one wonder whether
he had not perhaps personally experienced the sharpness of
Stub's pen at the expense of his Norwegian compositions.
Like Ibsen's dramatic and political articles in Christiania,
these essays are excellent examples of polemical writing,
clearly reasoned and precisely worded, and reading them a
century later one is again grateful for the fate that allowed
him no opportunity at this period of his life of taking up
journalism as a career.

Ole Bull had by now left Bergen; it had never been the
intention that he should do more than launch the theatre.
He had given two years to the scheme and the financial
sacrifice to himself, in loss of earnings, must have been considerable. From the time of his departure, things began to go
less well for the Bergen Theatre. The first play of the new
year, 1852, a Norwegian work entitled *The Christmas Guest*,
by C. P. Riis, was a fiasco; on the second night there was so
thin a house that the reviewer of *Theatervennen* commented: 'we can hardly remember having seen so few spectators in a theatre.' They had better luck with Ponsard's
Charlotte Corday, in which the young Louise Brun created
an excellent impression in the title role and a new actor,
Andreas Isachsen (with whom Ibsen was to have a long running feud, extending beyond his stay at Bergen), gave a fine
performance as Marat. Isachsen was the first *student* to join
the company (i.e., the first to have passed his matriculation,
then, as now, an important status symbol in Scandinavia),
and the advent of so qualified an intellectual into the theatrical profession created something of a sensation in the
town. *Charlotte Corday* opened on 1 February, and five days
later a topical new play, entitled *The First Jew*, also proved

successful. The entry of Jews into Norway for residential purposes had been forbidden until 1851, and the play dealt with the problems encountered by an early immigrant. The author's name was kept secret, but it was generally supposed to be the local magistrate, a lawyer of literary leanings named C. R. Hansson.

Although Ibsen's contract had specified that he was to 'assist the theatre as dramatic author', it was also intended that he should help with the work of instructing the actors and the rest of what would nowadays be called production. The theatre, however, already possessed an artistic instructor, a local schoolmaster named Herman Laading. Laading, at thirty-eight, was fifteen years older than Ibsen, and was quite a considerable person in Bergen. At Christiania University the subjects which he had read included law, medicine, theology and even mineralogy, all, apparently, to some effect. He was also a fine fencer and an excellent shot, and knew several languages. Laading had started his own school in Bergen in 1837, and continued to run it while working at the theatre; indeed, he ran it for fifty years, until his retirement in 1887. The Scandinavian theatres have always displayed what to other countries sometimes seems an exaggerated respect for the academic mind; however, in this instance the choice may have been justified, since the members of the company had, for the most part, scarcely any education at all, and in the performance of historical plays especially some kind of general background knowledge was plainly desirable.

The directors of the theatre were finding considerable difficulty in choosing plays that lay within the capabilities of their company and were suited to the taste of their audience. The French conversation pieces popular in Christiania made demands which the untrained actors of Bergen could not meet. (By one of the more chauvinistic of the Bergen Theatre's regulations not only the actors and instructors, but even the prompter, had to be of Norwegian birth.) The great classics were even more obviously outside the company's range; attempts that season to stage Calderon's *The Burgo-master of Zalamea*, Oehlenschläger's tragedy *Axel and Valborg*, and Garrick and Colman's *The Jealous Wife* all failed completely. In an enterprising effort to meet the situation, the board decided to send their new 'dramatic author', together with the two most talented younger members of the company, Johannes and Louise Brun, abroad, to study foreign theatrical methods and obtain new and suitable plays; and on 13 April 1852 Ibsen was given a new contract which included a travel grant of £50 'to visit, over a period of three months, certain foreign theatres, notably in Copenhagen, Berlin, Dresden and Hamburg, in order to acquire such knowledge and experience as may equip him to fill a position at the theatre as instructor, the work to include, in addition to the instruction of the actors, responsibility for everything pertaining to the furnishing, equipment and decoration of the stage, the actors' costumes, etc'. On return, he was to occupy this post for five years at an annual salary of £75, which was not bad by the Norwegian standards of those days; it was the same as the older and more experienced Laading was to receive, and represented an increase of 25 per cent on Ibsen's original salary. The board must have felt satisfied with and confident in their new recruit. Paris was not included in the itinerary, presumably because neither Ibsen nor the Bruns knew French.

On 15 April 1852, accordingly, Ibsen sailed from Bergen to see, for the first time, what the world looked like outside Norway. There was no direct route by ship to Copenhagen, so they travelled via Hamburg, which was linked with Bergen by a regular fortnightly service. Ibsen's companions were even younger than he was; Johannes Brun was twenty, his wife, whom he had married the previous year, twenty-one. They were two deeply contrasted characters. Johannes Brun was square-built, merry and spontaneous and, like Ibsen, extremely clothes-conscious and elegant in appearance; Louise, on the other hand, was rather reserved and formal, 'not handsome', and careless in her dress 'almost to the point of slovenliness'. Both were destined to reach the heights of their profession and to die while still in their prime, she at thirty-five, he at fifty-eight. Johannes Brun, indeed, was to become perhaps the most famous of all of Norway's actors, and to create several of Ibsen's most famous character roles, including the Old Man of the Mountains in *Peer Gynt*, Daniel Hejre in *The League of Youth*, and Ulric Brendel in *Rosmersholm*. His statue stands outside the National Theatre in Oslo only a few yards from that of Ibsen.

After a brief pause in Hamburg, of which Ibsen vexatiously records no impression, they reached Copenhagen on 20 April. The Danish capital still had oil lighting in the streets and watchmen shouting the hours, but its cosmopolitanism and elegance, and architectural pleasures, must, to the young provincial from Norway, have been a revelation. It possessed, moreover, in the Royal Theatre, Det Kongelige, one of the great theatres of Europe, with a fully international repertoire and actors and actresses comparable to the best of France and Germany, and better than those of England, where Macready had finished his career the previous year (though he was to live for another twenty-two, surely the longest time that any great actor has spent in unenforced retirement), and Irving was a boy of fourteen.

C. R. Hansson, the literary-minded Recorder of Bergen, had given Ibsen a letter of introduction to the director of the Royal Theatre, Johan Ludvig Heiberg, and this proved of great value. Heiberg, besides being a scholar, was a considerable poet and dramatist, and one of the very few authors whom Ibsen, in his maturity, admitted to admiring. Born in 1791, the son of a woman who later, as the Baroness Gyllembourg-Ehrensværd, was to achieve fame as a kind of Danish Mrs Gaskell, Heiberg had been elected to a lectureship in Danish at Kiel University at the age of thirty-one; but creative writing attracted him more than academic life, and three years later he returned to Copenhagen with the expressed intention of introducing vaudeville to the Danish stage. Vaudeville then meant not, as now, music hall, but comedies with music, with the characters, at climactic moments, breaking into songs consisting of new lyrics set to familiar tunes. Heiberg wrote a great many of these, based on French models but with Danish settings and topical Danish themes; Ibsen was to stage several of them in both Bergen and Christiania. The author of a number of comedies and straight plays, of which the best are perhaps *The Day of the Seven Sleepers* and *A Soul after Death*, Heiberg was also a poet, and a vigorous critic; and in 1847, five years before Ibsen met him, he had been appointed to his present position as director of the Royal Theatre. Since Oehlenschläger's death two years previously he was regarded as the most eminent man of letters not merely in Denmark, but in Scandinavia, more so than his juniors Hans Christian Andersen and Søren Kierkegaard. In many ways he must have seemed a pattern of what the young Ibsen might have hoped to become; his fields of activity and his critical, nonconformist standpoint were very much Ibsen's own.

Heiberg had now virtually retired from authorship and had become a formidable pundit. 'Standing in the centre of his office in the Royal Theatre', we are told, 'he would hold audience with his hands clasped behind his back, his legs parted, the upper half of his body swaying from side to side, as he fastened his stare, as cold as water, upon his unfortunate visitor, who as often as not would become confused and lose the thread of his discourse under the impact of that superior and ironic smile.' Hansson had, however, with lawyer's cunning, couched his introductory letter in terms highly flattering to Heiberg, describing Ibsen as 'a bright and gifted young man of more than common poetical talent' whom he had come to like, since he had 'found in him the same passionate admiration of you that formed one of the worthiest emotions of my youth'.

Hansson's letter seems to have had the required effect, for Heiberg immediately granted Ibsen and the Bruns free entry to the theatre each evening; disappointingly, however, he advised them not to bother to attend any rehearsals since, the season being so far advanced, nothing of interest was in preparation. He commanded his chief instructor, Thomas Overskou, who was also a playwright and translator of some repute, to show Ibsen round the theatre, drawing his attention in particular to the stage machinery, which was far in advance of anything that Ibsen had seen in Christiania or Bergen. Overskou, writing to his daughter at this time, described Ibsen as 'a little clenched Norwegian with alert eyes'.

Overskou was not, as a stage instructor, the best of models for a young man; even by the standards of those days, he was coming to be regarded as somewhat old-fashioned. However, he proved a friendly and helpful guide, as Ibsen's letters to his directors in Bergen (the first we have from his hand since those which he had written to Schulerud from Grimstad) show. On 25 April 1852 he wrote to them:

I am happy to be able to tell you that ... both Heiberg and Herr Overskou have received us with exceptional kindness, and through the latter I shall easily obtain all the information I require concerning the internal organization of the theatre. As regards the other matters you have instructed me to investigate, such as the procuring of a dancing teacher for Brun and his wife, etc., I have not yet managed to arrange this, but hope to do so within the course of the next week.

Three weeks later, on 16 May, he reported on the plays he had seen.

We have been very fortunate with the repertory. We have seen *Hamlet*, and several other plays by Shakespeare, and by Holberg ... I need hardly add that we acquainted ourselves with everything that might be of artistic interest. The Danes have in all respects shown us the utmost courtesy and good will and, so far from feeling any annoyance at our seeking to liberate ourselves from their influence upon our theatre, they only wonder that this has not happened long ago. I have made the acquaintance of H.C. Andersen; he advises me strongly, when I have finished in Dresden, to go on to Vienna to see the Burgtheater; he may be there himself then, in which case he will act as my guide; if not, I hope Professor Dahl may be able to assist me.

Hans Andersen was then forty-seven, and five years previously had paid a famous visit to Charles Dickens in London; but unfortunately, the directors of the Bergen Theatre decided that they could not afford to extend their young apprentice's tour beyond Dresden, so that the fascinating prospect of Hans Andersen showing Ibsen around Vienna never materialized. 'We feel', wrote the Bergen board on 28 May, 'that it will be much more rewarding for you to stay longer at a place such as Dresden than to move on from town to town.' They also warned him that 'we know from experience that living in Germany is very cheap, so that if you do not manage on your £50 we shall be forced to conclude that you have not arranged your economy wisely', and at first refused to refund him the £6 he had paid for dancing lessons, telling him that he and the Bruns were expected to pay for this out of their grants. Since neither he nor they could afford this, Ibsen had to write another begging letter to his board; not the last example he was to encounter of the parsimony of committees.

But these irritations must have been more than compensated for by the new horizons that were being opened for him theatrically and aesthetically. He was indeed, as he had told his board, 'very fortunate with the repertory'. During his six weeks in Copenhagen that spring he, who had never previously seen a Shakespeare play on the stage, saw four – *Hamlet, King Lear, Romeo and Juliet*, and *As You Like It*. He also saw four of Holberg's best comedies, *The Lying-In Room, Henrik and Pernilla, Pernilla's Brief Mistress-ship*, and *The Woman of Whims*; three Oehlenschläger tragedies, *Queen Margareta, The Vikings at Byzantium*, and *Earl Haakon the Mighty*; Mozart's opera *Don Giovanni*; and two of Heiberg's own works, including his best and most famous vaudeville, *No*. The actors, too, were far superior to any he had seen in Norway. The great tragedian Michael Wiehe was then at his peak, and a generation later Ibsen was to name him as still the finest actor he had seen. 'When I recall his performances', he said, 'it is as though I were walking

through a gallery filled with ancient statues. Pure *plastik!*
Pure beauty.'[1] He was also fortunate enough to witness, for
the first time, a major actress demonstrating her art: Johanne Luise Heiberg, whom he saw in one of her most
famous parts as Lucretia (the title role) in Holberg's *The
Woman of Whims*, a lady so moody and changeable that her
two lovers, ecstatically describing their mistresses to each
other, do not realize that they are speaking of the same
person. Fru Heiberg was to become a close friend of Ibsen in
later years, and he was to address to her one of his most
delicate poems.

In contrast to Wiehe, there was the young Fredrik Høedt,
who was to be the founder of a new school of acting, more
realistic and analytical, less inclined to the grand manner
and subtler in his appreciation of psychological nuances.
Ibsen saw Høedt as Hamlet, but admired him more as the
young lover, Grignon, in Scribe's *La Bataille des Dames*.
When one remembers the wretched plays that Ibsen had
seen in Christiania and, reading between the lines of his dramatic criticisms, the moderate talents of the actors there (to
say nothing of Bergen, where even the Bruns were still raw
beginners), one realizes what a revelation to him these evenings in the theatre at Copenhagen must have been. The
actors, he reported wonderingly to his directors in Bergen,
knew their parts before rehearsals of a play began.

Finally, and by no means least, it was probably during his
stay in Copenhagen that Ibsen happened upon a short book
written by a young German professor at Jena and published
only that year which was to have a considerable influence
upon his writing: Herman Hettner's *Das moderne Drama*.
Two aspects in particular of the book must have interested
him: the sections dealing with historical drama and with
Märchenlustspiel, or romantic fairy-tale comedy. Hettner
asserted that historical plays should be written so as to be
psychologically relevant to modern times; human character

1. Wiehe was only thirty-two when Ibsen saw him. He died at the
age of forty-four in 1864.

had not changed fundamentally over the centuries, nor, *mutatis mutandis*, had the issues of human conflict. Historical drama, in other words, should be written as psychological character-conflicts, and not, like Oehlenschläger's plays, as grand opera without music. Nor was there any place in serious drama, whether historical or modern, for the paraphernalia of coincidence with which (as in Scribe's plays) it was commonly cluttered: overheard conversations, intercepted letters, mistaken identities and the like. Such things were all very well in comedy; but in serious drama, what mattered (Hettner asserted) was conflict of, and development of, character. The lesson of Shakespeare had been largely forgotten; Hettner held up *Coriolanus* as a model.

As regards *Märchenlustspiel*, the important thing about this genre, it seemed to Hettner, was the fact that it dealt with two opposite worlds, that of everyday reality and that of fantasy; in the best plays of this kind, these two worlds are constantly being juxtaposed in such a way that the world of dreams is shown as a source of truth and wisdom, while that of everyday reality is made to seem comic and unrealistic. As a prime example of this type of play, Hettner instanced Shakespeare's *A Midsummer Night's Dream*. It is a genre that has always seemed to hold an especial appeal for Scandinavians – Oehlenschläger, Heiberg and Hostrup had all experimented in it, and so, in plays as well as in stories, had Hans Andersen. Ibsen's next five plays were to be either historical dramas or *Märchenlustspiel,* and in each of them he was to follow, or try to follow, Hettner's precepts – though here again, as with Kierkegaard, we must beware of assuming that Hettner did more than crystallize ideas that were already present in Ibsen's mind. Another demand which Hettner made, that dramatists should stick closely to historical facts, Ibsen was, like Shakespeare, to ignore.

Hettner also drew Ibsen's attention to a recent play by a young German dramatist, Friedrich Hebbel's *Maria Magdalena*, written nine years previously in 1843. Hettner thought this powerful melodrama, written in high-flown

prose about ordinary village people, worthy to stand beside
Sophocles' *Electra* and Goethe's *Faust* as an outstanding
specimen of the tragedy of ideas, and as an example of how
bürgerliche Tragödie need not be trivial, but may be both
profound and poetic. Several witnesses, such as John Paulsen
and Gunnar Heiberg, have testified to Ibsen's later admiration of *Maria Magdalena*,[2] and it seems probable that it
stemmed from this period; after reading Hettner's praise, he
is hardly likely to have missed the chance of studying it.
Hettner did not know of Alexander Ostrovsky's experiments
in the same field (his play *The Bankrupt*, though written in
1849, had been banned, and although he was to become
known in Russia in 1853 through *The Poor Bride*, it was to be
many years before his fame spread to western Europe). Nor
did Hettner know of Gogol or Turgenev, both of whom, like
Ostrovsky, would have supported his faith in the potentialities of *bürgerliche Tragödie*. Their examples would
have been useful to Ibsen; in the event, ignorant of their
experiments, he was, in his own good time, to follow the
path that they had trod, and go far beyond them.

Shortly before Ibsen left Copenhagen, Heiberg honoured
him with an invitation to dinner at his house; but the occasion proved something of an anticlimax. To Ibsen's disappointment, the great man discoursed on neither literature,
the theatre nor even politics, but solely on questions of gas-
tronomic interest; and he never saw Heiberg again before
the latter died in 1860, embittered at the constant sniping he
had had to undergo from his fellow-countrymen during his
last years. Ibsen (although Heiberg had by then rejected
The Vikings at Helgeland) wrote a handsome elegy in his
honour. 'He lit a torch in the land. You used it to burn his

2. 'The best evidence of how unforgettable an impression *Maria
Magdalena* made on him is the meticulous *précis* he dramatically
gave us of the plot. I saw the various scenes come alive before me, and
heard not without emotion the old father's last, despairing cry: "*Ich
verstehe die Welt nicht mehr!*" ["I understand the world no
longer!] – a sentence which had long haunted Ibsen.' Thus John
Paulsen; Gunnar Heiberg likewise records that Ibsen advised him to
read Hebbel.

brow. He taught you to wield a sword. You pressed it against his heart. Boldly he fought the trolls of his day. You crushed him between your shields.' The situation of the prophet who is without honour in his own country had, by 1860, already become familiar to Ibsen.

On 6 June, the Bruns having returned to Norway, Ibsen departed alone for Dresden. Here he found a helpful guide in a celebrated fellow-countryman, the old Norwegian painter J. C. Dahl. Ibsen was not able to obtain free tickets to the theatre, as he had done in Copenhagen, but he was lucky enough to see, and compare, two exciting actors of contrasting styles. One was Emil Devrient, a fine performer in the traditional classical manner (and son of the mighty Ludwig Devrient, who frequently collapsed in an epileptic fit while playing Lear); the other was an exciting young Polish actor, Boguwil Dawison, whose more modern approach, with its realism and subtlèty of characterization, resembled that of Fredrick Høedt. Ibsen saw Dawison play Hamlet, and much preferred it to Høedt's performance in the role which he had seen in Copenhagen the previous month.[3]

He studied the stage machinery at the Hofoper, where three years earlier the young Richard Wagner had been *Kapellmeister*, and spent many hours in the Dresden art galleries and museums. In those days photography was in its infancy, and until one saw the original works of a painter one knew of them, if at all, only by engravings or verbal description; the effect of the great galleries of Dresden on one who still cherished ambitions of his own in the field of painting can be imagined. When, a dozen years later, he visited Italy, it was the paintings and sculptures, more than anything else, that excited him.

Ibsen stayed in Dresden for about a month, returning to Norway some time in July. During his three months abroad,

3. The repertory also included, while he was there, *A Midsummer Night's Dream*, *Richard III*, Goethe's *Egmont*, and Lessing's *Emilia Galotti*, but we do not know how many of these he saw; probably, as will appear, at least the first-named.

he had completed a play which he may have begun at
Bergen in the spring: *Sancthansnatten* (*St John's Night*, i.e.
Midsummer Night). This is unique among Ibsen's plays in
being the only one which he refused to allow to be printed in
his lifetime. When, in 1897, his German editor (and, later,
executor) Julius Elias asked permission to include it in the
German collected edition of his works, Ibsen angrily replied
(19 September 1897): 'I neither will nor *can* permit the play
St John's Night to appear in any collection of *my* works. The
play is a miserable thing which is not really by *my* hand. It is
founded on a rough mess of a draft which I was given by a
student acquaintance, re-worked, and put my name to, but
which I cannot now possibly acknowledge as being mine.' In
accordance with his wishes it was not printed until after his
death, in 1909, and has been dismissed by most commentators as negligible. It is in fact a curiously engaging
work, considerably superior to *The Warrior's Barrow* and
The Feast at Solhaug, both of which he allowed to be
printed, and one imagines that his rejection of it stemmed
not from any lack of merit so much as from the almost
pathological horror which he showed throughout his life at
any suggestion that anything he had written owed anything
to any other author, living or dead. He was, indeed, probably
less influenced by other writers than any other great dramatist, but not as little as he made out.

He called the play an *eventyrkomedie*. *Eventyr* means,
roughly, fairy tale, so that *eventyrkomedie* is the Norwegian
equivalent of *Märchenlustspiel*. Four young people are
gathered in a house on Midsummer Night: Johannes and
Juliane, who are engaged but do not love each other; Julian
Poulsen, a student friend of Johannes; and Anne, Juliane's
step-sister, whose freshness and innocence contrast with the
sophisticated artificiality of the other three, and whom they
regard as 'fey'. A *nisse*, or goblin, lives in the loft; Anne
accepts his presence, sensing no difference between natural
and supernatural things; only she can see him. This goblin,
a kind of Puck, puts a potion into the bowl of punch which

the young people are about to drink; then, in a charming scene, they go up to the hilltop where the midsummer pyre is dying, and catch a glimpse of the other-world of the supernatural. But only those with poetic souls, Anne and Johannes, see and understand; to the two blinded by intellect, Julian and Juliane, it is an obscure and incomprehensible vision. Under the influence of the magic night, all four declare themselves to the ones they truly love, Johannes to Anne and Julian to Juliane. Next morning, they realize they are betrothed to the wrong people. At first, they resign themselves fatalistically to the apparently unavoidable; in the end, however, each gets his or her true partner.

St John's Night is written mainly in prose, with occasional excursions (as when the goblin speaks) into rhymed verse. It is very much in the romantic fairy-tale tradition which was popular in Scandinavia then – Oehlenschläger had written a comedy entitled *A Midsummer Night's Play*, and Heiberg a similar one, *The Day of the Seven Sleepers*; Hans Andersen had exercised himself in the genre and, Ibsen had seen an example, Jens Christian Hostrup's *Master and Pupil*, while in Copenhagen.[4] Ibsen's *St John's Night*, however, like Strindberg's later and remarkable essay in the same genre, *The Virgin Bride*, has a wit and individuality which lift it far above the rest of its kind; in this, his first essay in prose drama, he shows himself already able to write excellent colloquial dialogue, to create satirical characters, and to keep a complicated structure of plot and sub-plot continuously ticking. Julian Poulsen, quoting undigested gobbets of Heiberg and Kierkegaard, is the first of those pretentious charmers, vain, romanticizing and self-pitying, who were to become a feature of Ibsen's work, the forerunner of Falk in *Love's Comedy*, Peer Gynt, Stensgaard in

4. The action of these three plays by Oehlenschläger, Heiberg, and Hostrup takes place, as does *St John's Night*, on a summer night when the supernatural world reveals its secrets: and Heiberg, like Ibsen, suggests that only those whose souls are genuinely poetic can see that world.

The League of Youth, Hilmar Tønnesen in *The Pillars of Society*, Hjalmar Ekdal in *The Wild Duck*, and Ulrik Brendel in *Rosmersholm*. Through Julian, Ibsen ridiculed that exaggerated passion for all things national which had made it fashionable to admire everything rustic simply because it was, or seemed to be, untainted by Danish or Swedish influence, just as later, in other countries, it was to become fashionable to admire any literary work that was, or appeared to be, working-class. The attempt to create a new language (*landsmaal*) based on the country dialects became the subject of a questioning eyebrow, not for the last time in Ibsen's work; so, too, did the kind of bogus aestheticism which W. S. Gilbert was to caricature a generation later in *Patience*. *St John's Night* is too topical in its allusions, and too reminiscent of *A Midsummer Night's Dream* in certain phases of its plot, to stand much chance of proving more than an interesting curiosity if it were staged today; but the ridiculer of contemporary poses who was to hold an unflattering mirror up to his countrymen in *Love's Comedy*, *Brand*, *Peer Gynt*, *The League of Youth*, and *An Enemy of the People* is more clearly distinguishable in *St John's Night* than in any of the other plays of Ibsen's immaturity. And Julian, towards the end of the play, makes a point which Ibsen was to stress more sharply in *Love's Comedy* and which was especially to enrage contemporary opinion: the necessity of qualifying one's ideal of love when one gets married.

One of Ibsen's jobs at Bergen was to provide a new play to be performed each year on the anniversary of the opening of the theatre, 2 January, and that autumn of 1852 he offered as his contribution for the coming anniversary *St John's Night*. It was accepted, and thus became the second of Ibsen's plays to appear on the stage. Anticipation in the little town was great; the theatre-goers of Bergen were eager to see what their young 'dramatic author' could do. New decor, a luxury that the theatre could scarcely afford, was prepared, so that the play would not be seen in the familiar standard sets; it would not be quite true to say that no expense was spared to make the evening a success, but at least the few pennies that the theatre could disburse were freely given. The opening performance was sold out in advance, and many people were turned away without tickets. Alas, the occasion turned out a fearful failure. The first night audience so disliked the play that they whistled and hissed it; and at the second performance not merely seats but whole rows were empty. Word spread fast in a town that size. *Bergenske Blade* dismissed it as 'a somewhat unfortunate piece, though it contains some pretty fancies'. The management accepted the verdict of the public and withdrew the play, replacing it, ironically, with P. A. Jensen's *The Goblin's Home*, a tedious essay in rustic romanticism which Ibsen had damned as a drama critic in Christiania, and exactly the kind of play for which *St John's Night* had been intended to ring the death knell.

This failure must have been a bitter disappointment to the young dramatist, not merely in itself but in its implications. The Bergen public had shown that it preferred banal melodramas, superficial comedies, and mock-rustic folk tales to anything critical, novel, and unusual. Seldom can the prospects for experiment have seemed as unpromising to any writer as to the young Ibsen in Bergen. Even at this early stage of his career we find him challenging and experimenting; but he had neither the actors to carry out his wishes nor the public to appreciate them. It is not hard to imagine with what feelings he must have turned to the direction of the plays that formed the rest of the season, a list that makes the programme of the humblest modern provincial theatre or stock company appear almost astral by comparison.

It was an exceptionally bad period for the drama throughout Europe. During the half-century that had elapsed since the death of Schiller in 1805, a gap had opened between the theatre and the serious playwright. A number of interesting plays had been written, but most of them remained unperformed even in their own countries, let alone in so theatrically backward a land as Norway. The two most

exciting, Georg Büchner's *Danton's Death* and *Woyzeck*,
both composed in the eighteen-thirties before Büchner died
of typhoid at the age of twenty-three, were to remain for
many years unknown to anyone; neither play was staged
anywhere before the twentieth century. Nor, in Norway, was
anything to be seen before 1900 of either of those other
brilliant but tragically-fated young German dramatists of
the period, Friedrich Hebbel, whose *Maria Magdalena* Ibsen
had discovered through Hettner, or Christian Dietrich-
Grabbe (1801–36), the author of that eccentric but remarkable play *Comedy, Satire, Irony and Deeper Meaning*; nor
anything by Heinrich von Kleist, who had committed suicide in 1811 at the age of thirty-four, except *Kätchen von
Heilbronn*, and that not until 1868. The Russian realists,
Gogol, Turgenev and Ostrovsky, had equally long to wait.
Neither *The Government Inspector* (1836) nor *A Month in
the Country* (1850) reached Norway before 1890, nor anything by Ostrovsky until the present century. Alfred de
Musset's comedies of the eighteen-thirties were unperformed in Norway until the sixties, when Ibsen himself
directed *Un Caprice*. It is a commentary on the theatrical
taste of the period that the only contemporary plays in the
general European repertoire which have survived are the
farces of Eugène Labiche, such as *An Italian Straw Hat*
(1851). Zola was not to start writing for the stage till the
seventies, Becque till the eighties.

Nor, in Bergen, did Ibsen have the opportunity, which he
would have found in, say, Copenhagen or Stockholm, to
work on classical plays. No Greeks, no Shakespeare, no
Molière; even the few English Restoration playwrights who
reached him, and there were not many, did so in botched
adaptations hideously translated, and shorn of the elegance
of their prose they must have seemed pretty poor stuff. Only
Holberg and Heiberg can have had anything to teach him
that he did not already know about construction and characterization. From Scribe he could have learned no virtue that
was not better exemplified in both these writers; and what-

ever Ibsen's admiration for Oehlenschläger as a poet, he can hardly have been blind to his limitations as a dramatist.

Neither could the circumstances under which Ibsen worked as a director have been much less fortunately arranged. His duties were confined to deciding the decor and costumes and arranging the movements; the interpretation of the roles and the speaking of the lines were Laading's business. Not that this was an uncommon arrangement in those days. Even at the Royal Theatre in Copenhagen, Thomas Overskou limited his advice to visual matters, not bothering about the psychology of the characters, their relationships, or the way the actors spoke their lines. Such subtleties were not then regarded as necessary to a theatrical performance, any more than until very recently they were regarded as necessary in opera. Tragedy was, to repeat, a kind of grand opera without music, interesting only in so far as it afforded opportunities for sonorous declamations, spectacular outbursts, and striking visual effects; comedy was merely an excuse for individual inventiveness. Nobody except a very few innovators, such as Fredrik Høedt and Boguwil Dawison, expected a play to reflect real life, any more than they would have expected an opera to do so; what people wanted to see on the stage, in tragedy as in opera or musical comedy, was a world of fantasy. There was no such thing as what we today would call a straight play; there was tragedy, comedy, farce and melodrama, with or without music. Comedy might be in prose, but tragedy had to be in verse; the idea that a tragedy could be written in prose, or could be about people of humble birth and of ordinary human dimensions like the lower-paying members of the audience, would have struck both actor and public as absurd. (Even a play such as Hebbel's *Maria Magdalena* was in a high-flown prose, to modern ears uncomfortably close to the language of *Maria Marten*.) Such few attempts as there had been to break this rule had failed, which seemed to confirm its general validity. Büchner had succeeded, but nobody knew about Büchner; *Danton's Death* had been published in 1835, but in a version vulgarized almost beyond recognition, and the confused manuscript of *Woyzeck* was not to be discovered until 1879, the year in which, by a strange coincidence, Ibsen won international fame with *A Doll's House*, achieving, in his own way, what Büchner had sought to achieve forty years earlier – the writing of a major serious play in simple prose, employing characters who were not kings and princesses, nor even Capulets and Montagues, but ordinary people called Mr and Mrs, such as might live next door.

The actual stage conditions under which Ibsen operated at Bergen were some fifty years behind the times, and resembled those commonly to be found on the Continent and in England during the eighteenth century. The sets had no side walls, but a painted backcloth and a sequence of painted wings, with borders (i.e. hanging strips of cloth) overhead. The wings were mounted on wheels which rested in a kind of tramline, and were moved by a cranking device beneath the stage. Spectators sitting in the side seats could see through the gaps between the wings. The backcloth had to be rolled up like a home cinema screen before being hoisted into the flies to make way for another. The lighting consisted of chandeliers above the stage and auditorium, footlights, and lamps vertically arranged behind the various wings to give a primitive kind of side illumination. Gas was not introduced at the Bergen Theatre until 1856, the year before Ibsen left; until then, chandeliers, footlights and wing lamps worked on candles or petroleum. Little variation was possible, and such as there was was obtained by the use of movable coloured shades. Light and shadow were often painted on the decor. The front of the stage received the most light, thanks to the footlights and the extra illumination from the lamps and candles in the auditorium, and all dialogue scenes (as opposed to crowd scenes, mime, dances, etc.) were accordingly played downstage. In any case, words spoken upstage tended to get lost in the wings. The smoke, melted wax and spilt oil inevitably gave the decor, and especially the wing cloths, a soiled appearance. When, in 1848, the management had tried winching the main auditorium chandelier up to the roof, so as to give more effect to the stage lights, spectators complained that it was no longer possible to 'enjoy the diversion of looking at the audience when the plays or the performance were such that a broader field of view might prove less exhausting to the limbs and spirit than if eye and mind should be directed uninterruptedly towards the stage'.

New decor, when the theatre could afford it, which was not often, and then only in the case of a new Norwegian play such as *St John's Night*, usually consisted simply of one or more new backcloths. The wing sets were seldom changed, and included standard representations of *a street, a park, a church, winter, a grotto, a pillared hall*, etc. A French visitor to Bergen in 1841 had satirically inquired why the theatre's painter employed his talents on the faces of the actresses instead of on the scenery.

Doors, windows, furniture, vases of flowers, mirrors and so on were, as in other countries, normally painted on the wings and backcloth. Even in England and on the Continent it was not until well into the second half of the century that real furniture was used; as late as 1888 we find Strindberg, in his preface to *Miss Julie*, complaining that 'stage doors are made of canvas and flap at the slightest touch', and pleading that 'even if the walls have to be made of canvas it is surely time to stop painting them with shelves and kitchen utensils'.

The normal number of rehearsals judged necessary for a production when Ibsen was at Bergen was three to five. Such properties as could not be painted on the decor (chairs, tankards, etc.) were borrowed from well-wishers in the town; these even included eighteenth-century clothes, of which the citizens of Bergen, already famous for their thrift, had a surprising number in their family wardrobes. These were especially welcome when, as occurred once or twice a season, a play by Holberg entered the repertory.

The normal placing of actors at Bergen was in a horizontal bow, with its tips in the downstage corners and everyone facing the audience, even when they were meant to be speaking to each other. Ibsen's sketches in his prompt books show that he tried to get away from this convention; and when the company visited Trondhjem in 1856, his direction elicited some interesting praise from local critics. 'It deserves to be remarked', wrote one, 'that the actors have abandoned the stiff and unnatural old-fashioned custom of running right down to the footlights or turning to the audience whenever they have anything to say.' It was also noticed that 'the actors keep quite far upstage', and, amazingly, 'turn towards each other when conversing'. This was eye-opening stuff indeed for the provincial theatre-goers of Norway, and one assumes that it was one of the fruits of Ibsen's study trip to Copenhagen and Dresden.

But although Ibsen was a visually imaginative director, as befitted one whose early ambition had been to become a painter, and although he was in advance of his time in his meticulous attention (when the theatre could afford it) to costume detail, all reports agree that he was not a good instructor of actors. He was far too timid. Peter Blytt, a young member of the theatre board, relates:

There was not much about him to suggest the creative genius which he was later to display. This quiet, reticent, not very prepossessing, unassuming young man, with a glance that was usually half-veiled and seldom lit up, and then only briefly, rather gave the impression of being an exceedingly withdrawn and shy person. One knew he had a quick and fertile poetic talent ... but no one would have guessed that this pale, fully bearded face, with its tightly closed lips, concealed a mind of such quality ... He moved quietly, almost soundlessly, about the wings at rehearsals ... He not infrequently manifested a certain helplessness, and appeared embarrassed when forced directly to address any actor or, worse still, actress, in order to rebuke or even to correct them ... He carried the director's books without in the true sense of the word being a *director* ... He struck me as a naturally withdrawn personality who had difficulty, and even reluctance, in forming a close and intimate relationship with anyone. He preferred to wander around alone and unnoticed ...

It became repeatedly evident that economic calculations and estimates, which were naturally an essential part of his work, lay somewhat outside his range. But no one doubted his good will. Undemanding and retiring, he aroused in that easily emotional and often passionate theatrical world no enmity – though one might now and then perceive in him a certain indolence, doubtless the consequence of his quickly fermenting talent ... He was regarded with a certain shy veneration, and when, as stated, he moved soundlessly or, as the company sometimes put it, mooched around in the wings in his curious, capacious, and somewhat worn cloak, he was respected but won little sympathy. He made scarcely any intimate friends ... but he made no enemies either. He preferred to go his own way, taciturn, enclosed, little understood ... He did not often interrupt with instructions at rehearsals, and delivered no harangues, but when he did intervene his comments were perceptive, illuminating and to the point. His suggestions were brief, clear, precise, and helpful.

H. Wiers-Jenssen, the author of the play *Anne Pedersdotter* (known in England as *The Witch*, and brilliantly filmed by Carl Dreyer as *Day of Wrath* in 1943), records that an actress who had worked with Ibsen at Bergen, whom he does not name, told him how Ibsen would rehearse his actors either mooching soundlessly in the wings (she uses the same verb as Blytt) or sitting far back in the auditorium 'pulling at his beard and edging back if anyone came near. He would sometimes approach some young and as yet unintimidating beginner who happened to be sitting near him and, referring to the actress speaking on the stage, would say: "Don't you hear how falsely she said that line? And how untrue and unnecessary that movement was?" "But, Herr Ibsen, why don't you tell her?" "No, *you* tell her, Frøken Nielsen." ' They thought of him, she told Wiers-Jenssen, as someone who 'wouldn't frighten a cat'.

During the spring of 1853 Ibsen left Fru Sontum's and moved into an apartment in the rear annexe of the theatre, where he was looked after by the theatre's 'restauratrice', an old lady named Frøken l'Abbée 'with a red face and grey curls beneath her cap', who cooked him two meals a day. Many years later, Ibsen remembered the excellence of her cooking. 'Her fried cod', he told John Paulsen, 'was a master-piece.'[5] Sophie Monsen recalled that he 'always ate his meals by himself in his rooms in the rear annexe – and when he needed anything he would go across the courtyard to the woman who cooked for him rather than ring for and disturb the servant, who would then be eating himself. He was very thoughtful.'

The winter of 1852–3 had been a depressing one for Ibsen, with the failure of *St John's Night* and the dull and dismal list of plays. Spring, however, occasionally brings con-solations to the professionally unsuccessful, and it now did for Ibsen. He fell in love. At Fru Sontum's, shortly before he moved into the theatre annexe, he met a young girl named Rikke (i.e. Henrikke) Holst. She was only fifteen, ten years younger than Ibsen, and not yet confirmed, the niece, indeed, of that Sofie Holst for whom he had written his last Grim-stad poem, 'Moonlight Wandering after a Ball'. Rikke is re-puted to have drawn his attention to her by pertly throwing a posy of flowers in his face. Ibsen bought her cakes, sent her flowers, and went for walks with her; she was a merry, extro-vert girl and seems to have enjoyed his company. He wrote her several charming poems, including one entitled 'Earth Flowers and Potted Plants', in which he contrasts her fresh-ness with the sophistication of other young ladies, as a wild flower contrasts with a cultivated plant in a window.

Rikke seems to have reciprocated his love, and he spent a happy spring. On Whit Sunday, 15 May, he climbed with a group of young people up to Ulrikken. Rikke recalled the occasion thirty-six years later: how, when they had reached the top, they unpacked their picnic baskets, the musicians

5. Let no one whose experience of cod is confined to England or the United States sneer. The cod of Bergen, properly prepared, *is* a master-piece.

began to play, and Ibsen suddenly leaped to his feet and, standing there on the mountainside, declaimed an apparently spontaneous 'Ode to Joy'. Two days after the Whit Sunday excursion, he joined in the 17th of May celebrations, when the young actors of the theatre (the ladies were not allowed to partake in this ceremony) walked in procession through the town wearing the Hungarian *luva* of grey-green cloth with a tassel, to demonstrate their support of Kossuth's new uprising. Rikke remembered how he

descended from the mountain ... and delivered an eloquent speech about how Norway still lay in her swaddling-clothes; but development was near, and must surely come. This aroused great enthusiasm and he was greeted with joyful demonstrations ... It made him happy in those days occasionally to stand face to face with a crowd and feel that he had tamed it and was able to control it ... Even his friends sometimes felt it was embarrassing to walk with him across the street, for there was something strange about him, even the way he dressed. But once he began to talk, you forgot everything and were caught up by the fire that burned in him.

Early that June he asked Rikke to marry him. But her father refused to countenance any engagement before she was confirmed; furthermore, he forbade her to continue seeing this young poet, who was poor, of uncertain prospects, had failed his matriculation, held radical political views, and must altogether have seemed, to any respectable citizen, a singularly unpromising match. Despite this edict, they continued to meet, with her five-year-old brother as chaperon and a girl friend of hers as look-out, and plighted their troth in a time-honoured and romantic manner by joining their rings on a key-ring and throwing them linked into the fjord. Thus, according to an ancient tradition, the sea had joined them as surely as any priest. Unhappily, one day her father surprised them together. Many years later Rikke's little brother, then an old man, remembered the occasion: a clenched fist raised threateningly in the long avenue of trees, and his father's face 'green with anger'. A bolder lover might have braved it out; but Ibsen turned tail and fled. That was the end of things between Ibsen and Rikke Holst. Thirty years afterwards, when revisiting Bergen, he called on her; she was by now a comfortably married *hausfrau* with many children. The old warmth, we are told, rose again in him, and he asked wonderingly: 'I wonder why nothing ever came of our relationship?' She laughed as in the old days, and said: 'But, my dear Ibsen, don't you remember? You ran away!' 'Yes, yes,' he replied. 'I never was a brave man face to face.'

It is tempting to exaggerate the effect of the Rikke Holst affair on Ibsen's life. Most of us have loved and lost in our early twenties; it is an essential part of any artist's education; and at least his love had been reciprocated. It was probably at this time that he wrote at any rate the first draft of the long, brilliant and bitter poem, 'In the Picture Gallery':

> There dwells an ugly demon in my breast
> Who sometimes visits me in evil hours;
> In loneliness, or when life's joys are best,
> As when I dream, or, rhyming, sense my powers . . .

> 'Will you not realize', it whispers, gloating,
> 'How meaningless it is, your life's short span?
> Have you not lost your faith in God and man?

> Can you not understand, your hopes are nothing?
> Your ideals but a distant candle are;
> Your goal a meteor, and not a star?' . . .

> Outside my window stood an apple tree,
> Its branches filled with flowers and with fragrance.
> There a small bird sang for my ear alone,
> Singing of life's great glory and abundance.

> Now those bright flowers rot black against the roots.
> The once-green leaf rustles against the stone.
> A tempest snatched them from the stage of life,
> And the sweet singer of the spring has flown.

Now autumn reigns within me and without.
I press my forehead to the window, where
The frost makes foolish patterns on the pane.

What proof have I that once I saw the spring?
A withered leaf, a stump of memory;
That is the sum and total of life's gain!

Not surprisingly, his work at the theatre suffered, and on
30 July the board felt constrained to send him a letter demanding that he apply himself more actively to his duties:

It has come to the notice of the board that some of the responsibilities connected with your work have been postponed and
subsequently overlooked, while others have not always been carried out in the most desirable manner ... It would be to the
advantage of all parties if you could be more active in the theatre
... The board believes, however, that this neglect of duty stems
rather from lack of experience than from any want of ability or
willingness to perform your duties.

Ibsen should have written a new play that autumn for the
coming anniversary of the theatre's opening but, although
he wrote to Paul Botten Hansen on 5 August that he was
'pretty productive, as you will discover before the winter is
out', he in fact did no more than revise *The Warrior's
Barrow*, individualizing the characters more sharply, improving the motivation, reducing the mythological apparatus (rather to the play's detriment), and generally polishing
the verse. In this new form *The Warrior's Barrow* accordingly received its second production, at the Bergen Theatre
on 2 January 1854. Perhaps it was not unreasonable of Ibsen
to wish it to be performed again; after all, it had been sympathetically received in Christiania. But at Bergen it failed,
even more calamitously than *St John's Night*, for it was
dropped after a single performance. The local press did not
notice it at all.

5

Kid Gloves in Bergen
1854–7

THE effect of the failure of *The Warrior's Barrow* upon Ibsen's self-confidence can be measured by the fact that he offered his next play to the Bergen Theatre anonymously. In September 1854 Peter Blytt became chairman of the board; at thirty-one, he was only five years older than Ibsen. In his memoirs he records that a few weeks after his appointment to this post, Ibsen came to see him with a quarto notebook under his arm. 'I was immediately struck', notes Blytt, 'by the fact that he seemed more than usually ill at ease that day. After a few confused preliminary remarks he handed me the book, saying that it was a manuscript that had been sent him by a friend in Christiania, a historical drama or, if one preferred, a tragedy, which the author in question, who wished to remain anonymous, would like to be performed at the Bergen Theatre, should it be deemed worthy of acceptance. But before submitting it to the board he – Ibsen – desired me to read it through and give him my opinion.'

The play was entitled *Lady Inger of Østraat*. Blytt guessed from Ibsen's demeanour that he was probably the author; he read the play, liked it, and quickly put it into rehearsal. It was only a few days before the opening performance that Ibsen admitted to its authorship. Blytt tells us that at a rehearsal Ibsen, in his capacity as *sceneinstruktør*, suddenly rushed on to the stage, interrupted one of the actors in the middle of a long speech, and showed him with unusual feeling how it ought to be spoken. Blytt noticed that Ibsen did this without referring to the prompt book, and this confirmed his suspicion. Nevertheless, Ibsen remained adamant in refusing to allow his name to appear as the author on either the posters or the programme.

H. Wiers-Jenssen, quoting an actress who was in the company at the time, confirms this story with some interesting additional details. The speech about which Ibsen felt so strongly was the one in Act Three in which Nils Lykke says to Lady Inger's daughter, Eline:

> How often have you not sat here at Østraat, alone, your brain in a whirl . . . longing to get away, to flee far away, you know not whither? How often have you not wandered alone along the fjord, and a gilded ship with knights and ladies aboard, with harps and singers, has glided by, far from the shore; a faint echo of mighty deeds has floated to your ear; and you have felt a longing in your breast, an irresistible longing to know what exists on the other side of the sea? . . . When you dreamed of the many-coloured life out there in the wide world – when you dreamed of tourneys and merry feastings – did you never see in your dreams a knight standing with a smile on his lips and grief in his heart in the midst of the tumult – a knight who had once dreamed, as fairly as you, of a woman, noble and virtuous, and whom he had sought in vain among all those who surrounded him?

When (Wiers-Jenssen tells) Ibsen had sprung on to the stage and delivered this speech with a passion which astonished the actors standing silently around, he fell silent for a moment and then said to the actor who was playing the part: 'Well – you know – something along those lines – I think the speech will sound best if you say it that way – But if you don't feel – of course – then – it's you who are acting it – yes.' And he shuffled back into the wings.

Lady Inger of Østraat is set in Norway in 1528. Like *The Warrior's Barrow* and *St John's Night* (and, for that matter, his next two plays, *The Feast at Solhaug* and *Olaf Lilje-krans*), it conforms to the classic demand for unity of time, place, and action, for the entire story takes place during a single night in Lady Inger's castle. The plot is extremely complicated. Lady Inger, a rich and powerful noblewoman, is under persuasion to lead a Norwegian uprising against the Danish overlords. A Norwegian patriot, Olaf Skaktavl, tells her that a stranger will come to her castle that night; he is the son of a Swedish rebel murdered by the Danes, Sten Sture, and is preparing a rebellion which Olaf begs Lady Inger to support. Sure enough, a stranger arrives; but he is not Sten Sture's son, but a Danish intriguer, Nils Lykke, who has got wind of Sten Sturesson's plans and has come to intercept and kill him. Lady Inger, however, supposes him to be Sturesson. A sub-plot, beautifully worked into the main action, is that Lady Inger's eldest daughter Lucia had, some years before, been seduced by Nils Lykke, and had killed herself; but Lady Inger has never seen Lykke, and does not recognize him. She has a surviving daughter, Eline, whose ambition is to discover and revenge herself upon her sister's seducer; but she knows his face no more than her mother does, and she, like her sister, is seduced by him that night. Then a second stranger arrives at the castle, so late that everyone has gone to bed except Lykke, who is waiting to murder him. But this second stranger is not, as he had expected, Sten Sturesson, but his half-brother Sten Steensson, an illegitimate son of Sten Sture born to him long before by Lady Inger herself. Lady Inger, who has not seen him since childhood, supposes him to be his legitimate half-brother and thinks that if she can kill him she may pave the way for her own son to be king; herself unable to rule because of her sex, she has cherished a secret ambition to become the mother of a king. She has him killed, only to discover that he is her own son. At the same time, Eline discovers that her lover, Nils Lykke, is her sister's seducer. Lady Inger dies by her son's coffin, and Nils Lykke walks quietly out, his mission accomplished. Evil has triumphed.

Lady Inger of Østraat was the first of Ibsen's plays to be written entirely in prose; it is also the first that would stand up to performance today. In 1857, even after he had had a public success with *The Feast at Solhaug*, Ibsen, writing to

Paul Botten Hansen, twice referred to *Lady Inger* as 'my best play'. It is indeed, despite its obvious faults, a remarkably mature and powerful work. Not that it is to be regarded as a harbinger of the new drama; it is rather a brilliant essay in the old tradition. In it, Ibsen has retained, as yet without question, much of the old paraphernalia of plot which was still then supposed to be indigenous to tragedy, as to comedy – mistaken identities, intercepted letters, overheard conversations, lengthy monologues, and frequent asides (which last can be deleted from *Lady Inger* without in any way obscuring the action). The language, too, is often stiff, though of considerable quality and precisely phrased. But the characterization is much more searching than anything he had achieved previously, and the action moves towards its climax with that inevitability which we associate with his later and more famous works. Here, too, for the first time, we hear that tone of controlled yet searching self-analysis which we shall later come to recognize as the authentic Ibsen music. In particular, Lady Inger's conflict of courage and cowardice, her desire to act and her doubts that hold her back, was a theme to which Ibsen was to return again and again in his plays; it is the dilemma of Skule in *The Pretenders*, Mrs Alving in *Ghosts*, Ellida in *The Lady from the Sea*, Rebecca West in *Rosmersholm*, and Hedda Gabler.

It has been suggested that *Lady Inger of Østraat* was technically influenced by Scribe's historical drama *Les Contes de la Reine de Navarre*, which Ibsen had helped to direct that autumn, in October 1854. The rapid succession of short scenes, it is argued, and the various coincidences vital to the plot, are typical of Scribe. Have the critics who make such assertions never read Shakespeare? Mistaken identities, intercepted letters, overheard conversations, monologues and asides are all to be found in both *Hamlet* and *King Lear*, which we know Ibsen had seen in Copenhagen, and which he had almost certainly read; indeed, off-hand it is difficult to think of a Shakespeare play that does not contain them. And anyone who has ever acted in, or been associated with, a Shakespeare production knows how, with the free Elizabethan method of staging, Shakespeare was addicted to the frequent use of the short scene. Even if Ibsen had not learned all this from Shakespeare, he would have done so from Holberg. One repeats that the myth of Ibsen's debt to Scribe, of whom he never recorded a good word, needs to be exploded. Scribe, if shallow in characterization, was a skilful theatrical craftsman, but there is no evidence that he ever exerted the slightest influence upon Ibsen.

Lady Inger of Østraat might, if its reception had been different, have proved the first major turning-point in Ibsen's career as a dramatist; it was his first step on that road of high tragedy which he was ultimately to extend into previously uncharted country. As fate decreed, however, he was thrown smartly off that road, and it was to be another decade before he ventured to return to it. For *Lady Inger* was as big a failure with the Bergen public as *St John's Night* and *The Warrior's Barrow* had been. They received it so poorly at its first performance on 2 January 1855 that it was repeated only once; and even when, the following year, Ibsen had a success with *The Feast at Solhaug* and tried to persuade them to revive *Lady Inger*, the board refused. It is possible, of course, that it may, like so many plays that have failed critically and publicly, have won him the admiration of a discriminating few, but we have no evidence for this.

He does not seem to have found any replacement for Rikke Holst; those who knew him at this period say that he was preternaturally shy and had few friends. As far as we know it was to be almost three years before he again formed any close association with a girl, and then it was to be the one he was to marry. The over-all picture we have of Ibsen at this time is very different from that which Christopher Due paints of him at Grimstad only five years earlier, when he had, apparently, become infatuated fairly often. No love poems have survived from the years 1854 and 1855. But this, again, is not so inexplicable a phenomenon as some critics and biographers have tried to make out. Some young men

fall in love at the drop of a handkerchief, others rarely and
with difficulty, and it is not uncommon for a young man to
change in his twenties from one type to the other. Nor
should we be surprised that he, who had made several close
friends in Christiania, found none in Bergen. Although the
two towns were roughly similar in size, Bergen had no university and, as Lorentz Dietrichson has told us, little culture.
Ibsen was not the first man who, on leaving a university city
for a small provincial town, has found himself isolated and
friendless and sought in vain for someone to love.

Outwardly, too, and especially sartorially, Ibsen was very
different from the shabby apprentice, lacking socks and
overcoat, whom Due had known at Grimstad. True to the
child who, at Venstøp, had admired the sexton's father as
he arrayed himself in his fine clothes, Ibsen used what
must have been a largish proportion of his salary to dress
elegantly. Magdalene Thoresen, seeing Ibsen around 1870
in a velvet coat, 'was reminded of an earlier attempt at the
elegant which he once made in Bergen when, very smart, he
swung round a corner wearing light yellow kid gloves. In
Bergen!' she added uncharitably. Herman Bang, writing in
1889, quotes a description given him by someone who had
known Ibsen at Bergen: 'He was so soigné, almost precise
and finicky, in his dress. He wore elegant frilled poet's cuffs,
with lace edges extending over his hands. And on the street
he carried a short little cane. People thought he looked unimpressive, and he suffered from the consciousness of being
small – but those who dismissed him as insignificant had
never seen his eyes. They could catch fire and throw a glance
that pierced you, so that you remembered it long afterwards.'

That February, 1855, he wrote a pleasant epithalamium to
celebrate the marriage of another of his former landlady's
sons, Edvard Sontum: it is the only poem from Ibsen's pen
that has survived from this year, apart from those which he
was to insert into his new play. The same month, he directed
one of the few good plays (apart from Holberg's and his own)

which came his way at Bergen: Eugène Labiche's farce *An Italian Straw Hat*. Otherwise, the repertory made the usual dismal reading: Scribe, Bayard and Mélesville, with German, Danish, and (occasionally) Norwegian pieces of equal triviality and, usually, less expertise.

That others besides himself were dissatisfied with such dramatic fare Ibsen would have learned from a drama criticism by Bjørnson which appeared in *Aftenbladet* on 1 February that year. The starting-point of the article was a new French play, *Le Gendre de M. Poirier*, by a thirty-four-year-old dramatist named Emile Augier, which had been produced in Paris the previous year. Bjørnson wrote admiringly of 'the economy of the dialogue, the careful unfolding of character, so that even in the fourth act the author has new aspects of personality with which to surprise us', and of 'the perspective which is opened ... by the dialogue never illuminating the character directly but ... as it were, merely allowing it to be distantly glimpsed'. This new naturalism is generally agreed to have dated, as far as the French theatre is concerned, from the production of Musset's *Un Caprice* at the Comédie-française in 1847 (though in the novel it can be traced back at least twenty-five years, to Balzac's *Le Peau de Chagrin* [1830] and Stendal's *Le Rouge et le Noir* [1831], and was to reach its peak in Flaubert's *Madame Bovary* in 1856). Bjørnson, praising the psychological advance which Augier had made on Scribe, expressed the hope that the new movement might help 'to reform the taste of our time for characterless drama'.

But Ibsen was unable to read Augier because of his ignorance of French, and some time during the spring or summer of 1855 he made a literary discovery which excited him much more: the Icelandic Sagas. They were the first literature that had excited him for several years, since his discovery in his teens of Voltaire, Oehlenschläger, Holberg, and Heiberg, and the Shakespeare he had seen in Copenhagen and Dresden; and they were to be virtually the last. Once Ibsen had thrown off the not very inspiring influence

of Oehlenschläger and had absorbed what he could of
Shakespeare from seeing him and reading him in bad translations, he was never again to be seriously influenced by any
writer, dead or alive. He would sometimes pick up a thought
from Kierkegaard or Brandes, or a hint by Bjørnson, and
develop it; but he was, as Edmund Gosse observed, one of
the very few great writers who worked without a library. For
the last half of his life indeed, if not longer, Ibsen read little
but newspapers and the Bible (the latter, he would hasten to
point out, for the language only); but he read them, and the
newspapers especially, most minutely; his last twelve great
prose plays, from which the whole of modern prose drama
stems, are like fragments of newspapers written by some all-
seeing editor.

The sagas, however, fascinated him. It is remarkable that
he had not discovered them before; even such knowledge of
the Viking Age as he had required when writing *The Warrior's Barrow* had been gleaned from Oehlenschläger. It
was not that no good translations of the sagas were available
in Norwegian or Danish, for N. M. Petersen had produced
four excellent volumes between 1839 and 1844. But somehow
Ibsen had missed them. They excited him as the literature
and history of the Middle Ages, which he had studied when
preparing *Lady Inger of Østraat*, had failed to do.

At the same time, groping back into the literature of the
remote past, he happened upon two other forms that proved
a revelation to him: the medieval folk tale and ballad.
Twenty-eight years later, in a foreword which he wrote to
The Feast at Solhaug in 1883, Ibsen recalled the effect which
the discovery of this ancient literature had had upon him at
the time:

In the Icelandic *family* sagas I found in rich measure what I
required in the way of human clothing for the thoughts, moods,
and ideas which at that time were filling, or anyway running
around in my head ... In these family chronicles, with their
varied relationships and confrontations between man and man,
woman and woman, above all between human being and human

being, I discovered a rich, vital, and personal life; and from my encounter with all these intensely rounded and individual men and women there arose in my mind the first rough and misty outline of *The Vikings at Helgeland* ... But then something intervened. This was principally and decisively of a personal nature; but I think it was not without significance that I had at that time begun to study Landstad's collection of Norwegian folk ballads which had been published a few years previously. The mood in which I then found myself fitted better with the literary romanticism of the Middle Ages than with the deeds of the sagas, better with verse than prose, better with the linguistic music of the folk ballad than with the characterization of the sagas. So it happened that the shapeless, embryonic idea of *The Vikings of Helgeland* gradually transformed itself into the lyrical drama *The Feast at Solhaug*.

Ibsen wrote *The Feast at Solhaug* during the summer of 1855. It is partly in rhymed verse, partly in prose, and is set in the fourteenth century. A tedious melodrama about two sisters in love with the same man, it is, except possibly for *The Warrior's Barrow*, the worst play that Ibsen ever wrote. The plot and characterization are both extremely banal, and the only merit lies in some of the lyrical writing. The influence of the folk ballad is very apparent; both the style and the atmosphere of the play are full of echoes from Landstad's collection, and so are the characterization and motivation. If Ibsen had any illusions about the play's quality at the time, he soon abandoned them; writing to Peter Hansen in 1870 he dismissed it as 'a trifle that I no longer wish to acknowledge'.

But even the worst of plays may serve a purpose, and *The Feast at Solhaug*, as Ibsen was to discover when it was staged the following January, was to prove extremely important to him, for two reasons.

Meanwhile, he continued with his work as *sceneinstruktør*. On 30 September 1855, for the first and last time in his career, he directed a Shakespeare play – *As You Like It*, adapted by a Frøken S. Beyer and re-entitled *Life in the Forest*. The Bergen public did not appreciate it, and it was dropped after two performances. T. Blanc, the historian of the Bergen Theatre, comments: 'The play seems to have proved too difficult for the company's talents.'

That autumn, however, Ibsen had the honour of being elected to a fairly exclusive club, the 22 December Society. The name had no political significance, but arose merely from the fact that on 22 December 1845 twenty-five citizens had met in Bergen to found a literary society which was to meet every fortnight during the winter for lectures and readings; the playing of cards was to be strictly forbidden. The records of the society inform us that on 27 November 1855 'Instruktør Ibsen gave a lecture on W. Shackspear [*sic*] and his influence on Scandinavian Art.' Exasperatingly, the manuscript of this talk has not survived, and we have no record of anything that Ibsen said in it. One would give a lot to know.

On 2 January 1856 *The Feast at Solhaug* was performed, under Ibsen's direction, at the Bergen Theatre and, thanks to the debased taste of the public, was a success: the first, apart from the very limited praise accorded to *The Warrior's Barrow* in Christiania, that Ibsen had known. As much as the play itself, people admired the apparently authentic medieval peasant costumes and furniture, and the new decor which, like the costumes, Ibsen had designed, or at any rate co-operated on. In his 1883 foreword to the play, Ibsen described the first night reception:

I was at the time employed as stage instructor at the Bergen Theatre, and so personally supervised the rehearsals of my play. The performance was admirable, and of a rare warmth; acted with joy and devotion, it was received in the same spirit ... The performance ended with repeated calls for the author and cast. Later that evening the orchestra, accompanied by a large part of the audience, serenaded me outside my windows. I am not sure that I did not permit myself to be so carried away as to deliver a kind of address to the gathering. I know, at any rate, that I felt profoundly happy.

When, after a subsequent performance, one of the actors
made a speech in his honour, Ibsen thanked them for 'the
recognition that will strengthen me in my pursuit of the goal
towards which I am striving, and which I *shall* achieve'.
Later, he said it was the only really happy day he ever spent
in Bergen.

The Feast at Solhaug was repeated five times during the
next few months, a record previously achieved at the theatre
by only one play. Ibsen was by now nearly twenty-eight, and
he badly needed some kind of success; a poet or a novelist
can work unrecognized, but hardly a playwright. The occasion had, though, a side effect which in the long run was to
prove vastly more important to his writing.

Among the audience at the Bergen Theatre that January
evening in 1856 was a thirty-six-year-old authoress named
Magdalene Thoresen. Danish by birth, she had fled from
her native country to escape from a love affair with an Icelandic poet, and had married a twice widowed clergyman
seventeen years her senior, Hans Conrad Thoresen, the
Dean of Bergen. She was a beautiful and remarkable
woman, who had already achieved recognition as a novelist
and short story writer, and had both written and translated
plays for the Bergen Theatre, so that she had already met
Ibsen several times. Now that he was acclaimed as a successful playwright, she invited him to a literary evening at
her house, and he paid his first visit there five days after the
première of *The Feast at Solhaug*, on 7 January 1856.

Dean Thoresen's first wife, Sara, had died in 1841, aged
thirty-five, leaving him two daughters, Suzannah and
Marie. Suzannah, in 1856, was nineteen, eight years younger
than Ibsen. Her closest friend was a girl of the same age
named Karoline Reimers; they subscribed to the same lend-
ing library, and often sat back to back on a sofa reading
novels. They promised each other that if the one should
have a son and the other a daughter, the two should marry;

and so it turned out. Karoline Reimers was destined to become the wife of Bjørnstjerne Bjørnson; she lived into her ninety-ninth year, and gave her daughter, Bergliot, a vivid description of Suzannah as a girl, which Bergliot recorded nearly a century later:

The Dean's study was lined with books, and Magdalene Thoresen, being an authoress, gave the house an added literary atmosphere. But Suzannah Thoresen was not just generally interested in literature; she was a bookworm, with a voracious appetite ... She was especially interested in the drama, being herself of a dramatic temperament. Her descriptive power was on occasion so imaginative that both her sister Marie and her mother would burst into laughter; but then she would laugh herself, for she had a great sense of humour. But what was most deep-rooted in her nature was, and remained, her sense of the epic in life, her feeling for everything that was intense and powerful like herself, her understanding of the monumental and the tragic. No wonder that both her sister Marie and her friend Karoline began to whisper that the young dramatist at the city theatre, Henrik Ibsen, was the man for Suzannah.

Bergliot herself remembered Suzannah only as 'an old woman, crippled by gout, sitting motionless in a chair, sharp of feature and dim of eye'. But a photograph of her in her early thirties, fifteen years after Ibsen met her, shows a lively face, not classically beautiful but attractive and well-proportioned, with unusually fine eyes. She was famous for the beauty of her hair. 'Everyone in Bergen talked about it,' writes Bergliot Ibsen. 'Once it was even weighed on a festive occasion in the town; and it was so long that it stretched right down to her feet like a cloak, chestnut brown and splendidly wavy. Her figure had always been somewhat full, but the taste of the time was different from ours. Her sister Marie was the prettier, but Suzannah's face acquired a beauty from the strength and vitality that coursed through her.'

Suzannah's views on most matters were, partly no doubt thanks to the influence of her stepmother, advanced to the point of radicalism, and she was probably the first 'new woman', apart from Magdalene herself, whom Ibsen had ever met. It is easy to imagine the effect she must have made on the lonely and restless young poet; less easy to guess whether Magdalene, never averse to the admiration of young men (she was later to have a celebrated passion for Georg Brandes, twenty-two years her junior), was pleased to note this, or a little jealous. Ibsen, at any rate, was immediately attracted by Suzannah, and she by him. Their second and decisive meeting took place later that month at a ball in Bergen given by the local Philharmonic Society. Here, Bergliot tells us (and her mother and both parents-in-law were present on the occasion) 'he did not dance, and neither did she. They talked together deep into the night; and that same night he wrote to her that if she would join her destiny to his, he could become something great in the world.' Later he was to re-create the atmosphere of that evening in an exquisite love poem, entitled 'To the Only One'.[1]

Ibsen now became a constant visitor to the Thoresen household; which, as Bergliot Ibsen observed, presumably on her mother's information, 'must surely have both astonished and vexed the admired Magdalene Thoresen, to see the young Ibsen paying court to her stepdaughter and not to herself'. Before the end of the month he sought formal permission to ask for Suzannah's hand. Halvdan Koht, who knew both Ibsen and Suzannah and presumably had the story from one or other of them, or perhaps from Karoline Reimers-Bjørnson, tells what followed:

He went in his best clothes to receive an answer, and was shown into an empty room to wait for her. Time passed, and she did not come. He paced to and fro, sat down, got up, became more and more restless. Finally, in despair, he moved towards

---

1. He wrote several other poems to Suzannah during their courtship, but only one other has survived; she destroyed the rest, and also, it seems, all his early letters to her, shortly before her death. 'Our relationship', she said, 'concerns no one but ourselves.' She was, to the last, the most formidably inflexible of women.

the door. Then he heard a laugh from beneath the sofa, and a head peeped out; she had been hiding there all the time. She gave him her answer, and they became engaged.

His position and prospects were, however, not yet adequate to support a wife, and it was to be two and a half years before they could marry.

Magdalene Thoresen commented briefly: 'The engagement went off very quietly, and gave not the slightest occasion for strong outbursts of emotion.' Her attitude towards her future stepson-in-law remained, throughout her long life, curiously ambivalent. She went on to make an interesting comparison between Ibsen and another writer of genius whom she had met in her own country of Denmark.

One couldn't restrain an involuntary smile – and that awoke a memory. As a young girl I had once met Søren Kierkegaard. It now occurs to me that there was a striking similarity between these two great spirits. Outwardly the resemblance was small; Søren Kierkegaard was long-striding and gangling, while Ibsen took short paces and had the squat build of a miner. What similarity there was must, therefore, have lain deeper; and so it was. I have never seen in any other two persons, male or female, so marked a compulsion to be alone with themselves.

That spring of 1856 was a good one for Ibsen. On 13 March *The Feast at Solhaug* was produced in Christiania, and received a considerable ovation. Six days later it was published there – the first book by Ibsen to appear since *Catiline*, and the first to carry his name on the title page.[2] Critical opinion, admittedly, was less favourable than the reception by the first night audience had been; he was accused of having plagiarized both Henrik Hertz's *Svend Dyring's House*, an inferior melodrama written ten years earlier (and which Ibsen had directed on 24 February 1856 in Bergen), and Heinrich von Kleist's *Kätchen von Heilbronn* – a

2. It sold poorly, however; it took fifteen years to exhaust the small edition.

charge which Ibsen was angrily to rebut. One of the few critics to praise the play in print was Bjørnson who, we must remember, had at this time scarcely met Ibsen, and who wrote a dynamic notice of the work in *Morgenbladet*. It was repeated five times in Christiania that season, a sign of fair success for a comparatively serious work.

That summer the theatre at Bergen was honoured, and nearly bankrupted, by a royal visit. On the afternoon of Saturday 23 August, Prince Napoleon, the son of King Jerome Napoleon and nephew to Napoleon I, landed completely unannounced in the city, asked if it contained a theatre and, on learning that it did, 'thrice expressed the wish to see a performance' on the following day, before departing on the Monday. The theatre was by now closed for the summer recess, the actors were all holidaying out of town, and the Prince's request did not reach Peter Blytt until ten o'clock that Saturday night, when he was in bed with a painful attack of gout, and had to go to be presented to the Prince wearing one shoe and one galosh, the afflicted foot being too swollen to take any more elaborate form of footwear. Blytt did not quite see how the company could be reassembled and re-rehearsed in what was, after all, less than twenty-four hours; however, he said he would see what could be done, and sent a message to Ibsen telling him to come and see him at once.

Ibsen, who had also gone to bed, in due course appeared, 'evidently in no good humour', and told the board that what they were asking was quite impossible. Blytt asked whether, since most of the company, including the leading players, were known to be together at Kolstien just outside town, a messenger could not be sent to summon them back. Reluctantly Ibsen wrote a letter, asking them to return first thing in the morning; then, after it had been dispatched, 'became more abrupt and unforthcoming than usual. He spoke only when directly addressed, and made no suggestions as to how the various difficulties might be overcome. Suddenly he jumped up and said with vehement irritability:

"No, it's no good – I've just remembered. We have no orchestra. All the wind instruments have been commandeered for tomorrow by the steamer *Patriot* for its cruise to Hardanger. I'd forgotten." '

Blytt said that this could surely be countermanded. Ibsen still shook his head. Then Blytt had a brilliant idea. 'It would be a pity if we had to cancel the performance,' he said, 'for the play we had in mind to show His Royal Highness was *The Feast at Solhaug*. It is as Norwegian as anything in our repertory – Norwegian author, Norwegian subject, Norwegian costumes – all of which unfamiliar material cannot but enrapture Prince Napoleon.' At this, Blytt tells, 'a marked change became noticeable in Ibsen. He suddenly became transformed into a bundle of energy and vitality, and looked interested, happy, and hopeful. The difficulties began to vanish.' Ibsen promised to conduct a rehearsal at eight the next morning. The wives of the board, plus Magdalene Thoresen, were bidden to prepare a supper of, indigestible as it sounds, 'ice cream, cakes, fruit, confectionery and champagne', and to lend their best china and silver, there being no hotel in the town then'. Real gold and silver cups for use on stage in the performance were to be borrowed from local goldsmiths, and posters were to be run off by a relative of one member of the board who fortunately happened to be a printer, so that the citizens might be informed and a full audience assembled.

Early the next morning Blytt received a note from Ibsen telling him that 'the company had arrived early and in the best of spirits, delighted at the honour of being asked to play before Prince Napoleon'. And at seven o'clock that Sunday evening the performance took place. Prince Napoleon, who knew no Norwegian, had asked for a written synopsis of the play in French; but the few French and French-speaking people in the city were all engaged in the preparations for the banquet, except for the local barber who was regarded as unsuitable. Blytt, however, knew German and, on inquiring whether the prince understood that language, and finding that he did, having, surprisingly, taught it once in Alsace ('the reader of these lines may shake his head in doubt, but I can swear on my honour and conscience that Prince Napoleon actually told me this'), stood behind him throughout the performance, despite his gout (and still clad in a galosh?), giving the prince and his suite, which included Ernest Renan, a brief résumé before each act of what was to come.

During the second interval the author and his company were presented, whereupon

Ibsen offered the prince a handwritten copy of the play bound in red Morocco. He received it graciously, took wine with Ibsen, and promised that he would see that the play was translated into French and performed at the Imperial private theatre at St Cloud.[3] He also ordered a copy, exactly similar in colour and cut, to be made of the costume that Louise Brun had worn [as Margit], which, executed in silk and velvet, he proposed to present to the Empress Eugénie. This, before being dispatched, was exhibited in Bergen, and aroused much admiration.

The prince enjoyed his visit so much that he postponed his departure by a day, and attended a special ball hastily arranged by some local bigwigs, to which Ibsen and several of the company but, to Blytt's rage, on account of some private quarrel, none of the board were invited.

Some time during that summer or autumn Ibsen settled down, no doubt with greatly increased confidence, to write another play for the next January anniversary. After the success of *The Feast of Solhaug* it seemed obvious to attempt another comedy in the balladic manner; and he bethought himself of the theme on which he had begun to work during his first year at Christiania in 1850, and raked out the unfinished manuscript of *The Ptarmigan of Justedal*.

To complete this in its original metre would have meant abandoning the style which had served him so well in *The*

3. Neither of which things happened.

Feast at Solhaug, for *The Ptarmigan of Justedal* was, so far as
it went, written in unrhymed blank verse, and Ibsen wished
to use again a mixture of prose and rhymed verse of varying
rhythms as found in the ballads. He therefore rewrote it
completely, retaining only the original idea of a girl (still
named Alfhild) who was the sole survivor in a valley devas-
tated by the Black Death, and thus lived a wild, bird-like
existence uncontaminated by the materialism of civilization; and also the character of the wandering singer.
Apart from this he kept nothing. Not a single line of *The
Ptarmigan of Justedal* is carried over.

He found the theme for his new play in a ballad about a
character named Olaf Liljekrans who, while out riding the
evening before his wedding, is killed by fairies because he
will not let them seduce him into joining them. Ibsen set his
drama in the Middle Ages, in a village in the Norwegian
mountains. Two families have waged a vendetta for generations; now their two present heads, Arne of Guldvik and
Dame Kirsten Liljekrans, have decided to end the quarrel
and merge their fortunes by marrying Dame Kirsten's son
Olaf to Arne's daughter Ingeborg. In a spirited opening
scene, Arne and his followers, on their way to the wedding,
are met by Dame Kirsten in a state of great confusion; Olaf
has disappeared. Wandering in the mountains, he has met
the strange, half-elfin girl Alfhild, and has been bewitched
by her innocence (as Johannes, in *St John's Night*, was bewitched by the innocence of the unworldly Anne). Arne suspects trickery, and his daughter, Ingeborg, is furious; she is
in any case half-infatuated with her father's servant, Hemming. However, Olaf and Alfhild are now discovered, and
are persuaded to come down to the village; Dame Kirsten
thinks she can settle things by marrying off Alfhild to one of
her servants.

Alfhild is told that a wedding will be arranged for her,
and assumes in her innocence that her husband is to be Olaf.
He, meanwhile, back among civilized people, weakly agrees
to marry Ingeborg. When Alfhild discovers the truth, she

bars the doors and windows of the house, sets fire to it and flees back into the mountains. The guests manage to get out, and Ingeborg runs away with Hemming, also into the mountains; she no longer wishes to marry a man who does not love her. Dame Kirsten, Arne and their followers pursue Alfhild and capture her; then, on the mountain-side, Dame Kirsten, as is her right under feudal law, sentences Alfhild to be thrown to her death unless any man can be found willing to marry her. She proclaims this twice, and no one answers; at the third and final proclamation, however, Olaf claims her as his. Dame Kirsten has no alternative but to accept the situation, and Arne reluctantly has to agree to his daughter, Ingeborg, marrying his servant Hemming (being much more worried at the prospect of losing his best servant than at his daughter marrying beneath her).

Olaf Liljekrans was immediately accepted by the theatre for production the following January. During the last three months of 1856, before he got down to directing it, Ibsen found himself staging several worthwhile plays of a much better class than had usually fallen to his lot – none of them, needless to say, new. In October he produced two of Holberg's best comedies, *The Scatterbrain* and *Erasmus Montanus*; in November, Oehlenschläger's *The Vikings in Byzantium*; and in December, Scribe's best comedy, and perhaps the only play by him that stands revival today, *Une Verre d'Eau*, which is set at the court of Queen Anne and has as its main characters the Queen, Bolingbroke and the Duchess of Marlborough. (What with this play, Dumas's *Katharine Howard*, and two comedies by Alexandre Duval called *La Jeunesse d'Henri V* and *Edouard en Ecosse, ou La Nuit d'un Proscrit*, which he had directed earlier, Ibsen was learning a lot of bad English history.) He also busied himself with preparing a lecture on 'The Heroic Ballad and Its Significance to Modern Poetry' which he was due to deliver to the 22 December Society the following February, and which he later expanded into a lengthy essay.

After the success of *The Feast at Solhaug*, there was a

great rush for seats for *Olaf Liljekrans* when it was announced for 2 January 1857. According to *Bergens Tidende*, 'the demand was so great that only the stronger succeeded in forcing their way to the box-office, under the present somewhat unfortunate arrangements for the sale of tickets'. It was quite cordially received at its first performance, and the board rewarded Ibsen with an honorarium of £25, a large sum when one considers his salary; but after his previous play expectations had been high, and among the public, and even more so among the critics, there was a feeling of disappointment. Peter Blytt noted that it was 'little understood, and was not a success; the audience which had filled the theatre, hugely expectant, left in a cool mood'. Ibsen took a curtain call, and Marcus Grønvold, who was present, remembered him many years later 'pale, thin, and with a full black beard'. *Bergens Tidende* admired the 'pretty versification and often beautiful and poetic images', but plainly thought little of the plot, which it summarized disparagingly; and the correspondent of the Christiania *Aftenbladet* expressed himself bewildered by 'all the confusion' of the action. The play was repeated only once, on 4 January, and was never performed again in Ibsen's lifetime; nor was it published until shortly before his death, over forty years later. Ibsen himself rejected it as completely as *St John's Night*. When writing to Julius Elias in 1897 about his various early works, he deliberately omitted all mention of it, and subsequent commentators have rather slavishly accepted his judgement.

In fact, *Olaf Liljekrans* is by modern standards a much better play than *The Feast at Solhaug*, or indeed than any other play that Ibsen had yet written except *Lady Inger of Østraat*. The principal characters are all sharply drawn. The plot, which so confused the critic of *Aftenbladet*, is more complex than that of *The Feast at Solhaug*, which one would have thought a trifle uncomplicated even for the Bergen public, but is less unravellable than that of *Lady*

Inger; to a modern eye its complexity, yet lack of obscurity, is one of its virtues. The rhymed verse anticipates *Peer Gynt* in the freedom with which it changes from one rhythm to another. The main difficulty to a modern reader, and one which would probably prove insuperable upon the stage, lies in Alfhild herself. Two types of character are notoriously difficult to make convincing in the theatre, mad people and peasants, and a mad peasant-girl offers a formidable challenge to any actress and audience. Gerd, in *Brand*, can be made acceptable because she appears only in three brief scenes; but Alfhild is the leading character in *Olaf Liljekrans*, and Ibsen has, it must be admitted, put a deal of rather mawkish dialogue into her mouth. The play, depending as it does so much upon the lyrical quality and subtle rhyming of the dialogue, would be monstrously difficult to translate, and will probably never be adequately translated; but it is not to be dismissed as negligible.[4]

We know disappointingly little of Ibsen's activities during this, his last summer in Bergen. He must have felt that the little town had nothing more to offer him, artistically or materially. He could not marry Suzannah on any salary that the Bergen Theatre seemed likely to pay him in the foreseeable future; he badly needed the security of married life, they had already been engaged for a year and a half, and he must have felt that if this delay were to continue indefinitely, he might well lose her. Nor can the apparently unending prospect of directing Scribe and his followers have offered any incentive to remain.

Suddenly an avenue of escape appeared. On 18 July he left on a three weeks' visit to Christiania, 'chiefly', he wrote to

4. The prose, too, bears the marked and not altogether fortunate influence of the Icelandic Sagas (or Petersen's translation of them) in the frequent inversion of the natural word order – 'Little shall it boot you . . .', etc. The unnaturalness of verse works in the theatre; unnatural prose seldom does, except in comedy. But the discovery of this fact, and its corollary, that high tragedy could be written in ordinary colloquial prose, still lay many years ahead.

Paul Botten Hansen the previous day, 'to enjoy myself and see old friends again'. Five days later he wrote the following letter:

Christiania, 23 July 1857

To the Directors of the Norwegian Theatre at Bergen:

On my arrival in Christiania I saw in the newspapers a report which has probably by now also reached Bergen, and which I should accordingly like to correct. It asserts that the directors of the Norwegian Theatre in Christiania have entered into negotiations with me with a view to my taking over the post of artistic director at the Norwegian Theatre . . .

The reason, gentlemen, that I did not inform you of this situation lay simply in the uncertainty which I felt about the whole matter; I felt I had to come and assure myself at first-hand of the theatre's circumstances and prospects, etc. This I have now done, and I am now satisfied that the Christiania Theatre is as securely established as that of Bergen, and that here, as there, there is a chance that something may be achieved. I need not stress the advantages there would be to me in living in the capital; they are overwhelming and, painful as it would be to me to leave Bergen and the Bergen Theatre, I cannot but question whether it would not be indefensible of me to reject the opportunity which now presents itself of taking up a not unrewarding post. I speak in terms of salary and material advantages, but I am, please believe me, not merely being mercenary, or ungrateful. I shall never forget the debt I owe to the Bergen Theatre, but I also have duties towards myself, and I have long found working conditions at the Bergen Theatre oppressive; every way in which I might achieve anything has been barred to me, my hands have never been free, and I have as a result felt daily frustrated by the consciousness of having to work without being able to accomplish what I desired. In now addressing myself to you and asking whether, in the event of my agreeing terms with the Christiania Theatre, I may be released from my duties at Bergen, and how soon – I regard myself as appealing not merely to my superiors, but also to benevolent counsellors who will not refuse to look at the situation from what is, to me, its most important aspect. Should I be released from the remainder of my contract, I should naturally feel bound to refund my last month's salary, which has been paid in full. I need scarcely add that, offered equal conditions, I should prefer to remain at the Bergen Theatre, where I regard myself as having grown up, but I know that the theatre cannot stretch its resources further than has already been done, and I feel sure you will not be surprised that I feel compelled to seize this opportunity of a securer future. I await your reply eagerly.

> Your obedient servant,
> Henr. Ibsen

During the days of waiting to know their decision, he renewed his acquaintance with Bjørnstjerne Bjørnson, whom he had met occasionally during his student period in Christiania and who was just completing *Synnøve Solbakken*, the peasant novel that was to make him famous. 'Ibsen has come from Bergen – read his *Feast at Solhaug*!' wrote Bjørnson to the Danish critic Clemens Petersen on 2 August; adding: 'I love him!!' On 4 August Herman Laading replied to Ibsen on behalf of the Bergen directors

regretting that your application should come at a time when, as you must know, any reduction in the number of our instructors will be especially felt, since with the departure of Brun [in April] practically the whole of our repertory has been dislocated; but the board feel that the obvious advantages which must ensure to you from your new appointment and from living in the capital must override other considerations. We therefore release you from your contract with the Bergen Theatre, and wish you every luck in your work for your new theatre, whose goal is our own.

On 11 August 1857 Ibsen signed a contract with the Norwegian Theatre of Christiania. On 21 August *Morgenbladet* announced: 'Hr. Ibsen's appointment as stage instructor and artistic director at the Christiania Norwegian Theatre has now been confirmed. His salary is to comprise 7½ per cent of the theatre's gross takings against a guaranteed minimum salary of 600 specie-dollars [£150] per year. He has, as is well known, worked for five years at the Bergen Theatre, whither he has now returned to make preparations for his final removal. He is expected here at the end of the month.'

Ibsen left Bergen as unheralded as he had arrived – indeed, more so, for no newspaper thought it worth while to inform its readers of his departure, the date of which remains unknown. He said farewell to his fiancée and on 3 September took up his new post in Christiania.

He had, including his study trip to Copenhagen and Dresden, spent five years and ten months in Bergen. They had, after the first excitement, been extremely frustrating. As a director, his hands had been tied; as an author, he had repeatedly seen every attempt he had made to experiment and diverge from either the antiquated conventions of static verse tragedy, or the banalities of nationalistic rustic comedy, derided. His voyage abroad had opened his eyes to the potentialities of theatrical art; he had seen *Hamlet* and *King Lear*, met Heiberg and Hans Andersen, seen Michael Wiehe and N. P. Nielsen, Johanne Luise Heiberg and Frederik Høedt, Emil Devrient and Boguwil Dawison act. Bergen must have seemed more than usually provincial to him after that, and he must have been hideously aware of the inadequacy of the performances which he directed, whether of his own plays or of others.

Nevertheless, it is easy to over-stress his depression. He may well have felt that, in spite of everything, he had developed his powers not unprofitably during those five years. He had written four full-length plays in that time, and re-written a fifth; admittedly, all but one had failed, but there is some evidence that even the 'failures' were admired by a discerning minority. Some writers and artists, particularly if they are restless experimentalists, as Ibsen was to be all his life, are content with such recognition; conscious of the power and quality of their work, they know with the certainty of religionists that they are right and other people wrong. What they normally need is one other person who shares their faith in themselves; and this he had now found. As he packed his bags that August day in Bergen, Ibsen may well have felt that his time of fulfilment and recognition was at hand. If so, he was to be unpleasantly disillusioned. The six and a half years he was to spend in Christiania were to be far more chilling to his spirit than anything he had experienced in Bergen, or Grimstad, or Skien.

6

The Chicken Ladder
1857–9

THE Norwegian Theatre of Christiania, of which Ibsen in
the autumn of 1857 found himself artistic director, was a
more recent enterprise than its counterpart in Bergen. At
first a drama school, it had been founded in 1852 as an angry
reaction by a few extreme patriots against what they regarded as the failure of the Bergen Theatre to live up to its
expressed ideals.

The project of a Norwegian theatre had by no means been
received with unqualified enthusiasm in the capital. Knud
Knudsen tells in his memoirs how indignant the higher
stratum of Christiania society, 'more Danish than the
Danes themselves', was to find actors in the theatre at
Møllergaden speaking in the accent and idiom which Norwegians used, indeed, in private conversation, but regarded
as unsuitable for public occasions; just as, a century earlier
in Copenhagen, before Holberg had begun to write, we learn
that the Danish language was never heard in a gentleman's
house, and that polite Danes were wont to say that a man
wrote Latin to his friends, talked French to the ladies, called
his dogs in German, and used Danish only for swearing at
his servants. Particular offence was caused by the fact that
many of the actors at Møllergaden were from the eastern
country districts of Norway and spoke in the despised 'eastland' dialect. Bergenese was just acceptable, but eastland
dialect, no. This contempt of the educated public had a damaging effect on the Norwegian company, who soon realized
that if they were to progress in their career they would have,
sooner or later, to perform elsewhere in Danish, however fer-

vent their patriotism might be. Nor did the unfashionable situation of the new theatre help. Møllergaden was an ugly and dirty street, full of doubtful inns where drunken individuals engaged in horse-coping and similar ungenteel transactions. When the young Laura Svendsen was asked by a relative why she did not perform at the Norwegian Theatre, she replied that she would sooner beg in the gutter.

The Christiania Theatre (such being the official title of the 'Danish' Theatre at Bankpladsen) not surprisingly gave little encouragement to its new rival. An application from Knudsen and his committee for free tickets for their actors to the performances at Bankpladsen was refused; and whenever a promising player appeared at Møllergaden, the Christiania Theatre immediately tried to seduce him or her away with the carrot of higher pay. From the state, the new theatre received no more help than Bull had. Requests for financial support were repeatedly refused, the most recent appeal, only three months before Ibsen took up his post, having been rather unluckily rejected in the Storthing by 57 votes to 49, a majority of eight.

The Christiania Norwegian Theatre soon found, as the Bergen Theatre had, that to fulfil the ideals of experimentalism is easier in theory than in practice. Such new Norwegian plays as came their way were naïve and either undramatic or melodramatic. Nor could they follow the common practice of experimental theatres today when new plays fail, by taking refuge in the classics, firstly because the classics could not be translated into *landsmaal*, and secondly because the inexperienced actors were totally incapable of the heights demanded by classical tragedy or of the technique required for classical comedy. The translations, too, were mainly of poor quality, conveying little poetry or wit. Soon the directors found themselves compelled, like their fellows at Bergen, to fall back upon the staple diet of Danish vaudeville and French farce and musical comedy, so that it came to be said that a good singing voice was more likely to

get an actor a leading part than acting ability. The usual
evening bill consisted of two or three short pieces varied with
songs, declamations, and *tableaux vivants*. After five years
of activity no new authors had been discovered and neither
the repertory nor the talents of the company had been noticeably broadened. By the spring of 1857 things were so bad
that the committee considered winding up the whole project; but they decided to continue, and it was to remedy
matters that they imported Ibsen as artistic instructor. The
previous instructor, apart from being a Dane, had been an
actor very much in the traditional manner. They had appointed him because no qualified Norwegian existed; now
that, in Ibsen, one had arisen, they gave him the job.

Ibsen took lodgings in a house at the corner of Akersga-
den and Carl Johansgade, and got down to work at once.
Only a fortnight after his arrival on 18 September, a double
bill of two Norwegian plays was performed under his direction. Both were familiar works, by writers who had died ten
to fifteen years previously: Henrik Bjerregaard's musical, *A
Tale of the Mountains*, and Henrik Wergeland's sequel to
that play. Ibsen contributed a rhymed prologue in praise of
the two dead dramatists, and *Morgenbladet* remarked that
'the stage management showed evidence of considerable
care, and augurs well for Herr Ibsen's direction of the
theatre'. *A Tale of the Mountains* proved a public success,
and was performed twenty-two times that season.

Most of the repertory that autumn consisted of revivals of
plays produced in previous seasons – a fact that has surprised
some commentators, but which is simply explained in
Ibsen's report to his board two years later, on 2 July 1859.
'Nothing had been prepared ... and there was nothing new
to begin with.' The titles read dismally. *Cousin Lotta*, a
vaudeville by C. M. Wengel; *The Cobbler and the Countess*,
a musical by Ibsen's mentor in Copenhagen, Thomas Overskou, based on a French piece named *Riquiqui*; *A Foolish
Girl*, a vaudeville by Erik Bøgh, adapted from a French
comedy which had in turn been adapted from a play by Cal-

derón (*Casa con dos puertos mala es de guardar*); and J. H. Wessel's old musical parody, *Love without Stockings*. The only three new additions to the repertory before Christmas were on the same level: R. Benedix's comedy *Die Lügnerin*, which had to be withdrawn after one performance; *Lazarilla*, an operetta based on Scribe's comic opera *La Chanteuse Voilée*, which was a success and achieved sixteen performances before the summer closure; and Alexandre Duval's comedy, *La Jeunesse d'Henri V*, which Ibsen had already directed in Bergen, and which managed nine performances. A revival of Holberg's *Jeppe of the Hill*, an old favourite about a peasant who finds himself rich for an afternoon, was the only play of genuine distinction to be produced that season.

Not that the quality of the repertory at the Danish-controlled Christiania Theatre was any different, or any better. This was clearly what the public wanted. Ibsen, in addition to his work at the Møllergaden theatre, wrote occasional reviews for Botten Hansen's *Illustreret Nyhedsblad* of the productions at Bankpladsen, an arrangement which strikes a modern reader as somewhat unprofessional but which does not appear to have caused any surprise or offence then. An insight into his feelings at this time concerning the proper purpose of drama is given in a long review of over seven thousand words, which appeared in *Illustreret Nyhedsblad* on 20 and 27 December 1857. The subject in question was a historical drama, *Lord William Russell*, by Andreas Munch (1811–84), a reputable Norwegian writer who had sat with Ibsen and Bjørnson in the author's box at the première of the latter's *Between the Battles* the previous month. Lord William Russell was an English Protestant who was executed in 1683 for supposed complicity in the Rye House Plot to assassinate King Charles II, and it is apparent from Ibsen's very favourable review that both the theme and Munch's treatment of it had considerably excited him. Attacking 'the traditional demands which are made of tragedy in general', he writes: 'It has become customary to expect from tragic characters a loftiness, a purification, a greatness of thought and expression, will and action, that shall fulfil the function of the Greek cothurn – namely, to give us the feeling that we are outside the realm of everyday life. But this achieves the exact opposite of its purpose; the world portrayed by the dramatist is rendered completely foreign to the spectator, no bond exists between us and the protagonist as he struggles and is defeated, and so he cannot fully engage our sympathy.' One of the great virtues of Munch's play, Ibsen says, is that whereas 'traditional tragedy presents minor gods, A. Munch's work presents great mortal men'. Sixteen years later he was to explain his final abandonment of poetry as a dramatic medium in similar words.[1]

Ibsen then expatiates briefly on the proper treatment of symbolism, in a paragraph which should be compulsory reading for the many commentators who have written ignorantly about this aspect of Ibsen's work.

Every notable human being is symbolic, both in his career and in his relationship to history. But bad writers, misconstruing the theory that the significant phenomena of life should be intensified in art, make this symbolism conscious . . . Instead of it existing hidden in the work, like a vein of silver ore in a mountain, it is continually being dragged into the light of day.

One of the virtues of Munch's play, says Ibsen, is that

he has allowed the symbolism to stand there without commentary like a runic inscription, leaving it to each member of the audience to interpret it according to his or her individual needs . . . It is no conscious battle of ideas that enacts itself before us, any more than that ever happens in reality; what we see is human conflicts, behind which, yet interwoven with them, ideas conflict and conquer or are vanquished. And the play does not end at the fall of the curtain on the fifth act. The true end lies beyond; the poet indicates the direction in which we may seek; it is now up to each one of us to find his or her own way there.

1. 'What I sought to depict was human beings, and therefore I would not let them talk "the language of the gods" ' (Letter to Edmund Gosse, 15 January 1874).

These two ideas, that tragedy should present recognizable human beings rather than superhuman creatures, and that symbolism should be integral rather than overt, were, in time, to become two of his principal dogmas as a dramatist. At this early stage of his dramatic career, however, cut off by his ignorance of all foreign languages except German from practically all great specimens of drama, save in clumsy translations and adaptations, and blinded by the claims of the nationalistic movement and his excitement at the discovery of ancient Scandinavian literature, he was still groping inexpertly towards a satisfactory form. This isolation from the main tradition of classical tragedy was, eventually, to prove his strength, compelling him to strike out hugely on his own. But the confusion and uncertainty in which he now, at the age of twenty-nine, found himself are clearly shown in the play which he had completed a few weeks before writing the *Lord William Russell* review, *The Vikings at Helgeland*.

As explained, Ibsen had conceived this tragedy two years earlier in Bergen, as a result of reading N. M. Petersen's translation of the Icelandic Sagas, but had turned aside, under the influence of the folk ballad, to write *The Feast at Solhaug*. When he returned to it, during the spring of 1857, he began to write in verse, but abandoned that medium in favour of a prose based on the Homerically simple yet formalized language of the sagas. This incompatibility between saga material and dramatic form was a problem which Ibsen found himself unable to solve. The ancient Greek dramatists had solved it, but Ibsen knew no Greek and had very possibly never read a Greek play, even in bad translation; nor was the Norwegian theatre of the nineteenth century a medium remotely suited to epic presentation. *The Vikings at Helgeland* is a remarkable literary pastiche, and contains, buried in the impossible form of this pastiche, the kernel of what, over thirty years later, in a very different setting, was to become one of his greatest plays. It was the closest he had yet come to writing a great play; the construction, the consistency and development of the characterization, and the sense of an inevitable working out of destiny evolving directly from given characters in given situations, are for the first time in his work under mature and successful control. Only the remoteness of these ancient, heroic figures, and, more especially, of the conventions which governed their lives, defeated him.

The Vikings at Helgeland is set in northern Norway during the tenth century. As in *The Feast at Solhaug* (and, earlier, *Catiline*), the two principal women are diametrically contrasted characters: Hjørdis is a ruthless and formidable visionary, Dagny gentle, uxorious, and practical. Each is married to a man who is her own opposite: Hjørdis to the peaceful Gunnar, Dagny to a great warrior, Sigurd, Gunnar's foster-brother. Hjørdis despises her husband for his gentleness; only one thing binds her to him. As a girl in Iceland she had, in a splendid symbol, been guarded in her room by a huge white bear 'of the strength of twenty men'; no man might win her until he had killed this monster. One night, Gunnar had done this, and so she had become his wife; but their marriage has not been happy. She admires Sigurd, and he her, but he remains faithful to Dagny. During a feast, Hjørdis tries to start a quarrel between her husband and Sigurd; this so enrages Dagny that she reveals what Sigurd has told her, that it was he, and not Gunnar, who killed the white bear, in order that his foster-brother might win the woman he loved. Then, in the most effective, because it is psychologically the most modern scene in the play, Hjørdis and Sigurd, left alone, reveal their love for each other; neither has been happy in marriage; their good and gentle partners have not been what they wanted, and needed. Hjørdis tries to tempt Sigurd to kill Gunnar; but instead, he challenges Gunnar to single combat, knowing that, if he wins, the ancient laws of vendetta will compel Hjørdis to kill him. In the final act Hjørdis, believing that she and Sigurd can only be united in death, shoots him with her bow; but before he dies, he reveals to her that now they can never be together, since he, unknown to her, has embraced the Christian faith, and Christians and heathens can never meet after death. Hjørdis then kills herself in despair.

Thus bleakly outlined, *The Vikings at Helgeland* may seem little, if at all, superior to the static Viking dramas of Oehlenschläger; and the remoteness of the setting, the deliberate pastiche of the prose, and the Homeric simplicity of the characters make it unlikely that it could ever successfully be staged before a modern and sophisticated audience. In its own century it was to prove the most successful of Ibsen's early plays; the audiences who admired the Devrients and Frédéric Lemaître, Sarah Bernhardt and Henry Irving, liked their heroes and heroines to be huger than life, and *The Vikings at Helgeland* was to be performed more often in Christiania before 1900 than any of even his mature works. But for a play to work today one must be able to some extent at least to identify oneself with the characters; and the ethics and motivations of these mighty archetypal figures are wholly foreign to our own.

Nevertheless, *The Vikings at Helgeland* is of extraordinary interest to anyone who reads it with a knowledge of what Ibsen was later to write. Beneath the formalized characters of this ancient world with their strange conceptions of honour lies the story of [Hedda Gabler. Hedda, like Hjørdis, dreamed romantically of heroes, was guarded against them by a 'white bear' (in Hedda's case, a horror of things physical), married a gentle and unheroic man, was jealous of the tender and uxorious girl to whom her hero attached himself and, in her frustration, sent him to his death and took her own life. There is even a scene in the second act of *The Vikings of Helgeland* in which Hjørdis passionately seizes her rival, Dagny, and clasps her tightly, at which Dagny cries: 'Let me go! I don't want to listen to you!' just as Thea Elvsted, when passionately clasped by Hedda in the second act of that play, cries: 'Let me go! I'm frightened of you!' And the great scene in the third act when Hjørdis and Sigurd sit down quietly together and reveal to each other for the first time their mutual love that

can never find fulfilment, carries strong anticipatory echoes
of that famous scene when Hedda and Ejlert Løvborg pretend to peruse the photograph album. The sense, too, of fate
spinning her inflexible web around men, and of evil spirits
ruling their world – 'but their power is small unless they find
willing helpers within our hearts, and happiness is granted
to him who has the strength to fight against fate' (as
Hjørdis tells Sigurd) – is something with which we shall
become familiar in every mature play of Ibsen's from *The
Pretenders* to *When We Dead Awaken*. Structurally, too,
The Vikings at Helgeland shows an important advance on
his previous plays in two important respects. It is blessedly
free from the coincidences and improbabilities of *Lady
Inger* and *The Feast at Solhaug*; and it does not contain a
single monologue (though Ibsen was to revert to the monologue, with calculated effect, for a period later).

Ibsen's first months in Christiania during that autumn of
1857 must have seemed full of encouragement. Apart from
the relief of directing a theatre without having to share the
work with a *dramaturge* of superior upbringing and education, other irons were beginning to glow in the fire. On 4
November *The Feast at Solhaug* was performed at the Royal
Dramatic Theatre in Stockholm, the first time any of his
plays had been staged outside Norway, and it was well received. The same month, *The Vikings at Helgeland* was accepted by the directors of the Danish-controlled Christiania
Theatre for production the following spring. He had offered
the play to them rather than to his own theatre on the assumption, rightly as it turned out, that his own actors at the
Norwegian Theatre were as incapable of high tragedy as
the actors at Bergen had been. And as though his work at the
theatre were not sufficient to occupy him fully, he applied on
13 November for a university bursary in Scandinavian literature of £65 a year (largely, one imagines, on the strength of
his essay on the Heroic Ballad). In his letter to the authorities he admitted that he 'has indeed not much to plead in
support of his application, but ventures to nominate himself

since he has good grounds for supposing that other applicants find themselves similarly placed'. Two months later,
however, on 13 January 1858, he withdrew his application,
having presumably decided that the reorganization and direction of the Norwegian Theatre was not, after all, a part-
time job.

The newspapers, meanwhile, were taking notice of the improved standard of production at the Norwegian Theatre.
That February a correspondent in *Aftenbladet*, after complaining at the way in which the gallery is allowed to dominate the style of performance, so that 'inconceivable
exaggerations, vulgarities, and untruthfulness' evoke 'hysterical applause', praised the 'more faithful, if less technically skilled, interpretation of the author's ideas ... than is
often the case at the other, the Danish Theatre, despite the
larger size and superior experience of the company at the
latter'. If only, the writer continued, critics would give a lead,
the unfortunate public interruptions during performance,
which are at present in danger of destroying the good work
of the new artistic director, might cease. 'However, Herr
Ibsen will surely, being a man of creative power and sen-
sibility, be able to guard against the effect of this repeated
caterwauling on his sense of theatrical vocation; yet it needs
to be remarked that at present he stands virtually alone, and
alone in his vision; and it should not be so.' It was to remain
so for longer than the anonymous author of these lines could
have guessed.

Another article at about the same time in *Christiania-
Posten* gives an interesting picture of the difference between
the new Norwegian Theatre and the Danish-controlled one
at Bankpladsen. The audience of the one, we learn, comes in
'working clothes', the other in 'going-out dress'. In the
Danish Theatre the main purpose is to see and be seen, especially since it has acquired a new chandelier. 'In the Norwegian Theatre the lighting is not quite so bright; there are
no boxes to underline differences of class and wealth, and
the short jacket of the hill peasant may be seen side by side

with a coat of the most elegant cut. Yet if one of the regular
Thursday patrons of the Christiania Theatre were to visit
Møllergaden *incognito* he might find to his surprise that
the acting was not so bad nor the audience so obtuse as he
had confidently imagined.' By and large the repertories of
the two companies were very similar, since both depended
mostly on Danish adaptations of contemporary French and,
occasionally, German comedies, musical or not. In anything
requiring singing the Norwegian Theatre seems to have had
a slight edge over its rival; moreover, the playing there was
in general brisker, and so, we are told, was the scene-chang-
ing.

An interesting portrait of Ibsen at this juncture in his
career is provided for us by Bjørnstjerne Bjørnson, who
had recently returned from a year in Denmark and of
whom, for the first time, Ibsen had begun to see a good deal.
At the première on 27 October of Bjørnson's first play,
Between the Battles (a fine one-acter, set in a moment of
peace during a bloody civil war, and vitiated only by a certain glibness of climax which was to be one of Bjørnson's
besetting faults as a dramatist), Ibsen had sat beside him in
the author's box; and in a letter that November (which
Bjørnson, as so often, forgot or did not bother to date) to
the young but influential Danish critic Clemens Petersen,
Bjørnson, who had evidently read *The Vikings at Helgeland* in manuscript, gives his impressions of his fellow-
playwright. He found Ibsen, for his tastes, too derivative.
'I'm afraid', he wrote to Petersen, 'he must find a new and a
different road before I can have any faith in him. In *The
Feast at Solhaug* he has so buried himself in the heroic
ballad that he ended up by becoming a ballad incarnate. To
the point where he made the language his own. Then he
moved on to the saga, and now he's emerging from that with
all its expressions, its language, word for word, its least
nuance and its dead poetry ... He has a curiously dreamy
personality which can't immerse itself in life but only in
dead poetry.'

It is scarcely possible to imagine two more contrasted characters than Ibsen and Bjørnson. Even Dickens and Thackeray were less dissimilar. Ibsen was small, gauche, self-distrustful, shy of women, physically unattractive and, artistically, a slow developer. Bjørnson was tall, powerfully built, self-confident, gregarious, an intensive and successful womanizer, and a brilliant public speaker, who achieved literary fame in his middle twenties. For half a century a violent and extraordinary love-hatred relationship was to exist between them, harsh words and condemnations alternating bewilderingly with protestations of admiration and devotion. The wonder is, not that their friendship was so perpetually troubled, but that somehow, in defiance of all probability, it eventually managed to survive.

We have disappointingly few letters from Ibsen's hand during the six and a half years that he was now to spend in Christiania. He must, lamentable correspondent though he was, have written at least occasionally to Suzannah in Bergen during the nine months they were separated (from September 1857 to June 1858), but she apparently destroyed his early letters as she did his early poems. 'Our relationship concerns no one but ourselves.' The only letter of interest which we have during this period is one dated 30 January 1858 to a friend seven years younger than himself, one Carl Johan Anker, who was now serving in the Norwegian Guard in Stockholm and with whom he had gone on a walking tour from Bergen to Hardanger and back in the summer of 1856. After the usual apology for silence, with which so many of his letters were to begin, he recalled their excursion affectionately, and continued:

I have often wondered what you must have thought of me then, whether you didn't find me walled about with a kind of off-putting coldness which makes any close relationship with me difficult. And yet I found it incomparably easier to make contact with you than with anyone else, for I found in you a spiritual youthfulness, a joy in life, a chivalry of outlook which warmed my heart. Keep all this! Believe me, it is not pleasant to

see the world from an October standpoint; though, strangely,
there was once a time when I wanted nothing more. I have
passionately longed for, yes, almost *prayed* for, a great grief
which might fill my existence, give content to my life. It was
foolish, and I have fought my way out of that state of mind – but
the memory of it will always remain.

This is a very different Ibsen from the 'merry and vital'
young man whom Christopher Due remembered from
Grimstad. Yet we should not, as some commentators have
done, be unduly surprised at this. The shyest people
often have one or two friends from youth, usually (as Due
seems to have been) simple and warm-hearted extroverts,
who remember them as open almost to the point of ebul-
lience.

The first months in Christiania had been full of promise;
the New Year (1858) was to bring two sharp disap-
pointments. In February J. L. Heiberg refused *The Vikings
at Helgeland* for the Royal Theatre at Copenhagen. A worse
blow was to follow. On 9 March Ibsen learned that Carl Borgaard, the head of the Danish-controlled Christiania
Theatre, who had accepted the play for production that
spring, was proposing to postpone production for a year
'since the economic position of the theatre and its immediate
prospects do not permit of the payment of honoraria for
original works during the current season'.

Ibsen reacted promptly and furiously. The day after he
heard the news, on 10 March, he published a violent attack
on the Christiania Theatre in *Aftenbladet*. Ever since its
inception, he declared, the theatre had jealously clung to
everything Danish. The establishment of a Norwegian
theatre in the capital had now resulted in their deciding to
leave the production of all Norwegian plays to their rival,
although they well knew that certain works, especially those
written in the mould of classical tragedy, could be
adequately performed only by trained actors such as the
Danish, but not the Norwegian Theatre possessed. A reply
to Ibsen's accusation appeared in the *Christiania Post* from

the pen of one Richard Petersen, a civil servant who later, not inappropriately, became a prison governor. In a bitter personal attack on Ibsen, Petersen dismissed him as 'a small-time poet'. Ridiculing him for 'identifying himself with all native dramatic literature', he concluded:

Herr Ibsen is a playwright of gigantic insignificance, about whom our nation cannot with any enthusiasm plant a protective palisade. *The Feast of Solhaug* is altogether too lacking in originality to encourage any hopes for his future, and his next [*sic*] stage work, *Lady Inger of Ostraat* is devoid of idealism and poetry to a degree which can only be described as astounding. Every character in this play bears the stamp of baseness ... Under the circumstances Herr Ibsen should surely appreciate that the public no longer awaits his *Vikings* with any excitement, and that the present is not the most appropriate time to present a play of probably mediocre quality.

During this controversy, Ibsen had been directing the usual succession of appalling plays at the Norwegian Theatre: Thomas Overskou's *A Chapter of Misunderstandings*; *Uncle*, a musical comedy by R. Benedix; *Clifford le Voleur*, a drama by Mélesville and Dubetrier; and a French musical entitled *The Day before the Battle of Marengo*. Scribe had, naturally, been represented, by three works, *Les Premières Amours*, *La Marraine*, and *La Chanteuse Voilée*, the last-named, with its sixteen performances, proving the principal success of the season. Nothing of any quality had been performed since Christmas except Holberg's comedy *Henrik and Pernilla*, and that had been a revival of an earlier production. The only new play by a living Norwegian author had been Rolf Olsen's *Anna Kolbjørnsdatter*. Nevertheless, the season had proved, on the whole, not unsuccessful. The takings, which totalled some 9,000 specie-dollars (£2,250), had been higher than in the preceding year, and the theatre had more or less paid its way.

In June, a few days before the season at the Norwegian Theatre ended, Ibsen went to Bergen to marry Suzannah

Thoresen. The wedding was celebrated quietly on 18 June 1858, under melancholy circumstances, for only seven days previously her father, the Dean, had died at the age of fifty-two. His death cannot have been unexpected, for the obituary notice in *Bergens Adressecontoirs Efterretninger* speaks of 'grievous physical suffering'. No eyewitness account of the wedding ceremony has come down to us; small loss probably, for who ever reported anything interesting about a wedding? Ibsen took Suzannah back to share his life in Christiania, taking the opportunity as the steamer touched at Grimstad to introduce her to his old friend Christopher Due. Magdalene Thoresen, before very long, returned to her native Denmark, where the sorrows of widowhood do not seem greatly to have inhibited her.

On 23 August the new season began at the Norwegian Theatre. Both it and the Christiania Theatre had decided on a policy of more new plays, to the pleasure of the newspapers; and the open quarrel between Ibsen and Borgaard seems to have had a good publicity effect, for both theatres found themselves playing to increased business. Every week, we learn, the Norwegian Theatre presented something new, if only a one-acter. On 1 October Ibsen was praised by a critic in *Morgenbladet*, who pointed out that he was answerable not only for the staging of the plays but also for the coaching of the younger and less talented of his players, 'and has therefore much more responsibility than his Danish counterpart'. The plays were well rehearsed 'and the roles were memorized'. It is evident that Ibsen was, at this stage, pursuing his task with energy; and the public, too, was well pleased. Yet the plays themselves were little more exciting than before. The staple fare continued to consist of light comedy, musicals, and vaudevilles, mainly Danish adaptations from the French.

Ibsen now decided to risk his company in *The Vikings at Helgeland*, rather than wait a year in the uncertain hope of the more experienced Danish players performing it. *Morgenbladet* doubted the wisdom of attempting so difficult a play on so small a stage and with a company virtually devoid of experience outside comedy and vaudeville. However, in one of his letters to the press complaining of Borgaard's rejection of the play, Ibsen had observed that 'only by seeing their plays performed can dramatists discover their faults and learn for the future', and when *The Vikings at Helgeland* received its première at the Norwegian Theatre on 24 November 1858 the house was full and people had to be turned away.

The production, amazingly, proved a success. The management had gone to the expense of new decor and costumes, spending as much as 500 specie-dollars (£125) on the production. At the final curtain there was loud cheering, and 'the author, Herr Ibsen, was called for, and was thunderously applauded'. *Aftenbladet* remarked that the production was the first essay that the Norwegian Theatre had attempted in 'the higher dramatic art', and that the result exceeded all expectations. 'No effort had been spared by the actors to see that the play should succeed, and encouraging outbursts of applause occurred not infrequently. It did one good to hear the powerful language of the play spoken in the homely accents of our mother tongue.' Botten Hansen in *Illustreret Nyhedsblad* noted the significance of 'a national play being presented with every technical advantage that stage management can provide', and took the opportunity to quote a laudatory comment upon the play by a German critic.

The evening had, in fact, been a triumph for Ibsen, the last that he was to know for over five years. Both the play and his production of it had been acclaimed almost unanimously. The first four performances were well attended, with takings totalling 460 specie-dollars (£115), a quarter of which was allotted to Ibsen as honorarium. But in spite of the excellent reviews and the attractions of the new decor and costumes, the play proved to have a limited appeal. There was not the same public in Christiania for a tragedy as for a comedy or a vaudeville, and only four more performances were given that season, compared with twenty-one of a French comedy, *Les Jolis Soldats*.

Nevertheless, by the end of 1858 the hopes with which Ibsen had come to Christiania must still have been high. He had written a few poems for special occasions during the autumn – for the fiftieth anniversary of a society, for the inauguration of new school buildings in Lillehammer, for a student ballet performance, receiving as payment now a silver mug, now a punch bowl with matching glasses – and the tone of these is vigorous and optimistic, almost Kiplingesque in its naïve nationalism. In January of the New Year (1859) he revived two Holberg comedies, *Jeppe of the Hill* and *The Peasant in Pawn*, and in March he produced, for the first time at the theatre, a Molière, *Les Fourberies de Scapin*; though, characteristically, none of these proved as popular as a slight vaudeville by Erik Bøgh called *All Possible Parts*, based on a French original but set locally at 'the Hotel Nord in Christiania'. Then, emboldened by the reception of *The Vikings at Helgeland* (which had also been staged at Trondhjem on 10 February and at Bergen on 4 March, the latter production being directed by Bjørnson, though with no great success[2]), Ibsen decided to see what his company could do with *Lady Inger of Østraat*.

Unfortunately, *Lady Inger* defeated the talents of the Christiania actors as completely as it had those of the company at Bergen. More than any other of Ibsen's early plays, *Lady Inger* requires, especially in the title role, the

2. 'The play hasn't succeeded, though it may seem from a distance to have ... Ibsen has a little clique of admirers headed by *Nyhedsbladet*. But every time he has to face the general public everything goes wrong and I've had to go to his aid twice, because Ibsen despite his aberrations *is* a poet. And I hope some day to get him to be himself and turn away from all this damned pastiche. The day Ibsen admits *he is small* he'll become a perfectly enchanting poet ... The point is, he's a rather small and gnomish little chap, with no chest or rump, so he feels that as he has no other gifts he has to strain most frightfully when he writes. And so he doesn't write what he'd really like to, and could.' (Bjørnson to Clemens Petersen, Bergen, 5 March 1859.)

kind of acting between and against the lines that he was to demand in the prose plays of his maturity. This was something to which the inexperienced players of the Christiania Norwegian Theatre were not equal without the kind of forceful instruction which Ibsen was too shy to give them. Neither the press nor the public liked *Lady Inger* when it was presented on 11 April 1859, and the second performance, two evenings later, was so poorly attended that it was withdrawn and never revived. From the reviews of the play we learn among other things that contemporary Norwegian taste found it difficult to stomach what we would nowadays regard as a typical Ibsen ending; they wanted a play to conclude in calm and reconciliation. To remedy the financial loss incurred by this failure, the theatre engaged two English dancers, a pair of sisters named Agnes and Christine Healey, who filled the theatre night after night.

But if the results of the season had not satisfied Ibsen's 'higher ideals', they had, financially, proved highly successful.[3] The one hundred and thirty-one performances given had produced takings of just over 11,000 specie-dollars (£2,750), a much larger figure than in any previous year since the theatre had opened. Admittedly, this had resulted in a loss on the year of 1,048 specie-dollars (£262), but this was partly accounted for by the rebuilding of the stage machinery and various expenses inseparable from new productions, such as fees to authors and translators, new decor and costumes (on occasion), and the cost of gas for the many extra rehearsals.

That summer, after the season at the Norwegian Theatre had ended, Ibsen paid a brief visit to Skien, not to see his family but to ask for financial help from his half-uncle, and most prosperous relative, Christopher Blom Paus, a mer-

3. They were, in fact, doing better than the Bergen Theatre under Bjørnson, whom we find complaining in *Bergens-Posten* on 8 March 1859; 'Talent and enthusiasm have been wasted the whole winter on houses a half, a quarter, an eighth and even less full; the actors and the directors are losing heart.'

chant in the town. Hanna Olsen, at that time a maidservant of Paus, recalled nearly seventy years later how Ibsen had arrived in a top hat and frock coat. 'He looked sad and dispirited; his clothes were somewhat worn, but neat and well cared for, so that one did not immediately notice that they were far from new. In his whole demeanour there was a suggestion of suffering which we servants could not but mark. We realized that things were going hardly for him, and pitied him. When he left we stood in the window watching him go.' She added that he did not sleep at his uncle's, but ate his dinners there, and took many walks in and around the town, out to Venstøp and up to Bratsberg. He did not, she said, visit his parents; he had stayed in the neighbourhood about a week, and his uncle had suggested that he should come and work in his shop, but Ibsen had refused. 'As he walked through the streets, he kept to himself, seemingly deep in thought. It was as though he knew no one and no one knew him. But people turned and looked at him; for he stood out from the generality with his neat clothes and shrewd and learned mien.'

Ibsen himself never referred to this visit; in a letter to his sister Hedvig in 1891 he refers to having last been 'at home in Skien' in 1850 (on his way from Grimstad to Christiania). Halvdan Koht rejects Hanna Olsen's evidence on the strength of this statement and the fact that Ibsen and Hedvig, and his father and another uncle, Christian Paus, several times later write of having last met in 1850. But this proves nothing except that Ibsen did not see them during any visit he may have made, which falls in with Hanna's statement that he did not call on his parents; and Ibsen's letter of 1891 specifically states that 1850 was the last time he was *at home*. Koht, who had been appointed one of Ibsen's literary executors, was inclined to reject, sometimes rather high-handedly, anything that redounded to his old master's discredit. Hanna's account is very detailed, and Oskar Mosfjeld, who met her and was a critical judge of witnesses, found her testimony convincing. She also told him that

Christopher Paus visited Ibsen in Christiania later during the year and, on his return to Skien, reported that Ibsen was living in humble circumstances, with a 'chicken-ladder' leading up to his room.

7

The Thousand Beaks
1859–62

THAT summer of 1859 marks a turning-point during Ibsen's second sojourn in Christiania. Up to now he had faced the difficulties of trying to run a national theatre with inexperienced actors, and no worthwhile plays to produce, hopefully. From now on the obstacles became too much for him, and the next three years are a sad story of administrative failure and creative barrenness. He wrote no plays at all between *The Vikings at Helgeland* in 1857 and *Love's Comedy* in 1862, the longest period of inactivity as a dramatist that he was to know until the first of his strokes incapacitated him in 1900, six years before his death.

He staged nothing of interest at the Norwegian Theatre during the autumn after his return from Skien, preferring mainly to revive the light successes of the previous season. For this policy he was attacked in the press. Why, asked *Morgenbladet* on 9 September, did he allow his company to waste their talents on such trivialities as *Le Chevalier des Dames*, a farce by Marc-Michel and Labiche, and *Frontin, Mari, Garçon*, a vaudeville by Scribe and Mélesville? The fact that the public seemed to enjoy them, declared the critic, was no excuse. Thus Ibsen, for the only time in his life, found himself rebuked for truckling to the box-office.

Similar newspaper attacks continued throughout the autumn. On 9 October *Morgenbladet* declared that 'the so-called Norwegian Theatre no longer exists', and that the public was attending 'in blind devotion to the cause which the Norwegian Theatre is supposed to be advancing, but which it no longer raises a finger to support . . . It is declining

into a kind of amusement ground for the lower classes ...
We are amazed that the theatre should be allowed to slide
lazily and without apparent resistance on to the well-greased
chute of Danish mediocrity – under the guidance of a *Norwegian* poet.'

Ibsen retorted to these criticisms by producing, on 12 October, Holberg's five-act comedy *Jean de France*; but this
was the only play of any quality that he staged before the
end of the year, and the newspaper attacks were soon
renewed. Bjørnson defended him, with his usual eloquence,
on 26 November in *Aftenbladet*: on 7 December, however,
the most vituperative attack yet on the Norwegian Theatre
appeared in the form of a poem in *Morgenbladet* by one H.
Ø. Blom (ostensibly a farewell tribute to the Danish actor
Anton Wilhelm Wiehe, who was leaving the Christiania
Theatre). Ibsen replied in *Aftenbladet* three days later, likewise in rhymed verse; whereupon Blom came back at him
with another poem, of twenty-two strophes, using his seniority to deliver the magisterial rebuke:

> But here's the difference. I am H. Ø. Blom,
> And you are Henrik Ibsen, nothing more.

Blom had himself been at school at Skien, and may have
been hitting at Ibsen's being the son of a virtual bankrupt;
the lines quoted suggest a sense of more than literary su-
periority. Ibsen's reply was so violent that Bjørnson (now
co-editor of the paper) thought it best not to print it.

Of Ibsen's private life at this time, we know virtually
nothing; it remained, as it was always to remain, a closed
book to the outside world. Such scanty evidence as we have
suggests that, now as later, Suzannah was a source of extraordinary strength to him. 'She is just the kind of character I
need,' he wrote to Peter Hansen in 1870, 'illogical, but with a
strong poetical intuition, a bigness of outlook, and an almost
violent hatred of all things petty. My fellow-countrymen
understood nothing of all this.' And their son was to declare:

It is probably true, as has been suggested, that he sometimes rebelled against her will and wished himself far away so that he could lose himself in his daydreams. I am thinking particularly of their first years together. But if he had lost her for good he would have been inconsolable; he would have been miserable had she withdrawn her will. He was the genius, she was the character. His character. And he knew it, though he would not willingly have admitted it until towards the end. But she knew it the whole time, and so was unconcerned by what people said, and by the criticisms of friends and acquaintances. She knew what fate had entrusted to her care, and she regarded it as her life's task. Let them call her a kill-joy when bad friends, in my father's younger days, wanted to drag him out with them – or self-willed, when she was old, and kept the fire still burning in him. She knew that ultimately, her will was his will.

This son was born to them on 23 December 1859. They called him Sigurd, after the hero of *The Vikings at Helgeland*, and Bjørnson stood as godfather. Bjørnson's wife Karoline asserted to numerous acquaintances during the next three-quarters of a century (she died in 1934, in her ninety-ninth year) that, as they were returning from the christening, she heard Suzannah loudly declare that she would never have another child – a statement which, at that time, as Fru Bjørnson never failed to point out to her listeners, was taken to mean that a woman had decided to cease sexual relations with her husband. But there is no record that Fru Bjørnson began to spread this story until much later, when her dislike of Suzannah and jealousy of Ibsen had become marked; and her relish in the telling of disparaging stories about them once Ibsen's fame had begun to surpass that of her husband makes her not the most credible of witnesses. 'Anyone who has ever done me any wrong,' wrote Bjørnson of her on 5 March 1859 to Clemens Petersen, 'is immediately, and for ever, her most implacable enemy.' Whatever Suzannah Ibsen's faults may have been, disloyalty to her husband was never one of them, and it seems extraordinarily unlikely that, if she had decided to give up sleeping with her husband, she would have said so out loud in public, particularly with Karoline Bjørnson around.

During this winter, Ibsen began to frequent a literary circle which Paul Botten Hansen had gathered round him. Botten Hansen was a passionate bibliophile, who had already amassed a fine library when Ibsen had first met him in 1850; he had had to sell it all the following year to pay his debts, but in the eight years since, by assiduous attendance at book auctions, he had built up another, of no less than fourteen thousand volumes. With his 'pale, angular face and irregular gait', as Ludvig Daae describes him, he had a remarkable flair for discovering rare and often valuable books in the most unlikely places; it used to be said that the most obscure provincial could not die owning one worth-while book without Botten Hansen hearing of and acquiring it. 'Damn that Dutchman, he has his spies everywhere!' said Ludvig Daae of him, quoting Holberg. The name caught. Botten Hansen came to be known as 'the Dutchman', and his circle as 'The Learned Holland'. Its members were, in the main, critics and scholars rather than creative writers. A kind of cross between the Bloomsbury Set and the Fabian Society, they distrusted naïve plans for the future, and submitted them to sceptical analysis, being especially opposed to any form of chauvinism.

Holberg, the supreme iconoclast, was, not surprisingly, the principal idol of the group. Some of the members knew his comedies almost by heart, and his style and vocabulary influenced their conversation, so that they would often talk a kind of Holberg pastiche. They gave each other nicknames taken from his characters, and Ibsen became known as Gert Westphaler, after the talkative barber in the play of that name. This does not seem to have been applied to him in sarcasm; Christopher Due, Jonas Lie and Lorentz Dietrichson have all testified that, when the mood took him, he could, like many depressives, hold forth with passionate eloquence.

One of Ibsen's early biographers, Gerhard Gran, half a

generation younger than the Hollanders, knew most of them well and has left an interesting comment upon them.

They were, almost without exception, distinguished for learning rather than for original ideas, for intelligence rather than energy or vitality, for critical ability rather than creative fertility. The ideals they worshipped were old and dying ideals; they clung tightly to the old Danish traditions, from which others were seeking to emancipate themselves, they abased themselves before the classical education which even then was beginning to show cracks in its seams, they worshipped the concept of Scandinavianism, which was soon to be proved bankrupt. The river of progress passed them by, and, clinging to the past, they watched it glide – each according to his temperament, some in hopeless surrender, others bitterly resentful – certain that their country was moving swiftly towards perdition.

No wonder that Bjørnson hated them; but Ibsen, as Gran says,

felt at home in this atmosphere which Bjørnson found poisonous. Ibsen had no reason to look on life with a hopeful eye; the iron had, not unnaturally, entered deep into his soul, he had little faith left, and he was, like so many of those others, cynical; he shared readily in their causticity. There was in Ibsen's highly complex make-up a strong measure of conservatism . . . radical as he was in matters of the spirit and in his championship of individuality, he was indifferent, even antagonistic towards anyone with a bombastic passion for external reforms. He, who was so shy and silent, was by nature suspicious of facile enthusiasm and loud-mouthedness . . . Eloquence was to him an empty jingle, a politician synonymous with a self-seeker, a patriot with a screeching monkey; he hated nothing so much as silken phrases. One can easily understand why such a man found himself at home among the Hollanders . . . He shared their antipathies, at any rate to a degree. He found in their circle an echo of his contempt for the poverty of Norwegian political and cultural life.

Ibsen's sympathy with the Holland group is confirmation of his growing disillusionment with nationalism. Under the circumstances, it is hardly surprising that his work at the theatre was soon to deteriorate; a man can hardly be a good theatre director if he has doubts about its policy.

His associates in 'Holland' were in the main acquaintances rather than friends; he did not make friends easily, and that autumn he lost one of the few he had. Ole Schulerud, who had published *Catiline* at his own expense and shared his small means with Ibsen in their student days, died in October at the age of thirty-one. He was one of the few people with whom Ibsen had been, or was ever to be, really intimate, and Ibsen composed a simple and moving little poem to be sung at his graveside. Eleven years later, on 9 June 1870, he wrote Schulerud's widow a long and, for him, unusually personal letter recalling the debt he owed to her husband:

... He was a true friend to me, unstinting, unqualified, and loyal. When I look back, there was no one so closely bound up with my youthful development as he. And amid the successes which I have since achieved it has been a great grief to me that he could not be here among us and share my joy with me. He was the friend I needed in the days when one had to make certain renunciations and prepare oneself for the future; and how few such one has in times like those! There are plenty of people who take note of one when things go well; but the likelihood of failure was every bit as great as that of success when he joined his fortunes to mine with all his loyal and noble heart. Then our lives parted; we seldom wrote to each other; we didn't seem to need to; now that I think back, we never really exchanged a word about friendship or anything like that. What existed between us arose quite spontaneously and developed into something completely unforced, and it never occurred to us to think it could be otherwise. And then, when we met again, our time together was so sadly brief.

But a loss has its exaltation, as it has its grief. The sharpened memory, the inward truth, remain; what parting robs us of is inessential ... I should deeply love to have a portrait of Ole, if you can spare one; I have none ...

In warmest friendship,
Henrik Ibsen

The picture we have of Ibsen at this stage in his career, when he was approaching his thirty-second birthday, is of a writer distracted. At the age when an author is commonly at his most fertile, if not at his best, he found his creative energies diverted by the claims of two ideals which he was gradually finding to be false: the ideal of nationalism, and the ideal of creating a worthwhile theatre. Both demanded something that he lacked, and that Bjørnson revelled in: gregariousness, the love of being with and working with other people. To Ibsen, torn between his ideals and his daily work on the one hand, and his instincts and nature on the other, the problem was especially tormenting; and during the last months of 1859 he managed, heaven knows how, to find the leisure to write a long poem of three hundred and eighty-four lines in which he dramatized his dilemma. He called it 'On the Heights', and it is perhaps the finest of his non-dramatic works.

The narrator, a young man, leaves his mother 'with scrip on back and gun in hand' to seek solitude in the mountains. On the way he sees a girl, spends the night with her, and promises to return and marry her. But once in the mountains, he feels different:

> All passions dark, all wild desires
> Are driven from my thoughts.
> I'm born anew. Up here I stand
> Near to myself and God.

Among the peaks he meets a stranger. 'Tears play in his laughter. His lips, when silent, speak.' His eyes are like the mountain lake, born of, and caged by, the glacier. He teaches the young man a 'new wisdom'; the old desires and longings lose their power over him. On Christmas Night he looks down and sees his home burn, with his mother in it; but the stranger, by his side, views the scene through his hollowed hand and points out the beauty of the red flames in the moonlight. He loses all desire to return to the life of the valley below. Finally, at midsummer, he sees the girl he loves riding to church to marry another man, and shades his eyes with his hand, like the stranger, better to appreciate the aesthetic effect of the gay clothes against the white birch trees. He is now freed from all foolish emotional ties, and senses in his heart 'full evidence of petrifaction'. The poem ends:

> I am steeled. I am done with the lowland life.
> Up here on the heights are freedom and God.
> Men do but grope in the valley.

'On the Heights' is one of Ibsen's most personal poems; and again, as with so many of his best, the English poet whom it most calls to mind is Thomas Hardy, with its changing rhythms, frequent use of dactylic metres, strong dramatization, economy of narration, and extreme simplicity of statement that trembles on, yet never quite oversteps, the cliff-edge of banality. The problem of whether an artist should plunge into life or withdraw from it had been exhaustively and comparatively recently examined by Kierkegaard in (among other works) *Either-Or*; yet this temptation of total withdrawal is one that has confronted writers in every age, whether as Aestheticism (Kierkegaard), Apollonianism (Nietzsche), the Ivory Tower (Yeats) or, in our own time, non-commitment. At the same time, Kierkegaard was one of those thinkers whose ideas were certainly discussed in the Holland circle, and Ibsen may well, as at other times, have been infected by them at second-hand. The dilemma of commitment or non-commitment remained with him, as it had to while he continued with his grind at the theatre; and he now, in the first month of 1860, began to plan a play on the theme – *Love's Comedy*, which, however, he was not to finish until 1862.[1]

1. 'Not until I married', wrote Ibsen to Peter Hansen on 28 October 1870, did my life achieve a weightier content. The first fruits of this was a longish poem, "On the Heights". But the demand for freedom which runs throughout this poem did not find full expression until I wrote *Love's Comedy*.'

This question of Kierkegaard's influence on Ibsen is one that no student of either writer can sidestep. On the one hand, it has undoubtedly been exaggerated by critics who seem ignorant of the frequency with which authors distrustful of and hostile to each other's work have followed parallel paths to the same goal; and Ibsen, as we have seen, when questioned in later life as to this influence, replied testily that he had 'read little of Kierkegaard and understood less'. This statement was probably true, for Ibsen was never much interested in philosophical writing. On the other hand, he shares with Kierkegaard such striking similarities not merely of thought but of phrasing that the matter cannot be allowed to rest there.

Ibsen, though a free-thinker from a very early age, had, like Kierkegaard, been brought up in an atmosphere of deep pietism and, again like Kierkegaard, regarded the Christian doctrine with a mixture of fear and admiration. Julian the Apostate, in *Emperor and Galilean*, was to voice this duality: 'Whoever has once been in His power can never completely free himself from it.' Ibsen must often have felt, as Kierkegaard did, that he could never fight his way out of the stranglehold which the Galilean system of ethics had put on him; and Kierkegaard's stern conception of Christianity, contempt for the established church, and insistence that religion was a matter for the individual soul must have appealed very strongly to him. The two men had, moreover, much in common psychologically. Both were shy of close human relationships. Kierkegaard had written (in his journal for 1841): 'The curse which rests on me is never to be allowed to let anyone join themselves to me deeply and inwardly,' just as Ibsen had apologized to C. J. Anker in 1858 for being 'walled about with a kind of off-putting coldness which makes any close relationship with me difficult'. Both despised the masses, and were suspicious of so-called liberalism and all party lines; both tended to ask questions rather than give answers; both were oddly addicted to reading newspaper advertisements. Many ideas receive almost identical expression in their writings: Kierkegaard's 'Truth is in the minority' and Dr Stockmann's 'The minority is always right'; Kierkegaard's 'The great thing is not to be this or the other, but to be oneself, and of that every human being is capable if only he wills it,' and Brand's:

> To be wholly oneself! But how,
> With the weight of one's inheritance of sin? . . .
> It is not by spectacular achievements
> That man can be transformed, but by will.
> It is man's will that acquits or condemns him.

Kierkegaard had stressed, as Ibsen was frequently to do, the necessity of self-liberation as opposed to liberation from without, and the need for an artist to experience sorrow (though Keats had also stressed this, and he had died when Kierkegaard was eight). And Kierkegaard had stated, in 'A Seducer's Diary' (in *Either-Or*) that: 'When two people fall in love and decide that they are destined for each other, then they must have the courage to break it off. For to continue is to lose everything and win nothing'; which was to be precisely the theme of *Love's Comedy*.

Such similarities could be coincidental; Strindberg and Freud share as many, yet Strindberg almost certainly never read a word of Freud,[2] and Freud came to his conclusions without Strindberg's help. (As Coleridge remarked when Hazlitt accused him of plagiarizing Shakespeare: 'Is there no such thing as two men's having similar thoughts on similar occasions?') But many of Ibsen's friends were ardent Kierkegaardians. In June 1857, towards the end of Ibsen's stay in Bergen, Magdalene Thoresen wrote to a friend that

2. There is no mention of Freud in Strindberg's twenty thousand surviving letters, which are full of references to what he was reading, nor is there any work of Freud's in Strindberg's library; and he always bought rather than borrowed books, even when he could least afford them. Freud's *The Interpretation of Dreams* was scarcely reviewed at all when it appeared in 1900, and took eight years to sell its first edition of 600 copies, so that Strindberg, though he did not die till 1912, had probably never heard of Freud's name.

she read Kierkegaard 'unceasingly', so that Ibsen can hardly have avoided hearing a lot of him through her. Kierkegaard was also much discussed by Ibsen's friends in the 'Holland' circle; and the young priest Christopher Bruun, with whom Ibsen was to have close contact during his first year in Rome, was another enthusiastic disciple. In short, Kierkegaard's ideas were everywhere in the air around Ibsen during the latter's formative years and, bored and puzzled as he may have been by Kierkegaard's philosophical processes, he must have found many of his own half-formed thoughts crystallized there.

Meanwhile, now that he had written 'On the Heights', the Norwegian Theatre continued to occupy most of his time and energy. He had, as we have seen, been under fire from the press; but towards the end of 1859 the repertory began to show signs of improvement. On 11 December, the day after he published his long verse counter-attack on H. Ø. Blom (how on earth did he find the time for that during the last days of rehearsing a new production?), he staged Holberg's full-length comedy, *Jacob von Thyboe* (about a boastful soldier), and followed it ten days later with a new Danish one-acter, Carit Etlar's *When the Sun Goes Down*. On 3 February 1860 he directed *Ole Shut-Eye*, a comedy by Hans Andersen requiring elaborate staging and scenery, and this proved a popular as well as a critical success, being performed thirteen times that month and nineteen in all before the end of the season. Another new play, Thomas Overskou's *The Devil's Master* (after Mélesville's *Le Fils de la Vierge*), followed in March, and this, too, was a success; the critics went out of their way to praise the production, which included several tableaux of 'witchcraft', with 'Bengal candles'. 'The acting in general', wrote *Aftenbladet* (on 10 March) surveying the theatre's recent productions, 'bears witness to such conscientious instruction that the performances give considerable satisfaction.' Dumas *père's Les Demoiselles de St Cyr*, in April, achieved only two performances, as did Joseph Bouchardy's *Le Sonneur de St Paul* the following month. But no one could now complain that the theatre was not presenting new works, even if disappointingly few of the required quality were being written by native dramatists.

On 18 May the Storthing rejected another appeal from the theatre for a state grant. Some time during this summer Ibsen had again to humiliate himself by asking his uncle, Christopher Blom Paus, for money. He visited the latter at his country estate, Buslaaten, in Gjerpen, just outside Skien. We do not know whether he succeeded in his mission, and he does not seem to have visited his family on this occasion either. That summer there were floods in Skien which caused widespread destruction, and the last memory he took away of his native town (for he was never to visit it again) may have been of the great waters pouring through the streets. No wonder he later remembered Skien as 'the town of the storming, soughing, seething waters'. There is also a local tradition that at about this time he applied to the Skien town council for help; but many of the council papers were destroyed in the fire of 1886, so that this cannot be confirmed or denied.

On 1 July he wrote a song for the winners at the summer festival of a rifle club to which he belonged in Christiania; this was published in *Illustreret Nyhedsblad* on 8 July. On 6 August he applied, together with Bjørnson and Vinje, for state travel grants. Ibsen's application reads pathetically:

To the King!

Henrik Johan Ibsen most humbly begs that he may be granted a sum of 400 (four hundred) specie-dollars [£100] from the fund set aside for artists and scholars for foreign travel, for a six months journey to London, Paris, the larger German cities, Copenhagen and Stockholm, to study dramatic art and literature.

During ten years of literary activity, and an earlier period of preparation for this work, the study of dramatic art and literature, its principles, system and histories, has absorbed the greater part of my time and constituted my main occupation. The criticisms of my dramatic works which have during this period been published by foreign as well as native judges may, I trust, present sufficient testimony that these efforts have not been fruitless; as the sympathy with which the public has received my various plays, several of which have also been performed in Sweden and Denmark, may testify to a talent for the vocation which I have chosen . . .

Your Majesty's most humble servant,
Henr. Ibsen

The Akademiske Kollegium, to whom the applications of the three writers were referred, at first rejected them all. The head of the Ministry for Ecclesiastical and Educational Affairs, Christian Birch-Reichenwald, persuaded them to reconsider their decision in the cases of Bjørnson and Vinje, though each received only half the amount applied for (Bjørnson 500 specie-dollars instead of 1,000, and Vinje 250 instead of 500). But they steadfastly refused to make any grant to Ibsen, whose application had been the most modest of the three. It is interesting to speculate on the influence that a visit to London and Paris might have had on Ibsen at this stage of his career. The London theatre was undergoing a particularly lean period; Harley Granville Barker has described its state during the fifties and sixties as one of 'slovenly chaos'. There were no good playwrights; Ibsen would have been just too early for the 'realistic' plays of T. W. Robertson (who was to write *Caste* in 1867) and for W. S. Gilbert, whose first play, *Dulcamara*, would be produced in 1866; he would have seen nothing more interesting in the way of new plays than the comedies of H. J. Byron and J. R. Planché, which were no better than the trivia he had been directing at home. Nor was it a great period for English acting. Macready had recently ended his career and Henry Irving, though he had just started on his, did not play in London in either 1860 or 1861. The best that Ibsen could have seen would have been Charles Kean, J. L. Toole, Samuel Phelps, Helen Faucit, and Dion Boucicault, none of them major talents. Nor would Paris have had much more to offer. Rachel had died in 1858, and Sarah Bernhardt was

not to make her début until August 1862. Frédéric
Lemaître, now aged sixty, had gone into decline. Of the
French dramatists, Ibsen already knew about Dumas *père*
and Victorien Sardou; he had produced several plays by the
former, and was to stage the latter's *Pattes de Mouche* later
that year. He might have seen in Paris a revival of the
younger Dumas's *La Dame aux Camélias*, which had been
first produced in 1852 (but was not to reach Christiania until
1899). What would most have interested him, however,
would have been the plays of Emile Augier. Augier's plays,
with their contemporary themes and settings, such as *Gabrielle, Le Gendre de M. Poirier, Le Fils de Giboyer* and *Lions
et Renards*, today seem scarcely more 'realistic' than *La
Dame aux Camélias*, or *Caste*, or *The Second Mrs Tanqueray*. The characters seem shallow, the plots melodramatic. But they dealt, however superficially, with current
problems; they castigated contemporary morals, and even
introduced contemporary politics. No doubt Ibsen, even
without any French, would have been delighted to see such
things on the stage. But since he himself was to do exactly
these things in his next play, *Love's Comedy,* and since his
dramatic technique was already much superior to Augier's,
it is difficult to imagine that seeing the latter's plays acted
would have had much, if any, influence on him.

As things turned out, Ibsen was never to visit England;
nor, although he was to live for twenty-seven years in Italy
and Germany, was he to enter France, except to pass briefly
through in 1869 on his way to and from the opening of the
Suez Canal.

So he stayed in Norway, and on 17 August that year, 1860,
we find him again in the role of hack poet, writing a song to
greet visiting members of the Swedish Parliament. A week
later, on 25 August, J. L. Heiberg died, and Ibsen wrote a
moving elegy[3] to the memory of the man who had received
him courteously in Copenhagen eight years before, and
whose plays had been among the few that it can have given

3. See pp. 117–18 above.

him any pleasure to direct. Ibsen retained his admiration for
Heiberg, and for his actress wife, all his life. He also, in the
role of unofficial local laureate which he so curiously filled,
wrote a poem to be spoken on the day of the new King Carl
XV's coronation, and yet another greeting to the Swedish
M.P.'s, this time to a deputation from them which was visiting Trondhjem. All of these pieces, except the Heiberg elegy,
are naïvely, even (to an outsider) embarrassingly patriotic,
with frequent exhortations to 'Men of Norway' and 'Norway's Heroes'. Needless to say, they delighted most of his
contemporaries. 'Thank Ibsen for his poems!' wrote Vinje to
Botten Hansen (who had published three of the worst of
them in *Illustreret Nyhedsblad*) on 8 September. 'They are
the most Norwegian of all!'

Ibsen seems around this time to have become apathetic
about his work at the theatre. That summer the theatre was
being rebuilt, at considerable expense, and Knud Knudsen,
the language instructor who was also on the board, records
that Ibsen showed little interest in the theatre's affairs, was
lazy during August and September in rehearsing new plays
for the coming season (which did not open until the rebuilding was completed in October), and frequently absen-
ted himself from board meetings 'for no other reason than
that he knew he would be asked what he had done since the
last meeting. I remember we once found ourselves holding a
board meeting in a rear room at L'Orsa's café in Prindsensgade, because we had heard that he happened to be
there.' He recalled that at one board meeting this year he
'gave Ibsen a real dressing-down, the like of which he can
never have experienced before or since'; and that Joachim
Garborg, another board member, had told him (Knudsen)
that he had treated Ibsen 'like a truant schoolboy'. But, says
Knudsen, 'Ibsen took what I gave him without saying a
word'; and he adds that Ole Bull, now back from America,
who himself had spoken severely to Ibsen at the same meeting, told him: 'You've got to be tough with Ibsen if you're to
get anywhere.'

Evidence of Ibsen's apathy can be found in the fact that he chose as his second production of the new season a tedious nationalistic drama, *The Goblin's Home*, by P. A. Jensen, which he had condemned in violent terms as a student drama critic back in 1851. He may have thought his cynicism justified when the production received enthusiastic reviews and ran for ten performances. The enlarged stage and more elaborate scenic effects that could consequently be achieved were doubtless partly responsible; on 30 October, *Morgenbladet* noted with pleasure that it was no longer necessary for 'one step to signify four, or for lovers to crowd and buffet each other incongruously for lack of space'. In November Ibsen revived another play which he had seen as an undergraduate in 1851, a five-act German historical drama by Karl Gutzkow entitled *Zopf und Schwert* (Pigtail and Sword), set in the court of Frederick William I. It had been badly received then, but he had admired and defended it: 'When one has, like our public, inured oneself year in and year out to the dramatic candy-floss of Scribe & Co., cautiously seasoned with a ration of bogus poetry, it is not to be wondered at that this more solid German fare should prove indigestible even to the ostrich stomachs of Christiania audiences.' The play was newly translated by Suzannah Ibsen, and was sympathetically reviewed; but the public liked it no better than they had in 1851, and it was withdrawn after four performances.

No wonder Ibsen was feeling apathetic towards his work. The public had made it clear that it had little appetite for serious drama, and that what it wanted, and what the theatre needed if it was to remain solvent, was a virtually unbroken diet of comedy, preferably with music and dancing. Even Sardou's *Pattes de Mouche*, being without music, proved too much and ran for only three performances that November; and *The Foster Brothers*, an adaptation by J. L. Heiberg of a comedy by Karl Töpfer based on an adaptation by J. R. Planché of William Rowley's 1632 comedy, *A New Wonder, A Woman Never Vext* (the list of credits underlines the kind of material with which Ibsen had to work, even when the original was of some quality), managed only four in January. A reviewer of the Sardou complained that the actors seemed to 'lack instruction', to which Ibsen replied in *Aftenbladet* (5 December) that 'under me, no debutant has appeared on the stage without sufficient preparation. It is another thing for beginners to show lack of experience, which your reviewer has confused with lack of instruction.'

Bowing to the public taste, Ibsen presented in February a 'folk comedy' entitled *The Builders*, an adaptation of a French piece by Théodore Cogniard and L. F. N. Clairville, *Les Compagnons de la Truelle*. The play, as adapted, was set locally in Christiania, and this caused the greatest excitement. The public, we learn, were amazed and delighted to see 'their own windows' on the stage, and the presentation of Frederiksberg and the Klingenberg gardens with their famous Apollo *salon* evoked 'a storm of spontaneous enthusiasm'. There was a scene in Storgaden 'at eventide', another against the background of the fortress of Akershus and, the grand climax, a bird's-eye view of the whole city. *Morgenbladet*, which seems to have acquired a new and caustic reviewer at the beginning of this year, complained that this was merely 'the photographic language of reality . . . as if one were to present masons with chalk dust on their faces or a blacksmith with dirty fingers'; a reminder that every age has its critics who object to what they regard as excessive realism. The same gentleman also felt that the humble diction of the actors was unsuited to the representation of upper-class Christiania society, though he appears to have accepted it in the portrayal of foreign royalty and aristocrats. But the public liked the show, and it ran for twelve performances that season.

This was, however, almost the only success of the New Year, and attendances at the theatre declined badly.

Throughout this winter and spring of 1861 Ibsen was violently and repeatedly attacked in the press for his conduct of the Norwegian Theatre. His new enemy in *Morgenbladet* was particularly to the fore, criticizing 'the very bad plays which the artistic director thinks fit to present week after week. A visit to the Norwegian Theatre is like a kind of aesthetic visit to a hospital; to wander down the long empty corridors to the empty rows of stalls and boxes is "a journey through the abodes of misery and the vales of sorrow". Things could scarcely be worse if the artistic director strove his utmost to make the repertory as unattractive as possible.' On 28 May, the *Christiania Post* joined in the fray, complaining that 'one lacked any sense of direction, the theatre stood tottering, the acting was bad, the repertory bad', and concluding that 'Herr Ibsen is not the man to direct our theatre.'

The feeling that Ibsen had neglected his duties was evidently fairly widespread. Knudsen records in his memoirs that on 14 May Ibsen was rebuked by the board for holding no rehearsals at all between 29 April and 10 May; and a correspondent in *Morgenbladet* asked what Herr Ibsen had done with two new Norwegian plays which had been submitted to him as long ago as 1859 and which he had promised would be performed that season. 'Herr Ibsen has thus repeatedly discouraged his authors, flaunted his committee and vexed his public. One cannot but ask whether such behaviour is becoming in Herr Ibsen, who recently took such offence because the directors of the Christiania Theatre found themselves compelled to postpone for a few months the production of his own play, *The Vikings at Helgeland*.' An even more damaging attack, however, came in the form, not of an article, but of a lecture by a member of his own company named Døvle. While the five unpaid members of the board, asserted Døvle, had done all that could reasonably be expected of them, this could not be said of the sixth, paid, member, who was receiving a salary of approaching 1,000 [*sic*] specie-dollars a year, and whose direction of the theatre during the season had been 'somewhat negligent'. Another correspondent in *Morgenbladet*, in an article carrying the headline BRING BJØRNSON HOME! demanded that Ibsen be ejected from a post which he seemed to regard as a sinecure and that Bjørnson be put in his place.

To these last attacks Ibsen remained silent, and it fell to his old friend Paul Botten Hansen, in *Illustreret Nyhedblad*, to speak out in his defence. He made the interesting assertion that, apart from Døvle's lecture, all the attacks on Ibsen, while purporting to come from different sources, were in fact being written by the same pen, and declared that 'people are destroying the good name of the press by pretending to speak with a multitude of voices from selfish political motives'. The public, he went on, should not forget the difficulties under which Ibsen has had to work: 'box-office considerations, ideals, artistic considerations and unsuitable material all make their own special powerful demands.' He admits that Ibsen might perhaps show a little more energy; but whatever Ibsen may or may not have achieved for the Norwegian Theatre, he is not 'a man whom any schoolboy may treat as an equal, even if the wind of opinion should be blowing against him'. By writing such works as *The Vikings at Helgeland*, and others, Ibsen has laid claim to 'a position in our literature which demands a modicum of reason from his opponents, whether they be members of his own company or whether they be undergraduates'. Botten Hansen concluded: 'These vulgarians of art and letters who have spoken so scornfully of Ibsen should have sufficient insight into the future and sufficient sense of their own poverty of talent to realize that this man, so viciously attacked by them, will live in Norwegian literature long after moss and grass have grown over their own graves and nettles over their literary reputations.'

Nevertheless, even if all the newspaper attacks were, as Botten Hansen claimed, written by the same pen, it seems likely that they were at least in part justified. It must have been more than a mere difference of opinion that caused Døvle to speak out; Ibsen told Henrik Jæger that Døvle was angry because 'his wife was not getting enough to do', but one notes that no other member of the company raised his or her voice in public to contradict him. And Ibsen had, as we have seen, been rebuked by his board. Moreover, he was now drinking heavily. At least once students returning to their rooms at night saw his bearded figure lying senseless in the gutter.[4]

At the annual general meeting of the Norwegian Theatre on 19 September 1861, Ibsen presented his report in what must have been an uncomfortable atmosphere. Owing to the fact, he says, that his new actors were not engaged until the end of September, he was unable to plan his repertory ahead, since this was dependent upon what players he might have at his disposal. The departure of several members of the old company had meant that, whereas previously he had a repertory of about a hundred plays which he could revive at short notice, he was now left with only one which would not require recasting and, consequently, protracted rehearsals. Then, the old decor did not fit the new stage, and had to be 'enlarged and repainted', and was not ready until after it was needed. The company, with so many new members, was unused to playing together, and there had been a number of illnesses, as a result of which five performances had had to be cancelled and seven replanned. Despite all this, the theatre had presented more new plays during this seven-and-a-half-month season than in the previous season of nine months. As regards complaints about the economic situation, he presented figures to remind the board that takings had considerably increased since he had taken over the artistic directorship.

Ibsen's defence does not read altogether convincingly at

4. Told by H. Koht (whose father saw Ibsen thus) to A. E. Zucker, and recorded by the latter in *Ibsen, The Master Builder* (London, 1929), pp. 94 and 310–11 note. Professor Francis Bull writes: 'I realized how Ibsen was regarded by the bourgeoisie of Christiania in the eighteen-sixties when generalkonsul Andresen Butenschøn told me that as a young man, in 1864, he had been encouraged by his uncle to subscribe to a fund so that "the drunken poet Henrik Ibsen" might go abroad and be rescued from his misery.'

this distance of time. One cannot help feeling, and no doubt the board felt, that, while the difficulties had been considerable, they were of the kind with which a theatre director must more or less expect to be faced, and that a more energetic and resourceful man might have overcome them more successfully. Bjørnson's achievements during his two years as Ibsen's successor at Bergen had become a legend, fostered, we may be sure, by those actors who had recently joined Ibsen's company from there, and that newspaper headline BRING BJØRNSON HOME! must have been in the mind's eye of many a person present. The chairman of the board, Judge Hansteen, expressed his opinion that 'the artistic director has not shown the zeal that might have been wished for'.

Not surprisingly, the strain was beginning to tell on Ibsen. On 5 December a notice appeared in the press that the artistic director was ill and therefore unable to perform his duties. 'Ibsen is sick, I see?' wrote Vinje to Botten Hansen on 13 December. Magdalene Thoresen, as an old woman in the next century, recalled his illness in her novelettish style:

He had a violent attack of nervous fever. He, who had hitherto possessed a body of granite, resistant to all the buffets of fate, found himself for once in a situation in which he required care and nursing. He was now a married man with a home, so that all the help he needed was to hand. But he refused to accept any ... He left his home each morning and wandered around in the winter air, planless, alone, dazed. And he came through. The sickness gradually left him. But when ... he became himself again, it was as though he had covered a part of his journey as a writer underground, and had come up into the daylight again in another place. Henceforth Henrik Ibsen was to steer a new course. It is no longer in the open pages of history that he seeks his themes; from now on he follows a personal path, and strides forth as a cleanser, with a scourge in his hand.

Magdalene always, even as a young woman, preferred the melodramatic to the prosaic explanation. Ever since his teens, Ibsen had been intensely interested in contemporary problems, whether political, social or personal. It was the tide of nationalism, plus the convention that high tragedy usually concerned the dead, that had caused him to seek his themes in the pages of history; and in any event, it was to be another twelve years before he finally turned his back on historical drama. He had always been by nature a cleanser; it was simply that from now on, he was to use the drama instead of journalism as his medium for this.

The first work that he wrote after his illness, though, was as uncontemporary as it could be: a long, patriotic historical poem entitled 'Terje Vigen'. Set during the Napoleonic Wars, when Norway was blockaded by the Allies, it tells how a wild youth of that name was changed by the birth of a daughter into a responsible citizen. To save his wife and child from starvation, he tries to run the blockade in a rowboat, but is intercepted by an English man-of-war (the poem is studded with English words, such as 'Stop!', 'Mylord' [*sic*], etc.), and spends five years in prison. When he is freed, he returns to Norway and finds that his wife and child have starved to death. He becomes a pilot; and one night an English yacht is shipwrecked. Terje, by now grizzled, rows out to save the occupants, and who should they be but the English 'Mylord' who had arrested him, with his 'Mylady' and child? Conscience and the desire for revenge struggle within him; conscience wins, and he brings them safely to land, for, as he explains, 'the little one's sake'. If, without knowing, one were asked to guess the author of this curiously sentimental and conventional ballad, the last name that would come to mind would be Ibsen's; yet the poem, perhaps because it is one of the few tolerable patriotic works that he wrote, is held in Norway in extraordinary affection. Victor Sjöström, one of the pioneers of the silent cinema, made a film of it in 1916, only ten years after Ibsen's death.[5]

5. Sjöström lived long enough to act the leading role in Ingmar Bergman's film, *Wild Strawberries*, in 1957.

In the New Year of 1862, Ibsen presented several more new productions at the Norwegian Theatre: Mélesville's comedy *Sullivan*, Emile de Najac's *Une Croix à la cheminée, More than Pearls and Gold* (a romantic comedy freely adapted by Hans Andersen from both F. Raimund's *Der Diamant des Geisterkönigs* and *The Thousand and One Nights*), and two new Danish plays, J. C. Hastrup's *Night in the Mountains* and Meïr Aron Goldschmidt's *Rabbi Eliezer. More than Pearls and Gold* ran for seven performances, *Sullivan* for six; the others for only two, four and two performances respectively. Bjørnson's historical verse drama, *Lame Hulda*, in April, managed only three.

On 14 March, Ibsen applied to the Akademiske Kollegium for a stipend of 120 specie-dollars (£30) 'to make a journey during two of the summer months through outer Hardanger and the districts around the Sognefjord, northwards to Molde and back through Romsdal, to collect and annotate such folk songs and tales, old and new, as may still be extant'. On 24 May this application was granted, though the college cheeseparingly knocked 10 specie-dollars off the amount asked.

The economic position of the Norwegian Theatre was by now critical. On 18 March the board had to ask the actors to renounce their holiday pay during the summer, in return for being allowed to lease the theatre free during these months and share the proceeds. In April the orchestra announced that they would not perform until their wages had been paid. That catastrophe was averted; but Ibsen himself was being dunned by creditors, and on 14 May he wrote to J. B. Klingenberg, the treasurer:

If, as promised, you have met any members of the board or would be willing to act on your own account, you would do me the greatest possible service if you could possibly send me by messenger some of the money that is due to me. A warrant of distraint has been served on me for last year's tax (11–12 specie-dollars) [just under £3], and I am threatened with the removal of my possessions. This is more than hard, since I am owed a considerable part of my salary, and I therefore place my trust in you as the only person to whom I can turn.

Your obedient servant,
Henr. Ibsen

A sad note by Klingenberg that same day in the record books of the theatre shows that they had no more than 53 specie-dollars (£13) in the till. 'Last week,' concludes Klingenberg's note, 'I had to pay 126 specie-dollars from my own pocket to settle salaries and other essential debts concerned with the running of the theatre.'

But by now the Norwegian Theatre had reached the point of no return. The rebuilding operation, on which they had embarked with such hopes, had crippled them, and they now found themselves with debts amounting to 28,000 specie-dollars (£7,000). It was decided to file a petition of bankruptcy and Ibsen and his company were given notice as from 1 June.

So Ibsen's career as a theatre director ended. If his six years at Bergen had been hard, these five years at Christiania had been harder. For him of all people, so fastidious in his tastes and so shy of human contact, to produce this succession of featherweight farces and musicals with an inexperienced company, contemptible rehearsal time, and hopelessly inadequate financial and technical resources, abused in the press, attacked from within his own company and condemned by his board, it must indeed have been a protracted nightmare. His own dramatic talent, instead of flowering as he had hoped, had gone barren; and now, with a wife and son to support and no private means, he was without a job.

Moreover, he was now being blamed in some quarters for the theatre's failure. Knud Knudsen, in his unpublished memoirs, makes no bones about the matter. They should, he said, have got rid of Ibsen much earlier, and had only not done so 'because (1) we had no one else to turn to (2) we always hoped that the pressure exerted by the board must some time take effect (3) he undeniably *understood* the work better than anyone else we could possibly hope to get (4) we were unwilling to make a man, in other respects so deserving, jobless ... People would hardly credit that an author who could create so strong-willed a character as Brand could have been so slack and lethargical in practical matters.'

Knudsen's condemnation probably goes too far. We know that he and Ibsen had disagreed violently from the beginning about how far the theatre could go in being 'Norwegian'; Knudsen was a fanatic on this subject, and there is evidence that, in common with a curiously high proportion of linguists, he tended to become paranoiacally hostile to anyone who opposed him on his pet subject. If one peruses the newspaper reactions to the hundreds of productions which Ibsen presented at the Norwegian Theatre, one finds him praised more often than blamed; frequently we read that the scenic arrangements are 'especially handsome and tasteful', the ensemble playing excellent, the costumes attractive (he was always especially meticulous about other people's clothes as well as his own). Not only the standard of acting and production, but also the box-office takings improved markedly during his tenure of office, except during his last season, and the falling-off then was almost certainly directly due to his pursuing a policy of new plays on the orders of his committee. Under his direction, the Norwegian Theatre soon found itself able to compete on equal terms with, and sometimes even surpass, the Christiania Theatre, which had a better building and stage, a smarter position, much more experienced actors, and an established audience. When Ibsen arrived, the annual takings at the Norwegian Theatre had averaged 7,000 specie-dollars; during his first year this rose to 9,000 and over the next few years it rose to 12,000 – an increase of more than 70 per cent. If the board had not over-reached themselves by their decision to rebuild, and so saddled themselves with a debt they could never hope to pay off, they would probably still, eventually, have had to merge with the Christiania Theatre, because the city could not support two theatres running roughly similar repertories; but Ibsen would at least have been recognized as having done the job he had been appointed to do, namely, to raise the Norwegian Theatre to the same level as the Christiania Theatre. He was not the first nor the last theatre director to become a scapegoat for the failings of his committee and the preferences of his audience for light entertainment rather than serious drama.

Nowhere, probably, in Europe could he have found a less inspiring town to work in. 'Christiania during the late eighteen-fifties and early eighteen-sixties', wrote Gerhard Gran, 'must have been a sadly jejune place ... All observers from this time agree in their condemnation of its spiritual indifference.' J. E. Sars called it 'a temple of puritanism and narrow-mindedness, a community of the old, granting youth no rights whatever'. Henrik Jæger, writing in 1887–8, noted: 'It is significant that none of our living Norwegian authors choose to live in the capital. They have arranged to live in the country ... or have buried themselves in a small town. And usually they have chosen to exile themselves for a shorter or longer period.' The most eloquent condemnation of nineteenth-century Christiania, however, comes from one of Norway's most distinguished novelists, Henrik Wergeland's sister, Camilla Collett:

O great and little city! What cold and surly sky broods over you! You are great enough, with your thousand beaks! great enough slowly to peck to death the man who no longer diverts you, or against whom you bear a grudge. But not so great that one of these unhappy creatures can find a corner in which to hide ... You have all the consuming passions, yearnings and pretensions of a great city; and yet you are so small, and so petty, that you cannot gratify one of them ... We, your children, must live off one another, feed on one another ... [*The Judge's Daughters*, 1854–5].

In the long run, however, we must be grateful that things happened as they did. If Ibsen had been successful and happy in his work in Christiania he might, with his lifelong dislike of travel, never have uprooted himself from Norway and spent the greater part of his working life abroad; and, as with so many creative writers, it was only when he transplanted himself to foreign soil that his genius really began to flower.

8

Out of the Tunnel
1862–4

ON 20 June 1862 Ibsen signed a contract with Jonas Lie, who by now had taken over the ownership of *Illustreret Nyhedsblad* (though Botten Hansen was still its editor) for the publication of a new play, his first in five years; and on 29 June the magazine announced that 'a modern verse comedy in three acts by Henrik Ibsen' would constitute its New Year supplement. The idea for this play had first come to Ibsen as early as 1858, and in 1860 he had begun to write it under the title of *Svanhild* (the name of the heroine). About sixteen pages of this draft have survived; apart from a song which opens it, a solo with choruses, it is in prose, a modern satirical comedy set just outside Christiania. But during 1860 he had been overwhelmed by a general feeling of apathy towards his work, and had abandoned the project. Now, during either the spring or, more probably, the early summer of 1862, he had taken it up again, this time writing it in verse which, one can scarcely repeat too often, came to him as a young man more easily than prose, not least in the composing of dialogue. He re-titled it *Love's Comedy*.

On 24 June, he left Christiania on his trip northwards to gather folklore, for which the Akademiske Kollegium had granted him a stipend. He travelled partly by coach, partly on foot, partly by fjord steamer, and partly by rowboat. A brief diary which he kept during the first three weeks, barely a thousand words all told, was discovered as late as 1932, and enables us to follow him, in the company of a newly-engaged young law student and a stern Catholic priest, to Lillehammer, along the valley of Gudbrandsdal and across the

Sogne mountains; thence he voyaged along the Sognefjord, northwards through the spectacular landscape of Sunnfjord and Nordfjord, over the mountains from Breim to Sunnylven, by steamer to Søholt, on to Vestnes in Romsdal, and back through Gudbrandsdal to Christiania. The harshness of life in the remoter areas astonished him. He came to one valley where the parsonage had been destroyed by an avalanche. The wife, who had just given birth to a child, occupied a screened-off corner, while the husband transacted the business of the parish in the rest of the room. Another house lay at the foot of a precipice so sheer that the inhabitants had no fear of avalanches; the stones, they told him, always fell at a slight angle so that, hugging the rock, the house was safe. From the Jotunfjeld he looked straight down on a steeple hundreds of feet below, and could see no possible way of descent; but there turned out to be a path cut in the face of the precipice, and he descended this with his Catholic priest and a sick woman tied to a horse. He mistook two Swedish fellow-travellers in succession for the young Swedish poet Carl Snoilsky, who that year had published his first book of poems (and who was to become his close friend a quarter of a century later); was depressed by the heavy rain which followed him everywhere; commented on the varying quality of his lodgings; took showers when he could, bathed, fished, and collected stories.

Some of these he dismissed as fabrications, such as the sea-serpent caught in Lysterfjord and sold for 300 specie-dollars to an Englishman, who got his money back; 'for' (records Ibsen) 'he knew where the sea-serpent hides in its belly all costly objects of gold and silver which it swallows, and slit it open and took them'. But others seemed more authentic; and he scribbled down over a hundred pages of legendary anecdotes, most of them dealing with supernatural visitations. Many of these centred on an eighteenth-century priest named Peder Strøm; he had studied the 'Black Book' at Wittenberg, as was common among churchmen of those days, for the ability to perform seemingly impossible tricks enabled them to impress and convert otherwise sceptical peasants. Thus, Ibsen learned, Peder once sank an unbeliever in the earth up to his shoulders and freed him only when he had promised to follow the true faith. He terrified the local witches by telling them that, if they were.in league with the Devil, blood would run from their butter when he cut it with his knife; 'and those present saw a new sight, for the blood not only ran from the butter but drenched the whole table'. Then there was the story of St Olav's pig; the saint left it with a peasant, and at first the animal thrived, 'but as the rumour spread that the saint was dead, the pig began to pine, and finally so sickened that it turned into stone, and so it may still be seen standing there today'. There was the witch who, as they took her to the stake, swore that no living thing would grow for as far as she could see as she burned, 'wherefore they deemed it expedient to bandage her eyes'; and the ignorant charcoal-burner whose one desire was to become a priest, though he could neither read nor write. By a trick played on the king, he managed to obtain a living, but his ignorance was so patent that the parishioners petitioned the bishop to remove him. Knowing the bishop to be a lecher, he feigned death, having bidden his wife to sit alone with the bishop watching over his coffin. Then, as the bishop began to fondle her, the charcoal-burner rose from his coffin and denounced him, as a result of which 'the bishop had to let him remain as priest, although he could not read the Book'.

In addition to these notes, Ibsen made drawings of the landscape, and when he returned to Christiania in early August, four of these (two of Gudbrandsdal, one of Vestnes, and one of Nordfjord) were published in *Illustreret Nyhedsblad* – the only time, so far as we know, that he ever received payment for any artistic work. They are excellent realistic studies; Ibsen had continued with his painting all the time he had been in Christiania, even, when he could ill afford it, taking lessons from a feckless painter named Magnus Bagge who was to be one of the models (there were several, for it is a common enough Norwegian type) for Hjalmar Ekdal in *The Wild Duck*. He accompanied these drawings with stiff little descriptive sketches, of the kind expected from nineteenth-century travellers. He also wrote up for *Illustreret Nyhedsblad* four of the legendary anecdotes he had heard, and on 17 November signed a contract with the bookseller and publisher Johan Dahl to make a book of them, of two hundred and fifty pages, for an honorarium of 160 specie-dollars (£40) – a project which (surprisingly, in view of his need for cash) he never completed. Now that the Norwegian Theatre had closed he was without a job, and had to support his wife and son by casual journalism, plus whatever he may have saved from his travel stipend. There cannot have been much left from the 110 specie-dollars; but Ibsen (and Suzannah, too) were, all their lives, the thriftiest of people, and they seem to have managed somehow.

Ibsen wrote eight long articles for *Illustreret Nyhedsblad*, *Aftenbladet* and even *Morgenbladet* (which had been so hostile towards him) before the end of the year. The first two, on 'The Crisis in the Theatre' (that perennial subject) included, in addition to an indictment of the public for indifference, a bitter attack on the complacency of actors. 'Our players', he wrote, 'have not as yet experienced the blessing of privation, which no man escapes with impunity. The man of ideas who lacks the opportunity to starve or suffer is thereby deprived of *one* way of becoming great.' He went on to express his personal faith in a vivid image. 'When Vesuvius erupted and destroyed Pompeii with earthquake and ash, a Roman soldier stood guard at the temple. Slaves and anyone, anything that could flee, fled past him; but the soldier remained at his post, bound by his duty, guarding his trust. The rain of ash rose and rose around him, inch by inch, and rose so high that it buried him; he could not flee, for *he had not been dismissed*! Such action is spiritual, it is a revelation of the spirit that should rule in art as in the army or the Church ... to remain at one's post and guard one's trust.' He was, though he did not know it, about to be given a further opportunity to test the strength of his belief in his calling.

On 31 December 1862 *Love's Comedy* was published, as *Illustreret Nyhedsblad's* special New Year supplement for their subscribers. Ibsen received 100 specie-dollars (£25), 'at that time a goodish fee', noted Henrik Jæger. Apart from *St John's Night*, it was the first play he had written with a modern setting.

The action takes place in the garden of a villa just outside Christiania, owned by Mrs Halm, the widow of a civil servant. She has married off seven nieces from this house, and is anxious to do the same for her two daughters, Anna and Svanhild; which ambition seems about to be fulfilled, for they are being courted by her lively young student lodgers, Lind and Falk. Falk, however, believes that marriage and love are incompatible; marriage, he declares, is 'a galley of chains and thralldom', and as though to prove his point the local Pastor Strawman enters with his wife and eight of their twelve children. Once he had been a burning young idealist like Falk; now he has faded into dullness and conventionality, and the girl he loved has become a plump housewife. 'Everything's burned out, dead!' cries Falk. 'Where's the green joy of life?' He calls on Svanhild to join her life to his, but without the bond of marriage. 'If you must die, live first! Be mine, in God's green spring!' With her to inspire him, he knows he could become a great poet. Like the falcon whose name he bears:

> I must fly against the wind to reach the heights,
> And you're the gust to carry me . . .
> Be mine, be mine, until the world shall claim you!
> And when our tree grows bare, why, then we'll part.

SVANHILD
> You think of me as a reed that a child cuts
> Into a flute to play on for an hour,
> Then casts away.

FALK
> Better that than to stagnate in the marsh
> Till autumn comes and chokes you with grey fog.

But she, the first of those imaginative yet realistic girls whom Ibsen was to create, the predecessor of Agnes in *Brand*, Solveig in *Peer Gynt*, Dina Dorf in *The Pillars of Society*, Nora when the scales have fallen from her eyes, replies:

> You called yourself a falcon . . .
> Another image came into my mind.
> I saw you as no falcon, but a kite,
> A poet's kite of paper, that is nothing
> Without its string . . . impotently beseeching:
> 'Send me aloft, that the strong winds may bear me!'

She leaves him; and impulsively he decides that he must, after all, marry her.

But in the second act his disillusionment returns. His friend Lind, whom Anna has by now accepted, begins to show the marks of domesticity; and Pastor Strawman does not help by descanting on the joys of marriage. Falk, in exasperation, denounces marriage to the assembled company. Love, he says, anticipating T. S. Eliot, has to cross the desert; to marry is to turn one's back on that desert. Marriage is to love 'as is a potted plant to fresh field flowers'. The company is scandalized and departs into the house; only Svanhild remains, awed by his fury as Agnes was to be by Brand's, and says that, if he still wants her, she will go with him. He tells her that they will show the world that there is a love which marriage need not destroy, takes off his ring and puts it on her finger.

This is where most dramatists of the age would have ended the play; but Ibsen, even this early in his career, had something up his sleeve for the final act. Pastor Strawman, hitherto merely a figure of fun, tells Falk that the latter's denunciation of marriage has reminded him of his own lost ideals, and begs him, somehow, to give him (Strawman) back his faith. Falk says he cannot. But now Guldstad, a rich but kindly business man, and himself an admirer of Svanhild, steps in. He reminds Falk of what the latter had said yesterday, about the incompatibility of marriage and love; has he really changed his views? The only possible foundation for a happy marriage, says Guldstad, is the kind of love that is based on other things than passion; it is not inferior to passionate love, and it grows where the other fades. He leaves Falk and Svanhild alone to make their decision. Svanhild asks Falk if he would not still cherish her if and when his love died; to which he replies: 'No. When my love died, all else would die too.' She asks whether he can promise her that he will love her for ever. He answers: 'For a long time.' She says that the kind of love she and Falk bear for each other can only survive if the lovers part when it is at its full, and keep it as a memory. This memory will do more for Falk as a poet than if they should stay together and their love fade. She kisses his ring, throws it into the fjord, and tells Guldstad that she will marry him; and is left sadly seated as the others congratulate her, while Falk, free as he has always longed to be, goes off into the mountains with his illusions.

Love's Comedy was, both structurally and in the depth of its characterization, by far the best play that Ibsen had yet written. Why is it never acted today, in Scandinavia any more than elsewhere? The reason lies in the form which Ibsen employed. It is written throughout in rhymed verse, of remarkable concentration and ingenuity, but of an extreme formalism, as though by a modern Alexander Pope. Admittedly, Ibsen was to use rhyme throughout both *Brand* and *Peer Gynt*, but in both those plays he employed it far more flexibly than in *Love's Comedy*. In them the characters speak dialogue, in *Love's Comedy* they deliver set pieces packed with epigrams. To work on a modern stage, the play would have to be translated into free verse; and even then, the effect of set pieces would remain. Attempts to revive it in this century have never proved successful, and are never likely to; it remains a brilliant dramatic poem rather than a poetic play. It is crippled by the untheatricality of its form, just as *Olaf Liljekrans* is crippled by the untheatricality of the ballad form and *The Vikings at Helgeland* by that of the saga style.

The day after *Love's Comedy* was published, on 1 January 1863, Ibsen took up a part-time employment as *æsthetisk konsulent* to the Christiania Theatre, which had decided to bow to public opinion and go Norwegian. The Danish manager, Carl Borgaard, had been dismissed, and negotiations were in progress for the services of the actors of the Norwegian Theatre who, since that body had declared itself bankrupt, had been giving performances at the Møllergaden theatre as an independent company. Most of them were to move to Bankpladsen in the summer. Ibsen's duties in his new post included, as well as literary advice, supervision of the historical accuracy of the decor and costumes, and, when required, stage direction. His salary was pathetically small, 25 specie-dollars (£6.25) per month, and since even this small sum was dependent on the box-office takings exceeding a certain figure, he in fact received only a fraction of it.

On 8 January he offered *Love's Comedy* to the theatre at Trondhjem for the modest honorarium of 60 specie-dollars, and while he was awaiting their reply a notice appeared in *Illustreret Nyhedsblad*, on 25 January, to the effect that the play was shortly to be staged at the Christiania Theatre. But during February and March reviews of the most unfavourable nature began to appear in the press. Professor M. J. Monrad, who had welcomed the appearance of *Catiline* thirteen years earlier, warned Ibsen in *Morgenbladet* that he would destroy himself if he became 'a mouthpiece for the loose thinking and debilitating nihilism that is now fashionable'. The play, he asserted, was 'an offence against human decency ... The underlying theme, that marriage and love are irreconcilable opposites, is not merely basically untrue and, in the loftier sense of the word, immoral, in that it denigrates both love and marriage; it is also unpoetical, as any viewpoint must be which claims that idealism and reality are incompatible.' Botten Hansen, as always, attempted to defend his friend in *Illustreret Nyhedsblad*, but the public was left in no doubt that *Love's Comedy* was an immoral work (just as, eighteen years later, they were to receive a like warning about *Ghosts*). The Christiania Theatre, never (then or later) renowned for flying in the face of public sentiment, decided that they dare not perform it.

Ibsen never forgot the abuse with which his compatriots had received *Love's Comedy* and the effect it had had on him. When, three years later, following the success of *Brand*, *Love's Comedy* came to be reprinted, he decided to hit back at his attackers in a preface. 'I made the mistake', he wrote, 'of publishing it in Norway. Both the time and the place were ill chosen. The play aroused a storm of hostility, more violent and widespread than most books could boast of having evoked in a community the vast majority of whose members commonly regard matters of literature as being of small concern. This reception did not really surprise me ... When, in my comedy, as best I could, I cracked the whip over the problem of love and marriage, it was only natural that the majority should rush shrieking to the defence of those institutions. Not many of our critics and readers have acquired the intellectual discipline and training which enable a man to recognize delusions.' In a letter to Peter Hansen on 28 October 1870, he recalled: 'People brought my personal affairs into the discussion, and my reputation suffered considerably. The only person who approved of the play was my wife ... I was excommunicated. Everyone was against me.'[1] Perhaps partly because of the hostility of its reception, he retained a particular fondness for the play. 'Structurally', he wrote to Hartvig Lassen on 24 October 1872, 'I am more than ever convinced that it cannot be

---

1. 'They began, as is customary in such cases, to search into Ibsen's private life and investigate the nature of his own marriage. As Ibsen once put it to me: the printed criticism of the comedy might have been borne at a pinch, but the oral and private criticism was absolutely unbearable.' Georg Brandes, *Henrik Ibsen* (Copenhagen, 1898), pp. 57–8; Muir-Archer translation.

faulted, and has not in this respect been bettered in any of my other plays. All in all, I reckon *Love's Comedy* to be among the best things that I have done' – and this was after he had written *Brand* and *Peer Gynt*.

Ibsen's finances were now at rock bottom. They had, as we know, been bad enough when he was receiving 50 specie-dollars a month from the Norwegian Theatre; now he was forced to resort to money-lenders, and to making further applications for grants and stipends. On 6 March he applied to the Akademiske Kollegium for a renewal of the stipend allowed him the previous year for the collection of folklore. He asked 120 specie-dollars and was granted 100. Four days later he addressed a petition to the king: 'Henrik Ibsen', it begins, 'most humbly begs ... that he be granted an annual pension of 400 (four hundred) specie-dollars, to enable him to continue his literary activity.'

The document makes sad reading. Ibsen describes his career up to this point: how he had started work at fifteen, 'my parents being in needy circumstances'; how he had prepared himself for his matriculation; and then lists his publications and the plays which he has had staged, naming the various salaries he has enjoyed.

My salary at the Bergen Theatre amounted to 300 specie-dollars annually, and I was compelled to leave the city in debt. My appointment at the Norwegian Theatre of Christiania carried with it an annual salary of about 600 specie-dollars, but the theatre's bankruptcy involved me in a loss of over 150 specie-dollars, together with all permanency of occupation. At the Christiania Theatre I have been allotted a nominal salary of 25 specie-dollars per month, but the payment of this is dependent upon higher takings than the theatre has achieved during the current winter. My financially most successful work, *The Vikings at Helgeland*, which occupied me for nearly a year, brought me in all 277 specie-dollars. Under the circumstances I have incurred debts of some 500 specie-dollars, and since I have been unable to envisage any prospect of improving my financial situation in this country, I have felt compelled to make the necessary preliminary arrangements to emigrate this spring to Denmark. To leave my

native land and abandon a career which I have hitherto regarded, and still regard, as my true vocation, is, however, a step
which I find inexpressibly distressing, and it is in the hope of
avoiding this step that I now, as a last resort, most humbly be-
seech that a proposal signed by Your Majesty be laid before the
present Parliament granting me an annual pension of 400 specie-
dollars, whereby I may be enabled to continue a career in the
service of letters which I have reason to believe that the public
would not wish to see brought to an end.

> Your Majesty's most humble servant,
> Henrik Ibsen

This appeal was rejected; not, as some biographers have
suggested, because of *Love's Comedy* (though one member
of the grants board, a cleric named Riddervold, declared
that the man who could have written such a play deserved
not a grant but a thrashing). The records of the Department
of Education (who had, after all, granted his folklore application the previous year) show that in their report they admitted that 'the applicant's literary achievements must be
agreed to be of no small importance to our literature, and
would have wished that Ibsen could be granted support to
enable him to continue his work under more favourable circumstances; but, since we must hesitate before recommending new grants that are not of immediate urgency,
Parliament having been assembled for so long, we cannot
feel that there is the same urgency to make such a recommendation as in that of the grant for Bjørnstjerne
Bjørnson', who had applied simultaneously. The mem-
orandum added a reminder that Ibsen's request in 1860 for a
travel grant had not been acceded to, and concluded: 'We
feel it is probable that he will be favourably considered at
the next allocation of stipendia, though this statement naturally cannot be regarded as binding.'

On 27 May he made a further application, this time for a
grant of 600 specie-dollars 'to spend a year, principally in
Paris and Rome, studying art, art history, and literature'.
The petition continues: 'The many and great difficulties

with which an author has to contend in this country are
increased still further by the almost total absence of opportunity to obtain the necessary grounding in general culture
which everywhere else is regarded as an essential condition
for the successful and profitable continuation of the work
which I believe to be my vocation. I venture to observe that
travel grants of this nature have been granted to every Norwegian writer who has devoted himself exclusively to
authorship except myself.'

'Ibsen can rely on a bigger grant than Bjørnson, surely!'
wrote Vinje to Botten Hansen on 11 June; but he was wrong.
Although, on 12 September, the Akademiske Kollegium at
last acceded to his request, they did so as grudgingly as possible, giving him the last place on their list and recommending that the award be reduced to 250 specie-dollars. This
sum struck even the Department of Education as miserly,
and they recommended that it be increased to 400 specie-
dollars (£100) 'which, though considerably less than the
amount applied for, may be regarded as sufficient to ensure
some satisfactory return, which can scarcely be said of so
small sum as that suggested by the Kollegium'.

The result of this latest application was not made known
to Ibsen until mid-September, and he existed that summer,
we must suppose, largely on the 100 specie-dollars which he
had been granted to continue his study of folklore, and
which he in fact never used for that purpose. O. Arvesen
describes how Ibsen could be seen in his shabby clothes entering L'Orsa's café punctually at two o'clock each afternoon
to drink coffee and read the foreign newspapers, and adds:
'That this man with the threadbare coat, old, soft mormon
hat and profoundly unassuming mien would become one of
Norway's and Scandinavia's greatest men was an unim-
aginable thought.'

The tide was, however, about to turn.

In June Ibsen received an invitation from students to
attend a choral festival at Bergen, at which over a thousand

singers were to gather from various parts of Norway. He accepted, and wrote a song which the three choral groups from Christiania learned for the occasion. The news of Ibsen's imminent return aroused no enthusiasm in Bergen. A list of those requiring accommodation was posted in the town; those willing to offer hospitality were asked to sign against visitors whom they would like to have, and, we are told, Ibsen's was the last name to be taken up. Ignorant of this, he left Christiania with the three choirs by ship on 12 June, and reached Bergen two days later.

The voyage in the company of these people, and the festival itself (which lasted four days) had a remarkable effect on him. For the first time in his life, he was lionized. The critics, especially of late, had been hostile to his works, the cultural authorities had repeatedly turned down his applications, and, living, as he did now, a comparatively solitary life, he can seldom have heard a word of praise except from those he knew well, and one never quite believes that. But now, forced into the company of this largely youthful gathering, he, who had previously felt isolated and rejected, found himself surrounded by sympathy, friendship, and spontaneous admiration. One incident especially moved him. At a banquet in Bergen on 16 June, Bjørnson paid him a most generous public tribute, speaking out handsomely in praise of his writing and denouncing those people who had tried, as critics will in every age that contains writers of comparable stature, to turn them into adversaries. 'Have I not experienced,' cried Bjørnson, 'that my friend Ibsen has been held up against me for the purpose of disparaging me, and I against him, to disparage him?' His speech was followed by the song which Ibsen had written for the occasion, dealing, it so happened, with the importance of naturally dissimilar people living together in harmony – a coincidence which Ibsen, no more than anyone else, can have missed. Four days after his return to Christiania, on 25th June, he wrote to his host at Bergen, a shipping agent named Randolph Nilsen:

It is eight days to the hour since we said good-bye, and, God be praised, I still carry within me the spirit of the festival, and I hope I shall long keep it. My hearty thanks to you and your good wife for all the indescribable warmth and friendliness you showed me. The festival up there, and the many dear and un-forgettable people whom I met, are working on me like a good visit to church, and I sincerely hope that this mood will not pass. Everyone was so kind to me in Bergen. It is not so here, where there are many people who seek to hurt and wound me at every opportunity. This powerful feeling of elevation, of being en-nobled and purified in all one's thoughts, must I think have been common to all who attended the choral festival, and he would indeed have something hard and evil in his soul who could remain insensitive to such an atmosphere.

Further encouraging things were to happen that summer. On 18 July, the young Danish critic Clemens Petersen pub-lished a long review of *Love's Comedy* in the Copenhagen magazine *Fædrelandet*. It occupied half the issue, and was by no means altogether favourable; indeed, it summed the play itself up as 'a failure'. Petersen praised the skill of the verse, but thought, rightly, that there was too much virtuoso rhyming, and that the reasoning was sometimes glib. He also asserted, one would think less correctly, that Ibsen wrote well only when he wrote 'in the shadow of some accepted prototype', saying that he was 'unsure and hit-or-miss' when left to his own resources. Although, therefore, Petersen ul-timately came down against *Love's Comedy*, his review made it clear that he regarded Ibsen as a writer of both ac-complishment and promise, to be taken seriously; and this, from the most influential critic in Scandinavia, must have seemed praise indeed compared with the kind of criticisms which Ibsen had been getting in Norway.

The following day, 19 July, a long 'profile' of Ibsen was published in *Illustreret Nyhedsblad*. These weekly profiles were a feature of the magazine; notabilities thus honoured that summer included Lamartine, Liszt and Stonewall Jack-son, so that to appear in the series was something of a distinction. Paul Botten Hansen was the author, and the piece, some twenty-five hundred words in length, was accompanied by the first likeness of Ibsen to be printed, a clumsy linocut 'after a photograph by Petersen', not easily distinguishable from one of Vinje, similarly bearded and melancholy, which was published in the next issue, and much inferior to a large illustration of Princess Alexandra of Denmark's arrival in London for her wedding with the Prince of Wales which appeared in the same issue as Ibsen's profile. Pointing out that Ibsen now had no fixed income other than his uncertain salary as *aesthetisk konsulent* to the Christiania Theatre, Botten Hansen continued:

He is consequently mainly dependent on such honoraria as his writing may bring him. But this, Ibsen being the kind of author he is, can never prove a rich source, for he is one of those individuals whom external circumstances, and even privation, cannot readily incite, except as the expression of a temporary inspiration. The reason for this is a self-criticism which often rejects not merely long-matured plans, drafts and works already commenced, but even completed *œuvres* which, when he considers them coldly and at a distance, no longer satisfy him.

Botten Hansen went on to compare Ibsen's lyrics with those of Heine, but said that his dramatic works were his most important, and concluded with the information that Ibsen 'is at present busied with a new saga-play set in Norway in the Middle Ages'.

This 'saga-play' was to be Ibsen's first major dramatic work: *The Pretenders*.

He had begun to plan it as early as five years previously, in the summer of 1858. According to a letter which Ibsen wrote to J. B. Halvorsen (18 June 1889), he had also worked on it during 1860; but he had put the project aside, and it needed the tonic effect of the Bergen Festival, and his meetings there with Bjørnson, to get him into the mood to write it. He seems to have begun it almost immediately on his return to Christiania from Bergen towards the end of June (1863), and he completed it in six to eight weeks. It was published by the Christiania bookseller Johan Dahl towards the end of October (though, by an error, the date 1864 appears on the title page of the first edition).

The Pretenders is set in Norway during the first half of the thirteenth century. The King, Inge, has just died leaving no legal heir, and there are several claimants to the throne. Of these, the two strongest are Earl Skule, brother to the dead King, a famous warrior and a skilled statesman, and Haakon Haakonsson, a boy still in his teens who claims to be the dead King's illegitimate son. The Grand Council votes Haakon king; he, to win Skule's friendship, takes Skule's daughter to be his Queen, and gives Skule a third of his kingdom. But the villainous Bishop Nicholas, whom sexual impotence has twisted into evil, and who is anxious that 'there must be no giants in Norway, for I was never one', sows discord between them. He incites Skule to rebel against Haakon, hoping that they will destroy each other. Skule proclaims himself King, and civil war breaks out. At first, things go Skule's way. He is the more experienced soldier and statesman. But he has one fatal defect, and Haakon one supreme advantage. Skule has, when it comes to the crunch, no real belief in himself; he lacks single-mindedness. Haakon, on the other hand, never has a moment's doubt that 'he is the one whom God has chosen'. It has been Skule's fate, throughout his life, to vacillate when success was within his grasp; and so it is now. He is defeated and killed. Haakon is left King of, for the first time in its history, a united Norway.

Such is a brief outline of the plot, but it gives little idea of the richness and complexity of the play, of its intense poetic imagination (though it is written in prose) and epic sweep, working remorselessly towards the superb climax in the abbey, where Skule has taken sanctuary with Haakon's baby son as hostage and the peasants are waiting outside to lynch him. It contains, in Skule, Haakon and Bishop Nicholas, three characters comparable in stature with any that he was to create later, and a dozen splendidly drawn minor parts:

Peter, Skule's illegitimate son, a former priest whom blind belief in his father has turned into a ruthless killer; the lonely bard, Jatgeir; the young Queen, Margaret, torn between love of her husband and of her father; Ingeborg, Skule's former mistress and Peter's mother; and the Cassandra-like figure of Skule's sister, Sigrid. Ibsen's previous plays, from *Catiline* to *Love's Comedy*, had been rangefinders; *The Pretenders* is the first of the great epic quartet that was to embrace *Brand*, *Peer Gynt*, and *Emperor and Galilean*.

Stylistically, too, it marks an important stage in Ibsen's development as a dramatist. Of his previous nine plays, four (*Catiline*, *The Warrior's Barrow*, *Norma*, and *Love's Comedy*) had been written in verse, and three (*St John's Night*, *Lady Inger of Østraat*, and *The Vikings at Helgeland*) in prose (apart from songs, etc.), while *The Feast at Solhaug* and *Olaf Liljekrans* had been composed in a mixture of the two. Although he had managed here and there to achieve a colloquial prose, he had limited it to his peasants and lower class characters; his princes and chieftains had spoken a formal dialogue, and in *The Vikings at Helgeland* he had, as stated, deliberately imitated the antique language of the sagas. Bjørnson had disapproved of this experiment, and Ibsen himself, in a review of Bjørnson's historical drama *Sigurd Slembe* published in *Illustreret Nyhedsblad* on 21 December 1862, had expressed his conviction that the language of a historical play should be living and colloquial, whoever might be speaking. In *The Pretenders* he attempted to create such a dialogue, retaining formal language only when the characters used a deliberately formal mode of address – as in the opening exchange between Haakon and Skule – and occasionally for special effect. He succeeded, not indeed completely, but to a considerable degree.[2] The play is full of terse, colloquial statements that we do not find in

2. Not least in the delightfully easy rhymed verse given to the Bishop's ghost in Act Five, and dismissed by some critics as 'doggerel'. If this is doggerel, so is much of *Peer Gynt*.

Lady Inger or *The Vikings*, and that shock by their unex-
pectedness; as in the exchange between Skule, when his fortunes are at their height, and the bard Jatgeir:

SKULE (*passionately.*) I must have someone by me who will obey
  me instinctively, believe in me unflinchingly, stand close by me
  through good days and evil, live only to give light and warmth
  to my life – someone who, when I fall, must die! What shall I
  do, Jatgeir?
JATGEIR. Buy a dog, my lord.

In a sense, that line of Jatgeir's is the beginning of modern
prose drama.

   The Pretenders is one of Ibsen's most personal plays; there
can be little doubt that the conflict between Skule and
Haakon reflects Ibsen's sense of bitterness at the contrast
between his failure (at the time he wrote it) and the younger,
less gifted but utterly self-confident Bjørnson's success.
This contrast must have seemed especially painful in that
summer of 1863, when his fortunes were at their lowest, and
he portrayed it very recognizably in *The Pretenders*, in
which a man of great gifts invalidated by self-distrust is wor-
sted by a potentially lesser man who possesses the supreme
virtue of believing in himself. Bjørnson was very much the
model for Haakon (whom, incidentally, he had praised in a
speech at Bergen as 'Norway's best king'), and Ibsen put
much of himself into Skule and also, by his own admission,
into the bard Jatgeir. 'I know I have the fault', he was to
write to Bjørnson from Rome on 16 September 1864, echoing
the words he had used earlier to Carl Johan Anker, 'that I
can't make close contact with those people who demand that
one should give onself freely and unreservedly. I am rather
like the bard Jatgeir in *The Pretenders*, I can never bring
myself to strip naked. I have the feeling that, where personal
relationships are concerned, I can only give false expression
to what I feel deep down inside, to my true self, and that is
why I prefer to shut it up within me, and why we have sometimes stood as it were observing each other from a distance.'

And to Peter Hansen, on 28 October 1870, he wrote: 'The fact that everyone was against me, that there was no un-committed person who could be said to believe in me, could not but give rise to the strain of feeling which found utter-ance in *The Pretenders*.'

The Pretenders received mixed reviews when it was pub-lished in October 1863, including a disappointing one from Clemens Petersen; but the Christiania Theatre accepted it for production the following January. It was presumably this last turn of events which caused Ibsen to delay his departure for the south; on 8 October he had asked for an advance of 100 specie-dollars from his pension to send his wife and son to Copenhagen, to stay with Magdalene Thoresen, and on 27 October he applied for a further 300 specie-dollars, 'since it is my intention to leave during the next few weeks by steamer for Hamburg'. But a production of his new play was some-thing which he could not afford to miss.

Ibsen directed the production himself – the last time that he was ever to direct a play of his own or anyone else's – and it received its first performance at the Christiania Theatre on 17 January 1864. Although it lasted for nearly five hours – later they managed to reduce the playing time to four – we are told that 'from start to finish it was followed with excited attention' and that 'after the fall of the curtain there was a general cry for the author who, when he appeared, was re-warded with thunderous applause. . . . In less than two months [writes Halvdan Koht] *The Pretenders* was performed eight times, a success unique for a play as long and serious as this in a town as small as the Christiania of those days . . . Now for the first time he rested in a full and free confidence in his own ability to write, and in his calling as a poet.'

Between the writing of *The Pretenders* and its production, however, larger and more far-reaching issues had arisen to occupy Ibsen's mind.

On 15 November 1863 King Frederik VII of Denmark had died without male issue, and been succeeded by a collateral member of the family, Christian IX. The old and grisly problem of the Duchies of Schleswig and Holstein now reared its head. They disputed Christian's claim to be their ruler, since they had always accepted the Salic Law and denied claims through females. The German states, who had long resented the Danish suzerainty over the Duchies, maintained that the rightful ruler of them was now the Duke of Augustenburg, and Bismarck, supported by Austria, championed the German cause. In December the armies of the German League attacked Holstein; in mid-January the Prussians issued an ultimatum to Denmark; and on 1 February the Prussian forces invaded Schleswig. It was the first testing of Bismarck's new army, which Lord Palmerston had recently scorned ('all military men who have seen it at its annual reviews of late years have unequivocally declared that the French could walk over it and get without difficulty to Berlin'), and which Franz Josef and Napoleon III were similarly, and more disastrously, to under-rate.

The young king of Sweden and Norway, Carl XV, and his foreign minister, Count Manderström, had continuously and openly professed support for Denmark in this matter of the Duchies, and Manderström had made several pronouncements, notably one in July, which left no doubt in most Scandinavian minds, including Ibsen's that, if Danish independence were threatened, Sweden and Norway would come to her aid. A few days after Manderström's July statement, Carl XV offered Denmark a military alliance. But, not for the last time in Swedish history, strong forces within the government advocated a policy of isolationism, and the king found his hands bound. The Norwegian students held a big meeting on 12 December, at which they sent a declaration to the Swedish students asserting that all Scandinavians must now regard the Danish cause as their own, and a week later a gathering of three thousand citizens in Christiania sent the king a message of support for any military action he might take in support of the Danish cause. But the Storthing would go no further than to make a promise of financial aid to Denmark, and that conditional on one of the great western powers joining the alliance. Palmerston had declared in the House of Commons that autumn that any nation which challenged the rights of Denmark 'would find in the result that it would not be Denmark alone with which they would have to contend', but for any effective intervention the co-operation of France was essential, and Palmerston could not face the prospect of a French conquest of Prussia. When the crisis came, Denmark found herself alone.

Ibsen's feelings towards his countrymen, already strained, became considerably aggravated by this, as he thought, chicanery. He had had hard things to say about Denmark in the cultural field in recent years, but this example of aggression against a small neighbour by a bullying power angered him as much as that similar situation had done in 1848 when the Swedes and Norwegians had uttered professions of sympathy but had sent almost no help. On 13 December, the day after the student meeting in Christiania, Ibsen published in *Illustreret Nyhedsblad* a furious indictment of his fellow-countrymen. He called the poem simply 'To Norway'.

> Those generous words that seemed to gush
> From bold hearts swelling high
> Were but a flood of empty gush,
> And now their stream is dry!
> The tree, that buds of promise bore
> Beneath the banquet's light
> Stands stripped and smitten to its core,
> A graveyard cross upon the shore
> That's ravaged in a night.
>
> 'Twas but a lie in festal song,
> A kiss that Judas gave,
> When Norway's song sang loud and long
> Beside the Danish wave.[3]

The poem continued in such vehement terms that Botten Hansen, who wished to print it in *Illustreret Nyhedsblad*,

3. Edmund Gosse's translation.

asked Ibsen to tone it down; and a comparison of the Norwegian people to Cain was modified, as was a suggestion that they would do well in the future to deny their nationality since the stigma attached to the word 'Norwegian' would be such that even the country's flag would be shunned like a plague pennant. Ibsen has sometimes been condemned for compromising in this fashion, especially since his next play after *The Pretenders, Brand,* was largely an indictment of compromise; but in that tiny community it was fairly certain that no one but Botten Hansen would have published the poem in any form, and it was presumably a question of getting it printed in a modified version or not at all. And Botten Hansen, himself no coward, may have been right in thinking that the poem would be more effective if it made Norwegians ashamed rather than angry. It appeared in *Illustreret Nyhedsblad* on 13 December 1863 and shortly afterwards Ibsen wrote an elegy to King Frederik VII which developed into a moving expression of sympathy with the beleaguered Danes. This was sung at a meeting in the Christiania Students' Union on 13 January 1864 and printed in *Illustreret Nyhedsblad* four days later on the day of the première of *The Pretenders.*

Christiania was icebound that winter until early April, so that Ibsen had to kick his heels for ten weeks, separated from his wife and son, before starting on his journey. He occupied part of his time in planning a new historical drama to succeed *The Pretenders;* some notes have survived which he copied from history books about Magnus Heineson, a sixteenth-century freebooter from the Faroe Islands who ended his life on the executioner's block. But he never completed or, as far as we know, even began this work, though he was still talking about it as late as 1870. Meanwhile, Bjørnson, who had returned to Christiania the previous autumn, had, with characteristically impulsive generosity, set about raising a fund to augment Ibsen's small grant and, we may suppose, to help pay off his outstanding debts in Norway. He used his powers of eloquence to such effect that he managed to gather 700 specie-dollars (£175), and thus more than double Ibsen's finances. Johan Sverdrup, the future Prime Minister, was among the subscribers.

On 2 April the Learned Holland Group gave a banquet at the Hotel Nord, partly to celebrate Paul Botten Hansen's recent appointment (on 7 March) as university librarian, and partly to say farewell to Ibsen. Of this surely interesting occasion there is, infuriatingly, no record whatever. Three days later, in the early morning of Tuesday 5 April, Ibsen left Christiania with Botten Hansen in the first southbound steamer of the year. The next day he joined his wife and son in Copenhagen; it was to be ten years before he set foot in Norway again, and a further seventeen before he returned to live there.

On 17 April Ibsen wrote from Copenhagen to Bernhard Dunker, a lawyer who had helped Bjørnson to organize the fund for him,[4] thanking him for the money and adding: 'On Wednesday I leave for Lübeck, and shall proceed thence to Trieste. I have gained much pleasure and profit from my stay here; as soon as I reach Rome I shall work on a new five act play, which I hope to have ready by the end of the summer.' This, presumably, was the abortive project about Magnus Heineson.

The next day the Prussians stormed Dybbøl, and the brave Danish resistance was ended. Two days later, on 20 April, Ibsen sailed to Lübeck, leaving Suzannah and Sigurd to follow him later, and continued on to Berlin. There, on 4 May, he saw the Danish cannon captured at Dybbøl led in triumph through the streets while Germans lining the route spat at them. 'It was for me', he wrote a year later to Magdalene Thoresen, 'a sign that, some day, history would spit in the eyes of Sweden and Norway for their part in this affair' and the idea for a new play, unlike anything that he had hitherto written, grew in him 'like a foetus'.

From Berlin he took the railway to Vienna, and thence southwards across the Alps. Thirty-four years later, in a

4. He had been Marcus Thrane's defending counsel.

speech in Copenhagen on 1 April 1898, he was to recall his first sight of Italy. 'I ... crossed the Alps on 9 May. Over the high mountains the clouds hung like great, dark curtains, and beneath these we drove through the tunnel and, suddenly, found ourselves at Mira Mara, where that marvellously bright light which is the beauty of the south suddenly revealed itself to me, gleaming like white marble. It was to affect all my later work, even if the content thereof was not always beautiful.' He described his emotion at that moment as 'a feeling of being released from the darkness into light, of emerging from mists through a tunnel into the sunshine'. He travelled on through Trieste, Venice, Milan, Piacenza, Parma, Bologna and Florence; what impression these cities made on him we do not know, apart from the fact that he admired Milan Cathedral. Otherwise, of these six weeks in May and early June of 1864, when Europe was opening itself before him, no record exists; the letters which he must have written to Suzannah were, like all his early letters to her, destroyed. 'Our relationship concerns no one but ourselves.' At last, in the middle of June, he reached Rome.

PART TWO

Italian Spring

9

The New Michelangelo
1864–6

THE Italy which greeted Ibsen in the summer of 1864 was a country rejoicing in new-found unification and liberty. Here, if nowhere else in Europe, the hopes of 1848, that year of revolutions and disillusionments, had at last been fulfilled. In 1859, five years before Ibsen's arrival, Napoleon III had helped the Italians to drive their Austrian overlords out of Milan and Lombardy, and although, to the anger of his allies, he had then made peace with the young Emperor Franz Josef and left him in possession of Venice, the fires of rebellion had been ignited. One by one the little kingdoms of Modena, Parma and Tuscany had risen against and ejected their tyrants. In 1860 Garibaldi had liberated Sicily, taken Naples, and been dissuaded from marching on Rome only by the fear of provoking a clash with Napoleon; after which, in surely the most remarkable gesture that any conqueror has made, he accepted the sovereignty of the young King Victor Emmanuel of Piedmont-Sardinia and sailed away with a little borrowed money to a life of hard work, poverty and meditation on the island of Caprera. So Rome, when Ibsen entered it that June, was still an independent state under the once liberal but now reactionary Pope Pius IX, garrisoned and protected by French troops. It and Venice were the only parts of Italy that remained outside the new kingdom, of which Florence was the capital, and into which they, too, were to find themselves incorporated within four years.

Rome, which then contained some two hundred thousand inhabitants, was, more than Paris, the cynosure of contemporary writers and artists, and to Scandinavians especially it was the promised city. Its influence had been a decisive turning-point in the lives of Oehlenschläger, Thorvaldsen, Hans Andersen, Ole Bull, and many others, as it was to be in Ibsen's. Sir Rennell Rodd, who had been a boy there at the time, described Rome in the eighteen-sixties as 'changed but little from the Rome of the eighteenth century ... still lit at night by oil-lamps, with streets mostly innocent of sidewalks, but gay with the coloured hoods of the wine-carts and the coaches of the Cardinals with their big black horses and red trappings ... Only the uniforms of the French army of occupation struck a rather anomalous note.' The old ghetto still existed near the Cenci Palace, though its walls had been pulled down in 1848. Another Englishman visiting the city in 1866–7 noted the narrowness of the streets ('there are few, if any, in which three friends can walk arm in arm'); even the Corso was 'a very long, narrow and dirty lane with many turnings'. Compared with Florence, it was an evil-smelling city. 'The streets of Rome, the houses of Rome – to the very palaces and museums – reek with such horrible odours that you are very soon led to conjecture that the ever-quoted malaria from the Pontine Marshes has been made responsible for a great deal of which it is quite innocent, and that one of the chief predisposing causes of the Roman fever is the inconceivable filthiness of the people and their dwellings.' George Augustus Sala was not exaggerating, for Ibsen later recalled how 'the inhabitants were permitted to perform their necessary functions, for want of other arrangements, in the courtyards of the ancient palaces'. Nor did the method of supplying dairy products contribute to the general cleanliness, for the streets in the early mornings were commonly full of goats which would be milked outside any restaurant that needed that luxury, and were even led up two or three flights of stairs to individual customers.

Up to five years previously, visitors from the north had travelled the final stages of their journey by coach, keeping a sharp watch for bandits, and had ridden romantically in

through the Porta del Popolo; but in 1861 the railway had
been completed, so Ibsen arrived soberly by train – doubtless
to his relief, for the bandits still flourished, and tourists
unwise enough to stray outside the city after dark were liable
to be kidnapped and held to ransom.

Ibsen lost no time in acquainting himself with the Norwegian consul, a hook-nosed old Holstein Jew named Johan
Bravo. Born in the previous century, he had lived in Rome
since 1827 and was to prove a good friend and counsellor to
Ibsen over the next two decades. Early on the morning of 19
June, presumably the day of or the day after Ibsen's arrival,
Bravo took him along to the Circolo Scandinavico, or Scandinavian Club, a lively meeting-place with impressive quarters in the Palazzo Correa, which had been built into the
remains of the Mausoleum of Augustus. Bravo's young secretary, Lorentz Dietrichson, was librarian of the club, and
lodged there. He was in bed when his visitors arrived, but
Bravo roused him with a series of oaths and commanded
him to take the newcomer on a tour of the city.

Dietrichson, who was six years younger than Ibsen, was a
native of Bergen, where he had been a childhood friend of
Suzannah, and had known Ibsen slightly in Christiania.
After studying at the university, he had worked for a while
under Paul Botten Hansen on *Illustreret Nyhedsblad*, and
had then lectured for two years on Scandinavian literature
at Upsala University, where he had scandalized the Swedes
by denouncing their modern poets as sterile and backward-
looking and, worse, by bidding them turn to the tougher and
more realistic work being produced in Norway by such as
Ibsen and Bjørnson. He had now been in Rome for two
years, studying art history, a subject in which he was later to
become professor at Christiania University, and he proved
an excellent and sympathetic guide. It was a fine, hot
Sunday and, after witnessing High Mass at St Peter's –
almost the only recorded instance of Ibsen attending a
church service, except at weddings and funerals – they
walked to the Forum and examined its ruins. Then they

crossed the Tiber into the working-class quarter of Trastevere and climbed the Janiculum Hill, where Garibaldi had
made his stand for the republic against the papal troops in
1849, and whence they enjoyed a magnificent panoramic
view of the city. On the way down, they passed the oak tree
where Tasso was reputed to have found the inspiration
for his epic *Jerusalem* and, when evening came, sat down
to dine in a little garden restaurant by the Tiber named
Fornarina, after the baker's daughter of that name whom
Raphael loved and whom he was reputed to have first seen
there.

Forty years later, Dietrichson recalled in his florid style
the impression that Ibsen had made on him that first evening in Rome. He found him, to his surprise,

quite another person than the withdrawn and bitter man I had
left three years earlier. He had of course been deeply shaken by
the latest events in Scandinavia, and expressed himself with
burning indignation on the deceitful policies which had been
adopted towards Denmark and how, with suppressed anger, he
had seen the Prussians enter Berlin with their trophies from the
Schleswig campaign. But at the same time it was as though, on
his arrival into *la bella Italia* and *la Roma eterna*, he had put all
this behind him, and now wished only to live as intensively as
possible for his writing ... Now he was able to laugh at all the
dust which *Love's Comedy* had raised, and which had embittered
his life in Norway – now he was able doubly to rejoice in the ten
[*sic*] full houses which *The Pretenders* had achieved before he
had left. And when the sun went down and we felt the gentle air
of the Italian evening shimmer through the little garden where
we sat beneath the vine leaves in our pergola with a *foglietta* of
Roman wine before us – while the natives of Trastevere came to
enjoy the cool of the river flowing beneath the garden wall, and
the small dwarf improvised to his mandolin beneath the vines
that hung out over the river – while the lamps burned on the
garden tables and the lights on the far bank in the Palazzo Far-
nese and around the great and ancient city mirrored themselves
in the water – yes, then, for a moment, we were two young men
happy in the certainty that life was rich and beautiful and that

its finest fruits were beckoning to us from the future . . . With the aid of our *fogliette* we built our dream castles in the little garden, and when night fell we wandered home in the soft Mediterranean moonlight.

Ibsen spent the next few days in further sightseeing, spending much time, as befitted a painter, in the museums and galleries, where he formed impressions quite out of fashion with prevalent taste. Yet while he wandered the streets and hills of Rome, unembarrassed by the smells and enjoying the unaccustomed heat in which, like so many Scandinavians, he was always to revel, the indignation which was so inescapable a part of his character seethed unabated; and it was not long before it found expression. The Scandinavian community was about to break up and go into the countryside to avoid the worst of the summer heat, and they held a farewell party at Raphael's Vigne on the Aquiline Hill, on the then still completely rural Via Merulana between S. Maria Maggjore and the Lateran. Dietrichson describes the scene:

on an open loggia, where we ate our frugal dinner and drank a glass of wine under the sky. It was the first evening for some while that Ibsen had spent among Scandinavians, and he began to speak of the painful and disturbing impressions of recent events in the war which he had received on his journey. Gradually, and almost imperceptibly, his talk took on the character of an improvised speech; all the bitterness which had so long been stored up within him, all the fiery indignation and passion for the Scandinavian cause which he had bottled up for so long, found an outlet. His voice began to ring, and in the evening dusk one saw only his burning eyes. When he had finished, no one cried Bravo or raised his glass, but I think we all felt that that evening the Marseillaise of the North had rung out into the Roman night air.

According to another listener, Ibsen concluded his speech by banging on the table 'so that all the wine-glasses rattled', and vowing that 'never should his son set foot on Norwegian

soil before Norway had expiated the wrong that she had
done to Denmark'.

Dietrichson and his family had taken a villa at Genzano
on Lake Nemi, and Ibsen decided to join them there. After
watching the illumination of St Peter's and the fireworks on
Monte Pincio on St Peter's and St Paul's Day, 29 June, he
rode out to Genzano with the Finnish sculptor Walter Runeberg (son of the famous poet J. L. Runeberg) and took
lodgings with the village *caffettiere*, who leased them a room
in the billiards saloon. To protect himself against the sun
Ibsen had purchased a broad-brimmed soft hat with a sky-
blue lining, which earned him among the locals the nickname of *capellone* (big hat). 'Here', records Dietrichson, 'we
spent the summer in a delightful *far niente.*'

Also living at Genzano that summer was a Norwegian
lady named Lina Bruun, with her artist son Peter and her
daughter Thea, both suffering from tuberculosis, from
which they were both to die within eighteen months. Her
other son Christopher, a theological student, had accompanied them to Rome the previous year, but had returned north to fight with the Danes against their Prussian
invaders; he was to become a lifelong friend of Ibsen, and
was to provide one of the chief inspirations for his next play.
Ibsen saw a good deal of Lina, Thea and Peter Bruun at
Genzano, and on 4 July Lina wrote to Christopher conveying
her distaste for their new acquaintance. Ibsen, she wrote,
aroused 'evil feelings' in her; five days previously (i.e. within
twenty-four hours of Ibsen's arrival), they had had a set-to;
his genius, she explained, needed something to censure and'
chastise, and he had continually to be seeking targets for his
wrath. However, they got on better than she had anticipated.
On 5 August she wrote again to Christopher about Ibsen: 'So
dual a character it is difficult to imagine. To meet day by
day he is the most sociable, cheerful and friendly man you
could conceive.' But sometimes, she added, his eyes glitter
cruelly, and then all he wants is to play the devil. She added
a note on his drinking habits. 'He likes to take a glass of

wine, because it heightens his animal spirits, and, since they are already lively, it is easy to get a false impression ... But when he is writing, he drinks tea.' Ibsen assured Lina Bruun that if Christopher fell in the war he would raise a memorial to him in poetry. Christopher Bruun did not fall, but returned to point the finger of judgement at Ibsen, who raised a poetic memorial to him none the less.

Dietrichson tells how Ibsen and he spent their days in Genzano:

In the morning we worked. At noon we gathered to eat in a wine cellar, literally a cellar, an almost pitch-dark room filled with wine barrels and a huge basket containing a bitch with her litter. There was only one tiny window and when, as frequently happened, one of the village donkeys stopped outside to scratch itself against the wall, Ibsen or one of us had to run out and chase it away so that we could see to eat.

In the afternoon they lay reading or chatting under the trees on one of the hills overlooking Lake Nemi.

I remember especially that one day I was lying there reading Ammianus Marcellinus's account of Julian the Apostate's campaigns, and Ibsen became much interested in this. We began to talk of Julian, and I know that the idea of writing about this subject took root in his mind that day. At any rate, when I had finished reading, he said he hoped no one would write about it before he did ... Towards evening we either walked across the hill to Lake Nemi or descended to the lake, strolled along it and climbed up to Nemi through the bushes. There, many an evening, we good friends emptied a glass of Nemi wine on a pretty verandah with a splendid view across the lake, the village of Genzano, the *campagna*, and the sea, or inside in the little *locanda* where the cat rubbed itself against the foot of the old woman at her spinning-wheel and Piux IX smiled benignly down on us from a fearful painting on the wall, while the tiny Roman lamp was lit and the landscape outside with its lake, woods and *campagna* grew dim in the magic dusk of evening, which swiftly turned into the blackest night. And as we walked home we would usually meet the natives singing as they moved from Madonna portrait to Madonna portrait with their devout songs in the warm, dark summer night, while the lamps gleamed in the niches of the saints along the roadside and at street corners.

One day they heard that the Pope, whom Ibsen had not yet seen, was to pass in formal procession through the nearby village of Castelgandolfo on his way to his summer residence there, and they decided to have a look at him.

We acquired two donkeys and rode cheerfully off. As we approached the village we saw that its single long street was filled with people waiting to watch the procession and receive his blessing; they thronged the street on either side . . . We had no choice but to ride with as good a face as we could muster through the town gate and, like two *matti inglesi*, run the gauntlet of the laughing lines of people. For a few moments all went well, but then the donkeys broke into a violent gallop, and suddenly first one of them, then the other, were flat on their bellies in the middle of the street with us standing above them. The jubilation was immense. At that moment, the papal procession arrived. The donkeys were dragged out of the way, braying and protesting, and the Pope made his entry undisturbed by the Norwegian poet and his squire; nor did he withhold from us the blessing which he extended to his loyal disciples.

Which was just as well, for Pius IX was supposed to have the evil eye, to counter which many a peasant would hold a finger pointed towards him, in the cover of his pocket.

That summer at Genzano, Ibsen began to write a play in prose;[1] but he encountered a 'block', technical or psychological, and began to rework it as a long epic poem. This was the work the theme of which had been growing in him 'like a foetus' ever since that day in April when he had seen the Danish cannon captured at Dybbøl drawn in triumph through the Berlin streets and spat on by the watching crowds. He composed this poem in eight-line stanzas of

---

1. So states Martin Schneekloth in his diary for 6 February 1867, printed in Peter Schindler's moving memoir of Schneekloth, *En Ungdom* (Copenhagen, 1942), pp. 120–22.

rhymed pentameters, and clearly planned it as an indictment of his countrymen for their lassitude and materialism,
particularly as manifested in their non-assistance of the
Danes. The opening section, 'To the Accomplices', states the
theme:

> My people, my fair land, my northern home ...
> I'll sing you a sad song. Perhaps my last
> As Norway's bard. For no bard sings again
> Who has bemoaned the passing of his people.
> And the sickness has begun. I see a corpse
> Huge as a giant's, poisoning field and fjord.
> Deck it with Norway's flags, and sink it deep ...
> What is dead can't be lied back to life.
> What is dead must go down into the dark.
> The dead have only one task; to provide
> Soil and nourishment for the new-sown seed.

The second section shows two boys lying on a Norwegian
hillside. One is 'the kind that looks bright-eyed upon the
world'; the other 'faces north, his back towards the sun'. The
former, looking down into the valley, speaks of his happy
home; the other speaks of his, and tells how, when his father
died, he had dreamed he had seen his mother creep in and
strike her husband's corpse. Soon after this point the section
breaks off, apparently unfinished. The third section, entitled
'Across the Mountain', shows the happier of the two boys,
Ejnar, now a painter, with his fiancée, Agnes, taking farewell
of friends at a betrothal feast in the mountains. As they
leave, they meet the 'northward-facing' boy, Koll (later
altered to Brand), who is now a priest. From this point until
the fragment ends, the action closely corresponds to that of
the play which Ibsen was shortly to write. Brand denounces
Ejnar's lazy and self-indulgent hedonism as typical of their
countrymen, continues alone on his way, and comes to the
village where he was born. As he looks down into the valley
with its cramped church, a crazed peasant girl sees him and
says: 'Come to my church,' and leads him up the mountain
to a huge natural cave hollowed into the rock which local

people call the 'Ice Church'. Brand ponders the contrast between this awe-inspiring God-made church and the mean
building below. He descends to the village, where there is
famine. The mayor is doling out meagre rations to the
people; he appeals to Brand to give food or money, but Brand
tells them that the famine is God's judgement on them for
their materialism and lack of spirituality. The poem breaks
off in the middle of his sermon.

It measures, to this point, just over two hundred stanzas,
or sixteen hundred lines. With its splendidly Byronic opening denouncing his compatriots, its fine descriptions of natural ščenery and the powerful rhetoric of Brand's
condemnation of Ejnar and, later, of the villagers, it was
certainly the most powerful and exciting poem that Ibsen
had yet written. Yet it made painful progress; he was at one
of those critical stages in a writer's career when he realizes,
slowly and unwillingly, that he is writing in the wrong
medium. The composition of these two hundred stanzas
took him over a year before he finally abandoned the work
in its epic form and began to rewrite it as dialogue.

Meanwhile, as a distraction during that summer of 1864,
he composed three short poems, all in something approaching his best manner. 'In Time of Dybbøl' tells how,
on the ship from Norway to Denmark the previous spring,
the passengers had begun to talk of the Dano-Prussian war,
and one old lady had said with a calm smile: 'I do not fear for
my son.' Ibsen admired her courage until he learned the
reason for it; her son was a soldier in the Norwegian army,
and so stood in no danger of being involved in the fighting.
'The Power of Memory' describes how an animal trainer
teaches a bear to dance; he ties it in a copper which he heats,
and then, as it begins to burn the bear's feet, plays a tune on
his barrel organ. The bear dances with pain; afterwards, by
association, it dances whenever that tune is played. So, continues the poem, I too must dance whenever I hear the tune
that reminds me of the time when 'more than my skin was
burned'. The final verse runs:

> Whenever I hear an echo from that time
> It is as though I were bound in a burning copper.
> It pierces me like a needle under my nails
> And makes me dance in verse.

The third poem was a lyric of twelve lines entitled 'Gone', and is traditionally supposed to have been written for Thea Bruun:

> We followed the last
> Guest to the gate.
> The night wind stole
> The syllables of farewell.
>
> The garden and house
> Where sweetest sounds
> Had drugged my senses
> Lay deserted.
>
> It was but a feast
> Before the black night.
> She was but a guest
> And now she is gone.

In Genzano that July, Ibsen received a letter from Richard Petersen, the chairman of the Christiania Theatre who six years earlier had publicly denounced him as 'a playwright of gigantic insignificance', inviting him to become the theatre's artistic director. The post had been offered to Bjørnson, but he had demanded powers the board regarded as too sweeping. The temptation to Ibsen must have been considerable for, cheap as life was in Italy, his grant was insufficient to provide him with more than the barest necessities. But he had had enough of the 'daily abortion' of running a theatre, and Italy had given him a peace he had not previously known and was not prepared to surrender. He declined the offer.

In September Ibsen returned, like the other Scandinavians, to Rome, and on the 16th of that month he wrote a long and revealing letter to Bjørnson in Christiania, the first we have from his hand since his arrival in Italy. Bjørnson had learned of the Christiania Theatre's offer to Ibsen and, not unreasonably, had written to Dietrichson asking for clarification. Ibsen, to whom Dietrichson had passed on the message, explained that Petersen had assured him that negotiations with Bjørnson had broken down, and had urged: 'since *you* would not take the job, I *must* ... I rejected the offer, rejected it totally and unreservedly, and without implying that any change of circumstances could ever alter my position ... So you see, my dear Bjørnson, that in this matter you have done me an injustice by nurturing the mistrust which is apparent in your letter to Dietrichson ... I cannot, though, deny that I can think of an explanation for this mistrust, and that I blame you less than myself for it.' He then allowed himself a rare moment of self-revelation, which has been quoted earlier but bears repeating in its original context. 'I know I have the fault that I cannot make close contact with people who demand that one should give oneself freely and unreservedly. I am rather like the bard in *The Pretenders*; I can never bring myself to strip naked. I have the feeling that, where personal relationships are concerned, I can give only false expression to what I feel deep down inside, to my true self, and that is why I prefer to shut it up within me, and why we have sometimes stood as it were observing each other from a distance.' The letter continues:

Please accept my thanks for all the beauty I have drunk in on my journey; I can tell you, it has done me good. Here in Rome especially much has been revealed to me; though I can't yet get to terms with classical art, I don't really understand its relevance to our time, I lack the illusion and, above all, the sense of personal and individual expression in the subject as in the artist, and I cannot help often seeing (as yet, anyway) mere conventions where others postulate laws. It seems to me that the classical plastic works of art are, like our heroic ballads, the products of their age rather than of this or that master; which may perhaps be a reason why so many of our modern sculptors fail when they persist, today, in trying to create heroic ballads in clay and marble. Michelangelo, Bernini and his school I understand better; those fellows had the courage to commit a madness now and then. The architecture has impressed me more, but neither the classical style nor its later offsprings attract me as much as the Gothic; to me, the cathedral in Milan is the most overwhelming thing I can imagine in this field; the man who could conceive such a work must have been capable in his spare moments, of creating a moon and tossing it into the heavens. I know you won't agree with much of what I have loosely indicated here, but I think it is consistent with my general standpoint, and that my appreciation of art will develop along these lines.

Here in Rome there is blessed peace for writing; I am now working on a longish poem, and am planning a tragedy, *Julian the Apostate*, a task which I embrace with inordinate enthusiasm and which I think will bring me joy. My wife and small son will be coming here this autumn; I hope you approve of this arrangement ... Dietrichson will be leaving Rome in the New Year, and I shall be taking over his job [as librarian of the Scandiavian Club], which will mean free furnished lodgings and a small salary too; I can live a year in Rome on 400 speciedollars.

Political events at home have grieved me sadly, and have much clouded my happiness. So it was all lies and dreams. These recent happenings will have a considerable effect on me. We must now draw a line through our ancient history; the Norwegians of today clearly have no more connection with their past than the Greek pirates have with the race that sailed to Troy and fought beside the gods ...

Ibsen's first reaction to classical art closely reflects his feelings about drama – the need to get away from the generalized and the heroic towards the human and the individual. The ancient Greek statues in Rome must have seemed to him like the characters in Oehlenschläger's plays, devoid of personality; he preferred, as Shelley had done half a century earlier, the Roman busts, which portrayed recognizable human beings. For the same reason, he was disappointed in the paintings of Raphael, whom his fellow-Scandinavians idolized. In Michelangelo, on the other hand, then fashionably regarded as extravagant and barbaric, rather as Shakespeare had been during the previous century, he must have recognized a kindred spirit, one of those bleak and lonely artists who tower above their age like a snow-capped mountain, as Dante, Milton and Wordsworth had done, and as Ibsen himself was to do. During his visit to Florence on his journey south, Ibsen can scarcely have missed seeing Michelangelo's unfinished statues, then in the Boboli Gardens, and those mighty figures straining to free themselves from the imprisoning marble must have seemed to him a mirror of his own struggle as an artist. In the plays to come, from *Brand* to *When We Dead Awaken*, he was to create similar gigantic and tormented prisoners. More than any writer, Michelangelo was to be Ibsen's master; the one was to create in words what the other had created in stone. Ibsen's equally unfashionable admiration of the Gothic (Milan Cathedral) and the Baroque (Bernini) was also logical in the man who was shortly to write *Peer Gynt*.

When Suzannah and Sigurd arrived, Ibsen moved into an apartment at 55, Via Capo le Case, a house (now demolished) on the corner of the Via Due Macelli. The hoped-for librarianship, with its free lodgings, did not materialize, and they remained in the Via Capo le Case until they left Rome four years later. Dietrichson relates that for several days before the arrival of his wife and son Ibsen was 'restless with excitement', and that when they finally met, an occasion at which Dietrichson was present, few words were exchanged, but no one could have doubted that 'these two highly individual people belonged intensely to one another. And I said to myself: "She and no one else is the wife for him; the only one. Only someone like her, with her strong, masculine love of truth and her deep, feminine devotion, can guide him to fulfilment." '

By October Ibsen had exhausted his grant, and only a timely draft of 100 specie-dollars (£25) from Bjørnson, tireless as ever in whipping up money for worthy causes, saw him through the last ten weeks of the year. He was earning nothing, and his expenses in Rome came to 40 scudi (40 specie-dollars, £10) a month. Bjørnson's letter of 5 October enclosing the money contained a few home truths:

> Your whole life has been such that the sun never reached it, and under such circumstances plants absorb more water than light and acquire more mud than colour. What you lacked was affection, love, a calm view of essentials. Now, God be praised, you have all that, and we shall have the fruits! ... There are many goblins in your head which I think you ought to placate. But, as I'm sure I have often told you, they are a dangerous army to have around; they're like the Praetorians and medieval mercenaries; after routing their enemies, they turn on their masters and plunder them ... I understand your admiration for the Gothic; but you'll see it differently when you get home ... As regards classical art, I think you'll soon perceive the individualism behind the convention; but it's true, our senses have to be attuned first ... Here ... the theatre has stood empty for six weeks and is expected to go bankrupt, which would be the best thing for everyone ... I enclose 100 specie-dollars. When you want more, you must tell me.

Ibsen did not acknowledge this gift for two months, a delay which seems ungracious even for him. To make matters worse, his letter went astray and was never delivered.

Ibsen led a gregarious life that autumn and winter in Rome, as indeed he was to do during the whole of his stay there. But he limited himself to his fellow-Scandinavians; he does not seem to have made any Italian friends, nor did he meet any of the foreign celebrities living there, such as Franz Liszt, or the aged English consul Joseph Severn, in whose arms John Keats had died nearly half a century before. He became a regular habitué of the Scandinavian Club, which had an excellent library; it had just received a big grant of books from the university library in Christiania and possessed six thousand volumes. The register shows that Ibsen borrowed, among others, the following books during these four years in Rome – and although the list gives no positive clue to his reading, since most were probably taken out for Suzannah, a far more avid reader than he, at least we can be sure that she would have discussed them with him: 1864, Becker's *World History*, and several volumes of Goethe, including *Wilhelm Meister*; 1865, more Goethe, including *Faust*, several of Scott's novels, including *The Heart of Mid-lothian*, *Waverley* and *The Bride of Lammermoor*, Dante's *The Divine Comedy* in Danish (in May, borrowed again in October), two volumes of Goldoni's comedies, and Garibaldi's autobiography; 1866, Aristophanes' *The Birds*, a book about Euripides by Christian Wilster, novels by George Sand, Dickens, Dumas and Maria Edgeworth, and *Faust* again; 1867, more Goethe, Eckermann's *Conversations with Goethe*, two volumes of Shakespeare, *Don Quixote* and *David Copperfield*. At various times he also borrowed several volumes of Ludvig Holberg's plays.[2]

Ibsen's name appears frequently in the Club's suggestion book, demanding that the lamps be cleaned, that a packet of glue be removed from the pedestal of a bust of a dancer, that 'the dancer's big left toe be restored', that a map of the papal state be procured and hung, and that the newspaper *Osservatore Romano* be provided. On 6 December he was elected a member of the newspaper committee; on 20 January 1865 he proposed 'That Germans be not permitted entry into the Club', a motion which was rejected at an extraordinary general meeting on 6 February with only two votes in its favour; and on 13 February he was put in charge of the library accounts (why he was not, as he had hoped, appointed librarian is not clear). He was invited to serve on the

2. Ibsen seems to have visited Italian theatres at least occasionally during this stay, for in 1877 he remarked to Didrik Grønvold that Italian actresses swooned realistically 'whereas in his time in Norway actresses always swooned according to fixed rules, always on the left of the stage and always with a handkerchief in their left hand'.

general committee, but refused, explaining: 'I must belong to the opposition.'[3] He was not the most clubbable of members. One of his fellows recalled how, in his 'single suit of shabby leek-green cloth, he used to stalk sullenly up and down ... not speaking a word to anyone until supper-time, when he would empty a flask of thin red wine and slowly brighten up, not into geniality exactly, but into loquacity, and dart the scathing bolts of his sarcasm ruthlessly in all directions'. One day, finding in an illustrated magazine a portrait of Count Manderström, the Swedish foreign minister and an advocate of non-intervention, he drew a halter round the count's neck; when, at the next meeting of the Club, the offender was challenged to reveal himself, Ibsen silently rose from his chair.

He often dined with his fellow-Scandinavians at an *osteria*, the Cucina Tedesca, or 'Deutsche Küche', a very humble place at the junction of the Via Felice and the Via del Tritone, which in addition to the usual Italian dishes served sauerkraut and pancakes; Lepre, on the corner of the Via Condotti and the Via Mario dei Fiori, where the wine waiter, Marco, had been a famous bandit; Mangani, outside the Porta Pia; and, especially, Il Genio in the Due Macelli. The wine waiter here, Evangelista, had been one of Garibaldi's thousand, and they had a table permanently reserved for them in the far left-hand corner. A meal with half a *foglietta* of wine at any of these places cost 1½ paolo (threepence); or you could buy your own food from shops and stalls, washing your vegetables in the nearest fountain, and the *osteria* would provide salt, pepper and oil and, most importantly, wine, and cook what needed to be cooked. A Danish acquaintance of Ibsen who came to Rome the following year describes one such shopping expedition in detail.

3. Though when the committee decided to revise the rules, Ibsen 'moved, with statesmanlike dexterity, behind the chairs, dropping a word here and there which seemed to have its effect'. (Frederik G. Knudtzon, *Ungdomsdage* [Copenhagen, 1927], p. 165.)

You saw a *pizzicarolo* and went in and bought a sardine –
soldo[4] – or, better still, tunnyfish (3 or 4 soldi) – and cheese
(1 or 2 soldi). Then the butcher, who for 5 soldi would sell you a
veal chop, and the greengrocer, where you could get a lettuce
head for 1 soldo. At the entrance to the *osteria* sat a man crying
'*Uova dure! Uova toste! Un soldo l'uno!*', so you bought an egg
Another man would be sitting in the doorway working a ma
chine, specially designed for the purpose, which, disagreeable a
it sounds, treated artichokes with lard so that they absorbed i
completely. He cried '*Carciofi romani!*', and sold you one for a
soldo. Then you entered the front room of the *osteria*. Behind a
counter stood a handsome, blonde, Junoesque creature. You gave
her your salad to prepare and your chop to fry. To the right a
door led into a larger room, where a long table was reserved
for the Scandinavians. You ordered *mezza foglietta, bianco* ..
With the wine arrived two glazed clay plates, one bearing
the fried chop, the other the salad; also a tin fork, its thin
teeth splayed in all directions, a knife, and a napkin of un
bleached linen. One now had a splendid dinner: *entrée*, sardine
or tunnyfish; *pièce de resistance*, chop with salad, including
egg; vegetable, artichoke; and, finally, cheese – stracchino, gor
gonzola, or parmigiano. The preparation of the salad cost
soldo, the frying of the chop the same, and the wine 6–7 soldi.

They usually dined between seven and eight, and took thei
coffee at the century-old Café Greco in the Via Condotti, a
Oehlenschläger, Thorvaldsen and Hans Andersen had
done, smoking long pipes or bad papal cigars.

As always, Ibsen took many long walks, alone or in the
company of Suzannah and Sigurd, the latter often carried
upon Walter Runeberg's shoulders, 'walks', recalled Diet
richson, 'that usually ended in some rustic *osteria* on the
Ponte Molle or in the Moletta at the foot of the Palatine
Hill'. Among the other writers and artists whose acquaint
ance he now made was the young Swedish poet Car
Snoilsky, who had arrived in Rome that September and with
whom Ibsen was later to enjoy a close friendship. Aged
twenty-three, and in appearance not unlike Robert Loui

4. A soldo was worth about one fifth of a penny.

Stevenson, Snoilsky had already won himself a reputation as one of the most gifted poets in Scandinavia, and as a romantic and successful lover.

Snoilsky and Walter Runeberg were both ten or so years younger than Ibsen who, living up to his Learned Holland nickname of Gert Westphaler, the Talkative Barber, would sit at the centre of the table as they dined, wearing his broad-brimmed hat and leading the discussions in Socratic vein, pressing the arguments of the others to their often uncomfortable conclusions, challenging and bantering. Once when someone, galled by this insistent cross-examination, declared that the truth was as clear as that two and two make four, Ibsen asked whether one could in fact be sure that two and two would make four on, say, Jupiter? One question to which he obsessively returned was how far an artist ought to reject the demands of society and live according to his own creed and morality; he enjoyed citing the example of the English poet Thomas Chatterton, who had starved to death, swallowing (according to legend) even his doorkey, rather than take an ordinary breadwinning job. Ibsen declared that Chatterton had been right, and that he himself would choose the same course; it is ironical to reflect that, unknown to him, his friends in Christiania were at this time trying unsuccessfully to get him an assistant librarianship and, of all things, a post in the customs, the latter of which professions a writer of Ibsen's own temperament and stature on the other side of the world, Herman Melville, was shortly to embrace (and to remain in for nineteen years). Snoilsky remembered Ibsen at these dinners, 'the lightning flashing from beneath the enormous hat'.

The topic which obsessed Ibsen most, however, was still the old question of the Dano-Prussian war, and the failure of Norway and Sweden to help their neighbour. Again and again in his letters and recorded utterances he returns to the subject. 'The significant and decisive thing for me', he wrote to Magdalene Thoresen (3 December 1865), has been that I have got far enough away from our country to see the hollowness behind all the self-created lies in our so-called public life ... How often do we not hear people in Norway speak with intense complacency of our Norwegian 'good sense', which really means nothing but a tepidity of spirit which makes it impossible for those honest souls to commit a madness [the phrase is the one he had used in praise of Michelangelo and Bernini] ... Down here, I assure you, it is different!

In a Norwegian paper he had read of a boy who had cut off a finger to avoid military service.

I know mothers in Piedmont, in Genoa, Novara, Alessandria, who took their fourteen-year-old sons from school that they might join Garibaldi's adventure in Palermo; it was not so much a question of liberating their country as of realizing an idea. How many of our politicians do you suppose will do likewise when the Russians invade Finnmark? ... I was in Berlin at the time of the triumphal entry, I saw the people spit on the cannon from Dybbøl, and it was to me a sign that history will spit in the eyes of Sweden and Norway for their part in that affair. Here in Rome I find every kind of spiritual squalidity among the Scandinavians. What do you think of the fact that during the war Danish men and women sat on Sundays among the Germans in the chapel of the Prussian embassy and listened piously while the Prussian priest prayed from his pulpit for victory for the Prussian armies in their just war against the enemy? But I have raged and scourged, believe me; for down here, I fear nothing; at home I was afraid when I stood in that clammy crowd and sensed their ugly smiles behind me ... I had to get away from all that swinishness up there to become cleansed. Up there I could never achieve any coherent inner life; so that I was one thing in my work and another outside it; and so that my work, too, never achieved any real entity.

Yet as Ibsen mocked his fellow-Scandinavians for their cowardice under the Italian sky, there was one man who did not quail before his onslaughts, and whose presence must have nagged Ibsen like a Banquo – the young theological student Christopher Bruun, newly returned to Rome that autumn from the Danish war, having made the journey through Europe on foot. At a meeting of the Christiania Students' Union three days before Ibsen left Norway, which Ibsen did not attend, being otherwise occupied with his Learned Holland friends, Bruun had exhorted his fellow-countrymen to volunteer with him and thereby 'testify by action that idealism, truth, and justice are not mere subjects for speeches on festive occasions, but things for which a man should be prepared to live, fight and, if necessary, die'. He had been much disillusioned with the Danish army, finding little idealism or patriotism, but mainly a desire to return safely home; on one occasion he had been warned not to shoot lest he 'irritate the enemy'. He had signed off from the war, and had arrived in Rome a deeply disappointed man, very different from the idealist who had set forth from Christiania. One day when Ibsen brought the Danish war up for discussion Bruun asked him why, if he felt so strongly, he had not volunteered. 'We poets have other tasks to perform,' Ibsen replied, but a doubt remained in his mind. He wondered whether he had been right to compromise, and with this doubt was linked another. Was he right to believe so inflexibly in his calling and thus, in all probability, condemn his wife and child to continued poverty?

So this breakaway year of 1864 ended in a mood of, if possible, more than usual doubt. The new year was ushered in by a buoyant letter from Bjørnson who, notwithstanding his earlier protestations, had finally accepted the directorship of the Christiania Theatre and had forgiven Ibsen the latter's apparent failure to acknowledge his previous letter and draft. 'How often I long for you, Ibsen!' he declared (19 January). 'I always do when I am parted from you, even when you were in Bergen and I was here – but when we meet, things go wrong. Why? ... Stay down there as long as you can, and go to Naples and Sorrento as soon as you can manage after Easter.' He added a suggestion which was to have far-reaching and beneficial consequences for Ibsen. 'Let me put you under Hegel's wing! He'll gladly send you an advance, which I shall guarantee on your behalf.'

Frederik Hegel, the first great Scandinavian publisher, had been born the illegitimate son of a servant-girl and her employer's son, Frederik V. Mansa, later to become a well-known doctor and medical historian. One of Mansa's patients was a certain Jacob Deichmann, the head of a small Copenhagen publishing house named Gyldendal, and at Mansa's suggestion Deichmann took Hegel into his employ when the latter was fifteen. In 1850, at the age of thirty-three, Hegel became head of the firm, and within fifteen years had transformed it from its modest beginnings into the distinguished house which it has since remained. Bjørnson had lately become one of his authors, and had found him a wise and generous counsellor; an opinion which Ibsen, after an unfortunate preliminary misunderstanding, was permanently to share. His association with Hegel, on whose advice he came to rely not merely in literary but also in financial matters, was to give him that feeling of trust in his publisher which can be, as it was with Ibsen, such a stabilizing influence on an author's career.

This last letter of Bjørnson crossed with one which Ibsen wrote to him on 28 January confirming Bjørnson's prediction that his senses would gradually become attuned to classical art and sculpture. Its beauty, Ibsen confessed,

grows more and more on me, as you said it would. It comes in flashes, but a single flash throws light over whole vistas. Do you remember the 'Tragic Muse' which stands outside the hall in the Rotunda in the Vatican? No sculpture here has yet been such a revelation to me. I may even say that it is through this that I have understood what Greek tragedy was. The indescribably calm, noble and exalted joy in the expression of the face, the richly laurelled head containing within it something supernaturally luxuriant and bacchantic, the eyes that look both inwards and at the same time through and far beyond the object of their gaze – such was Greek tragedy. The statue of Demosthenes in the Lateran, the Faun in the Villa Borghese, and the Faun (of Praxiteles) in the Vatican (*bracchio nuovo*), have also opened great windows for me into Greek life and the Greek character, and have enabled me to understand what imperishability in beauty really is. Pray heaven I may be able to use this understanding for my own work. Michelangelo's Moses in S. Pietro in Vincoli I had not seen when I last wrote to you; but I had read about it and built up an expectation which has not quite been fulfilled – however, I have only seen it once.

How glorious the landscape is down here; in both forms and colours there is an indescribable harmony. I often spend half the day lying out among the graves on the Via Latina or the old Via Appia, and think it an idleness but no waste of time. Caracalla's Baths are another place which holds some especial attraction for me . . .

That spring of 1865 Ibsen struggled with three projects: *Brand* (as an epic poem), *Emperor and Galilean* (as a prose drama), and another epic poem set against the background of a Seventeenth of May celebration in Norway. He read Dietrichson a song from the last of these which, however, he abandoned and rewrote four years later as a prose play, *The League of Youth*. The two other projects, likewise, made painful progress. The relaxing atmosphere of Rome, 'its ideal peace, the carefree companionship of the artistic world, an existence comparable only to that of Shakespeare's *As You Like It*', as he was later to describe it, was totally different to the conditions which had stimulated his writing in Norway, and it took time for him to assimilate it. *Emperor and Galilean* he was already finding too big a theme to fit into the span of a normal play. 'Why can't one write a drama in ten acts?' he asked Dietrichson one day. 'I can't find room in five.' *Emperor and Galilean* was in fact to occupy ten acts and to take him eight more years to complete; the malaise of contemporary Europe, and of Norway in particular, obsessed him too much for him to concentrate on the problems of Julian the Apostate. The subject uppermost in his mind, as with those two other exiles half a century later, James Joyce and D. H. Lawrence, was the complacency and narrowness of his fellow-countrymen, with their failure to support the Danes as the indelible symbol.

Yet his own failure to have acted may have been responsible for the writer's block which he now experienced.

On Good Friday, 14 April, John Wilkes Booth fired a pistol into a box at Ford's Theatre in Washington, and the event roused Ibsen to compose a striking poem, one indeed of his finest, 'The Murder of Abraham Lincoln'. Characteristically, he directed his indignation not, like the rest of the world, at Booth, but at what he regarded as the hypocrisy of human reaction. Why such anger now? he asks. Was this worse than the Prussian action at Dybbøl, the Russian rape of Poland, England's bombardment of Copenhagen in 1801 and 1807? These broken promises and betrayals have 'manured the soil of history'; could anyone expect a sweeter harvest? But, the poem ends, I shall not cry woe over every poisoned blossom that opens on time's tree. Let the worm gnaw; there can be no rebirth till the skull is clean. Let the mockery of our system be exposed. Nemesis will the sooner sit in judgement on our hypocrisy.

In late June Ibsen left Rome for the countryside, this time to Ariccia, fifteen miles to the south-east in the Alban mountains. Ariccia was, and still is, an idyllic little town, containing several fine works by Bernini, including the main piazza, its two fountains and the magnificent Chigi Palace. The Ibsens lived, as Suzannah later described it to her daughter-in-law, 'not just humbly, but like paupers ... Sigurd can tell you how he used to go each afternoon and buy three soldi-worth of bread and three soldi-worth of Caceotto cheese; this, with half a carafe of red wine, was our dinner.' The work continued to go painfully, and Ibsen needed all the encouragement that Bjørnson could give him:

Copenhagen, 25 July 1865

Why the devil don't you write? You don't need to frank them ... From Trondhjem a provisional 'No', i.e. you applied too late as always, they had made their allocations, but I've spoken to one of them, written again, and something'll happen soon, so don't lose heart if it comes a bit late ...

Your prospects now are:

> What you can earn yourself
> What I can raise (*very* little)
> 300 from Trondhjem Society (am of course asking 500)
> 400 from Storthing
> A performance at the theatre (if Dunker agrees)
> Whatever you get when you come home from the theatre or the university library (I'm trying to get you something there whether you like it or not) ...

But the problem is, you need money *now* ... Can't you start sending the MS for printing? Then you can ask a bigger advance. If you can't do that yet I'll have to resort to murder ... Don't lose heart, don't lose faith in your friends, or in your admirers – but, my dear Ibsen, why all these gloomy words? Hasn't everything gone splendidly for you (a few misfortunes apart, which were your own fault partly) since you came to Christiania [!] – you are now regarded as one of the leading poets in Scandinavia, respected, your work eagerly anticipated, you are in Italy, you are liked down there (I hear that from Bloch), you have a handsome and assured future (assured both by the State and by your own dramatic talent), you have young people around you, and you have me!

Your most affectionate
Bjørnstjerne

P.S. Stay in Rome and Italy till everything is settled here, the Storthing, Trondhjem, maybe the library or the theatre too, if you'd prefer that. If you'd like to *run* the theatre, that too; I'll soon have had enough. But my advice is: don't, or at most for a limited period like me ... I'll tell them it's a question of money or life – 'A poet is dying!' Though you won't b— die, you're tough, brave, lazy – such people never die.

But by the time this letter reached Ibsen, the longed-for breakthrough had come. Ibsen described it in his reply to Bjørnson:

Ariccia, 12 September 1865

My dear Bjørnson!

Your letter and the draft from Hegel came at a good time. Thank you, my dear, blessed friend, for both! But affectionate and kind as your letter was – indeed, all the more therefore – I have read it with self-reproach because of the worry and anxiety you have endured on my account. Thank you for this too! It all adds up to one thing, by far the most important thing for me and for my calling in life – the fact that I have met and really found you – this I can never repay except by a devotion which neither my friends nor your enemies will ever be able to alter. I know you will understand that it is not Bjørnson the fund-raiser whom I have in mind. Well, more of this when we meet; now I can speak openly to you, I could never do so before. Everything is going well for me now, and has really been so the whole time, except for isolated periods when I didn't know which way to turn, not only as regards money, but because my work would not progress. Then one day I went into St Peter's – I had gone into Rome on some business – and suddenly everything I wanted to say appeared to me in a strong and clear light. Now I have thrown overboard the work with which I had been torturing myself for a year without getting anywhere, and in the middle of July I started working on something new which has been making such progress as no other work of mine has ever done. New, I mean, in the sense that I only then began to write it, but the matter and mood have been weighing on me like a nightmare ever since those many distasteful happenings at home which forced me to look into myself and our life there and think seriously about things which have previously passed me by and about which I didn't seriously bother. It is a dramatic poem, of serious content; contemporary theme; five acts in rhymed verse (but no *Love's Comedy*). The fourth act is almost finished, and I feel I shall be able to complete the fifth in a week. I work both morning and afternoon, which I have never been able to do before. It is blessedly peaceful out here; no one I know; I read nothing but the Bible – it is powerful and strong!

If I were to name the most important result of my coming here, I should say that it was that I have rid myself of that aesthetic attitude, that forcing of oneself into isolation and self-sufficiency, that formerly held sway over me. Aestheticism in this sense now seems to me as great a curse to writing as theology is to religion. You have never been troubled by aestheticism in this sense, you have never looked at things through the hollow of your hand. Is it not an indescribable joy to be able to write? But it carries with it a great responsibility, and I now have sufficient earnestness to realize this and be stern with myself. A Copenhagen aesthete once said when I was there: 'Whatever else one may feel about him, Christ was the most interesting phenomenon in the history of the world.' The aesthete relished him as the gourmet relishes the sight of an oyster. I have always had the strength not to become that kind of cartilaginous animal, but God knows what all those spiritual asses might not have made of me if they had had me to themselves, and what prevented them from having me, my dear Bjørnson, was you . . .

You say the Storthing will approve my grant. Do you think so? I have a suspicion that my new work will not dispose the members more charitably towards me, but may God punish me if, for that reason, I cut a single line, whatever those pygmy souls may feel. Let me rather be a beggar all my life. If I cannot be myself in what I write, then my work would be nothing but lies and humbug, and our country has had enough of that without handing out grants for more . . .

I don't think the theatre could stage my play – if I were on the board I would have to vote against it. But if you can use it, that's another matter; it's dramatic all right; but whether it is performable on other grounds you must judge for yourself . . .

> Our warmest regards to you and yours,
> Your affectionate
> Henr. Ibsen

The new version of *Brand* was in the form of a poetic drama and, as the above letter indicates, Ibsen wrote it at an extraordinary speed. We do not know the exact date of his visit to St Peter's, but even if it took place within a week of his leaving Rome it means that he composed nearly three and a half thousand lines of rhymed octosyllabics in, at the most, ten weeks, a rate of fifty lines a day, and it is a measure of his new-found confidence that he was expecting to complete the fifth act in a week. In the end it took him longer, for it extended to seventeen hundred lines, or one-third of the play, but he wrote it at the same rate, finishing it in a little over a month.

Dietrichson has described Ibsen's working routine at Ariccia. 'He liked to rise at 4 a.m. and take a stroll in the woods or the great Chigi park before the day grew hot. As the sun rose higher in the heavens he sat down at his desk, where he would work more or less uninterruptedly until the day ended; and in the evening he liked to sit and enjoy the cool on the big flight of steps in front of the church.' 'I was,' Ibsen wrote to Bjørnson the following March, 'despite my poverty and tribulation, so indescribably happy, I felt such a crusading joy within me, that I do not know the thing I would have lacked the courage to tilt at.' On another occasion he used a less Bunyanesque image to describe his mood of that summer. 'At the time I was writing *Brand* I had on my table a scorpion in an empty beer glass. From time to time the brute would ail; then I would throw a piece of ripe fruit in to it, on which it would cast itself in a rage and eject its poison into it; then it was well again.' Ibsen's euphoria and venom both found vent; the play is at the same time an exultation and an indictment.

Brand marks an extraordinary leap forward in Ibsen's development as a dramatist, and the chief reason is clear. He was not writing for performance, and was thus able to work uninhibited by the limitations of practical staging (and we have seen how severe these were in the middle of the nineteenth century). He wrote it, as Alfred de Musset and Turgenev had written their plays (even *A Month in the Country*), and as Thomas Hardy was to write *The Dynasts*, to be read, and so was able to include, *inter alia*, a storm at sea and an avalanche. But there are other reasons for the immensity of *Brand* compared with any of his previous works. The distance and relaxation he had found in Italy offered ideal circumstances for the expression of that *saeva indignatio* from which his poetry welled; and his first sight of Italian Renaissance art and, more particularly, sculpture and architecture, especially that of Michelangelo, had given him a new standard at which to aim. His former masters, one must remember, had been Oehlenschläger, Holberg, Heiberg, the sagas and ballads, and Shakespeare glimpsed through the mist of dull translation; now he had Michelangelo. It is significant that his revelation of how the play should shape itself had come to him in St Peter's, under Michelangelo's dome. *Brand* is a mighty cathedral of a play, and Brand's God, 'young and strong like Hercules', is an exact description of Christ as painted by Michelangelo in the Sistine Chapel. The same taste that disparaged Michelangelo and Milan Cathedral and admired Raphael dominated Scandinavian taste in drama; it was the dogma of aestheticism which Heiberg had laid down and which no critic had yet authoritatively challenged, though Georg Brandes was shortly to do so. No wonder Ibsen had told Bjørnson that he regarded ridding himself of his aestheticism as the most important result of his coming to Italy. Michelangelo, Bernini and the unknown architect of Milan Cathedral had what Ibsen recognized as 'the courage to commit a madness now and then', and *Brand* is the direct result of their influence. Its power is not static but dynamic; each scene, superb in itself, moves irresistibly on to the next, culminating in what is arguably the greatest final act that any dramatist had written since *King Lear*.

The story of the play is that of the epic Ibsen had left unfinished, lopped of its introductory section about the boys on the hillside, and carried to its terrifying logical conclusion. Brand, the young priest, walking in the mountains, meets (as in the poem) his old schoolfriend Ejnar with the latter's fiancée, Agnes. He denounces their materialistic hedonism in words that uninhibitedly reflected Ibsen's opinion of his countrymen.

> You separate
> Faith from doctrine. You do not want
> To live your faith. For that you need a God
> Who'll keep one eye shut. That God is getting feeble

> Like the generation that worships him.
> Mine is a storm where yours is a gentle wind,
> Inflexible where yours is deaf, all-loving
> Not all-doting. And he is young
> And strong like Hercules. His is the voice
> That spoke in thunder when He stood
> Bright before Moses in the burning bush,
> A giant before the dwarf of dwarfs. In the valley
> Of Gideon He stayed the sun, and worked
> Miracles without number – and would work
> Them still, if people were not dead, like you . . .

EJNAR　(*waves him away*).　Turn the world upside down.
　　　　I still have faith in my God.
BRAND　　　　　　　　　　　　　　　Good. But paint him
　　　　With crutches. I go to lay him in his grave.

Brand goes on his way and meets the mad girl Gerd, who is
pursued in her imagination by a hawk that is for ever diving
and clawing at her. She tries to lead him to her Ice Church
among the peaks:

> 　　　　　　　　　　　Come with me!
> Up there, cataract and avalanche sing Mass.
> The wind preaches along the wall of the glacier
> And the hawk can't get in. He swoops down
> On to the Black Peak and sits there
> On my church steeple like an ugly weathercock.

He descends instead to the village where he was born,
which is gripped by famine, and tells the people that their
plight is God's judgement on their lack of faith. Agnes, inspired by his words, and by his courage in sailing across the
storm-tossed fjord to shrive a dying man, leaves Ejnar and
joins him. Brand warns her what life with him will mean:

> Young woman, think carefully before you decide.
> Locked between mountains, shadowed by crag and
> 　　peak,

	Shut in the twilight of this ravine
	My life will flow like a sad October evening.
AGNES	The darkness no longer frightens me. A star
	Pierces through the night.
BRAND	Remember, I am stern
	In my demands. I require All or Nothing,
	No half-measures. There is no forgiveness
	For failure. It may not be enough
	To offer your life. Your death may be required also.
EJNAR	Stop this mad game, leave this man of dark law.
	Live the life you know you can.
BRAND	Choose. You stand at the parting of the ways.

She marries Brand, and he remains in the village as priest.
They have a child who, the doctor warns them, will die if
they stay in this cold place which 'the sun never warms'.
Brand sees this as a temptation to abandon his calling; he
stays and the child dies; as a result, Agnes dies too. Then
Brand sees his whole life as a failure and leads the villagers
up into the mountains to find God (as Lammers the revivalist
had done with the people of Skien). There they lose heart,
revile and, finally, stone him. Abandoned, he is joined by the
mad girl Gerd who, seeing the blood on him, thinks he is the
Saviour and kneels down and worships him.

GERD	Priest, you're limping. Your foot's hurt.
	How did it happen?
BRAND	The people hunted me.
GERD	(*goes closer*). Your forehead is red.
BRAND	The people stoned me.
GERD	Your voice used to be clear as song.
	Now it creaks like leaves in autumn.
BRAND	Everything – everyone –
GERD	What?
BRAND	Betrayed me.
GERD	(*stares at him*). Ah! Now I know who you are!
	I thought you were the priest.
	Fie upon him and all the others!
	You're the Big Man. The Biggest of all.
BRAND	I used to think I was.

GERD   Let me see your hands.

BRAND   My hands?

GERD   They're scarred with nails. There's blood in your hair.
They thorn's teeth have cut your forehead.
You've been on the cross. My father told me
It happened long ago and far away.
But now I see he was deceiving me.
I know you. You're the Saviour Man!

BRAND   Get away from me!

GERD   Shall I fall down at your feet and pray?

BRAND   Go!

GERD   You gave the blood that will save us all.
There are nail holes in your hands. You are the Chosen
One.
You are the Greatest of all.

BRAND   I am the meanest thing that crawls on earth.

As the sun rises, Brand sees that they are standing in the
Ice Church, symbol of the cold and grandiose emptiness of
his life. Gerd fires her rifle at the imaginary hawk which she
still thinks pursues her, and this brings down the Ice Church
in an avalanche, killing them both. As it engulfs them,
Brand cries in despair:

> Answer me, God, in the moment of death!
> If not by will, how shall Man be redeemed?

And a voice replies through the thunder:

> He is the God of love.

The character of Brand himself, while probably owing
something to hearsay memories of Lammers at Skien, was,
by Ibsen's own admission, largely based on Christopher
Bruun, whose deep religious feeling, distrust of the established Church and contempt for compromise had made so
profound an impression on Ibsen during the past months in
Rome. Ibsen, however, confessed that he had put a good deal
of himself into the part. 'Brand', he once remarked, 'is
myself in my best moments.' He later told Georg Brandes

that he could as easily have made Brand a sculptor or a politician, or even Galileo – 'except that then of course he would have had to have held strongly to his beliefs, and not pretended that the earth stood still'. It is also worth noting that in the spring of 1865, when he was wrestling with *Brand*, Ibsen had found 'joy and strength' in reading Bjørnson's play *Mary Stuart in Scotland*, one of the central characters of which is the Calvinist preacher John Knox, a figure with whom Brand has much in common. Another historical figure who probably contributed to the portrait of Brand was Garibaldi, who, when he led the last forlorn hope out of Rome in 1849 to continue his resistance in the Italian mountains, had said to his followers 'I offer neither pay, nor quarters, nor provisions. I offer hunger, thirst, forced marches, battle and death' – words markedly similar to those used by Brand to his parishioners on the mountain in Act Five – and we know that Ibsen borrowed Garibaldi's autobiography from the Scandinavian Club library during the year he wrote *Brand*.

He wrote the play in rhymed four-beat verse, using both iambics and trochees, iambics mainly for colloquial or argumentative dialogue, trochees for scenes of passion, poetry, or vision. 'I wanted a metre', he told William Archer, 'in which I could career where I would as on horseback', and he achieved a marvellous flexibility, moving without incongruity between colloquialism and high poetry. Archer perceptively observed of *Brand* that it contained 'the prophetic fire of Carlyle fused with the genial verve and intellectual athleticism of Browning, and expressed by aid of a dramatic facility to parallel which we must go two centuries backwards'.

A great deal has been written about the symbolism of *Brand*, and the different significances that might be attached to the hawk, the Ice Church, and so on. Dr Arne Duve, in his stimulating book *Symbolikken i Henrik Ibsens skuespill*, suggests that the hawk represents the life of the emotions, or love, and that it is Brand's fear of the powers of life and light that make him, in Act Five, dismiss the hawk contemptuously as 'the spirit of compromise'. The Ice Church, thinks Dr Duve, represents the opposite of the hawk, the negation of love. Gerd, like Brand, fears and distrusts love (like him, she is the child of a loveless marriage), and Brand's negation of love finally leads him, too, to the terrible citadel of the Ice Church; what Ibsen, thirty years later in *John Gabriel Borkman*, was to term 'the coldness of the heart'. The Ice Church finally killed Brand, just as the coldness of the heart killed John Gabriel Borkman.

Michael Elliott, who directed the justly-celebrated production of *Brand* in 1959 in London, has expressed the view that the hawk represents nothing as specific as love but rather, in a general way, 'whatever one rejects', just as Room 101 in George Orwell's *1984* contained 'the worst thing in the world', whatever that might be for each individual. I agree with this theory, and believe that the Ice Church stands for the false citadel that each of us builds in his own imagination as a refuge from his particular hawk.

Brand was published in Copenhagen on 15 March 1866, and created an immediate and widespread sensation throughout Scandinavia. As he was so often to do in the future, Ibsen had touched his contemporaries on their most sensitive spot; the movement towards liberalism and individualism was just approaching its climax, and the call to follow one's private conscience, avoid compromise and 'be oneself', answered a general and unspoken need. *Brand* established Ibsen in Scandinavia as the pioneer of revolt against dead thought and tradition. It had the same explosive effect in Norway, Sweden and Denmark which, eleven years later, *The Pillars of Society* was to have on German audiences and, later still, *A Doll's House* on thinking people throughout the western world.

To modern readers *Brand* is a mighty, Lear-like poetic tragedy of a lonely, misguided and tormented spirit. To the

Scandinavia of 1866 it was before all else a gauntlet thrown down to authority, an attack on complacency and conventionality, whether in the field of religion, of patriotism, or of human relationships. Orthodox Christianity, as preached by the established church, was of course a prime target (in this respect, the play did for Scandinavians what the new scientific teaching and Bible criticism were doing in England), but unthinking humanism, as represented by Ejnar and to some extent by the Mayor, also came under fire. Truth, the play stressed, was something which every man must find out for himself, and every woman too. And the character of Brand himself – narrow, intolerant, harsh to his wife and child as to his flock and himself – was a new kind of hero, new at any rate since *Coriolanus*, and as unfamiliar and refreshing to readers in the eighteen-sixties as another kind of anti-hero was to be to European theatre audiences ninety years later.

Illustreret Nyhedsblad of 29 April 1866 quoted *Morgenbladet*'s Copenhagen correspondent on the book's reception in Denmark: 'Of the new literary works that have lately appeared, *Brand* takes a pre-eminence which few poetic works have previously been able to claim. It is read with the greatest interest, its praise is in all men's mouths, and its powerful words in all men's thoughts.' Paul Botten Hansen added an editorial comment: 'That this picture is not exaggerated is confirmed by private information from Denmark. Wherever people meet, the talk is only of *Brand* ... The interest in *Brand* has also led men of letters to read Ibsen's earlier works, such as *Love's Comedy*, and they have marvelled greatly that such a book managed to create so little effect up here as to pass virtually unnoticed.' In Sweden it was the same. The poet Gustaf af Geijerstam recalled: 'It would be vain for me to attempt to describe the passion with which we young men read and discussed the great poet.' The reading of Ibsen, he explains, became a bond of unity between friends and lovers. 'No more sacred gift could be offered to anyone than *Brand*.' August Strindberg, who was seventeen when *Brand* appeared and twenty when he read it belatedly in 1869 (and wrote a play that year, *The Free-thinker*, which bears evident signs of its influence), described it as 'the voice of a Savonarola'.

Brand was, in short, discussed and debated as no previous book had ever been in Scandinavia – including Kierkegaard, for *Brand* was written in more accessible and less abstract language. Sermons were preached about it; more importantly for Ibsen, it sold. Within two months Hegel ordered a reprint of five hundred copies; a third edition followed in August, and a fourth in December. Yet nobody dared to stage it. Act Four was performed at the Christiania Theatre on 26 June 1867 (after an amateur performance at the Students' Union), and was successful enough to take its place in the general repertory; but it was to be nineteen years before the play was presented in its entirety. But Ibsen, who had not written it for the theatre, cannot have been surprised or disappointed at this.

Together with the critical and popular success of the book came relief from financial worry. Bjørnson, though personally hostile to *Brand*, had not relaxed his efforts to raise money for Ibsen; indeed, he decided with his usual naïvety that a sense of security was the most likely thing to give Ibsen 'that clear and moving view of life which alone makes a man a poet'. He asked Riddervold, the minister in charge of the Ecclesiastical Department (which administered grants to authors), to give Ibsen the same civil list pension which he himself had received; but Riddervold, perhaps remembering *Love's Comedy*, refused. Undeterred, Bjørnson approached friends in the Storthing, and together they collected twenty-eight signatures to a motion demanding that a pension be allotted 'which, by assuring Ibsen of future means, will surely honour and reward us as much as it will him'.

The sponsors of this motion were not sanguine as to its chances, but by good fortune Riddervold fell ill and his place in charge of the ecclesiastical department was taken by another parliamentarian, Frederik Stang, who let it be known that he would treat any application relating to Ibsen sympathetically. On 19 April Ibsen's friend Michael Birkeland, by now state archivist, sent Stang a formal plea on Ibsen's behalf signed by three others of the Learned Holland Circle, O. A. Bachke, Jakob Løkke and Paul Botten Hansen. This was approved within two days and forwarded to the king in Stockholm for ratification. Birkeland had already telegraphed Ibsen advising him to write personally to the king, and on 15 April, four days before Birkeland formally handed his appeal to Stang, Ibsen posted his petition to Carl XV. 'I am', he wrote, 'not fighting for a sinecure existence, but for the calling which I inflexibly believe and know that God has given me – the calling which I believe to be the most important for a Norwegian, namely, to wake the people and make them think big ... It rests in Your Majesty's royal hands whether I must remain silent and bow to the bitterest deprivation that can wound a man's soul – the deprivation of having to abandon one's calling in life, of having to yield when I know I have been granted the spiritual armoury to fight, and this would be tenfold grievous to me; for to this day I have never yielded.'

His request was modest: an annual pension of 400 specie-dollars (£100). On 12 May this proposal was put before the Storthing and was approved with only four dissenting votes. A few days earlier the Trondhjem Society for Knowledge had allotted him a single grant of 100 specie-dollars, and on 28 July the government gave him a new travel stipend of 350 specie-dollars – a total of 850 specie-dollars. The first edition of *Brand* had brought him 200 specie-dollars, so that he, who for the past year had lived on loans, now found himself with 1,050 specie-dollars (over £260) to his credit, a sum so far in excess of his modest requirements that on 21 May he wrote to Hegel that he did not need to avail himself of the latter's offer of an advance on the second edition.

A letter which Ibsen addressed to Michael Birkeland on 4 May thanking him for organizing the petition expresses the euphoria he now felt.

I had not expected that my book would be so favourably received. I have been sent many expressions of admiration and good will from Denmark ... also various invitations, etc., which make me happy, since I am thinking of making Copenhagen my future home ... I have such a lust for work, such strength, that I could strangle bears. I went round wrestling with that play of mine for a year before it took shape, but once I had it I wrote from morning till evening and finished it in under three months. About Rome it's impossible to write, especially when one knows it inside out as I do. I have wandered through most of the Papal States at various times, on foot with a knapsack on my back. The brigand situation isn't as dangerous as people at home imagine ... Inwardly I think I am in certain respects much changed; yet I feel I am more myself than ever before. Outwardly I've grown thin, which I shall prove with a photograph.

This new security and euphoria found visible expression. During the months of nervous waiting for the publication of *Brand* he had, as in those months of despair in Christiania, neglected his dress and appearance, and walked around with untrimmed beard, shoes worn to their uppers and holes in his leek-green coat. When the Norwegian colony in Rome held a vote for the worst-dressed member among them, they unanimously elected Ibsen. The first thing he did when he learned of the money that was coming to him was to reform his dress to the smartness for which he had been noted in Bergen. One day in May of 1866 he set out with friends on a walking tour in the mountains around Rome, but at the first *osteria* at which they halted a mood came over him, he decided to go no farther, and they proceeded without him, leaving him unkempt, shaggy and silent over a *foglietta* of wine. When they returned a few days later they found him elegantly clothed, shod and barbered – as a photograph taken that year, probably identical to the one promised to Birkeland, bears witness. Another piece of evidence exists in

the form of a clothes list written in Ibsen's hand on the back
of a letter to him from Consul Bravo:

8 shirts	16 scudi
8 pairs socks	3
1 pair boots	3
2 woollen vests	3
1 frock coat	14
2 waistcoats	4
1 pr. black trousers	6
1 pr. coloured ditto	6
1 overcoat	14
1 hat	3
2 cravats	1
cuff-links	3
watch	10
lorgnette	2
	88 scudi

His son Sigurd later remembered that when the advance
for *Brand* arrived, his parents were so overwhelmed by the
'enormous sum' that they did not know what they would do
with it all. And Kristofer Janson (later to be the partial
model for Hjalmar Ekdal) records that, finding himself
short of money that summer, he asked Ibsen for a loan, and
Ibsen opened a drawer, took out a sock, and gave Janson
some silver from it, explaining that 'this was the fruit of
Brand, and that he was so well off that he had been able to
put some in the bank'.

In such a mood Ibsen felt disinclined to rest on his newly
won laurels. 'I will let you know shortly which work I shall be
embarking on next,' he wrote to Hegel on 21 May. 'I feel
more and more inclined to get down in earnest to *Emperor
Julian*, which I have been thinking about for two years.'
Magnus Heineson, the sixteenth-century freebooter, had
been pushed into the background. But as things turned out
the Emperor Julian was to join him there. A new and
hitherto unmeditated theme began to preoccupy Ibsen's
mind.

10

Peer Gynt
1866–8

EARLY in June 1866 Ibsen left Rome to spend the summer
in Frascati, a few miles to the south-east. 'I live out here
among the mountains, see no newspapers, and know nothing
of what is happening outside,' he wrote to Hegel on 9 June.
'It is miraculously beautiful.' A week later he, who had written so many letters begging for help, received one himself.
Edvard Grieg, not yet twenty-three, had spent five months in
Rome that winter and spring; like Ibsen, he claimed, and
was proud of, Scottish ancestry, which in his case was less
remote, his grandfather having emigrated after the battle of
Culloden in 1746. Ibsen and Grieg had got on well (they had
even considered collaborating on an operatic version of *Olaf
Liljekrans*), and now, on 10 June, Grieg wrote to Ibsen from
Christiania asking him to recommend him for the job of
Kapellmeister at the Christiania Theatre. Would Ibsen drop
a line to the artistic director, Bjørnson, who had not
answered Grieg's application of six weeks previously?

'He may not be able to stand me, I may be being stupid
about the matter, but I hope you will be able to put things
right ... I have read your splendid *Brand*; it's a strange
thing about truth, people can take it in poetry, it doesn't go
too near the knuckle, whereas in plain prose, as Kierkegaard
has said, it's too close, too cheeky. How else explain the
tremendous furore *Brand* has created, the huge numbers
who daily gulp it down?'

Ibsen tried to help, but Grieg never got the job; instead, he
became *Kapellmeister* at the Philharmonien. But he remained grateful for Ibsen's assistance and encouragement

('Don't say your whole future depends on this,' Ibsen wrote to him on 24 August. 'No, my dear Grieg, your future will be bigger and better than a musical directorship.') and a decade later their friendship was to ripen into a successful if mutually uncomprehending partnership.

Ibsen enjoyed Frascati. He wrote to Paul Botten Hansen on 22 July:

We live in an old palace of the nobility, the Palazzo Gratiosi, inexpensively and in splendour. Frascati lies below ancient Tusculum where, as you know, Cicero had his great villa and wrote his Tusculan letters; the ruins of the villa are still standing; his little theatre, probably the same as what he called his *schola*, where he used to give lectures to a chosen circle of guests, remains almost intact. It is indescribably beautiful to sit up here of an evening, two thousand feet above sea level, with a view far out over the Mediterranean, the *campagna*, and Rome; eastwards the whole mountainous Sabine country, with the Apennines, and southwards the Volscian mountains rising on the Neapolitan frontier. From the windows of my study I can see in the furthest distance Mount Soracte towering in solitary splendour across the limitless plain. In short, whichever way one turns it is as if one were surveying the battlefield where the Goddess of History staged her greatest events. Soon, now, I shall write in earnest; I am still wrestling with the material, but soon, I know I shall have the beast under me, and then the rest will glide forwards of its own volition.

He was still undecided whether to stay away from Norway.

When I shall return I can't say; I am already known, and feel at home, here; but I must go back some time. I can live on my pension here, since life is very cheap, and the climate suits us all well.

Whether the 'beast' referred to was *Emperor and Galilean* or the old Magnus Heineson project we do not know, but whichever it was it continued to resist him, and on 22 August he had to tell Hegel that he was doubtful whether it would be ready by the autumn, suggesting instead a re-issue of

Love's Comedy 'as a Christmas book', and hopefully observing, as a bait, that 'it may be regarded as a forerunner of *Brand*'. Hegel accepted the idea, and Ibsen spent the next five weeks revising the play and removing some of the more specifically Norwegian words so as to make it more palatable to Danish readers (and thereby, it has been suggested, indirectly indicating his contempt for the campaign in his own country to purge the Norwegian language of its foreign influences, a campaign which he was shortly to castigate in a more outspoken and vehement fashion).

In the first week in October he returned to Rome; and his financial position was now so secure that he was able to ask Hegel (5 October) 'not to send me the honorarium for *Love's Comedy* when it falls due, but to hold it over till next summer, or such time as I shall need more than serves my ordinary purposes'. He was planning to use this money, he informed Michael Birkeland the same day, 'to pay a visit next summer to Paris, and then to Greece' – the latter perhaps to gather background material for *Emperor and Galilean*, part of which is set there (though as things turned out, when the summer arrived he found himself writing a different play, and he never to the end of his life visited Greece, a country which would surely have excited him). He also decided to risk a little gentle speculation and requested Hegel to buy him some tickets for the Copenhagen lottery: 'I hold no hope of winning, but there is an excitement in it which I enjoy.' He was in fact to win two small prizes within the year.

The following month came disagreeable news; a Christiania solicitor named Nandrup, who had lent Ibsen money in 1862, had obtained a warrant of distraint on such few of Ibsen's possessions as remained in Norway, and had sold them by auction. 'I don't', he wrote to Bjørnson, 'mourn the loss of my furniture, etc., but to know that my private letters, papers, drafts, etc., may be in anyone's hands is a most vexatious thought, not to speak of the loss of many things which had a more than material value for me. You were not told the truth when they said the auction was held because I had not surrendered possession of my lodgings; it was because Nandrup, from the time I left, was discourteously rebuffed at Dunker's[1] office – I won't bother you with the details.' In the same letter he hinted for the first time that his stay in the south might be more than temporary. 'In a year or two I plan to come north, but scarcely farther than Copenhagen. If I can now and then make a summer trip to Norway, I think that will be the best arrangement.'

On 2 November he told Hegel he was still meditating the Magnus Heineson play, but added a rider: 'Whether this work will be the *first* I shall complete I am not yet certain. I have a couple of other themes in my head; but this very division of interest means that none of them has yet sufficiently matured; however, I feel sure this will soon happen, and hope to be able to send you the completed manuscript during the spring.' As the three themes jostled for precedence in his head that November and December, he completed his revisions for *Love's Comedy* and, painfully, composed the foreword.

That December a young Dane named Frederik G. Knudtzon, later to become a distinguished publisher, visited Rome, and his memoirs, published long after his death, give a vivid picture of Ibsen in his new role of established author in exile, a picture which interestingly contrasts with that left by Lorentz Dietrichson of those first eighteen months of struggling poverty. Recalling that Ibsen once described these years as his '*Sturm-und-Drang* period', Knudtzon continues: 'There was so much conflict within him that he could never appear a harmonious person. His high ideals, his extraordinary narrow-mindedness in social matters, his joy in Italy and in art, his residue of bitterness towards Norway, the financial difficulties which he had only recently overcome, and his secret need to keep a strict discipline – all this and much more that simmered within him meant that he

---

1. Bernhard Dunker, who had several times helped Ibsen with money, was acting as his lawyer in Norway.

was liable to explode to this side or that, and he moved among the Scandinavians like a lion of whom most of them were terrified. There was a *noli me tangere* quality about his personality, as about his dress; a long, buttoned tail coat, an elegant cravat – everything impeccable. The previous year, I was told, he had walked around with holes under his arms, as though indifferent to such trivia.'

The character of the Scandinavian Club had changed somewhat during the past year; several of the livelier members, including Bruun and Snoilsky, had returned home, and memories of the Danish war had receded. Even Ibsen seemed to have got a good deal of it out of his system with *Brand*. A few days after Knudtzon's arrival in Rome he attended a Christmas party at the Club with Ibsen present, and has left a pleasant record of the occasion. 'It was the custom for every guest to bring a little gift for the Christmas tree. When the dance round the tree was finished, the gifts were shared out, so that everyone went home with something other than what he had brought ... We ate rice porridge, and duck had to serve for the goose we would have enjoyed at home ... In the absence of a fir, a laurel had to serve as Christmas tree.' Then Consul Bravo, the badness of whose Danish was a perpetual source of joy to the members, rose as he had done for years to propose the health of 'the three Norwegian kingdoms'. What he meant was the three Scandinavian kingdoms, but he had (surprisingly, considering his position as consul) never mastered the difference between *nordisk* (Scandinavian) and *norsk* (Norwegian), and it had long been agreed that no one should spoil this annual delight by telling him.

During the dinner, however, there was trouble. The new arrivals included Kristofer Janson, the young novelist to whom Ibsen had lent money from his sock. Janson was a fervent devotee of the *landsmaal* movement, of which Ibsen was an equally fervent opponent, and he announced to the gathering that after the meal he proposed to read one of his stories in *landsmaal* aloud; at which Ibsen declared that if

Janson did this he, Ibsen, would leave. Janson saved the situation by reciting a poem by Bjørnson; not, one might think, the most tactful alternative, but one that passed off without ado.

Knudtzon gives several further examples of Ibsen's pepperiness that winter. One evening in the Club some well-meaning member proposed a toast to the two members who had chosen the food and wine, Ibsen and an old Danish painter named Lars Hansen. 'Hansen rose, ready to drink. But Ibsen suddenly stood up, stamped his foot, and said: "No one is going to drink my health as a member of the food committee."' On another occasion a Swedish nobleman, Count von Rosen, entered the Club with an effeminate young guest whom he introduced as Herr Sverdrup. When the two had left, Jerichau, the sculptor, remarked that the guest was evidently a girl. Most of the members, writes Knudtzon, thought this a fair joke, but 'Ibsen felt deeply offended on behalf of the fair sex ... He declared to all and sundry that the Scandinavian Club should not tolerate such behaviour; ladies were not admitted into the Club except on special occasions; Rosen and Sverdrup should be banned. Ibsen felt that the insult touched him most deeply as a *paterfamilias* – he was worried more on Fru Ibsen's account than on that of the Scandinavian ladies in general. He lived at the time in a state of permanent anxiety at not being sufficiently appreciated *qua familie*.' It turned out that Rosen's companion was indeed a girl, named Emma Toll, and Ibsen started a campaign to get her and Rosen excluded, writing letter after letter to Consul Bravo, and then to a Docent Landmanson who was acting on Rosen's behalf. Landmanson diplomatically managed to delay the explosion until Rosen and Emma had left Rome, and Ibsen was very annoyed with the Norwegians and Danes for their lack of co-operation.

These memoirs of Knudtzon are the earliest record we have of a trait which Ibsen appears to have developed after achieving fame, and which was to remain his most unappealing characteristic. Throughout the rest of his life he maintained an monarchical sensitivity in matters of protocol. Amazingly for one who so despised convention, and who was to bring such enlightenment to his contemporaries, he was, in his contacts with other human beings, to remain always a *nouveau riche* (or anyway a *nouveau* well-to-do, for his capital was never to exceed eleven thousand pounds) of the most aggressive and hypersensitive kind. The root lay deeper in time than Knudtzon knew, in his father's bankruptcy and the rumours of his own illegitimacy, those twin themes which haunt his plays so obsessively. Kristofer Janson noted: 'As long as one took care not to touch on those old and hated memories, Ibsen was friendly and amiable. But [he adds, and it is a point which others were to make] you had to be alone with him.'

Ibsen spent the last weeks of 1866 completing his foreword to the new edition of *Love's Comedy*, which he posted to Hegel on 5 January 1867, complaining that 'these few lines have caused me a bigger headache than the whole play. I have rewritten it innumerable times and finally settled for the first version.' He had, though, more important news. 'At last I can tell you that my new work is well under way and will, if nothing untoward happens, be ready early in the summer. It will be a long dramatic poem, having as its principal a part-legendary, part-fictional character from Norwegian folklore during *recent* times. It will bear no resemblance to *Brand*, and will contain no direct polemics or anything of that kind. I have long been pondering the theme;[2] now I have the whole plan worked out and on paper, and have begun the first act. It grows as I work on it and I am confident that you will be satisfied with the result. Please keep this secret for the time being.'

2. As early as 16 March 1866, the day after the publication of *Brand*, he had written to Anton Klubien: 'In the summer I shall go to Sorrento, where I plan to write a new play; I must be near the sea to get the right air into it.' And as things turned out he was (thanks to an earthquake) to write the last two acts of *Peer Gynt* there.

This new play was *Peer Gynt*; though, if we are to believe the dates inscribed by Ibsen on his manuscript, he did not in fact begin it until 14 January, nine days after his letter to Hegel. He had a tendency, not unique among authors, to tell white lies to his publisher. He composed it, as he had composed *Brand*, in rhymed verse, but of a far greater variety, in both octosyllabics and decasyllabics, not merely iambic ($\smile$—) and trochaic (—$\smile$), but dactylic (—$\smile\smile$) and anapaestic ($\smile\smile$—) too, and even, for those interested in these things, amphibrachs ($\smile$—$\smile$). He completed Act One in six weeks, on 25 February. Six days later, on 3 March, he started on Act Two. On 8 March he wrote Hegel what must have been another slight untruth, that he had 'now reached the middle of the second act', adding: 'it will comprise five [acts] and as far as I can calculate will occupy about 250 pages. If you wish, I shall be able to send you the manuscript as early as July.'

The play continued to make good progress, for on 27 March he was able to tell Hegel that he had finished Act Two. Then there was something of a hold-up, for by 2 May he had no further progress to report than that 'the plan for the rest of the play is completely clarified and worked out. Here in Rome,' he added, 'I scarcely think I shall be able to manage any more on it; for I feel a restlessness in my blood and, still more, the need for greater isolation.'

A week after Ibsen wrote this letter, the 'restlessness' to which he referred manifested itself in an unpleasant incident which showed him at his ugliest. Knudtzon tells that on 10 May the Scandinavians were having a party at an *osteria*, and a young painter named August Lorange, who suffered from tuberculosis (he was to die of it eight years later), was helping old Lars Hansen to add up the bill.

Ibsen suddenly stood up and began a speech which gradually turned into a brutal attack on Lorange. He was irritated partly because Lorange was helping to add up the bill, partly because he was generally hostile to the young man both as an artist and as a person; he was a poor painter, very untalented and unstable. He was (thus Ibsen concluded his speech) 'not worthy to walk on

two feet, but ought to crawl on four'. We were all left speechless
at such an attack on an unoffending and defenceless man, an
unfortunate consumptive who had enough to contend with without being banged on the head by Ibsen. But then Vilhelm Bissen[3]
intervened and told Ibsen it was wrong to suggest that Lorange
had interfered about the bill, since he himself had heard Hansen
ask Lorange to help him. Ibsen became a little calmer; but the
insult to Lorange had been delivered and could not be withdrawn. And the worst of the matter was that most of what Ibsen
had said about Lorange both as an artist and as a person was true
– though clearly it should not have been said so brutally, least of
all to an unfortunate invalid. When Ibsen had been silent for a
while, he rose again, and now, after the storm, the gentleness in
his nature found expression. He proposed a toast to a young man
who was an example of the best kind of artist, Ludvig Abelin
Schou [a Danish painter]. In handsome and well-chosen words
he praised Schou's talent, his truthfulness and industry, and we
emptied our glasses to his future.

When the party broke up, several of the diners went off
with Lorange to console him, and Ibsen, Knudtzon, and a
journalist named Jørgen Meincke were the last to rise.

But alas! It now became apparent that Ibsen could not steer his
own course. So Jørgen took him by the right arm and I by the
left, and we started on our way home. This afternoon walk with
the great poet was not of the shortest. On the road a few remarks
passed, but not many. At Ibsen's door I asked him to give me his
key so that I could let him in. This he did; but when we made to
accompany him up the stairs to his apartment he resisted violently. Beyond doubt Ibsen's brain was functioning much better
than his legs. He pondered, made up his mind, and gravely expressed his thanks to us.

Ibsen was evidently (there are other witnesses to the fact)
one of that not uncommon tribe who, when drunk, become
cruel, lose the use of their legs, yet remain mentally clear. It
was not until Ibsen attempted to walk that Knudtzon realized he was drunk; perhaps that was why he remained at
the table till most of the others had left.

3. A sculptor who executed a bust of Ibsen around this time – as did
Walter Runeberg. The two worked simultaneously in Bissen's studio.

Eleven days after this incident, on 21 May, Ibsen left Rome with Suzannah and Sigurd for the island of Ischia, where he lived for three months in the little town of Casamicciola on the northern side of the island, near the extinct volcano of Epomeo. The weather was exceptionally hot, even for the natives, but Ibsen seemed to revel in it; he completed Act Three in as little as two and a half weeks, on 2 July. Vilhelm Bergsøe was his companion throughout his stay, and noted his routine. He rose early, took a walk, drank coffee and wrote from ten till two. Then he had a siesta and, in the late afternoon, read through what he had written and fair-copied it. For relaxation he went on long, silent walks with Bergsøe, often saying nothing. He wrote, as the speed of his composition confirms, at intense pressure; he told Bergsøe that he felt 'like a rearing stallion about to leap', and later recalled to William Archer that his head was so full of verses that he would sometimes rise in his nightshirt to write them down – though, as so often happens in such cases, these sometimes turned out in the morning to be 'the veriest nonsense'.

In the beginning of July the sirocco arrived, and lasted ten days, tearing the roofs off houses, scattering the chairs and tables, and leaving, when it departed, the air filled with a fine yellow dust through which the sun glowed dully, casting no rays. They scattered ice on the stone floor to give a little cool as it melted, but Ibsen continued to work uninterruptedly. One day, while walking with Bergsøe, Ibsen suddenly asked: 'Can one put a man on the stage running around with a casting-ladle?' 'Yes, why not?' 'But it will have to be a big ladle – big enough to recast human beings in.' 'It'll look rather strange,' Bergsøe ventured, to which Ibsen replied, 'Yes, I think so too, but I don't think the play's for acting.'

Bergsøe's portrait of Ibsen during these months on Ischia is vivid and detailed. He cites several examples of that physical cowardice which has already been remarked. 'He had a curious fear of anything that might bring death or misadventure. This fear was not grounded in the thought of losing his life, but in a terror lest he might not achieve the artistic goal he had set himself.' Once Bergsøe took him to a crevasse named *valle del tamburro*. 'As one penetrates more deeply the crevasse changes character, the vegetation becomes sparse, the walls narrow, the light fades and ... finally one has to walk on the big stones that lie in the hot water. When we reached this point Ibsen exclaimed in alarm: "Where are you taking me, do you want me inside the mountain? I won't go any farther. It might close over us." When I said this was impossible he cried: "But a rock might fall and crush us! I want to get out, I want to go home!" Ignoring my assurances, he hastened off, and that afternoon I saw him no more.'

A similar thing happened when they climbed Punto Imperatore, a hill with a fine view over the sea. 'The last part of the way I had almost to drag Ibsen with me, for he repeatedly asserted that the cliff might fall, and when I objected that we were in proportion to the cliff as a fly to a tower he made the curious observation that even a fly could bring down a tower if it were on the point of falling.' Unable to persuade him further, Bergsøe climbed alone to the cliff's edge and surveyed the view. 'Now and then I seemed to hear Ibsen's voice, but because of the roar of the sea I could not distinguish what he was saying. When I finally turned around, I saw him lying with his face to the ground, clasping a rock with both hands. "You will kill me!" he cried furiously. "Why didn't you come when I called? I shall never go on one of your so-called nature walks again!" '

Even now their troubles were not over, for on their way down they found their path barred by a large dog. 'There is a dog,' said Ibsen, and stopped. Bergsøe assured him that it had no hostile intentions. 'You cannot know,' replied Ibsen. 'I am not going near it.' Bergsøe said there was no danger as long as Ibsen did not appear afraid. 'I am not afraid,' said Ibsen angrily, but moved over to the other side. 'So we walked briskly towards the dog, which stood there calmly enough; but just as we were about to pass it Ibsen made a movement as though about to break into a run, and immediately the dog jumped at him and bit him in the hand. A well-aimed blow from my stick sent it yelping off, but Ibsen went as white as a corpse and stared at his hand. I looked at it and found only a tiny scratch, but Ibsen cried: "The dog is mad, it must be shot, otherwise I shall go mad too." In vain I explained to him that there was no evidence that the dog was mad, and that it was a groundless superstition that a human being could catch hydrophobia if, long after biting him, a dog developed the disease. He was foaming with rage, and it was several days before his fear departed.'

Bergsøe noted (as Knudtzon did) Ibsen's habit of interlarding his conversation with phrases from Holberg, especially from *Jeppe of the Hill* – '*Hej, Jakob Skomager! Er Du optaaen? Lukk op, Jakob! Hej, Jakob Skomager, nu ska vi mare have os en Dram!* [Ho, Jacob Cobbler! Are you up? Open up, Jacob! Ho, Jacob Cobbler, let's have a dram!]' – and the meticulous care with which he recorded even the smallest purchases. Once he bought two cheap local cigars, took out his notebook, and carefully wrote down their price. ' "Do you make a note of things like that?" I asked in amazement. "Yes," he replied, "I have to keep a very careful account of my expenses now I am married. I didn't when I was young." '[4] Sometimes he would behave in an unexpectedly schoolboy fashion. When a copy of *Fædrelandet* arrived with a hostile criticism of Bergsøe's work in it, Ibsen astonished the townspeople by rolling it into a trumpet and hooting through it as he trotted across the square. On the subject of his mother country he was very haughty. 'I shall not go back to Norway,' he told Bergsøe, 'until Norway calls me.'

At the beginning of August the sirocco returned even worse than before, and the temperature rose to no less than

---

4. Similarly, John Paulsen saw the accounts Ibsen had kept at Aricia while working on *Brand*, and noted that one item read: 'Bought an orange, 1 bajoc [one fifth of a penny]. To a beggar, 1 bajoc. A glass of lemonade, 2 bajoc.'

37° Réaumur or 115° Fahrenheit (46° Centigrade), making it almost impossible to breathe. Nevertheless, on 8 August Ibsen was able to write to Hegel:

I have today sent you, via Consul-General Danchertsen in Naples, the manuscript of the first three acts of my new work, entitled *Peer Gynt*, a dramatic poem. This section will come to around 120 printed pages, and the remainder will add up to about the same. I hope to be able to send you Act Four towards the end of the month, and the rest not long afterwards. In case it should interest you, Peer Gynt was a real person who lived in Gudbrandsdal, probably around the end of the last century or the beginning of this. His name is still famous among the people up there, but not much more is known about his life than what is to be found in Asbjørnsen's *Norwegian Fairy Tales* (in the section entitled 'Stories from the Mountain'). So I haven't had much on which to base my poem, but that has meant that I have had all the more freedom with which to work on it.

On the night of 14 August there was a slight earthquake on Ischia. The next day Ibsen and Bergsøe walked down to the church in Casamicciola, where a crack broad enough for a man's hand to enter had opened in the tower. Ibsen put his hand in the crack, looked at it, looked at Bergsøe and left the island next day for Sorrento.[5] Here he remained for two months, writing the last two acts. There was no earthquake to trouble him, but in nearby Naples there was an outbreak of cholera, and at one time he thought Suzannah had caught it; but this fear proved to be unfounded. We do not know when he began the long fourth (African) act, but he completed it on 15 September and posted the fair copy to Hegel three days later, adding: 'If the printing of the *dramatis personae* could be delayed until I have sent you the rest of the play, I should be grateful, since I might possibly wish to add a few minor ones; but this isn't important.' The next day, 19 September, he began the great final act, which he completed, amazingly, in twenty-five days on 14 October –

5. For once Ibsen's fears were to prove not altogether groundless. Sixteen years later Casamicciola was destroyed by an earthquake.

over a thousand lines of rhymed verse, at the rate of forty a day. Four days later he posted the fair copy of this to Hegel – 'and may luck attend it!'

The Ibsens spent a week relaxing in Sorrento; then, towards the end of the month, left for Pompeii, where they stayed for two days. From there they moved on to Naples, now free of the cholera. Bergsøe tried to persuade Ibsen to take a trip with him in a fishing boat to Capri, but Ibsen refused. 'I won't go out with these Neapolitans. If there's a storm they lie flat in the boat and pray to the Virgin Mary instead of reefing the sails.' Bergsøe adds, however, that Ibsen's fear in this context was, again, not without foundation, since a boat with a young girl in it had recently overturned in the bay – 'whereupon the fisherman swam ashore, and the young girl was found drowned the following evening'.

At the end of October they set out from Naples for Rome. but politics intervened; a week previously Garibaldi had invaded the Papal States, fighting was in full progress, the railway was cut, and the Ibsens and Bergsøe found themselves stuck at San Germano, a few miles short of the Papal frontier. For a professed champion of liberty, Ibsen showed a disappointing lack of enthusiasm for his hero's cause, very different from his mood of two years earlier. 'Damn all war!' he wrote to Consul Bravo in Rome from San Germano on 4 November, two days after Garibaldi had been defeated at Mentana by the French and Papal forces. 'We have been sitting here, a few miles from the Papal frontier, since Wednesday, in the continued but as yet vain hope of being able to proceed to Rome.'[6] At length, on 8 November, the trains started running again and he was able to return.

6. Edmund Gosse rightly observes that in his attitude of passive appreciation Ibsen resembled Walter Savage Landor rather than those other illustrious exiles such as Stendhal, Lamartine, Ruskin and the Brownings, who had 'spent nights of insomnia dreaming of Italian liberty'. Landor had died in Florence three months after Ibsen's first arrival in Rome.

Rome presented a strangely changed appearance. 'The Corso', writes Bergsøe, 'was almost empty, and the few people I met were foreigners. Many of the great palazzos seemed deserted, there was quiet in the small streets, and instead of the conversing groups usually to be found on the Piazza Colonna one now saw bivouacking soldiers, their rifles piled in pyramids, guarded by sentry posts at each corner of the square. Patrols moved ceaselessly through the streets; but when the French bugles sounded, the Romans stared at the red-breeched troops with a mixture of hatred and contempt, remembering that it had been a French general who had defeated Garibaldi at Mentana.' At night 'numerous patrols roamed in long grey coats and with rifles over their shoulders. When an Orsini bomb exploded they placed themselves back to back and fired at random in all directions, regardless of where the shots might land.'[7]

On 14 November 1867, six days after Ibsen had returned to Rome and less than four weeks after Hegel had received the final section of the manuscript, *Peer Gynt* appeared in the Scandinavian bookshops. Ibsen was delighted at its being out in time to catch the Christmas sales. 'Let us hope the critics will be kind to us,' he wrote to Hegel on 23 November. 'I think the book will be much read in Norway.'

Peer Gynt, however – the tale of a man the exact opposite of Brand, a compromiser who thinks only of himself, shuns work and suffering, and (it is hinted) typifies the most common Norwegian failings – had a mixed reception in Scandinavia. The first omens were good; Hegel sent word that the first edition of 1,250 copies had sold out almost at once, and that a second edition of 2,000 was in the press. Three days after publication Bjørnson, that most patriotic of poets who more than most might have been expected to take offence at the fun poked at Norwegian nationalism, especially since Peer was the exact opposite of Bjørnson's own

7. Felice Orsini had tried to assassinate Napoleon III by throwing a bomb (made in Birmingham) at his carriage in 1858, and had been executed.

romanticized peasant heroes, wrote Ibsen a letter full of admiration: 'I love your spleen, I love the courage with which it has armed you, I love your strength, I love your recklessness – oh, it turned all my thoughts to laughter, like the smell of the sea after the closed air of a sickroom,' and ending: 'this is a love letter, and nothing else . . . *Peer Gynt* is magnificent, Ibsen! Only Norwegians can see how good it is!' He reviewed the book in *Norsk Folkeblad* on 23 November, describing it as 'a satire in Norwegian egotism, narrowness, and self-sufficiency, so executed as to have made me not only again and again laugh till I was sore, but again and again give thanks to the author in my heart, as I do here in public',[8] and dispraising nothing but the over-exuberance of detail and certain aspects of the versification. He especially admired the threadballs scene.

So far, so good; but the most influential critic in Scandinavia was Clemens Petersen, and his long notice in *Fædrelandet* (30 November), though granting the play some merits and admitting its 'often surprising brilliance', ultimately rejected it on doctrinaire philosophical grounds. The article, a formidable specimen of woolly-mindedness and dogmatism, condemned *Peer Gynt* as lacking in idealism, objected that the characters were not fully rounded or alive and that the play contained 'riddles which are insoluble because they are empty', dismissed Peer's identification of the Sphinx with the Boyg as 'an intellectual swindle', and ended by categorizing the play as political journalism, declaring that 'it is not poetry, because in the transmutation of reality into art it fails to meet the demands of either art or reality'.

Hostility to *Peer Gynt*, it gradually became apparent, was widespread. Hans Andersen hated it. 'Ibsen is repellent to him', wrote Edvard Grieg to Bjørnson, 'and *Peer Gynt* the worst that he has read.' Camilla Collett, the pioneer of women's independence in Norway, was offended by the passivity of Solveig's character, declaring that a more forceful

8. William Archer's translation.

female would have shown Peer the error of his ways much earlier. A reviewer in *Nordisk Tidskrift* thought the play had 'too much thought'; another, in the Danish newspaper *Berlingske Tidende*, thought it 'not truly aesthetic'. Even Georg Brandes, in his notice in the Copenhagen *Dagbladet* on 16 December, joined in the condemnation. While granting Ibsen's 'incredible gift for versification' and 'wonderful command of language', he found the theme and its treatment ethically offensive. 'What great and noble powers are wasted on this thankless material! ... It would be unjust to deny that the book contains great beauties, or that it tells us all, and Norwegians in particular, some important truths; but beauties and truths are of far less value than Beauty and Truth in the singular, and Ibsen's poem is neither beautiful nor true. Contempt for humanity and self-hatred make a bad foundation on which to build a poetic work.'[9]

On 30 December *Morgenbladet* printed a letter from its Copenhagen correspondent summarizing critical reaction in Denmark: 'The verdict on this remarkable work, which was at first uncertain and much divided, now seems more or less agreed that a writer of such great gifts, mastery of form and intellectual depth ought to abandon the moralizing and polemizing in which he has indulged in his latest works and serve with a larger sense of beauty and discrimination the Muse of Poetry who has elected to bless him with her patronage.'

Petersen's review, from which Ibsen had hoped so much, drove him into a fury, not merely because it was hostile (Brandes's was almost equally so), but because it represented just that kind of pompous mental rigidity which he most detested and which he was to spend his life castigating. He received a copy of the notice just as he had composed a letter

9. Archer's translation. It is much to Ibsen's credit that he did not let these adverse reviews spoil the friendship which was shortly to develop between him and Brandes. He recognized the difference in quality between Brandes's mind and Petersen's. Brandes was later to recant his condemnation of *Peer Gynt*, except concerning Act Four.

of thanks to Bjørnson for the latter's praise of the play, and
was so enraged that he tore this letter up and wrote another.
His redrafted letter reveals that manic side of his character
which he rarely allowed to appear in his writing but which,
as we have seen, not infrequently emerged in social intercourse. 'Dear Bjørnson', he wrote on 9 December,

What is this curse that at every juncture interposes itself between us? It is as though the Devil came in person to cast his
shadow over us ... An hour ago, I read Hr. Clemens Petersen's
review in *Fædrelandet* ... If I were in Copenhagen and anyone
stood as near to me as Clemens Petersen does to you, I would
have struck him senseless before allowing him to commit so calculated an offence against Truth and Justice ... My book *is*
poetry; and if it isn't, it will become such. The conception of
poetry in our country, in Norway, shall shape itself according to
this book ... However, I am glad that this injustice has been
flung at me; it is a sign of divine aid and dispensation; anger
increases my strength. If there is to be war, then let there be war!
If I am not a poet, what have I to lose? I shall try my hand as a
photographer, I shall deal with my contemporaries up there, each
and all of them, one by one, as I have dealt with these language
reformers; I shall not spare the child in its mother's womb, nor
any thought nor feeling that may have motivated the actions of
any man who shall merit the honour of being my victim ... Do
you know that all my life I have turned my back on my parents,
on my whole family, because I could not bear to continue a relationship based on imperfect understanding?

He did not post the letter at once, but added a postscript
the following day: 'I have slept on these words and read
them again in cold blood. The mood they express is that of
yesterday; I shall send them, nevertheless.' After another
hysterical outburst ('Do not underrate my friends and supporters in Norway; the party whose paper has allowed its
pages to carry an injustice against me shall realize that I do
not stand alone ... My enemies shall learn that if I cannot
build I have at least strength enough to destroy'), he ended
on a scarcely appeasing note: 'I reproach you merely with
inactivity. It was not good of you to permit, by doing

nothing, such an attempt to be made in my absence to put my reputation under the auctioneer's hammer.'

Bjørnson accepted this abuse calmly, and wrote Ibsen a letter (16 December) of splendid generosity and exhortation, begging him to 'be just towards us and have faith in yourself'. This letter, which ran to 3,500 words, reached Ibsen on Christmas Day and so mollified him that in his reply, of 28 December, he actually asked Bjørnson to give Petersen his regards. But his old feeling of resentment soon returned, and it was to be ten years before he wrote to Bjørnson again.

After his first outburst of fury, Ibsen accepted the criticisms calmly. 'How goes it with *Peer Gynt*?' he asked Hegel on 24 February 1868. 'In Sweden, as far as I can tell from the newspaper reviews, it has been very well received; but has it sold accordingly? In Norway I gather the book has caused a great rumpus; which bothers me not in the least; but both there and in Denmark, people have discovered much more satire than I intended. Why can't people read the thing as a work of fiction? That is how I wrote it. The satirical sections are pretty isolated. But if, as seems to be the case, the Modern Norwegian recognizes himself in Peer Gynt, that is those good gentlemen's own funeral.'

Surprisingly, in view of the controversy surrounding it, *Peer Gynt* did not sell particularly well; the second edition, printed immediately after publication, was not exhausted until 1874, by which time *Brand* had entered its seventh edition. It was nine years before anyone staged it, and thirteen years before Ibsen received a request for translation rights.

Like *Brand*, Alfred de Musset's comedies, Turgenev's *A Month in the Country* and (probably, for Büchner's exact intention regarding his plays is unknown) *Woyzeck* and *Danton's Death*, *Peer Gynt* was written with no thought of performance; and the consequent rejection of the accepted limitations of stagecraft proved, as with *Brand*, tremendously liberating. It was not merely that Ibsen felt free to move uninhibitedly in time and space (*Peer Gynt* contains forty scenes). He had done that in *Brand*. More importantly, he felt free to ignore other frontiers, the frontiers between reality and fantasy, between (as we should now say) the conscious and the unconscious. Nobody, one hopes, any longer takes the last act of *Peer Gynt* at its face value, as the return of an old man to his youthful love; such an ending would have been, for Ibsen, most untypically banal and sentimental, two adjectives which recur frequently in contemporary criticisms of it. Whether one regards Peer as having died in the madhouse at the end of Act Four, or in the shipwreck at the beginning of Act Five, we must surely take that fifth act as representing either the unreeling of his past life in his mind at the moment of death or (which is perhaps the same thing) as the wandering of his soul in purgatory, '*limbo patrum*, nigh to hell'. Viewed thus, the last hour of the play is Peer's life seen in a distorting mirror, just as the troll scene in Act Three is the wedding party and Peer's hopes and fears concerning it dreamed by a drunken and confused man: the desirable yet (once he has got her) repulsive girl, the wrathful vengeance-seeking father, the conflict between lust and conscience. To present *Peer Gynt* on a purely realistic level, as still, alas, occasionally happens, is to reduce it to an amiable and confused pantomime with a facile ending, an interpretation to which Grieg's music, for all its intrinsic merits, has lent authority. Ibsen was not Freud's darling playwright, and Joyce's, for nothing; he understood, as few of their predecessors did, the power of the unconscious, the truth behind dreams and nightmares, the higher reality of what most of his contemporaries dismissed as unreality; and *Peer Gynt* may be regarded as the first prolonged exploration, whether deliberate or unconscious, of this field, to which, nearly twenty years later, he was to return with such effect in *Rosmersholm*, *The Lady from the Sea* and the powerful and, to his contemporaries, scarcely intelligible plays which followed. *Peer Gynt* is the direct ancestor of Strindberg's *A Dream Play*. But at the time of its appearance, as Ibsen complained, it was regarded mainly as a satire.

Yet in one sense at least Ibsen's critics came nearer the truth than some of the play's later admirers. They were right to find it disturbing, discordant and offensive. It is one of the most upsetting and uncomfortable plays ever written. Trolls, properly understood, are not mere goblins but, as Professor Francis Bull has written: 'the evil forces of Nature ... embodying and symbolizing those powers of evil, hidden in the soul of man, which may at times suppress his conscious will and dominate his actions ... By ever pandering to his evil instincts and desires they have come to be really his rulers – mysterious powers that make him afraid of himself.' This is what *Peer Gynt* is really about – the struggle between the divine purpose and our undermining passions and egocentricities, between man's deeper self and his animal, or troll, self; in Stekel's phrase 'how the soul, oppressed by the primal passions, struggles to escape the hell of the instincts'. The Boyg, the Greenclad One and the Strange Passenger are, like the Thin Person, lackeys of the Enemy; as is Peer himself, apart from the image of him which Solveig keeps

> With the mark of destiny on his brow
> As he sprang forth in the mind of God.

Ibsen himself thought *Peer Gynt* too Norwegian ever to be appreciated abroad, much as Synge felt about *The Playboy of the Western World* (a character who has much in common with Peer, as the styles of the two plays have much in common, with their ebullient rhythms and extravagant imagery). 'Of all my books', Ibsen wrote to a would-be German translator, Ludwig Passarge (19 May 1880), 'I regard *Peer Gynt* as the least likely to be understood outside Scandinavia ... You know the people and the personalities one finds up there. But is not all this necessary if one is to find any real flavour in the poem?' Ibsen's doubts were to prove unfounded, for *Peer Gynt* has become the best known of his works outside as well as inside Scandinavia. Peer himself has everywhere been accepted as a national prototype; a Japanese critic has described him as 'typically Japanese'. As Bernard Shaw wrote: 'The universality of Ibsen makes his plays come home to all nations.'[10]

In a later letter (16 June 1880) to Passarge, who, despite the warning, had translated the play, Ibsen made it clear, if any confirmation were needed, that *Peer Gynt* is a self-analysis. Referring specifically to this play, he stated: 'Everything that I have written is most minutely connected with what I have lived through, if not personally experienced; every new work has had for me the object of serving as a process of spiritual liberation and catharsis; for every man shares the responsibility and the guilt of the society to which he belongs. That is why I once inscribed in a copy of one of my books the following dedicatory lines:

> To live is to war with trolls in heart and soul.
> To write is to sit in judgment on oneself.'[11]

If, as Ibsen once remarked, Brand was 'myself, in my best moments', Peer was the other side of the medallion.

Ibsen's letters from Rome during the last months of 1867 show him toying with the idea of returning to Scandinavia. Several times he hints that Copenhagen may be the answer; Norway still seemed out of the question. 'I can never make out how you endure it up there,' he wrote to Magdalene Thoresen on 15 October. 'Life up there, as I now see it, seems boring beyond description. It bores the soul from one's body, it bores the marrow from one's will; that's the damnable thing about petty surroundings, they make a man's soul

10. But there is some evidence that Ibsen in later years rather took against *Peer Gynt*. P. G. la Chesnais tells that, to a French visitor who began to praise the play in 1900, Ibsen replied (I quote la Chesnais's version; Ibsen would not have said it in French): 'Bah! Une oeuvre de jeunesse! Ce fut mon Manfred. Qui sait s'il n'a pas persisté en moi un byronien attardé?'

11. William Archer's translation.

petty!' And in his last letter to Bjørnson on 28 December he had said: 'Where we shall spend next winter, I don't know. I only know it won't be in Norway. If I went home now, one of two things would happen. Either I'd make an enemy of everyone within a month, or I'd bury my head in the sand again and become a lie to myself and others.' After warning Bjørnson not to continue in theatre management ('Working in the theatre is for a writer a daily repeated abortion'), he exhorted him: 'No, come abroad, *carissimo*! Both because distance gives one a broader perspective, and because one is out of people's sight.' In a similar mood at this time he told Frederik Knudtzon: 'One should live down here and rule them all.'

But his son was now eight, and there was his schooling to consider; for all his hatred of Norway, Ibsen was unwilling that Sigurd should be educated as a foreigner. He did not know enough Italian, anyway, to go to an ordinary local school, and such foreign schools as there were in Rome at this time could not take a child who was fluent only in Norwegian; so on 24 February 1868 we find Ibsen asking Hegel to send him 'a geography book, a general world history, an arithmetic book, and books containing the elements of religious instruction, all suitable for an eight-year-old child ... My little boy has read a lot, especially history (both general and biblical), but as yet quite unsystematically, and it must not continue so.' By the spring he was beginning to accept that, if for this reason only, he would have to return to Norway. 'What it will be like to live outside Italy, and above all what it will be like to live in Christiania,' he wrote to Magdalene Thoresen on 31 March, 'I can scarcely imagine. However, I suppose I shall have to. But one will have to isolate oneself totally up there (I shall, anyway), if I am not to make an enemy of everyone ... The best that could happen to our country would be a great national calamity. If one can't survive that one has no right to live. I have witnessed sacrifices down here which make me draw comparisons from which our country does not emerge with honour.'

Early in 1868 Ibsen had resumed work on *Emperor and Galilean*, but after *Brand* and *Peer Gynt* he found himself wanting to write for the theatre again, as opposed to the printed page, and on 28 February he told Hegel: 'My next work will probably be a play for the stage, and I hope it will not be long before I begin to work seriously on it.' Another plan had occurred to him. 'I have been thinking of making a collection of my various unpublished poems, but I can't do that down here, as they must be ferreted out of various newspapers, etc. But some time I shall have to come north again, and I suppose make a detour to Christiania, in which case I could start things moving.'

That spring, Ibsen seems to have been in an unusually prickly mood. His marriage may have entered upon a difficult phase. Martin Schneekloth, a young Dane whom Ibsen found sympathetic and who, like so many of those young Scandinavians in Rome, was shortly to die of consumption, noted in his diary, which was to remain unpublished for three-quarters of a century:

To find that one does not really love the woman one has married, that one's requirements for a happy co-existence are so opposed to one's wife's that no reconciliation is possible, must be a desperate situation for a man, and that is Ibsen's. He is a domineering character, egocentric and unbending, with a passionate masculinity and a curious admixture of personal cowardice, compulsively idealistic yet totally indifferent to expressing these ideals in his daily life, restlessly questing, confused, yet striving for clarity. *She* is unwomanly, tactless, *but* a stable, hard character, a mixture of intelligence and stupidity, not deficient in feeling but lacking humility and feminine love. They cannot find peace through love, so they wage war on each other, ruthlessly, coldly, and yet she loves him, if only through their son, their poor son, whose fate is the saddest that could befall any child, to see divided what should be reconciled in him. Whose is the fault if not the man's? He took her from her father's house, led her out into the strange world, and instead of devoting his life to finding some form of reconciliation he gives all his mind and passion to a demonic pursuit of literary fame. It is disturbing to hear him describe his plans to send his wife and child home so that he may work in peace abroad. He lacks the courage to pursue his career without abandoning his domestic responsibilities, to face up to the consequences of his ambition, to work incessantly to give her life fulfilment, to suffer and strive to educate his son. Thus he, who so loudly and brilliantly condemns the cravenness of our age, who in mighty poems proclaims the strength of human will, is himself a craven, a vacillating weakling.

This formidable indictment is reinforced by a later entry for the same month:

Does Ibsen love his wife? I don't know, but she loves him, but is not happy in her love. Ibsen himself is so obsessed with his work that the proverb 'humanity first, art second' has practically been reversed. I think his love for his wife has long vanished, and been replaced by a mood of resignation, if such is possible in so restless a character. His crime now is that he cannot discipline himself to correct the situation, but rather asserts his moody and despotic nature over both her and their poor, spiritually warped, terrified son.

Schneekloth might almost have been prophetically describing the marriages of the Master Builder, John Gabriel Borkman, or Arnold and Maja Rubek in *When We Dead Awaken*; and the theme of at any rate the last two plays is indeed 'humanity first, art (or ambition) second'. Yet Schneekloth's account, though probably accurate, gives only half the picture, the surface half which so many other acquaintances of the Ibsens were to record. Unlike Solness, Borkman, and Rubek, Ibsen was dependent on and devoted to his wife, as the statements of their son and daughter-in-law, and the frequent references in his own letters, show. Ibsen was, like Milton, Dickens, Tolstoy, Dostoyevsky, Shelley, Carlyle, D. H. Lawrence and Joyce (to say nothing of numberless great painters and composers), monstrously egocentric and frequently cruel; yet if he had survived Suzannah and recorded his private thoughts about her, it is difficult to imagine that they would have greatly differed from those of Thomas Carlyle about his Jane, another

couple whom their contemporaries supposed to live in a state
of permanent mutual torment.

Frederik Knudtzon recounts an anecdote from this spring
of 1868 which vividly illustrates the duality of Ibsen's nature,
and the suddenness with which he would switch from one
mood to another. One Sunday afternoon, while accompanying the sculptor Frederick Stramboe to the latter's
studio, Knudtzon saw Ibsen on the other pavement in the
Via Felice, together with Lars Hansen and the Norwegian
sculptor Ole Fladager.

As soon as Ibsen caught sight of us he crossed the street
towards us and cried 'Ih, mare,[12] Knudtzon! You must come
out with us to La Baracca.' 'But I've promised Stramboe I'd go to
his studio.' That could be done tomorrow, said Ibsen; we must
join him; it would be a delightful walk. So we turned round,
introduced ourselves to his companions and joined them. It soon
became apparent that Ibsen had been lunching with them and
had come straight from the table. We arrived at the Piazza Barberina. There were several cabs there, and Ibsen made straight
for them. As he seized on the first, Fru Ibsen announced that she
would not accompany us. Ibsen protested at this, but she maintained that she would not come. 'Get up into the cab!' thundered
Ibsen with all his might, if somewhat indistinctly. It was very
disagreeable for the four of us to listen to. But the moment the
words were out of his mouth Fru Ibsen climbed up and took her
seat in the cab. Ibsen and Fladager followed, we three others
jumped hastily into another cab, and the two vehicles rolled off.
After a quarter of an hour we trundled into the spacious courtyard of La Baracca, with its splendid view towards the blue
Alban mountains. Our little Sunday symposium was about to
begin; but the violent scene in the Piazza Barberina had undeniably given us the feeling that there was thunder in the air.
Under the great tree where we usually sat there was ample
room. I came first to the table, and as the Bodega simultaneously
presented himself I ordered un mezzo, but Ibsen was just behind
me, and when he heard my order he shouted in a leave-this-to-
me voice: 'Due mezzi!' This meant three mezzi, i.e. six fogliette,

12. An exclamation much used by Jeppe of the Hill in Holberg's
play of that name, roughly equivalent to 'What cheer?'

which if equally divided would mean a whole *foglietta* each ...
However, we drank and chatted and the wine effected a considerable change in the atmosphere. Ibsen seemed from the start
to have some worm of indignation in the depths of his soul, an
indignation which grew as the tempo heightened under the
influence of the wine and the general euphoria increased. This
indignation weighed on him and demanded an outlet. It may
have been connected with Ibsen's sense of responsibility and calling as a poet; he once told me he saw his ideal of a poet in the
Old Testament prophets. Perhaps ... his prophetic indignation
had built up until it could find vent only through an explosion.

However, as we sat under the great tree looking now at each
other, now at the blue Alban mountains, everything still went
agreeably. I think we emptied most of the three *mezzi*, and as
darkness fell we prepared to leave. But now the same happened
as the previous year; Ibsen's brain was found to be functioning
better than his legs. Had we been wise we would have sent for a
carriage. But we failed to take that precaution. We moved off,
Fru Ibsen going ahead with old Hansen and Fladager. Ibsen followed some distance behind, with Stramboe and myself on either
side; we kept a good hold of him under the arms and started to
walk slowly and carefully. But when we had come about a third
of the way, something on the other side of the road caught
Ibsen's attention. Behind an iron gate in a wall surrounding one
of the big villas we saw a huge dog, which barked angrily at us.
Ibsen quickened his pace – he had to go over to it, in other words,
we had to go over, and soon the three of us were standing at the
gate. Ibsen had a stick in his hand, which he now began to poke
at the dog, one of those gigantic brutes that resemble small lions.
It came closer, and Ibsen poked and struck at it, trying in every
way to madden it, and succeeding. It rushed at the gate, Ibsen
prodded and struck it anew, and worked it into such a rage that
without doubt, had not the solid iron gate stood between it and
us, it would have torn us apart. This, I realized, was the explosion
of violence which resulted from the enjoyment of the wine, and
which had been the cause of the attack on Lorange. But it lasted
longer. Ibsen must have stood teasing the dog for six to eight
minutes. At length he grew bored with the sport. Then his eye
chanced on two Italian children who, attracted by the furious
barking, were standing by his side, two enchanting children in

national dress with fresh, red cheeks, a sight in complete contrast to the raging dog. Ibsen looked down at them, and with an astonishing glow of kindness and gentleness in his eyes took between two of his fingers a little pinch of each child's cheek, and released it – a gesture of love that was expressive of both human kindness and the need to protect. It was an *adagio* after the storm, like the speech to Ludvig Abelin Schou after the outburst against Lorange. Now both his prophetic indignation and his benevolence had found expression, and we continued on our way.

People still occasionally write about Ibsen as though he were a figure of Olympian calm and detachment. It cannot be over-emphasized that, while his writing was indeed detached, in the sense of being supremely objective, it was a detachment born of a fearful discipline exercised over a manic depressive temperament. Ibsen never spoke more truly than when he likened himself to an Old Testament prophet. Isaiah, dressed in a tall hat and morning coat, would surely have looked and talked like Ibsen.[13]

On 9 May 1868 Ibsen, Suzannah, and Sigurd left Rome, 'to spend the summer', as he informed Hegel on 27 April, 'in northern Italy or the Tyrol', probably with the intention of proceeding to Christiania in the autumn. For the time being, at any rate, on account of Sigurd's schooling, they had put Italy behind them. They spent eight days in Florence, two in Bologna, eight in Venice and eight in Botzen (now Bolzano) in the Tyrol. In the middle of June, riding in an old-fashioned coach with the postilion blowing his bugle, they reached the little Bavarian resort of Berchtesgaden, where they settled for the summer (and to which they were frequently to return). 'I don't know if you are familiar with this place,' Ibsen wrote to Consul Bravo on 22 June. 'If not, it is worth discovering. It is the most beautiful country I have seen north of the Alps, cheap, easy of access, pleasant in

13. The Swedish writer Ola Hansson once remarked that Ibsen always had 'something of Moses on Sinai with the tablets of the law in his hand.' Cf. also Ibsen's own insistence that he was a passionate writer, p. 757 below.

every way ... I have started a new work, which I hope to complete here ... When we shall return to our home in Rome is still uncertain; but some time we shall come back, or anyway I shall, life and health permitting.' On 28 July he wrote to Hegel: 'We shall spend the winter in Munich and Dresden, and shall then probably come home. I have not yet got down seriously to anything big, but I shall soon ... The landscape here is splendid, but the weather changeable; I miss my beloved Italy in more respects than one.' He visited Salzburg, and in August spent eight days walking to Gastein and back. By this time, his new play was beginning to mature in his mind. 'My new dramatic work (written for the theatre, and wholly realistic, influenced no doubt by the heavy German air) occupies all my thoughts,' he told Hegel on 20 August.

At the end of August they left Berchtesgaden and proceeded to Munich. They stayed there a month, in an apartment at Maximilianplatz 13, 'the whole time under a blessedly Italian sky, rejoicing in the city's wonderful art treasures and in the local populace's hatred of all things Prussian', as he informed Hegel on 22 September. In the first days of October they arrived in Dresden, where they were to spend the next six and a half years.

PART THREE

German Seed-Time

11

Dresden: *The League of Youth*
1868-9

A CENTURY earlier the poet Johann Gottfried von Herder, fresh from introducing the young Goethe to the beauties of Shakespeare and Gothic architecture, had described Dresden as 'the German Florence', and the compliment, if not strictly accurate, was still reasonably deserved. Surrounded by blue hills, and traversed by the curving Elbe with its ancient bridges and terraces, the city greeted the traveller with a picturesque skyline of green copper roofs, spires and cupolas. In 1868 Dresden was still, despite the bombardment it had suffered in 1760, largely of the seventeenth and eighteenth century, with many fine medieval buildings in the Altstadt or Old Town, which Canaletto had so admired. It was a favourite resort of foreigners, partly for the splendour of its art collections and historic buildings, and partly, for those with children, on account of the famed excellence of its educational facilities – an important consideration for Ibsen, whose movements in Europe over the next decade and a half were largely to be dictated by the needs of his son.

He took furnished lodgings in a small two-room apartment on the first floor at An der Frauenkirche 6, shown in contemporary photographs as a pleasant, tall house, and settled down to complete his plans for his new play. On 10 October, less than a week after his arrival, he asked Hegel to send him regular copies of the Danish newspaper *Dagbladet*, 'not to satisfy an idle curiosity for news ... but because I shall thereby be drawn more closely and intensively into life in Norway, and thus feel strengthened for my work'. He was determined to make his play nothing if not realistic.

He began his first draft on 21 October, and completed Act One in five days. On the last of the month he was able to report happily to Hegel that 'the play makes swift progress. All this summer I have been turning it over in my mind without actually writing; now the whole draft is ready and on paper, Act One is finished, Act Two will be in a week, and I hope the whole play will be completed by the end of the year. It will be in prose, and written entirely with the stage in mind. The title of the play is *The League of Youth*, or *Our Lord & Co*; a comedy in five acts. It deals with frictions and currents in modern life. I find myself in a calm and happy frame of mind, and write accordingly.' He was finding Dresden 'very pleasant and very cheap', and concluded: 'I go much to the theatre. It is one of the best in Germany, but far, far behind that of Copenhagen in taste and accomplishment. But that is so everywhere in Germany' – an opinion which Hans Andersen had expressed twenty years earlier. One would like to know which plays Ibsen saw but, unhelpful as so often, he names none.

Hegel had expressed doubts about the propriety of Ibsen's suggested sub-title for his new play; he feared that some might think *Our Lord & Co* blasphemous, and Ibsen agreed to alter it. 'I was myself half of the same opinion', he told Hegel in the same letter, 'though the expression would not have offended anyone *once they had read the play*. It contains no word on religious matters; but people can't know that in advance, and the sub-title might well cause offence; so, away with it! The play will be the most artistically finished work I have yet written ... I hope to send you the fair copy in February.' He was less good than his word; he did not complete even his first draft until 28 February. 'It is a blessed feeling', he wrote to Hegel that day, 'to be done with something which for a whole year now has never for a single day been out of my thoughts.'

The fair-copying of his manuscript took him a further nine weeks, a long time, one might think, even allowing for a certain amount of rewriting. A more cogent reason for this apparent dilatoriness, however, may have been his reluctance to return (as he would then have had to have done) to the heart-searching labour of *Emperor and Galilean*, that burden which had for so long been on his back. Replying on 23 March to Martin Schneekloth, the young Dane who had so sharply observed his marriage, and who had inquired about the progress of the Roman play, Ibsen wrote: 'I am not thinking about "Julian" for the moment, and don't want to bother about him in the near future; to be honest, I shrink from both the man and the theme ... We visit the theatre regularly ... Life is fabulously cheap here. In the New Year Sigurd became a pupil at Dr Holbe's famous school, which is principally attended by foreigners, Americans, English, Russians, Poles, etc ... We shall stay here at least a year.'

Sigurd later recalled to his wife Bergliot how poor his parents were during those first months in Dresden. He himself was looked down on by his schoolmates because he was so ill-dressed; Suzannah made his clothes out of his father's old ones, and cut them big enough to allow for growth. His trousers were too long, and the boys in the street used to run after him shouting: '*Du tretst in deine Hosen! Du tretst in deine Hosen!* [You're treading on your trousers!].' Once, when Ibsen suggested that Sigurd should bring some of his schoolfriends home, he told his father that he 'didn't want to', ashamed that they should see how humbly his parents lived; at which his father gave him 'a long, wounded, and questioning look' which left such an impression on him that 'I would have given years of my life to have unsaid it.' The neighbours' children mocked him too, and he had to make up fantastic tales to impress them, such as that his mother (who had been ill for some weeks, and had left the shopping to him) was a Negress who never went out of the house, and that he had a brother whom his parents kept in a box. Suzannah brought him up austerely, continually drumming into him the importance of duty; once when he had cut his head so that it bled and he was running a fever, Suzannah simply bandaged it and sent him to school as usual.

When there was some occasion for celebration, such as the anniversary of their wedding, or Suzannah's or Sigurd's birthday, Ibsen would design an imitation banknote for a certain sum, to be cashed when sufficient funds should be in hand. Several of these banknotes have survived, the earliest from 1867 when he was on Ischia writing *Peer Gynt*, and continuing as late as 1875, after the move to Munich. Most of them contain drawings of either a cat or an eagle – both nicknames that he had affectionately coined for Suzannah. (His own nickname in the family was 'The Tiger' or 'The Bear'.) He also on occasion awarded them medals, often copied from real medals, and sometimes amused himself by sketching these in the margins of his manuscripts.

Sigurd remembered too how Suzannah used to force Ibsen to write, when the mood was not on him. Gradually he realized that she was right. 'When you are not in the mood to write', he told Sigurd many years later, 'you must nevertheless sit down calmly at your desk, and the inspiration will come of itself.' Bergliot (who recorded her husband's memories) adds an interesting note on Suzannah which needs to be measured against the detractions of casual observers. 'From the very beginning of their marriage she tried to keep away friends or acquaintances who might distract him ... She let nothing and no one disturb him ... Nor could anyone give him enthusiasm as she could. When he was depressed she knew how to ignite his courage. One needs to have personally heard her proclaim her fanatical faith to understand the strength she gave him through the years. When hostile criticism depressed him she did not lose courage. Her eyes blazed and she said: "With your genius, what should you care what this rabble writes?" And it always ended with his walking calmly into his study.'

He still, even after he had come to Dresden, hankered after painting, and it cost Suzannah much effort to dissuade him from pursuing it seriously. 'I had to fight with him', she told Sigurd, who commented to Bergliot: 'The world can thank my mother that it has one bad painter the fewer and got a great writer instead.'

About this time, Ibsen spotted an item of news in the Danish press which must surely have caused those tight lips to allow themselves the luxury of a small smile. To few authors is it granted to see a hostile critic of their work publicly humiliated; but in March Clemens Petersen, whose review of *Peer Gynt* had so enraged Ibsen, became involved in a homosexual scandal concerning some boys at a school where he had been lecturing, and had to leave hurriedly for the United States, where for the next thirty-five years he devoted himself to religious journalism among the Scandinavian-Americans, a fate which even Ibsen himself might have hesitated to wish on a leading literary critic. 'This is a dreadful business about Clemens Petersen,' he wrote to Hegel on 7 April. 'I have always had strong suspicions about his character; but such a thing – !' Petersen's passionate admiration of Bjørnson, which may have had a sexual element in it (not that Bjørnson would have approved of or been likely to perceive that), was probably partly responsible for his denigration of Ibsen's work; Ibsen may well have appeared to him principally as a challenger to his idol. As soon as he left Denmark, Petersen's name became taboo and his influence ceased. His friends subscribed to bring him home in 1904, and he died ten years later at the age of eighty-four, almost forgotten.

During 1869 the rift between Ibsen and Bjørnson gradually widened. They had not corresponded since the end of 1867, and their letters to third parties show that a mutual distrust had developed. 'From Ibsen', wrote Bjørnson to Hegel on 25 February, 'I've heard nothing but a discourtesy which he sent me through someone else. Whether I have deserved it, I don't know, nor care; for now I'm tired; he must sail his own moody sea.' And on 15 July Ibsen cynically observed to Brandes, with whom Bjørnson had likewise recently quarrelled: 'For him [Bjørnson] there exist only two kinds of men, those whom he might use and those who embarrass him' – an ungrateful and untrue remark. More accurately, he added: 'However good Bjørnson may be at analysing his own characters, he is a poor psychologist when it comes to dealing with real people.'

The exact cause of their alienation remains unknown; but that it should have happened when the two were separated by half Europe is hardly surprising. Both were sharptongued, free in their condemnation of other human beings, inordinately sensitive to any kind of criticism and, as such men are, more than usually ready to believe gossip. Even if they did not say caustic things about each other, and they pretty certainly did, we may be sure that rumours of such remarks reached both pairs of ears. 'Have I not experienced', Bjørnson had publicly declared at Bergen six years earlier, 'that my friend Ibsen has been held up against me for the purpose of disparaging me, and I against him to disparage him?' If they had been able to meet, the differences might have been resolved, as they were when, many years later, they did at last see one another. But Ibsen's suspicions were intensified by something, whether true or false we do not know, which his old Holland acquaintance Jakob Løkke told him in Stockholm later that summer. Bjørnson tried to mend things by writing Ibsen a friendly letter in September, ten days before the publication of *The League of Youth*, saying that he was looking forward to reading the play; but the implied insult to him contained in the character of Stensgaard, and the continued success of the play on the stage, widened the gap impossibly; and although Ibsen told Hegel in December that he would like a reconciliation, it was to be eight years before they corresponded again and fifteen before they met.

Hegel held *The League of Youth* over until the autumn, when the publication of the play and its stage première would conveniently coincide, and Ibsen spent the summer relaxing. 'I lead a pleasant and carefree life', he wrote to Lorentz Dietrichson on 28 May, 'and plan to get down to

"Julian" in the autumn.' Asking Dietrichson to write a brief biographical sketch of him to preface a German translation of *Brand* which was to be published that autumn,[1] he exhorted him to 'forget the starving poet stuff; tell rather how the government and Storthing have granted me a pension, how I travel, am happy in *dem grossen Vaterlande,* etc.' Dietrichson has recorded how, on receiving this letter, he failed to recognize the neat, elegant handwriting, so unlike the scratchy script of Ibsen's earlier correspondence; and a photograph which followed three weeks later, with the words: 'I enclose the requested likeness of my phiz; I don't know whether you will recognize me from my bearded period,' surprised him equally with its trimly barbered head, mutton-chop whiskers and assured expression in the eyes. Ibsen's letter included a defensive note on *The League of Youth*: 'The play is a pure comedy and nothing else. People in Norway may say that I have portrayed specific persons and circumstances, but this is untrue; though I have used models, which is as necessary for a writer of comedy as for a painter or sculptor.'

During the spring of 1869 Ibsen had applied to the Norwegian government for a stipend of 300 specie-dollars (£75) to enable him to spend a year in Sweden studying the art, literature, and other aspects of that country's cultural life. This was granted him; meanwhile he received an invitation to take part in an orthographic conference in Stockholm, convened in order to agree on a unified spelling for the three Scandinavian countries (a purpose in which it failed signally). After changing his lodgings in Dresden to a first-floor apartment at Königsbrücker-Strasse 33, he departed for Stockholm on 20 July.

1. As things turned out, although the translator, P. F. Siebold, a travelling salesman from Kassel, completed his translation that autumn, he did not succeed in getting it published until 1872, when it marked the first appearance of any of Ibsen's plays in a non-Scandinavian language. John Grieg, the brother of Edvard Grieg, had translated *The Pretenders* into German as early as 1866, but never managed to find a publisher.

Stockholm was then, apart from its impressive public buildings, still largely a town of small wooden houses; a piped water system had only just been introduced, and men and girls with buckets on yokes could still be seen selling water from the wells. Citizens were awakened at night by the collectors of night-soil, thumping on the door with their long poles. As the closets were usually in the attic, the soil was commonly thrown out of the windows into, or at, the carts; foreign travellers compared Stockholm to Constantinople for its combination of beauty and filth.

Ibsen took lodgings at Herkulesgatan 5, a narrow street just across the bridge from the royal palace, and was regally entertained. 'I live here', he wrote to his brother-in-law, J. H. Thoresen, on 2 August, 'in an endless round of festivities. I have not had a single day when I have not been invited to dinner or something.' The other delegates to the conference included Knud Knudsen, his old enemy from the Norwegian Christiania Theatre, and Jakob Løkke of the Learned Holland circle, who widened the rift between Ibsen and Bjørnson by telling the former of some unkind things the latter had reputedly said of him. He saw a good deal of Lorentz Dietrichson, and renewed his acquaintance with Count Snoilsky, to whom he apologized for the halter incident in Rome. He had, he said, changed his mind about Manderström, who was Snoilsky's uncle, and had come to the conclusion that he was not really to blame. 'Then we are still as far apart as ever on this subject', replied Snoilsky, 'for I have come to the conclusion that he was.' Ibsen spent several days with a family named Limnell, who had a villa on Lake Mälaren. Herr Limnell held a high position in the railways, and his wife, the widow of a famous newspaper editor, was the centre of a literary circle; Ibsen was to thank her for her hospitality in one of his best longer poems. He met writers, actors, and politicians, one of whom, a lively young liberal named Adolf Hedin, rebuked him for his conservatism – an incident which was later to provoke another interesting poetic declaration.

Ibsen's appearance and demeanour caused astonishment. 'People had expected the author of *Brand*', writes Dietrichson, 'to be an earnest, severe old ascetic, and there appeared an elegant, youngish man in a velvet coat, refined, lively and likeable. People could not reconcile *Brand* with its author,[2] and several people openly expressed their amazement, amounting in some cases to downright disappointment; but soon he had taken them all by storm, especially the ladies.' On 22 September, two months after his arrival, he told Hegel: 'My stay in Sweden has been, and still is, one long festivity. From all sides I meet a courtesy and friendliness which cannot be described ... I have plenty of plans for new works; but to get down to them I must find solitude again; I cannot write here.'

Thus Ibsen, for the first time in his life, found himself lionized; and the experience was not distasteful. King Carl XV, who, in his enjoyment of the company of writers, artists, and pretty women, much resembled our own Charles II, invited him several times to the palace, where (he later related to John Paulsen), he spent 'unforgettable' and highly informal evenings, continuing long after midnight, with champagne and merry stories, 'not always for dainty ears'.

Shortly before he left, the director and actors of the Royal Theatre held a farewell dinner for him and Dietrichson (who was leaving at the same time) at the Hôtel du Nord in Carl XII's Torg. The actor Daniel Hwasser, proposing Ibsen's health, recited a poem in Swedish which Ibsen only gradually recognized as a very free translation of one of his

2. August Strindberg, who in 1869 was twenty and had just failed his medical exams and concluded his brief and calamitous career as a professional actor, did not meet Ibsen (then or ever), but eight years later he recalled the impression Ibsen made in Sweden: 'Who does not remember the famous poet's appearance when he visited Stockholm a few years back? Dressed in a velvet jacket, a white waistcoat with black buttons, and a cape of the latest fashion, with an elegant cane in his hand and a protective self-mocking curl to his lip, he went his way, avoiding all deep subjects of conversation.'

own songs from *Love's Comedy*. 'It was very droll', recalled
Dietrichson, 'to see Ibsen's expression as, towards the conclusion of the first verse, he recognized his own child.' Dietrichson wrote an article about him in the leading Swedish
illustrated weekly, *Ny Illustrerad Tidning*, describing him
as 'one of the greatest poets of our time, if not absolutely the
greatest'; and so considerable was the impact Ibsen made on
Stockholm that someone advised the king to recommend
that he be chosen to represent his country that autumn at
the official opening of the Suez Canal. Ibsen received the
invitation with unmixed delight. 'I get everything free', he
wrote happily to J. H. Thoresen on 24 September, 'the trip
from Paris and back included.' And on his last evening in
Stockholm, Carl XV invited him to the palace and personally invested him with the Order of Vasa, the first of
those many medals he was to receive and in which he took so
curious and childlike a pride.

On 29 September Ibsen left Stockholm for Dresden. The
next day, while he was en route, *The League of Youth* was
published in Copenhagen.

The importance of *The League of Youth* to a modern reader
lies in the fact that it was Ibsen's first attempt to write a play
entirely in modern colloquial dialogue. The plot must be
briefly summarized, since the play is little known, though its
complexity is such that any summary must seem bewildering. The scene is a market town in south Norway, generally thought to have been modelled on Skien. Stensgaard,
an ambitious young liberal politician, in a burst of enthusiasm at an Independence Day celebration, founds an anti-
capitalist party which he christens the League of Youth. In
the course of his speech he delivers an eloquent attack on the
local ironmaster, Brattsberg; he does not name him, however, and Brattsberg thinks he is referring to a landowner
named Monsen, whose daughter, Ragna, Stensgaard has
been courting. Fickle in love as in all else, Stensgaard now
takes a fancy to Brattsberg's daughter, Thora, and to restore

himself to favour makes a public apology to her father, who shows him the door in a fury. Then Stensgaard learns that Brattsberg's son, Erik, has forged a bill, realizes that Brattsberg may be disgraced too, and turns his attentions back to Ragna Monsen. But he hears that Monsen may likewise be involved in the scandal, so proposes to a rich tradesman's widow named Mrs·Rundholmen. Then he finds that Monsen was involved but not Brattsberg, and renews his interest in Thora. She no longer wants him; in despair, he announces his engagement to Mrs Rundholmen; but she has accepted someone else, and he is left with nobody. Yet his future is by no means gloomy. 'Mark my words,' says someone at the end of the play. 'In ten or fifteen years Stensgaard will be in Parliament or the Privy Council'; and another character adds a quotation from Napoleon: 'Double-dealing is the stuff of which politicians are made.'

Ibsen had for some time sensed that the dialogue of drama must move towards a greater colloquialism, as the novel had been doing, and Bjørnson had shown him the way four years earlier in a two-act comedy called *The Newly Wedded Couple*, a slight piece about a young wife bound to her parents of which Ibsen, on reading it, is said to have remarked: 'This is how we must write modern drama.' He tried, in *The League of Youth*, to escape as far as possible from all the old conventions of artificial drama (as witness his proud claim to Georg Brandes that he had completed it 'without a single monologue or aside'). Having raised poetic drama to its finest peak since Shakespeare (for *Brand* and *Peer Gynt* are greater *plays* than anything by Racine, Goethe, or Schiller, none of whose works is tolerable in the theatre if performed in any language but its own), he had set himself to cultivate, as he was later to phrase it, 'the much more difficult art of writing the genuine, plain language spoken in life'. As William Archer observed: 'Having now outgrown his youthful romanticism, and laid down, in *Brand* and *Peer Gynt*, the fundamental positions of his criticism of life, he felt that, to carry that criticism into detail, he must come to closer quarters with reality; and to that end he required a suppler instrument than verse.'

Over the next thirty years *The League of Youth* was to prove the most popular (if judged by the number of performances given) of all Ibsen's plays in Norway. Since 1900, however, it has been staged less often than any other of his established plays, there as elsewhere. Edmund Gosse dismissed it as 'the most provincial of all Ibsen's mature works', an adjective that was often later to be aimed at Ibsen by his denigrators. In fact, *The League of Youth* is no more provincial than *The Pillars of Society* or *An Enemy of the People*, which likewise have as their themes the petty-mindedness which prevails in small communities; and anyway the word 'provincial' has ceased to be pejorative when applied to drama. The real reason for posterity's lack of interest in the play lies, despite Ibsen's professed aim in writing it, in the outdatedness of its technique. The synopsis given above is much simplified; it omits (otherwise it would have been as unravellable as those verbal cats'-cradles which confront us in opera programmes) a mesh of sub-plots which depend for their working on the old-fashioned machinery of misdirected letters, overheard conversations and the like which Ibsen had inherited from Holberg and which commentators have so often mistakenly attributed to his supposed admiration for Scribe. Holberg's plays, Ibsen wrote to Lorentz Dietrichson on 28 May 1869, shortly after sending the last pages of *The League of Youth* to the printers, were 'almost the only book I never tire of reading'; but the conventions of mannered comedy, amusing in their proper context, are destructive to any play that sets out to impress by its realism. They did not bother nineteenth-century audiences, but they bother us. To keep a tightly knit plot (as opposed to the looser, freer and more modern structures of *Brand* and *Peer Gynt*) running was something that Ibsen was not yet able to manage without recourse to the rusty starting-handle of coincidence.[3] The play is, moreover, full of topical references

3. 'It is much easier', he told William Archer 'to write a piece like

which were a source of delight and fury to Ibsen's contemporaries, but which would be lost on a modern audience.
As Archer remarked, it was essentially an experimental
transitional work; and by the time Ibsen became known
abroad, ten years later, its technique was already outdated.

With all its faults, however, it was an advance on the technique of the day. The plot never stops moving – something
that can scarcely be said of any other comedy of the period,
apart from the farces of Labiche – and, like every other play
Ibsen had written since *St John's Night*, it contains a galaxy
of minutely observed characters. Unlike Strindberg, who was
often perfunctory in his drawing of secondary personages,
Ibsen never, in his maturity, created the smallest role that
was not worth the playing. Stensgaard, the leading character, has been well summed up as 'Peer Gynt as a politician'.
An 'inescapably split personality', as Dr Fjeldbo describes
him in the play, he is another in the long line of self-deceiv-
ers which began with Julian Poulsen in *St John's Night* (or
even with Severus in *Norma*), and was to continue through
Karsten Bernick, Torvald Helmer, Hjalmar Ekdal and Ulrik
Brendel to its culmination in John Gabriel Borkman and
Arnold Rubek. Ibsen once admitted that Stensgaard contained a good deal of himself, a curious confession, one
might think, from the writer who, above all others, has come
to be associated with a hatred of self-deception. But Brand,
we must remember, Ibsen had declared to be himself 'in his
best moments', and Stensgaard, like Peer Gynt, presumably
represented those qualities in himself of which he was
ashamed and which he sought, not always successfully, to
subdue – cowardice, readiness to compromise when faced
with unpleasant realities, and facile eloquence. Bjørnson,
while possessing many qualities which Ibsen envied, at the
same time personified one of the subtlest snares that can

Brand or *Peer Gynt*, in which you can bring in a little of everything,
than to carry through a severely logical scheme, like that of *John
Gabriel Borkman*, for example.'

destroy a writer: the temptation to give full rein to those gifts which bring the easiest and most immediate success; and in this sense Ibsen may have been speaking honestly when, later, he asserted that Stensgaard was not (as his contemporaries assumed) a portrayal of Bjørnson, Johan Sverdrup, or any other specific individual. The real model for Stensgaard, as for Peer Gynt, was any Norwegian with charm and eloquence, which in practice meant, then as now, almost any Norwegian, including Ibsen himself.

Of the other characters, Daniel Hejre, a clever and malicious man who has lost his money but retained his wit, is generally accepted as being a portrait of the dramatist's father; and Aslaksen, a timid and bibulous printer who was to re-appear, still timid but now a teetotaller, in *An Enemy of the People*, seems to have been based on N. F. Axelsen, the publisher of the student magazine *Andhrimner*, who, like Aslaksen, apparently disapproved of provocative young writers. The most important character for Ibsen's future and the future of drama, however, was the minor figure of Selma Brattsberg, the ironmaster's young daughter-in-law who, chafing against the bonds of marriage, complains to her husband: 'You dressed me up like a doll; you played with me as one plays with a child.' When Georg Brandes read the play he suggested in his review that she, or a character like her, might make a good central figure for a later work, a suggestion which ten years later was to bring forth remarkable fruit.

The League of Youth received mixed notices in the Scandinavian press. Ibsen's old friend Aasmund Vinje probably summed up the general feeling when he wrote in *Dølen*: 'Those who think that they or their friends are portrayed in the play complain and find it bad; but those who enjoy seeing these people so caricatured are happy, and find it a good piece.' As one of the former, he compared Ibsen to Don Quixote, expressed indignation at Ibsen's mockery of his country, and hoped that he would soon get bored with 'acting Brand'.

Ibsen, however, saw none of these reviews until several weeks after they had appeared, for on his return to Dresden at the beginning of October he had departed almost immediately by train for Paris on the first stage of his journey to Suez. What impression did Paris make on him? We do not know, for of this, as of his first sighting of Venice and Florence in 1864, he has left no word. With the other delegates from northern Europe he entrained for Marseilles, and thence, on 9 October, he sailed on the SS *Moeris* for Alexandria.

12

Egypt
1869

THERE were eighty-six guests of the Khedive aboard the *Moeris*: Frenchmen, Germans, Dutchmen, Spaniards and Scandinavians, but no Englishmen; they followed with the Russians and others in another ship the next day. Surprisingly few of the names of Ibsen's fellow-travellers mean anything today; one exception was Théophile Gautier, who fell down the steps to the dining saloon on the first morning, dislocated a shoulder and spent the rest of the voyage with his arm in a sling. Ibsen's ignorance of French prevented him from holding any conversation with him. The only other Norwegian delegate was an Egyptologist, Professor J. D. C. Lieblein, who had condemned *Brand* as an insane work, but got on with its author well. Lorentz Dietrichson should have accompanied them, but was prevented by illness. Ibsen, as usual, kept mainly to his fellow-Scandinavians throughout his holiday. These included a pleasant young Danish literary historian, Peter Hansen (later to become director of the Royal Theatre in Copenhagen), and a Swedish army captain, Oscar von Knorring, who had served as a volunteer in the first (1849) Schleswig-Holstein war, was something of a composer, and later published a naïve but readable account of his visit to Suez. He noted as his first impression of Ibsen that he had 'elegant manners and an agreeable social tone'.

The voyage across the Mediterranean was rough, and Lieblein, who sent regular and lively dispatches back to *Morgenbladet*, reported on the second day that 'there has been some distress among the bulk of the passengers'.[1] They sailed between Sardinia and Corsica, the high mountains of which reminded Lieblein, and doubtless Ibsen too, of the Norwegian coast; then, the next day, they passed close to Caprera, where Garibaldi was living in retirement, and wondered which of the buildings there was 'the home of the great adventurer and republican'. They skirted Sicily, and admired Stromboli; the Plough sank towards the horizon and the moon rose higher towards her zenith as they proceeded south. The weather remained rough all the way, so that 'several of the party were unable to take full advantage of the Khedive's hospitality', which included four meals a day. At last, on 13 October, after four days at sea, they reached Alexandria.

Ferdinand de Lesseps, the creator of the Canal, was there in person to greet them, and they were escorted to the Hôtel d'Europe, where 'the best rooms and carriages with dragomans' were placed at their disposal. They spent two days in Alexandria, visiting among other memorabilia Pompey's Pillar and Cleopatra's Needles (not yet removed to the Thames Embankment and New York's Central Park) and were banqueted in the Khedive's garden, where they were entertained with European military music and 'somewhat monotonous Arab melodies'. At eight in the morning of 17 October they left Alexandria and, five hours later, arrived in Cairo.

The guests stayed five days in the Egyptian capital, luxuriously accommodated at the Hôtel de l'Orient, where von Knorring notes that he and Ibsen 'spent many hours under palm trees on a terrace. I take this opportunity', he added, 'publicly to record my gratitude for the many interesting and delightful moments which the amiable and truly cul-

1. Except where otherwise specified, all quoted references to the Egyptian journey are from Lieblein's dispatches to *Morgenbladet*, printed on 21 October, 6, 14 and 24 November, and 5, 17 and 23 December 1869.

tivated Henrik Ibsen's company afforded me during both my journey to Egypt and our passage up the Nile.' They walked through the bazaars, 'streets too narrow for any vehicle to enter', were shown the mosques and the citadel, from which they could distantly glimpse the Pyramids, and made expeditions to the museum at Bulak, old Cairo, where they saw the tombs of the Mamelukes, and Heliopolis, whence Ibsen sent Suzannah some flowers. The day after their arrival, the Khedive, 'a little, fat, powerfully built man in European dress', received them at his palace, Kasr-el-Nil; he was 'friendly, and talked with everyone … in fairly fluent French', which must have been lost on Ibsen. Von Knorring had an introduction to de Lesseps, who gave him a signed photograph; whether Ibsen accompanied him on his visit to the great man he does not say.

Not content with paying his guests' passages from Paris and back ('Who will finally foot the bill for all this hospitality may be questioned,' reflected Lieblein. 'Probably the unfortunate fellah, who is already poor enough without our coming and eating his last sheep'), the Khedive, Ismael Pasha, had arranged a three-week expedition for them up the Nile under the guidance of his conservator, the French Egyptologist Mariette Bey, who eighteen years earlier had discovered the subterranean catacombs of the Apis bulls. On the morning of 22 October they set off in three steamers, each towing a *dahaby*, or barge, covered by an awning for the greater comfort of the passengers. Ibsen and von Knorring shared a cabin on the SS *Ferus*, which also carried Lieblein, a Swiss, a Dutchman and seventeen Germans, whose behaviour was to earn them a derogatory simile in a poem which Ibsen later wrote about the trip and which was to involve him in a controversy in the German press. They tried to insist that the German flag be hoisted on the ship, ' "Scandinavians, Dutchmen and Swiss being of course pure Germans"; but this was luckily prevented, and we still sail under the crescent of Turkey, whose guests we are. The Germans are frightened lest the French hear of their failure, but the secret is already abroad ... The French and German guests are on very uneasy terms.' Lieblein found the Prussians 'more overbearing than ever after their military exploits of recent years'; only nine months were to elapse before the outbreak of the Franco-Prussian War.

Several of the places they had hoped to visit en route were unfortunately rendered inaccessible by heavy floods, including Gizeh, so that Ibsen, who had written about the Sphinx in *Peer Gynt*, glimpsed it only from afar; also Memphis, Sakkara, the tombs at Beni-Hasan, and the ruins of Abydos. On the second day von Knorring and Ibsen intervened to save an aged Arab from being flogged by the ship's dragoman for idleness, an action which earned them the good will of the crew for the remainder of the expedition. One imagines that Captain von Knorring did most of the intervening. That same day they were surprised by a visit from Coptic monks from a monastery, who swam out to them, 'climbed up on the stern and asked for *baksheesh* ... Since they presented themselves to the passengers in a state of the utmost primitiveness, they had nothing to put the money in but stuffed it all, silver and copper alike, into their mouths.'

On the third day they stopped at Roda, where they were shown round a sugar factory employing five thousand workers by the English manager, 'with great courtesy'. At Assiut they inspected the great tombs. As Ibsen and Lieblein were returning, they 'walked along the river bank and came to a great white brick house. Outside the entrance sat two distinguished-looking Arabs. They seemed glad to see us, offered us chairs, and had us served with coffee.' One of the Arabs spoke fluent French and explained that this was a school and they the teachers; they invited Lieblein and Ibsen in, and the pupils demonstrated their skill in French and mathematics. Lieblein wrote a message of thanks on the blackboard. Upstairs they were shown a dormitory with a hundred and fifty beds; the pupils wore a kind of military uniform after the French pattern.

In the evening the travellers were entertained, on sofas, to a 'Fantasia by Torchlight', songs and dances performed by five expensively dressed and bejewelled girls. 'Since this was ... enacted in the open air', comments Lieblein prudishly, 'the dance was reasonably decent, though certain wild Frenchmen did everything to persuade the performers into the licentiousness with which such dances customarily end.'

The heat grew intense as they approached the 26th parallel, reaching 28° Réaumur (95° Fahrenheit). The natives hereabouts wore nothing but fig leaves, 'a fashion which the Europeans observed with envy, making a few, admittedly incomplete, attempts to imitate it'. They visited Kena, where there was more torchlight dancing, and the Hathor Temple at Dendera, and spent the last three days of October in Thebes. Here Ibsen and his companions walked round the twin cities, the Temple City on the east bank and the City of the Dead on the west; they saw the huge statue of Rameses the Great, eleven times life-size, the Temple of Amon Ra with its one hundred and thirty-four pillars, the Temple of Rameses III at Medinet Habu, the Memnon statue of which Ibsen had written in *Peer Gynt*, and the great tombs. Arabs offered them pieces of mummy for sale, and Ibsen bought a little woman's hand with a scarab ring. 'It must have come from a grand lady,' he later reflected, 'perhaps from one of the ancient noble houses of Egypt, and now her hand was being sold for a shilling.'

On the third day, 31 October, the Empress Eugénie arrived at Thebes amid spectacular ceremony. 'It was towards sunset,' Ibsen recalled twenty-four years later. 'Far in the distance a pillar of smoke approached, rising from the polished river. A handsome great Nile ship glided towards us. This must be the empress. But she was not there. Far, far away, a new pillar of smoke. An even larger ship, white, with silken banners. This *must* be she. No. A new Nile ship, bigger than the others, rose-pink. *Here* she sits, clothed in white, beautiful as Cleopatra, while the setting sun casts its gold over the banners and carpets and silken tents of the ship. Before a year had passed, she would be no mightier than the kings we had just visited.'

She was greeted by a firework display and, at six o'clock, a banquet in a specially erected tent which all the guests attended, while the crews and servants were given sheep to roast. They left Thebes the next day, and continued as far as the great cataract, pausing at Esna, Edfu, Gebel, Silfilis, Kom Ombo and Assuan, whence they rode on donkeys a short way into Nubia, through the desert to the Isle of Philae, in a temperature of over 100° Fahrenheit. At last, on 6 November, they returned towards Cairo.

From Assuan northwards, with the following current, they travelled 'almost with the speed of a railway'. The floods had by now subsided sufficiently for them to be able to visit some of the places they had missed on the outward trip, including Luxor and Girgeh, where they had another donkey-ride, this time to inspect the ruins of Abydos. They stopped at Beni-Hasan and Gizeh, where they spent their last night aboard the *Ferus*; next morning, they visited the Great Pyramids and Sakkara, the necropolis of Memphis, to see the Step Pyramid, the oldest of them all. At last, on the evening of 13 November, after twenty-three days on the river, they arrived in Cairo, where they rested for thirty-six hours before leaving by train for Alexandria, early on the morning of 15 November.

There, trouble awaited them. A hundred guests needed transport to Port Said, where the Canal was to be ceremonially opened, and the steamer was found to have room for only fifty. No extra ship could be organized before the following day, so Lieblein and some others, including Ibsen, persuaded the authorities to lay on a special train to take them overland to Ismailia. It arrived there in oriental style six hours behind schedule, but by sailing up the still officially unopened Canal they managed to arrive at Port Said in time for the beginning of the festivities on 16 November. These were inaugurated with a double religious service, Catholic and Muslim, attended by the Empress Eugénie and the Emperor Franz Josef of Austria. The following day, Wednesday, 17 November, the Suez Canal was declared open.

At nine in the morning the procession of ships began to enter the Canal, led by the Empress in *L'Aigle*. The Scandinavians travelled in the Danish corvette *Nordstjernen*; this should have gone with the second group of ships, but to their annoyance they had to wait while the third, fourth and fifth groups steamed past, 'doubtless', comments Lieblein, 'because the small nations have to stand aside for the big'. They did not get started until the next day, when further trouble awaited them, for the Egyptian ship in front of them went aground twice, so that the journey to Ismailia, which should have taken seven to eight hours, occupied three days. Determined not to miss the celebrations at Ismailia, the Scandinavians abandoned the Danish vessel and transferred to a barge towed by a small steamer, which, proceeding at 'the pace of a tortoise' got them there just in time.

Lieblein describes the scene at Ismailia as being 'like a story from the Thousand and One Nights', a phrase which Ibsen was later to borrow. 'The whole town and harbour [writes Lieblein] glittered with light and colour. Ships, quays and the town were brilliantly illuminated, fireworks were exploded, and everything was decked with the flags of all the nations.' Tents had been erected everywhere; the huge crowds included people of 'every race and country'; there were carriages, camels, donkeys, European brass bands, orchestras playing dance music, and Asian flutes and pipes. In the evening a great ball was held in a palace specially built by the Khedive for the occasion; some of the furnishings had evidently arrived only just in time, for the huge wall mirrors from Europe were 'still uncleaned and bearing the makers' labels'. The dancing continued until three in the morning.

All this must have been heady stuff for Ibsen; and shortly

before he had left Port Said to sail down the Canal, a letter
had been handed to him on the quayside which, in that setting at that moment, must more than ever have underlined
the narrowness and pettiness of life back home in Norway.

A month earlier, on 18 October, the day after Ibsen had
first arrived in Cairo, *The League of Youth* had received its
first performance at the Christiania Theatre. The political
implications of the play, which by then had been in the
bookshops for nearly three weeks, were already one of the
chief talking points in the capital. Ibsen was later to protest
that his characters were not meant to represent specific individuals ('There is a big difference between using someone as
a model and directly portraying him'), but it had become a
parlour game in Christiania to try to identify the models,
and it was of little comfort to those selected that traits of
other politicians were to be found in the same character.
Stensgaard's facile eloquence, his readiness to make a patriotic speech at the drop of a hat, and his repeated invocation
of the Almighty, were irresistibly reminiscent of Bjørnson;
and his penchant for proposing to rich ladies was a well-
known characteristic of another of the liberal leaders, Ole
Richter. Johan Sverdrup, who shared Bjørnson's love of
speechifying, was declared by others to be the original of
Stensgaard; and Lundestad, the rich farmer, was generally
assumed to be a caricature of Ueland, the leader of the
Peasants' faction in the liberal party.

The play, in short, as William Archer observed, offended
the entire progressive front. Ten days before its publication
Bjørnson had broken his silence towards Ibsen by writing to
him to tell him how much he was looking forward to reading
it; but when he did, it struck him, not unnaturally, as a stab
in the back for freedom. '*The League of Youth*', he declared
later, 'tried to paint our young freedom-loving party as a
mob of speculating mountebanks,' and he expressed his resentment to Sverdrup in an eloquent verse:

> If poesy's sacred grove be made
> The assassin's hiding-place, if this

> The new poetic fashion is
> Then I for one renounce its shade.[2]

Ibsen's apparent betrayal of the progressive cause seemed all the more ungrateful when it was recalled that Bjørnson had organized the fund for Ibsen five years earlier, and that both Richter and Sverdrup had been among the subscribers, as well as signing the petition for him to be awarded a Civil List pension. To quote William Archer, the cleavage between the right and the left was now at its sharpest in Norway, not merely in politics but also in religion, literature and even art; no one was regarded as an independent, and so Ibsen, to his embarrassment, found himself hailed as a champion of conservatism, a charge which had also (as we have seen) been levelled against him in Stockholm. As a consequence, the atmosphere on the opening night resembled that of a political meeting. This is how Suzannah described it in the letter which Ibsen received on the quayside at Port Said:

Dresden, 29 October 1869

Dear Ibsen,

I have received your letters, from which I see that you are having the best possible time. Sigurd says it is that thought which comforts him, and I say the same, take and enjoy everything which is offered you, one is not a king's guest every day.

But while you are enjoying the splendour of the south, there is a terrible storm in Christiania over *The League of Youth*. The first evening the first three acts were greeted with loud applause, but in the fourth act when Bastian says his line about what the nation is,[3] the gallery started to whistle, led by a few students who are fighting for the new language. What do you think of that?

According to *Morgenbladet* the evening went brilliantly, Krohn's and Isachsen's performances were works of art, all the company were called, *Morgenbladet* printed several excellent reports. The evening ended with thunderous applause.

2. Edmund Gosse's translation.
3. 'The people who have nothing and are nothing, who lie in chains.'

But then came the second evening, your benefit performance. They had already decided in advance that things were going to start now; the house was sold out, as soon as Lundestad finished his first speech the whistles began, time after time they were drowned by applause, but they would not stop. The curtain had to come down. The director had to step forward and ask for quiet so that the play could continue, and the commotion so grew that after the performance was over the lights had to be put out ... But your play has not suffered ...

Indeed it had not. Within ten days of the première, the sales of the book had been such that Hegel had already brought out a second edition; and so heavy was the demand for tickets at the theatre that seats were even sold in the space normally reserved for the orchestra. The violent demonstrations continued, however; the atmosphere in the theatre was that of an angry debating-chamber. Ibsen's later plays were to arouse far more widespread debate than *The League of Youth*, but none was to provoke audiences to such immediate and noisy enmity. Ibsen carefully kept every hostile criticism. 'My enemies have helped me so much,' he is said to have remarked. 'They protested so much that in the end people wanted to know who this man was whom everyone was always abusing.' On his return to Dresden, he recorded his reaction to these events in a poem, 'At Port Said':

> The eastern dawn
> Rose on the harbour.
> The flags of the nations
> Hung from the masts.
> The sound of music
> Preceded the hymn;
> A thousand cannon
> Baptised the Canal.
>
> The steamers moved
> Past the obelisk.
> Whispers reached me
> In my mother tongue.

The mirror I had polished
For male coquettes
Had been dirtied there
By a shower of saliva.

The gadfly bit me;
Memories stirred.
Bright star, I thank thee!
My home hasn't changed.
We hailed the frigate
From our small deck.
I waved my hand
And saluted the flag.

To the feasting, on!
Though the snake spit venom.
A chosen guest
Through the Bitter Lakes.
As the day dies, quenched,
Dreaming I slumber
Where Pharaoh drowned
And Moses passed over.

By the time he reached Ismailia, Ibsen had had enough of Egypt. Leaving Lieblein and von Knorring to enjoy another month of the Khedive's hospitality, he returned to Cairo, took the train to Alexandria and embarked for Marseilles. By the end of November he was back in Paris, where he stayed for a fortnight at his own expense. These two weeks provide another infuriating lacuna in our knowledge of Ibsen's life. No letters from him while he was there have survived; we know only that he spent much time visiting art galleries and exhibitions. What did he see? He was five years too early for the first Impressionist exhibition, but he might possibly have noticed the odd painting by Manet or Monet, who had begun to exhibit in 1861 and 1865 respectively; and one would like to think that he may have wandered in for a drink at the Café Guerbois on the Avenue de Clichy, where the future Impressionists (the name had not yet been coined) habitually gathered that year. But art galleries and exhibitions close soon after dark; how did he spend his later hours? Did he (we must remember his almost total ignorance of French) go to the theatre? Did he visit other, less decorous, places of entertainment? We do not know. He told no one; or if he did, they have not told us. In the middle of December he rejoined Suzannah and Sigurd in Dresden.

13

Doubts and Hesitations
1870

WHATEVER the limitations of Ibsen's physical courage may have been, he revelled in hostile criticism. 'The reception of *The League of Youth*', he wrote to Frederik Hegel on 14 December 1869, shortly after his return to Dresden, 'delights me. I was prepared for opposition to it, and would have been disappointed had there been none ... I will write to him [Bjørnson] today or tomorrow, and hope the affair will, despite all our differences, end in a reconciliation.' But he does not seem to have written any such letter, and it is difficult to imagine that by this time it would have had any effect, except to add fuel to the flames. He was already meditating a successor to *The League of Youth*: 'I am planning a new, serious, contemporary drama in three acts; I expect to start work on it in the very near future.' Of his visit to Egypt he had little to say. 'I had a pleasant journey. I got right down into Nubia and the Red Sea, underwent many experiences and met many interesting people. But it is best to sit quietly at home and look back on it all.'

'I shall probably come up to Christiania in the summer,' he informed his brother-in-law, Johan Thoresen, on 17 December. Year after year he toyed with the idea of revisiting Norway, without bringing himself to take the plunge. The reaction to *The League of Youth* must have confirmed his conviction that a writer did best to study his subject matter from a distance. 'From the attacks that I read,' he wrote to Jonas Collin on 4 January 1870, 'it seems that in Norway people regard empty phrase-making, hollowness and mean-mindedness as national characteristics which are therefore sacrosanct. But none of this bothers me in the least.'

Ibsen was not the only foreign writer who was studying his subject matter from a distance in Dresden that year. One wonders whether he ever noticed a short, bearded Russian, even smaller than himself,[1] who haunted the art galleries and theatres (which he found poor), and consumed in the cafés great quantities of ice cream, for which he had a passion. From August 1869 until July 1871 Fyodor Dostoyevsky was living in Dresden, at Viktoria-Strasse in the English quarter, not very far from Ibsen, writing *The Possessed* and heartily disliking both the city and its inhabitants, who were for ever short-changing him in the shops and restaurants and misdirecting him in the streets. 'Dresden is a very dull place,' he complained to a friend in December 1869, the month Ibsen returned from Egypt. 'I can't bear these Germans.' His working routine was very different from Ibsen's, though equally rigid. 'I get up at one o'clock in the afternoon because I do my work at night. I work from 3 to 5 p.m., then go for half an hour's walk to the post office and back through the Royal Gardens – always the same route. We dine at home and then I go out for another walk and back home through the Royal Gardens again. At home I have tea and at half past ten sit down to work and usually write till five o'clock in the morning. Then I go to bed and punctually on the stroke of six fall asleep. That is my life.'

Since Ibsen, too, liked to walk in the Gardens, and both men frequented the cafés on the Brühl Terrace, the two must surely have seen each other; but Dostoyevsky would not, any more than most other non-Scandinavians, have heard of Ibsen, and although Ibsen must at least have heard of Dostoyevsky, who had already published *Crime and Punishment* and *The Idiot*, the latter's presence in Dresden seems to have been known to very few. Nearly thirty years

1. Dostoyevsky stood five feet six inches, Ibsen about five feet seven and a half.

later Ibsen was to name *Crime and Punishment* as the Russian novel which attracted him most – and he was a great admirer of the Russian novelists, especially of Turgenev and even (despite Tolstoy's hatred of him) of *Anna Karenina*.[2] But we do not know whether he had yet read Dostoyevsky when they were neighbours in Dresden.

The 'contemporary drama' referred to in Ibsen's letter to Hegel of 14 December must have been *The Pillars of Society*, for his first notes for that play date from this year. 'The main theme', he recorded, 'must be how women sit modestly in the background while the men busily pursue their petty aims with an assurance that at once infuriates and impresses.' But he found unusual difficulty in (as he had written in another context) 'getting the beast under him'. On 25 January he informed Hegel that he hoped to have it ready by the following October, but two and a half months later he had to tell him that it had not yet got beyond the draft 'and since I have to put my travel notes in order it looks like being delayed for some time'. (He had promised articles on Egypt to both *Morgenbladet* and *Dansk Tidsskrift*, but never completed them.) When October arrived, far from having the play ready he could only tell Hegel that it had 'sufficiently developed in my mind for me to hope that any day now I may be able to start writing it'.

It was in fact to be a further seven years before he completed this next work, an extraordinary period of silence for one who had written three successful plays in five years and who was to be so prolific for the remainder of his life. Nor can it be explained away by the stumbling-block of *Emperor and Galilean.* This long gestation has been much debated by commentators; *The League of Youth*, it has been argued, shows that he had already and painlessly made the decision to abandon poetic drama for prose. Yet the reason is surely plain to see, and Georg Brandes, whose entry into Ibsen's life at this period was to be so important to both of them, stated it. Ibsen's artistic instincts, Brandes wrote in his auto-

2. For Tolstoy's opinion of Ibsen, see pp. 623–4.

biography, 'were unconsciously leading him in the direction of modern prose drama. He was to remain silent for several years while these new efforts were taking shape within him. Admittedly he had written the sharply modern satire, *The League of Youth*, in 1869, but without the intent of striking out a new path; which was why he straightway turned back to the distant past (in *Emperor and Galilean*).'

The key word here is *unconsciously*. Commentators may argue whether *The League of Youth* is the first of Ibsen's 'new' dramas, or a bridge between the old and the new. The point is that Ibsen himself did not yet know in which direction he was moving. He had not yet taken the decision to abandon poetry for prose; he was to arrive at that standpoint slowly and agonizingly over the next few years, and the long gestation of *The Pillars of Society*, the gathering, revision and publication of his poems, and the unusually flawed quality of *Emperor and Galilean*, are all evidence of the struggle within him, and of the hesitation with which he took that momentous step. Abandoning poetry, in which he felt so free, for prose, in which he felt so constricted, was for Ibsen like abandoning the Mediterranean to return to Norway. Georg Brandes was to remark that 'some time during the battle of life, a lyrical Pegasus must have been killed under him'. It would be truer to say that he shot it himself, and that from the action, much as we may regret that *Brand* and *Peer Gynt* were to have no successors, the whole of modern prose drama was to stem.

Ibsen's shortage of acquaintances in Dresden, which had chafed him during his first months there, seemed now not to bother him. On 6 March 1870 he addressed a few words of fatherly advice on the subject to Georg Brandes, now being reviled in Copenhagen for his open liaison with Caroline David, a lady who had left her husband (and whose daughter Marie, twenty-one years later, was to be accused by Strindberg, possibly for once justifiably, of having a Lesbian affair with the latter's wife Siri). Brandes's letters to Ibsen have, like so many others which Ibsen received, disappeared, but he had evidently pictured himself as a kind of Ishmael.

'You say you have no friends at home,' wrote Ibsen. 'I have often supposed this to be the case with you. When one stands, as you do, in so intensely personal a relationship to one's life-work, one cannot really expect to keep one's friends. But I think it is, in the long run, good for you that you are setting out[3] without leaving any friends behind. Friends are an expensive luxury; and when one invests one's capital in a calling or mission in this life, one cannot afford to have friends. The expensive thing about friends is not what one does for them but what, out of consideration for them, one leaves undone. Many spiritual ambitions have been crippled thus. I have been through this, and that is why I had to wait for several years before I succeeded in being myself.'

He returned to this theme in other letters that spring and summer, and the unusual emotion with which he, normally so uncommunicative a correspondent, expatiated on it seems further evidence of the split which was beginning to widen in his creative personality. On 29 May he warned Magdalene Thoresen (from whose clutches Brandes had only recently escaped, and who was now unsuccessfully refocusing her attentions on Bjørnson) against being over-sensitive to criticism. 'Most critical objections', he assured her, 'boil down to a reproach against the writer for being himself, thinking, feeling, seeing and writing as himself, instead of seeing and writing as the critic would have done, had he been able. The essential thing is to protect one's essential self, to keep it pure and free of all intrusive elements, and to draw a clear distinction between what one has merely experienced and what one has spiritually *lived through*; for only the latter is proper matter for creative writing.'

During the spring, a young Norwegian girl named Laura

3. Brandes was about to embark on a long and fruitful European tour, which was to bring him the friendship of Taine, Renan and, especially, John Stuart Mill.

Petersen had published an emotional contribution to the debate on women's rights in the form of an imaginary sequel to *Brand* entitled *Brand's Daughters*. She sent Ibsen a copy, which one would have expected him to ignore or, at best, formally acknowledge; but young girls sometimes brought out the cavalier in him, or anyway the father-figure, and on 11 June he wrote her a long and kindly reply. 'Are you thinking of continuing to write?' he inquired. 'Much more is needed than mere talent. One must have something to create from, some genuine experience. If one lacks that, one doesn't write in the true sense, one just makes books ... Intellectually, man is a long-sighted animal; we see most clearly from a distance; details distract; one must remove oneself from what one wishes to judge; one describes the summer best on a winter's day ... The main thing is to be true and faithful to oneself. It is not a question of willing to go in this direction or that, but of willing what one absolutely must, because one is oneself and cannot do otherwise. The rest is only lies.'

To be true and faithful to oneself, to will what one must; this, more perhaps than anything, was to be the theme of all Ibsen's future work. Nora gave herself at any rate a chance of salvation by following her own convictions; Mrs Alving was destroyed because she did not follow hers, but stayed with the husband she despised. Yet Ibsen, even this early in his career, knew that to follow one's convictions may end in self-destruction; Julian the Apostate and Rebecca West destroyed themselves thus, and who knows whether Nora's life ended more happily than Mrs Alving's? To write in verse for the printed page, as in *Brand* and *Peer Gynt*, which had brought him fame with a comparative minimum of controversy, or to write in prose for performance, which had stirred up a hornets' nest about his head? To remain in exile or to return home? The easy course would have been to continue in the medium of verse drama for reading, but in artistic matters Ibsen was never to take the easy course, any more than he was ever to take the easy way out of a fifth act. He

was never to write the same play twice, never to repeat a
success; he was to remain for ever the most restless of experimentalists.

The problem of whether or not to return to Norway crops
up as frequently in Ibsen's letters of this period as the importance of being oneself, a question of which, in Ibsen's
case, it was of course part. He knew well that he could never
deny the Norwegian in him, or turn his back, as other self-
exiled writers had done, on the country that had at first
rejected and now at last acclaimed him.[4] 'I long to come
northwards,' he wrote to Ole Schulerud's widow on 9 June (in
the letter already partly quoted),[5] 'if only for a short while – I
have grave doubts about settling permanently up there. I
fear it would cramp my activity ... Everything that is irrelevant or transitory acquires undeserved significance when
one stands in the midst of the tumult; or so I have always
felt. I have wandered widely since we parted. I have lived
and travelled in Italy for about five years; then two years in
various places in Germany. I have, as you may perhaps know,
also been in Egypt; have travelled all the way down into
Nubia; have sat by the Red Sea and looked across to Sinai.
Yet I feel more Norwegian in my soul than ever before; you
must not believe, as so many do, that I feel hostile towards
my native land. It is the excrescences on our social existence
which I hate; but they are not organic to it.' And he concluded his letter to Laura Petersen: 'Sooner or later I shall
come to Norway ... You must not think me so ill-disposed
towards my countrymen as many assert; and in any case I
can assure you that I am no more tolerant towards myself
than towards others ...'

4. He retained, like so many exiles, a nostalgic longing for the
simple food of his homeland. Several times in his letters he begs
friends to send him *gammelost*, the pungent Norwegian cheese, and
on 22 January 1871, complaining of the lack of fresh fish in Dresden, he
asked a chemist acquaintance in Trondhjem to send him a cask of a
north Norwegian speciality: 'a very delicate fish called redfish,
rosefish, rose-perch or some such name'.

5. See p. 183.

If Ibsen was getting nothing written that spring and summer of 1870, at least *The League of Youth* was being more widely performed than any of his previous plays. On 11 December it had been staged in Stockholm, at the Royal Theatre, and had been a success, for Sweden too had its Stensgaards in political life. In Copenhagen it at first seemed no more likely to get produced than anything else he had written. The censor of the Royal Theatre, old Carsten Hauch, an early befriender of Brandes but somewhat conservative in his literary judgements, reported to his board that the author had 'adopted an unfortunately fragmentary style which constantly, as it were, chops the dialogue into pieces', complained that 'one has to know about all the humbug which can be performed with false bills of hand, and the mysteries of fraud, to be able to follow the action and fully comprehend it', and concluded: 'The play is totally unsuited to the theatre.' But the board, doubtless mindful of the full houses the play was attracting in Christiania, asked Hauch to think again, whereupon he grudgingly admitted that, despite the 'chaotic obscurity and formlessness from which the play, in my view, so sadly suffers', since the board felt that 'the play must possess some significance as a political satire which it lacks aesthetically', he would not oppose its production. Johanne Luise Heiberg herself directed it, and it received its première in Copenhagen on 16 February 1870, the first Ibsen play to be performed in Denmark; and here, as in Christiania and Stockholm, despite some critical disapproval, it proved a success.

Ibsen spent the spring in a leisurely revision of *The Pretenders* for re-publication by Gyldendal, a task which principally involved amending the spelling so as to conform with the recommendations of the Stockholm orthographic conference. He also altered a few phrases to read more particularly and less generally, in defence to an objection Brandes had made on that score. When July came he packed Suzannah and Sigurd off for a holiday in Teplitz and, doubtless encouraged by his reception in Stockholm the pre-

vious summer and by the success of *The League of Youth*
in Denmark, went off to be lionized in Copenhagen. He
sailed from Lübeck on 19 July, a momentous day for
Europe, for it marked the outbreak of the Franco-Prussian
War. Brandes, unfortunately, was in England, being
horrified by the poverty, disappointed with Oxford and with
the theatres and ladies of London, enjoying the Zoo and
Kew Gardens and talking French (since his English was
poor) with John Stuart Mill at Blackheath. But Ibsen met his
publisher, Frederik Hegel, for the first time, and renewed
two acquaintances which he had fleetingly made on his
study visit eighteen years before, with Johanne Luise Heiberg and Hans Christian Andersen.

Hegel had received a neurotic letter from Bjørnson warning him about his guest and concluding: 'Beware of Ibsen!
He is ungrateful, and a man who is that is capable of anything!' But he had by now doubtless learned to discount
whatever the two writers said about each other, and he took
excellent care of Ibsen throughout the latter's stay, though
he never, during their long friendship, managed to penetrate Ibsen's reserve. 'Ibsen is an extremely courteous man
and pleasant to do business with,' he wrote eleven years later,
'but very cautious and withdrawn, and I have the feeling
that I haven't got any closer to him now than in 1866 when I
had the honour to publish *Brand* for the first time – and that
saddens me.'

Hans Andersen[6] was eager to meet the new dramatist,

6. Edmund Gosse, who met Andersen at the Melchiors' two years
later, recorded a vivid impression of him: 'a very tall, elderly gentleman, dressed in a complete suit of brown, and in a curly wig of the
same shade of snuff-colour. I was almost painfully struck, at the first
moment, by the grotesque ugliness of his face and hands, and by his
enormously long and swinging arms; but this impression passed away
as soon as he began to speak ... Gentleness and ingenuousness
breathed from everything he said ... He had but to speak, almost
to smile, and the man of genius stood revealed.' Andersen read a story
to Gosse but lost his voice during the conversation that ensued and
had to be 'conducted to his bed with infinite precautions'. Gosse

having apparently forgotten their brief encounter in 1852.
On 11 August he noted in his diary: 'Fru Melchior told me
that the poet Ibsen was dining today with Carl Bloch, and
expressed surprise that I had not been invited. I was put in a
bad humour by the thought of how little attention B. had
paid to me.' 'I wasn't there,' he wrote the next day to Henriette Collin, 'but would have liked to have been invited, to
see at last this Norwegian poet who doesn't like the Norwegians.' A week later he got his wish, when Moritz Gerson
Melchior, a politician in whose eighteenth-century house
overlooking the Sound Andersen had, by a generous arrangement, a permanent suite of three or four rooms, gave a
party for the two writers. Andersen tried to prepare himself
for the meeting with a little homework, and the result depressed him. 'Read *Peer Gynt*,' he noted in his diary for 18
August, 'which is written by a mad poet. One goes crazy
oneself reading this book. The poetry isn't good either, there
is something sick and distraught about the whole thing. Am
sorry I read it, as Ibsen is coming here this evening for the
first time. I've never seen him; he's said to be taciturn and
gloomy.' But the occasion passed off unexpectedly well, for
the diary continues: 'After dinner he arrived with Bloch,
and made a good impression ... He talked well and amiably.
We all liked him.'

Andersen's diary conceals how close the evening came to
being a disaster. According to John Paulsen, who had the
story from Ibsen himself:

Many of the city's most notable personages were among the
guests. Everyone had arrived and was ready to sit down, but no
Andersen descended from his rooms upstairs. A quarter of an
hour passed, half an hour; a nervous restlessness settled on the
company, and the hostess looked unhappy. Message after message was sent up, but he still did not appear. The hostess quietly

---

especially remembered his 'amazingly long and bony hand – a great
brown hand almost like that of a man of the wood – grasping my
shoulder as he read to me'.

went upstairs, but returned with a more worried expression than
before. He would not come down. No one said anything to the
guest of honour, but Ibsen sensed what was afoot. Andersen did
not like to be with people of whose sympathy he was not sure.
When people mentioned strange authors he would naïvely ask:
'Does he admire me?' The atmosphere grew more embarrassed.
It was now three-quarters of an hour past the appointed time for
supper. The host and hostess were at a loss what to do. Were they
to sit down without Andersen?

Then Ibsen saved the situation. He took his host aside and asked
to be allowed to go up to Andersen's room and speak with him.
The host nodded and showed him the way. A minute later, to the
joyful surprise of the company, the two great writers entered the
room arm in arm, Andersen evidently deeply moved, smiling
through his tears. He was like a small child who has got his way.

'But what happened between you and Andersen in his room?' I
asked Ibsen. Ibsen smiled at the memory. 'I embraced him and
paid him a casual compliment. He was moved and, as he returned
my embrace, asked, "Then you really like me?" ' Ibsen added: 'It
was one of the pleasantest evenings I have ever known. Andersen
could be lovable and entertaining as few other men when he
wanted to be.'

Andersen was delighted with his new acquaintance. He
wrote to a friend that he had found Ibsen 'very amiable,
unassuming and pleasant. I like him a lot, but *Peer Gynt* not
at all.'

Johanne Luise Heiberg, whose acting had been such a revelation to Ibsen on his previous visit, invited him to dine with
her at her home, the beautiful seaside villa (not far from the
Melchiors') where her husband's conversation had so disappointed Ibsen in 1852, and where he now, in turn, disappointed her by his taciturnity, a fault for which he was to
make handsome amends in a poem the following year. Sadly
for him, she had retired from the stage, and of the other
actors whom he had admired then Michael Wiehe and N. P.
Nielsen (whom he had seen as Lear) were both dead; but
there was an exciting new talent to enjoy in Emil Poulsen. Fru
Heiberg arranged a special performance of *The League of*

Youth in Ibsen's honour. Stensgaard was played by Anton Wilhelm Wiehe, whom Ibsen had known and respected in Christiania – an unexpected but shrewd piece of casting, for Wiehe specialized in strong romantic roles, such as Oehlenschläger's heroes, and, as Edvard Brandes observed, 'all his faults as well as his virtues helped him in the part' of Ibsen's narcissistic hypocrite.

The documentation of these weeks is scanty. The only letters of Ibsen which have survived, apart from a brief note thanking Wiehe for his interpretation, are two which one would be happy to do without, revealing as they do one of the quirkiest and least attractive aspects of his character. Addressed (9 and 12 September) to a Danish lawyer named Anton Klubien whom he had known in Rome, they ask him to use his influence to obtain for the writer the Order of Dannebrog which, Ibsen reminds his correspondent, had been awarded to his fellow-countrymen Welhaven and Andreas Munch. 'I must tell you', runs the first of these embarrassing documents, 'that I am greedy for any recognition that I can receive from Denmark. You have no conception of the effect this kind of thing has in Norway ... A Danish decoration would much strengthen my standing there ... Seriously – the matter is important to me.' One might have thought that the success of *The Pretenders, Brand, Peer Gynt* and *The League of Youth,* his selection as delegate to Suez and the Swedish Order of Vasa would have been enough. But medals were always to hold some especial significance for Ibsen.

While he was in Copenhagen Ibsen received two letters from Suzannah in Dresden. The first of these, undated, is worth recording if only to underline the genuineness of the affection which bound this remarkable and difficult couple, and which many casual acquaintances (such as Martin Schneekloth) and envious gossips failed to appreciate:

Dear Ibsen!

We returned here on Thursday evening, and found your letter. I was very happy, for I had been longing to hear from you.

I would have replied at once but I have had such bad pains that I have not been able to hold a pen for four days. I am glad to learn that you are so happy, but you must go to Norway too, my dear Ibsen! Do not put it off for another year! It will look like indifference, and I am afraid may do you harm. You can make it a short visit, but overcome your reluctance and go there. Once you are there I am sure it will do you good.

We had a very nice time in Bohemia. Each day we received an excellent Viennese newspaper which was filled with nothing but telegrams about the war, as much about France as Germany. Here it is quite different, as you can imagine, everything from one side, France, its emperor, empress and prince all mocked in the most common lampoons, caricatures of them in the windows, that is what one sees here. In Bohemia everyone's sympathies were with the French. The people hate the Prussians, there was *great* sorrow when the news came of France's defeat.

The woman we lived with was quite fanatical, she said she could not sleep night or day; and she and Sigurd argued so, it was a delight to hear them. He is all for the French, and champions his cause each day with his fists at school, he is a real war-hero, there is no room for hesitation in this matter, he says.

The boys told Herr Elbe that Sigurd was for the French. 'Das ist nicht gut, mein lieber Sigurd.' 'Aber Norwegen-Schweden hält auch mit den Franzosen, und ich will keine Ausnahme machen,' the boy replied.

This is now your son's creed, I am myself horribly depressed by what is happening. The city is filled with wounded. Many Frenchmen. Otherwise, flags, cannon, victory celebrations. I have before me a special edition of a newspaper dealing with the victory at Metz; in a few days they will be in Paris, I cannot think of it, it hurts me so. The way is now open for the Prussians to take what they want.

Dear Ibsen, your long letter made me so happy, and I often long deeply for you, but of course it is much more important that you are where you are now.

Give my best greetings to Mother ... After paying Herr Berger I still have sixty thalers left.

Be happy, my dear Ibsen. Warmest greetings from

Your affectionate
Suzannah Ibsen

Another letter from her tells how Sigurd had been beaten up daily for a fortnight 'because he would not declare himself pro-German'. She had complained to the headmaster, who had promised to see that the bullies were punished. 'It would look bad for his school, where over half the pupils are foreign, if such treatment were permitted; so now we have peace . . . Herr Elbe is quite mad; instead of religion he talks only politics and the wickedness of the French. The French teacher could not stick it, so they have had to engage an Italian . . . Last Saturday was a sad day for us. At eight in the morning we received telegrams announcing the fall of Napoleon. Huge crowds gathered, and there were horrible scenes, cheering and hooting. Marie and I were quite frightned to speak on the street, as all foreign tongues jar in their ears. All their flags made me quite sick. You cannot imagine what it is like to live here among such a coarse bawling mob.' Dostoyevsky was suffering similarly a few streets away. 'Even the German shopkeepers', he recalled a year later in his *Writer's Diary*, 'when talking to a Russian customer, invariably put in the remark: "Now that we've finished with the French, we're going to start on you." '

Ibsen returned to Dresden towards the end of September. 'I had intended', he wrote to Johan Thoresen on 3 October, 'to visit Norway too, but the war made things so uncertain that I feared I might not be able to get back here, and when things were all right again the autumn was so far advanced that I decided to postpone my visit until next spring.' The excuse rings rather feebly; despite Suzannah's exhortations, he was still reluctant to see Norway again, and four more years were to pass before he did. 'Life here just now', the letter continues, 'is anything but pleasant. The city is full of prisoners and wounded, and the atmosphere feverish and oppressive.' A week later (10 October) he informed Hegel:

The city is filled with sick and wounded; at any hour of the day one can be sure of encountering a military funeral, or waggons filled with new patients for the hospitals. We have, besides, several thousand French prisoners; some of them walk around freely, enjoy good treatment and seem contented enough. There is no sign of enthusiasm for the war; what the papers say about this is completely untrue.[7] The country is suffering dreadfully; half-grown boys and middle-aged fathers are called to the colours and sent to France; almost every family wears mourning for someone; many have lost all their relatives; all this despite the fact that no casualty lists have been published for the past six weeks. As I say, it is horrible living here . . .

On 28 October he wrote a long letter to Peter Hansen, his companion in Egypt, supplying information for a short biographical note which the latter was writing for a book entitled *Scandinavian Writers of the Present Century*, due to appear that Christmas. Most of the matter in this letter has already been quoted,[8] but two passages especially reflect the mood of this year of 1870. 'Everything I have written', runs the first paragraph of the autobiographical section, 'has had its origin in a mood and situation in which I found myself; I have never written anything because I had, as the saying goes, "found a good subject".' And the section concludes: 'The locality in which one writes has a great influence on the form through which the imagination works. May I not, like Christoff in [Holberg's] *Jacob von Thyboe*, point at *Brand* and *Peer Gynt* and say, "Such are the effects of wine"? And is there not in *The League of Youth* something which smacks of *knackwurst* and beer? I don't mean thereby to rate the play lower; I mean that my standpoint is different because I live here in a society well-ordered to the point of tedium. What will happen when I finally come home? I will have to seek peace in distance, and then I intend to get down to *Emperor Julian*.' The letter also contains those words on Suzannah which bear repeating: 'She is just the kind of

7. Ibsen's impression here is curiously at variance with that expressed by Suzannah in her letters to him; though, since Saxony had fought against Prussia in the Austro-Prussian War of 1866, any absence of enthusiasm would hardly have been surprising.
8. See pp. 141, 179, etc.

character I need, illogical but with a strong poetical intuition, a bigness of outlook and an almost violent hatred of all things petty.'

The contemporary drama which Ibsen was planning still eluded him. On 6 November he wrote Hegel that he felt a 'strong inclination' to write an opera libretto for the Danish composer Peter Heise, based on the saga of Sigurd Jorsalfar. He got as far as completing a draft synopsis, from which it appears that among other things it was to deal with the difference between the northern and southern temperaments, the one dominated by a sense of duty, the other by *livsglæde*, the joy of life. But he abandoned the idea (though coincidentally Bjørnson wrote a play about the same character the following year). In a desultory way he began to think again about preparing a collection of his shorter poems; the appearance in 1870 of such a collection by Bjørnson, plus his lack of inspiration for any larger project, encouraged him to pursue the idea to the extent of asking Jacob Løkke to get hold of and copy as many of his poems as the latter could find in Norwegian newspapers and periodicals. His own copies had disappeared during the auction of his goods in Christiania and, surprisingly, he seems to have taken none to Italy.

The question of medals cropped up again that autumn. On 23 November Ibsen addressed a supplicatory letter on the subject to a shadowy character in Stockholm named Ohan Demirgian, an Armenian who had brought some Berber horses as a gift from the Khedive of Egypt to Carl XV, won that genial king's favour, and landed the job of royal stablemaster (but evidently made enemies somewhere along the line, for he was sacked as soon as the king died in 1872). The letter is couched in similar terms to the one written to Klubien; after stating that he had learned while in Egypt that he was to receive a decoration, Ibsen continues:

This honour was in the highest degree flattering to me, *as too it would be of the greatest help to my literary standing in Norway.* It would likewise have been a consolation to me for the neglect I

have endured at home, where the Order of St Olaf has been given
to several artists, painters and musicians, while I have been
passed over – and that despite the fact that I faithfully support
the government, with my pen and all my talents . . . The [Egyp-
tian] decoration would have been regarded in my country as
proof of the favour of my king and would have been doubly
precious to me.

Of all the begging letters addressed to patrons from Grub
Street (and a list of signatories would include most of the
great writers of the world up to that date), this is one of the
least appetizing. A man may be forgiven for humbling himself to obtain money, but not in order to get a medal, and a
foreign one at that. It is not easy to see how the award of an
Egyptian or Turkish medal (in the end it turned out to be
Turkish, since Egypt was still part of the Ottoman empire,
and the delay was due to the fact that the matter had to be
referred to Constantinople) could have been regarded in
Norway as 'proof of the favour of my king'. What is particularly nauseating is Ibsen's statement that 'I faithfully
support the government', not because the supporting of
governments is necessarily wrong but because it was untrue.
Ibsen supported the government no more than he did the
opposition; his political position was one of genuine independence, and one would have expected him to be proud of
it. This passion for medals and willingness to demean
himself in order to acquire a further specimen is a trait
in Ibsen's character with which it is difficult to feel any
sympathy.

Ibsen, however, felt no qualms about his position, and defended it eloquently in another poem stemming from his
Swedish visit, which he addressed to a young liberal politician he had met there, Adolf Hedin. Hedin, a gifted and
imaginative statesman who should have become his
country's prime minister, but was kept out of office by the
personal animosity of Carl XV's successor, Oscar II, had accused Ibsen of becoming reactionary. Ibsen entitled his reply
'To My Friend Who Talks of Revolutions':

You say I've become a conservative.
I am what I have been all my life.

I've never been one for shifting pawns.
Blow the board to glory – *then* I'm your man!

I can only recall one revolution
That wasn't scamped half-heartedly.

It makes all subsequent lettings of blood
Seem small – I refer of course to the Flood.

Though even then Satan was left the poorer;
It was Noah who ended up as Führer.

All right, let's do it again, my friends!
But let's not scamp to achieve our ends.

You unleash the waters to make your mark.
I set a torpedo under the Ark.

The last verse summarizes the attitude Ibsen was to hold towards reform for the rest of his life: that it was a writer's duty to aim at a bigger and more basic explosion than politicians could dare to envisage. He believed that politicians, once they had achieved power, invariably compromised with their ideals and that the only way to avoid doing the same was to keep oneself free from all party loyalties. Such compromise might be permissible in a politician if he were to achieve practical reforms, but for a writer it was not permissible; he must be totally independent and never sacrifice his integrity. It was an attitude which, seventy years later, George Orwell was to adopt, and which Ibsen himself was to epitomize in a phrase which is less un-Orwellian than might at first sight appear: 'The minority is always right.' At this early stage of its development he elaborated the theory in a letter dated 20 December 1870 (three months before the explosion of the Paris Commune) to Georg Brandes, then in hospital in Rome recovering from typhus:

That glorious yearning for liberty – that is now past. I must
confess that the only thing I love about liberty is the fight for it;
for the possession of it, I care not . . . The old France of illusions
is broken in pieces; and now, too, the new pragmatic Prussia is in
pieces, so that suddenly we find ourselves at the start of a new
era. How the ideas tumble about us now! And indeed it is time.
All that we have been living on until now is but scraps from the
table of the last century's revolution, and that gristle has been
chewed and re-chewed for long enough. The ideas need to be
scourged and re-interpreted. Liberty, equality and fraternity are
no longer the same as they were in the days of the lamented
guillotine. That is what the politicians refuse to understand, and
that is why I hate them. These fellows only want individual revolutions, external revolutions, political, etc. But all that is just
small change. What matters is the revolution of the spirit, and
you must be one of those who march in the van.

'The revolution of the spirit' – the phrase epitomizes what
Ibsen was striving to achieve and, more perhaps than any
man of his century except Karl Marx, was to achieve. And it
is worth noting that Ibsen's distinction between freedoms
and Freedom was one which Marx (whose first volume of
Das Kapital had appeared in 1867, the year of *Peer Gynt*)
was also to make.

Ibsen's restlessness with Bismarck's Prussia expressed
itself in a letter he wrote the same day as the one to Brandes,
to his old friend Consul Bravo. 'My wife and I both long
deeply for our beloved Rome, and we shall probably be
taking up residence there again. The only thing which
makes me hesitate is whether there is any good Protestant
school in Rome.' The answer was apparently no; once again,
the question of Sigurd's education was to determine the residence of his parents.

That December the Christiania Theatre mooted the possibility of a stage production of *Peer Gynt*, and Ibsen wrote to
Johan Thoresen, who was now managing his affairs in
Norway, suggesting as terms the net takings of the first performance, with a minimum guarantee of 150 specie-dollars

(£42).[9] But the project fell through, and *Peer Gynt* was not staged until 1876.

In 1870 Ibsen had begun to keep an account book, in which he meticulously noted (in careful copperplate) details of his income and investments. He continued to do this until his first stroke in 1900, and these two black books, now in the possession of his grandson, Mr Tancred Ibsen, provide fascinating statistics. For the year 1870 Ibsen's earnings were as follows:

	specie-dollars	£
Fee for *The League of Youth* at Christiania Theatre	301	84
Fee for *The League of Youth* at Royal Theatre, Copenhagen	600	168
Fee for 2nd edn of *The Pretenders*	200	56
	1,101	308

In addition to this, there was his Civil List pension of 400 specie-dollars (£111) and a balance of 100 specie-dollars (£28) which he had apparently managed to save from his Swedish travel grant. He had a balance of 282 specie-dollars (£78) to his credit with Hegel from previous years, and he notes that at the beginning of the year he had 74 specie-dollars (£21) in his *huskasse*, or domestic money-box. It is a measure of how cheaply he lived that he was able to ask his publisher to hold money for him; as he built up a small reserve, he was to invest all that he could possibly spare in the soberest and least speculative securities. He had no intention that he and his family should ever be faced with the spectre of bankruptcy as his father had been. Once, later, when Sigurd asked his father whether they could not occasionally eat a little less frugally, Ibsen replied, 'It is better to sleep well and not eat well, than to eat well and not sleep well.'

9. From 1870 until Ibsen's death in 1906, the exchange rate of the Norwegian crown varied between 18 and 18.80 to the pound, i.e. a lower rate than earlier in the century. (At the time of Ibsen's birth it had stood at over 25 to the pound.) For the purposes of conversion after 1870, I have calculated at 18 to the pound.

14

The Farewell to Poetry
1871

THE New Year brought a change of heart about the Danish medal, and on 8 January Ibsen wrote to Anton Klubien asking him to forget about it. The circumlocution of the language is evidence of Ibsen's embarrassment at the importunity he had previously shown.

My dear Klubien,

There is nothing for it; I must write to you while there is still time.

When I was in Copenhagen this summer, so close to my own country, it seemed to me so pre-eminently desirable to be able to return home under conditions which I regarded as essential that I expressed a wish which, could a calmer mood have prevailed, I would have left unsaid.

I now see clearly that I cannot explain this matter to you in any way which will acquit me of the charge of unpardonable vanity. Nor, consequently, will you have been able to evoke any other reaction in the people you would have had to approach.

This has troubled me since; I have felt as though I were walking unwashed on the street.

This I cannot bear; I must restore my self-respect. I therefore entreat you to forget the whole matter, and to strive your utmost to restore my standing in the eyes of those people whose respect I feel I cannot do without. All other considerations must, compared with this, be regarded as secondary . . .

There! Now I feel better. Remember me once more as your old Roman *carissimo* and devoted friend

Henrik Ibsen

Ibsen's change of heart came too late to affect the issue, however, for Klubien had talked to Fru Heiberg who had talked to the Minister of Justice who had talked to the Minister of Culture, and the machinery, as Ibsen was shortly to discover, had already been set in motion.

On 11 January the Royal Theatre in Copenhagen, encouraged by the success of *The League of Youth*, staged *The Pretenders*, and this, too, was well received. 'The audiences have not poured in to admire the brilliant acting of Mr A. or Miss B.,' reported Johanne Luise Heiberg, who had directed it, to Ibsen on 25 April. 'It is the great play itself that has excited their wonder . . . Not since 1807, when [Oehlenschläger's] *Earl Haakon* received its première, has any tragic drama gripped audiences as *The Pretenders* has done.' Hans Andersen went to the opening, and quite enjoyed himself, though he had doubts about the production. 'There was too much music', he wrote in his diary that evening, 'so that it became almost melodramatic. It's a rambling piece, but with some splendid lines. It's the best thing I know of Ibsen's.'

Early that January Ibsen had received the copies of his lost poems which he had been awaiting from Jakob Løkke. 'They make a thick book,' he informed Hegel on 8 January. 'But I am throwing out three fourths of them and rewriting the rest.' Løkke had collected fifty-two poems – eight from the student magazine *Andhrimner*, five from *Aftenbladet*, three from *Morgenbladet* and no less than thirty-six from Botten Hansen's *Illustreret Nyhedsblad*. Ibsen set to work on them at once, as though happy to get away from the play that was tormenting him, and on 21 January he sent Hegel the first batch, promising to post 'a similar batch each week' (an undertaking which, for once, he kept). Further instalments followed on 31 January and 8 February, with requests concerning the typography. 'I earnestly beg that the printer see carefully to it that the verses lie in the centre of the page, with no greater a margin on one side than the other; this is not always done, and the appearance suffers. And I greatly love the big French typefaces; I have never seen anything more beautiful for poetry; and, what is more important, they seem to me to match exactly the character of my poems. Printed thus they will be twice as good!'

He seems to have kept no copies even of the poems (or some of them) which he had written in Rome, for he had to ask Hegel to get hold of the elegy on Abraham Lincoln 'which appeared in *Fædrelandet* in either March or April 1865', the drinking song from *Love's Comedy* 'since I don't have the book', and a dirge from *The Vikings at Helgeland* which he appears not to have had either. Has any other poet, major or minor, when preparing a collection of his own work for the press, been so dependent on friends to supply him with the material?

On 16 February he sent two more poems, which 'I supposed lost, and couldn't remember [!]; finally I found them among my travel papers'. Both were unusually personal statements (which some would say was a cause of his supposing them lost and being unable to remember them). One was a confession of the bond he still felt with Norway. He called it 'Burned Ships':

> He turned his ship's
> Prow from the north,
> Seeking the trail
> Of brighter gods.
>
> The snow-land's beacons
> Quenched in the sea.
> The fauns of the seashore
> Stilled his longing.
>
> He burned his ships.
> Blue smoke drifted
> Like a bridge's span
> Towards the north.
>
> To those snow-capped huts
> From the hills of the south
> There rides a rider
> Every night.

He placed this poem last in the book, as though to remind

his compatriots that, whatever thunderbolts he might send from the south, his roots remained fast in the country which had rejected him. The other new poem, for Suzannah, he entitled simply 'Thanks':

> Her grief was the sorrows
> That cobbled my path.
> Her joy the spirits
> That lifted me o'er them.
>
> Her home lies here
> On Freedom's sea
> Where the poet's ship
> Finds its mirror.
>
> Her children are
> The shifting figures
> Who glide, waving
> Flags in my song.
>
> Her goal is to fan
> My vision's embers
> So that none knows
> Whence the fire cometh.
>
> And because she asks
> And expects no thanks,
> I give her now
> Thanks in a song.

The task of revising his earlier poems proved much more arduous than Ibsen had imagined. Never the man to skimp a job, he went through every poem he had decided to include, cutting away anything that now struck him as conventionally poetic or self-indulgent, making the language more natural and less redolent of Wergeland and Welhaven, his two earliest influences, and sometimes deleting whole sections of a poem which one is rather sorry to lose. The twenty-three sonnets which comprise 'In the Picture Gallery', for example, he omitted altogether, though he used five of them as the bases for new poems. Among these was

the Hardyesque 'In the Gallery', the mood and language of
which were near-perfectly caught by a Victorian translator,
F. E. Garrett:

> With palette laden,
> She sat, as I passed her,
> A dainty maiden
> Before an Old Master.
>
> What mountain-top is
> She bent upon? Ah,
> She neatly copies
> Murillo's *Madonna*.
>
> But rapt and brimming
> The eyes' full chalice says
> The heart builds dreaming
> Its fairy palaces.
>
> The eighteenth year rolled
> By, ere returning,
> I greeted the dear old
> Scenes with yearning.
>
> With palette laden
> She sat as I passed her,
> A faded maiden
> Before an Old Master.
>
> But what is she doing?
> The same thing still – lo,
> Hotly pursuing
> That very Murillo!
>
> Her wrist never falters;
> It keeps her, that poor wrist,
> With panels for altars
> And daubs for the tourist.
>
> And so she has painted
> Through years unbrightened,
> Till hopes have fainted
> And hair has whitened.

> But rapt and brimming
> The eyes' full chalice says
> The heart builds dreaming
> Its fairy palaces.

On 13 February Ibsen received 'an exceedingly beautiful document' announcing that he had been made a Knight of Dannebrog. The chain of action started by that word to Klubien in Copenhagen had had its effect, and his qualms seem to have vanished. 'Now,' he assured Hegel on 16 February, 'my compatriots will think my poems twice as good as they would otherwise have done!'

'Since Christmas', he wrote the next day to Georg Brandes, who was still in the hospital in Rome, 'I have been occupied practically day and night preparing this collection. It has been a damnable job to relive all those attitudes which I long since left behind. But together they form a kind of whole.' He returned to the obsessive question of freedom and its true meaning. 'I shall never agree to identify Freedom with political freedom. What you call Freedom I call freedoms, and what I call the battle for Freedom is nothing but the continuous pursuit of the idea of Freedom. He who possesses Freedom otherwise than as something to be striven for possesses something dead and meaningless, for by its very definition Freedom perpetually expands as one seeks to embrace it, so that if, during the quest, anyone stops and says: "Now I have it!" he shows thereby that he has lost it.' Ibsen found Brandes's suggestions for political reform inadequate, as he had found Adolf Hedin's, and was now (he, the most ordered of men!) suggesting that the only solution was anarchy. 'The state must be abolished!' he concluded in the same letter. '*There's* a revolution to which I will gladly lend my shoulder. Abolish the conception of the state, establish the principle of free will and all that is spiritually akin to it as the one prerequisite for a universal brotherhood – *there* is the beginning of a Freedom that is worth something!'

This was a bit much even for Brandes. 'His radicalism really exceeds all conceivable bounds,' he wrote to a friend on 22 February. 'My head grows dizzy with reading of all he wishes to revolutionize. I am afraid that had he power commensurate to his genius, or had he lived in another era, he would have been regarded as a greater radical than Marat in one field, Proudhon in another. Not only does he reject the established concepts of religion and morality, he even rejects the concept of the state.' Ibsen's ideas as expressed in this letter are so close to those of Proudhon, who had died only six years earlier ('Government of man by man in every form is oppression,' Proudhon had written. 'The highest perfection of society is found in the union of order and anarchy') that one wonders whether Ibsen may not have been reading him, or anyway had Suzannah read him and pass on the gist; but such ideas were, like those of Kierkegaard, so much a part of everyday conversation among thinking people then that he would have been a dull and out-of-touch fellow who had not absorbed something of them.

In that same letter of 14 February to Brandes, Ibsen cited the Jews as an example of the advantages of abolishing the state. 'How is it they have kept their place apart, their political halo, amid surroundings of coarse cruelty?' he asked. 'By having no state to burden them. Had they remained in Palestine, they would long ago have lost their individuality in the process of the state's construction, like other nations.'[1] He referred to the Jews as 'the aristocracy of the human race'. This need for an aristocracy, not of birth but spiritual, was something that Ibsen was increasingly to stress, notably in *An Enemy of the People*, and it made him many enemies among Scandinavian liberals. Even today (as this writer knows from experience) Dr Stockmann's demand for this kind of aristocracy upsets many a liberally inclined director and actor working on the play.

On 25 February Ibsen sent the (as he thought) last pages of his poems to Hegel, but as late as Easter week he composed a long and, again, technically intricate piece, 'Rhymed

[1]. I quote William Archer's incomparable translation of this difficult passage.

Letter to Fru Heiberg', which Georg Brandes, a quarter of a century later, was to describe as Ibsen's most artistically accomplished poem. In this exquisite work, two hundred and eighty-two lines of astonishing variety, Ibsen stated his attitude towards the rival media of verse and prose in a sentence that anticipated his imminent abandonment of the former for the latter. 'Prose is for ideas, verse for visions. The joys and sorrows of the soul, grief that snows upon my head, indignation's lightning bolt – these I endow most fully with life, and express most freely, in the bonds of verse.' The renunciation of this medium, in which he moved so easily, was to be a continuation of the austere process which he had begun with the astringent revision of his poems.

The 'Letter to Fru Heiberg' ends with an expression of faith, unfashionable for the period, that things created in the theatre may perhaps last longer than works which never leave the printed page. Ibsen intended this as a compliment to the great actress now living in retirement, but it plainly expresses a conviction which he himself possessed, and which is a little surprising when we remember that his two triumphs, *Brand* and *Peer Gynt*, were still both commonly regarded as unstageable.

Ibsen's *Poems* were published on 3 May 1871. The edition was a large one, 4,000 copies (the equivalent, counting Norway and Denmark as one, of something approaching 50,000 in modern Britain). The reviews were generally most favourable, though Bjørnson, predictably, disliked it. 'As with almost everything by Ibsen', he wrote to his wife Karoline on 14 May, 'I am left so empty afterwards. His standing *vis-à-vis* his country is becoming almost comic.' The man about whose opinion Ibsen was most anxious, Georg Brandes, did not review the book until the autumn, by which time he had met Ibsen, and his review was to reflect that meeting.

That first fortnight in May was a good one for Ibsen, for on 9 May, six days after the publication of his *Poems*, he at last received his longed-for Medjidje Order, 'a handsome object', he informed Hegel the same day, 'together with a large and unintelligible diploma from the Grand Turk himself'. With unusual (on this subject) candour he admitted that the main reason for his getting the decoration was that 'we brought a lot of Swedish and Norwegian decorations for Egyptian bigwigs, and this courtesy was merely being reciprocated.'

Down in Rome, Georg Brandes had at last left hospital after five months, his attack of typhus having been followed by a blood clot in the leg. Brandes's sense of kinship with Ibsen had been deepened by their correspondence; from his sickbed earlier in the year he had written a poem entitled 'To Henrik Ibsen', describing his lonely struggle and his longing for a comrade in arms:

> Brother! I found thee. What care I
> That thou art a matchless chieftain, I
> But an armourer? Our souls are kin.
> We shall sound a spiritual call to arms.

Ibsen reciprocated the younger man's feeling; and so, as Brandes's biographer Henning Fenger has put it, 'these two lonely men joined hands'. None, alas, of Brandes's letters to Ibsen has survived, but Ibsen's side of the correspondence is proof of the warmth which already existed between them:

Dresden, 18 May 1871

My dear Brandes!

... Well, I never really believed you were in danger; one doesn't die in the first act;[2] the great world *dramaturge* needs you for a leading role in his *Haupt- und Staatsaction*[3] which He is now doubtless preparing for our respected public.

2. A reference to the Strange Passenger's cold comfort to Peer Gynt: 'One doesn't die in the middle of the fifth act.'

3. 'A type of entertainment popular in Germany in the seventeenth and eighteenth centuries, consisting of a chronicle play, improvised farce and spectacular effects. The chronicle play presented the extravagant and absurd adventures of an emperor or general over a period of many years.' (Evert Sprinchorn, *Ibsen's Letters and Speeches* [New York, 1964], p. 11.)

Warmest thanks for your portrait! ... I always like to have a physical likeness to hang my conception on. I shan't rest till I have met you, when I think we shall prove to have more in common than a liking for velvet jackets.

During this somewhat long interval I have managed to persuade myself not to write to you. I sensed from your last letter that you were a little angry with me, and since my poems were about to be published I didn't want to do anything which might look like an attempt to conciliate you before you should read them. I know you would not let this affect your judgement, but a kind of diffidence bade me avoid even the appearance of having supposed any such thing. My dear friend, you will understand what I mean.

I trust you will long since have received the *Poems* from Hegel. It contains both old and new material, and much that I no longer set much store by; but it all belongs to the story of my development. So tell me what you think of it; I attach the greatest importance to your judgement.

And what are you up to now, down there in beautiful, warm Italy? Your illness will perhaps have had one good result, I mean, that you may have to spend a summer there. I think of you daily; sometimes I see you in Frascati, sometimes Albano or Ariccia. Which is right? And what new work are you preparing down there for our spiritual enlightenment? I am sure something must have matured during your long sickness. One of the blessings of being ill is that it gives a kind of purity and stature to so much which otherwise would not blossom. I have only once been really ill; but that may be another way of saying that I have never, perhaps, been totally well. *Chi lo sa!*

Is it not wretched of the Paris Commune to have gone and spoiled my excellent theory of the State – or rather, of the No-State? Now the idea is ruined for ages; I cannot even decently write a poem about it. But the idea is sound, of that I am sure, and some time it will be achieved without caricature.

I have often thought about what you once wrote, that I had not taken up the standpoint of modern scientific knowledge. How could I overcome this failing? But is not each generation born with the prejudices of its time? Have you never noticed in a painting of a group from some previous century a curious kind of family likeness between people of the same period? So it is in the field of intellect too. What we profane creatures lack in knowledge I think we possess, to a certain degree, in intuition or instinct. And a writer's task is essentially to *see*, not to mirror; I am conscious of a particular danger to myself in indulging the latter tendency.

Dear Brandes – it is always a relief to me to talk to you, and a great, great joy to hear you talk, if only on paper. So give me that pleasure again soon.

Your affectionate
Henrik Ibsen

Brandes was overwhelmed. 'I received an extremely charming and flattering letter from Henrik Ibsen', he informed his family on 26 May, 'almost too flattering for me to believe that he was being completely honest.' Visiting Walter Runeberg's studio in Rome he was interested to see the latter's 'remarkable bust of Ibsen, fiery yet overcast'.

Meanwhile, Ibsen had at last broken the creative block that had been tormenting him. 'I have now begun my big play, *Emperor Julian*,' he wrote to Johan Thoresen on 26 June, 'and hope to have it ready by Christmas ... I work blazingly fast, but only for a few hours[!] each day.' On 12 July he told Frederik Hegel: 'I am well into *Emperor Julian*. This book will be my masterpiece, and occupies all my thoughts and all my time. The positive view of things which the critics have so long demanded of me they will find here.'

At last, on 14 July 1871, Ibsen and Brandes met. Brandes had arranged his homeward journey to Copenhagen so as to pass through Dresden, and had arrived there the previous night. His autobiography contains a vivid account of his first sight of Ibsen:

As I approached the house, which lay in an avenue, Dippoldiswaldærstrasse, I saw him, easily recognizable from his portrait, leaning out of the window in his shirtsleeves. But when I entered he had put on a velvet jacket. He hugged me to his breast, almost suffocating me. I found him handsome, with an incomparable forehead, clear eyes, long curled hair. I was surprised how handsome I found him.

They talked for two or three hours, 'partly of his work, partly of conditions at home, much of me'. Ibsen was wearing an order ribbon in his buttonhole, which slightly disturbed Brandes. Later that day Brandes returned, and Ibsen took him to the Waldschlösslein 'where we ate and drank beer ... Ibsen told me how Bjørnson had tried to persuade him to avoid all contact with me, and promised to show me letters the following day. He told me how they had demanded, in the most shameless manner, that he should become co-editor of [the literary magazine] *Idea and Reality*, demanded it of him as his *duty* ... He had replied that he felt no inclination to occupy a seat that was still warm from Clemens Petersen.' They discussed Danish writers. Brandes asked Ibsen if there was any one he cared about. 'After letting me guess for some while in vain, he answered: "Once upon a time, somewhere in Zealand, there walked behind his plough an old man in a smock frock who had looked upon men and things until he was wroth at heart. That is a man I like." ' They agreed in their admiration of Heiberg and shared a feeling that Scandinavia was sadly backward in its cultural development. 'Ibsen was full of plans and hopes, and overflowing with the spirit of battle. "You needle the Danes, I'll needle the Norwegians!" were the last words he smilingly addressed to me.'[4]

Brandes, no doubt, told Ibsen of the exciting actors and actresses he had seen in Paris the previous summer – Ristori as Lady Macbeth, Mounet-Sully as Hernani, Coquelin in Ponsard's *Gringoire*, the young Sarah Bernhardt in George Sand's *L'Autre*; no doubt, too, they argued about John Stuart Mill, whom Brandes so revered and whom Ibsen found tedious. Ibsen left no record of their meeting, but a vivid impression of how Brandes looked and behaved at around this time survives from a young Englishman who made his acquaintance three years later, Edmund Gosse. Gosse found Brandes

4. The poet-ploughman was Christian Hviid Bredahl (1784–1860).

a tall, thin young man ... gentle and even mild in appearance, pale, with a great thatch of hair arched over a wide forehead ... I never met anyone more impatient than Brandes, and this probably had something to do with the atmosphere of anger and suspicion which he had created around him in Copenhagen. He not merely did not bear fools gladly, but he was easily driven to distraction, and to the visible stamping of feet, by those who were not, even in his own measure, fools, but merely less arrowy in their mental movements than himself. Thus I immediately fell under his ban because I spoke Danish so slowly ... Brandes went pacing, infuriated, between the sofa and the door, and snapped his long tapering fingers.

Gosse's account of the distrust with which Brandes was regarded by his fellow-countrymen helps us to understand why he and Ibsen, two difficult men whose views on literature and other matters often differed so widely, were drawn to each other. Brandes was, writes Gosse, 'the only man in Denmark who represented the spirit of modern Europe in *belles-lettres*', and the Danes were angered by his cultivation of friendships with German authors such as Paul Heyse – hostility towards Germany still being fierce in Denmark – and his attempts to impose their writings on Danish readers.

It was difficult to account for the repulsion and even terror of Georg Brandes which I heard expressed around me whenever his name came up in the course of general conversation ... Brandes was a Jew,[5] an illuminated specimen of a race little known at that time in Scandinavia, and much dreaded and suspected. That a scion of this hated people, so long excluded from citizenship, should come forward with a loud message of defiance to the exquisite and effete civilization of Denmark was in itself an outrage ... There was something exasperating, too, in the lofty tone which Brandes adopted. He did not spare the susceptibilities of his countrymen ... 'How these Christians hate me!' he could not help saying. He belonged to the race of iconoclasts, like Heine

5. His father had been born Cohen, but the family name was changed to Brandes when Georg's grandmother remarried with a man of that name.

before him, like Nietzsche after him, and he was expected to disturb all the convictions of his contemporaries. In religion a deist, in politics a republican, in ethics an extreme individualist, Brandes seemed at that time prepared to upset every part of the settled and convenient order of things.

In other words, Brandes was, as a critic, doing for Denmark what Ibsen, as a creative writer, was doing for Norway, and what August Strindberg, then a twenty-two-year-old student at Upsala, was shortly to do for Sweden: in Ibsen's own phrase, to 'wake the people and make them think big'.

The meeting with Ibsen had given Brandes the stimulation he had been hoping for, and the next months were for him a time of violent fermentation, as his diaries for August and September show. On 20 September he noted: 'Towards 2 a.m. I wrote a long, violent and ardent letter to Ibsen. Surely this will inflame him? Thought him worth more.' Doubtless he compared Ibsen with John Stuart Mill, whom he was to describe in his autobiography as 'the incarnation of the ideal I had drawn for myself of the great man . . . His boldness was not of the merely theoretic kind; he wished to interfere and remodel.' Ibsen was in fact to interfere and remodel contemporary thought at least as much as Mill; what must have disappointed Brandes was Ibsen's lack of inflexibility and his willingness (like Schopenhauer) to compromise in his private life. Brandes's letter to Ibsen of 20 September has disappeared, but we have Ibsen's answer, from which it is evident that Brandes had tried to persuade him to play a less detached and more active and committed role.

Dresden, 24 September 1871

Dear Brandes!

It is always with curiously mixed emotions that I read your letters. They are more poems than letters; they come to me like a cry for help from a solitary survivor in some immense and lifeless desert. I cannot but rejoice and thank you for addressing this cry to me. Yet it worries me, for I ask myself 'To what will such a mood lead?' I can only comfort myself with the hope that it is merely transitional. It seems to me that you now find yourself in the same crisis that I was in when I wrote *Brand*, and I am sure you too will find the medicine to drive the sickness from your body. Energetic creation is an excellent remedy. Above all, I would wish you a full-blooded egotism, to persuade you for a while to rate yourself and your thoughts as the only things that have any value or significance and everything else as non-existent. Do not regard this as a sign of brutality in me! You cannot serve your community better than by minting this metal which lies within you. I have never really had any strong liking for solidarity; I have always regarded it as just another traditional dogma – and if one had the courage completely to disregard it one might perhaps be rid of the ballast which weighs heaviest on a man's individuality. There are times when the whole history of the world seems to me but a mighty shipwreck, and the only sane course to save oneself. I hope for nothing from isolated reforms. The whole human race is on the wrong track; that is the situation. Is there really any hope in the present state of affairs, with these unattainable ideals, etc.? Human history seems to me like a young man who has left his work-bench and gone to the theatre. We have made a fiasco of everything, both as lovers and as heroes; the only role for which we have shown a faint talent has been that of the fool; and with our increasing sophistication we shall no longer be able to play that. Nor do I think things are better arranged in other countries; the masses, whether at home or abroad, have no understanding of higher things.

And so I am to try to raise a banner? Alas, my dear friend, that would be like Louis Napoleon's arrival at Boulogne with an eagle on his head. When his hour of destiny eventually struck, he needed no eagle. Working on *Julian* has made me something of a fatalist; but this play will be a kind of banner. Don't fear, however, that this will be a tendentious work; I explore the characters, their conflicting plans, their story, and do not try to seek a moral – always remembering that one must not confuse the moral of a story with its philosophy; for it is inevitable that a philosophy must emerge as the final judgement on the conflict and the victory. But all this can be illustrated only in practice . . .

I have received your book [*Criticisms and Portraits*]. I can only say that it is something to which I return again and again. Yes, my dear, splendid Brandes, I cannot understand how *you* can be despondent. You have received a spiritual summons as clearly and unmistakably as is granted to few people. So why this gloom? Have you a right to feel thus? Though don't imagine that I don't fully understand you ...

Finally, hearty thanks for the visit you paid me in Dresden; those were festive hours for me. Good luck, courage, good health and good everything!

Your affectionate
Henrik Ibsen

We have no record of Brandes's reaction to this letter, but his diaries of the period show how continuously Ibsen was in his thoughts. On 21 September, presumably just after he had sent his letter, Brandes noted: 'If only Ibsen would write me a powerfully *poetic* reply! Were he a ready and fertile writer he could hardly not do so.' And the next day: 'Is it I who am to raise the battle cry, is it really I who am the sole chieftain of the young? I feel like Moses and Jonah when the Lord chose them and they prayed for strength ... Ought I to hold a lecture in the Students' Union to sound a trumpet call for the young? I think I *must*, I think it my duty.' On 30 September: 'Still no letter from H. Ibsen. I am hurt and indignant.' The same day he began to write a review of Ibsen's volume of poems, and a day or two later he received Ibsen's reply of 24 September which must have struck him as disappointingly evasive, and which inspired him to the deeply personal statement which that review, published in *Illustreret Tidende* on 22 October, represents – a wonderfully mature assessment which repays quoting *in extenso*. After apologizing for writing about the volume so long after its appearance, Brandes continues.

'The book is in no way very rich, and does not contain many poems that broaden the soul ... but ... it brings us a message from a spirit who has the rare characteristic of being a warrior, in the fields of both artistic and human endeavour ... Despite its faults, it is so passionate that it contains passion, and one likes to write about something by which one has been powerfully moved.' Ibsen's poetry is 'the poetry of loneliness, portraying the lonely need, the lonely strife, and the lonely protest'; as examples, Brandes names 'The Miner', 'The Murder of Lincoln' and 'On the Heights'. 'It is out of isolation that Ibsen writes. It is irrelevant that he isolated himself partly out of discontent at not being able to carry the public with him. It was loneliness that first drove Ibsen to become a poet, and this collection of poems mirrors in microcosm the whole development of Ibsen's life, beginning as it does with a series of works of no marked individuality.' There are those who attain to self-knowledge and originality almost at their first contact with the world, with its society and personalities so different to their own. 'But others, the lonely ones, achieve this only by the gradual rejection of bonds and scruples, as being ever more weighty and useless ballast. I remember I once heard a man of this ilk say: "It is good to be without friends. Friends are an expensive luxury, and when one invests one's capital in a mission, a calling in this life, one cannot afford to keep friends" ... Ibsen is like this man; he became himself by becoming a solitary.'

One of the tasks of poets, continues Brandes, is to give the lead in ideas to the young – not that the young do not know what their password must be,

but they wish to hear it uttered, for the first time, by inspired lips. If the poet does not, at the right moment, give the answer that is awaited from him, it forms itself without his help in the mouths of the young, and then it is the poet himself who is challenged and asked if he knows the password; if he does not, the young will strike him down and proceed. But where scattered yearnings do not work towards a single goal and seek a central point, no rallying cry can be expected, and then the poet withdraws into himself. Ibsen's character fits such a situation and draws strength from it. His strength depends on the night-stillness around him, on the calm darkness in which alone he can freely breathe. Not the twelve fair hours of the day but the dark hours of the night stand godparents to his poetry. Alone, he divides more than he unites. He shows each man the way back to the powers which he may discover within himself when, without fear or scruple, he follows his own nature and his own star. But a star shines only in the night. It is useless to ask Ibsen to raise a banner. He writes only for himself and for those who are created like him; to them he offers not a banner but an example . . . He, the enemy of apathy and sloth, is alarmed and indignant at seeing his people sit out the sword-dance, retreat like Peer Gynt, turn their backs on the opportunity to be tested, and this mood has called forth a string of his most notable works.

As examples, Brandes cites *Brand* and *Peer Gynt*, 'The Murder of Lincoln' and 'A Brother in Need'.

In such protests the poet's genius stands forth in its full strength; the axe glints, the torch glitters in his hand. The axe and the torch! These are his emblems. One recalls those words of Hippocrates which Schiller set on the title page of *The Robbers*: 'What medicine cannot cure, the iron will heal; what the iron cannot heal, will be cured by fire.' Can this lonely and passionate spirit seriously be regarded as one who delights in annihilation and renunciation?

Wise readers, explains Brandes, find this kind of destroyer easy to understand, and such an instinct, Ibsen's character being what it is, natural. He quotes the anecdote from Lamartine's *Jocelyn* about the travellers who, desiring to cross a river in flood, laid their axes to the trees under which they had just rested, to the amazement and consternation of the birds and beasts of the forest; but by destroying these trees they were able to build a bridge, cross the river, and continue their journey. 'Thus the human spirit fells what had once sheltered it, and thus it progresses over the corpses of what it has destroyed.'

Regarding Ibsen's supposed lack of faith, Brandes asserts that: 'Faith consists in believing in truth though untruth reign and lies triumph and drug men's minds. In believing in justice though injustice inflict one defeat after another, in believing in the future despite the present.' There are, he concludes, two kinds of unbelievers. On the one hand, there are those who regard themselves as believers, but whose ideals lie

not before them, but behind them, like some physical, tangible object of the past ... While mankind strives forward, these men, calling themselves philanthropists, liberals, men of the future, cling on with all their might to protect what has fallen, shore up what is crumbling, curse the presumption of those who demolish and deny, lend all their strength to reaction. In contrast to these, those whose highest ideals lie not behind them but ahead of them, in the future which they are preparing, build bridges over the abyss from the trees which they have felled and, in the darkest night, believe, with all the passion with which they have demolished and denied, in the dawn and the sunrise.

The poet of loneliness, of iron and fire, the divider not the uniter, the believer in truth and justice who 'shows each man the way back to the powers he may discover within himself' – has any critic in the century since Brandes penned these words more penetratingly epitomized what Ibsen stood for, even though the judgement was delivered before Ibsen had written most of the work on which his fame rests? No wonder that, however fallible Brandes's judgement may have been concerning individual plays, not only Ibsen, but Strindberg also, regarded him as the one contemporary critic whose opinion they could respect.

That autumn and winter, Ibsen plodded ahead with *Emperor and Galilean*. 'My new play', he wrote to Hegel on 27 December, 'goes forward unceasingly. Part One, "Julian and the Friends of Wisdom", comprising three acts, is already finished and *fair-copied* ... I am now busily engaged on Part Two, and this will go more quickly and be much shorter. Part Three will, though, be somewhat longer; the whole thing will probably run to between 280–300 pages, all in prose, in a style mainly approximating to that of *The Pretenders*.' Camilla Collett, the novelist champion of women's rights, was now in Dresden. 'She is thinking of proceeding to Rome.' Ibsen told Hegel, 'but I doubt if she will get any farther, for she has no idea how to arrange a journey.' She was hopelessly unpractical and kept her gold coins in a matchbox. She and Ibsen met often and indulged in many lively debates; she was scandalized at what she regarded as the old-fashionedness of his ideas about woman's place in society. Her forthrightly expressed views on the subject were to have a considerable influence on him.

1871 had been another thin year financially, even worse than 1870. *Poems* had earned him 562 specie-dollars (£156); a sixth edition of *Brand* had brought a welcome 212 specie-dollars (£59); and *Morgenbladet* had paid him 25 specie-dollars (£7) for a poem – a total of 799 specie-dollars (£222). His only other source of income had been his pension of 400 specie-dollars. But this was enough for his very modest requirements. 'Everything has become dreadfully expensive here in Germany since the recent war,' he wrote to Consul Bravo on 16 February 1872. 'Luckily my income has risen proportionally, so that we can live without worry; new editions of my books are appearing regularly[!] and I am always busy with something new.' He was miserly with his money, but not for selfish reasons. 'The little capital which I have succeeded in amassing during these years', he told Johan Thoresen on 22 February, 'must be further increased, if Suzannah and Sigurd are to be reasonably secured against all eventualities. This consideration precedes all others, as far as I am concerned. Nor can I be certain that my literary talents may not decline with time; I cannot rely on new editions of my books being printed every year.' He badly needed to complete *Emperor and Galilean* during the next twelve months; in the event, he didn't, and 1872 was to prove, financially, a lean year indeed.

15

An English Admirer; and a New Friendship
1872-3

ON 24 February 1872 Ibsen made a fresh monetary application to the Ecclesiastical Department in Christiania, this time for a stipend of 450 specie-dollars (£125) to enable him 'by comprehensive research in the Berlin Museum of Egyptology to complete my knowledge of Egyptian architecture and sculpture, and their connection with corresponding ancient forms of art in Europe. Next year family considerations will compel me to return home, I had planned to do so this year, but a big new work on which I am engaged makes this impossible. The mental disturbance inseparable from a change of residence and a re-entry into an environment which, after an absence of more than eight years, has in many respects become foreign to me, could not but leave an unfortunate mark on an uncompleted work.' What these 'family considerations' were is not clear, unless Sigurd's independence of outlook had been running him into further trouble at school. In any case, Ibsen's application was refused.

That month P. F. Siebold's German translation of *Brand* was at last published, the first foreign version of any of Ibsen's plays to be thus honoured. It was rapidly followed by German translations of *The Pretenders* and *The League of Youth*; and before they appeared, on 3 March, his name was printed for the first time in English.[1] The periodical was the

---

1. At any rate in England. But some time in 1872 (I have not been able to ascertain the month) a native of Bergen named Johan Dahl published there his own English translations of *Norwegian and Swedish Poems*, including (together with items by Wergeland, Welhaven,

Spectator, the article a review of Ibsen's *Poems*, and the author a twenty-three-year-old member of the cataloguing department at the British Museum. While on a visit to Norway two years previously, Edmund Gosse, who then knew no Norwegian, had gone into a bookshop at Trondhjem to buy an English novel, entered into conversation with the manager, H.L. Brækstad, and asked him whether Norway had any poets. Brækstad (who later became Norwegian vice-consul in London and translated Hans Andersen into English) showed Gosse a copy of Ibsen's *Poems* newly arrived that day from Copenhagen. 'I put the small green volume in my pocket and left the shop. Of course I could not understand one word, but I could see that the versification was singular and good, and altogether felt much attracted to the unknown poet.'

There was no Danish or Norwegian grammar or reader available in English then, and on his return to London Gosse taught himself by going through a Danish novel with an English crib. He then managed to work his way through the poems, and wrote the review. As well as dealing with the poems, the article naturally referred to Ibsen's dramatic achievements; and Gosse, always an assiduous cultivator of the great, sent a copy, with an accompanying letter, to Ibsen in Dresden, and received a gratifying reply:

Dresden, 2 April 1872

Most honoured sir!

Some days ago I had the great pleasure to receive your very

Andreas Munch, J. L. Runeberg, Esaias Tegnér, the National Anthem and a prose story by Bjørnson) 'Terje Vigen'. This brave effort is not always successful; for example:

> The sea rushed in thro' the opening broad,
> In two feet of water it sunk.
> And gone was the precious barley-load.
> But not so our hero's spunk.

This volume is sometimes stated to have been published in 1874, but the title-page and preface are both dated 1872.

flattering letter, accompanied by your kind review in 'The Spectator'.

My knowledge of the English language is unfortunately not such that I dare attempt to write it, so I hope you will forgive me if I use my native tongue to express my deepest and most heartfelt thanks for the generous way in which you have written of my work.

I could not wish to be introduced to a foreign public better or more sympathetically than in your excellent article; nor is there any public by whom I should be prouder to be read than the English. Should this, thanks to your kind and perceptive assistance, come about, I shall feel boundlessly and permanently indebted to you . . .

The English people are so close to us Scandinavians spiritually, intellectually and emotionally – for which reason it has been especially painful to me that language should set a barrier between my writing and the whole of this great related world. So you will appreciate the pleasure you have given me by the prospect of removing this barrier.

Here in Germany several editions of my books are in preparation. A translation of *Brand* has been published in Cassel, but I am not satisfied with it. Another translation of the same play is announced in Berlin. Also in Berlin there have appeared German versions of *The Pretenders* and *The League of Youth*, both excellently rendered by Dr Adolf Strodtmann, the admirable translator of Byron and Tennyson. Dr Strodtmann is currently engaged in translating my shorter poems.

To be introduced to the English reading public is, though, my chief concern, and the sooner this could happen the happier I should be . . .

Your most respectful and obliged
Henrik Ibsen

Gosse's reply is not extant, but he must have explained that his contribution to the campaign would mainly be in the form of articles and reviews, for on 11 April Ibsen informed Michael Birkeland: 'The translations are to be executed by various hands, and Mr Gosse, though in charge of the enterprise, is not likely to be most active in this side of the work, but will do his utmost to advance the cause by placing articles in the English newspapers.' Gosse kept one-half of his promise,[2] for he published a review of *Peer Gynt* in the *Spectator* on 7 July, another of *The Pretenders* in the *Academy* on 1 August, an article on 'Norwegian Poetry since 1814' in the October issue of *Fraser's Magazine* and, in January 1873, a long article in the *Fortnightly Review* entitled 'Ibsen, the Norwegian Satirist'. But in his attempts to arrange translations, he was less successful. He completed a blank verse version of *Love's Comedy* in the spring of 1873, but failed to find a publisher, and (not surprisingly, considering how few English people knew Norwegian, and the indifference shown to his own single effort) does not seem to have found any willing collaborators.[3] No English version of an Ibsen play was to appear before Catherine Ray's translation of *Emperor and Galilean* in 1876.

While Gosse was learning Norwegian in London and introducing Ibsen's name to a tiny section of the English public, Ibsen's Danish champion had been running into trouble in Copenhagen. On his return there the previous summer after the meeting in Dresden, Georg Brandes had applied for a position at Copenhagen University, where it was obvious that a successor would soon be needed to the octogenarian Carsten Hauch as Professor of Aesthetics.

2. Not without difficulty. 'I had an introduction to the *Saturday Review*, so I submitted a longish article on *Peer Gynt*. Mr Harwood, who was then the editor, said that I had used terms of so warm an eulogy that he could not publish the article unless I could find some other witness to the merit of this strange piece by an unknown foreign writer. But no sponsor for Ibsen's poetic respectability was forthcoming, and the review did not appear. A little later on I tried the same editor with an article on *The Young Men's League*, which was tartly rejected ... I wrote more articles, which were rejected ... Mr Archer is the host, and his the guests and dances; but it was I who swept the floor and lighted the candles.' (An article by Gosse congratulating Ibsen on his seventieth birthday, printed in the *Sketch*, 23 March 1898.)

3. Gosse also translated 'The Poet's Song' from *Love's Comedy* and 'Agnes' from *Brand*, and included them in his own collection of poems, *On Viol and Flute*, published in London in 1873.

Hauch himself had been an early champion of Brandes, and the latter was asked to give a series of lectures to show his qualifications. He chose as his subject *Main Currents in Nineteenth-Century Literature,* and delivered his first lecture on 3 November 1871.

The hall was filled, one-third of the audience consisting of women; not only was Brandes the translator of Mill's *The Subjection of Women,* he was also known to have been the lover of a married woman with six children.[4] The lectures were a tremendous turning-point in Scandinavian culture. Brandes declared that Danish thinking was half a century behind the times, that it was reactionary and divorced from reality instead of, like French literature (which Brandes, fresh from his meetings with Taine and Renan, took as his model) dealing with contemporary social problems. Danish literature, he asserted, lived in the past; it was the duty of writers to live in the present and the future. Harmless as these sentiments appear today, they infuriated the powerful conservative element in Danish society and its press organs. In November Brandes wrote a satirical piece about a modern Red Riding Hood, a free-thinking girl who is gobbled up by the *opposition* press (he despised the official opposition party in Denmark as much as Ibsen did its counterpart in Norway). For this he was violently attacked in *Fædrelandet;* it and the other newspapers of the capital closed their columns to him, and to reply to the attack he had to insert a paid advertisement. When the first volume of Brandes's lectures was published in February 1872 it, too, was violently abused in every Danish newspaper; and when Carsten Hauch died in March, his recommendation that Brandes should be his successor was ignored. Brandes wrote to Ibsen, pouring out his troubles; the letter has perished, but we have

4. On these lectures, see Evert Sprinchorn's excellent note in his edition of *Ibsen's Letters and Speeches,* pp. 120–21. I do not like Mr Sprinchorn's translation of the letters, except where it follows the Maurvik-Morison version of 1905, but his notes are informed and illuminating.

Ibsen's reply, the rough comfort of a battle-scarred veteran to a subaltern enduring his first experience of shellfire:

Dresden, 4 April 1872

Dear Brandes!

I have this moment received your letter, and am replying immediately.

But what unbelievable news you tell me! And I imagined you revelling in success and triumph. Surely, though, you must have an army behind you. Remember that these are but recruits whom you are leading into battle. The first time, they will retreat; the second time, stand their ground; and after that they will follow you to victory.

So the liberal press has closed its doors to you. But of course! I once expressed to you my contempt for political freedom. You thought me wrong on that occasion. From your story of *The Red Hat* I see you have gained some experience. My dear friend, the liberals are the worst enemies of Freedom. Spiritual and intellectual freedom flourish best under absolutism; that was proved in France, then in Germany and it is now being proved in Russia.

But I must turn to what for these past weeks has continually filled my thoughts and disturbed my nightly rest. I have read your lectures.

A more dangerous book could never fall into the hands of a pregnant writer. It is one of those books which set a yawning gulf between yesterday and today. When I was in Italy I could not understand how I had managed to exist before I went there. In twenty years people will not understand how anyone managed to live spiritually in Scandinavia before these lectures . . . Your book is not literary history in the accepted meaning, neither is it cultural history; what it is, I shall not attempt to describe. It is to me as the goldfields of California were to those who discovered them; they either made men millionaires or ruined them. Now, is our spiritual constitution in the North strong enough to survive this shock? I don't know; but it doesn't matter. Whatever cannot sustain these new ideas must fall.

You say everyone in the faculty of philosophy is against you. My dear Brandes, would you have it otherwise? Are you not fighting to destroy the philosophy of that faculty? A war such as yours cannot be waged by a crown servant. If they did not bar the door against you, it would show that you had failed to frighten them.

As regards this agitation which is being worked up against you, all these lies and calumnies and so forth, let me give you a word of advice which I know from experience to be sovereign. Be an aristocrat! Aristocracy of the spirit is the only weapon against this kind of thing. Appear indifferent; never write a word of reply in the newspapers; if you polemize in your writings, never direct your polemic against this or that specific attack; never write a single word which could make it seem as though your enemies had found their mark; in short, act as though you had no idea that anyone was opposed to you. What power of survival do you suppose your enemies' attacks will have? In the old days when I read an attack on me in the morning, I used to think: 'Now I am finished, I shall never be able to hold up my head again!' But I did; no one any longer remembers what was written, and even I myself have long forgotten it. So, don't cheapen yourself by getting involved in mud-slinging. Start a new series of lectures, unperturbed, unmoved, maddeningly indifferent, cheerfully contemptuous of everything that is crumbling around you. Do you think that what is rotten to the core has any powers of resistance?

How this mortal combat between two epochs will end, I do not know; but anything is preferable to the *status quo* – of that I am certain. I do not promise myself that victory will result in any permanent improvement; every historical development has been but a lurch from one delusion to another. But the battle itself is good, healthy and invigorating; your revolt is a mighty and emancipating declaration of genius. When these old men complain that you mock God, they should reflect that they themselves are the mockers. The Great Aforesaid created you for a purpose.

I hear you have founded a society. Do not rely implicitly on everyone who joins you; what matters is whether they do so for the right reason. Nor am I sure that this will strengthen your position; my own conviction is that the strongest man is he who stands most alone. But I sit here outside it all while you stand there in the midst of the storm; that makes a big difference.

Au revoir, my dear Brandes! Keep a friendly place in your heart for me and mine, next to what must henceforth be the only important thing to you, because it is your own child in spirit and in truth.

Forgive the haste and incoherence of this letter!

> Your affectionate
> Henrik Ibsen

No wonder that Ibsen was so excited by *Main Currents*, which still reads wonderfully well today. The theme, as stated in Brandes's introduction, is 'the revolution waged by the first decades of the nineteenth century against the literature of the eighteenth, and the victory of that revolution', as reflected in French, English and German literature up to 1848; in other words, the gradual conquest of liberal ideas through such writers as Byron, Hugo, Lamartine and Heine. It is easy to realize what a revelation this brilliant survey of Ibsen's spiritual ancestors must have been to one ever conscious of his imperfect education and inability to read French and English.

Meanwhile, *Emperor and Galilean* was grinding slowly on, for ever falling further behind schedule. On 19 January he had told Hegel that he hoped to have the whole play finished by June; on 24 April he was still optimistic enough to write: 'I shall soon be ready with Part Two of *Julian*. The third and final section will go easily. The spring has now arrived here, and I always work best in warm weather.' He was not in fact to complete even Part Two until August, nor the whole play until the following February. 'We have had the pleasure of seeing several Danish travellers,' continued this last letter to Hegel. 'H. C. Andersen is now here.' Andersen and Ibsen met on 22 April, and evidently got on well again, for Andersen (though he continued to spell his new friend Ipsen) sent him a copy of the final volume of his *New Tales and Stories*, which had appeared that year. An undated letter from Ibsen, or rather a fragment of it, has survived: 'Thank you for your visit to Dresden; thank you for the book; thank you for everything else ...' The rest of the letter has been cut away.

Some time early in July Ibsen moved from Dippoldiswal-dær-Strasse to a new apartment at Grosse Plauenche Strasse 9, and on the fifteenth he took Suzannah and Sigurd for a holiday to Berchtesgaden, where they had enjoyed themselves four years previously. There he received a request from Brandes to help him and his brother Edvard in a new magazine they were planning, to be named *The Nineteenth Century* and to be published by Gyldendal. Ibsen replied (23 July) that he was thinking of writing some more rhymed epistles on the lines of the 'Letter to Fru Heiberg', 'concerning our position, and that of our age in general, vis-à-vis politics, literature, etc. They would be a kind of declaration of faith.' But he refused to associate himself more actively with Brandes's project. 'I must confine myself within my own chosen sphere; here, all my thoughts are concentrated. Its range is not wide, but I exploit it as best I can ... I do not in the least fear being regarded as holding partisan sympathies,' he concluded surprisingly. 'I cannot understand why people now regard me as having no party allegiances.' Presumably he meant by this last sentence that his criticisms of the faults of the left did not imply that his sympathies lay elsewhere, and that one could owe allegiance to a party without toeing the line, just as a man can regard himself as a good Catholic while retaining the right to independent criticism.

On 18 July Norway celebrated her thousand years as a kingdom, and Ibsen wrote a special poem for the occasion which the university library in Christiania printed on the day. It contained one of the most disturbing messages of thanks that any country or individual can ever have received. Edmund Gosse was not always the most accurate of translators, but his rendering of the first two verses of this poem will hardly be bettered:

> My countrymen, who filled for me deep bowls
> Of wholesome bitter medicine, such as gave
> The poet, on the margin of his grave,
> Fresh strength to fight where broken twilight rolls –

My countrymen, who sped me o'er the wave –
An exile, with my griefs for pilgrim-soles,
My fears for burdens, doubts for staffs, to roam –
From the wide world I send you greeting home.

I send you thanks for gifts that help and harden,
Thanks for each hour of purifying pain;
Each plant that prospers in my poet's garden
Is rooted where your harshness poured its rain;
Each shoot in which it blooms and burgeons forth
It owes to that grey weather from the north;
The sun's fire loosens, but the fog secures.
My country, thanks! My life's best gifts were yours.

He worked hard on *Julian* in Berchtesgaden, and on 8 August he was able to write joyfully to Hegel that he had completed Part Two and assure him that the third and final part 'is so clear in my mind that it will go very much quicker than the others'. On 30 August he left for Dresden where a fortnight later, he was joined by Georg Brandes. This time, Brandes stayed a month, during which period he saw Ibsen almost daily, and his autobiography contains some vivid reminiscences of their meetings:

Each day I walked from the small, very bad hotel which he had recommended to me nearby, and collected him for a walk, often broken by a visit to an inn, where the waiters were impressed by the barbaric splendour of his buttonhole, but invariably ending with tea at his apartment. I received a new impression after the year that had passed since I had last seen him. Not very tall, but handsome, athletically built, with a mighty head, big neck, powerful shoulders – he looked as though one would need a club to overpower him. He spoke, in general, little, though he was communicative to me; but the curious thing about his speech was its calm and slowness, and the fact that he never smiled except when the person to whom he was talking smiled first. This sometimes had an effect that was almost of timidity. Yet if one had to choose a single adjective to describe him, it would be menacing. He could look terrifying, as he sat with his watchful eyes. Then he resembled a judge. He looked a man who was accustomed, in intercourse with other men, to occupy the standpoint of a schoolmaster confronting his pupils, and to instil fear. For all his hostility towards the Norwegians he was, in essence, very Norwegian.

There lay stored within him twenty-four years of bitterness and hatred; his contempt for humanity knew no limits. He was an aristocrat to his fingertips, with all that that implied. It was an article of faith with him that all politicians – parliamentary politicians, that is, not men such as Bismarck – were hypocrites, liars, drivellers, dogs ... His hatred for false freedom movements was supplanting his interest in genuine ones ... The true freedom was social freedom, spiritual freedom, freedom of thought, freedom of conscience ... He hated the liberals of Norway,[5] and regarded most Norwegian peasants as sordid and self-seeking ... He laughed at Bjørnson's rustic tales; he chortled over the space that love occupied in them, saying that nothing bothered the Norwegian peasant less, unless one used the word 'love' in its crudest sense. A youth of twenty would gladly marry a woman of sixty if she were well-to-do. Let Bjørnson but continue till his hero Arne got into Parliament, and we should see that fellow in his true colours. Many years later I learned from Ibsen's letters that he at times felt friendly towards Bjørnson, even infatuated. But on this occasion, and others, I heard him name Bjørnson only with the most vehement distaste and contempt. The violence of his fanaticism struck me one day when in an angry outburst he decried Magdalene Thoresen's writings, damned their language, called them artificial and false, and then broke off to remark: 'Mind you, she has more talent than that Bjørnson.' One must, however, add that, as Christian Rickardt once rightly observed, Ibsen never spoke as disparagingly of Bjørnson as the latter did of him.

Walking out towards Plauenscher Grund he said: 'Scandinavia lies outside the cultural mainstream. The unhappy consequence is that we never get anywhere until the rest of Europe has moved on ... It is as though one were to introduce astronomy into Mada-

---

5. 'In political matters he is very conservative, or rather absolutist ... The political liberals are almost illiberal in intellectual matters, and he says it is better to be under the rule of one big tyrant than several little ones.' (Letters from Brandes to Hans Brøchner, 29 September 1872.)

gascar and begin with the Ptolemaic system ...' He spoke of the importance of written work having 'an intense connection with the author's spiritual life', and thought the major advance of the age was that poetry was becoming more and more psychological, and not merely poetry but all literature. 'What will ensure your latest book a future life is that it reveals how *you* have regarded things. If you want objectivity, then go to the objects. Read me so as to get to know *me!*' He thought that this was the great literary revolution that he was attempting.[6]

Of *Emperor and Galilean*, Brandes recalled:

At first he could not be persuaded to read a line of it to me. When he wanted to rewrite a scene to refine the dialogue, he would not let me see its first, inferior form. He said: 'I never write a line without asking myself: "What will G.B. think of this?" So how could I let you see it in the rough?' However, he shortly afterwards read me long extracts, including the scene between Julian and the mystic Maximus. His quiet voice lent itself well to the expression of what was powerful and disturbing.

He took Brandes to more than one meeting of the Dresden Literary Society (where, says Brandes, Ibsen regularly attended lectures); among other subjects, they heard a talk on Tieck's essay on the monologues in *Hamlet*, 'of which, strangely enough', comments Brandes, 'I was the only person present who had foreknowledge.'

Another Danish visitor to Dresden that month was Meïr Aron Goldschmidt, founder of *The Corsair*, the magazine on which, twenty years earlier, Botten Hansen and Vinje had modelled *The Man*, to give Ibsen his first opening in journalism. Goldschmidt invited Ibsen and Brandes to dinner at the Hotel Berlin. The conversation turned to religion. Goldschmidt denied that Voltaire was an atheist, and

6. Another example of Ibsen's imperfect acquaintance with literary history. 'Read me so as to know *me*' had been one of the principles of the Romantic movement throughout Europe at the beginning of the century, as one would have expected him to know from his acquaintance with Byron's work.

suddenly asked Ibsen if he believed in God. Ibsen 'replied in astonishment at this inquisition: "Certainly." "Then I don't see how you can associate with someone like Brandes who doesn't believe in any God ..." Ibsen replied in rising displeasure: "I have no idea what Brandes believes in or doesn't believe in. I have never discussed it with him, and feel no cause to." '

Ibsen does not record what Brandes said to him during these meetings in Dresden; but some things, at least, we can guess at, and if we are correct, they were to bear importantly on Ibsen's future work. As Dr Henning Fenger, the distinguished Brandes scholar, points out, Brandes had that spring followed up his lectures of the preceding winter with a series of six on the development of French drama from Beaumarchais to Dumas *fils*. In these lectures, Brandes had shown especial interest in the connection between money and morality – the way French dramatists regarded money as playing a vital role in determining human destinies, the way false share dealings are brought to light, and so forth. This interlocking of money with morality was something that was to feature strongly in *The Pillars of Society* and *A Doll's House*. Moreover, from these unpublished lectures Dr Fenger quotes Brandes's description of the new type of woman who was threatening to replace the traditional romantic heroines:

This young girl is no longer ignorant of life and the world. She walks forth into it self-possessed and sceptical. She does not throw herself at the first man who asks her. Even in extreme youth, she has a character of her own. She has a man's seriousness, power of decision, and will.

These words exactly describe the 'heroines' (did anyone then, in conversation if not in print, ever refer to them as anti-heroines?) whom Ibsen was henceforth to create, beginning with Dina Dorf, Nora and Petra Stockmann, and of whom Selma in *The League of Youth* was, as we have seen, in a small way (for she has very few lines) the forerunner.

Brandes also, in his lectures, praised Dumas *fils* for his realism and 'physiological, clinical view of human nature ... a directness, a brutality, but at the same time a truthfulness of expression hitherto unparalleled'.[7] One must assume that Brandes expatiated on this to Ibsen during their Dresden walks; and any writer knows how immensely stimulating and strengthening it is when, apparently ploughing a lonely furrow, he meets someone who can crystallize in clear language his own unstated intuitions.

Most importantly, perhaps, Brandes had demanded in his lectures that the Scandinavian dramatists should employ 'careful and truthful study of human character' *in the service of liberal thought* – in other words, not stand objectively and ironically aloof, as Ibsen had done in *The League of Youth*, but use the drama as a pulpit for preaching the ideals of the new age. Dr Fenger rightly comments that to Ibsen this uncompromising demand that he should commit himself must have come as manna from heaven. 'Here was the answer to the problems he had wrestled with in 1869–70 ... A whole-hearted commitment to the ideals of the new age was something that would lift and animate the most realistic portrait of actuality.' Remembering that these lectures of Brandes were (and were to remain) unpublished, the conversations that Ibsen had with him in Dresden that September may well have been vital in stimulating Ibsen to make the leap from the uncommittedness of *The League of Youth* to the committed progressiveness of *The Pillars of Society* and its great successors.

Some time during November Ibsen moved for the second time that year, from Grosse Plauensche Strasse to a first-floor apartment at Wettiner-Strasse 22. He had a welcome visitor that month in Lorentz Dietrichson, whom he had not seen since his visit to Stockholm three years earlier. Dietrichson, like Brandes, enjoyed the unusual pleasure of hear-

7. It is interesting that, according to the French scholar P. G. la Chesnais, Dumas *fils* was probably partly responsible for the first (private) staging in France of *A Doll's House* in 1891.

ing Ibsen read Part One of *Julian*, and remembered the
disappointment of the thirteen-year-old Sigurd at being
ordered into another room to do his divinity homework instead of being allowed to listen. 'I think there's as much
divinity in father's plays as in my homework,' he pleaded,
but in vain. 'Although Ibsen has no outstanding talent for
reading [writes Dietrichson], it was a rare and exquisite delight to hear him read his drama in his pleasant voice and
noble, totally unaffected diction.' It was nearly midnight
before Ibsen read the final line: 'For Thine is the Kingdom,
the Power and the Glory'; and Dietrichson walked home
'quite shaken, and convinced that I had heard one of the
most remarkable tragedies written since the time of Shakespeare. Its mighty figures haunted me even in my dreams.'

Dietrichson (again like Brandes) was amazed that Ibsen
had not made the acquaintance of Hermann Hettner, whose
Das moderne Drama had so excited the dramatist twenty
years earlier, and who was now living in Dresden. 'I tried to
bring them together, but did not succeed in the few days I
could spend in Dresden. Hettner knew Ibsen's name well,
indeed, almost everyone I met in Dresden was aware that a
great Norwegian writer was dwelling in their midst; but very
few then knew his work, and those who had read his *Brand*
in Siebold's translation ... could not really get a grip on the
work; they could of course sense the grandeur of its scope,
but found its full meaning, to put it mildly, obscure.'

Ibsen's avoidance of Hettner may have been conscious; as
we have seen, he had a neurotic fear of admitting that he
owed a debt to anyone, a feeling which is perhaps tied up
with his obsession about bankruptcy. He may, too, have felt
that he had outgrown Hettner's teaching and would gain
little from a meeting, for Hettner had written nothing very
interesting since (though Brandes had met him several times
and found him rewarding). The other fact which Dietrichson mentions, that Ibsen's German literary acquaintances had to take his reputation on trust – in the next five
years, only *The Vikings at Helgeland* and *Lady Inger of*

Østraat were to be translated, in addition to the three plays published earlier that year, and of his best work, *Brand* was most inadequately translated and *Peer Gynt* not at all – no doubt helped to increase his already formidable reserve.

Ibsen spent the last months of 1872 combining Parts One and Two of his *Julian* trilogy into a single part of five acts, and beginning the draft of his final section (the ultimate Part Two). The great work was at last approaching its end; indeed, it was urgent that it should, as Ibsen must have realized when making up his balance sheet for the year. His total earnings for 1872 were the 200 specie-dollars (£56) which he had received for the third edition of *The Pretenders*. And this was five years after the publication of *Peer Gynt*.

16

The End of Several Phases
1873–5

1873 opened propitiously for Ibsen, in several respects. On New Year's Day the *Fortnightly Review* in London published a long article by Edmund Gosse entitled 'Ibsen, the Norwegian Satirist', the first full assessment of Ibsen in English. 'Where shall we look for a young great poet among the continental nations?' asked Gosse. 'It is my firm belief that in the Norwegian, Henrik Ibsen, the representative of a land unknown in the literary annals of Europe, such a poet is found.' News also arrived from Hegel that reprints were in hand of both *Brand* and *Love's Comedy*; and Ibsen himself had good tidings to send in reply. 'I have the great joy', he wrote on 6 February, 'to be able to inform you that my great work is finished, and more happily so than anything I have previously written. The book is entitled *Emperor and Galilean; A World Drama in Two Parts*. It contains: Part One: Caesar's Apostasy, a play in five acts (170 pages). Part Two: Emperor Julian, a play in five acts (252 pages). Do not let the description "World Drama" frighten you! I shall begin fair-copying the play in a week and shall send you a weekly batch of 48 pages ... This has been a Herculean labour for me; not the work itself, that has gone easily, but the pain it has cost me to live myself freshly and vividly into so distant and alien an age.'

Ibsen at first kept pretty well to his timetable for the fair-copying; he posted batches of forty-eight pages to Hegel on 22 February, 1 March and 9 March. Then there was a gap until 22 April, but further instalments followed on 30 April, 9 May, and finally 24 May. 'There is much self-anatomy in this book,' he told Edmund Gosse, who used the information to publish a brief note about its imminent appearance in the *Academy* on 1 April; and to Ludvig Daae, who was helping him with the spelling of the Greek names, he wrote: 'The play deals with a conflict between two irreconcilable powers in human life which will always be repeated, and that is why I call it "A World-Historical Drama".' It would, he assured Daae, 'be my masterpiece'.

Even the Dresden Literary Society began to take notice of him, thanks to Strodtmann's translations of *The Pretenders* and *The League of Youth* and his praise of Ibsen in a series of articles in the *Hamburg Correspondent*. The articles especially, he told Strodtmann (20 March) 'have added immeasurably to my standing here. They have been the subject of three separate lectures in the Literary Society, together with the two plays you translated. This has put me back into a good humour with my surroundings, so that I now feel happy again in Dresden – the only home I can imagine for myself north of the Alps.' Yet he concluded his letter: 'I stand unspeakably alone, today – which happens to be my birthday – more than ever.'

He tried to read Georg Brandes's translation of Mill's *Utilitarianism*, but found it, like most theoretical writing (apart from Brandes's own), unsatisfying. He wrote to Brandes on 30 April:

I don't know whether I dare express an opinion on a subject on which I have no professional expertise. When, however, I reflect that there are writers who lay down the law about philosophy without any knowledge of Hegel or German thought in general, it seems to me that anything is allowed. So I must honestly tell you that I cannot see any hope of progress, or any future at all, in the way Stuart Mill describes. I don't see why you have bothered to translate this book, the philistine sophistry of which harks back to Cicero or Seneca. I am convinced you could have written a ten times better book yourself in half the time it must have taken you to translate it . . . Come here soon! I long to see you, despite our many differences of opinion.

Brandes, he must have felt, was the only person who could relieve his loneliness.

While he was awaiting the publication of *Emperor and Galilean*, a pleasant diversion offered itself. He was invited to attend the International Exhibition in Vienna as representative for Denmark and Norway on the jury which was to award the prizes in the painting and sculpture sections. The Exhibition opened on 1 May, but Ibsen's services were not required until the following month. He left Dresden by train on the evening of 12 June, and the day after his arrival in Vienna he wrote to Suzannah. It is the earliest of his letters to her that has survived:

Vienna, 14 June 1873

Dear Suzannah!

A few hasty words, just to put you in the picture. I arrived here yesterday morning at nine o'clock, and was met at the station by Thomas,[1] who brought me word from Tobias Møller that I could have a room next to his, which he strongly recommended. I could not have done better! The house, which is near the Exhibition, only fifteen minutes' walk or five minutes' ride for five *kreutzer*, is an excellent and respectable hotel in the most elegant part of the city. The first floor, which I have rented, overlooking the street, or avenue, belongs to a baroness, who has left town and instructed her *Wirthschafterin*, or housekeeper, to rent out the room for the summer. She is an absolute pearl of amiability, honesty and helpfulness. Hildur[2] is enthusiastic about her, and rightly. For my room, with service, cleaning and valeting, errands within the city, etc., I pay 80 *gulden* a month, i.e. about 2½ *gulden* a day. She brings me coffee when I require it, with rolls and butter for breakfast, all for 30 *kreutzer* or 6 *groschen*. I ate breakfast here this morning, beautifully served on a silver tray with a cloth and napkin, a whole small pot of coffee, lots of milk, bread, butter, and sugar all of the best quality, and delicious.

1. The elder of Magdalene's two sons by Dean Thoresen. They both died at the age of thirty, Thomas (who was a successful writer of vaudevilles) in 1876, Axel in 1881.

2. The daughter of Randolph Nilsen, with whom he had stayed at Bergen in 1863.

I visited the Exhibition yesterday, but cannot of course yet venture any opinion on it. I live next to the Møllers. Our admirable landlady lives quite alone in the house and sees to everything herself.

Møller and I have to go out now to pay our official respects. It is said to be expensive here, but I have found that I can manage economically for lunch, etc.

This must be all for today. Be patient in my absence and write soon to

Your affectionate
Henrik Ibsen

When you write you can until further notice use the address I gave you. My lodging is: Augarten Allée-Strasse no. 23, first floor.

Suzannah's birthday fell on 26 June, and Ibsen dutifully remembered it:

Vienna, 25 June 1873

Dear Suzannah!

Now that the good time approaches when there will be roasting and frying for three days on end, and the coffee-pot will simmer unceasingly from early morning, I write you a few words to wish you many happy returns of the day. The only handsome present that I can offer you for the moment is the enclosed banknote, which I beg that you will not disdain, and which you will be able to change immediately into Prussian currency. Had Thomas not been inaccessible these past days, I would have sent some small thing with him. But he remained invisible, and left without saying goodbye. So you must be patient, dear cattttt!

The jury work has now started in earnest, so you must not expect long letters from me for a while. I have become a juror for both painting and sculpture, and have therefore double duties. My timetable is as follows: in the morning I rise at 6, and by 8 have completed my toilet, eaten breakfast, read the newspaper and smoked my morning pipe. Then I go out to the Exhibition, where the painting jury meets from 9 to 12. As soon as this is finished, I go to a restaurant nearby, where I eat a good meat dish, with admirable beer. At 2 the sculpture jury's meetings begin, and these last till 4.30 or 5. These meetings are, however, not always confined to the table; for example, these last days we

have been walking round the huge Exhibition buildings studying the works of art. There has of course been no question of any
midday siesta since I arrived in Vienna. When the jury meetings
are finished I am, as you can imagine, tired. Then I sit down in
one of the many open-air restaurants in the Prater and look at
the thousands of people driving along the avenue while I eat my
evening meal, comprising bread and cheese, with excellent beer.
At 9 I go home and, immediately, to bed. I greatly enjoy this life
here. They have not yet begun to offer hospitality to the jury-
men, though I hear this is to come later ... Each day I find
myself in the company of many notables, and all the officials at
the Exhibition have instructions to show us the greatest respect.

Write again soon ... I shall celebrate tomorrow by indulging
in some luxury.

> Happy birthday!
> Your affectionate
> Henrik Ibsen

Ibsen stayed in Vienna until the end of July. One of his
fellow-jurors was a Swede, Fritz von Dardel, a gifted cari-
caturist (and much besides) whose diaries are an endless
source of fascination to anyone interested in the Scand-
dinavia of those years. In addition to a lively drawing of
Ibsen, Dardel (to whom, almost alone among his fellow-
jurors, Ibsen's name was known) noted in his diary:

The black clothes and white cravat which he always wore, and
the searching, penetrating glance which issued from behind his
spectacles, gave him the appearance of a French notary rather
than an artist. Throughout all our meetings he remained completely silent, spoke to no one and avoided all opportunity of
making the acquaintance of his fellows, who were mostly eminent persons. When the rest of us went to take lunch together in
the restaurant, Ibsen retired to the beer-hall, where he sat quite
alone emptying his tankards. I joined him there a couple of
times, and found much interest in his conversation. My fellow-
jurors were amazed when I told them that their supposed notary
was a famous dramatist.

On 8 July the jurors were presented to the Emperor Franz

Josef, whom Ibsen had seen from a distance at the Suez opening; and four days later, they were taken by train to Murz to be dined by Baron Schwarz-Senborn, the director of the Exhibition. 'At every station where the train halted,' the *Illustrated London News* of 19 July 1873 reported, 'troops of little children came running up with baskets of wild strawberries, bouquets of Alpine flowers, and jugs full of fresh, cool water from the mountain springs ... At the repast which followed the greatest convivality prevailed.' Six days later Ibsen was awarded another medal to add to his collection. On 18 May the new King of Sweden and Norway, Oscar II (the younger brother of Carl XV, who had died of syphilis without legitimate male issue), having been crowned in Stockholm in May, was crowned again before his Norwegian subjects in Trondhjem. In the ensuing welter of decorating Ibsen received the coveted Order of St Olaf. On 26 July the jurors were invited on a trip to Budapest along the Danube, but Ibsen, surprisingly, seems not to have gone; at any rate there is no mention of it in his letters. It is possible that he had, by then, already left; the date of his departure from Vienna is not known.

He wrote a short report on the Exhibition for *Morgenbladet*, which that newspaper published on 30 August. What impressed Ibsen most were the entries from Eastern Europe. The Exhibition, he writes, 'will dispel certain prejudices which have hitherto existed; I refer especially to the outdated superstition that the Slav peoples have little or nothing to contribute to the great common task of civilization. The acquaintance which Europe has made in recent years with Russian writing should have ended such an attitude; but I have no doubt that the Vienna Exhibition will lead to a quite different and juster appraisal. It teaches us that in every sphere of graphic art Russia stands among the leaders of our age.' Ibsen concluded by asserting that Russia possessed 'a school of painters fully comparable with those of France, Germany, or any other country' – a judgement hardly confirmed by posterity – and suggested that young Norwegian artists should be given grants to enable them to visit Vienna.

Ibsen's taste in painting was less discriminating than his taste in literature; for, explaining that 'medals could only be awarded to living artists and then only for works completed since 1867, a condition to which several countries, notably England, paid scant attention', he adds: 'Thus the English exhibits, though almost exclusively comprising master-pieces, gained comparatively few medals.' What were these 'masterpieces' provided by England? Ibsen does not name them, but a list is given in the *Official Catalogue of the British Section at the Vienna Universal Exhibition, 1873* (London, 1873). Turner, who had been dead for over twenty years, was represented by 'Walton Bridges', Whistler by six etchings, and Cruikshank by five. Otherwise, there was W. P. Frith's 'Ramsgate Sands' and 'Lord Foppington Relating His Adventures' (from Vanbrugh's play, *The Relapse*); Millais's 'Portrait of Miss Nina Lehmann' and 'The Sisters'; G. F. Watts's 'Portrait of Robert Browning' and 'The Angel of Death'; Landseer's 'The Sanctuary' (lent by Queen Victoria) and 'The Arab Tent' and 'Self-Portrait' (both lent by the Prince of Wales); and Thomas Woolner's bust of Charles Darwin, lent by the subject. Also in the oils section were Mrs E. M. Ward's 'The Tower, Ayè, the Tower' and 'The Last Sleep of Argyll'; W. B. Richmond's 'The Lament of Ariadne'; George A. Storey's 'The Shy Pupil'; C. V. Cope's 'Othello Relating His Adventures to Desdemona'; John Pettie's 'Touchstone and Audrey'; and Sir G. Harvey's 'School Dismissing'.

It is a melancholy comment on Ibsen's taste in painting, which was always to remain curiously conservative (to the end of his life there is no record of his taking any interest in Impressionism), that he should have described this collection as 'almost exclusively comprising masterpieces'. Nor could they even be defended on the ground of realism; they were the visual equivalent of exactly the kind of sentimental melodrama that he was trying to lead the theatre away from.

A seventeen-year-old Scot, also in Vienna that August, making his journalistic debut as a roving correspondent for the *Alloa Advertiser*, condemned the whole of the English art section as 'glaringly inferior'. But the two men did not meet; William Archer had not yet heard of Ibsen.

Nor, one supposes, had a young Jew who left school in Vienna that summer and was likewise to become a passionate admirer. Sigmund Freud was then just seventeen, and in some ways his and Ibsen's lives and personalities were curiously similar. 'I could tell you about my long years of honourable, but painful, loneliness that began for me as soon as I got the first glimpse into the new world; of the lack of interest and understanding on the part of my nearest friends; of the anxious moments when I myself believed I was in error and wondered how it was going to be possible to follow such unconventional paths and yet support my family ... and of the calm certainty which bade me wait until a voice from beyond my ken would respond.' That is Freud writing to Jung in 1910, but the words could have been Ibsen's; and in a few years Ibsen might have echoed: 'I understood that from now onward I belonged to those who have "troubled the sleep of the world", as Hebbel says, and that I could not reckon upon objectivity and tolerance.' To Freud too, as to Ibsen, Rome 'became the symbol for a number of warmly cherished wishes', and a source of 'great happiness and even exaltation ... experienced on every visit'. And one suspects that Ibsen, like Freud, had a 'confessed need for periodic experiences of intense love and hate'.

One interesting relic of Ibsen's stay in Vienna has survived in the form of a photograph of the art and sculpture jury, twenty-five formidably bearded and whiskered figures. Ibsen, looking much the youngest (as, at forty-five, he probably was) is seated noticeably apart from the others, neatly barbered, in frock coat and spats, an order in his buttonhole, a top hat on his knee, and a rolled umbrella between his legs.

There was an outbreak of cholera in Dresden that July, so on leaving Vienna Ibsen spent a few weeks at Pillnitz, an hour from Dresden by steamer. Suzannah and Sigurd joined him there, and he had two other visitors. Lorentz Dietrichson, who had missed him in Vienna, dropped in on his way north, and found him more grandly dressed than when they had last met in Dresden. 'His outward appearance had undergone a change; instead of his smart short velvet jacket he was now wearing a long black coat that reached beneath his knees, of a very severe character.' Dietrichson was not surprised when Ibsen told him that during their summer in the Tyrol the local children had kissed his hand and asked for his blessing, taking him for a Catholic Priest.

Ibsen's other caller at Pillnitz was Ludvig Josephson, a young Swede who had succeeded Hartvig Lassen as artistic director of the Christiania Theatre. In Stockholm, Josephson had enjoyed considerable success as a dramatist, and had been director of both the Royal Theatre and the Opera, but had had to leave because the Swedish actors disliked being ordered about by a Jew. In Christiania he had an equally rough baptism; as he tells in his memoirs, 'one director after another had been forced to resign because of the savage press criticisms and public hostility', and there was additional feeling against Josephson because he was (in addition to being a Jew) a Swede. The première of his first production that February had been repeatedly interrupted with boos, hisses, and cries of 'Out with the foreigner!' and the police had to be called to restore order. He stuck to his post, however, and during his four years there raised the artistic standard of the theatre to a height it had never previously attained, as the list of plays that he presented bears witness. Josephson may be ranked as the earliest of those imaginative young directors, after Duke Georg of Saxe-Meiningen and his lieutenant Ludwig Chronegk, who saw in Ibsen's plays the dawn of a new era in the theatre. He was the forerunner of August Lindberg, André Antoine, Otto

Brahm, Aurélien Lugné-Poe, Konstantin Stanislavsky and J. T. Grein.

Josephson was anxious to make the acquaintance of the author of *Love's Comedy*, which was on the theatre's schedule for the coming season, and wrote diffidently to ask if he might visit him. Ibsen assented; and

as the steamer approached the humble jetty, I saw a solitary figure walking to and fro on the shore, dressed in black with medal ribbons in his lapel, kid gloves, and a tall black hat – a costume which suited neither the season nor the shabby surroundings . . . I recognized him immediately from the portraits I had seen. My astonishment at his dress and the formality of his manner (a weakness which never left him once he had gone abroad) vanished as soon as we had exchanged preliminary courtesies. Soon the total unpretentiousness of the man became clear to me beneath the formal surface, and I found him the most friendly, kind and unpretentious [Josephson repeats the word, *ansprākslös*] great man that I had ever met among famous authors. I have often since wondered at this curious passion of Ibsen's for appearing, if I may say so, dressed up. The appearance he chose for himself was more suited to a rich merchant or banker than to a philosopher and a poet.

Josephson accompanied Ibsen back to Dresden at the beginning of September, and they spent a good deal of time together, both in the cafés and at Ibsen's home. Josephson noted with curiosity the relationship between father and son. He found Sigurd 'handsome and elegant' but 'very strange, withdrawn, and brooding'.

I observed with surprise that the young Ibsen would at mealtimes make his entry at the last moment, bow deeply like a stranger to his parents, and seat himself silently at table. In that house, where everything happened silently, scarcely a word was ever exchanged between father and son in a stranger's presence, and when the father or mother did speak, the son always replied in a very few words, very slowly and formally . . . After eating, the young man retired immediately with the same stiff ceremonious bow . . . We were happiest when we sat over our coffee and in the evening, when he had a great glass jug of ale brought in, which stood beside him on the floor and from which he himself filled our glasses ... But I never saw his study ... and I don't think many of his visitors were more favoured than I in this respect.

His favourite cafés, Josephson remembered, were those on the Brühl Terrace, the restaurants near the Wildsrufferplatz, and the Café Français in the Old Town, where there were Scandinavian newspapers available.

Ibsen liked the young Swede. On the whole, dare one say, he got on better with Swedes than with his own countrymen; the Swedish formality suited him, and he felt free of the reproach, unspoken or expressed, of being a 'bad Norwegian'.

He restlessly awaited the publication of *Emperor and Galilean*. 'I hear from Norway', he wrote to Georg Brandes on 8 September, 'that Bjørnson, although he can know nothing of the book, declares it to be "Atheism", and says it was inevitable that I should come to that.' Bjørnson's hostility towards Ibsen had doubtless been sharpened by the latter's acceptance of the Order of St Olaf, and although he was in Dresden that autumn he did not contact Ibsen.

On 2 October Hegel wrote that 'the orders for your new book have been so large that I have had to have no less than eight hundred copies bound', and that as an honorarium he had credited Ibsen's account with 3,200 riksdollars (£356). Ibsen replied on 6 October asking Hegel to invest the whole sum in gilt-edged securities 'giving an interest of at least 4 per cent'. His letter ended with a reference to 'new literary plans which have begun to stir in me'. These, again, probably (though not certainly) refer to *The Pillars of Society*, though it was to be four painful years before he completed it; its gestation was to be almost as difficult as that of *Emperor and Galilean*. A few days later he learned from Hegel that, despite the first printing of four thousand copies (twice that of *The League of Youth*), a second edition was already being prepared; he greeted this good news soberly by asking Hegel to use the new advance to buy Swedish railway shares, adding: 'More profitable shares are nothing to have if one is disinclined to speculate.'

Emperor and Galilean was published on 16 October 1873. 'The booksellers were so interested in this work', Hegel informed Bjørnson, who cannot have been overjoyed at the news, 'that the large edition ... was almost entirely subscribed, and the rest were taken by the Copenhagen booksellers on the day of publication.'

Of all Ibsen's plays, including even *When We Dead Awaken*, *Emperor and Galilean* is the one most under-rated by posterity; indeed, it is unique among his major works in having been admired less by posterity than by his contemporaries. Ibsen himself several times referred to it as his masterpiece; most subsequent commentators have rejected it as a worthy failure. But few Ibsen commentators can have seen it, and fewer still seem able to read a play as a play, mentally excising (as a director of Shakespeare likewise must) what on the stage would be tedious and superfluous – for we must remember that *Emperor and Galilean*, like *Brand* and *Peer Gynt*, was written not for the spectator but for the reader. *Brand* was regarded as unactable in England until 1959, *When We Dead Awaken* until 1968; in some countries they are still regarded as such, awaiting the director who can reveal their profound and exciting theatricality. The same is true of *Emperor and Galilean*. It has longueurs, especially in the first half of Part Two, but so have *Brand* and *Peer Gynt*; once one has stripped away the superfluous detail, a play is revealed which is a worthy successor to those two great dramas.

The action of *Emperor and Galilean* covers twelve years, from A.D. 351 to 363. Julian, who is nineteen when the play opens, and his brother Gallus live in terror of the mad Emperor Constantius, their cousin, who has already had their parents and nine other kinsmen murdered. Julian, like the Emperor, is a Christian, but is restless in his faith; under the influence of the philosopher Libanius ('There is a whole glorious world to which you Christians are blind') he goes to Athens to study the pagan religion. But in Athens he becomes equally disillusioned with paganism and longs for a vision to show him his way. He hears of a mystic, Maximus, who claims to have power over ghosts and spirits, and visits him in Ephesus. There, Maximus expounds his philosophy to Julian: 'First, there is the kingdom founded on the Tree of Knowledge. Then the kingdom founded on the Tree of the Cross. The third kingdom is the kingdom of the great mystery, which shall be founded on both the Tree of Knowledge and the Tree of the Cross ... It's life-spring has its source beneath Adam's grove and Golgotha.' In other words, Julian must combine the wisdom of Christianity and the wisdom of paganism.

Now Maximus summons up the spirits of three men who, as unconscious instruments of the world-will, most altered the course of history: Cain, Judas Iscariot, and – but the third does not appear. Then Maximus realizes that this third is either Julian or himself; which, he does not know. Julian believes that he could alter the course of history, granted the companionship of a 'pure woman'. Then he hears that the Emperor has offered him his sister Helena as wife. This seems to him a further sign that he has been chosen by destiny.

The Emperor sends Julian to Gaul to quell a rebellion. His brother Gallus has been executed at the Emperor's orders, so that now Julian is the last of his line. He knows he is being spied on, and that the Emperor has sent him to Gaul so that if he fails at least the Emperor will be rid of him. When he defeats the rebels, a tribune comes from the Emperor to arrest him, lest he should march on Rome. Helena is pregnant; the tribune brings her a gift of peaches from the Emperor; she eats them and is poisoned – the Emperor's precaution lest she should bear Julian an heir. In her delirium before she dies, she reveals that the child she is carrying is not Julian's. This extra disillusionment dispels Julian's last scruples; he decides to lead his army against Rome; but before doing so, he denies Christ and, under the guidance of Maximus, embraces paganism and appears before his soldiers smeared with the blood of the sacrifice. Here Part One ends.

In Part Two, Julian is Emperor, Constantius having died before Julian reached Rome. He proclaims a regime of tolerance; although he himself is a pagan, the Christians will be granted freedom of worship. But the Christians will not permit a return to paganism; they destroy the temples, and Julian is forced to take repressive measures against them. He becomes a worse tyrant than Constantius, because on a wider scale. He leads an army against the Persians, and is killed in the desert by a Christian who had been his friend but who now sees him as the anti-Christ. As he dies he realizes that by his tyranny he has roused the Christians from their apathy and advanced their cause. Like Cain and Judas he has unwittingly, and in the opposite direction to which he intended, altered the course of history.

Emperor and Galilean is full of extraordinary scenes: the opening in Constantinople, with Julian and his brother waiting for the mad Emperor's hand to fall on them as on their eleven murdered kinsmen; Julian's confrontation with the philosopher Libanius, who tempts him to forsake the church for the debating-halls; Maximus's evocation of the ghosts of the 'corner-stones' of history, and Julian's sudden realization that he himself is to be the third of these; Helena's revelation that she is pregnant by another man, and Julian's order to the doctor not to save her; and the great climax to Part One, when Helena's body lies in the church and the army outside grows mutinous while Julian hesitates to lead them against Rome until he has taken the final step of renouncing Christianity; he learns that Helena's body is working miracles because she was 'the pure woman' and, maddened by the falsity of this, he makes the sacrifice and appears with the blood of the beast on his forehead. The first three acts of Part Two mark a certain slackening of tension, and are over-weighted with grubbed-up knowledge which

Ibsen does not carry very lightly; in any production, they would profit most by cutting. But the last two acts are of the quality of the whole of Part One; Julian's gradual submission to the force on which he has turned his back but which he cannot evade is as powerful and moving in its inevitability as the final acts of *Brand, Peer Gynt,* or any of the great prose plays.

Emperor and Galilean marks a vital turning-point in Ibsen's development as a dramatist. Although it is on an epic scale like *Brand* and *Peer Gynt,* he wrote it in prose; it is both the last play of one period and the first of another. The conviction which had been growing in him for several years that he must abandon the poetic medium in which he had gained his greatest triumphs found expression in a letter he wrote on 15 January 1874 to Edmund Gosse. Gosse, in a review of the play published in the *Spectator* on 27 December 1873, had regretted Ibsen's abandonment of verse; and we must be grateful to Gosse that he wrote as he did, for his remarks stimulated Ibsen to a clear statement of his new policy in play-writing. He informed Gosse:

The illusion I wanted to produce is that of reality. I wished to produce the impression on the reader that what he was reading was something that had really happened. If I had employed verse, I should have counteracted my own intention, and prevented the accomplishment of the task I had set myself. The many ordinary and insignificant characters whom I have introduced into the play would have become indistinct, and indistinguishable from one another, if I had allowed all of them to speak in one and the same rhythmical measure. We are no longer living in the age of Shakespeare. Among sculptors, there is already talk of painting statues in the natural colours. Much can be said both for and against this. I have no desire to see the Venus de Milo painted, but I would rather see the head of a Negro executed in black rather than white marble. Speaking generally, the style must conform to the degree of ideality which pervades the representation. My new drama is no tragedy in the ancient acceptation; what I desired to depict were human beings, and therefore I would not let them talk in 'the language of the gods'.[3]

In other words, *Emperor and Galilean* is at the same time Ibsen's farewell to the epic drama (at any rate until the final act of *John Gabriel Borkman* and *When We Dead Awaken*), and the forerunner of those naturalistic prose plays which were shortly to explode upon the nineteenth century like a series of bombs.

Despite the seeming remoteness of its theme, *Emperor and Galilean* is one of Ibsen's most personal statements, as self-analytical as *The Pretenders*, *Brand*, *The Master Builder*, or *When We Dead Awaken*. Somewhat unexpectedly, he took pains to establish this fact. 'I have put a good deal of my own inner life into the play,' he had written to Gosse on 14 October 1872, and again to Gosse on 20 February 1873: 'There is much self-anatomy in this book.' Three days later he told Ludvig Daae that it contained 'more of my own personal experience than I would publicly admit'. The problem that baffled and finally destroyed Julian was one that was always at the back of Ibsen's mind, though he seldom if ever mentioned it; where to find a faith to replace the Christianity of his upbringing. The third quarter of the nineteenth century was, more than preceding ages, a time of revolt against conventional religious thinking, with Bible criticism and natural science marching hand in hand, and *Emperor and Galilean*, in its search for a 'third kingdom' (a phrase which had not yet acquired a sinister significance), was as much a book of its era as *The Origin of Species*, Renan's *Life of Jesus*, and *Das Kapital*. 'He who has once been under Him [Christ] can never be free,' says Julian, and they are words that Ibsen himself, and many of his contemporaries, might have spoken.

It is a cliché that man is attracted by the qualities he lacks, and Ibsen's plays are permeated by a longing for what, in *Ghosts*, he was to term *livsglæde*, the joy of life. He deplored

3. Edmund Gosse's translation.

its absence in contemporary Christian teaching, which he probably (and with reason) blamed for his own inability to experience that joy; Brand and Pastor Manders, and those daunting lay preachers Rørlund, Gregers Werle, and Kroll, denounce it as a sin; Bishop Nicholas and John Rosmer would like to enjoy it but cannot, as though castrated by their own church upbringing. To find a religion which would combine Christian ethics with the joy of life is a problem that has troubled many a piously educated man and woman; it was a problem which Ibsen personally was never to solve and it is the central theme of *Emperor and Galilean* as it was to be the theme (or part-theme) of so many of his plays, whether explicitly as in *Ghosts* and *Rosmersholm*, or implicitly, as in *The Master Builder*, *John Gabriel Borkman* and *When We Dead Awaken*.

When Ibsen said that *Emperor and Galilean* contained 'more of my own personal experience than I would care to admit', I do not think there is much doubt that he was referring to the emotional strait-jacket in which he found himself confined, and from which, as from his childhood Christianity, he could never escape. It is relevant to add here a remark that Professor Francis Bull once made to this writer: that his father, Edvard Bull, who was Ibsen's doctor during his last years, once told his son that Ibsen was preternaturally shy about exposing his sexual organs even during medical examination. There was, indeed, much of Hedda Gabler in her creator.

Critical reaction to *Emperor and Galilean* was generally favourable, though somewhat bewildered. Arne Garborg published a long pamphlet on the play before the year was out, and it is an interesting example of the kind of grudging admiration with which so many of Ibsen's contemporaries regarded him. 'He is read with interest, even greedily,' Garborg admitted. 'His books are gutted with an eagerness otherwise unknown in our literary circles. As soon as the rumour spreads that a new work is expected from his pen,

the public gets worked up into an anticipation which sometimes reaches fever pitch, and once it has been published
and read it is discussed to the exclusion of all else for a long
time afterwards in the circles where such interests hold
sway.' Yet with all this, continues Garborg, Ibsen is not the
usual idea of a 'popular' author. He only asks, he gives no
answer, he is but a seeker, and so people call him negative.
'Ibsen has somewhere said that the "gift of doubt", too, can
make a man a poet. But this is unhappily where Ibsen is
wrong. Doubt is not a gift, it is a standpoint – nay, more, it is
only a temporary standpoint. As long as a soul doubts it
is not yet fully developed, not free, and however mighty its
talent it will stand impotent before its calling. Ibsen is an
example of this. He has received the gift of creativeness in
the richest measure, but doubt destroys his song. His poetry
... cannot achieve full beauty because it is bounded by obscurity and darkness, and lacks reconciliation and harmony.
This is the main reason why people are reluctant to acknowledge him. They are conscious of the sickness which lies at
the heart of his work.' Similar objections were to be raised
against Ibsen's plays as they gradually came to be translated
and staged in other countries.

Ibsen's fellow-authors were full of doubts. J. P. Jacobsen,
the Danish novelist whom Rilke so revered, disliked it:
'There's no pace in the play, it's cold, the characters are without character.' So did Bjørnson. 'I've read Ibsen's *Emperor
and Galilean*,' he wrote to H. E. Schirmer from Florence on
19 November. 'It was a great disappointment.' But he added
a perceptive prophecy: 'I think he's finished with *Brand*-style
writing ... and that we shall henceforth have what he will be
a master at – plays of plot. We need them!'

'I was especially pleased to hear that the first edition of the
book has sold out so quickly,' Ibsen wrote to Hegel on 13
November. 'And I am happy that the second edition can be
expected so soon; for should the bookshops be without it any
longer, every day would have reduced the advantage which
we both might have had from its publication. I know my

countrymen; they will save their money by borrowing it, and then not buy it. But this can't be helped; for who would have supposed that the whole large first edition would so soon disappear? From many letters from Norway I gather that none of my previous books has aroused such a stir up there. It has established itself in circles not normally concerned with literature.' Yet despite its (one would have thought) obvious dramatic possibilities, *Emperor and Galilean* was not to be performed even in part until 1896, when an adaptation was staged at the Leipzig Stadttheater. The first attempt to stage any of it in Norway was in 1903, when Part One was produced at the National Theatre in Christiania.

Ibsen had a row that November with Andreas Isachsen, the actor who had been the first 'student' to join the Bergen company back in 1852. Without asking Ibsen's, or indeed anyone's permission, Isachsen gave a public reading of *Emperor and Galilean* in Christiania, in two parts, on 1 and 8 November. Ibsen read an advertisement of this event in a newspaper, and on 4 November he penned Isachsen a furious letter. 'You will doubtless recall', he reminded him, 'that I have repeatedly impressed on you the need of foreign travel. Being abroad does not merely develop one's artistic outlook; it also teaches one the requirements needful to behave like a gentleman ... You can scarcely deny that every penny you get from publicly reading my book you take from my pocket ... And what is one to say to your presuming after so few days to seek to interpret by a public reading a work such as my latest? I can assure you that you need longer to get to the bottom of it.' The incident, trivial in itself, underlines a problem which Ibsen was to face for the whole of his career: lack of copyright protection. Ibsen's letter to Isachsen is scarcely pricklier than what a modern playwright would write under similar circumstances to someone who had given an unauthorized performance of his work, and modern playwrights are not, as Ibsen then was, dependent on book sales for the bulk of their income.

That same month, on 24 November, *Love's Comedy* received its first performance, eleven years after publication. This, again, was thanks to Ludvig Josephson, the new director of the Christiania Theatre, who had just opened his second season that September with a revival of *The Pretenders*. There was much curiosity to see how *Love's Comedy* would act, the general opinion being (not unreasonably) that it was 'scarcely suited to the stage'; but the result exceeded all expectations, even though Sigvard and Laura Gundersen, as Falk and Svanhild, lacked the youth that these two roles demanded. Johannes Brun, however, was excellent as Pastor Strawman, and so, despite his strained relations with Ibsen, was Isachsen as Guldstad. The play at once became a regular item in the theatre's repertory, and in the next twenty-five years was performed there seventy-seven times.

As the year drew to its close, Ibsen heard from Johan Thoresen that his debts in Norway had finally been paid off. 'I am particularly happy', he wrote to Thoresen on 12 December, 'that the business with Nandrup[4] has at last been settled. I am clear of debt and have several thousand crowns invested in the public funds, which Hegel has arranged for me over the years, and which steadily increase in value, so that I look forward to the not too distant time when we shall be able to live exclusively on my interest and my pension.' When he came to make up his accounts for the year, he found it had been by a long way his best yet:

	crowns	£
3rd edn of *Love's Comedy*	645	36
1st edn of *Emperor and Galilean*	6,400	355
Ditto (supplementary fee)	640	35
2nd edn of *Emperor and Galilean*	3,200	178
2nd edn of *The Vikings at Helgeland*	609	34
3rd edn of *The Vikings at Helgeland*	609	34
Fee for performances of *Love's Comedy* in Christiania	1,200	67
	13,303	739

4. See p. 272 above.

With his pension of 400 specie-dollars (£111), a grant of 100 specie-dollars (£28), which he had received for his trip to Vienna, and interest on his Danish and Swedish shares of 107 specie-dollars (£30), Ibsen's total income for the year amounted to £908. This was excellent by the average standard of Norwegian salaries. In 1870, a Professor ordinarius in Christiania received a basic salary of £250, rising to a ceiling of £333; a headmaster earned £300. At the same time, it was pathetically little compared with what leading authors of a stature comparable to Ibsen's were getting in the larger European countries. Anthony Trollope, for example, earned at his peak £4,500 annually. John Ruskin averaged £4,000 from his book royalties during his later years. George Eliot had refused £10,000 for the copyright of *Romola* in 1862, and *Middlemarch* brought her £9,000 in seven years. Ibsen only started to earn one thousand pounds a year regularly when he was well into his sixties, long after he had become world famous; and, as we shall see, he often, thanks partly to his refusal ever to repeat the pattern of a success, made barely half that amount, sometimes less. Although he lived parsimoniously until his death and eventually sold his copyrights, he left only a fractional sum compared with his peers abroad. Yet so humble was the rate of earning in Norway that the myth that he was a rich man has survived there to this day.

Still, 'This has been a good year for me,' he was able to tell Hegel on 30 December, adding: 'I have something new in my head and it grows clearer all the time, so that I think it cannot be long before I begin to write.'

The success of *Love's Comedy* on the stage stimulated Ibsen to think afresh about the possibility of a production of *Peer Gynt*, and on 23 January 1874 he wrote to Edvard Grieg asking him if he would consider providing a musical accompaniment and suggesting cuts, some of them surprising:

Act One should be retained in its entirety apart from some thinning out of the dialogue ... The wedding scene on p. 28 can

be made much more of, with the help of ballet, than appears in
the text ... In Act Two the incident with the three peasant girls
on pp. 57–60 should receive whatever musical treatment you feel
appropriate; but there must be devilry in it! ... There will have
to be some kind of musical accompaniment to the scene in the
troll palace, though here too the dialogue must be considerably
thinned out. The scene with the Boyg, also, which should remain
uncut, must have music; the Bird Voices to be sung, the church
bells and psalm singing to be heard in the distance ... Pretty well
the whole of Act Four will be omitted in performance. In its place
I thought we might have a great musical tone-picture to suggest
Peer Gynt's wanderings in the wide world, with American, English and French melodies interwoven as changing and disappearing *motifs* ... Act Five must be shortened considerably ...
The scenes on the upturned boat and in the churchyard will have
to go ... The scenes with the Button Moulder and the Old Man
of the Mountains must be trimmed down. On p. 254 the church-
goers sing on the forest path; church bells and distant psalm
singing should be indicated in the music during the dialogue
which follows until Solveig's song concludes the play, at which
point the curtain will descend while the psalm singing is heard
again clearer and louder. That is roughly how I have imagined it
... If you agree to come in with me on this, I shall immediately
approach the management of the Christiania Theatre, send them
an acting script and ensure that the play is guaranteed a production. As a fee I propose to ask 400 specie-dollars (£111) to be
shared equally between the two of us. I think it certain that we
can also reckon on the play being performed in Copenhagen and
Stockholm.

Grieg accepted the invitation, though not with unmixed
delight. 'It's a dreadfully intractable subject,' he wrote to his
friend Frantz Beyer that August. 'Except for certain passages – e.g. the part where Solveig sings – I've done that all
right. And I've made something of the Old Man's palace in
the mountains, which I literally can't bear to listen to, it
stinks so of cow dung and Norwegian insularity and self-
sufficiency! But I think people will sense the irony behind it.'
On 12 September Grieg complained to Bjørnson, who had
told him that he was wasting his time: 'I can't but admire

the way from start to finish it [*Peer Gynt*] splutters with wit and venom; but it will never win my sympathy. Though I think it the best thing Ibsen has written. Am I not right? But you don't imagine I had a free choice in the matter! I got the offer from Ibsen last year [*sic*], and naturally baulked at the prospect of putting music to this most unmusical of subjects. But I thought of the 200 [specie-dollars] and of the voyage, and made the sacrifice. The whole thing sits on me like a nightmare.'

Grieg continued to grouse privately about the task, and it was not until eighteen months after he had accepted the commission, in August 1875, that he finished the music. Ludvig Josephson, on the other hand, to whom Ibsen broached the project in a letter on 6 February after having received an affirmative answer from Grieg, reacted enthusiastically to the proposal, begging him only not to omit the whole of Act Four, and suggesting instead several extra cuts, to which Ibsen agreed.

It was in fact only by the chance of a lost manuscript that Grieg was invited to compose the music for *Peer Gynt*. Ludvig Josephson tells in his memoirs how a gifted Swedish composer, August Söderman,

had so fallen in love with *Peer Gynt* that, soon after its publication, he began to compose music for the play; and I still happily remember the many occasions when, sitting at the piano beside him, I went through scene after scene to the accompaniment of Söderman's personal performance of all the accompaniments he had provided to Ibsen's masterpiece. Unfortunately this composition could not be found at Söderman's death. It is known that in his lifetime he lent this work to various people, but when, later, *Peer Gynt* came to be staged, Söderman was dead and no one knew where his music was. So it fell to Edvard Grieg to set his great compatriot's ideas to music.

Admittedly Ibsen offered the idea of a stage production to Josephson on the basis of Grieg's promise to write the music; but the idea of a performance was already on the Christiania files when Josephson took over, and I think there is little doubt that had Söderman's score been available Josephson, being familiar with and enthusiastic about it, would have suggested a production before Ibsen did. And even after getting Ibsen's letter, he would probably have succeeded in persuading the unenthusiastic Grieg to withdraw from the project had a good score already been available.

Meanwhile, another continent was beginning to show a flicker of interest in the new dramatist. 'I am especially glad', Ibsen wrote to Hegel on 10 February, 'that a new market has been opened up for us in America. I think that *Brand, Peer Gynt* and *The League of Youth* will all, for different reasons, appeal to the taste of American Scandinavians. The only pity is that the sending of books there will involve so much extra expense.' The interest seems, however, to have been limited to those Americans who were able to read Ibsen in his own language (of whom there were already several thousand, after the large-scale immigrations of the past two decades). There was to be no American translation or performance of Ibsen for several years to come.

Georg Brandes visited Ibsen for a couple of days in June and was disturbed at what seemed to him Ibsen's eccentric and conservative opinions. As an example, he recalled that Ibsen was 'loud in his praise of Russia. "A splendid country," he said with a smile. "Think of all the grand oppression they have." "How do you mean?" "Only think of the glorious love of liberty it engenders. Russia is one of the few countries in the world where men still love liberty and make sacrifices for it. That is why she holds so high a place in poetry and art. Remember that they possess a writer such as Turgenev; and they have Turgenevs too among their painters, only we don't know them; but I have seen their pictures in Vienna." '[5]

Brandes thought that one reason for Ibsen's partiality for Russia lay in the fact that the country had no parliament. 'Ibsen's whole character presupposes a distrust of and ill-will

5. From Brandes's 'Second Impression' of Ibsen, written in 1882 and reprinted in his book *Henrik Ibsen* (1898). Muir-Archer translation.

towards parliamentarianism. He believes in the individual, in the single great personality; the individual, and he alone, can accomplish everything. Such a body as a parliament is, in Ibsen's eyes, a mere assembly of orators and dilettanti.' Like so many liberals who were working actively against conservatism in literature and politics, Brandes felt that Ibsen, by his contempt for practical politics, was not helping their cause; and it explains that growing coolness towards Ibsen which has already been noted. A couple of months after their meeting he was to describe Ibsen to a friend as 'remarkably receptive to every kind of reactionary influence'. One can sympathize with Brandes's distress; ironical paradoxes of the kind with which Ibsen had loved to taunt his companions in Rome are infuriating to the earnestly committed. But that summer Ibsen was to undergo a series of experiences which were to alter his course sharply from the conservatism to which, as Brandes had observed, he was beginning to lean.

He had at last, under the influence of Suzannah's constant urging, taken the decision to do what he had been planning, and putting off, for so many years: to revisit Norway. He made the journey with the utmost trepidation; as he sailed up the fjord, he was to recall ten years later, 'I literally felt my chest tighten with a feeling of sickness and unease.' It was ten years and one hundred and five days since he had last set foot on native soil when, at six o'clock in the evening of Sunday 19 July 1874, he disembarked with Suzannah and Sigurd in Christiania from the SS *Aarhus*.

They lodged modestly at a pension in Pilestrædet, in the centre of town, and stayed two and a half months, apparently spending the whole time in Christiania apart from a week in Stockholm during August to attend an archaeological congress. The experience left him with, if possible, even more confused feelings towards his country than before. The people of whose friendship he had felt surest had, he found, become remote; and those about whose feelings towards him he had least evidence, and perhaps cared most, acclaimed him as a champion.

The first to seek him out were, naturally, his old friends from the Learned Holland Circle, Michael Birkeland, Olof Rygh, Jacob Løkke (who had helped him with the poems), and Jonas Lie. But the decade that had elapsed since he had last seen them had separated their viewpoints, and he found himself much less in sympathy with them than before. Their cynicism, which he had previously found stimulating, now seemed to him to have stiffened into an extreme conservatism which he found distasteful. Moreover, he found that, thanks to *The League of Youth*, those right-wing elements which ten years earlier had scorned and excommunicated him now hailed him as a champion of the established order. The medals he had sought so assiduously in the hope that they would give him a position in Norwegian eyes had had their effect, and he found the result not altogether to his liking. Ibsen had no desire to be regarded as a pillar of society. The experience must surely have reminded him that, although he had mocked the pretensions of the left in *The League of Youth*, and stood aloof from the liberal party, his political sympathies still lay to the left of centre, and with the young rather than with the old; and when he read in the right-wing newspaper *Morgenbladet* an editorial demand that a candidate for a professorship at the university should be rejected on the ground that he was a free-thinker, he seized the opportunity to advertise his independence. He withdrew his subscription to *Morgenbladet* and changed to the left-wing newspaper *Dagbladet*. The uneasiness of the conservatives on hearing this would have been considerably increased if they had known what he was preparing for them.

This distant attitude towards his old friends was, by some at least of them, reciprocated. 'Ibsen is in town,' wrote Jonas Lie to Bjørnson on 4 September. '... [He] has become a somewhat elderly gentleman with fixed opinions and personality,' and he went on to describe Ibsen as 'Bismarckian'.

But if Ibsen's old friends in Norway greeted him with reserve, the general public did not. The Christiania Theatre put on special performances of *Love's Comedy*, which Ibsen had not seen before, and *The League of Youth*. He attended on both occasions, and was loudly cheered in the theatre which had so repeatedly humiliated him as a young man. After the performance (appropriately) of *The League of Youth* on 10 September, the Students' Union and Choral Society honoured him with a torchlight procession. They sang a song for him and thrice cried: 'Welcome home!' – words which ten years earlier he could hardly have expected ever to hear in Christiania. In reply he delivered a speech of thanks, in which he squarely identified himself with the young against the old.

Ibsen made one friendship during this visit which, two decades later, was to have much meaning for him. Annette Sontum, the daughter of his old landlady at Bergen, had married an engineer named O. M. Andersen; he struck up an acquaintance with them and he enjoyed their company, and, too, that of their ten-year-old daughter Hildur, who already showed signs of becoming a talented musician. When he returned to Norway for good seventeen years later, Hildur was to become a considerable factor in his life.

'I have', he wrote to Hegel on 16 September, shortly before he left, 'been received with extraordinary friendliness by everyone. All earlier unpleasantness is now past. I am thinking of exploiting these good times by indulging in a little property speculation. Several of my friends have become well-to-do by this means, and I think things might turn out well for me too.'[6] But this did not mean that he was thinking of settling there himself. Ludvig Josephson, who saw Ibsen several times during his stay, recalls that he 'sensed that Ibsen did not yet really feel at home or at ease in his

6. In the end he decided against it, and instead bought 1,000 specie-dollars worth of shares in the new Christiania railway company.

native capital, nor, to speak plainly, that he was happy. I and
his wife had unceasingly sought to persuade him to return to
Norway for good, but he disliked having the matter raised,
and was disinclined to consider it, the more so since this visit
had failed to convince him that the move would bring him
pleasure, fertilize his imagination, or help him to reflect and
meditate as he loved to do.' Josephson adds that he thought
Ibsen would have missed the art galleries and ancient buildings of Germany and Italy.

Ten years later, Ibsen confirmed Josephson's impression.
In the letter to Bjørnson already quoted[7] in which he told
how, on his journey up the fjord, he felt his chest tighten
with sickness and unease, Ibsen continued: 'I had the same
sensation during the whole of my stay there; I was no longer
myself with all those cold and uncomprehending Norwegian
eyes staring at me from the windows and pavements.' While
his country had to some degree atoned for the neglect and
contempt with which it had treated him during the first half
of his life, he had not felt totally accepted there, in the way
he had been in Stockholm and Copenhagen. He was to continue his voluntary exile for the best part of two decades.
Some hard truths remained to be uttered, and Ibsen preferred to ponder and utter them from a distance.

On his return to Dresden at the end of September, Ibsen
settled down to rewrite *Lady Inger*, interrupting it briefly to
compose an epithalamium for the wedding of Hegel's son
Jacob on 9 October. On 22 October he posted the final instalment of *Lady Inger* to Gyldendals, and Hegel published
the play in November in an edition of four thousand copies,
together with a new edition of *The League of Youth*. Both
were virtually fully subscribed before publication; and
Hegel had the further good news for him that both *Catiline*
and *Poems* were to be reprinted early in the new year. He
needed the money. 'This has been an expensive year for me,'

7. See p. 408.

he had written to Hegel when sending him *Lady Inger*. 'I am almost frightened to look at my account books.' For the financial promise of the previous year had not been fulfilled. This year, he had earned less than half as much:

	specie-dollars	£
7th edn of *Brand*	255	71
3rd edn of *Peer Gynt*	247½	69
3rd edn of *The League of Youth*	215½	60
2nd edn of *Lady Inger of Østraat*	568	158
Extra royalties from Christiania Theatre	200	55
	1,486	413

With his state pension, dividends from his gilt-edged and railway shares, and a win of £5 in the Danish state lottery, Ibsen's total income for 1874 had been £576; not much for a man approaching his forty-seventh birthday who was the most talked-of writer in Scandinavia and one of its best-sellers.

That winter Ibsen made up his mind to leave Dresden, for several reasons. One was, again, Sigurd's education. 'The school which Sigurd has been attending here', he wrote to Ludvig Daae on 4 February, 'has done away with its two senior *gymnasialklasser*, and the state schools of the city seem to me, in their general method and organization, unsuitable for foreign pupils. Besides, I have again begun to feel the wanderlust, and during this past year more and more foreigners have been leaving Dresden. My move will, I fear, take me somewhat farther from home; but as compensation for that I shall be a little nearer Italy, and shall moreover have the pleasure of living among Catholics, who in Germany are unquestionably preferable to the Protestants.' A further reason was that of economy. 'Dresden, when I first went to live there in 1868', he told Jonas Lie (25 May 1879), 'was a cheap place to live in; but after the war, rents and all other necessities so rose that in the last years we were there, up to the spring of 1875, we spent twice as much as when we first came'; and to Johan Thoresen, on 20 February, he complained: 'Dresden has now become the most expensive place to live in in all Germany.' He added: 'I have recently drafted the plan for a new five-act modern drama, which I hope to complete during the summer. I much look forward to getting down to this work, which has long been fermenting in my mind and has at last matured.'

On 13 April 1875, Henrik, Suzannah and Sigurd Ibsen left Dresden. The seven years he had spent there had not, on the surface, been particularly fruitful compared with his four years in Italy: two plays (one of them, admittedly, of double length), and a handful of poems. *The League of Youth* and *Emperor and Galilean* had both been successes, and his earlier plays were being steadily reprinted; but his reputation still rested principally on *Brand* and *Peer Gynt*, and many of his admirers must have felt, like Edmund Gosse, that the brilliant achievement of those two plays had not quite been followed up. At forty-seven his prospects must have appeared, possibly even to himself, not quite so glittering as they had been at forty, and if it had been known that he would never again write a poetic drama he might well have been written off as having passed his seemingly brief peak. But the apparently barren years of a writer's life are often, when viewed in retrospect, the most fruitful. *Brand* and *Peer Gynt* may, in themselves, be Ibsen's greatest plays, but his main contribution to the future of drama still lay ahead of him. Neither *Brand* nor *Peer Gynt* was to inspire many notable successors; whereas the 'contemporary' drama which he had been brooding on for nearly five years and was now, at last, about to write was, though it is seldom performed today, to be the foundation-stone of most of the plays that anyone has written since.

On 1 May 1875, after a fortnight's house-hunting in Munich, the Ibsens moved into a ground-floor apartment at Schönfeldt-Strasse 17, yet another corner-house, gloomy and barrack-like to judge from a contemporary photograph. The same day, in Christiania, the Storthing rejected by 54 votes to 42 a motion to increase his state pension.

PART FOUR

The Critic of Society

17

Munich and Gossensass
1875–6

IBSEN found Munich much to his liking. 'Many Norwegians live here', he reported to Johan Thoresen on 21 May (how that recommendation would have surprised his countrymen!), 'and I find the air much fresher and more invigorating than in Dresden, a natural result of the proximity of the Alps.' Ibsen had an almost English passion for fresh air, as visitors to his apartment occasionally discovered to their discomfort. 'He needs good air in quantity,' Hans Midbøe was to note twelve years later. 'Lofty, airy rooms are an absolute necessity to him.' He was a great one for leaving windows open.

Soon after his arrival, two unexpected windfalls came his way. *The League of Youth* in Stockholm and *The Vikings at Helgeland* in Copenhagen had both proved so successful that both theatres sent him an extra honorarium, and he found himself with an extra 500 specie-dollars to his credit. Thanks to this he was able to contribute to a wedding present for Edmund Gosse, for which a whip-round was being organized among Scandinavian writers. He also learned (through reading about it in *Morgenbladet*) that as an additional commemoration of his twenty-five years of authorship he had been awarded a special gold medal by King Oscar, from whom, on his last day in Dresden, Ibsen had received 'a very friendly letter in his own hand'. Moreover, Sigurd, he was ably proudly to inform Thoresen, had, 'after an exhaustive examination', been accepted into the top form but one of the Royal Maximilian Gymnasium, 'although all acceptances should have been closed by last October'. Altogether, it was a good month.

Ibsen's fondness for versification was dying hard, and he wrote three poems that spring. He had been invited to attend a meeting of students from the various Scandinavian countries at Upsala, and although he refused he sent them, to excuse his absence, an 'Ode to Sweden' – a conventional piece stressing the importance of looking forwards and not backwards, and declaring his belief that a new age was dawning. This was not much better than the hack celebratory poems he had turned out during his lean years in Christiania; on reflection, the sentiments he had expressed struck him as hollow, and he considered the subject more cynically in the first of the intended series of 'rhymed letters' he had proposed to Brandes for the *Nineteenth Century*: thirty couplets of iambics and anapaests entitled 'A Distant View' (*Langt Borte*). Hopes similar to those at Upsala, he recalls, had recently been voiced in Italy and Germany, but 'the ghosts of old grey men' had appeared to quench them. Nevertheless, the young men of these countries had eventually triumphed; 'they *willed* their dream', and so Europe grew up. We in the north, Ibsen concluded, must learn these hard lessons.

He posted this poem to Brandes on 8 June, promising to send a further poem each month 'unless unforeseen obstacles prevent me' (which they did). The following month, however, he developed the same theme in a longer poem simply entitled 'A Letter in Rhyme', which, he told Brandes, had occupied him 'exclusively for four weeks'. Why, the poem begins, does modern man seem oppressed by restlessness and apathy, so that he is incapable of either true joy or true grief? As so often in his work, Ibsen chose as his central symbol a voyaging ship, but a ship with a difference. Sometimes, he says, a vessel will set forth, and all seems well. Then, suddenly, in mid-ocean, a blackness settles on her and on all aboard her; the sail falls slack, even the sea-birds' cry seems to bode ill. When this happens, sailors have a saying

that 'there is a corpse in the cargo'. So, suggests Ibsen, it is
with us today. A voice has whispered in his ear: 'I think
we're sailing with a corpse in the cargo.'

What this corpse is, Ibsen does not say:

> I only ask. My task is not to answer.

–a line that his enemies were often to use against him, apparently unaware that great writers very rarely answer the questions they ask, unless it be to preach resignation. In fact,
however, Ibsen was to state clearly and repeatedly what he
believed the corpse to be: a willingness to let oneself be
dominated by one's past. The idea that we can only become
ourselves, true individuals, if we slough off the past was a
theme he was to develop throughout his final twelve plays
from *The Pillars of Society* to *When We Dead Awaken*,
finding its fullest and most vivid expression in *Ghosts* and
Rosmersholm.

This 'Letter in Rhyme' was not merely the last of Ibsen's
promised contributions to the *Nineteenth Century*. It was to
be the last poem of any length which he was ever to write.

Another event that summer of 1875 strengthened Ibsen's
conviction that prose was the path which he must now
follow. The previous year Bjørnson, in Rome, had completed two new plays, *A Bankrupt* and *The Editor*, both
written in prose on contemporary themes (he had begun *A
Bankrupt* first, but finished it after *The Editor*). Both had
been printed in the summer of 1875, but their publication
had been held back to coincide with their production, an
event which turned out to be considerably delayed. The
Christiania Theatre refused to stage *The Editor* on the
grounds that the main character, a ruthless journalist who
comes to a bad end, too obviously represented the then
editor of *Morgenbladet*, Christian Friele, and indeed it was
not performed in Norway until 1917, seven years after
Bjørnson's death. Indignant at this censorship, Bjørnson
offered the two plays to Nya Teatern in Stockholm, which
accepted them, performing *A Bankrupt* in January 1875 and

The Editor in February. Georg Brandes was greatly excited, and wrote: 'At last it seems as though we of the north, too, are to have plays in which those two great forces, the present and reality, demand respect and enter into their right.' He noted, correctly, that Ibsen had sketched both an editor and a bankrupt in *The League of Youth*, but thought that Bjørnson's were the first genuinely modern realistic dramas; and Strindberg (then twenty-six) later described them as 'signal rockets'.

Neither *The Editor* nor *A Bankrupt* reads very well today. *The Editor* is impossibly melodramatic and is hardly ever performed even in Norway; *A Bankrupt* works reasonably until the last act, when it declines into one of those facile happy endings to which Bjørnson was so fatally prone. (He defended it on the ground that 'it is good for people to know that a man can raise himself up again', and that 'it shows a true family life, good, happy people', confusing, as he so often did, art with morality.) Ibsen had treated contemporary problems far more profoundly in *Love's Comedy* and *Brand*, but these had been in verse; and although *The League of Youth* nowadays strikes one as both more serious and more penetrating than *A Bankrupt*, it was, ostensibly at any rate, a comedy, and comedies were expected to be in prose. *A Bankrupt* and *The Editor* dealt with contemporary problems seriously and in everyday prose, and as such represented, at the time of their writing, an important breakthrough not merely in Scandinavian but in European drama.

Brandes's claim on behalf of the plays needs some qualification. Gogol and Ostrovsky had both written plays at least as modern and realistic as Bjørnson's; but these were as unknown in western Europe as *Woyzeck* and *Danton's Death*. And in 1873, the year before *The Editor* and *A Bankrupt*, Emile Zola had written *Thérèse Raquin*, so often named by historians as the first proletarian stage tragedy. Zola was indeed fully conscious of the need to do away with the artificially 'well-made' play. 'I have no taste for watch-making, and a great taste for truth', he had written as early as 1865, two years after the Goncourt brothers had written *Henriette Maréchal*, which Zola himself regarded as the first naturalistic play. But although *Thérèse Raquin* represented a considerable step forward from the old Scribean dramas of intrigue, its language was highly melodramatic, running directly counter to Zola's demand that actors should not act but *live* before the audience (a theory which André Antoine was to put into practice at his Théâtre Libre a decade later). Zola wanted the drama to do what the naturalistic novel had done, as in Flaubert's *Madame Bovary* and his own works. But, unlike Bjørnson, Zola did not know much about writing plays; his own dramas, *Thérèse Raquin* included, are much less interesting than his prefaces and programme notes.[1]

The success of *A Bankrupt* in Scandinavia quickly spread to Germany, where before the end of the year it was performed in practically every town that boasted a theatre. Bjørnson was never to have another success to equal it in that country. Ibsen asked Hegel to send him a copy when it at last got published in 1875, and in June he saw it acted in Munich. Its success gave him the stimulus he had been needing to get his own new play off the ground. On 22 August he was able at last to write to Hegel from Kitzbühel in the Alps, where he had gone to escape the city heat: 'I have now completed my plan for the new five act play about contemporary life which I have long been thinking of writing, and which, if nothing unforeseen happens, I shall finish during the winter.' The block that had obstructed him for so long seemed to have been broken. 'My new work is progressing swiftly,' he wrote Hegel on 23 October from Munich. 'In a few days I shall have completed the first act,

1. Of the other early realistic prose dramas which have survived, Henri Becque's masterpiece, *Les Corbeaux*, was to be completed in 1876 but remained unperformed until 1882. Tolstoy's *The Power of Darkness* was written in 1886, and Strindberg's first effective modern play *The Marauders* (later rewritten as *The Comrades*) in 1886–7.

which I always find the most difficult part. The title will be *The Pillars of Society*, a play in five acts. In a way it can be regarded as a counterblast to *The League of Youth*, and will touch on several of the more important questions of our time.' On 25 November he wrote: 'Act 1 of my new play is finished and fair-copied; I am now working on Act 2,' and by 10 December he was 'working at it daily and am now doubly anxious to get the manuscript to you as quickly as possible.'

So 1875 ended on a hopeful note. He was busy with, and excited about, his new play; a new production of *The Vikings at Helgeland* had opened in Stockholm on 3 November, and in Christiania preparations were under way for the first stage production of *Peer Gynt*, Edvard Grieg having finished the music that July. Moreover, the first complete book about him had appeared: *Henryk Ibsen, poeta norwegski*, published in Warsaw, and written by Count Lars von Engeström, a Pole of Swedish descent. And the first days of 1876 were to see the first publication of an Ibsen play in English – Catherine Ray's translation of *Emperor and Galilean*. It created little stir; of the three reviews which appeared, one was signed by Edmund Gosse and the other two, which appeared anonymously, were probably also by him; still, it was a beginning.

When Ibsen totted up his earnings for 1875, they amounted to £548, made up more or less equally of performing fees and reprints. This, though better than the previous year, was nothing like as good as 1873. His stocks and shares at the end of this year amounted to over £1,300, but this was the result of considerable parsimony; his *huskassebeholdning*, or money in hand, was only 25 specie-dollars, a little under £7.

Posterity must be grateful that Ibsen was never able, like his more fortunate fellow-dramatists in countries where there was copyright protection, to rest on the laurels of his past successes. He could not afford either to slow down his production or to let his quality decline. It was plainly necessary that he should complete his new play with all possible speed. Asking Hegel to advance him the 400 crowns due to him as interest on his investments, he explained (10 December): 'You will think that I have become a spendthrift or that life is very dear in Munich, since I am spending so much money here. But neither is the case; the fact is that we have been compelled to part-furnish our present apartment, which we have now done, so that in future we shall live more cheaply. But this has been an expensive year for me.' He ended the letter on a nostalgic note. 'This time ten years ago I was uneasily awaiting the publication of *Brand*. Thank you for all that has happened since! No one has contributed as much as you to the difference between my situation as it was then and as it is now. Be sure that I shall never forget this.' Nor did he.

By now Ibsen was making friends among the local Germans, something he seems never to have done in Dresden. 'I have begun to mix in a large literary group,' he informed Johan Thoresen on 6 February 1876, 'where I have been greeted with exceptional kindness and courtesy.' This group was known as the Crocodile, and its members included several well-known German literary figures: the poets Hermann Lingg and Karl Streler, the comic writer Ferdinand Bom, Franz Grandaur, dramaturge and director of opera at the Munich Hoftheater, and, the most talented among them, the novelist and short story writer Paul Heyse, who had recently published two acclaimed novels, *Kinder der Welt* and *Im Paradiese*, the latter being a *roman à clef* about writers and artists in Munich. (It is a pity Ibsen did not come to Munich a year earlier, or he might well have appeared in it.) Heyse was also a prolific dramatist (though he was less successful in this field), a fluent linguist (ultimately he even learned Norwegian), and a distinguished translator of, among others, Shakespeare and Leopardi. 'Visit him often,' Ibsen was later to advise John Paulsen. 'You will always learn something from this excellent and artistic writer.' Two years younger than Ibsen almost to the day, Heyse was (though he disapproved violently of *Ghosts*) to maintain a long friendship with him – and he was to achieve one literary feat which Ibsen never did, for in 1914 he received the Nobel Prize for Literature, although, as with so many recipients of that prize, posterity has not confirmed the verdict of the Swedish Academy.

Among the younger members of the Crocodile was a writer named Paul Lindau, who forty years later recalled their meetings. He remembered that Ibsen looked much older than his years and that he combed his hair frequently and never tired of looking at himself in mirrors. In the street he would stop before every mirror and comb his hair back from his forehead. Although Ibsen enjoyed jokes, he disapproved (surprisingly, for so ostentatious a free-thinker) of any jests concerning religion. Once when Lindau made such a jest, Ibsen became very tight-lipped, snapped: 'There are some things one doesn't make fun of,' and left the table. Lindau also recalled that Ibsen once told him that every time he finished a play he felt it was the last he would write, because he had said in it everything that he had to say.

The Crocodile used to meet daily at noon, first at the Café Probst, subsequently at their favourite rendezvous, the café of the Hotel Achatz in the Maximilianplatz. Another member was a young Norwegian painter named Marcus Grønvold, whom Ibsen liked and who has left an interesting account of him at this period. According to Grønvold, Ibsen at first attended these gatherings regularly, and even stood a couple of parties himself at a restaurant – 'but since he was afraid that his work might suffer and social life gain the upper hand, he later began to attend less regularly'.

Grønvold describes Ibsen's routine. He would breakfast simply on a small cup of black coffee and a roll, and would then work till one. After lunch he would rest, and then walk in the streets,

his sharp eyes perceiving everything, however buried in his own thoughts he might seem. People, shop windows, even dogs, were the objects of his attention. Sometimes he pondered what he would put on paper the following morning. On winter evenings his figure would appear like a phantom in the dark arcades of the Hofgarten. On these walks Ibsen did not like to be disturbed; he was as scant of speech then as, at other times, he could be communicative. When he returned home he again usually remained silent, and after his evening meal would walk up and down the room, smoking his pipe and listening to the conversation. But he listened carefully, taking pleasure in it, and sometimes partaking greedily, especially when eccentric characters whom he had known in his youth, gifted wrecks, were mentioned – characters such as he was to create in the persons of Ulrik Brendel and Ejlert Løvborg. He once referred to such a man as 'an ex-human being'.

As in the old days in Rome, Ibsen loved to start an argument, but when he got bored with it he would break it off curtly, saying: 'Well, there are two sides to every question.' He loved to question people about their jobs, 'but if he saw that they had come to study him or were expecting witty or Sphinx-like utterances, he withdrew into his shell'. He enjoyed stories and anecdotes, especially *risqué* ones; 'he regretted that one could not use such stories and events in one's writing, since they were usually the best' (a pleasant corrective to the customary picture of Ibsen as a puritan). He also once remarked to Grønvold how difficult it was to finish a play when the spiritual process was already completed and other ideas were beginning to crop up. 'It demands so much self-discipline *properly* to complete a work,' he said, 'for interest ceases at a comparatively early stage.' He added: 'At the moment of conception one must be on fire, but at the time of writing, cold.'

Like so many of those who knew Ibsen well, as opposed to his casual acquaintances, Grønvold speaks very highly of Suzannah. He calls her 'understanding, warm-hearted and moreover . . . free from all pettiness and narrow-mindedness, intellectually independent . . . a woman of aristocratic intelligence'.

On 24 February *Peer Gynt* was at last staged, at the Christiania Theatre. It was the most expensive production hitherto attempted in Norway, and proved a tremendous success. The reception at the première, recorded Ludvig Josephson, who directed it, was 'such as I have rarely experienced'. The play seems to have been produced with the accent on the lyrical rather than the satirical aspects (as it was to be for many years to come and, sadly, still often is). Few musical scores can have so softened an author's intentions as Grieg's *Peer Gynt* suite, which turns the play into a jolly Hans Andersen fairy tale; but Ibsen was too unmusical to perceive this, and was delighted with the result, though he might have been less so had he seen it. 'Thank you for *Peer Gynt!*' he wrote to Josephson on 5 March. 'The outcome of this bold enterprise by your theatre has exceeded all my expectations.'[2] The play was performed thirty-seven times during the next ten and a half months, an unprecedented number for so serious a work, when one remembers that *The Pretenders* was reckoned to have done creditably with eight. It would have continued longer had not a fire destroyed the expensive scenery and costumes the following January.

Munich theatrical circles had, meanwhile, begun to take note of the foreign dramatist in their midst, and on 10 April the Hoftheater (thanks perhaps to its dramaturge's acquaintance with Ibsen in the Crocodile) staged *The Vikings at Helgeland*, the first performance of an Ibsen play outside Scandinavia. 'The house was virtually full,' Ibsen reported to Hegel the following day, 'and the play was received with a storm of applause. I watched the performance from the wings, and was called on to the stage five times. After the performance the writers of Munich [presumably his colleagues in the Crocodile] improvised a party for me, which continued long into the night.' He even received a congratulatory letter from that passionate theatre lover Ludwig

2. But Ibsen seems to have had second thoughts about Grieg's score (see pp. 777–8).

II, the mad King of Bavaria, Richard Wagner's friend, who was to kill himself (and his doctor) ten years later.

The success of *The Vikings* was good enough, but better was to follow. 'I have this moment', Ibsen informed Hegel on 30 May, 'received an invitation from the Duke of Meiningen to go to Berlin, where on Saturday his company is to act *The Pretenders* for the first time ... The story that a Danish paper printed about the play being acted in Meiningen and receiving no applause is untrue. It was only a trial performance without the new décor and without any cuts.' To appear suitably dressed at so important an occasion required more money than Ibsen had to hand, and he begged Hegel to send 450 reichsmarks (£22) to him in Berlin and a like sum to Suzannah in Munich. This was hardly a loan, for Hegel had that amount to Ibsen's credit from the Stockholm production of *The Vikings*, and the interest on his shares was due in June. Hegel obliged as always, and so Ibsen saw for the first time the greatest theatrical company of his age.

The influence of the 'Meiningers' on the technique of stage production was almost as great as that of Ibsen on the technique of dramatic writing, and we may pause for a moment to consider it. André Antoine, who saw them in Brussels in 1888, and Konstantin Stanislavsky, who spent a year with them, have both described how the Meininger productions opened their eyes to the possibility of a theatrical realism of which they had never dreamed. Stanislavsky, indeed, recalled that it was their appearance in St Petersburg which first fired him to enter the theatre. The company was the creation of the new ruler of Saxe-Meiningen, Duke Georg II. Meiningen itself was a tiny town of only seven thousand inhabitants, but Duke Georg was no dilettante; the great Viennese actor, Josef Levinsky, described him as 'the finest theatrical director Germany has ever known', adding significantly: 'His deep understanding of dramatists' intentions is far more important than any amount of splendid décor.'

Many of the innovations which we today accept as a natural prerequisite of any good production, and which are commonly attributed to Antoine, Stanislavsky, Reinhardt and Granville Barker, were introduced by Duke Georg in the eighteen-seventies. Ensemble acting; the conception of décor as an integral and imaginative part of the production instead of a mere background; intelligent and searching characterization, instead of the kind of theatricality that uses the text as a trampoline; and above all, the treatment of crowds as so many individuals and not as a dumb and uncomprehending collection of extras – these were the innovations (or rather, since nothing is wholly new in the theatre, the recreations) of Duke Georg which astonished and excited his contemporaries. What these methods meant to an imaginative man of the theatre may best be evoked by quoting the reactions of Antoine and William Archer on seeing them for the first time. Here is Antoine writing to the critic Francisque Sarcey after seeing the Meiningers in Brussels in 1888:

They showed us things absolutely new and very instructive. Their crowds are not like ours, composed of elements picked haphazard, working men hired for dress rehearsals, badly clothed, and unaccustomed to wearing strange and uncomfortable costumes, especially when they are exact. Immobility is almost always required of the crowds on our stage, whereas the supernumeraries of the Meininger crowds must act and mime their characters. Don't understand by that that they force the note and that the attention is distracted from the protagonists. No, the tableau is complete, and in whatever direction you may look, you fix your eyes on a detail in the situation or character. At certain moments, its power is incomparable.

The troupe of the Meininger company contains about seventy actors of both sexes. All those who do not take a part are expected to figure in the play, and every evening too. If there are twenty actors occupied, the fifty others, without a single exception, even in the case of the leading players, appear on the stage in the tableaux, and each leading actor is the chief, the corporal, of a group of real supernumeraries, whom he directs and watches as long as the company is under the eye of the

public. This obligation is such that the wife of Hans von
Bülow,[3] one of the stars of the Meininger, having refused to
perform this service, which she considered beneath her talent,
was dismissed, although her husband had the title and functions
of *Kapellmeister* to the Duke of Saxony. In this way they obtain
ensembles that are extraordinarily true to life ... Mlle Lindner,
their star, playing in *A Winter's Tale*, took a silent part in the
tableau of the seat of Justice, and mimed a woman of the people
as conscientiously and as carefully as she interpreted on the following evening the important role of Hermione in the same
piece.[4]

William Archer covered the company's visit to London
in June and July, 1881, as a young critic of twenty-five for
the *London Figaro* (4 June and subsequent issues). Of their
opening production, *Julius Caesar* (in which Bjørnson's son,
Bjørn, the only non-German member of the group, acted
Casca), Archer noted: 'In the first scene already, a peculiarity of stage management is noticeable. The crowd does not
remain *au deuxième plan*, acting as a background to the tri-
bunes. On the contrary, Flavius and Marullus mix with it
and elbow with it, sometimes almost hidden in its midst. It
has all the uncertain fluctuations of an actual crowd. Its
splendid drill produces the effect of absolute freedom from
drill.' Of the scene when Antony addresses the crowd in the
Forum, Archer wrote that the actor, Ludwig Barnay, 'did
not address himself to the imagination of the audience, but
to the living and moving populace before him ... It is rather
by inference than by personal sensation or intuition that we
recognize the power of Mark Antony's oratory. We see how
it moves the crowd, and by an act of judgement we decide
that it should and must be so moved ... The scene is presented in a manner far surpassing anything of the kind as
yet attempted in England. Indeed, I search my memory in
vain for anything with which to compare it even for an instant.'

3. Marie Schanzer. Bülow's first wife, Cosima, had left him to
become the mistress, and later the wife, of Richard Wagner.
4. S. M. Waxman's translation.

Of their décor, Archer wrote: 'They take the trouble to distinguish between tree and tree, whereas our scene-painters have one recipe for every species of foliage, varied only by a dash of red-brown when an autumn landscape has to be depicted. Their handling of tree-stems and bark struck me as particularly admirable.' In their production of *William Tell* ('a marvellously fine and thoughtful presentation'), he noted the effect of rain which they achieved by 'a peculiar arrangement of light, and some motion in the backcloth'; the use of steam to represent dust when the Swiss tear down the Austrian castle; the small boys with beards on scaffolding at the back of the stage to give the effect of perspective; their presentation of the figure of Time as a young girl; and the care and individuality of their make-up. And they were far in advance of other European companies in their treatment of comedy; Archer thought that their *Malade imaginaire* 'need not shrink from comparison with the Comédie-française itself', though he had seen Coquelin in the part. Henry Irving saw them during their visit, and admired, and was influenced by, their crowd work and lighting.

The Meininger production of *The Pretenders* in Berlin was a great success; how one would love to have seen what Duke Georg did with the crowd scenes[5] in which the play abounds, and especially his treatment of the battle scenes. Writing to Ludvig Josephson on 14 June, Ibsen described the performance as 'brilliant and spectacular. The play was received with great applause, and I was repeatedly called. I don't think this much pleased the Berlin critics, most of whom are themselves playwrights. However, the play has run for nine successive performances, and would have continued longer had the Meiningers not been scheduled to end their season on the 15th. After the opening performance I

5. Bjørn Bjørnson records that when they acted in Meiningen the Duke used real soldiers from his own army for the crowd scenes, and that when they played in big theatres they would have five or six hundred people on the stage.

was invited by the duke to visit him at his summer palace at Liebenstein in Meiningen, where I have been staying until I came back here [to Munich] the day before yesterday.' And as if that was not enough: 'On my departure he decorated me with the Knight Cross of the Saxon-Ernestine Order, First Class. *The Pretenders* is to be given in Schwerin too, and *The Vikings* has been accepted by the Burgtheater in Vienna, where Charlotte Wolter is to play Hjørdis.' Ibsen got on well with monarchs, and the duke, who plainly liked Ibsen, as Carl XV and Oscar II had done, invited him to come back in the winter. Indeed, the time was to come when Ibsen had to give up visiting a certain resort because Duke Georg, who had a place in the vicinity, so pestered him with invitations as to make it impossible for him to work.

Did the Meininger methods influence Ibsen's future writing? It is possible; the realism of that production of *The Pretenders* may well have had its effect on *The Pillars of Society*, which he was at last to complete during the following year. Their methods must have given him the assurance that a technique of production and acting was developing which might eventually be equal to the demands he was planning to make.

On 5 August Ibsen took Suzannah and Sigurd for their usual holiday in the mountains, but this year, instead of Berchtesgaden, they tried somewhere new. 'We shall be staying', he informed Edvard Grieg, who was in Bayreuth for the opening of the Festspielhaus with the first complete performance of Wagner's *Ring*, 'at Gossensass, a country town near the Brenner railway, between Brenner and Sterzing. You must come via Munich, Rosenheim and Innsbruck, it being only three or four hours by rail from the last-named town to Gossensass. We shall probably be lodging at the Brauhaus Inn – in any case, you will find out where we are even if you don't warn us of your arrival. You will be most warmly welcome, and I hope you won't make too brief a stay. After the exhausting pleasures of Bayreuth you will need fresh mountain air, and you will find it up there.'

Grieg duly arrived in Gossensass, bringing with him a young writer from Bergen named John Paulsen, who had accompanied him to Bayreuth. Paulsen, then twenty-five, had published a few things, including some poems which Grieg had set to music, and he was to become a prolific, if not greatly talented, novelist and playwright. His poems and novels are scarcely read today, and his plays will never be performed again, but in a series of memoirs he was to leave one of the most vivid and intimate pictures of Ibsen that we possess. He was inclined to romanticize when reporting from hearsay, but his first-hand observation was perceptive and lively.

Paulsen had his first sight of Ibsen as he and Grieg walked from the station into the little town. They had not warned Ibsen of their arrival, and chanced on him as he was taking a walk.

Ibsen ... reminded me of a bridegroom going in his best clothes to meet his beloved. The black tail-coat with order ribbons, the dazzlingly white linen, the elegantly knotted cravat, the black, correct silk hat, the precise movements, the reserved expression, all put me in mind of his poem:

> I shrink from the mob.
> I have no wish to be clasped to their hot bosom.
> I shall await whatever time may bring
> In a well-pressed morning coat.[6]

Grieg introduced me. The conventional courtesies were exchanged. Ibsen's face expressed neither joy nor displeasure at seeing us. Gradually I studied his remarkable physiognomy – the small, blue-grey eyes behind the gold spectacles, the high, unusually broad brow, seemingly gnarled with thought, the long grizzled whiskers, the fine, pursed mouth, thin as a knife-blade ... I stood before a closed mountain-wall, an impenetrable riddle.

Paulsen could not help contrasting this figure with the poet in his Christiania days as described to him by an un-

6. From Ibsen's poem, 'Balloon Letter to a Swedish Lady' (1870).

named friend who had known Ibsen then: 'seated alone at
one of the humbler cafés, his cheek resting on his hand and
a careworn expression round his mouth, his beard allowed to
grow unchecked, his hair an unkempt mane, on his head an
old slouch hat'.

Each evening they ate together in the Brauhaus,

the cosy little room with the Madonna painting on the wall, the
friendly young Tyrolean landlord who knew Latin and Italian
... the meal, which usually consisted of ham and fried eggs, with
home-brewed beer or *vin ordinaire*, and a bunch of grapes for
dessert, the itinerant zither-player who occasionally appeared to
my delight and Grieg's distress ... All day Ibsen would be silent
and unapproachable. He often invited me to accompany him on
his walks, but never uttered a word ... Yet when we parted he
never failed to thank me for my 'pleasant company' ... In the
evenings he usually thawed and became communicative and
cheerful.

Grieg, adds Paulsen, had 'a particular talent for getting him
going'.

Lorentz Dietrichson joined them at Gossensass, with his
wife and daughters; he too (noted Paulsen) was good at 'getting Ibsen going'. One morning the four men left the ladies
and went for a walk; but a flurry of snow caused them to
seek shelter in a small wooden pavilion. Paulsen slipped back
to the hotel to fetch some brandy, hot water, sugar, and
glasses, and they sat in the pavilion drinking toddy and telling stories. Paulsen was surprised to discover (as Marcus
Grønvold had done) that Ibsen enjoyed slightly *risqué* anecdotes, which he would acknowledge with 'silent, chuckling
laughter'. Ibsen himself told one about an unnamed author,
then much admired, 'one of those hyper-aesthetic characters
whom Germany possesses in such abundance, who would
like to forget that we humans, for all our spiritual qualities,
share certain needs with animals'. Once, while travelling by
rail (related Ibsen), this gentleman was afflicted with a painful stomach-ache and, unhappily, the train possessed no
W.C. In addition to the hat he was wearing he had in his

trunk a *chapeau-bas* 'which, since he was fortunately alone in the compartment, was now pressed into service'. It having served its purpose, the man threw it out of the window; but he had unluckily forgotten that the hat carried his visiting-card in the inside band. The train was a slow local, and when it reached the station of the tiny town where he lived, and of which he was the leading inhabitant, the station-master ran up as the great man emerged with dignity on to the platform and proffered the hat with a respectful bow, it having been found on the line and rushed to its famous owner. The author was furious, at first denied that the hat was his, and ended by throwing it in the station-master's face.

Grieg talked of Wagner and Liszt, whom he had seen at Bayreuth, especially of Liszt, whose warm testimonial had been largely instrumental in Grieg's receiving a civil list pension from the Storthing. He also surely (though Paulsen does not mention it) told Ibsen of Wagner's experiments in staging at Bayreuth, such as his plunging the auditorium into total darkness throughout the performance, something that had not been done in the theatre before (though the Meiningers were to follow suit), and his concealment of the orchestra, so that the audience was separated from the stage by a 'mystical abyss'. But even the shortest concert bored Ibsen, and he never visited Bayreuth.

They discussed German women, and Ibsen remarked that 'a German lady in *grande toilette* always reminds me of a prize cow with gilt trappings and paper flowers between its horns'. He added that he thought animals realized that such decorations were a token of praise, since they resisted when anyone tried to remove them. On the subject of Bjørnson he observed: 'Bjørnson and I are not enemies, as many people believe. It is our disciples who are enemies.' At this interesting stage in the conversation the ladies surprised them over their glasses, and the three famous husbands were led back to the hotel 'with their tails between their legs'.

Grieg said that he was looking for a new subject for an opera. Ibsen suggested *Olaf Lilekrans*, but this did not appeal to Grieg, who suggested that Ibsen should write something new for him; but Ibsen said he was too preoccupied with his new play.

In September Ibsen and his companions moved south from Gossensass to the little town of Kaltern on the Italian border, where the Ibsens lodged with the burgomaster. They several times went fishing in a boat. 'Ibsen', writes Paulsen, 'turned out to be a passionate fisherman, and had miraculous luck. Every time he casually, and as though absent-mindedly, cast his line, a big fish immediately bit at the hook. In the space of half an hour he had caught a dozen ... This put him in an excellent humour. His success as a sportsman pleased him more than if he had achieved some great artistic triumph.'

Meanwhile, the success of *The Vikings* in Munich and of *The Pretenders* in Berlin had led to a rapid and widening increase in performances of Ibsen's work in the theatres. On 15 September he reported to Hegel:

The Vikings is to be staged at the Burgtheater in Vienna in October; I have received an official invitation to attend, as also in Schwerin, where *The Pretenders* is to be done in November. *The Vikings* is to be performed at the Dresden Hoftheater in a few weeks; the same play is also in rehearsal at the Stadttheater in Leipzig, and is now being acted again with great success in Munich. From all of these theatres I receive ten per cent of the gross takings from all performances during my lifetime, and my heirs for a further fifteen years. This is undeniably a great deal better than what Herr Berner thinks proper to offer me, and people will now understand why I regard it as pre-eminently important to make my work profitable here. A German translation of *Lady Inger* is already completed in manuscript, and will be performed, for a start, in Meiningen and Munich. My preoccupation with all these matters has necessitated my postponing the completion of my new play; but on my return to Munich at the beginning of next month I intend to get it finished, although it is not very tempting to write for the theatres at home ... I have long been waiting to see the new edition of *Peer Gynt* advertised; I hope it will soon appear. And perhaps there might be a call for a new edition at Christmas of one of my other books? I should be very happy if this were possible; for I need money, and theatre royalties down here are only paid quarterly or half-yearly. May I therefore, notwithstanding my debt to you, ask you to be so kind as to send me 450 reichsmarks [80 specie-dollars, £22] at the above address? You would be doing me a great service, and I sincerely hope it will not be long before my account with you is balanced.

Ibsen's reference to the lack of temptation to 'write for the theatres at home', and to the importance of making his work 'profitable' for the German theatres, may partly explain the apathy he had been showing towards *The Pillars of Society*, on which he had been working with such enthusiasm the previous autumn and winter. His successes in Germany had been with sweeping historical plays in the grand manner (*The Vikings at Helgeland* and *The Pretenders*) and, despite the success of Bjørnson's *A Bankrupt*, *The Pillars of Society*, with its very parochial and Norwegian atmosphere, must have struck Ibsen as unlikely to appeal either to German theatrical taste or to that country's traditional style of acting. It was with reluctance and doubt that he was to finish *The Pillars of Society*; but his fears were to prove totally unfounded, and it was to set the style for all his future work. Not only was he always thereafter to write in prose and on contemporary themes; he was never to set any more of his plays outside Norway, though he took good care to give his characters names that could easily be pronounced by foreigners.

Ibsen left Kaltern at the end of September; apart from other considerations, Sigurd had to be back at school in Munich by 1 October. Paulsen accompanied them back to Munich; as the train drew in, Paulsen exclaimed 'What a big city!' and Ibsen surprised him by replying: 'One can't live anywhere smaller.'

Ibsen's letters during the last three months of 1876 contain, significantly, no reference to *The Pillars of Society*. Even when writing to Hegel he avoided the subject. In October *The Vikings at Helgeland* was performed in Vienna, Dresden and Bergen, and in November *The Vikings* was revived at the Royal Theatre, Copenhagen. A fourth edition of *Peer Gynt* appeared this autumn; German translations of *Lady Inger* and *Brand* (the third German version of that work, this time by Baron Alfred von Wolzogen) were promised for the winter, and Ibsen was able to report to Hegel that the German edition of *The Vikings* was almost sold out. The inexpensiveness of book production in Germany amazed him; the first thousand copies of *The Vikings*, printed on 'very handsome paper', cost only 325 reichsmark (£16). Unfortunately, such fees as he might expect from all this lay in the future, and he had to ask Hegel to advance him another 400 crowns (£22).

Paulsen stayed in Munich until December, and recorded some further perceptive notes about Ibsen's routine in that city. In some respects his habits had changed since the early days in Dresden. He never now went to the theatre, unless to see one of his own plays; such as *The Vikings*, to which he took Paulsen, who found the production 'exciting and spectacular', especially 'a grand snowstorm'. The picture galleries which had attracted him as a young man he no longer visited, nor the studios of the numerous Norwegian painters who were in Munich at that time (and who included such distinguished artists as Erik Werenskiold, Eilif Peterssen, Christian Skredsvig and Gerhard Munthe). He isolated himself more and more, and was now even reluctant to accept invitations to dinner in other people's houses. 'Social life does not merely steal one's time,' he told Paulsen. 'It stultifies. An author who wants to achieve anything must isolate himself. Live alone in his thoughts and for his work.' He remarked of a Norwegian novelist (unnamed) who always allowed himself to be taken to dinner: 'When does that man write? I wonder he manages to accomplish anything.' But unwilling as he was to partake in social life, he was very curious to know what went on there. When Paulsen had attended any such dinner, Ibsen would question him minutely about everything that happened – what topics had been discussed, what the hostess had worn, even how much people had tipped the footman.

Arriving punctually at his fixed hour at the Café Maximilian, he would (Paulsen noted) always seat himself opposite a large mirror which reflected the door.

Here, without needing to turn his head, he could observe everything in the mirror, and sat there behind his big newspaper like some fiction detective. Nothing escaped his sharp eyes. He noticed, not merely people's appearance and habits . . . but picked up bits of their private conversations, and noted characteristics which were peculiar to them and which he had not perceived elsewhere . . . He also learned much from the newspapers. There he found the answers to so many of his unuttered questions about the people among whom he lived . . . From a small article or advertisement which other readers overlooked he could learn more than they from years of study . . . But Ibsen was no ordinary newspaper reader. He read the advertisements minutely, and remarked that they were not the least informative section of the paper. He began reading from the title at the top of page one and read right through to the names of the printer and publisher at the foot of the final page.

Paulsen was surprised to find that Ibsen liked to do as many domestic tasks as possible himself. If a button came loose on his trousers, he would 'go into his room, close the door firmly and, after various preparations as humorous as they were unnecessary, would sew on the button with the same care with which he would fair-copy a new play'. One of Ibsen's convictions was that 'women never know how to sew on a button so that it stays, whereas when he sewed one on himself it remained fast for ever'. Suzannah, however, told Paulsen that after Ibsen had sewed on a button she would stitch it, 'which Ibsen always forgets, and which is the most important thing. But let him go on believing it, it makes him so happy.'

On the other hand, Ibsen hated seeing his wife doing anything manual such as knitting, and Paulsen says he never saw Suzannah thus occupied because she knew her husband's aversion to such things. This business of independence Ibsen carried to unexpected lengths. One morning he startled Paulsen by asking him 'with an earnest and worried expression' whether he polished his own boots. Paulsen confessed that he did not. Ibsen said :'But you must ... One should never let another person do for one what one can do for oneself.' He was even, unexpectedly, something of a cook, and especially liked making soups.

As Paulsen had discovered at Gossensass, Ibsen could, when the mood took him, be an excellent raconteur. But despite his enjoyment of risqué anecdotes, 'Ibsen, with a bashfulness unusual among writers, avoided all sexual topics.' On this subject he was evidently inhibited to a degree unusual even for the nineteenth century; and he once astonished Paulsen by declaring that there were three things that meant nothing to him: flowers, music, and children. The last part of this claim is contradicted by several witnesses, such as Johanne Lie and Bolette Sontum, who have testified to the kindness and affection he showed them when they were small. His indifference to music has already been remarked; I do not know of any other evidence of his feeling for or against flowers. What is perhaps most interesting about Ibsen's claim, however, is not whether it is true, but that he should have made it. It is very much the statement of a man who has turned his back on all things of the heart.

Ibsen was almost theatrically fortunate in being permitted to witness the humiliation of former enemies. Clemens Petersen's fate has been related; and one day after dinner in Munich, Paulsen was standing at the window with Ibsen looking out into the street when they noticed a curious old man dressed like a priest in black with a white cravat slouch past. 'Did you ever meet him in Bergen?' Ibsen asked. He had identified him as Poul Stub, the pedant who had corrected Ibsen's Norwegian essays when he was studying in Grimstad, and had attacked the policy and inexperience of

the Bergen company shortly after Ibsen's arrival there in
1851. 'I looked long at the old, bowed schoolmaster, once
Ibsen's merciless critic, now pensioned and, for economical
reasons, compelled to live in Munich because of its cheap-
ness. I thought how differently their lives had shaped themselves since their clash in Bergen. Ibsen sat there, a famous
man in an elegant home, while Poul Stub was – still Poul
Stub.'

Paulsen noted, as Vilhelm Bergsøe had on Ischia, Ibsen's
physical timidity. 'In windy weather he was always appre-
hensive lest a tile might fall on his head, and it always
amused me to see how he glanced up over his gold spectacles
at the threatening rooftops. His fear of dogs was also
marked; he moved quickly aside if a bulldog approached.'
Paulsen comments that in this respect, as in the contrast
between the conventionality of his life and the uncon-
ventionality of his thought, Ibsen resembled Goethe.
Another weakness was his unwillingness that strangers
should know of his liking for a nap after lunch. 'When Fru
Ibsen once mentioned his long afternoon sleep, he got angry
and declared: "It isn't true. I merely lie on the sofa and
reflect." "How can you say such a thing, my dear Ibsen?"
said Suzannah. "You sleep so heavily that we can hear your
snores in the living-room." At this Ibsen left the room without speaking, evidently insulted.' Suzannah also confided in
Paulsen that Ibsen 'likes us to have maids who look pretty;
he can't stand old, ugly ones', adding: 'Though he never
looks at them – that is, he looks at them, but only aesthetically, as one looks at a statue or a painting.' One is reminded of
Irene's accusation of Rubek in *When We Dead Awaken*.

Ibsen had an extraordinary dislike of using Christian
names, even with his close friends; Suzannah told Paulsen
that Ibsen had addressed her as 'De' (the Norwegian equivalent of *vous*) throughout their engagement, 'which caused
much amazement in the circles in which the young couple
moved'. He used affectionately to address Suzannah as 'the
cat' or 'the eagle', the latter name having been given her

long ago by her brothers and sisters because of her bold character (hence his drawings of these creatures on the family's home-made banknotes). Sigurd he called 'the old one'; and he amused Paulsen by exhorting him not to disturb the boy at work, for Paulsen knew that 'Sigurd's "studies" just then consisted of smoking cigarettes and reading a novel by Zola, which on his father's approach he would hastily conceal behind a large dictionary'.

As regards Ibsen's method of work, Paulsen relates that he would (like so many writers) break off at an appointed hour even if in the heat of composition or in the middle of a scene, since 'instead of the mood evaporating it would carry over to the following day, when he would find the inspiration still fresh and could continue immediately without having to search for the central thread'. He once surprised Paulsen by declaring that 'the creative function operates exactly like the stomach. One receives certain material from without, digests it, and excretes it – *voilà tout!*' Nevertheless, Suzannah told Paulsen that Ibsen 'always approached his desk like a sanctuary, *soigné*, in a "well-pressed morning coat"'.

In December, Paulsen departed for Rome. 'Promise me you won't write a line the first year you are in Italy,' was Ibsen's advice to him as they said farewell. 'Just take in impressions.'

Considering that he had not completed any new work during the year, 1876 had, thanks mainly to the continued success of *The Vikings at Helgeland*, the Christiania production of *Peer Gynt*, and the reprints of *Peer Gynt* and *Brand*, been financially fair: he had earned £474.

18

The Pillars of Society
1877–8

IBSEN opened the New Year, 1877, with an eloquent appeal on 4 February to Johan Sverdrup, as President of the Storthing, for an increase in his pension, and his letter again underlines the disadvantage he suffered through Norway and Denmark not having copyright agreements with other European countries:

As a result, our books can be translated without let or hindrance anywhere and by anyone. And this is happening all the time. In England the whole of *Emperor and Galilean* was translated and published last year; I had not at that time the money available to arrange this at my own expense; now the translator and publisher take the profits; I get nothing. In Berlin, A. Strodtmann has taken my poems from me, as well as my plays *The Pretenders* and *The League of Youth*. Now these works are being widely read and performed in Germany, which brings money to the translator but not to me. The same has happened with *Brand*, of which three separate German translations now exist without providing me with a penny. Even in Sweden the situation is the same for us; we have no legal right to payment either from the theatres or from the publishers who have us translated. One Swedish translation of *The Vikings at Helgeland* has already appeared and another is in the press. All I have managed to keep for myself has been the editions I commissioned personally of *The Vikings at Helgeland* and *Lady Inger of Østraat*, but these editions cost me a considerable outlay which I can expect to regain only gradually over the years.

I appreciate that the Norwegian government cannot consider entering into cultural agreements with the great countries of literature. The advantage to us of the present anarchic situation is so evident that none of us, out of respect to our general reading public, would wish it altered. Should free access to foreign literary works be denied us, the source of intellectual progress and freedom in virtually every walk of life would be blocked, or at any rate rendered less accessible to us. Of that there must be no thought. But, Mr. President, I appeal to your sense of justice whether it is fair that the financial loss resulting from such an arrangement should be borne by us four or five writers? Give each of us an extra 200 specie-dollars (£55) supplement to our pensions as compensation for what we lose on the majority's behalf. With this extra help we could at least save some of our works from falling into the hands of foreign translators; we could keep them for our own benefit, and thereby also ensure that our literature is presented to foreign readers in a more correct form than is now commonly the case.

Eleven days later Sverdrup moved in the Storthing that all pensions of composers and authors should be raised by a total sum aggregating 800 crowns (£44). This modest proposal was rejected. Ibsen's finances were now so low that on 27 February he had to ask Hegel to advance him the honorarium due on the forthcoming reprint of *Love's Comedy*, and Hegel generously obliged with 1,000 specie-dollars (£278). With this, plus a windfall of 400 crowns (£22) from the Bergen Theatre for *The League of Youth*, which had opened there on 25 February, Ibsen was able to look round for new lodgings (he explained to Hegel on 27 February) 'where I can work undisturbed, my present apartment leaving much to be desired in this respect'. On 1 May he moved to a first-floor flat at Schellingstrasse 30.

Meanwhile he had at last begun to make progress with *The Pillars of Society*. 'I shall have it ready during the summer,' he told Hegel, who must have received the news with scepticism. But by 20 April it was 'moving rapidly towards its conclusion', and on 24 June, for once on schedule, he was able to report: 'Today I take advantage of a free moment to tell you that on the 15th inst. I completed my new play and am now going ahead with the fair-copying.' He posted the fair copy to Hegel in five instalments between 29 July and 20 August.

While he was engaged on the copying, Georg Brandes visited him for one evening, accompanied by his wife; for the previous summer he had married Gerda Strodtmann, the ex-wife of Ibsen's German translator. The hostility towards Brandes in his native country had reached such proportions that he had decided, as Ibsen had done, and as Strindberg was shortly to do, to go into exile – though in his case (unlike theirs) his departure was regretted, for forty-five eminent Danes published a joint letter thanking him for what he had done, and even Bjørnson, who had quarrelled so deeply with him, added his thanks in an article in a Danish newspaper. Brandes was struck by the impersonality of Ibsen's living conditions, an impression which other observers were to record of his various dwellings. 'Since 1864', Brandes was to write five years later, 'he has not had his feet under his own mahogany, nor slept in his own bed . . . He has lived as though in a tent, among pieces of hired furniture, which could be sent back on the day appointed for his departure . . . When I last visited him [on this occasion in 1877], on my asking whether nothing at all in the apartment belonged to him, he pointed to a row of paintings on the wall. They were the only things that were his own . . . He feels no longing to possess a house and a home, still less a farm and lands like Bjørnson.'

This unhomeliness which was always so characteristic of Ibsen's apartments is especially curious in a writer whose plays are so often permeated by a deep sense of home. Fifty years ago Gunnar Heiberg (a distinguished director of Ibsen's plays) pointed out how important it is when staging *A Doll's House* that the audience should have the feeling that a *home* is being broken up, and the same is true of *An Enemy of the People* and *The Wild Duck*. Unless Dr Stockmann's house is given the feeling of a home, the effect of the last act when we see it with the windows broken is greatly minimized. And one has seen productions of *The Wild Duck* ruined by a failure to present the four Ekdals as a closely knit family. By contrast, there are other plays, such as *Ghosts*, *The Master Builder* and *When We Dead Awaken*, in which the characters sadly remark on the fact that the house they live in is not in the fullest sense a home (as is also implied in *Hedda Gabler*, *Little Eyolf* and *John Gabriel Borkman*). Neither Ibsen nor Suzannah, for all their strong sense of family, seems to have had the gift of making the place they lived in homely – which need cost very little, as anyone who has lived in a bed-sitting room can testify. One remembers Ibsen's admission of his indifference to flowers.

Another visitor to Ibsen that summer was Ole Bull, making what proved to be his last concert tour. They spent an evening together reminiscing over old times, and Marcus Grønvold, who was present, noted Ibsen's amusement that Bull expressed such pleasure in *Peer Gynt*, for which he himself had been the part-model.

A week after he had sent the final instalment of *The Pillars of Society* to Hegel, Ibsen left for Sweden, having borrowed 600 crowns (£33) from his ever-willing publisher to pay for the ticket. The cause of his visit was an agreeable one; Upsala University, the oldest in Scandinavia, was celebrating its four hundredth anniversary, the occasion was to be marked by festivities, including the awarding of honorary degrees, and Ibsen was to be made a doctor of letters. (For this he had to thank Lorentz Dietrichson, who had been informed that he was to receive a doctorate and suggested that Ibsen should be similarly honoured.) Suzannah took the opportunity to pay a visit to Norway, taking Sigurd with her and leaving Ibsen to fend for himself for ten days in Munich before leaving – which, in his way, he managed to do, as appears from the following letter:

Munich, 21 August 1877

Dear Suzannah!

As soon as I received your letter and Sigurd's yesterday I telegraphed that everything was all right here, and I hope the telegram reached you safely. I am glad the sea trip went so well, and I hear from Sigurd that you praised your own dress at the dinner table![1]

The whole manuscript is now dispatched, and I am making preparations for my departure, which will probably be on Monday. I don't expect to be away longer than strictly necessary, i.e. about a fortnight. Here everything is as usual. Helene is very good, makes good coffee and does all her work very punctually and exactly the way she has seen that I want it. I usually dine at Schleich's, which is better than the Museum and not wickedly dearer. For 1.75 [about three pence] I get an excellent soup, fish, two meat dishes with all kinds of vegetables, and a compote, followed by pastries, cheese, bread and butter. This is pretty well my only meal, for I always stay at home in the evenings and then eat only a sandwich. Vullum has also been eating at Schleich's till yesterday, when he left. I have been with Grønvold once or twice and intend to invite him to dinner, since his brother has been so kind to you in Bergen.

I hope you are enjoying yourselves up there; but don't run any risks, and take good care of Sigurd and of your money and don't let the locals rob you.

I will write again from Sweden and hope to receive another letter from you there. No more for today. Enjoy yourselves.

> Your
> Henrik Ibsen

He enclosed a Polonius-like letter to Sigurd, exhorting him to 'be sure to be careful both ashore and at sea; the least carelessness can bring consequences ... Don't go out too much on the water, and not in a sailing boat!'

Ibsen spent a fortnight in Sweden. After a few days in Stockholm, he accompanied the other guests to Upsala, fifty miles north of the capital, on 4 September. 'The aquavit will begin to flow,' he wrote to Grønvold, 'and I don't expect to get any peace for letter-writing during the next few days.' The festivities in Upsala began on the 5th with a dinner. On

---

1. Forgetting that she was among Scandinavians, Suzannah had said at dinner the first day aboard the ship: 'I think my dress is much smarter than the other ladies'.'

the 6th the honorary degrees were handed out, and Ibsen had a laurel wreath placed on his head by the archbishop. That afternoon a banquet was given in the Botanical Gardens, attended by fifteen hundred people, the doctors still wearing their laurel wreaths; in the evening there was a firework display and torchlight procession, and the finance minister, Hans Forssell, who was also a distinguished man of letters, gave a party attended by several of the leading Swedish writers of the day. 'Within five minutes', says Dietrichson, who was there, 'it was Ibsen who led the conversation and made it interesting. How Ibsen has acquired the reputation of being so excessively silent I have never been able to understand.'

The following evening there was a ball in the Botanical Gardens in a specially created building, looking (to judge from an engraving in *Ny Illustrerad Tidning*) remarkably like Paddington Station. During these days at Upsala, Ibsen had several meetings with King Oscar II, who had already shown him several marks of his favour, and got on with that bluff but prickly giant nearly as well as he had with his much more open and attractive brother, Carl XV.

When the Upsala celebrations had ended, the king gave a farewell banquet for the guests at his palace at Drottningholm, just outside Stockholm, with illuminations in the park; and the Royal Theatre honoured Ibsen with a special performance of *The Vikings at Helgeland*. It is curious to reflect how antiquated that play, now twenty years old, must have seemed to the man who had just written *The Pillars of Society*.

On his way back to Munich, Ibsen spent a couple of days in Copenhagen, where Hegel put him up in style at the Hotel d'Angleterre opposite the Royal Theatre, refused to let him pay for anything, and gave a party in his honour at his villa. Unwittingly, however, Ibsen offended Georg Brandes by not contacting him, having been wrongly informed that Brandes was out of town. Brandes, as touchy as any of the many touchy persons in this narrative, was mortally offended. 'Ibsen and I', he wrote to Bjørnson the following June, 'have been good friends for so many years that I am unwilling to say any hard or unfriendly words about him. He seems to me to be an enclosed, shy person who has difficulty in finding words, is reluctant to open himself, and is full of suspicion and distrust, even to those who have never done him anything but good' (a sad case of the pot calling the kettle black). Amazingly, Ibsen seems to have been unaware of Brandes's change of attitude towards him; a year and a half later, on 18 February 1879, thanking Hegel for Brandes's book on Disraeli, he was to praise it as an 'absolute masterpiece' and to ask Hegel to convey to Brandes his admiration and best wishes. But he did not write direct to Brandes for four years, from 1877 to 1881 (for which the blame must largely rest with Brandes; their correspondence had always in the main been a case of Ibsen replying to Brandes's letters); and this silence unwittingly fed Brandes's suspicions that Ibsen's feelings towards him had cooled. So there was another friendship down the drain.

By 20 September Ibsen was back in Munich, whence three days later he again wrote characteristically to Suzannah:

... You must have read in the newspapers how hugely I was feted in Upsala. The Danish papers say I was the most feted of all the guests in Upsala, and this was indeed the case. But now I am content to be at peace again, although things are not very comfortable; it is tiresome to have to eat out every day, the food does not suit me, the evenings are long, cold, and gloomy. I sit here alone since Grønvold is in the country ... If you could find the time to buy me six pairs of gloves in Copenhagen, I should be grateful; they must be of fine, thin leather, preferably dark brown, size 8½; I bought a pair there for 1 kr. 70 øre [twenty pence] in a shop on the corner of Østergade and Kongens Nytorv. Perhaps Sara [Suzannah's sister] could help you with this; but pack them deep in your trunk, for the customs inspection.

As he awaited the appearance of *The Pillars of Society*, Ibsen learned to his annoyance that John Paulsen had passed on to a Norwegian journalist a few facts about the play which Ibsen had confided to him, and that the journalist had printed these, getting many of the details wrong. Among other errors, the title of the play was given as *Samfundets Piller* (*piller* is an archaic word for 'pillars', but more commonly means 'pills'). Didrik Grønvold (the brother of Marcus) visited Ibsen at Schellingstrasse just after he had discovered this, and found him 'walking up and down his room like a lion in its cage, sparking with anger, not so much at the leak of information as at the mutilated title'.

Ibsen had been painted that summer by Julius Kronberg, wearing his new doctor's cloak – a portrait which Ibsen kept until his death. Strindberg, a much better painter and judge of painting than Ibsen, saw this portrait at an exhibition in Stockholm, and wrote an eloquent description: 'The face is Brand's; the high, broad brow of the fanatic, the strong mouth of the witness whose lips have never uttered the truths that his hand has penned, the cold, determined look that never wavered when it stared "the spirit of compromise" in the face; that is Ibsen, the fanatical sceptic . . . so impressive and terrifying, so repellent, so attractive!'

On 11 October 1877 *The Pillars of Society* was at last published, and achieved an immediate and widespread success. The first edition of 6,000 copies sold out within seven weeks, and a further 4,000 had to be printed. A German translation appeared before the end of November.

Since *The Pillars of Society* is an indictment of a particular kind of right-wing figure, contemporary opinion naturally varied according to the political views of the reader; the liberals and radicals hailed it with the same delight with which the conservatives had greeted *The League of Youth*. Curiously, the Christiania papers scarcely noticed it at all; it was reviewed less in the capital than any play Ibsen had written since he had left Norway in 1864; not only the right-wing *Morgenbladet* but (inexplicably) the liberal *Dagbladet* ignored it. Indeed, only three Christiania publications printed reviews, and two of these were disparaging. The provincial newspapers were more perceptive; Nordahl Rolfsen, in *Bergens-Posten*, was shrewd enough to see that *The Pillars of Society* was more than a mere political salvo. 'It will help', he wrote, 'to dispel the idea that Ibsen is primarily a polemical writer. The real targets of Ibsen's indignation are mean-mindedness and pettiness, wherever they may be found.' The Danish reviews were all good, apart from an anonymous complaint in *Fædrelandet* that 'one hears too seldom the beating of a great and warm heart'. The writer of light vaudevilles, Erik Bøgh, generously acclaimed the new dramatist whose fame was so far exceeding his own:

It is a mighty test of strength that Henrik Ibsen has essayed in trying a fall with one of 'The Pillars of Society' ... He has gone about it like a Samson, and even if his shaking has not brought about the upheaval which levelled the Temple of Dagon, several Philistine hearts must surely have trembled as it groaned to its foundations in his mighty grip ... Ibsen does not suffer from the Danish malaise of never doing anything whole-heartedly [a disease which Ibsen had in fact condemned in *Brand* as being peculiarly Norwegian]. If falsehood is to be stripped bare, he will work at it till its fine feathers cling protectively to the wearer's skin like the shirt of Nessus. If necessary, he will remove the skin too, and should a little flesh be adhering to the skin, that will not deter him.

Like Rolfsen, Bøgh compared the play favourably with Bjørnson's *A Bankrupt* ('Ibsen never perpetrates a fifth act showing his hero restored to prosperity and converted as Bjørnson did'), and concluded with a shrewd criticism: 'there are too many speeches which delay the fall of the curtain after the action is finished and the play is over'. It was an error which (except in *An Enemy of the People*) Ibsen was never to commit again; anyone who has tried to cut one of his plays (for television, for instance) knows that, while a good deal of the exposition can usually be thinned out from the first act, and a certain amount from the middle, there is scarcely a line in any other of his last acts from *A Doll's House* onwards that will bear removal.

Surprisingly, especially for men of their political leanings, neither of the Brandes brothers liked it (which may be the reason why neither reviewed it). 'Ibsen is so anxious to provoke,' wrote Edvard to Georg on 30 November, 'that there is nothing *big* about his play. It's a big problem seen small and treated small.' And Georg wrote to J. P. Jacobsen on 16 December, 'Ibsen's play is technically fine, but it taught me nothing.'

The Pillars of Society is not often performed today on the professional stage, though in England, at least, it pops up frequently in the drama schools. The reason in both cases is the same: the size of the cast. There are nineteen characters, not including the crowd at the end, an advantage to students and amateurs but an expensive obstacle to any unsubsidized company. *Peer Gynt* needs as many actors, but *Peer Gynt*, like Shakespeare, can usually be sure of an audience. This neglect of *The Pillars of Society* is sad, for until the last five minutes it holds the stage splendidly, quick-moving, strongly plotted, sharply characterized, and full of feline wit. Were it not for those last minutes – but since the play is generally little known, one must pause briefly to outline its plot (a procedure which will not invariably be inflicted on the reader when more famous plays come to be discussed).

It is set in a small port. The chief character, Karsten Bernick, a wealthy shipowner, has (like John Gabriel Borkman) married a woman he does not love, to further his career. His life has been a series of successes founded on double-dealing, sometimes above the law, sometimes not. Caught in an actress's bedroom while still engaged (fifteen years before the play opens), he allowed his fiancée's brother Johan to take the blame. Planning a railway to the town, he has secretly bought up all the land through which the line will pass. When Johan returns from America and threatens to expose him, Bernick lets him go to sea in a ship he knows is rotten and must sink – only to find, seemingly too late, that his own son has stowed aboard. In the unconvincing ending, the ship is discovered not to have sailed, and Bernick in his relief confesses his crimes and is left not only unpunished but rather better off than he was before.

Such a summary omits the various sub-plots and several of the play's best characters: Lona Hessel, Bernick's former love, returning robustly (with a knapsack on her back) from America to let fresh air into the closed society of the little town; the narrow-minded schoolmaster, Dr Rørlund; Dina Dorf, the young orphan daughter of Bernick's former mistress, and his ward; Aune, the shipyard foreman, fearful of the unemployment that new machines may bring; Hilmar Tønnessen, Mrs Bernick's cousin, an indolent aesthete; Martha, Bernick's sister, who has loved Johan and waited for his return only to find that he has no eyes for her, but only for Dina who is half her age; and Bernick's three shifty capitalist associates and their gossiping wives. The pettiness of provincial life, which was one of the things Ibsen hated most about Norway (in its capital no less than in its small towns) is mercilessly detailed; and in two important respects the play marks a notable advance over *The League of Youth*.

One is the clarity with which the sub-plots are interwoven with the main plot, instead of the play being a Congrevian maze; the other is the sharpness with which individual modes of speech are differentiated, something which was to be one of Ibsen's supreme strengths, and one of his main contributions to the technique of prose drama. Lona Hessel, for example, fresh from America, has a breezy, slangy way of speaking which contrasts markedly with the prim speech of the local stay-at-homes; and Hilmar Tønnessen talks in an extraordinary, fanciful manner, over-loaded with adjectives and ridiculous flights of imagination, like Hjalmar Ekdal in *The Wild Duck*. Ibsen was a wonderfully minute observer of the way people talked (as of the way they looked and dressed), even to noting that we speak differently at different times of the day, and that women phrase their sentences differently from men. Other playwrights, such as Bjørnson, had attempted to differentiate the speech of their characters, but their efforts are crude compared with Ibsen's. These different modes of speech are one of the most difficult problems that face a translator; if one fails, one deprives the actor of his subtlest weapon.

The play dealt with two problems of especial topicality for the eighteen-seventies. One was the question of women's rights; the other, that of 'floating coffins'. Controversy over the former problem had reached its height in Norway (as elsewhere) during the seventies; in 1876 Asta Hansteen, a great champion of the cause, began a series of lectures on the subject, but was so furiously assailed that in 1880 she emigrated to America. She was the original of Lona Hessel (Ibsen at first gave the character the surname of Hassel, but changed it, presumably so as to avoid too direct an identification with Hansteen). Camilla Collett, the novelist, another doughty warrior, had probably exerted a good deal of influence on him when they had met in Dresden in 1871 and in Munich in 1877, when he was writing the play and they had many arguments about marriage and other female problems; and Suzannah, too, had long felt strongly about these things. Ibsen had already touched tentatively on the subject in *The League of Youth*, and he was to deal with it more minutely in his next play. His original intention in *The Pillars of Society* had been to be even more outspoken than he finally was, for in his first draft Dina announces her decision to go off with her lover, Johan, without marrying him; but he evidently doubted whether the theatres would stage a play which suggested anything quite so daring, and legalized their relationship.

The question of the 'floating coffins' was first forced upon Ibsen's attention by an English Member of Parliament. In 1868 Samuel Plimsoll had sought in the House of Commons to have the state interfere against the cold-blooded and unscrupulous sacrifice of human life by sending men to sea in rotten ships. In 1873 he succeeded in getting a law passed to enforce seaworthiness; but this proved too slack. On 22 July 1875 he created a tremendous commotion in Parliament by a boldly outspoken attack on the people responsible for such a policy; he called the owners of such ships murderers and the politicians who supported them scoundrels. This so roused the conscience of the nation that a temporary bill went through in a few days, and its principles were made permanent by the Merchant Shipping Act of the following year. Plimsoll's protest echoed throughout the world, and in a seafaring country such as Norway it rang especially loudly. A particularly scandalous case had occurred in Christiania during Ibsen's visit there in 1874. On 2 September of that year, at the annual general meeting of the shipping insurance company Norske Veritas, questions were asked about a ship which, after having been declared seaworthy, sprang a leak while at sea and was shown to be completely rotten. At the annual general meeting a year later two similar cases were mentioned, and a storm of indignation was aroused. The matter was reported in detail in the newspapers, and Ibsen can hardly have failed to read about it.

The presentation in a dramatic form of problems that were urgent and topical rather than eternal was not unprecedented; it was the depth and subtlety of Ibsen's characterization, his psychological insight and ability to strip respected people and institutions of their masks, that made *The Pillars of Society* a revelation to its contemporaries, especially the young, in a way in which *The Editor* and *A Bankrupt*, *La Dame aux Camélias* and *Thérèse Raquin*, for all their theatrical effectiveness, had never been. Two of the rising stars of the German theatre, then both in their early twenties, have recorded the effect that the play had on them.

'Our young eyes', recalled Paul Schlenther, 'were opened to the false tinsel of the theatre that was being offered to us. We thrilled with joy. We returned incessantly to the theatre where it was being played; when it was full, we read the play in Wilhelm Lange's terrible translation. Until then Ibsen had been but an empty name to us. It was this play that taught us to love him, a love that lasted for life. I can testify on behalf of many of my generation that under the influence of this example of modern realism there was implanted in us, at that formative age, an orientation of taste which was to be decisive for the whole of our lives.'

And Otto Brahm, at twenty-two a year younger than Schlenther, wrote: 'It was there that we gained the first inkling of a new world of creative art, first felt ourselves face to face with people of our time, in whom we could believe, and with a criticism which embraced the whole society of our time.' In a few years Schlenther and Brahm were to be leading spirits in the founding of the Freie Bühne, which was to do for the German theatre what Antoine's Théâtre Libre was to do for the French.

So exciting and new were the qualities of *The Pillars of Society* that Ibsen's contemporaries as a whole (political opponents and the Brandes brothers excepted) forgave the weakness of the last act; but it is a weakness we find less easy to forgive. It has been suggested that this ending possesses 'ironic potential'; that Ibsen, by showing how a double-dealer can survive exposure and remain at the helm, underlined the danger that such men are to the society they control. The idea may indeed have been at the back of his mind; and if it was, and if he betrayed his real belief by settling for a happy ending, this may explain why that ending is so unconvincing. Erik Bøgh, in the review quoted above, wrote: 'Ibsen never perpetrates a fifth act showing his hero restored to prosperity and converted, as Bjørnson did [in *A Bankrupt*],' but this in fact is exactly what Ibsen does in the final act of *The Pillars of Society*, and no sophistry or skilful acting can conceal it. Yet the rest of the play is so fine that with a good production we forgive this unlikely ending, as we forgive the equally unlikely ending of (for example) *A Winter's Tale*.

The Pillars of Society was not (as it is sometimes claimed to be) the first realistic prose play. Nor was it even the first that Ibsen had written in colloquial prose; he had done that in *The League of Youth* (and to some extent in *Emperor and Galilean*). But it can be fairly claimed to have been the first (always excepting Büchner and Gogol) to combine the three elements of colloquial dialogue, objectivity, and tightness of plot which are the requirements and characteristics of modern prose drama. And it is the first in which we can identify several of those elements which we nowadays instinctively associate with Ibsen's name – a marriage founded on a lie, passionate women stunted and inhibited by the conventions of their time, and an arrogant man of high intellectual and practical gifts who destroys, or nearly destroys, the happiness of those nearest to him. It also exhibits, unlike his earlier plays, what Henry James admiringly described as 'the operation of talent without glamour . . . the ugly interior on which his curtain inexorably rises and which, to be honest, I like for the queer associations it has taught us to respect: the hideous carpet and wallpaper (one may answer for them), the conspicuous stove, the lonely central table, the "lamps with green shades" . . . the pervasive air of small interests and standards, the sign of limited local life.' Above all, *The Pillars of Society* has, despite its overtones of comedy, that peculiarly Ibsenish quality of austerity which contrasts so sharply with the exuberant cornucopia of his earlier work; what Henry James, on another occasion, described as 'the hard compulsion of his strangely inscrutable art'. No wonder, when we remember the technical problems imposed by this new form, that *The Pillars of Society* took Ibsen longer to write than any of his other plays except the triple-length *Emperor and Galilean*. As *Peer Gynt* had been a farewell to the old drama, so *The Pillars of Society* was the harbinger of the new.

By the end of 1877, *The Pillars of Society* had received three separate productions, at the Royal Theatre in Copenhagen on 18 November, at the Bergen Theatre on 30 November, and at the Royal Theatre in Stockholm on 13 December. The

Christiania Theatre, however, had incurred Ibsen's wrath by permitting a performance that June of Act Four of *Brand* without reference to him and, worse, forcing the resignation of Ludvig Josephson, who had done so much for him (and for the theatre) over the past four years. 'The board would have acted more in the interests of the theatre if . . . they had sacked themselves,' Ibsen wrote to Hartvig Lassen on 2 November. '. . . And what kind of a successor have you appointed! This successor was here in Munich last summer, and talked about his job like a five-year-old child. How long do you suppose this miserable and totally useless fellow will survive? He won't last the season.' Ibsen added sadly that Josephson had had plans to stage a shortened version of *Brand*, and Part One of *Emperor and Galilean*. Not only did Ibsen allow the Bergen Theatre to give the first Norwegian production of *The Pillars of Society*; he rubbed in the lesson a year later by permitting a Swedish company to act it in Swedish at the old Møllergaden theatre in Christiania (on 6 November 1878), and it was not performed in the capital in Norwegian until the following March, seventeen months after publication.

Ibsen marked the appearance of *The Pillars of Society* by sending a copy of it to Bjørnson with a brief but affectionate note, the first contact between the two for eight years. The chief reason for this olive branch was, ironically, Bjørnson's public declaration of thanks to Georg Brandes, whom Ibsen, though he did not realize it, had himself now mortally offended. 'This one step [of Bjørnson's]', Ibsen wrote to Hegel on 28 October, 'in my eyes greatly expiates much else; it was a noble action. I should now like to bring about a closing of the gap between him and me, and therefore beg you to send him the enclosed note with a copy of *The Pillars of Society*.' The note read:

Munich, 28 October 1877

To Bjørnstjerne Bjørnson!

Your utterance on the occasion of G. Brandes's departure has delighted and deeply moved me. This is the true you. Will you be so good as to accept the enclosed book from me and give it to your wife?

H.I.

The olive branch was rejected. 'He has sent me a warm message of thanks and his last book because of what I wrote about you in D.F.,' Bjørnson informed Brandes on 10 June 1878. 'I didn't answer him, for I find his conduct towards me shabby. I think he's a pipsqueak with his titles and decorations and nauseating letters to every little person who praises him in the tiniest newspaper ... People excuse Ibsen because he comes from "simple folk". He needs it for his self-esteem. Well, well!'

When, at the end of 1877, Ibsen reckoned up his accounts, he had reason to feel satisfied; his earnings for the year had risen to £772. It is noteworthy that despite the greatly increased number of theatrical productions, nearly two thirds of this sum was from book sales in Scandinavia. For many years yet, performance rights were to remain a subsidiary source, and foreign translations, as he had complained to Sverdrup when appealing for an increase in his pension, were seldom to bring him anything at all.

This fact was exemplified at the beginning of 1878. The success of *The Pillars of Society* in the three Scandinavian countries did not pass unnoticed in Germany where, in the absence of copyright protection, translators and theatre directors fastened upon the play like vultures. In addition to the translation authorized by Ibsen, two pirate versions appeared before the end of January. One was by a man named Emil Jonas, whom Ibsen described to Hegel (28 January) as 'a frightful literary bandit', and to whom, ten days earlier, he had addressed one of those formidable rebukes which he so well knew how to word:

Munich, 18 January 1878

Herr Emil Jonas,
Berlin

In reply to your communication I must remind you of a fact of which you cannot be unaware, namely, that I myself, at the beginning of November last, published with Messrs. Theodor Ackermann a German version of my play, *The Pillars of Society*. A translation from your hand is therefore utterly superfluous, and I must totally disassociate myself from any adaptation such as you envisage.

Your suggestions for cuts in Act One are quite senseless and show that you have totally failed to understand this work which you regard yourself as worthy to adapt. Even to the most ignorant literary hack I should have thought it obvious that in this play no roles can be omitted and not a single line deleted. The play has already been accepted in an unabridged and unbowdlerized form by many German theatres . . .

If, in spite of me, you permit the proposed monstrosity to be put before the public, you at least owe it to me to clear my name by seeing that the placards outside the theatre carry the caption 'Travestied by Emil Jonas'.

Faithfully,
Henrik Ibsen

The extent to which this pirating cut into Ibsen's earnings soon became clear. In February *The Pillars of Society* was performed at five separate theatres in Berlin alone within a fortnight. Before the end of the year, it had been staged at no less than twenty-seven theatres in Germany and Austria. But financially, these productions brought Ibsen little joy. The play was performed almost exclusively in pirated versions. In a letter to a paper the following March Jonas, defending his adaptation by declaring that it 'suited German taste', pointed out that it had been accepted for performance by thirty-two German theatres, whereas Ibsen's authorized translation had been played only at the Nationaltheater in Berlin and the Munich Hoftheater. (Even the other pirated version, by Wilhelm Lange, had been performed at four theatres.) Most of Ibsen's German royalties and fees (excluding those from the Munich Hoftheater and one or two other theatres which had honourably offered to deal with him direct) were henceforth collected for him by the German Society of Dramatists, and appear only as unitemized lump

sums in his account books; but from these twenty-seven
productions, excluding Munich, he earned that year only
£35 plus another £14 which arrived early the next year.
Most of the German theatres do not appear to have paid him
anything at all. Georg Brandes reckoned that Ibsen was
robbed thus of £738 which he should have earned from *The
Pillars of Society* in this year alone – 'and his [German] publisher has lost much, much money, for three [*sic*] other
pirate publishers sold it for 2 groschen while his own publisher was asking 2 marks'. How much Emil Jonas made
from the play is not on record.

In England, however, he had a new admirer, and one who
was to do far more for him than Edmund Gosse, whose
interest in Scandinavian literature had rapidly faded.[2] William Archer, now twenty-two, had spent much of his childhood in Norway and had grown up bilingual in English and
Norwegian (his grandparents had settled in Larvik in 1825
and spent the rest of their lives there, and one of his uncles,
Colin Archer, was to build Nansen's famous ship, the *Fram*).
Archer had first made the acquaintance of Ibsen's work in
1873 (the year in which he had, unknowingly, been in
Vienna at the same time as Ibsen), and at once became an
addict.

A *chokolade-selskab* [chocolate party] was going on, and I, a
boy of seventeen, sat listening to the chatter of a lot of ladies.
One of them, whom I never saw before or since, but whose face I
remember as though I had seen it yesterday, said '*Jeg synes*
Kjærlighedens Komedie *er saa glimrende vittig*' ['I think *Love's
Comedy* is so brilliantly witty']. 'Hullo,' I thought, 'have they got
anything *glimrende vittig* in Norwegian? I must look into this' –
and forthwith went and bought the book. Then I read *Kongs-*

2. After contributing over twenty essays or reviews concerning Ibsen
to English periodicals between March 1872 and March 1878, Gosse
was to write nothing about Ibsen for five years. During these years the
only two other articles, etc., published in English about Ibsen were an
account by Edith Pradez of Ibsen's 1874 visit to Norway in the
Academy, 10 October 1874, and Archer's review of *The Pillars of
Society* in the *St James's Gazette* in 1878.

emnerne [*The Pretenders*], *Hærmænderne* [*The Vikings*], and all that he had written up to that time, with increasing delight.

When *Emperor and Galilean* appeared that autumn of 1873,

> I remember locking myself up in a little bare hutch of a bathing-house by the fjord in order to devour its ten acts in the luxury of unbroken solitude ... I laid in provisions to enable me, if necessary, to stand a siege. Even in those days, you see, Ibsenite and Ishmaelite meant much the same thing.

Archer waited impatiently for the publication of Ibsen's next play, and when *The Pillars of Society* at last appeared it so excited him that he made a hurried translation (rather uninspiredly entitled *The Supports of Society*), and on 2 March 1878 published an analysis of the play, with extracts from his translation, in *The Mirror of Literature*. He tried to interest publishers in his translation, but 'no publisher would look at it' and people 'used to jeer at my rapture over this incomprehensible Hyperborean'. With Scottish resolution, he settled down to prepare another, more careful version which, eighteen months later, was to meet with better luck.

A young Norwegian woman named Laura Kieler, whom Ibsen had met a few times over the past seven years, now re-entered his life, with results which were to prove significant for both of them. As Laura Petersen, a decade previously, she had written a sequel to *Brand* in the form of a novel entitled *Brand's Daughters*; then, in the summer of 1871, she had visited Dresden for a couple of months and had called on him. He must have liked her, for they saw a good deal of each other during her stay; he called her his 'skylark', and encouraged her to write more.

She married a Danish schoolmaster named Victor Kieler, and in 1876 visited Ibsen again, in Munich. She now had a sad story to tell him (or rather, she told Suzannah, and Suzannah told Ibsen). Her husband had contracted tuberculosis, and she had been advised that the only way to save his life was to take him for a while to a warmer climate. They lacked the means for this and, since Kieler became neurotically hysterical at any mention of money, she took it on herself secretly to obtain a loan, for which a friend stood security. The trip (to Italy) had been successful, for Kieler, unluckily for Laura, lived for another forty years; but the matter weighed on her mind, and Ibsen noticed sadly that his little skylark 'could no longer sing her happy songs'.

During the first months of 1878 Suzannah received a letter from Laura enclosing the manuscript of a novel she had written and begging Suzannah to ask Ibsen to recommend it to Hegel. Ibsen found himself embarrassingly placed, for the book struck him as really bad; any writer who has been asked by a friend to pass on a poor manuscript to a publisher will sympathize with his position. He replied on 26 March, in stern but kindly terms, telling her that he could not possibly recommend it.

> You speak of circumstances which compelled you to write this book under pressure. I do not understand. In a family where the husband is alive it can never be necessary for the wife to sacrifice her heart's blood as you have done. I am amazed that he should permit you to do so. There must be something which you don't tell me and which colours the whole situation; that is my impression after several readings of your letter . . . It is unthinkable that your husband knows everything; so you must tell him; he must take on his shoulders the sorrows and problems which now torment you . . . Hegel would never have accepted your manuscript even if I had recommended it . . . Confide all your troubles to your husband. He is the one who should bear them.

She had, indeed, not told Ibsen the full story; perhaps she feared he might take it as an attempt to touch him for a loan. Repayment had been demanded of the money she had borrowed to take her husband to Italy two years earlier. She did not have it, and dared not tell her husband because of his neurotic attitude towards such matters; worse, the friend who had stood security had himself fallen into straits, and told her he would be ruined if pressed for payment. Laura, who had published a book of sketches and a novel (*Everil*, about an unhappy marriage), had seen no way out but to write another book and hope for an unusually large advance; hence the hasty and unfortunate manuscript. Ibsen's reply (though he can scarcely be blamed) was to have disastrous consequences.

The success of *The Pillars of Society*[3] not surprisingly stimulated Ibsen to think immediately about following it up with another play in the same genre, just as the success of *Brand* had stimulated him to follow that work with another drama-for-reading. On 5 May, he informed Hegel: 'I have begun to busy myself with plans for a new play with a contemporary setting; it will, like the last, be in four acts. When it will be ready, however, I can as yet have no idea.' His own letters of that spring and summer deal exclusively with business matters. He was to ponder his theme for another twelve months before writing the first line of dialogue – a routine he was to adopt with every play he subsequently wrote, with but one exception.

That summer Sigurd took his matriculation, and passed with high honours. He was a far better student and examinee than his father had been; but he had been better taught. Now that the boy's schooling was finished, Ibsen felt free to do what he had been longing to do for several years: to return to Italy. He had enjoyed his three years in Munich, but the Mediterranean beckoned to him, and on 2 August he wrote to Hegel:

Towards the middle of this month we shall be leaving for the south; we plan to spend the winter in Rome, where I hope to find time and peace to complete my new work. The weather here has

3. Not that the conservatives liked it any more in Germany than they had in Norway. Karl Frenzel, the influential critic of *Deutsche Rundschau*, who had written of *The Pretenders* that Ibsen was poor at dramatic construction and did not know how to work out a plot, found *The Pillars of Society* an effective criticism of social conditions but reiterated that Ibsen was 'no dramatist'.

been beastly the whole time, so that we have had no real summer. I greatly long to get across the Alps . . .

Mrs Laura Kieler has, as you probably know, suffered a sad calamity. Her husband informed us rather curtly that she had been admitted into a mental clinic. Do you know the exact circumstances of this, and whether she is still there? . . . As soon as I have settled in at Florence, where we expect to spend a couple of months, you will hear from me again. Sigurd . . . will probably continue his studies at the university here [in Munich] when we return next autumn.

When the full news of the Kieler affair reached Ibsen, it must have shaken him. On receipt of his letter of 26 March she had burned the manuscript and forged a cheque. The forgery was discovered, and the bank refused payment; whereupon she told her husband the whole story. He, regardless of the fact that she had done it purely for his sake, treated her like a criminal, told her she was unworthy to have charge of their children and, when she in consequence suffered a nervous breakdown, had her committed to a public asylum (where she lived in a ward among lunatics) and demanded a separation so that the children could be removed from her care. After a month she was discharged from the asylum and, for the children's sake, begged her husband to take her back, which he very grudgingly agreed to do.

The story must have seemed especially relevant to a writer whose last play had dwelt upon the unequal position of woman in contemporary society, and Georg Brandes's advice nearly a decade earlier that he should make such a woman the chief character in a play must have come to his mind, if it had not already done so (we do not know how far the news changed Ibsen's plans).

On their way south, the Ibsens visited Gossensass, and remained there for several weeks till the last days of September. Ibsen wrote to Nils Lund on 23 September cancelling the *gammelost* which he had asked the latter to send him as early as 25 March, and which seems to have been a long time coming (not that a few months one way or the other would have made much difference to that pungent delicacy), They forsook their original plan to stay in Florence 'since I greatly long for familiar surroundings, so as to find peace for work',[4] and by the end of September, for the first time in ten and a half years, Ibsen was back in Rome.

4. Letter to Hegel, 8 October 1878. John Paulsen observed that Ibsen seemed to feel the same indifference towards Florence as Goethe, who likewise never stayed long there but always moved on quickly to Rome.

[19]

A Doll's House
1878–80

WITHIN three weeks of his arrival in Rome Ibsen, installed in an apartment in a pleasant, five-storied corner house next to the church on the Via Due Macelli, jotted down the following:

Rome, 19. 10. 78

NOTES FOR A MODERN TRAGEDY

There are two kinds of moral laws, two kinds of conscience, one for men and one, quite different, for women. They don't understand each other; but in practical life, woman is judged by masculine law, as though she weren't a woman but a man.

The wife in the play ends by having no idea what is right and what is wrong; natural feelings on the one hand and belief in authority on the other lead her to utter distraction.

A woman cannot be herself in modern society. It is an exclusively male society, with laws made by men and with prosecutors and judges who assess feminine conduct from a masculine standpoint.

She has committed forgery, and is proud of it; for she has done it out of love for her husband, to save his life. But this husband of hers takes his standpoint, conventionally honourable, on the side of the law, and sees the situation with male eyes.

Moral conflict. Weighed down and confused by her trust in authority, she loses faith in her own morality, and in her fitness to bring up her children. Bitterness. A mother in modern society, like certain insects, retires and dies once she has done her duty by propagating the race. Love of life, of home, of husband and children and family. Now and then, as women do, she shrugs off her thoughts. Suddenly anguish and fear return. Everything must be borne alone. The catastrophe approaches, mercilessly, inevitably. Despair, conflict, and defeat.

But although he told Hegel on 7 December that he was 'concerning myself only with the preparations for my new play', it was to be another six months before he wrote the first line. Meantime, as was his wont, he pondered the theme and characters until he knew them in depth. One day he surprised Suzannah by saying, 'Now I've seen Nora. She came right up to me and put her hand on my shoulder.' 'What was she wearing?' asked Suzannah, as a woman should; to which Ibsen 'with great earnestness' replied: 'A blue woollen dress.'

'A lot of Scandinavians have arrived here, but we have got to know few of them at all well,' he wrote to Marcus Grønvold on 30 December. 'On the other hand, we have made several acquaintances among German and Italian scholars, artists and writers, whom I meet frequently. Sigurd attends lectures at the university here, and has already pretty well brushed up his old forgotten Italian; he follows the lectures completely and without trouble. We shall stay in Rome until the university holidays begin in June or July; we have made no plans beyond that, but intend to return to Munich in early October.'

Lady Inger of Østraat had just received its first German production in Berlin. But when he made up his accounts for 1878, a year in which his most recent play had been performed at over thirty theatres in Scandinavia and Germany, they offered no scope for extravagance. With only one new reprint, and that a small one, the improvement of the last three years had not been maintained; at £421, his earnings had been little more than half of the previous year's.

Ibsen was touchy and nervous that winter in Rome. 'We live in general pretty quietly,' he wrote on 22 January to Marcus Grønvold. 'Lunch is brought in to us, and our landlady prepares our breakfast and supper. Everything is much cheaper here than in Munich, and wine especially is to be had for practically nothing this winter, so that in the Sabine villages one can buy excellent wine for 3 soldi [less than a penny] a litre!' Despite his poor earnings for the past year and his habitual economy, he now indulged himself in an unexpected direction. 'I am taking the opportunity', he informed Grønvold in the same letter, 'to buy old paintings, and have already purchased eleven, all good and valuable and at a comparatively modest price. I intend to buy more, so that I shall be able to furnish my next apartment in Munich solely with works of art. If only I can find somewhere suitable!' These paintings, or most of them, came from the collection of a recently deceased cardinal, and included a supposed Titian. Lorentz Dietrichson, who, as a professor of art history, ought to have known, refers to them as 'important pictures, especially by the older Italian masters'. One would like to know more about them.

He visited the Scandinavian Club regularly, but mainly to read the newspapers; although he occasionally entered into a conversation, he was evidently in one of those long combative moods which periodically settled on him for weeks on end. Once he got into a violent argument about religion with two Danish theologians after drinking Swedish punch. He attacked the teachings of the orthodox church as being slanted to prop up an antiquated society, got angrier and angrier, and had to be supported home in the small hours by the Danish novelist and botanist J. P. Jacobsen and a young Norwegian named Gunnar Heiberg, later to become one of his country's best theatrical directors and a distinguished playwright. On the way he grew more and more abusive of the human race and its aims and ambitions; and when Heiberg tried to mollify him by suggesting that at any rate Ibsen himself had written some great truths, and started to quote from his 'Balloon Letter' poem, Isben roared contemptuously: 'Verse, verse! Just verse!'

It was in this prickly mood that, on 28 January, he put two proposals before the club: that the post of paid librarian (which he had coveted himself fifteen years earlier) should be thrown open to women, and that women should have the right to vote on all club matters. When these proposals came to be debated on 27 February, he delivered a lengthy and impassioned speech; Sigurd, who was present, tells that he got so worked up that he occasionally abandoned his prepared text and improvised with that eloquence which, when the mood was on him, he knew how to command. Even his written text (which has survived) was fiery enough, if ill-calculated to gain support from the older members who formed the majority:

Is there anyone in this gathering who dares assert that our ladies are inferior to us in culture, or intelligence, or knowledge, or artistic talent? I don't think many men would dare suggest that. Then what is it men fear? I hear there is a tradition here that women are cunning intriguers, and that therefore we don't want them. Well, I have encountered a good deal of male intrigue in my time, not least recently ... Is it perhaps the supposed unpracticality of women in matters of business? Even if women were as unpractical as many an unpractical gentleman would like to suppose, are artists so especially practical in business matters? No, gentlemen, I think not. I hold it to be good and profitable that we should have ladies present at our annual general meeting just as I hold it good and advantageous that we should have young people there, those young people whose presence is now threatened by a proposal that the vote should only be allowed to those who have been resident for a year in Rome. I repeat that I am not afraid of these so-called unpractical women; women have something in common with the true artist, just as young people in general have – something that is a good substitute for worldly understanding. Look at our student societies in Norway! Matters are decided there which are ten times more complicated than ours; yet do not they manage well, although youth, untried, unpractised and unpractical youth, there enjoys an overwhelming majority? And why? Because youth has this instinctive genius which unconsciously hits upon the right answer. And it is precisely this instinct which women share with youth, and with the true artist. And that is why I want us to allow women to vote at our annual general meeting. I fear women, youth and inexperience as little as I fear the true artist. What I do fear is the worldly wisdom of the old; what I fear is men with little ambitions and little thoughts, little scruples and little fears, those men who direct all their thoughts and actions towards achieving certain little advantages for their own little and subservient selves. Should the affairs of this club fall into such hands, I should greatly fear for its survival, at any rate as a society of artists. And that is why I wish to have ladies included at our annual general meeting, so that they, together with the young, may see to it that power is placed into true, and truly artistic, hands.

The first of Ibsen's motions, concerning the librarianship, was accepted; but the second failed by a single vote to get the necessary two-thirds majority. Ibsen was furious.[1] He left the club immediately and sat alone in a café, refusing to speak to anyone who had voted against him. Some days later, however, to the general amazement, he attended a gala evening at the club, and Gunnar Heiberg, who was present, has left a picturesque account of what happened:

No one would have guessed it – but Ibsen came. He looked magnificent, in full panoply, with medals to boot. He ran his hand ceaselessly through his rich, grizzled hair, greeting no one in particular, but everyone in general. There was a deep peace in his face, but his eyes were watchful, so watchful. He sat alone. We all thought he had forgiven his fellow mortals, and some even supposed him penitent. This helped the atmosphere to be unusually gay and euphoric. Then, suddenly, he rose and stepped forward to a big table, so that he was facing the whole ballroom with its dancing couples.

'Ladies and gentlemen!' It was a tense and dramatic moment. What was going to happen? Was he about to admit the error of his ways? Surely he was not going to propose a toast? ... He stroked his hair calmly. Then he began, softly, but with a terrifying earnestness. He had recently wished to do the club a service, he might almost say a great favour, by bringing its members abreast with contemporary ideas. No one could escape these mighty developments. Not even here – in this community – in this duckpond! He did not actually use the word duckpond,

1. Feelings evidently ran high on both sides, for J. P. Jacobsen, who supported Ibsen's motion (as did the Swedish painter Ernst Josephson), relates that a captain of marines all but challenged Ibsen to a duel on the matter.

but the contempt around his mouth proclaimed it loudly. And how had his offer been received? As a criminal attempt! Rejected by a paltry couple of votes. And how had the women reacted – the women for whom his gift had been intended? They had intrigued and agitated against him. They had thrown his gift into the mud. What kind of women are these? They are worse – worse than the dregs, worse than scum –

Now he was no longer speaking calmly, no longer thoughtfully stroking his hair. He shook his head with its grey mane. He folded his arms across his breast. His eyes shone. His voice shook, his mouth trembled, and he thrust out his underlip. He resembled a lion, nay, more – he resembled that future enemy of the people, Dr Stockmann. He repeated and repeated: what kind of women are these, what kind of ladies, what kind of a sex, ignorant, in the truest sense ill-bred, immoral, dregs, contemptible –

Thump! A lady, Countess B., fell to the floor. She, like the rest of us, flinched from the unspeakable. So she took time by the forelock and swooned. She was carried out. Ibsen continued. Perhaps slightly more calmly. But eloquently and lucidly, never searching for a word. He intoxicated himself with his rhetoric against the ignorant, contemptible, and rigid resistance that mankind, and especially women, was attempting to offer to these new ideas, whose purpose was to make people bigger, richer, and better. He looked remote, ecstatic. As his voice thundered it was as though he were clarifying his own secret thoughts, as his tongue chastised it was as though his spirit were scouring the darkness in search of his immediate spiritual goal, his play – as though he were personally living out his theories, incarnating his characters. And when he was done, he went out into the hall, took his overcoat, and walked home. Calm and silent.

In February Hegel sent him the good news that fresh editions of both *The Pretenders* and *Poems* were in preparation; the fifth of the former and the third of the latter. Spring arrived. 'The almond trees have already blossomed,' he wrote to Marcus Grønvold on 9 March. 'The cherry trees are in full bloom, and all the fields are covered in fresh green grass and violets.' Yet something was missing in Rome. He no longer found the same excitement there which had so stimulated him fifteen years earlier. 'I have often thought of sending Sigurd back [to Munich] to continue his studies alone,' he wrote in the same letter. 'But in various respects it is desirable that I should get back into German literary life. Down here one is in most respects too much outside the movements of the times.' Was it, he may have wondered, that he was no longer as young as he had been? Edvard Brandes, meeting him this spring, was surprised by the venerability of his appearance. 'I spoke a few words with Henrik Ibsen in the street,' he wrote to his brother Georg on 1 May. 'How old he is! I'd imagined him different, alert.'

Old he may have looked; but the following day, he began the first draft of his new play and, as usual, once he had started the work went swiftly. He finished the first act in three weeks. The second act took him six weeks, but was interrupted by a holiday move. 'We had at first thought to go to one of the mountain villages around Rome,' he told Hegel on 19 June, 'but the sanitary conditions there leave much to be desired [he had grown fastidious since the old days at Genzano and Ariccia] and so we have decided to retire to Amalfi, on the coast south of Naples, where there are facilities for sea-bathing.'

He left for Amalfi on 5 July, armed with an inscribed copy of Edmund Gosse's *Studies in the Literature of Northern Europe*, published that February, and containing an essay on Ibsen (a revised reprint of Gosse's article in the *Fortnightly* in 1873, plus his reviews of *The Pretenders* and *Emperor and Galilean* and an account of *The League of Youth*). 'English causes me some difficulty,' he had written to Gosse the previous day. 'But when we leave tomorrow . . . your book will be about the only one I shall take with me.' At Amalfi they had 'two small rooms with three plain iron bedsteads' in the Albergo della Luna, an old monastery converted into a hotel, situated (still) on a cliff overlooking a sheer drop into the sea. There he was well cossetted by the proprietress, Marietta Barbaro; he had an ante-room where he could write, and the desk at which one of the most influential of all plays came to be written may still be seen there. When not working he bathed in the sea and took long walks in the hills.

Shortly before he finished Act Two, he received a letter from Bjørnson, the first for nine years, seeking to enlist his support in a campaign to remove the mark of union with Sweden from the Norwegian flag. A more unfortunate subject for the reopening of correspondence between the two men could hardly have been chosen. The business of the flag lay very close to Bjørnson's heart, and was exactly the kind of concern that Ibsen regarded as chauvinistic and irrelevant. 'I have not much sympathy for symbols,' he replied on 12 July, a remark that many an Ibsen critic might ponder. 'Let the mark of union remain, but take the mark of monkishness from people's minds; take away the mark of prejudice and narrow-mindedness and short-sightedness and subservience and unthinking trust in authority, so that every individual can sail under his own flag ... I don't think it is our job to make ourselves responsible for the liberty and independence of the state, but rather to awake as many individuals as possible to liberty and independence.'

Ibsen's dismissal as trivial of this question of the 'pure flag' deeply offended Bjørnson, to whom it was a matter of almost religious significance, and the gap between the two men, which had seemed about to close, now became so wide as to be all but unbridgeable. Georg Brandes tells how he found himself next to Karoline Bjørnson at a dinner at Hegel's around this time and asked her if she could not use her friendship with Suzannah to bring her husband and Ibsen together. The next day Bjørnson came to Brandes in a great rage and 'rode his hobby-horse, his contempt for decorations; Ibsen had his chest covered with orders, and a whole dog-collar around his neck. Bjørnson thought it disgusting; rather than offer him his hand he would plunge it into a toadstool.'[2]

2. In fairness to Bjørnson, however, one must remember that the

Having got the matter of the Norwegian flag off his chest, Ibsen returned to the more important business of finishing his play. He started Act Three on 18 July and completed it in less than three weeks, on 3 August. 'I cannot recall any work of mine', he informed Hegel on 15 September, enclosing the fair copy, 'that has given me more satisfaction in the solving of specific problems.' And indeed, the technical advance on *The Pillars of Society* is enormous; no one could complain of *A Doll's House* that it was let down by the final act.

He left Amalfi at the end of September, with the plan for a new play already in his head, and stayed a week in Sorrento, at the Hotel Tramontano. Another guest at the hotel was Ernest Renan, the great French orientalist whom Ibsen had met briefly in 1856, when Renan had visited Bergen as a member of Prince Napoleon's suite. Renan was now working on the final stages of his *Origins of Christianity*, and in view of what Ibsen had just written to Bjørnson about the Church's perversion of Christ's teaching they might have found much common ground; but Ibsen's ignorance of French and shyness of strangers inhibited him from introducing himself (though since Renan was equally shy, conversation might anyway have been difficult). On leaving Sorrento, Ibsen spent a week in Rome, and by 14 October was back in Munich, where he moved with his Italian paintings

---

years 1875–85 were a peculiarly frustrating time for him, especially coming as they did just after the success of *A Bankrupt*. Of the plays that he wrote during this decade only one, *Leonarda*, was immediately accepted for production in Christiania. *The New System* had to wait eight years, *A Glove* three, while *The King*, *Beyond Mortal Power, I* (his finest play) and *The Editor* never got staged until the National Theatre opened its doors there with his son as director in 1899. His plays were similarly rejected in Copenhagen, including even *Leonarda*. He was attacked continuously by the press in Norway, Denmark and Sweden, suffered from a deep sense of persecution, and around 1880 was in such financial straits that he even tried to sell his beloved home at Aulestad. The success of *The Pillars of Society* and *A Doll's House* must have been galling to him, especially that of the latter, overshadowing as it did *The New System* published only six weeks earlier.

into a new and larger apartment in an elegant house at Amalienstrasse 50.

That autumn Magdalene Thoresen visited them; and
Bjørnson, too, came to Munich. He stayed a stone's throw
from the Ibsens, at the Hotel Bambergerhof, and John Paulsen, also back from Rome, tells how Ibsen and Suzannah sat
hoping that he would visit them, but in vain. Sigurd, who
was Bjørnson's godson and had not set eyes on him since
childhood, went along to the Café Probst to see what the
great man looked like. When he returned, and Paulsen
asked him how Bjørnson looked, Sigurd replied, 'An Emperor! An Emperor!' Ibsen's friend Paul Heyse gave a dinner
for Bjørnson during his visit, but (according to Georg
Brandes) disliked the 'missionary and world-improver' in
him.

In November an old painter named Knud Både died in
Munich, and Ibsen attended the funeral. Paulsen, who was
present, noted: 'I shall never forget the manner in which he
approached the open grave and cast a handful of earth on
the coffin. He did it with a solemnity and deep intensity
which moved us all and brought tears to my eyes ... Ibsen
must have been a deeply religious person; no one who saw
him at this moment could doubt that.' His demeanour put
Paulsen in mind of Brand. Living painters seemed to concern Ibsen less; when Paulsen took him to the studio of one
Nils Hansteen, Ibsen showed less interest in the paintings
than in the model of a ship which hung from the ceiling.
On the way home he told Paulsen that if he ever
returned permanently to Norway he would live in a fjord
town smelling of pitch and seaweed where he would be able
to see many ships and shipyards, 'especially the latter'.

On 4 December 1879 *A Doll's House* was published in Copenhagen, in an edition of 8,000 copies, the largest first printing yet of any of Ibsen's works. Its success was immediate
and sensational. Despite its size, the first edition sold out
within a month; a second edition of 3,000 copies appeared on
4 January, and a third of 2,500 copies on 8 March. Such sales

(proportionately equivalent to something around 150,000 in the United Kingdom today) were without precedent for a play in Scandinavia; and certainly no play, in Norway or anywhere else, had had quite such an effect. 'A Doll's House', recalled Halvdan Koht, who was a child when it appeared, 'exploded like a bomb into contemporary life. *The Pillars of Society* ... though it attacked reigning social conventions, still retained the traditional theatrical happy ending, so that it bit less sharply. But *A Doll's House* knew no mercy; ending not in reconciliation, but in exorable calamity, it pronounced a death sentence on accepted social ethics.'

Several times during that famous last act Ibsen seems about to settle for a happy ending – when Krogstad promises Mrs Linde to take back his letter, when he returns Helmer's I.O.U., and when, in the closing moments of the play, Helmer remembers and echoes Nora's words: 'The miracle of miracles—?' But the terrible offstage slamming of that front door which brings down the curtain resounded through more apartments than Torvald Helmer's. No play had ever before contributed so momentously to the social debate, or been so widely and furiously discussed among people who were not normally interested in theatrical or even artistic matters. Even Strindberg, who disapproved of it as being calculated to encourage just the kind of woman he dreaded most (and was infallibly drawn to), and attacked it in his volume of stories, *Marriage* (1884), admitted in his preface that, 'thanks to *A Doll's House*, 'marriage was revealed as being a far from divine institution, people stopped regarding it as an automatic provider of absolute bliss, and divorce between incompatible parties came at last to be accepted as conceivably justifiable'. What other play has achieved as much?

So explosive was the message of *A Doll's House* – that a marriage was not sacrosanct, that a man's authority in his home should not go unchallenged, and that the prime duty of anyone was to find out who he or she really was and to become that person – that the technical originality of the play is often forgotten. It achieved the most powerful and moving effect by the highly untraditional methods of extreme simplicity and economy of language – a kind of literary Cubism. Erik Bøgh, perceptive as usual, spotted this when *A Doll's House* received its first performance, at the Royal Theatre in Copenhagen on 21 December.[3] 'It is long', he wrote in *Folkets Avis*, 'since any new play was awaited with such excitement, and even longer since a new play brought so much that is original to the stage, but it is beyond memory since a play so simple in its action and so everyday in its dress made such an impression of artistic mastery ... Not a single declamatory phrase, no high dramatics, no drop of blood, not even a tear; never for a moment was the dagger of tragedy raised ... Every needless line is cut, every exchange carries the action a step forward, there is not a superfluous effect in the whole play ... the mere fact that the author succeeded with the help only of these five characters in keeping our interest sustained throughout a whole evening is sufficient proof of Ibsen's technical mastery.' *The Pillars of Society* had used nineteen characters. And there are other ways in which *A Doll's House* marks a considerable technical advance over *The Pillars of Society*. The characters do not (as occasionally happens in the earlier play) tell each other what the listener already knows for the benefit of the audience; points once made are not drummed home in the manner beloved by politicians; the final curtain is not tediously delayed after the climax has been reached (an elementary fault which every playwright learns reluctantly to avoid, the more reluctantly if he has ever written a novel, in which such rapid wind-ups seem melodramatic). Only in the sub-plot of Krogstad does a trace of the old melodramatic machinery remain.

It is a tragedy of books carrying a particular message for

3. Despite the fact that the Royal Theatre's censor, Christian Molbech, had only grudgingly recommended it, finding the break-up of the Helmers' marriage 'not merely painful and unsatisfying but psychologically somewhat inexplicable'.

their times that they tend to be remembered by posterity for the wrong reasons. *A Doll's House* and its successor, *Ghosts*, are particular examples; critics still occasionally write about *A Doll's House* as though it were a play about the hoary problem of women's rights – an attitude largely conditioned by the habit, among British and American critics, of consulting Bernard Shaw's *Quintessence of Ibsenism*, that brilliantly misleading book which should have been called *The Quintessence of Shavianism*, before writing about any Ibsen play. *A Doll's House* is no more about women's rights than Shakespeare's *Richard II* is about the divine right of kings, or *Ghosts* about syphilis, or *An Enemy of the People* about public hygiene. Its theme is the need of every individual to find out the kind of person he or she really is and to strive to become that person. Ibsen knew what Freud and Jung were later to assert, that liberation can only come from within; which was why he had expressed to Georg Brandes his lack of interest in 'special revolutions, revolutions in externals', and had declared that 'what is really wanted is a revolution of the spirit of man'. The effect of *A Doll's House* in the theatre today is less explosive than when it was written, but scarcely less hypnotic, because there is hardly a married woman in the audience who does not sometimes want (or has not at some time wanted) to leave her husband. The unspoken thoughts in the cars and taxis returning from a modern performance of the play cannot vary much from those in the returning carriages of a century ago.

One woman to whom *A Doll's House* did not bring joy was Laura Kieler. Her tragedy was known to enough people in Copenhagen for them immediately to realize that Ibsen had based Nora's story very closely upon hers (except for the ending), especially as she had been proud to advertise her friendship with him; and the link soon became common knowledge. It must have made the situation between her and Kieler, which was already bad enough, even less tolerable; and she was also much hurt by the reference in Act Three to the 'recklessness and instability' of Nora's father.

Yet it is hard to blame Ibsen. The play is an admiring vindication of her conduct, and he may well have supposed that
she would be happy to be recognized as the original of so
sympathetic and courageous a character, as later Julius
Hoffory was proudly (and with much less reason to be proud)
to advertise that he was the original of Ejlert Løvborg in
Hedda Gabler. It is ironical that the play which established
Ibsen as the champion of women should have been so deeply
resented by the woman who had inspired it.

A Doll's House was to make Ibsen internationally famous.
But this (contrary to popular supposition) did not happen at
once, or even quickly. It was to be two years before the play
was performed outside Scandinavia and Germany, and ten
years before a recognizably faithful version was seen in England or America, although perverted adaptations were to
make brief and unsuccessful appearances.[4] France, even
further behind the times, did not see the play until 1894. By
the time it took its place in the general European repertoire,
Ibsen was over sixty and had moved on to a very different
kind of writing.

A Doll's House in book form made 1879 a somewhat
better year for Ibsen financially, though considering the
impact of the play his earnings remained unremarkable:
£778.

1880 opened with what must by now, for Ibsen, have been
the familiar mixture of public acclaim and stolen rights. On
8 January the Royal Theatre in Stockholm presented *A
Doll's House*, and Christiania and Bergen followed suit
within the month. In all three cities the play was a triumph,
(though Edvard Brandes, on a visit to the Christiania production, was shocked to hear how the two principals, Johanne
Juell and Arnoldus Reimers, 'both rephrased in the most
shameless manner practically every line'). The Germans,
however, were, as usual, treating him badly. Wilhelm

4. It is significant that even Bernard Shaw does not mention Ibsen in
his letters before 1889.

Lange's authorized translation was being freely sold in Copenhagen at a lower price than the original – a serious matter in a city where educated people read and spoke German as readily as educated Russians spoke French. 'I receive no payment from the publisher,' Ibsen complained to Hegel on 22 January. 'The translator has to give me such copies as I need for the German theatres, and that is all.' Hegel estimated the Danish sales of this German version to be as high as 2,000 copies. However, he was able to comfort Ibsen with two good pieces of news, that a fourth edition of *The League of Youth* and a fifth of *Emperor and Galilean* were in preparation, and that 'the last five performances of *A Doll's House* [at the Royal Theatre, Copenhagen] have brought you an honorarium of 2,270·12 [crowns] [£126] i.e. 3,904·99 [£217] in all. The next five performances will bring you a third of the takings, excluding subscription seats: so far the play has been sold out for every performance.'

But far worse than the undercutting of his book sales was what was about to happen to *A Doll's House* on the German stage. A well-known actress of the day, Hedwig Niemann-Raabe, had announced her intention to present the play with herself in the leading role, but she refused to act the final scene as written, on the grounds that '*I* would never leave *my* children!' In the absence of copyright protection, Ibsen's hands were completely tied; and he decided that, as the lesser of two evils, a 'happy' ending written by himself would be preferable to one by another hand which could be published and performed at other German theatres. 'To forestall any such possibility,' he explained in an open letter (17 February 1880) to the Danish newspaper *Nationaltidende*, 'I sent my translator and agent for use in an emergency a drafted emendation in which Nora does not leave the house but is forced by Helmer to the doorway of the children's bedroom; here a few lines are exchanged, Nora sinks down by the door and the curtain falls. This emendation I have myself described to my translator as a "barbaric outrage" on the play ... But if any such outrage is threatened, I prefer, on the basis of previous experience, to commit it myself rather than submit my work to the treatment and "adaptation" of less tender and competent hands.'

Frau Niemann-Raabe accepted this distorted version and acted it in February at Flensburg and later in Hamburg, Dresden, Hanover and Berlin. In the last-named city there was a public protest at the perversion (though when, subsequently, the original ending was used, there were further protests on the ground that the play had obviously been shorn of its fourth act!). The 'happy ending' was never a success, and eventually Frau Niemann-Raabe reverted to the original text. Meanwhile, on 3 March, an unbowdlerized production took place at the Munich Residenztheater, with Ibsen himself in the audience. John Paulsen accompanied him, and recorded his reactions. Ibsen had attended several rehearsals; the play was, to Paulsen's mind, well acted, and went down excellently with the public. After the première, Ibsen thanked everyone who had taken part in the production warmly. But afterwards, at home, he was full of criticisms, not merely of the interpretation of the play and the various roles, but of details such as that Nora had the wrong-sized hands (whether too big or too small Paulsen could not remember), and that the colour of the wallpaper in the Helmers' apartment was wrong and conveyed a false atmosphere. Paulsen wondered that Ibsen had not mentioned at any rate this point during rehearsals; but the actors later told Paulsen that Ibsen had 'neither praised nor blamed, but just remained silent', and that when they asked him if they had fulfilled his intentions, he merely complimented them, which frustrated rather than pleased them 'since they knew they were far from perfect'. Even now that he was famous, and anything he said would have been obeyed, Ibsen was as reluctant to offer advice as in the old days in Norway. Paulsen recalled that the Norwegian actress Lucie Wolf told him that, when a director in Christiania, Ibsen had 'always seemed happy with what we had done, though this was often moderate'.

A Doll's House had a mixed reception in the German theatres, and was in general coolly received by the German critics. Karl Frenzel reiterated in *Deutsche Rundschau* that Ibsen was poor at dramatic construction, and added that he seemed to love the repulsive; and Paul Lindau (later to become an admirer and friend of Ibsen) declared in *Die Gegenwart* that the ending as originally written was both illogical and immoral. Georg Brandes sadly commented that Ibsen would never be understood in Germany. But if he was not understood, he was immensely discussed. 'Down here,' he wrote to Hegel on 14 April, '*A Doll's House* has excited as much controversy as at home. People have taken sides passionately either for or against the play, and it has hardly ever happened before in Munich that any play has aroused such lively discussion.'

One extraordinary version of *A Doll's House* appeared this year in the form of an English translation by a Danish schoolteacher named T. Weber, published in Copenhagen, surely one of the most sustained specimens of unconscious humour in all literature. The final scene contains the following examples:

NORA. Don't utter such stupid shuffles ... Doff the shawl ... From this moment it depends no longer on felicity; it depends only on saving the rests, remnants, and the appearance.

HELMER. You are first of all a wife and mother.
NORA ... I believe that I am first of all a man, I as well as you – or at all events, that I am to try to become a man.

NORA. As I am now, I am no wife for you.
HELMER. I have power to grow another.

HELMER. Change yourself in such a manner that –
NORA. – that cohabitation between you and me might become a matrimony. Good-bye.

Of this last line, Harley Granville Barker wrote that he was 'not indisposed to offer a prize at the Royal Academy of Dramatic Art to the student who could manage to speak [it] without making the audience laugh'.

During the early months of 1880, Ludwig Passarge asked leave to prepare the first German (or, indeed, foreign) translation of *Peer Gynt*. Ibsen, as we have seen, was dubious about the possibility of the play succeeding with any but a Scandinavian public, but granted permission. In Finland, meanwhile, a young scholar named Valfred Vasenius published the second book to be devoted entirely to a study of Ibsen's work, a not unperceptive doctoral thesis covering the plays up to and including *The Pretenders*. In Sweden, the Gothenburg Theatre acquired the rights to *A Doll's House* (for an outright payment of £25), and in Stockholm Ludvig Josephson, now doing his best on a shoestring at the little Nya Teatern, asked permission to present not merely new productions of *The Vikings at Helgeland* and *The Pretenders*, but also the first Swedish production of *Love's Comedy*, and the first production anywhere of *Catiline*. Ibsen granted him the rights in return for outright payments of £5 (!) for each of the first two plays and £20 for the other two.

Knowing that he would not start on a new play before the following year, and anxious to have a new work in the bookstores by Christmas, Ibsen suggested to Hegel on 31 May that he might prepare 'a small volume of 10–12 signatures' [160–192 pages] consisting of prefaces to his various plays on the lines of the one he had written for *Catiline*. 'For *Lady Inger* and *The Vikings* I could describe my time in Bergen; for *The Pretenders* and *Love's Comedy*, the years that followed in Christiania; my life in Rome while I was writing *Brand* and *Peer Gynt*, etc., etc. ... I plan to spend the summer doing this, for I don't intend to write another play this year and have nothing else with which to occupy my time.' Surprisingly, Hegel dissuaded him from this project, on the grounds that 'your works stand on their own as clear and characteristic entities, the significance of which does not need to be tied to such slight footnotes which would unconsciously work themselves into the consciousness of their readers and introduce a new and distracting element ... It would be quite another matter, I feel, if you ever wanted to write an *aus meinem Leben*, in which these fragments would then appear in context and thereby cease to be fragments. But I think you would be wise to postpone writing such a work just yet ...' Worse, when, eighteen months later, Ibsen suggested writing just such an autobiography, Hegel again dissuaded him. Ibsen meekly accepted his advice, and the details which he could have given us about the gestation and composition of his plays remained unwritten.

Ludvig Josephson visited Ibsen in Munich that summer, on the way home from seeing the passion play at Oberammergau, and enjoyed the interesting experience of accompanying him on a visit to his tailor, where Ibsen ordered a black velvet coat and amazed Josephson by the minuteness of his instructions to the man. Ibsen, he noted, now usually wore a white cravat and white gloves with his invariable black coat, and a tall, shiny felt hat with a very broad brim, which with his 'long dark hair, not yet grizzled or white' gave him rather the appearance of a sectarian minister.

As a companion, Josephson had taken to Oberammergau a young Swedish actor-director named August Lindberg, who had just acted a remarkable Hamlet for him at Nya Teatern and who was to become one of the foremost interpreters of Ibsen's plays, both as actor and as director. He advised Lindberg, who was returning later than he, to visit Ibsen, warning him that Ibsen was 'an odd person, difficult to make conversation with'. 'Don't talk to him about the theatre,' advised Josephson, 'nor about plays, his or anyone else's.' 'As I had just come from Oberammergau,' records Lindberg, 'I began to talk of Jesus, Mary and all the apostles in the moving drama I had seen amid the mountains, but it was heavy going, and in the end I sat silent on a rock, and when I left retained only the memory of a pair of spectacles.'

In three years' time Ibsen was to have cause to be profoundly grateful to Lindberg.

In the beginning of August, Suzannah and Sigurd went to Norway, partly so that Sigurd could investigate the chances of his being able to study law at Christiania without going through the preliminary examinations; and Ibsen, shortly before they left, addressed a letter to King Oscar pleading, unsuccessfully as it turned out, that his son should be granted exemption. While awaiting the royal reply, he made preparations to leave with John Paulsen for a holiday in Berchtesgaden.

The preparations for this excursion, which would have occupied most people for perhaps a couple of hours, caused Ibsen extraordinary distraction. A week before they were due to depart Paulsen chanced to visit him at Amalienstrasse and found him walking up and down in great agitation with an open trunk on the floor. 'When Ibsen was going away,' Paulsen explains, 'he began to pack, not a day or two, but a whole week ahead, and, for fear of arriving late, would come to the station at least an hour before the train was due to leave.' When the day came, 'although I reached the station in good time, Ibsen was of course waiting, dressed in a new, elegant travelling suit and a big broad-brimmed felt hat which rendered him half unrecognizable'. They took the train as far as Salzburg. There, while they awaited the diligence which was to convey them to Berchtesgaden, Ibsen showed Paulsen round the town, 'the white houses with their flat roofs and green awnings, the marble buildings, the numerous churches, fountains and palaces, and the archbishop's ancient palace,' though not, which seems strange even when one remembers Ibsen's indifference to music, Mozart's house. When they reached Berchtesgaden, they had to share a bedroom for the first night at the Salzburger Hof; but, to Paulsen's surprise and relief, Ibsen 'slept as silently as a child'.

Living *à deux* with Ibsen was less difficult than Paulsen had feared. He took an inordinate time to dress in the morning, often an hour or more – 'and when he was ready, there was nothing particularly special about his appearance; he was attired like everyone else'. He was inclined to be testy during the morning, and did not much like being spoken to before noon. But 'later in the day he would begin to talk a little; after lunch he became amenable and friendly, and in the evening warm and lovable'. He bought a coloured feather and stuck it in his hat, which caused the local children to stare after him. He was brooding on his next play, and once in bad weather, when Paulsen tentatively asked him about it, he replied, 'It is a family story as sad and grey as this rainy day.'

Paulsen noted with interest the respect which Ibsen showed towards priests, despite the contempt with which he portrayed them in his plays. Whenever a priest passed them on their walks Ibsen would bow respectfully. At the hotel, he got annoyed because another guest kept taking the copy of *Berliner Tageblatt* which was reserved for him; but when he learned that the offender was a priest, Ibsen offered him the newspaper next morning with a deep bow. In contrast to this, he showed little respect for actors. A young German-American actor who was staying at the hotel and was an admirer of Ibsen tried to strike up an acquaintance, but Ibsen ostentatiously avoided him. He enjoyed, however, talking to artisans about their work. One day on their walk he saw a cobbler working outside his house and engaged him in a lengthy conversation. 'He took the boot, examined the leather and stitching carefully, and asked in surprise, "Does one do that now? In my day one did so-and-so." ' When they left, the cobbler bade farewell to Ibsen 'with the respect of a fellow craftsman'.

He ate little, but extremely slowly, chewing each mouthful almost as many times as Gladstone. They spoke of literature. Paulsen, while in Paris, had met Turgenev and his platonic mistress, Pauline Garcia-Viardot, and declared his amazement that any woman could have so 'demonic an influence' on a man that he could become her slave. This interested Ibsen. 'A man is easy to study', he said, 'but one never fully understands a woman. They are a sea which none can fathom.' He expressed to Paulsen (as he later did to William Archer) his admiration for Turgenev and the Russian writers in general; we know from other sources that these included Dostoyevsky and Tolstoy, but his opinion on Gogol (whom one would expect him especially to have enjoyed), Pushkin and Ostrovsky is not on record. Of French literature, on the other hand, Paulsen found that Ibsen was largely ignorant. He had read nothing of George Sand, despite Suzannah's admiration of her (she read *Consuelo* almost annually) and the only thing he knew about Madame de Staël was her remark '*Tout comprendre est tout pardonner*', on which he commented that anyone who had written that must be 'an unusual woman'. He praised Paul Heyse's work, especially the elegy for his dead child and his stories, *The Last Centaur, Salamander* and *The Widow of Pisa*, and exhorted Paulsen to read Kleist's conte, *Michael Kohlhaas*, 'which he averred to be a true masterpiece'. But he spoke contemptuously of Heine as a poet for adolescents. Goethe and Schiller he admired as poets but not as dramatists, and when anyone spoke, as Germans often did, of Goethe's *grosse, reine Liebe* (great pure love), Ibsen would laconically comment, 'That d—d old goat!' As regards Italian authors, Paulsen 'gained the impression that he had in his time studied Dante in translation', but 'the modern Italian writers, such as Verga, Edmondo De Amicis, Fogazzaro and Gabriele D'Annunzio were merely names that Ibsen had seen in the newspapers'. English authors he does not seem to have been reading at all. One would have expected Suzannah to have admired George Eliot (who was to die this year) and Thomas Hardy, who at forty had already published several of his finest novels, including *Far from the Madding Crowd* and *The Return of the Native*; but there is no record of Ibsen ever mentioning either writer.

On the subject of other Scandinavian authors, Ibsen expressed little sympathy for Henrik Wergeland, whose early influence he had long since rejected, but considerable admiration for his old professor J. S. Welhaven, both as a poet and as a man. He told how once, after a particularly brilliant lecture by Welhaven in Christiania, he had been surprised, when standing outside the lecture hall, to hear the great man complain to his wife as he emerged that his trouser buttons were loose and he had spent the whole hour wondering if they would fall off. He also related with approval a story of how Welhaven (who, like Ibsen, could be rude to people who bored him) once attended a party at which the hostess was a very fat lady with an enormous double chin and, exhausted by her conversation, put his finger to the crease between her chins and said, 'Couldn't you manage one little smile?' Of Alexander Kielland, whose proletarian novels Ibsen regarded as meretricious, he remarked, 'I have the impression that after a good dinner he suddenly remembers, over his coffee and Havana cigar, that there are poor people in the world, takes out a sheet of vellum and writes with a golden pen of their needs, thus, by the law of opposites, increasing his gourmet's pleasure in the moment.' He praised Carl Snoilsky's poetry, and also mentioned approvingly Strindberg's novel about Bohemian life in Stockholm, *The Red Room*, which had appeared the previous year (and which contains a scene in which the young hero is struck dumb with admiration on meeting a publisher who has been permitted to address Ibsen as 'Du'). This was the book which established Strindberg's reputation and probably provided Ibsen with his first introduction to an author whose work, despite Strindberg's oft-declared hostility to him (mainly because of his championship of women), he was to read with continued interest and respect.

On 17 August, Ibsen's old mentor Ole Bull, who had given him his first job in the theatre, died at the age of seventy. He had lived a full life to the last (at the age of fifty-eight he had married an American girl of nineteen, and that was by ·no means the last of his conquests). Marcus Grønvold relates how, on hearing that Bull, on his death-bed with a sprig of heather in his hand, had thanked God for everything, Ibsen remarked with a quiet smile: 'Ah, he thought he'd get away with it all!'

Ibsen often spoke to Paulsen of Sigurd and, when Paulsen remarked on the young man's talent for languages, declared, 'He has inherited that from me.' 'But', ventured Paulsen, 'you are poor at languages, Herr Ibsen, you have said so yourself.' 'Yes,' replied Ibsen, 'but I flatter myself that I know *our* language minutely – and this feeling which I have toiled to perfect I have passed on to my son.' Ibsen related with relish how Sigurd, as a small boy, on being spanked and ordered from the room, had turned on his father and shrieked: 'Poet! Poet! All you know is how to tell lies and rubbish!' 'Ibsen rubbed his hands as he told this story. It evidently amused him that the title which in the eyes of Europe was a term of honour was used by his small son as a term of abuse.'

One day a letter arrived at Berchtesgaden from Sigurd telling his father that there seemed little chance of his being excused the preliminary examinations before being admitted to read law at Christiania University, and that he would probably be required to study there for eighteen months first. Paulsen was with Ibsen when he received this letter. 'He sat silent, angry and tight-lipped . . . I scarcely dared to look at him. He refused the food that was brought to him and limited himself, with a martyr's expression, to eating a little bread and salt. I can still hear the rasping sound of the salt crystals as he crushed them with his knife . . . After a long and indescribably oppressive silence, he said: "But I shall raise a memorial to that black band of theologians who rule in Norway. They shall remember how they have treated me." ' A foolish priest was to be one of the central characters of the play he was meditating, and was to dominate it to the point of imbalance.

This decision of the Ecclesiastical Department, which controlled matters of education in Norway, affected Ibsen's own future as well as that of his son. Bergliot Ibsen says that had

Sigurd been accepted at Christiania University Ibsen would have settled there himself so as to be near Sigurd. As things were, he was to spend a further eleven years in exile.

Paulsen recalled of this summer:

> His mood could change like an April day. He could be uncommonly gentle and irrigate one with his calm smile, his good humour and his merry Peer Gynt-like fantasies, but he could also be dark and angry ... There were times when the satirist in him awoke and his sharp tongue spared nothing ... And he had other, huger moments when, filled with a holy indignation at the meanness and unjustness of humanity, he could thunder like Brand or an Old Testament prophet. By nature he was talkative, but if an unexpected reverse met him which awoke bitter memories of the old days, his mouth shut tight in bitterness as though padlocked, and there emanated from him an icy coldness which silenced everything about him. And once I caught a glimpse of the bird of prey in him, as later portrayed in Solness and Rubek, the falcon questing for a victim, some poor fellow-human whom he could dissect and then throw away.

Sometimes he would indulge a macabre humour. When, for instance, he related the story of a German painter who had tried repeatedly to commit suicide in different ways and had succeeded only at the fourth attempt,

> Ibsen told these horrible details with a merry laughter, as though the story were funny rather than tragic ... At such moments there emerged a demonic side to Ibsen's character which he normally concealed.

Rather than waste a year and a half on formal and useless studies, Sigurd suggested to his father that he should abandon all thought of trying for a legal degree in Norway and should instead continue his education in Italy. Ibsen telegraphed his approval and followed his telegram with a letter. 'Since I received the Ecclesiastical Department's reply,' he wrote on 18 September, 'I have naturally given much thought to the matter, and have come to the conclusion that you are probably best served by the turn which, thanks to our imbecile and superannuated regulations, events have taken. What would it have profited you to have studied law in Norway? It was not your intention to become a civil servant up there. The only positions which attract you are still within your reach: you can become a professor or enter the diplomatic service without taking any civil service examination; for we have foreign professors at the university ... But don't think further ahead than studying abroad; you should wait before deciding whether it would be advantageous to become an Italian citizen.'

Ibsen's old fellow-student from Christiania, Jonas Lie, by now a distinguished novelist, was spending the summer in Berchtesgaden with his wife Thomasine (who was also his cousin) and their children. Success had come late to Lie, as it had to Ibsen; but during the past decade such novels as *The Visionary*, *The Pilot and His Wife* and *Adam Schrøder* had established him as an imaginative portrayer of human relationships. The Lies were living in a small white house in which Ibsen himself had stayed during his first visit to Berchtesgaden in 1868, and he visited them every Saturday evening, sometimes with Paulsen. Lie's son Erik, then a boy of twelve, recorded his father's memories twenty-eight years later, and added his own in another and equally rewarding book.

Jonas and Thomasine Lie were the kind of warm-hearted, sensitive people with whom Ibsen found it most easy to relax. In their company 'he talked away about everything, told anecdotes, enjoyed himself to the full and never left before three in the morning'. 'I have never seen that closed face which people attribute to Ibsen,' Lie once remarked (and he must have been almost the only acquaintance who never did). 'When we were together in Berchtesgaden I always had the impression, as we sat together of an evening, of two front teeth which appeared more and more often as time went on – two front teeth with a gap between. And the higher his humour rose, the more he laughed and glowed, till at last he sat there like a good prattling midwife.' The observation about the gap between the teeth, surprising at first sight, reminds us that there exists no photograph or portrait of Ibsen with his mouth open. Apart from those Saturday evenings Ibsen and Lie virtually never saw each other, by mutual agreement, since Lie was working on a new novel. But, the latter remembered, 'more than once Ibsen walked past the house where we were living, and it was observed that he often paused before the lighted windows on the ground floor and peered tentatively in at the family as we sat at our evening meal'.

Ibsen's passion, already remarked, for sewing on his own buttons manifested itself during this holiday. Jonas Lie recalled:

> One morning Ibsen suddenly appeared and asked to speak to my wife. She was not to disturb me; it was only a trifling matter, to wit, a button. He had brought needle and thread. 'But may I not sew it on for you?' asked Thomasine. No, he wanted to do it himself. 'But what's the matter, then?' 'I wondered if you could help me to thread the needle. I have tried and tried, but I must confess it is a more difficult art than I had imagined.' Fru Lie of course immediately helped him. A week later she asked him if there was nothing else she could help him with. To thread another needle, perhaps? 'No, thank you,' replied Ibsen. 'Once I had the thread in, I took enough to last me the whole summer.'

The Lies particularly recalled Ibsen on his country walks, 'following the same precise routes along the rustic roads as, later, he was to do down Carl Johan [in Christiania] to the Grand Café'. As soon as a cart appeared Ibsen would move off the road until it had passed and the dust had settled. 'He would then take out the silk handkerchief which he carried in his left breast-pocket, wipe his spectacles, and carefully refold it ... and walk on with his small, tripping steps, elegant and finical, despite the green Tyrolean hat which he had acquired soon after his arrival, and into which he had put a cock's feather which nodded at every step.' Erik Lie also remembered how Ibsen loved to sit among the village children watching Punch and Judy shows, continuously wiping his spectacles as the puppets killed each other; how he rebuked John Paulsen angrily for making jokes about a dowager duchess; how he once remarked that he would ideally like to live on an island guarded by two hungry bloodhounds; and how little Elizabeth Lie, Jonas's elder daughter, on hearing her parents refer admiringly to Ibsen's *Doll's House*, supposed him to be a toymaker and was bitterly disappointed that he never brought any present for her. The youngest daughter, Johanne, recalled that he was 'nice, and very kind to children', and (confirming Paulsen's observation) that he loved to talk with the local cobbler, Jacob Hasenknopf.

Ibsen, as far as we know, did no writing that summer at Berchtesgaden. It was to be the last time he visited the little town; they had recently extended the railway to it, and the seclusion he so prized was gone. At the end of September or the beginning of October he returned to Munich whence, on 25 October, he informed Hegel that 'we are now returning to Rome, where he [Sigurd] will complete his legal studies, and then become naturalized'. Whether he had in fact taken this decision or whether it was still under discussion, we do not know. Ibsen went on to repeat, almost precisely, the words he had used to Paulsen on first hearing the news of the rejection of Sigurd's petition. 'To the black band of theologians who temporarily rule in the Ecclesiastical Department, I shall in due time raise a fitting memorial.'[5]

That October Ludwig Passarge's German translation of *Peer Gynt* appeared. On 2 November the Ibsens left Munich, arriving in Rome (the journey took thirty-one hours) on the 4th. They stayed the first week in a hotel, and on the 11th moved into 'a very handsome and spacious, but somewhat expensive apartment' at 75 Via Capo le Case, close

5. The similarity of the phrasing has led some critics to doubt the truth of Paulsen's reminiscence. But Ibsen often used in his letters (and plays) phrases which he is known previously to have used in conversation.

to where they had lived twelve years earlier. The description occurs in a letter Ibsen wrote to Hegel the next day asking him to send £90, adding, however, that 'luckily accommodation is practically the only thing which can be called dear down here'. He added that he was 'turning over new literary plans, which I hope will have sufficiently matured within the next few months for me to begin on the actual writing'.

Ibsen received evidence that autumn of how his plays could be misinterpreted. A Scandinavian lady appeared in Rome with her lover. Having found her marriage unsatisfactory, she had left her husband and children. The Norwegians in Rome condemned her action as unnatural; and Ibsen, when asked his opinion, said: 'It is not unnatural, but it is unusual.' When the lady sought out Ibsen at a public function, he treated her rather coolly; and when she complained that she had only behaved as his Nora had done, he replied: 'But my Nora went alone.'

The English theatre at last paid brief and belated recognition to Ibsen's existence that winter. On the morning of 15 December 1880 William Archer's revised translation of *The Pillars of Society* was given a single performance at the Gaiety Theatre in the Strand, the first in England, amateur or professional, of any Ibsen play – though Ibsen might have had some difficulty in recognizing it as his, for it was much abridged and adapted, and was entitled *Quicksands*. Charles Archer, in his biography of his brother William, describes how the play at last found its way on to the stage:

Having failed to find a publisher for his translation of *The Pillars of Society*, Archer had set himself, as the only way of bringing Ibsen to the front, to adapt the play for the English stage; for in those days it was unthinkable that a faithful translation, even of a French piece, much more of a play by an unknown Hyperborean dramatist, should ever make its way on to the London boards. By the end of 1878 an 'adaptation', which might better have been described as an abridgement, had been accepted by Mr W. H. Vernon, who was much struck by the part of Consul Bernick. But Mr Vernon had no theatre at his disposal, and negotiations for a London production dragged on for nearly two years. At last, since no better might be, the piece was produced experimentally at a Gaiety Theatre matinée on 15 December 1880 – and fell perfectly flat. The production, as a whole, was inevitably scrambling and ineffective. But the best setting and acting could not have made the play a success with the English critics and audiences of that day. Ibsen's time was not yet come.

The *Athenaeum* praised the play as 'a good and telling story which introduces some novel, if not very powerful, types of character ... extremely fine comedy ... we shall be glad to know more of its author's workmanship'. The *Theatre* described the performance as 'tentatively produced and fairly successful', but felt that 'Bernick's cold-blooded villainy appears somewhat inadequately punished'. The Danish correspondent of a Copenhagen newspaper reported that at the final curtain the audience called loudly for the author, 'a request which was readily met, without any trace of embarrassment or reserve, by Mr Archer, the English translator'. Archer's translation was not published until 1888, and then in a much revised form.

At the end of 1880 Ibsen found that he had, for the first time, earned over a thousand pounds in a single year – £1,196. Several features of this year's accounts are interesting. For once, book sales constituted a minority of his income. Performing rights represented approximately five-sixths of it, and these were almost entirely from a single play, *A Doll's House*. The fees from the Royal Theatre in Copenhagen alone (£487) exceeded his total income for many a previous year, and underline how much he lost by not getting similar royalties from all theatres. The German theatres, be it noted, paid him a total of £28.

But if Ibsen supposed that a period of financial affluence lay ahead of him, he was to be disillusioned. It was to be another ten years before his annual income again reached £1,000. The decade from 1881 to 1890, which was to see the composition of *Ghosts, An Enemy of the People, The Wild*

Duck, Rosmersholm, The Lady from the Sea and *Hedda Gabler*, was to bring him a total income of under £6,500 – less than what playwrights of far inferior stature in larger countries, such as Scribe, W. S. Gilbert and Pinero, would expect to make in a single year.

20

Ghosts
1881-2

IBSEN, as he approached his fifty-fourth birthday, was becoming, if not an international figure, at any rate one of the few Scandinavians whom other countries bothered to consider at all. The January 1881 issue of *Unser Zeit* contained a long essay on him by Eugen Zabel – the first, other than reviews of individual plays, to be devoted to him in a German paper. It was by no means wholly favourable; drawing parallels between Ibsen's philosophy and German pessimism, Zabel thought that both *Brand* and *Peer Gynt* had much in common with Goethe's *Faust,* but declared that Ibsen's imagination, although fertile, was enclosed in a frigid sheath of intellect, and that much of *Peer Gynt* belonged to the realm, not of poetry, but of pathology – an unconsciously penetrating observation.

At the same time, a far shrewder and more balanced assessment of Ibsen's work was placed before the English reading public in the form of two articles by William Archer in the January and February issues of the *St James's Magazine.* Instead of condemning Ibsen, as so many of his critics were doing, for pessimism, discord, and 'lack of idealism', Archer, familiar with the novels of George Eliot and Thomas Hardy, recognized that in these supposed defects lay much of Ibsen's strength. 'His countrymen', wrote Archer, 'admire, fear, and hate him. The lash of the satirist has fallen heavy upon them as a nation ... While admitting his greatness, they maintain that the negativeness of his aims detracts from or almost nullifies it ... [But] Ibsen depicts a real world, not the ideal where satisfaction and reconcili-

ation are possible ... The old theory that all great work
comes from a positive age is rapidly dying away. Ibsen is one
of the great negative voices of a negative age which tries in
vain, by shrieking in falsetto and thundering in the deepest
bass, to convince itself that it is positive.'

This was remarkably mature criticism from someone aged
barely twenty-four; and before the year was out Archer was
to introduce Ibsen's work to a chance acquaintance who was
to become, not merely his most influential apologist, but also
his most distinguished disciple as a dramatist. 'In the winter
of 1881-2', Archer recalled, 'I used to go almost every day to
the British Museum Reading Room in London. I frequently
sat next to a man of about my own age who attracted my
attention, partly by his peculiar colouring – his pallid skin
and bright red hair and beard – partly by the odd combination of authors whom he used to study – for I saw him,
day after day, poring over Karl Marx's *Das Kapital* and an
orchestral score of Wagner's *Tristan und Isolde*. How we
first made acquaintance I have forgotten; but one did not
need to meet him twice to be sure that George Bernard Shaw
was a personality to be noted and studied ... We became fast
friends.'

Not only did Archer introduce Shaw to Ibsen; he also got
Shaw his first critical work, first as a book reviewer, then as
art critic and finally as music critic. The debt of English and
Irish literature to William Archer is inadequately realized;
he was also one of the first people to encourage the young
James Joyce.

In America, too, that February, Ibsen's name was praised,
the first record of its mention in the New World. The writer
was none other than Bjørnson who, having delivered an
oration at Ole Bull's funeral in Bergen, had been invited by
Bull's young widow to visit her in Boston, and had stayed in
the States for seven months. In the course of a long article
entitled 'Norway's Constitutional Struggle' in *Scribner's
Monthly*, Bjørnson declared: 'I do not hesitate to say that
in my opinion Henrik Ibsen possesses the greatest dramatic

power of the age. I am so much the more certain of my judgement from the fact that I do not always like his dramas. It is surprising to me that he is not translated in America. He is one whom his contemporaries should know.' This was an extraordinarily generous tribute from a man whose own star was sliding into eclipse.

Several of Ibsen's old friends and acquaintances were in Rome that winter, including Lorentz Dietrichson, Camilla Collett and Kristofer Janson; and among the newcomers whom he met was a young Swedish poet, Verner von Heidenstam, later to become a Nobel prizewinner, but at this early stage in his career still regarded as a rich dilettante. John Paulsen, who was there too, records that Ibsen used to go every day to the Café Artisti, where the Scandinavians gathered, to see if anyone new had arrived. He began, too, to hold soirées, 'cosmopolitan rather than homely, but very agreeable. One arrived between nine and ten, and an Italian servant offered tea. On the sideboard stood wine, fruit, and cakes, to which one helped oneself during the course of the evening. Ibsen, dressed in a black frock coat without decorations, received the guests with a calm and impressive dignity.'

Paulsen, who was there on a travelling scholarship from the Norwegian government, which he had received largely thanks to Ibsen's recommendation, achieved something of a record on his arrival by becoming, surely, the only man ever suspected of being Suzannah Ibsen's lover. Calling at the Ibsens' apartment, he found them out and asked the Italian maid to tell Suzannah that her *amico* was in Rome and would return in the afternoon. The maid conspiratorially warned Suzannah on her return, knowing that then *il signor commendatore* (a title by which Ibsen was known among the Italians, because he was a Commander of the Medjije Order) might be at home, and adding delightedly: 'How rash of the young man!' The incident became, as long as their friendship with Paulsen lasted, a standing joke in the Ibsen household.

Among the other Scandinavians then in Rome was the Swedish painter Georg Pauli, who was amazed one day to see a figure walking towards him down the street wearing medals – 'not ribbons, but medals'. The two became acquainted, and it was not long before Pauli, like others before him, found himself assisting Ibsen back to his apartment, with the help of the Norwegian painter Christian Meyer Ross. 'We supported the great man on either side', Pauli noted in his diary, 'and he showed his gratitude by incessantly giving us his confidential opinion of our insignificance. I, he said, was a "frightful puppy", and Ross "a very repulsive character".' On another occasion Pauli asked Ibsen what books he was reading and was surprised to receive the answer: 'I don't read books, I leave them to my wife and Sigurd.' But Pauli, like other observers, confirms that Ibsen read the newspapers most minutely. Pauli noted that Sigurd, now twenty-one, was very much his father's son, meticulous in dress and demeanour, reserved, buttoned-up and 'seldom ungloved, even on the most informal occasions'.

Ibsen's dislike of reading books has disturbed many a man of letters, starting with Edmund Gosse; but it is not surprising that he, whose principal interest was modern people and modern ideas, should have found the newspapers more rewarding. They kept him better abreast of his subject. 'He has often seemed to me', wrote Georg Brandes in an essay published the following year, 'to stand in a sort of mysterious correspondence with the fermenting, germinating ideas of the day. Once or twice I have even had a distinct impression that new ideas, which were on the point of manifesting themselves publicly but were not yet perceived by others, had been preoccupying and indeed tormenting him'; and he added in an eloquent phrase that Ibsen possessed the true poet's ear for 'the low rumble that tells of ideas undermining the ground . . . for the throb of their pinions in the air'.

Not long after Ibsen's arrival in Rome the two Swedish princes Oscar and Carl visited the city. The Scandinavian Club gave a fancy-dress ball in their honour, which Ibsen attended, not, sadly, in fancy dress (what could he have gone as but himself?), but in, as the saying was, full gala, with his decorations on his chest and a *chapeau-bas* in his hand. King Oscar had given the princes a letter to Lindstrand, the Swedish minister in Rome, commanding him to introduce them to Ibsen, 'from whom they might learn much'; but Lindstrand, instead of inviting Ibsen to the dinner he gave for them, merely asked him to join them for tea afterwards. Ibsen, well able to answer one snub with another, replied by sending his visiting card bearing the brief message: 'I do not drink tea.' The princes took the hint and invited Ibsen to dinner the following day.

One day John Paulsen risked promulgating some theories about Ibsen's work and received a warning against 'looking for obscurities in his work where none existed'. Ibsen complained that 'critics were eager to find a double meaning, a hidden symbol, in every word or action', a tendency that has not lapsed with the years. He quoted as one example a Swede's assertion that Nora's extravagant tip to the porter of a crown, which he had intended merely to exemplify her carelessness with money, signified her desire to level the relationship between capitalist and worker; and told how another scholar had discovered a deep meaning in his choice of the name Makrina (which in Greek means far-sighted) for a character in *Emperor and Galilean*, whereas he had only used it because he had found the name in an old book and liked it.

He also gave Paulsen some stern advice about writing. 'Fixing me with a glance over his gold spectacles, he said, "You mustn't walk around dreaming. Use your eyes. That is doubly necessary for anyone who wishes to become an author ... Tell me," he asked suddenly, "what colour is the wallpaper in your room?"' Paulsen had to confess that he did not know. '"You see!" cried Ibsen triumphantly, as always whenever he discovered anything which confirmed his suspicions. "I was right. You don't notice anything. Though how a human being with normal senses can live in a room without noticing the colour of the walls ... When I enter a strange house I note the tiniest detail, nothing escapes me. Yes," he added quietly, more to himself than to me, "I see everything." '

He gave proof of his visual memory that winter when a Norwegian lady named Fanny Rijs, on being presented to him at one of his own receptions, said, 'There is no need to introduce us. We danced together in Bergen.' Ibsen replied curtly (and untruthfully), 'I have never danced,' and walked away into his study. But a few minutes later he emerged, said, 'You are right,' described precisely what she had been wearing at the dance twenty-five years before, and even sketched a necklace she had been wearing. When she left on 28 February, Ibsen gave her a signed photograph of himself bearing the inscription: 'Do not forget Rome.'

During the spring of 1881 Ibsen, still smarting under the treatment accorded to Sigurd, seriously pondered giving up his Norwegian citizenship. 'He [Sigurd] is intending to become naturalized here,' he wrote to Johan Thoresen on 9 March. 'He speaks and writes French, German and Italian like a native, is well versed in both politics and economics, and so feels confident that he will be able to make a career without having to resort to Norway. The question is whether I too shall not feel occasioned to expatriate myself. There will be many advantages for me in becoming an Italian or German citizen, and now that the Ecclesiastical Department has dispossessed my son I don't know what further business I have up there. We are exceptionally contented here in Rome.' He was never in fact to make so final a break with Norway, thanks largely perhaps to Suzannah's influence; but the mood expressed in this letter was shortly to find dramatic expression.

He had not, hitherto, been lucky in his translators in any country, but he all but acquired what would have been a very interesting one that spring. Ludvig Josephson had, as we have seen, conceived the idea of staging *Love's Comedy* in Stockholm, and he approached no less a person than

August Strindberg to translate it. Although Strindberg, then thirty-two, had written eight plays, none of these ranks among his best; his great days as a dramatist still lay ahead of him. Josephson's suggestion tempted him. 'I have looked at Ibsen's *Love's Comedy*', he replied on 14 March. 'It will be a long and expensive job. If you want me to translate it, make me a formal offer and name a deadline, for I daren't risk attempting so big a task for nothing.' Unfortunately Josephson could offer very little, and the project lapsed (it was to be eight years before *Love's Comedy* was seen in Sweden). One wonders what Strindberg, whose marriage to Siri von Essen had not yet begun to strain at the seams, would have made of this particular play, with its message that love and marriage are incompatible.

That spring of 1881 Ibsen spent a couple of days with Lorentz Dietrichson revisiting the country places they had explored together seventeen years earlier. They took the train to Frascati and Tusculum and rode on donkeys, as before, across to Grottaferrata and Castelgandolfo, this time without mishap. They spent a night at Albano and the next morning walked to Genzano, looking in at the café in which Ibsen had lived and strolling down to Lake Nemi. In Olcanda all was unchanged except that the portrait of Pope Pius IX had been replaced by those of Victor Emmanuel, Cavour and Garibaldi. During this trip Ibsen, after bewailing the inability of governments to put big ideas into practice, suddenly broke off and said: 'People think I have changed my views as time has passed, but that is quite wrong; my development has been wholly consistent ... I am jotting down a few notes which will show the world how precisely similar I am now to what I was when I first discovered myself.' Dietrichson comments that this seems to be evidence that Ibsen was already preparing the autobiography from which Hegel was so unfortunately to dissuade him. It may have been of this project that Ibsen informed Hegel on 22 March: 'I am writing a new book which will be ready in the summer ... This work interests me much, and I feel convinced that it will also be received with interest by the public. But I won't for the moment tell you its theme; later, perhaps.' (But it may also have been *An Enemy of the People*, which he completed with unwonted speed the following year and which may already have been in his thoughts.)

Meanwhile, John Paulsen had been running into trouble as an author; his latest novel had been refused by Hegel, and he seems to have become swollen-headed. His relations with Ibsen had taken a marked turn for the worse. 'I am not surprised that you do not wish to publish it,' Ibsen wrote to Hegel on 21 April. 'I am afraid Paulsen is falling more and more into the bad habit of over-rapid and slipshod composition. No properly prepared plan, no rounded, lifelike characters. But I've grown tired of warning him against this path which he has chosen to follow, as I see it bears no fruit and, besides, he takes it amiss. He has an immense and unmannerly confidence in himself.' Ibsen's doubts about Paulsen's character were shortly to receive painful confirmation.

On 18 June Ibsen informed Hegel: 'There has been a change in my literary plans for the summer. I have temporarily shelved the work I previously mentioned to you, and early this month embarked on a theme which has long occupied my thoughts and which at length forced itself so insistently upon me that I could no longer ignore it. I hope to be able to send you the manuscript by the middle of October. I'll tell you the title later; for the moment I shall merely say that I describe it as "a domestic drama in three acts". I need hardly add that this play has no kind of connection with *A Doll's House*.' This last remark was in reply to a letter from Hegel telling him that there was a rumour in Copenhagen that he was working on a sequel to that play.

That month John Paulsen left Rome; he and Ibsen were never to meet again. On 28 June Ibsen moved with Suzannah and Sigurd to Sorrento on the west coast, where they stayed, as they had two years previously, at the Hotel Tramontano and where Dietrichson and his family shortly joined them. The weather was tremendously hot. 'My wife

suffers more than us from the heat, and especially the sirocco', he wrote to Camilla Collett that August, 'but she
manages to survive with the help of a daily sea-bathe. I don't
think you could have survived the summer down here. To
walk is almost out of the question; one must just sit as still as
possible.' Despite these conditions, he was able to write to
Hegel on 30 September: 'I take advantage of a free moment
to tell you briefly that on the 23rd inst. I finished the first
draft of my new play and on the 25th began my fair copy.
The play is entitled *Ghosts: A Domestic Drama in Three
Acts.* If possible you shall have the whole thing by the end of
October.'

This 'fair copy' in fact took the form of a new draft, and as
time was getting short if the book was to catch the Christmas sales Ibsen revised Act One (the draft of which he
finished on 4 October) and posted off the fair copy of it to
Hegel on 16 October. Working feverishly against the clock,
he completed the draft of Act Two (which he had begun on
13 October) in seven days, and that of Act Three in four
days. On 4 November he posted off the fair copy of Act Two
plus the first page of Act Three to Hegel, promising that 'the
remainder will be sent to you with all speed from Rome,
whither we return tomorrow'.

On 23 November, writing from Rome, he uttered a mild
warning to Hegel. '*Ghosts* will probably cause alarm in some
circles; but that can't be helped. If it didn't, there would
have been no necessity for me to have written it.' He was
already, he added in the same letter, 'planning a new four-
act comedy which I had thought about before but put aside
to make way for *Ghosts*, which was obsessing me and mon-
opolizing my thoughts'.

Ghosts – the story of a woman who leaves her husband, is
persuaded by the Pastor (whom she loves) to return home,
does so, and bears a son who turns out to have inherited his
father's syphilis – was duly published by Gyldendal, in an
edition of ten thousand copies (two thousand more than *A
Doll's House*) on 13 December 1881, and at once aroused a

consternation and hostility beyond anything Ibsen had envisaged. At first he accepted this calmly; he knew there were small prospects of its being performed in either Scandinavia or Germany, but reckoned it would, like *Brand* and *Peer Gynt*, make its effect on the reading public. On 22 December he wrote to Ludwig Passarge, 'My new play has come out, and has created a violent commotion in the Scandinavian press. Every day I receive letters and newspaper articles, some for, some against. A copy will be sent you very shortly; but I feel it is quite impossible that the play should be performed in any German theatre at this time; I hardly think they'll dare to stage it even in Scandinavia for some little while. Incidentally, it has been printed in an edition of 10,000 copies, and there is every prospect that a new edition will be required soon' – a forecast that was to prove sadly incorrect, though on the strength of it he had, two days earlier, asked Hegel to invest almost the whole proceeds of the first edition, £342, in gilt-edged securities at 4½ per cent.

Replying to a toast at the Scandinavian Club on 20 December, he remarked that Christmas, which to most people brought joy and peace, to him usually brought battle, since it was at this season that his books appeared; but that to him battle was a joy, and peace merely a breathing-space until he could take up the struggle anew. Nevertheless, when he added up his accounts for 1881, he must have hoped hard for that second edition, for he had earned only £626, barely half as much as in the previous year. Apart from his advance of £342 on *Ghosts*, reprints of *Brand* and *Peer Gynt* had brought him £150, performing rights (mainly for German productions of *A Doll's House*) a further £134.

However, on 2 January 1882, he wrote in buoyant mood to Hegel: 'The violent criticisms and insane attacks which people are levelling against *Ghosts* don't worry me in the least. I was expecting this. When *Love's Comedy* appeared there was just such an hysterical outcry in Norway as there is now. They moaned about *Peer Gynt* too, and *The Pillars of Society* and *A Doll's House* just as much. The commotion will die away this time, as it did before.' Only as an after-thought did he add: 'One thing worries me a little when I think how big an edition you printed. Has all this fuss damaged the sales of the book?'

Hegel replied on 10 January:

Dear Dr Ibsen,

... You ask: has all this to-do damaged the sales of the book? To this I must decidedly answer: Yes.

As you will know from the reviews, *Ghosts* has caused a great sensation and has been the literary event of the winter, like *A Doll's House* two years ago. This is only as one would expect. But, amazingly, there ensued almost at once great indignation at the circumstances which are portrayed in *Ghosts* and which people wish at all costs not to have in family literature. The effect of this became noticeable immediately. Of the large edition a not inconsiderable number of copies had been subscribed in advance, partly by the provinces, partly by Norway and Sweden.

From several of the booksellers outside Copenhagen, notably from Chr-a, Bergen, and Stockholm, where the papers have openly opposed the sale of the book, I have already been informed that they could not find the expected sales for *Ghosts* and have therefore asked me to take back large quantities of the book, not merely those they had on sale or return, but also some that they took on the normal terms and which should not normally be credited. In view of the need to maintain a good relationship with my colleagues I felt it wisest to make them this concession.

Here in Copenhagen the sales of *Ghosts* have been markedly smaller than those of your earlier books. And the whole business has had a damaging effect on *their* sales. I usually sell a not inconsiderable number of your works each Christmas, but this year the figures have been noticeably smaller.

I felt bound, my dear Herr Ibsen, to tell you this plainly ...

Your most affectionate

Fr. Hegel

August Lindberg has described the scene in Stockholm on the day of publication. 'There was a rush to the bookshops. But the excitement vanished in silence. Absolute silence. The newspapers said nothing and the bookshops sent the book back to the publisher. It was contraband. Something which could not decently be discussed.' And Alexander Kielland informed Georg Brandes that Cammermeyer, the leading bookshop in Christiania, had returned no less than five hundred copies to Gyldendal.[1] *Ghosts*, in short, was not a book to have about the house. It was not merely that it attacked some of the most sacred principles of the age, such as the sanctity of marriage (*A Doll's House* had done that), and the duty of a son to honour his father. Far worse, it referred unmistakably (if not by name) to venereal disease, defended free love, and suggested that under certain circumstances even incest might be justifiable. Even some of Ibsen's strongest supporters were antagonized. When Lindberg asked Ludvig Josephson, who had championed Ibsen's cause so ardently in Christiania, whether he would not consider presenting *Ghosts* at his theatre in Stockholm, Josephson refused point blank. 'The play', he told Lindberg, 'is one of the filthiest things ever written in Scandinavia.' And Erik Bøgh reported to his board at the Royal Theatre, Copenhagen, that *Ghosts* was 'a repulsive pathological phenomenon which, by undermining the morality of our social order, threatens its foundations', and advised its rejection, a recommendation with which the board concurred.

It was, however, in Norway itself that *Ghosts* was attacked most violently. Ibsen had expected the conservative papers to dislike it, but he was shocked to discover that the liberal press denounced it with even greater fervour. The left-wing *Oplandenes Avis* set the tone when it declared that 'complete silence would in our opinion, be the most fitting reception for such a work'. Despite this recommendation, the reviewer went on to describe it as 'the most unpleasant book we have read for a long while', drawing some comfort from

---

1. Kielland added interestingly that he liked *Ghosts* 'less for its own sake than for the insight it gives me into this elegant, cautious, decorated, slightly snobbish person who, like Nora, has always had a secret desire to say: "Damn and blast!" in the midst of all his elegance – and has now acquired the courage'.

the fact that it was 'in our humble opinion at least, much worse written than the author's previous works'. An anonymous reviewer in *Dagbladet* wrote: 'It is as though Ibsen had taken enjoyment in saying all the worst things he knew, and in saying them in the most outrageous way he could conceive.' The author of these words, Arne Garborg, had, ironically, just published a story entitled 'The Freethinker'. The ageing Andreas Munch published a poem in *Morgenbladet* called 'A Fallen Star', likening Ibsen to a star which has allowed itself to be lured down into 'the region of mists', has there turned into a meteor which has buried itself in 'the black earth, swollen with corpses', and lies there giving off 'an evil stench of corruption'. An editorial in the same paper on 18 December concluded: 'The book has no place on the Christmas table of any Christian home.' Even such progressive writers as Jonas Lie and Alexander Kielland privately raised their eyebrows; and Henrik Jæger, who six years later was to write an admiring biography of Ibsen, lectured at Christiania University attacking the play, and toured the country repeating his opinions (which he later recanted).

A few bold spirits championed the play. Hans Jæger, later to be imprisoned for writing a supposedly pornographic novel, the young director Gunnar Heiberg, and those two formidable suffragettes Amalie Skram and Camilla Collett, all defended it in *Dagbladet*; so did Bjørnson, who, despite the recent bad friendship between him and Ibsen, praised it as 'free, brave and courageous'. 'That is like him,' wrote Ibsen to Olaf Skavlan on 24 January 1882. 'He has in truth a great imperial spirit, and I shall never forget this.' And P. O. Schjøtt, the Professor of Greek at Christiania University, writing a year later in *Nyt Tidsskrift*, compared the play to the ancient Greek dramas:

When the greatest tragic and comic poets of Athens presented the political, ethical and religious ideas of their age, and even their champions, on the stage, someone no doubt denounced them and called their work tendentious. But posterity saw this as quite normal practice. When the ancient art of dramatic writing stood at its zenith, in that golden age, it was this realism or, if you will, this tendentiousness, which gave it its vitality and character ... We generalize thus with particular reference to Ibsen's latest play ... For of all the modern dramas we have read, *Ghosts* comes closest to classical tragedy ... When the dust of ignorant criticism has subsided, which we trust will happen soon, this play of Ibsen's, with its pure, bold contours, will stand not only as his noblest deed but as the greatest work of art which he, or indeed our whole dramatic literature, has produced.

Schjøtt's last sentence was a reference to a review of the play by Georg Brandes, who, in *Morgenbladet* (the Danish, not the Norwegian newspaper of that name), had declared it to be 'not the most perfect play he has written, but the noblest deed in his literary career'. Brandes was almost the only Dane to come out in the play's favour; his review delighted Ibsen, and re-established good relations between the two men.

In Rome, Ibsen read the various comments with increasing indignation. 'What is one to say of the attitude taken by the so-called liberal press?' he wrote to Brandes on 3 January 1882 (his first letter to Brandes for over five years). 'These leaders who talk and write of freedom and progress, and at the same time let themselves be the slaves of the supposed opinions of their subscribers?' Three days later he wrote to the Danish writer Sophus Schandorph: 'I was prepared for some such commotion. If for nothing else, certain of our Norwegian reviewers have an undeniable talent for completely misunderstanding and misinterpreting the authors whose books they presume to judge.' After protesting that the views expressed in *Ghosts* were not necessarily his own ('In none of my plays is the author so totally detached and uncommitted as in this'),[2] he went on to deny

2. This assertion was denounced by Strindberg in a letter to Edvard Brandes, 18 February 1882 ('Isn't Ibsen cowardly?'). But Strindberg admired the play, telling Brandes to thank his brother for the latter's defence of it, and even in 1884, when he had become violently hostile towards Ibsen, he admitted: 'But he has written *Ghosts*. I mustn't hate him.'

that *Ghosts* advocated nihilism. 'The play is not concerned with advocating anything. It merely points to the fact that nihilism is fermenting beneath the surface in Norway as everywhere else. It is inevitable. A Pastor Manders will always incite some Mrs Alving into being. And she, simply because she is a woman, will, once she has started, go to the ultimate extreme.'

On 28 January he wrote to another Danish writer, Otto Borchsenius: 'It may well be that in certain respects this play is somewhat audacious. But I thought the time had come when a few boundary marks had to be shifted. And it was much easier for me, as an elder writer, to do this than for the many younger writers who might want to do something of the kind. I was prepared for a storm to break over me; but one can't run away from such things. That would have been cowardice. What has most depressed me has been not the attacks themselves, but the lack of guts which has been revealed in the ranks of the so-called liberals in Norway. They are poor stuff with which to man the barricades.'

On 8 March he wrote a letter of warm thanks to Bjørnson 'for so openly and honourably standing forth in my defence at a time when I have been attacked from so many quarters. It was of course only what I would have expected from your bold warrior spirit ... Rest assured that I shall never forget you. I have also noticed that during your stay in America you wrote kind words in my praise. Thank you for that too ... I heard you were ill there, and when you were on your way home I read of storms at sea. Then I suddenly and vividly realized how immensely much you mean to me, as to all of us. I felt that if anything should happen to you it would be a great disaster for our land and I should lose all joy in creating.'

So far from discouraging him from further writing, the smell of battle stimulated Ibsen. On 16 March he informed Hegel that he was 'fully occupied with preparations for a new work. This time it will be a peaceful play, which cabinet ministers and wholesale merchants and their ladies will be able to read, and from which the theatres will not need to shrink ... As far as *Ghosts* is concerned, comprehension will seep into the minds of the good people of our country, and that in the not too distant future. But all these fading and decrepit figures who have spat upon this work will one day bring upon their heads the crushing judgement of future literary historians ... My book contains the future.'

The Christiania Theatre and the Royal Theatre in Stockholm followed the example of the Royal Theatre in Copenhagen and Nya Teatern in refusing to stage the play. On 20 May, however, *Ghosts* at last received its world première in, of all places, Chicago, where it was presented in the original language at the Aurora Turner Hall before an audience of Scandinavian immigrants with the Danish actress Helga von Bluhme as Mrs Alving, the other parts being taken by Danish and Norwegian amateurs. This production – the first on record of any Ibsen play in America – subsequently toured Minneapolis and other cities of the Middle West which contained large Scandinavian populations. But it was to be over a year before the play was performed in Europe, and even when the scandal had died down and it was being acted before respectful audiences it was thirteen years before a new edition was required. It remained a book not to be seen about the house.

But if *Ghosts* shocked the literary and theatrical establishment of Scandinavia, it made an immediate and stimulating impact on the young. Herman Bang, then aged twenty-five, and later to become a celebrated Danish novelist and one of Ibsen's most influential pioneers in France, describes how it excited his generation even before it became a subject of scandal.

The play was distributed to the booksellers towards evening. The keenest buyers ran out in the dark to get it. That evening I visited a young actor who had just read *Ghosts* ... 'This', he said, 'is the greatest play our age will see.' The debate had already started by the next morning. An extraordinary number of people seemed to have read the play that night ... One or two restless people who had nothing to lose, having no good name to be smeared by associations with *Ghosts*, gave public readings. People flocked to the obscure places where these readings took place, out by the bridges, far into the suburbs. A group of unwanted actors determined to take it on tour. They wanted to act the play in the provinces.

But, Bang adds, 'good society knew its duty', and the project had to be abandoned. Nevertheless, it 'was performed semi-privately, in I know not what impossible places', and all but achieved a professional production in Copenhagen within weeks of publication, for Theodor Andersen, the head of the Casino Theatre, 'read it twenty times before finally rejecting it'.

In Germany, once the play had been published (which did not happen until 1884), the same pattern was repeated. Bang was in Germany then and tells of a performance of *A Doll's House* at Meiningen, with the celebrated actress Marie Ramlo as guest artist. The theatre was full of young students.

Frau Ramlo was excellent, but it was not she who held their attention. The young people barely heard her. They read when the curtain was down, and they read when the curtain was up. They read furtively and amazed, as though fearful, read, as the book was passed secretly from hand to hand, a little, humble, yellow, paperbound volume of a hundred pages bearing the title *Gespenster* [*Ghosts*]. What a strange evening when all those hundreds of young people read as one the play about the sins of their fathers, and when, as a drama about marriage was being acted behind the footlights, that other drama of parents and their children forced its way up from the auditorium on to the stage. They did not dare to read the book at home, and so they read it secretly here.

Bang adds that young actors and actresses used *Ghosts* as an audition piece long before it was allowed to be played in Germany (in 1886, and then only privately), and that 'young beginners acted the play secretly in suburban halls far out on the fringes of civilization, as in Norway'.

Ibsen's contemporaries saw *Ghosts* primarily as a play about physical illness, just as they had seen *A Doll's House* primarily as a play about women's rights. With few exceptions, they failed to realize that the true subject of *Ghosts* is the devitalizing effect of a dumb acceptance of convention. As Halvdan Koht has written: 'Oswald is branded with disease, not because his father was a beast, but because Mrs Alving had obeyed the immoral ethics of society'[3] – in other words, *Ghosts* is a play about ethical, not physical debility. The importance of waging war against the past, the need for each individual to find his or her own freedom, the danger of renouncing love in the name of duty – these are the real themes of *Ghosts*, as they are the themes of every play Ibsen wrote from *A Doll's House* onwards. And the targets are the same as those he had attacked in *A Doll's House* and, before that, in *The Pillars of Society*, and which he was to go on attacking until the end of his life – the hollowness of great reputations, provincialism of outlook, the narrow and inhibiting effect of small-town life, the suppression of individual freedom from within as well as from without, and the neglect of the significance of heredity – a problem much discussed among the Scandinavians in Rome, one of whom, the botanist and novelist J. P. Jacobsen, had translated Darwin's *Origin of Species* and *The Descent of Man* into Danish. Zola, of course, had hastened to exploit Darwin's thesis that man, like other animals, must adapt himself to the environment in which he lives; but Ibsen hated being compared with Zola, for whom he had a low regard. 'Zola',

3. In view of the frequently repeated complaint that syphilis cannot be inherited from one's father, it is worth pointing out that a baby can be infected by its mother, and that a woman can have syphilis without realizing it or suffering any particular discomfort. In other words, and this is a far more frightening explanation of Oswald's illness than the usual one, Mrs Alving could have caught syphilis from her husband and passed it on to her son. Dr Jonathan Miller has pointed out to me that Oswald could also have been infected by smoking his father's pipe when a child. Ibsen knew more about medicine than some of his critics.

he once remarked, 'descends into the sewer to bathe in it; I, to cleanse it.'

How much Ibsen had actually read of Zola is not clear. In 1882 he told William Archer he had read nothing, but in 1898 he informed a Swedish journalist he had 'read much of him, though not his great cycle of novels', and described him as 'clearly and beyond doubt a great talent'. But this was during his seventieth birthday celebrations, when he was being polite about everybody. Zola's opinion of Ibsen seems to have been equally ambiguous. Zola was largely responsible for the first French production of him in 1891, by reminding Antoine of *Ghosts* (Antoine had thought of doing it, but had dropped the idea; Zola had read an essay by Jacques Saint-Cères in the *Revue de l'art dramatique* describing Ibsen as a naturalist, and felt he had found a fellow-warrior). On the other hand, when asked his opinion of the influence of Ibsen on the French stage (and of Tolstoy on the French novel), Zola is said to have replied 'that he did not attach much importance to the question, for he held that the ideas which were supposed to rain on Paris from the north were in reality French ones which had been disseminated by French writers and had come back to their place of origin, occasionally crystallized or intensified by the more sombre imagination of Scandinavian or Russian writers'. The legend of Ibsen's supposed debt to Scribe, Dumas *fils*, George Sand and the rest died hard.

In one important technical respect *Ghosts* anticipates the later plays, and that is in the density of its dialogue. *The Pillars of Society* and *A Doll's House* are both simply written (and comparatively easy to translate), because for most of the time the characters say what they mean. But in *Ghosts*, Mrs Alving and Manders especially spend much of the time circling round a subject to which they dread to refer directly, and at these moments the dialogue is oblique, sometimes even opaque. This double-density dialogue, when the characters say one thing and mean another, was to be one of Ibsen's most important contributions to the technique of prose drama. He knew that when people talk about something concerning which they feel a sense of guilt, they cease to speak directly and instead talk evasively and with circumlocution; and actors, when they are playing these lines, have to speak the text but act the sub-text, the unspoken thoughts between the lines. One of the greatest problems that faces a translator of Ibsen is to convey this meaning behind the meaning; if this is not indicated (as Ibsen himself indicates it) it is practically impossible for an actor to convey that sense of guilt and evasion from which almost all of Ibsen's major characters suffer, and which is so often at crises the mainspring of their actions, or their failure to act.

Historically, *Ghosts* occupies a position of immense importance. Julius Hoffory remarked in 1888 that much of its effect on Ibsen's contemporaries was due to the fact that here was a play comparable to those of Aeschylus and Sophocles, but about modern people; a fact easily forgotten by us, to whom it is as much a costume play as the *Agamemnon*. *Ghosts* was the first great tragedy written about middle-class people in plain, everyday prose. *Danton's Death* and *Woyzeck* are composed in a high-flown prose which frequently, and splendidly, overlaps the frontier of poetry; and while other playwrights had attempted to do what Ibsen achieved in *Ghosts*, none had succeeded. Time has not dulled its impact (though it sometimes, in England and America at any rate, suffers from being publicized as 'the play which shocked our grandfathers'). Indeed, it gains enormously by not having, as so often in the last century, a declamatory and melodramatic Mrs Alving. Ibsen's plays needed, and helped to nurture, a new kind of player with the strength of restraint, life-size, not Wagnerian. Bernhardt and Henry Irving rejected his works; Duse embraced them.

21

An Enemy of the People
1882

DURING the winter of 1881–2, when the hubbub about *Ghosts* was at its height, Ibsen met for the first time his energetic new Scottish champion. Young William Archer had been ordered south for his health, and after walking from Cannes to Leghorn he proceeded by train to Rome. One of his first objects there was, naturally, to secure an introduction to the author whose work he so admired, and he described the meeting in a letter to his brother Charles, written in December 1881:

The great event has come off, satisfactorily, but not in the manner I expected ... I had been about a quarter of an hour there [at the Scandinavian Club], and was standing close to the door, when it opened and in walked unmistakably the great Henrik. My photograph is very good as far as the face is concerned, but it gives you the idea of broader shoulders and a fuller chest than he really has. He is of middle height, rather under than over – at any rate in talking to him I feel noticeably taller. [Archer stood around six feet] ... He went around for a while talking to different people, and gave you the impression, which I was prepared for, of extreme quietness. The red ribbon which excited young [*sic*] Bjørnson's contempt was very prominent in his buttonhole. After a while I got Professor Ravnkilde [the Danish composer and chairman of the club] to introduce me to him. I saw at once that he did not connect my name with *Samfundets Støtter* [*The Pillars of Society*], so after a little I told him about it. He had heard of the production, but not my name, and took my rather lame excuses for not having got his permission very readily ... He invited me to call at his house, which I shall do some day this week; and besides, I shall see him again at the [club], when I hope to get a little more under the surface, if it is at all possible . . . He does not read any of the French dramatists, and moreover he hardly ever goes to the theatre – and small blame to him in Italy, say I, though he says there are some very good Italian actors, besides the famous ones. Altogether, the interview was a success. Though I can't say that L's description of him as a *spidsborger* [*petit bourgeois*] is quite justified, he certainly is not the man you would imagine to have written Agnes's death-scene and the fourth act of *Brand* . . . At first sight there is an absence of anything Titanic about him . . . However, for the present 'the old min's friendly'[1], and that's the main point.

A few weeks later Archer wrote to J. M. Robertson that he was seeing Ibsen 'almost every day at a café which he and I both frequent for an afternoon glass of vermouth, and I have a yarn with him occasionally'. This was the Café Nazionale at the corner of the Corso and the Via della Mercede. Ibsen must have liked Archer, for he invited him to his home, which Archer found 'comfortable, yet comfortless . . . well furnished, but with no air of home about it . . . His writing-room was very bare and painfully orderly.' When Archer left Rome on 4 March Ibsen gave him an inscribed photograph; and when he returned in April, 'the old min was not only friendly but effusive'. Archer wrote an article entitled 'Henrik Ibsen at Home in the Via Capo le Case' and offered it to Edmund Yates, the editor of the *World* (a periodical of which Archer was to be the dramatic critic for twenty-one years); but Yates (who had once been the occasion of a quarrel between Dickens and Thackeray) rejected it, it was never published and, sadly, it has not survived among Archer's papers.

A Danish scholar, Harald Høffding, also met Ibsen for the first time that winter. 'He looked almost like a boatswain; broad and big-boned, brown in the face, he sat motionless and with half-closed eyes.' When he met him again ten years later Høffding received a very different im-

1. A reference to Dick Swiveller's question ('Is the old min agreeable?') in *The Old Curiosity Shop*.

pression, of 'an elegant little man'. '*À deux*', he added, 'Ibsen was very loquacious, though he avoided any discussion of his writings.' Georg Pauli confirms this last point; whenever anyone tried to probe Ibsen about his plays, Pauli says he would reply with a question, such as: 'How long have you been in Rome, madam?' – 'Did you have a good journey?' etc. And Fritz von Dardel, whom he had met at the Vienna Exhibition and who was now in Rome, confirms Høffding's impression of the new darkness of Ibsen's complexion, though he implies another cause than sun. 'He has fattened,' noted Dardel in his diary, 'and has developed a high facial colour. To any query why he did not have his son educated in Norway, he replied, "Because he can have a pleasanter life almost anywhere else." '

On 2 June 1882, a fortnight after the Chicago première of *Ghosts*, the first American production in English of an Ibsen play took place, though he might have had difficulty in recognizing it as his. The place was Milwaukee and the play *A Doll's House*, re-entitled *The Child Wife*, and freely adapted from the German by a schoolmaster named William M. Lawrence. Lawrence set the play in England, introducing an Irish widow to give the play some humour, and of course using the happy ending. In the second act, one of Nora's (or, as Lawrence called her, Eva's) children sang a pretty song, which the audience enjoyed so much that she had to repeat it. 'Love is the theme,' noted one reviewer, 'yet not a line of the play is impure.' Another critic named Lawrence as the author, while a third referred to the *play* as 'Henry Ibsen'.

Meanwhile, during that spring and early summer of 1882, while the storm over *Ghosts* still raged, Ibsen went ahead with his new play, which progressed with unwonted speed. No working notes or preliminary draft have survived, so we do not know, as we do for most of his plays, how long he took to write each act, or what alterations he made from his original conception; but on 21 June he was able to inform Hegel: 'Yesterday I completed my new dramatic work. It is entitled *An Enemy of the People*, and is in five acts. I am still a little uncertain whether to call it a comedy or simply a play; it has much of the character of a comedy, but there is also a serious basic theme.' At the beginning of August he left Rome for Gossensass, whence on 9 September he posted the fair copy of the final act to Hegel. 'It has been fun', he wrote, 'working on this play, and I feel a sense of emptiness and deprivation at being parted from it. Dr Stockmann and I got on most excellently; we agree about so many things; but the Doctor has a more muddled head on his shoulders than I have, and has beside certain characteristics which will permit people to tolerate things from his lips which they might not accept so readily had they issued from mine. If you have begun to read the manuscript, I think you will share this opinion.'

The speed with which Ibsen completed *An Enemy of the People*, without the usual eighteen months of cud-chewing ('He has never been so quick before!' commented Georg Brandes to Alexander Kielland on 30 June), suggests that this must have been the work he had conceived and pondered before putting it aside for *Ghosts*, as described in his letters to Hegel of 12 November 1880 and 22 March 1881. Moreover, Lorentz Dietrichson and Kristofer Janson both record earlier conversations with Ibsen in which he expressed many of the opinions which he was to put into Dr Stockmann's mouth. On New Year's Eve, 1880, Janson noted in his diary:

Today Ibsen and I discussed French politics, especially the expulsion of the monks from their monasteries. Ibsen deplored this greatly, and said: 'Haven't I always said that you republicans are the worst tyrants of all? You don't respect individual freedom. Republicanism is the form of government in which individual freedom has the least chance of being respected ... What is the majority? The ignorant mass. Intelligence always belongs to the minority. How many of the majority do you think are entitled to hold any opinion? The only people I have any real sympathy with are the socialists and nihilists. They want something wholeheartedly and are consistent.'

And Dietrichson recalled: 'The ideas which he expressed

in *An Enemy of the People* were already fully developed by the spring of 1881 and were aired in almost every conversation we had at that time.'

The reception of *Ghosts* in Norway had brought Ibsen's distrust of popular opinion and contemporary liberalism to the boil. 'What is one to say of the attitude taken by the so-called liberal press?' he had written to Georg Brandes on 3 January 1882.

These leaders who talk and write of freedom and progress, and at the same time allow themselves to be the slaves of the supposed opinions of their subscribers? I become more and more convinced that there is something demoralizing about involving oneself in politics and attaching oneself to a party. Under no circumstances will I ever link myself with any party which has the majority behind it. Bjørnson says: 'The majority is always right.' As a practising politician I suppose he has to say that. But I say: 'The minority is always right.' I am of course not thinking of the minority of reactionaries who have been left astern by the big central party which we call liberal; I mean the minority which forges ahead in territory which the majority has not yet reached. I believe that he is right who is most closely attuned to the future ... For me freedom is the first condition of life, and the highest. At home people don't bother much about freedom but only about freedoms – a few more or a few less, according to the party standpoint. I feel most painfully affected by this vulgarity, this plebeianism in our public attitude. In the course of their undeniably worthy efforts to turn our country into a democratic community, people have unwittingly gone a good way towards turning us into a mob community. The aristocracy of the intellect seems to be in short supply in Norway.[2]

An Enemy of the People tells the story of a doctor at a

2. Several of the phrases Ibsen used in this letter recur in *An Enemy of the People*. 'When my new play reaches you,' he wrote to Brandes on 21 September 1882, shortly after finishing it, 'you will perhaps be able to understand what interest and, I may add, fun it has given me to recall the many scattered and casual remarks I have made in my letters to you.' Didrik Grønvold recalls that Ibsen had spoken to him of the necessity of having an aristocracy to educate a nation as early as 1877 in Munich.

small spa who discovers that the Baths, on which the livelihood of the town depends, are contaminated. At first the
locals praise him as a public benefactor, but when they learn
that the baths will have to be closed for several years and
their income affected, they turn against him and, when he
calls a meeting to put his views to them, brand him as an
enemy of the people. In this famous fourth act, Dr Stock=
mann utters many of the opinions Ibsen himself had been
expressing in Rome:

> I can't stand politicians! I've had all I can take of them!
> They're like goats in a plantation of young trees! They destroy
> everything! . . .

> The most dangerous enemies of truth and freedom are the
> majority! Yes, the solid, liberal, bloody majority – they're the
> ones we have to fear! . . . Who form the majority in any country?
> The wise, or the fools? I think we'd all have to agree that the
> fools are in a terrifying, overwhelming majority all over the
> world! But in the name of God it can't be right that the fools
> should rule the wise! Yes, yes, you can shout me down. But you
> can't say I'm wrong! The majority has the power, unfortunately
> – but the majority is not right! The ones who are right are a few
> isolated individuals like me. The minority is always right! . . .

> I'm not so forgiving as a certain person. I don't say 'I forgive
> ye, for ye know not what ye do!'

Dr Stockmann's first reaction as his daughter is sacked, his
patients refuse to employ him, and the mob breaks his
windows is to take his wife and children away; but he finally
decides to stay and try to re-educate the townspeople, beginning with the lowest and poorest:

DR STOCKMANN. . . . I'm going to experiment with mongrels for
     once. They've good heads on them sometimes.
EILIF. But what shall we do when we've become free men and
     aristocrats?
DR STOCKMANN. Then, my boys, you'll chase all those damned
     politicians into the Atlantic Ocean!

MRS STOCKMANN. Let's hope it won't be the politicians who'll chase you out, Thomas.

DR STOCKMANN. Are you quite mad, Catherine? Chase me out? Now, when I am the strongest man in town?

MRS STOCKMANN. The strongest – now?

DR STOCKMANN. Yes! I'll go further! I am one of the strongest men in the whole world ... Hush! You mustn't talk about it yet. But I've made a great discovery!

MRS STOCKMANN. Not again!

DR STOCKMANN. Yes – yes! (*Gathers them round him and whispers to them.*) The fact is, you see, that the strongest man in the world is he who stands most alone.

The plot of *An Enemy of the People* had its origin in two actual incidents. Alfred Meisner, a young German poet whom Ibsen knew in Munich, had told him how, when his father had been medical officer at the spa of Teiplitz in the eighteen-thirties, there had occurred an outbreak of cholera which the doctor felt it his duty to make known publicly. As a result the season was ruined and the citizens of Teiplitz became so enraged that they stoned the doctor's house and forced him to flee the town.

Then there had been the case in Norway of a chemist named Harald Thaulow. For nearly ten years Thaulow had furiously attacked the Christiania Steam Kitchens for neglecting their duty towards the city's poor. He had delivered a violent speech on the subject in 1874, during Ibsen's visit to Norway; and on 23 February 1881, only a fortnight before he died, Thaulow had attempted to read a prepared speech at the annual general meeting of the Steam Kitchens. The chairman of the meeting tried to prevent him from speaking, and eventually the public forced him, amid commotion, to withdraw. Ibsen read a report of this meeting in *Aftenposten* (24 February), just at the time when his indignation at the reception of *Ghosts* was reaching its climax, and he must have recognized in the eccentric old chemist a spirit very kindred to his own.

As with *The Pillars of Society*, an English Member of Parliament may also have contributed something to the play. Charles Bradlaugh, having narrowly escaped imprisonment for his part in a pamphlet advocating birth control (he had actually been sentenced, but had been acquitted on appeal), had been elected Radical M.P. for Northampton in 1880, but had been barred from taking his seat on the ground that, since he was a confessed free-thinker, the oath would not bind him. New elections were held in Northampton, and he was returned each time, but was still excluded; in 1881, he was forcibly removed from the House by ten policemen. It was not until 1886 that a new Speaker granted him the right to take the oath and sit.

'You should hear Ibsen on Bradlaugh – he has the most vivid sympathy for him,' wrote William Archer to his brother Charles on 14 March 1882, when Ibsen was about to start writing *An Enemy of the People*; and Bradlaugh obviously has a good deal in common with Dr Stockmann. So, it has often been pointed out, do Bjørnson and Jonas Lie, both intellectually confused, warm-hearted, eloquent and impatient men, with strong family feelings and an infinite capacity for moral indignation. But, as Ibsen hinted in his letter to Hegel of 9 September 1882, he himself was probably the chief model for the character, at any rate in Act Four; and it is worth remembering that the house in Skien in which Ibsen was born was called Stockmannsgaarden.

After posting the final pages to Hegel on 9 September, Ibsen remained for a month in Gossensass, staying, as he was to do on future occasions, at the friendly Gröbner family hotel. While there he received, and granted, a request from America for the right to translate and publish *The Pillars of Society*, *A Doll's House* and *Ghosts*. The request came from Rasmus B. Anderson, Professor of Scandinavian Languages at the University of Wisconsin, who that year published a review of *Brand* in the *Literary World* and an essay on Ibsen in the *American*, the first articles about him to appear in America apart from Bjørnson's panegyric. Anderson was to supervise the project, and Ibsen, in his reply of 14 September, begged him to see that 'the language of the translation be kept as close as possible to ordinary everyday speech; all the turns of phrase and expressions which belong only to books should most carefully be avoided in dramatic works, especially mine, which aim to produce in the reader or spectator a feeling that he is, during the reading or performance, witnessing a slice of real life'.

It was advice that many of his translators, recent as well as contemporary, would have done well to heed. But these translations, if completed, never appeared – fortunately, since the translator was that William M. Lawrence who had been responsible for the travestied version of *A Doll's House* produced in Milwaukee. Henrietta Frances Lord's version of *A Doll's House* was published by Dutton's of New York the same year; *The Pillars of Society* and *An Enemy of the People* had to wait until 1888.

On 9 October (the snow must have come later than usual to Gossensass that year) Ibsen left Gossensass and moved south to the little town of Brixen, where he put up at the Hotel Elefant, 'the best hotel in the Tyrol', as he described it to Hegel on 28 October. He had intended to stay there only briefly, but heavy floods cut the roads and railways to the south, and it was not until 24 November that he was able to return to Rome.

When he got there he found an unpleasant surprise awaiting him. John Paulsen had published with Gyldendal a novel called *The Pehrsen Family*, and one can only suppose that Frederick Hegel had (as with *Brand*) not read the manuscript before sending it to press or in proof. The book deals with a middle-aged couple and their only son. The father, a self-made tradesman, is short, domineering, emotionally buttoned-up, contemptuous of his country, and obsessed by a secret passion to gain a medal, an end towards which he has done some careful lobbying. He has a drunken old father of whom he is ashamed, and walks with his hands behind his back. As a young man, he had been very poor and taken refuge in alcohol, and there had been a whip-round among his acquaintances to help him out. His wife, an avid novel-reader whose 'weak health had been broken in the struggle with this hard man', had seen him through this crisis; the lower he had sunk, the higher she had risen; Paulsen calls her 'Murillo's Madonna', the painting named by Ibsen in his poem 'In the Gallery'. Pehrsen becomes prosperous and tries to be aristocratic (Paulsen uses the adjective *fornem* which had begun to recur somewhat frequently in Ibsen's letters and conversation, and which is held up as an ideal by Dr Stockmann in *An Enemy of the People*). But the humiliations which he suffered in youth have left him with a feeling of inferiority from which he cannot escape. The son dreams of a diplomatic career, and the family emigrates to Rome (of whose social life Paulsen paints a lively picture). The book has Paulsen's usual virtues and defects; it is extremely readable (even today), written with an eye for detail and a sense of atmosphere, and ends the way his books usually end, in rubbishy and unconvincing melodrama.

It seems inconceivable that Paulsen did not intend to portray the Ibsens, or that he could have been unconscious that his readers would assume them to be the originals; it also seems extraordinary that he could have wished to libel a man whom he genuinely admired and who had been particularly kind to him. Yet perhaps Paulsen was being no more naïve than Ibsen had been in assuming that Bjørnson would not be offended by *The League of Youth*. He wrote Ibsen a letter assuring him that he had intended no harm, to which Ibsen replied with an open card addressed care of the Scandinavian Club and bearing the one word 'Scoundrel!' with his signature. And that was the end of that friendship.

An Enemy of the People was published on 28 November 1882, in an edition (despite the calamitous sales of *Ghosts*) of ten thousand copies. Its reception was mixed. Not surprisingly, Dr Stockmann's hard remarks about political parties offended all the reviewers who belonged to either;

Danish liberal circles were very cool. Edvard Brandes, greatly piqued, began his review in *Dansk Morgenbladet* by calling it 'a disappointment', sharply criticized several of Dr Stockmann's remarks, and ended by characterizing the play as 'a mere dramatized newspaper article written in answer to some poor newspaper scribblings [i.e., the attacks upon *Ghosts*] which weren't worth a ha'porth of gunpowder, let alone a literary reply from a great author'. Strindberg, whose political feelings were equally fervent, also disliked it. 'I begin to hate Ibsen after *An Enemy of the People*', he wrote to Bjørnson on 4 May 1884. 'There's something insufferably *aesthetic* about him' (the modern word would be 'uncommitted'). Much the most percipient review came from Erik Bøgh who, with a fellow-craftsman's percipience, praised Ibsen's ability to 'treat a genuinely tragic theme with no trace of tragic apparatus, no pathos, employing everyday circumstances with everyday people speaking everyday prose ... presenting his hero not merely without an idealized costume but without any pretence at an idealized personality'.

The theatres seized eagerly upon the play. The Christiania Theatre and the Royal Theatres of Copenhagen and Stockholm, all of which had rejected *Ghosts* as unfit for public presentation, immediately acquired production rights of *An Enemy of the People*, apparently unembarrassed by the fact that its theme was the unworthiness of those who 'do not dare'. Hans Schrøder, the director of the Christiania Theatre, telegraphed Ibsen for permission to give the first public performance of the play, and Ibsen agreed, stinging them for a lump payment of £222; he had let them have *A Doll's House* for £139.

The prospect of increased performance fees, and of a normal sale for the book, must have comforted Ibsen, for 1882 had been an even worse year financially than 1881. Apart from Gyldendal's advance on *An Enemy of the People* (£467), and the reprint of *Poems* (£53), he had earned only £63: a total of £583. Yet, although by the beginning of the year his share holdings had amounted to over £3,600, he nevertheless asked Hegel on 2 December to buy him a further £220-worth of securities. Few writers can ever have saved so high a proportion of what they earned.

An Enemy of the People is less frequently performed today than most of Ibsen's mature plays, for two principal reasons. One is, simply, the size of the cast. A crowd costs money, and without a crowd the great fourth act loses much of its impact (and a small crowd is almost worse than no crowd at all). The other problem is ideological. Some of the opinions expressed by Dr Stockmann, especially his demand for 'aristocrats', his contempt for the masses, and his assertion that 'the minority is always right', strike an illiberal note in modern ears. On these points Ibsen was in fact expressing a commonly shared attitude; Mill, Tocqueville, Dickens and most liberal thinkers of the time distrusted the tyranny of the common majority. 'Those whose opinions go by the name of public opinion ... are always a mass, that is to say, collective mediocrity,' wrote Mill in his great essay *On Liberty*. 'No government by a democracy or a numerous aristocracy, either in its political acts or in the opinions, qualities, and tone of mind which it fosters, ever did or could rise above mediocrity, except in so far as the sovereign Many have let themselves be guided (which in their best times they always have done) by the counsels and influence of a more highly gifted and instructed One or Few. The initiation of all wise or noble things comes and must come from individuals; generally at first from some one individual.' That is precisely Dr Stockmann's message. But it is an unfashionable viewpoint to put forward in an age of universal suffrage.

The play has, also, suffered worse than most from the dead hand of academic criticism. The kind of commentator that dismisses *Emperor and Galilean* as 'stone-cold', *Brand* as 'ambiguous', and *Little Eyolf* as 'a falling-off' (to quote from a recent and embarrassing English book intended as a vindication of Ibsen) has tended to reject *An Enemy of the People* as 'thin'. It lacks, indeed, the extra density and overtones of Ibsen's later works; but there are precious few other plays outside the Greeks, Shakespeare and Chekhov with which it need fear comparison. The truths it expresses have not dated, and are not likely to as long as there are town councils and politicians. Even when only adequately performed, it is one of the most accessible and compulsive of Ibsen's plays; and Dr Stockmann is one of the half-dozen greatest male parts he wrote.

Of all the roles that Konstantin Stanislavsky acted, by any author, this was his favourite, and when he acted it in Petrograd in 1905 for the Moscow Arts Theatre it was the scene of a remarkable demonstration. Stanislavsky has described the occasion in his autobiography:

In that time of political unrest – it was but a little while before the first revolution – the feeling of protest was very strong in all spheres of society. They waited for the hero who could tell the truth strongly and bravely in the very teeth of the government. It is not to be wondered at that the image of Dr Stockmann became popular at once in Moscow, and especially so in Petrograd. *An Enemy of the People* became the favourite play of the revolutionists, notwithstanding the fact that Stockmann himself despised the solid majority and believed in individuals to whom he could entrust the conduct of life. But Stockmann protested, Stockmann told the truth, and that was considered enough.

On the day of the well-known massacre in Kazansky Square, *An Enemy of the People* was on the boards of our theatre. The average run of spectators that night was from the intelligentsia, the professors and learned men of Petrograd. I remember that the stalls were filled almost entirely with grey heads. Thanks to the sad events of the day, the audience was very excited and answered even the slightest hints about liberty in every word of Stockmann's protest. In the most unexpected places in the play the thunder of applause would break in on the performance ... The atmosphere in the theatre was such that we expected arrests at any minute and a stop to the performance. Censors, who sat at all the performances of *An Enemy of the People* and saw to it that I, who played Dr Stockmann, should use only the censored text, and raised trouble over every syllable that was not admitted by the censorship, were on this evening even more watchful than on other occasions. I had to be doubly careful. When the text of a role is cut and re-cut many times it is not hard to make a mistake and say too much or too little.

In the last act of the play Dr Stockmann, putting into order his room which has been stoned by the crowd, finds in the general chaos his black coat[3] in which he appeared at the meeting the day before. Seeing a rent in the cloth, Stockmann says to his wife: 'One must never put on a new coat when one goes to fight for freedom and truth.'

The spectators in the theatre connected this sentence with the massacre in Kazansky Square, when more than one new coat must have been torn in the name of freedom and truth. Unexpectedly, my words aroused such a pandemonium that it was necessary to stop the performance, into which a real mob scene was interpolated by impromptu. There had taken place the unification of the actor and the spectators, who took on themselves the role of chief actor in the theatre, that same mob action of which so much is said by the theoreticians of art. The entire audience rose from its seats and threw itself towards the footlights. Thanks to the fact that the stage was very low and there was no orchestra before it, I saw hundreds of hands stretched towards me, all of which I was forced to shake. The younger people in the audience jumped on to the stage and embraced Dr Stockmann. It was not easy to establish order and to continue with the play. That evening I found out through my own experience what power the theatre could exercise.[4]

There will always, somewhere in the world, be a Kazansky Square[5]; and the historical importance of *An Enemy of the*

3. More accurately, his trousers.
4. Stanislavsky based his physical appearance in the role on Rimsky-Korsakov, and borrowed several gestures and characteristics from Gorki.
5. When it was staged in Paris at the time of the Dreyfus affair everyone identified Stockmann with Emile Zola. Its first performance there became linked with riots in the city (see pp. 748–9 below) and it was deliberately chosen for the first Ibsen production in Spain, at the Teatre de Novetats in Barcelona on 14 April 1893, to help organized opposition to the established order in government and industry.

People lies in the fact that it is, except for *Danton's Death*, which no one then knew about, the first political debate which succeeds in remaining a great play. It possesses, too, a wit and lightness which people do not usually associate with Ibsen, though he had both qualities at his command, as *Peer Gynt* and *The League of Youth* bear witness. It is the most Shavian of Ibsen's plays; and the last act is one of his finest. What, one might ask on finishing Act Four, *can* he write that will not seem an anti-climax after this? Yet when one has read or seen that final act, one wonders how else one could possibly have supposed that he would end the play – the surest test of dramatic inevitability.

Some months after the publication of *An Enemy of the People* Georg Brandes wrote to Ibsen, apparently (the letter is lost) rebuking him for isolationism and not putting his shoulder to the progressive wheel. Ibsen replied (12 June 1883):

You are of course right when you say that we must all try to spread our opinions. But I firmly believe that an intellectual pioneer can never gather a majority around him. In ten years the majority may have reached the point where Dr Stockmann stood when the people held their meeting. But during those ten years the doctor has not stood stationary: he is still at least ten years ahead of the others. The majority, the masses, the mob, will never catch him up; he can never rally them behind him. I myself feel a similarly unrelenting compulsion to keep pressing forward. A crowd now stands where I stood when I wrote my earlier books. But I myself am there no longer, I am somewhere else – far ahead of them – or so I hope.

To the end of his literary career, which spanned fifty years, Ibsen was to keep moving relentlessly forward, never repeating the pattern of an earlier success. Just as, fifteen years previously, he had abandoned the epic form of poetic drama which had established him, so now he was to abandon the type of (to use a loose term) sociological drama which was to spread his fame throughout the western world, and with which his name is still principally and misleadingly linked. Having exposed the hollowness of a certain kind of left-wing politician in *The League of Youth*, he had gone on to expose the equal hollowness of their right-wing counterparts in *The Pillars of Society*; having questioned the sanctity of marriage in *A Doll's House*, he had questioned it yet further, together with several other equally sacred cows, in *Ghosts*. Then he had returned to the field of politics, broadening his sights so as to include the ordinary voter in his line of fire. *An Enemy of the People* is an attack, not merely on those who lead people by the nose, but on those who allow themselves to be thus led. These four plays, for all their differences, share one theme: the necessity of discovering who one really is and of trying to become that person. In his next play, he was to question even this belief.

22

The Wild Duck
1883–4

1883 opened for Ibsen with a series of productions of *An Enemy of the People*, which he had completed the previous June. The première took place at Christiania on 13 January; Bergen followed suit on 24 January, Gothenburg and Helsinki in February, and Stockholm and Copenhagen in March. In Germany, strangely considering the success there of *The Pillars of Society* and *A Doll's House*, it had to wait four years before being staged. Its reception was everywhere cordial but nowhere enthusiastic. Carl Georgsson Fleetwood, a young Swedish diplomat, probably hit on the reason for this when, after seeing the Stockholm production, he noted in his diary: 'It is a mirror in which our age *could* see itself, but which it does not really understand. The audience tonight did not grasp what the play was really about ... From the moment I read it ... I realized how lonely and uncomprehended a man like Ibsen must be, and tonight confirmed my conviction.' Ibsen's main appeal in every country was to the young, to men like Fleetwood, Otto Brahm and Paul Schlenther, Herman Bang, William Archer, Konstantin Stanislavsky and Aurélien Lugné-Poe, and the views of the young, the ones who are about, in Dr Stockmann's words, to 'ginger up the future', are often unreflected in the columns of established reviewers. 'Ibsen showed us our problems,' recalled another member of the new generation, Gurli Linder, 'our doubts, the injustices of our age, how dead tradition survived in a living shape, our belief in the future, in a just world built upon truth.'

An Enemy of the People had scarcely appeared before

Ibsen began to think about its successor, for as early as 11 January 1883 he wrote to Hegel that he was 'already planning a new drama about contemporary life. It will be in four acts, and I hope to be able to get down to the actual writing within a couple of months at most. The Italian air, and the pleasant way of life down here, greatly increase my eagerness to create. I find it much easier to work here than in Germany.' He seems at first to have been projecting another broadside of sociological criticism, for his preliminary notes include caustic observations on marriage ('has set the mark of slavery on everyone'), Christianity ('demoralizes and inhibits both men and women'), modern society ('merely a society of males'), and one splendid aphorism which deserves to figure in any anthology of quotations: 'Our best thoughts are thought by our worst scoundrels.' But instead of dashing off this play at once like *An Enemy of the People*, he returned to his old routine of brooding on it for a year, and by the time he got down to writing the dialogue of *The Wild Duck* social criticism had faded into the background, where it was to remain for the rest of his life.

As a subsidiary occupation and more immediate source of income, he suggested to Hegel that he might revise, and write a preface to, *The Feast of Solhaug*. 'The rewriting of this old play', he assured Hegel on 21 February, 'will not seriously delay the new work I am planning.' Hegel replied on 1 March accepting the idea enthusiastically and suggesting an edition of 4,000 copies against a fee of 80 pence a page. As with his *Poems* thirteen years previously, Ibsen had no copy of his own to work from, in print or in manuscript, and had to ask Hegel to try to obtain one for him from a second-hand bookshop. The work went rapidly (how can he have thought that dull old play worthy of a reprint?), and he posted off the final instalment on 6 April.

Early in May the actress Lucie Wolf, who had worked under him in Bergen and Christiania, asked him to write a verse prologue for a jubilee performance being arranged to celebrate her thirty years on the stage. Any plea to return to poetry touched him on a sensitive nerve, like a plea to return to Skien, and he replied on 25 May with a peppery re-statement of his position:

> Your prologue must naturally be in verse, for such is the ac-cepted convention. But I cannot conspire to keep this convention alive. Poetry has caused dreadful damage to the art of acting. A theatrical artist who seeks his repertoire in contemporary drama should not willingly let a line of verse pass his lips. Poetry will scarcely find any place worth mentioning in the drama of the immediate future; for the creative intentions of the future will certainly not be reconciled with it. I myself have during the past seven or eight years hardly written a single verse, but have de-voted myself exclusively to the incomparably more difficult art of writing in the consistently true language of reality.

The new edition of *The Feast at Solhaug* appeared in June, and at the same time Ibsen learned that a sixth edition of *The Pretenders*, one of his steadiest sellers, was in the press. He also heard from Georg Brandes that the latter's most recent essay on him (later published as the 'Second Impression' in Brandes's 1898 book on Ibsen) was to appear in Germany, which must have gratified him, since he re-garded it as the most penetrating and sympathetic study of his work yet to have appeared.

The Ibsens had now begun to hold weekly soirées, and visitors who had been daunted by tales of their prickliness, and of the Webb-like plainness of the fare they had pro-vided in Munich, were often pleasantly surprised. A young Norwegian named Kristian Gløersen who attended these gatherings speaks of Suzannah's 'always ample and taste-fully decorated table, at which a relaxed and witty atmos-phere invariably prevailed', and praises both her and Ibsen's excellence as hosts, their attention to even the humblest guests and their skill at arranging congenial little groups within a party, not always a Scandinavian (or for that matter an English) talent. He also refers to Ibsen's 'personal ami-ability', remarking that 'despite his withdrawnness, his *noli me tangere*, his often chilly mask and eruptions of vehement bitterness, there appeared frequent glimpses of a warmth of heart and of a fine and noble character, doubly winning because of his anxiety to conceal it'. Gunnar Heiberg, too, confirms Ibsen's skill as a host:

It was an especial pleasure to see Ibsen speak with and entertain the many old or aging ladies who came there. He sat down among them and talked of his experiences, his books, his travels. One evening, I well recall, he spoke in great detail to three old ladies about his trip to Egypt. He gesticulated and talked vividly. He let himself be carried away. It was as though he were describing the events for the first time, as though the words were only this moment forming on his lips ... The old ladies' eyes shone with intense gratitude. I remember this sight of Ibsen creeping out of his marble shell in honour of a few old ladies who he thought needed a little sparkle and happiness in their eyes.

Gløersen, who saw a lot of Ibsen in 1882 and 1883, records how he enjoyed, as of old, provoking people by the Socratic use of paradox, often pushing his listeners' arguments to the point of absurdity. He 'liked to be opposed when he came out with his most audacious paradoxes, which were perhaps directed to that end'. Thus, late one night at the Café Nazionale, after a ball at the Scandinavian Club, he declared: 'They should guillotine the bourgeoisie as a hundred years ago in France they guillotined the aristocrats.' No one in Norway who called himself a liberal or a republican was prepared to make any personal sacrifices. They would give nothing, sacrifice nothing, to enable the poor to be equal with them. If it came to the crunch, none of them would man the barricades. There must be a revolution, everything existing must come down, down. 'The Right, did you say? My dear fellow, I want nothing to do with them, one can't count them any longer. They don't belong to the saga of the future. The only useful thing they do is undermine their own position and show us the best way through the ruins. In that respect the reactionaries are our best allies.' No wonder the young Bernard Shaw, to whom William Archer was at this time reading Ibsen's plays, translating off the cuff as he went, felt that he had discovered a kindred spirit.

A similar account of Ibsen in provocative mood that year comes from Ingvald Undset, father of the novelist Sigrid Undset, who wrote home to a friend:

Ibsen is interminably radical; I have now got to know him and his opinions better. One evening I went out with him and the writer N.N., who is also here this winter, to a restaurant. Late at night – somewhere around the sixth glass – Ibsen really started talking, and you should have heard him. Ibsen refuses to acknowledge nationalism or anything any more; he is a complete anarchist, wants to wipe everything out – put a torpedo under the ark – mankind must start from the foundations to rebuild the world – and they must begin with the individual! . . . Society and everything else must be wiped out, wherever it in the smallest degree hampers our work; then possibly some kind of insurance companies may be allowed to emerge in place of the present societies and states. Or else – well, that will be society's problem, to decide what is to emerge; the great task of our age is to blow the existing fabric into the air – to destroy . . . He is remarkable, a titanic character! I mentioned the 'sixth glass', but I don't think Ibsen often drinks that much; only, now and then, when he's with someone he likes talking to, he enjoys going into a café and arguing late into the night. But this happens only seldom, and doesn't affect his life or his serious work.

Dr Undset's comment on Ibsen's drinking habits is confirmed by two reliable observers. William Archer wrote: 'The oft-repeated stories of his over-indulgence in stimulants were, to the best of my belief, such gross exaggerations· as to be practically falsehoods . . . In Germany, in Denmark, in Norway, I have been with him repeatedly, have seen him evidently pursuing his daily habit in the matter of spirituous liquors, and have always noted the moderation of that habit. On one public occasion when it was afterwards spread abroad that he had conspicuously exceeded, I both walked and talked with him, and can positively assert that there was no truth whatever in the scandal.' Bergliot Ibsen confirms

this: 'I have seen him sit for hours on end sipping at a glass
of red wine. In the same way, he used to sip at the famous
glass of brandy at the Grand, which people transformed into
a "regiment of nips". People assumed it must always be a
new glass, since it always seemed full. When in his old age
Ibsen's complexion became ruddy, the gossips found fresh
grist for their mill ... In fact, Ibsen suffered from a nervous
eczema ... When he died his physician, Dr Bull, told me he
had never seen a better preserved constitution.' The idea that
Ibsen was a semi-alcoholic for most of his life is another of
the myths that need to be exploded.

Ibsen was sometimes inclined to hold forth on subjects of
which he was largely ignorant. Thus, Gunnar Heiberg records, he liked to expatiate on science, although

he was ignorant of the most elementary principles thereof ... He
talked of flying machines and electricity with a buoyant enthusiasm which deceived us laymen but shocked professionals, or even
people with a sound general education. A Danish engineer, un-
impressed by Ibsen's literary renown told him in round terms
that he lacked the most elementary knowledge and was talking
plain rubbish. Ibsen did not like this, but continued. It often
seemed as though he preferred to acquire the rudiments of
knowledge in this way rather than by reading, which he did not
much enjoy ... J. P. Jacobsen often shook his head when Ibsen
touched on his particular field of botany; he smiled his wise,
gentle smile and said that he knew many small boys who knew
more about botany than this ex-apothecary.

Heiberg adds, probably correctly, that he felt that 'scientific
phenomena in themselves interested Ibsen less than how the
various people present treated them, the temperament
and tempo with which they dismissed them', Gløersen, too,
noted Ibsen's analytical interest in people's ways of speech;
he would often ask a question *à propos* of nothing, directed
now to a man, now to a woman, to see how they replied. He
once asked Gløersen: 'Have you ever noticed how in conversation a woman usually ends a remark with a word of two
or three syllables, a man with a monosyllable?' Gløersen

thought this absurd, but on testing Ibsen's theory was astonished to find it correct. Ibsen once similarly surprised John Paulsen, before their quarrel, by saying, 'Has it ever occurred to you that the lines in a play should sound different according to whether they are said in the morning or the evening?'

Gløersen noted Ibsen's routine. He liked to take a morning walk up the Via Sistina to Monte Pincio. Between twelve and one he would drop in at the Café Nazionale, where he had a special seat in which he liked to sit, though it was not reserved for him as at the Café Maximilian in Munich and, later, the Grand in Christiania. He was annoyed if he found it occupied. He lunched at two or two-thirty 'since he could not reconcile himself to the custom then most followed abroad of two meals a day, lunch at twelve to one, and dinner at seven to eight.' He often urged Gløersen to settle in Rome, since he knew of nowhere else that was so good for writing. 'Here I can write a book every year,' Ibsen said to him in the euphoric mood of *An Enemy of the People*. 'At home there would be a gap of five years. Why go home and let yourself be button-holed by hundreds of people, scarcely one per cent of whom you have any use for?' He added that (as he had told Laura Kieler) he preferred to live far from Norway when writing a play with a Norwegian setting. 'Life and its phenomena are best viewed by a writer at a distance, in both time and space.' He assured Gløersen that he was quite indifferent to what critics wrote about him, but Suzannah said (in his absence) that this was quite untrue and that he minded a lot.

At the end of June, Ibsen left with Suzannah for Gossensass, and while he was there *Ghosts* received its first European performance. The main Scandinavian theatres still fought shy, but August Lindberg, the young Swede who had found Ibsen so taciturn in Munich three years earlier, and had unsuccessfully tried to persuade Ludvig Josephson to stage the play in Stockholm, asked Ibsen's permission to set up a production to tour Sweden, Norway and Denmark.

Ibsen agreed, adding some advice on the translation: 'The language must sound natural and the mode of expression must be distinctive for every character in the play; one human being does not express himself like another ... The effect of the play depends greatly on the audience feeling that they are listening to something that is actually happening in real life.' He also stressed (a reminder of the immense length of time that nineteenth-century audiences liked to spend in a theatre) that *Ghosts*, 'although only three acts, fills a whole evening', and that 'nothing else must be acted either before or after the play. I should also like this work of mine to be staged everywhere without the employment of an orchestra, either before the performance or during the intervals.'

Ghosts runs (if one allows for two ten-minute intervals) for about two and a half hours, nearly half an hour less than *A Doll's House*, which was itself much shorter than any of his previous plays; one of Ibsen's forgotten contributions to the theatre was to remind audiences of a fact forgotten since the Greeks, that a tragedy need not fill five acts. Strindberg, within the decade, was to prove that it need fill no more than one.

Lindberg coaxed a once-famous actress named Hedvig Charlotte Winter-Hjelm out of retirement to play Mrs Alving and, to prepare himself for the role of Oswald, visited a hospital in Copenhagen to study children who were insane as the result of inherited syphilis.

Down the steps came a procession of the living dead. Small children, lying in their beds and mechanically playing with a little bell which each held in his or her hand. The procession passed on either side of us. Some were carried in nurses' arms, some ran, but most were pushed in their chairs. I bowed to the doctor, ran down the stairs more quickly than I had ascended them, and returned to Hälsingborg. But I never forgot the sight.

The rehearsals had a deeply disturbing effect on the

players. Lindberg himself suffered from repeated nightmares, and when he rehearsed with Fru Winter-Hjelm's
understudy the scene in which Oswald tells his mother of his
illness, the effect was such that she had to leave the stage.

Ghosts opened at Hälsingborg, on the Swedish west
coast, on 22 August 1883. The press and audience came expecting to be scandalized; but the play which respectable
citizens had refused to have on their shelves proved, in performance, to scandalize no one. Lindberg telegraphed
Ludvig Josephson that the atmosphere in the theatre had
been like a 'a new Oberammergau'. The Danish newspaper
Dagbladet's reporter wrote an ecstatic notice and was rewarded with the sack, the editor being of the opinion that no
decent theatre ought to perform the play. Six days later Lindberg's production crossed the Sound and played for ten
nights at the Folketeater in Copenhagen, where the effect
was the same. 'The excitement in the auditorium,' Lindberg
recalled, 'rose as though in small cyclones. Fru Winter-
Hjelm whispered at one stage: "Dare we go on?" ' The audiences found themselves unshocked, moved and gripped, and
the production played to full houses each night at double
the usual prices. '*Ghosts*', wrote Lindberg to Josephson, 'is
causing an excitement which spreads from house and home,
from street and café, to the box-office at Folketeater.'

Josephson, his fears allayed, signed up the production to
visit his theatre in Stockholm in September, where it was so
well received that the Royal Theatre, a few hundred yards
away, followed with a production of its own within the
month. Then on 17 October, Lindberg's company presented
the first performance of *Ghosts* in Norway at, appropriately,
the old Møllergaden theatre where, a quarter of a century
earlier, Ibsen had, as artistic director, suffered his long series
of humiliations. William Archer happened to be in Christiania at the time and attended the première.

I was present, and well remember the profound impression it
made on the crowded and enthusiastic audience. By this time the
reaction in favour of the play had fairly set in. It happened that

on the same evening a trivial French farce, *Tête de Linotte* (known in English as *Miss Featherbrain*) was being played at the Christiania Theatre; and the contrast could not but strike people. They saw a masterpiece of Norwegian literature acted by a foreign (Swedish) company at a minor playhouse, while the official theatre of the capital was given over to a piece of Parisian frivolity. The result was that on the following evening, and for some nights afterwards, demonstrations were made at the Christiania Theatre against the policy of the management in rejecting Ibsen's play ... Fru Winter-Hjelm's performance of Mrs Alving was exceedingly powerful, and Lindberg seemed to me an almost ideal Oswald. In his make-up, I remember, there was a strong suggestion of the portraits of Edgar Allan Poe.

Lindberg himself has left an interesting impression of the Christiania première as it seemed to someone on the other side of the footlights. 'When the curtain was raised, it felt as though the public held its breath. The scenes of the play unfolded in a silence worthy of a spiritual séance. When the final curtain fell, the silence continued for a good while before the ovations started.' The Norwegian Gunnar Heiberg commented: 'Pastor Manders, Engstrand, Helmer and several other gentlemen had leagued together to prevent *Ghosts* from being staged ... A foreigner had to bring us our own play. What the Swede Lindberg did remains one of the great occasions in the history of the Norwegian theatre.' And Lindberg himself wrote to Ibsen:

It was high time that *Ghosts* arrived, for the theatres up here have lived for so long on French comedy that we are well on the way to becoming monkeys instead of men. But now we see the truth, and the clowning and smirking are past. Real tears now fall on the stage, and that with no sense of shame. It is something new and splendid to assist in the re-introduction of nature to the stage.

Altogether, Lindberg's company performed *Ghosts* seventy-five times during this tour, and he returned with the production to Christiania several times over the next few years. The following year, a Danish company toured with the play through the Norwegian provinces (to give them credit, they and another Danish company had applied for permission to stage *Ghosts* before Lindberg had his première), but the main Scandinavian theatres (outside Stockholm) still fought shy, and it was not until 1890, nine years after its publication, that *Ghosts* was acted by a Norwegian company, at the Bergen Theatre. Schrøder, the director of the Christiania Theatre, steadfastly refused to let it be performed there as long as he remained in charge, and it was not played by Norwegians in their own capital until 1900 (when the Christiania Theatre had been replaced by the National Theatre), nor at the Royal Theatre in Copenhagen until 1903. In Germany, police censorship prevented any public performance being given for many years, although a number of private performances took place in various cities after 1886. England and France were not to see the play until the nineties (and no public performance was allowed in England before 1914).

In early October Ibsen left Gossensass for Botzen near the Italian frontier, proceeding to Rome at the end of the month. From Rome, on 30 November, he addressed a final appeal through his old friend O. A. Bachke to the Norwegian Ecclesiastical Department to admit Sigurd into his country's diplomatic service. The way now lay open, he explained, for Sigurd to make a career in the *Italian* foreign service;

but before this can happen, he will have to be naturalized. And this is the step which we find it so difficult to take. To cut oneself wholly off from one's country – that is a serious matter. I, therefore, on my son's behalf, make this last effort to keep him a Norwegian citizen by asking if you would and could extract a promise from the government that my son will be considered for a post as attaché when one next falls vacant . . . I am reluctant to believe that, as some have suggested, I should be such a *bête noir* to certain members of the government that they will totally refuse to meet me in this matter. I know well what I can expect from the head of the Ecclesiastical Department, but fortunately his voice is not decisive in this case.

The likelihood of any politician doing Ibsen a favour after *An Enemy of the People* must have seemed more than ever remote; but who can foretell the ways of statesmen? Bachke lost his job as Minister of Justice the following spring, so Ibsen approached the Prime Minister, Sverdrup, and when the following summer Sigurd called on Sverdrup in Christiania he so impressed him that Sverdrup pulled the necessary strings. So Sigurd got into the Norwegian consular service and remained a Norwegian. Future prime ministers, unfortunately, were less ready than Sverdrup to appreciate Sigurd's qualities.

So 1883 ended. Thanks mainly to the various productions of *An Enemy of the People*, which brought in £480, it had been a better year: he had earned £819. In the same year Henry Arthur Jones, an indifferent English playwright who had just achieved his first success with a melodrama called *The Silver King* (and who that winter was to adapt *A Doll's House* for the English stage), earned £3,398.

1884 began with a letter from Bjørnson urging Ibsen yet again to return and take over the directorship of the Christiania Theatre. But the offer held even less attraction for him than when it had last been made, and he replied on 9 January:

My experiences and memories of the theatre in Norway are not such that I feel any inclination to repeat them. I might, it is true, sense some twinge of duty and responsibility in this connection if I thought I could achieve anything of value for our theatre; but of that I have the gravest doubts. Our actors, etc., are demoralized, they will not accept discipline and unqualified obedience, besides which we have a press which is always ready to champion rebels against their leader. This is the main reason why we, unlike other countries where anarchic tendencies are less developed, can never achieve any real ensemble playing. I don't think I could improve matters in this respect; it is too closely tied up with our whole national attitude towards life; and anyway, my liking for the practicalities of theatre work is too small ... I am by no means sure how sincerely the Christiania public feels any need for good theatre. The packed houses on which the operettas and equestrian performances at Tivoli can always rely, and the interest with which dilettante productions of students and shop assistants are received there, seem to me to indicate a cultural outlook that is not yet ripe to appreciate genuine dramatic art.

Ibsen's visits to Norway had not mellowed his attitude towards his compatriots.

His new play, for which he had laid the first plans over six months earlier, had made negligible progress. 'I have had one of those periods', he wrote to Laura Grundtvig on 22 January, 'when I can only with the greatest reluctance sit down at my desk. But today I have been out and bought new paper, new ink and new pens in honour of a new play which I have been turning over in my mind.' Yet he seems to have done nothing for the next three months but make notes; it was 20 April before he began to write any dialogue.

On 8 February 1884 Ibsen was acted in Russian for the first time (though he had been performed in Russia in Polish and also in Finnish), when *A Doll's House* was staged in St Petersburg. But the play seems to have made less impact there than in other countries, and it was to be eight years before they staged another of his plays.

That spring Ibsen came as near as he ever did to meeting Strindberg. 'Surely I should visit Ibsen in Rome?' wrote Strindberg on 12 February from Ouchy in Switzerland to Bjørnson and Jonas Lie, who were together in Paris. 'Will you be kind enough to ask him to receive me, for if he shows me the door I shall feel hurt? I want to see the angriest man in Europe before I die!' But although Strindberg set off for Italy on 1 March he got no farther than Genoa, where the weather was so bad that he turned in a temper for home. 'All water is blue when the sky is blue,' he wrote to his friend Carl Larsson on 8 March. 'Eva [his children's nursemaid] and I have searched in vain for that damned blue in both

sky and water. Humbug, Sir![1] The olive trees are horribly
grey. The landscape like a garden and uglier than the oil
paintings. Pine trees are the same everywhere. And the
people? Moleskin and slouch hats! Not at all picturesque,
old chap! The old houses daubed with red, green and yellow!
... The whole coast here is occupied by factories and wharves
so that we can't get to the beach. The hills covered with
villas! Nature is dead here! No walks possible! The roads
dusty! Oh, how dusty it is here!' At least it does not seem
to have rained much; still, it is a sad thought that had the
sun shone in north Italy that week, a meeting would probably have taken place between these two extraordinary men,
and one suspects that they might have got on rather well,
for Strindberg, when his black mood was not on him, was a
tremendous charmer, and he was the kind of emotional individualist (like Brandes) whom Ibsen found stimulating. And
when Ibsen liked someone and put his own charm forward,
there were few who could resist him. Who but Strindberg
would have been unlucky enough to spend a spring week in
Italy without seeing the sun? By August, sadly, his hostility
towards Ibsen as a champion of feminism had become set,
and he was describing the latter's writing as 'swinish'.

Meanwhile, on 3 March, Ibsen's name had appeared for
the first time (apart from that single matinée of *The Pillars
of Society* in 1880) in the West End of London, though scarcely in a manner to cause him joy. Henry Arthur Jones,
together with a collaborator named Henry Herman who had
helped him with *The Silver King*, had been approached by
the Polish actress Helena Modjeska to adapt *A Doll's House*
into English. Between them they produced an even freer
adaptation than the one seen in America, and re-entitled
it

BREAKING A BUTTERFLY
(Founded on Ibsen's *Norah*)

1. The words 'Humbug, Sir!' are in English; Strindberg, unlike
Ibsen, was an accomplished linguist, and mixed up all his languages
in his letters.

and presented it at the Prince's Theatre in Coventry Street (now the Prince of Wales's Theatre). Harley Granville Barker gives an interesting account of their improvements on the text:

The scene is laid in some English town. Nora becomes Flora and, to her husband, rather terribly, Flossie. He is Humphrey Goddard and we find him gifted with a mother (quite unnecessarily) and a sister (wanted for the piano-playing, *vice* Mrs Linde, who disappears). The morbid Dr Rank is replaced by a Charles-his-friend, called, as if to wipe out every trace of his original, Ben Birdseye! He is not in love with Nora-Flora, of course; that would never do. But Dunkley, alias Krogstad, had loved her as a girl, when Humphrey Goddard stole her young heart from him; so love has turned to hate and revenge is sweet. Observe the certainty with which our operators in the English market fasten on the flawed streak in Ibsen's play and cheapen it still further. The tarantella episode, of course, will be the making of the whole affair (such was many people's judgement then, and now we find it rather marring), and this is left intact. But the third act sees the parent play stood deliberately on its head, and every ounce of Ibsen emptied out of it. Burlesque could do no more. Torvald-Humphrey behaves like the pasteboard hero of Nora's doll's-house dream; he *does* strike his chest and say: 'I am the guilty one!' And Nora-Flora cries that she is a poor weak foolish girl, '. . . no wife for a man like you. You are a thousand times too good for me,' and never wakes up and walks out of her doll's house at all.

A distinguished cast had been assembled, including Kyrle Bellew as Goddard/Helmer, Beerbohm Tree as Dunkley/Krogstad, and Alice Lingard as Nora/Flora. 'The result', noted William Archer, 'was à nice little play, standing to *Et Dukkehjem* somewhat in the relation of Mr Gilbert's *Gretchen* to Goethe's *Faust*; and even so, it did not succeed.'

Such was the introduction of Ibsen to the English theatre – a single matinée of *The Pillars of Society* in 1880, and this scarcely recognizable perversion of *A Doll's House* in 1884, from which, needless to say, Ibsen did not receive a penny.

Apart from an amateur charity performance of *A Doll's House* the following year, there were to be no further productions of Ibsen in England before 1889, when the dramatist was sixty-one. Two years after the Prince's Theatre travesty, however, there was a private reading of *A Doll's House* with, in retrospect, though none of the names meant anything then, a distinguished cast. This, according to Bernard Shaw, took place 'on a first floor in a Bloomsbury lodging-house. Karl Marx's youngest daughter played Nora Helmer; and I impersonated Krogstad at her request, with a very vague notion of what it was all about.' The date was 15 January 1886 and the place 55 Great Russell Street, opposite the British Museum. One would like to know whether Eleanor Marx-Aveling, shortly to translate (rather badly) *An Enemy of the People* and *The Wild Duck*, ever mentioned Ibsen to her father before he died in 1883.

On 20 April Ibsen began writing *The Wild Duck* and by 28 April (each act of the manuscript is dated) he had completed the first act. On 2 May he began Act Two; but when he was halfway through it he stopped, and started to rewrite the play from the beginning. By 24 May he had completed Acts One and Two in their new form. The last three acts took him less than a week each: 25–30 May, 2–8 June, and 9–13 June – a measure of how carefully he had worked the play out in his mind before putting pen to paper. On 14 June he wrote to Hegel:

I am glad to be able to tell you that yesterday I completed the draft of my new play. It comprises five acts and will, as far as I can calculate, occupy some 200 printed pages, perhaps a little more. It still remains for me to make the fair copy, and I shall start on that tomorrow. As usual, however, this will involve not just copying the draft but a comprehensive rewriting of the dialogue. So it will take time. Still, unless some unforeseen obstacle presents itself I reckon the whole manuscript should be in your hands by mid-September. The play doesn't touch on political or social problems, or indeed any matters of public import. It takes place entirely within the confines of family life. I dare say it will arouse some discussion; but it can't offend anyone.

As so often, his optimism was to prove unfounded.

This 'comprehensive rewriting' he described more precisely in a letter of 27 June to Theodor Caspari, a young poet who had addressed a lyric to him, as 'the more energetic individualizing of the characters and of their modes of expression' – a problem, which, as we have seen, particularly obsessed him. He added a remark which contains the central theme of *The Wild Duck*. Caspari had evidently taken Ibsen up on the latter's abandonment and apparent condemnation of verse, and Ibsen replied:

You are quite wrong in supposing that I should wish you to break your lyre ... I have long ceased to make universal demands of people because I no longer believe that one has any inherent right to pose such demands. I believe that none of us can have any higher aim in life than to realize ourselves in spirit and in truth. That, in my view, is the true meaning of liberalism, and that is why the so-called liberals are in so many ways repugnant to me.

One of the central characters in *The Wild Duck* was to be just such a 'so-called liberal', making blind 'universal' demands of people and so destroying their illusions and their happiness. Ibsen concluded his letter:

To find the necessary peace and solitude for this work, I am going in a few days up to Gossensass in the Tyrol. My wife and son will, at the same time, leave for Norway. Would I could have come with them! But it must not be. At my age one must use all one's time for work; one will never finish it all. One 'will not find time to finish the last verse';[2] but one wants to get down as much as possible.

2. A quotation from Holberg's *Jacob von Thyboe*, the Cyrano-like hero of which play needs only one word, rhyming with 'fool', to finish his letter to his beloved.

Ibsen left Rome on 30 June, and stayed a full four months in Gossensass. It was the longest period he had been separated from Suzannah during the twenty-six years of their marriage, and is consequently the best documented, for he wrote to her and Sigurd almost weekly.

Gossensass, 4 July 1884

Dear Suzannah!

Thank you for your card from Basel, which I received this noon. Your cards from Rome arrived yesterday, together with a couple of newspapers. Of the last-named I have so far received only *one* number of *Dagbladet* direct from Christiania, nothing from *Aftenposten*, though I informed them in good time of my change of address. The scoundrels at *Aftenposten* are of course too conservative to change an address,[3] and from their drunken friends at *Dagbladet* one can expect nothing but chaos and Norwegian slovenliness.

I am happy that you have reached Basel safely, and I trust that by tomorrow, or perhaps even today, you will reach Copenhagen.

As far as I am concerned, all is as it should be. The journey here was as usual; from Modena by night, and as far as Ala, I had to keep my overcoat on; thereafter I didn't need it; exceptionally beautiful weather and fresh air all the way up the valley here. The sandwiches proved most useful: they were my only food throughout the journey; I ate the last in Verona, for breakfast, with a cup of black coffee which was brought to me in the compartment; in Florence I had taken only half a bottle of wine, at Ala in the morning nothing; I shall always take sandwiches when I travel; I can eat them with pleasure at any time.

I was heartily welcomed here, but they were much surprised at my arriving alone. I chose the isolated room upstairs in the little annexe, similar to the one Sigurd had downstairs in previous years; no verandah outside, as this room does not stretch so far, and no connecting door with the next room, so that no noise is audible; I am excellently contented here.

Hitherto I have risen at 6.30, breakfasted in my room half an

3. *Aftenposten*, originally an unpolitical newspaper, had recently become right-wing, like *Morgenbladet*. *Dagbladet* and *Verdens Gang* represented the left.

hour later, gone out while they do the room, and then written from 9–1. Then lunch with a ravenous appetite. In the afternoons, too, I have managed to write a little, or at any rate do groundwork. The second act will be ready in five or six days. I am not drinking any beer; which suits me well. But I am drinking milk and a little – not much – white wine, with water. A light evening meal at 7.30. So far I have been in bed each evening by 10, and have been sleeping well.

He bade them 'profit from the good, nourishing Norwegian food', and to eat much fish, especially salmon; and announced that 'I have had to give up the white Tyrol wine, which did not suit me, and now drink an excellent Hungarian Carlowitzer which, surprisingly enough, costs exactly the same.' Pedantically, he noted his changes of routine:

In the morning I drink tea at seven o'clock precisely; rise each day at six at the latest, often earlier, and find this suits me excellently, though I do not now retire before eleven. For my admirable, isolated and peaceful room I pay this year only 60 kreutzer a day. All my expenses, including tobacco and laundry, come to 50 francs a week. Each Sunday morning I change a 50-lire note, and manage with that until exactly the following Sunday.[4]

His peace was disturbed by a hailstorm, which he describes in this same letter of 20 July:

The hail flew straight through the windows of the dining-room as we sat there; such was their force that they did not smash the panes but made round holes in them of their own size. And what a size! Many were larger than the largest hen's eggs I have ever seen; we collected a lot of them; they were of the hardest ice and polished like glass; I made pencil outlines of two of them. At midnight a new storm burst, and a third at 3 a.m. The church bells rang, incessantly, and most of the guests here stayed up all night; at three I too arose; but then went back to bed. The

4. In 1884 the Austrian gulden (100 kreutzer) was worth 8p, so that Ibsen's room cost him only 5p a night. The exchange rate of the French and Swiss francs and the Italian lira was in each case approximately 25.45 to the pound; thus his other expenses (including food) came to under £2 a week.

two following days we had heavy rain and yesterday, Saturday, morning there was a real cloudburst; towards noon the Eisach overflowed its banks ... and threatened Gossensass where, however, in the end all turned out well. Further down things were worse. You remember the little stream which comes from '*Wasserfall*' and flows out under the road to Sterzing, just at the curve where there stands a cross to a murdered man. This stream became a mighty, powerful and destructive current, carrying away the highway so that the whole bend is now a great gaping abyss. The railway beneath got covered with mud so that yesterday the trains from the north could not reach here. All the southbound passengers had to seek refuge in our hotel, where a great disturbance resulted.

Young Marcus Grønvold, the painter, had joined him, and his appetite worried Ibsen ('I think he must be suffering from some kind of illness'). An English lady fell and broke her leg, a schoolboy from Berlin cut his hand badly. He warned Suzannah and Sigurd not to bathe ('The water is cold and can easily bring on a fatal attack of cramp'), not to stand behind the horses of Trondhjem 'which are well known for their habit of kicking', and, above all, to avoid anyone carrying a gun. 'In almost every Norwegian newspaper I read of accidents caused by the careless use of loaded rifles. I shall be exceedingly displeased if you do not keep well away from people carrying such weapons. Should an accident happen I must be informed immediately by telegram.' His vanity was gratified by his noticing that 'several copies of Passarge's book about me, and of Brandes's essay in *Nord und Süd*, accompanied by an excellent engraving of my likeness, are circulating among the guests. Almost all of them, I suppose, know my plays in German.' Ludwig Passarge himself paid a visit with his wife; they 'said they only live and breathe in my books'. Grønvold's appetite continued to worry him. 'It is not just that he eats excessive quantities; everything must be of the best and most expensive, and that for both lunch and dinner; he spends twice as much each day as I do.'

Meanwhile, he worked steadily revising *The Wild Duck*,

taking about a fortnight over each act. On 2 September he
was able to write to Hegel:

I enclose the manuscript of my new play, *The Wild Duck*,
which has occupied me daily for the past four months, and from
which I cannot now part without a certain feeling of loss. The
characters in it have, despite their many failings, grown dear to
me as a result of this long daily association. But I cherish the
hope that they will also find good friends and well-wishers
among the great reading public and, not least, among theatre
people; for they all, without exception, offer rewarding opportunities. But the study and representation of them will not be
easy ... This new play occupies, in some ways, a unique position
among my dramatic works. Its method differs in certain respects
from that which I have previously employed. However, I don't
wish to enlarge on that here. The critics will, I trust, see this for
themselves; they will anyway find something to argue about,
something to construe. I believe, too, that *The Wild Duck* may
possibly tempt some of our younger dramatists to explore new
territories, and this I regard as a desirable thing.

In the middle of September, Ibsen received the letter he
had been awaiting for so many years: an invitation from
Bjørnson to visit him and his wife at Schwaz, where they
were holidaying, two or three hours by rail from Gossensass.
Bjørnson had got to know Strindberg in Paris the previous
December, and had spent the spring raising funds for him as
energetically as, twenty years earlier, he had done for Ibsen.
Ibsen accepted his invitation eagerly; so, for the first time in
nearly twenty years, these two old friends and enemies met,
and spent three days together. Ibsen described the occasion
in a letter to Suzannah on 17 September:

I would not for anything have missed this meeting. I will be
better able to tell you the details when we meet; here I shall
merely mention a few external circumstances. Bjørnson and his
son met me at the station; a room was prepared for me at the
Gasthaus where they are staying; but I preferred to lodge at
another hotel where, likewise, there awaited me for the occasion
an enormous room, very handsome and comfortable. At the

hotel I of course paid for my board and breakfast; but I ate lunch and dinner with the Bjørnsons and was with them for almost the whole of the rest of the time; they could not do enough for me. Bjørnson has gone grey, but looks strong. Fru B. is likewise somewhat greyed, and has grown rather deaf, but in other respects is as bright and lively as before and has developed into an excellent person. Both their daughters are uncommonly handsome, well brought up, unaffected and straightforward; I also much like Erling, their son. I did not see Jonas Lie, since he is so far behind with his novel. But this meant that B. and I were able to talk all the more undisturbed, and this we did, about political, literary, and many other matters. B. was often much struck by my remarks and frequently returned to them. In one respect I have, by my visit, prevented a true misfortune from befalling our country. But I don't want to put anything on paper about this . . .[5]

Here everything is as usual; many of the summer guests have now departed; but there are still a lot here, and newcomers arrive daily for brief visits. The weather is now as warm and beautiful as one could wish . . . Frøken Schirmer from Munich is occupying herself with spiritism [*sic*], or whatever it is called. She has the power of being able, by touching another person, to make her do what she wishes. Here she found a very ready medium in a Frøken von Pfeuffer, a nervous young lady, with whom she has undertaken a series of the most unlikely experiments, and subsequently with other people; she has now left.

This is the first reference in Ibsen's writings to an interest which was becoming widespread in Europe at this time and which was to manifest itself powerfully in Ibsen's next four plays: the ability of one human being to gain a supernatural power over the mind of another. Sigmund Freud, then a young neurologist of twenty-eight, had already seen hypnotism therapeutically used and probably made his own first experiments with it the following year; and Strindberg was to employ it with terrifying effect in his play *Creditors* three years later.

5. The nature of this national calamity which Ibsen claimed to have averted has never been identified; Halvdan Koht thinks it may have been a projected blind attack on the left-wing government.

'Schwaz', continued Ibsen's letter to Suzannah, 'is quite a town, with six thousand inhabitants. It was generally known there that I was visiting B., and the locals saluted us when we appeared, whether together or singly. One family sent Fru B. a fine haunch of venison, another game, others had sent excellent Moselle, and yet others old rum and other good things. I saw friendly, contented faces in the doors of the shops and in the windows round about. There has been a lot written about me in the newspapers of Innsbruck and other Tyrolean towns this summer.' One of Bjørnson's daughters, Bergliot, aged sixteen, particularly impressed him. When he saw Suzannah he told her: 'Now I have seen Sigurd's future wife', and he was to be proved right.

Bjørnson gave his impressions of their encounter in a letter to Hegel. 'Ibsen', he wrote (21 September), 'is now a good, well-meaning old gentleman, with whom I disagreed on many points regarding ends and means, but with whom it was in the highest degree interesting to exchange views. His intellect, circumspection and wisdom are remarkable. Yet his intelligence is not of the all-round kind, any more than his knowledge.' He expanded this last observation in a letter to Jonas Lie. 'You and I see more, and we see it better. Our intellectualism is incomparably greater. But he so adjusts himself to his that it gives a pretty good dividend.' Bjørnson was not far from the truth; Ibsen's intelligence was, like that of so many creative writers, intuitive and limited; he lacked many of the advantages of a trained mind; on many aspects of life and knowledge he was, as we have seen, almost childishly ignorant. Yet great creative minds are often thus: of Ibsen's contemporaries, Tolstoy, Dickens, Dostoyevsky, Herman Melville and Tennyson shared equal areas of ignorance and blindness.

Unfortunately for Bjørnson, no sooner had he become reconciled with Ibsen than he fell out with his new friend Strindberg. Strindberg, who was prosecuted that autumn for alleged blasphemy in his volume of short stories, *Marriage*, resented some fatherly advice Bjørnson chose to offer him,

and poked fun at the latter's new play, *A Gauntlet*, for demanding that men should, like women, stay chaste until
marriage – a particularly incongruous suggestion from a
man hardly famous for marital fidelity. 'Be immoral,
Bjørnson, as you were when you were young!' Strindberg
exhorted him on 14 October 1884. 'The virtue which comes
when a man is fifty is not worth preaching!' The advice was
no better received than Bjørnson's to Strindberg had
been.

The renewal of acquaintance between Ibsen and
Bjørnson did not lead to a complete reconciliation. Karl
Konow, who knew them both, was probably right when he
wrote: 'They respected and venerated each other, they met
and talked, but never more than that . . . Several times I have
heard [Bjørnson] express regret that he could not get closer
to him, and I think Ibsen felt the same. But the differences
were too great. They could talk together, but not feel
together. In a way they enjoyed each other's company, but
they did not understand each other.'

As there was an outbreak of cholera in Italy, Ibsen stayed
in Gossensass until the end of October. Suzannah and
Sigurd joined him there in the middle of the month ('Should
the weather be bad, stormy or foggy when you leave Christiania', he had warned them on 24 September, as neurotic
about their safety as he was about his own, 'do not take the
steamer but go by land via Sweden.'). Sigurd had learned on
his return to Christiania that his appeal to Sverdrup had
been successful, and that he had been appointed to the
consular office in Stockholm; he stayed only a few days with
his father before returning north. Thoughts of a new play
had already begun to crystallize in Ibsen's mind. 'I felt
pretty nervous and overstrained when I had finished my
manuscript', he wrote to Hegel on 18 October, 'and decided
to rest for a year. But this will not happen. I have already
worked out plans for a new play in four acts and hope, before
long, when I have settled down in Rome, to be able to start
work on it.' On 1 November he and Suzannah left Gos-

sensass and, after a few days at Botzen, arrived back in Rome on 13 November.

Two days earlier, *The Wild Duck* had been published, in a printing of 8,000 copies, 2,000 less than *Ghosts* and *An Enemy of the People* (but this was probably due to the fact that there had been a recession in the book trade rather than to any fear that it might prove less popular than its predecessors). The reaction among the critics and the reading public was principally one of bewilderment – which, indeed, was to be the general reaction to his remaining plays. Modern opinion regards these eight final plays as Ibsen's greatest period, or at any rate greater than the middle period of his 'social dramas' from *The Pillars of Society* to *An Enemy of the People*. His contemporaries in Scandinavia felt otherwise. From now on, we find him repeatedly accused of being a 'riddling Sphinx', of being obscure for obscurity's sake, and of concentrating on the sordid. Only his increasing fame abroad saved his reputation from going into a sharp decline at home.

'The public does not know what to make of it,' commented the *Christiania Intelligenssedler* on *The Wild Duck*. 'One paper says one thing and the other just the opposite.' *Aftenposten* complained: 'One may study and study to find what Ibsen wants to say and not find it.' *Morgenbladet* found the plot, 'as queer as it is thin ... One has an undeniable impression of something artificial and contrived ... The total impression can hardly be other than a strong sense of emptiness and unpleasantness.' Georg Brandes did not review it, but he confided to J. P. Jacobsen that '*The Wild Duck* was only a half-pleasure,' and he never rated it among Ibsen's masterpieces. 'Ibsen's [book] made a glum impression on me,' he wrote to Alexander Kielland on 13 November. 'I thought it rather empty. Why bother exclusively with such totally insignificant people? His contempt for humanity seems perpetually on the increase.'

Again, however, we must remember that the young, to whom Ibsen principally appealed, were inadequately (if at all) represented among the critics. Carl Georgsson Fleetwood in Stockholm must have been speaking for many of his generation when he noted in his diary on 7 December 1884 that *The Wild Duck* was all the more exciting ('A new book by Ibsen is always an exciting event') because he had heard it described as inferior 'by the very people who sing the praise of "fearless" Ibsen – probably because he has been fearless enough to expose the nakedness of the new gods too!'

Across the North Sea, Ibsen's English admirers were as baffled as their Scandinavian counterparts. Edmund Gosse condemned it four years later in the *Fortnightly Review* as 'a strange, melancholy and pessimistic drama, almost without a ray of light from beginning to end ... There is really not a character in the book that inspires confidence or liking ... There can be no doubt that it is by far the most difficult of Ibsen's dramas to comprehend.' William Archer also failed to understand it at first (though he came to admire it greatly once he had seen it staged). Arthur Symons thought it 'a play of inferior quality', and Havelock Ellis dismissed it as 'the least remarkable' of Ibsen's recent plays. Almost the only British critic (Ireland being then a part of Britain) to see the point of the play during the next ten years was Bernard Shaw, who devoted to it one of his most penetrating passages in *The Quintessence of Ibsenism*:

After *An Enemy of the People*, Ibsen ... left the vulgar ideals for dead and set about the exposure of those of the choicer spirits, beginning with the incorrigible idealists who had idealized his very self, and were becoming known as Ibsenites. His first move in this direction was such a tragi-comic slaughtering of sham Ibsenism that his astonished victims plaintively declared that *The Wild Duck*, as the new play was called, was a satire on his former works; while the pious, whom he had disappointed so severely by his interpretation of *Brand* ... began to hope that he was coming back repentant to the fold.

Shaw concluded with a remark which strikes surely to the heart of the play: 'the busybody [Gregers] finds that people cannot be freed from their failings from without. They must free themselves.'

Despite the general bewilderment, however, the book sold remarkably well in Scandinavia. Four days after publication *Dagbladet* announced that the first edition had sold out, and a second impression of two thousand copies was in the shops by early December. The principal Scandinavian theatres wasted no time in buying the performing rights, and productions were already in rehearsal in Christiania, Bergen, Copenhagen, Stockholm and Helsinki. 'If there is any living dramatist', reported Erik Bøgh, the censor of the Royal Theatre in Copenhagen, to his board on 17 November, 'whose plays the public demand to see performed, whose earlier plays have brought so much honour and profit as to pioneer a path for his successors . . . it must, before all others, be Henrik Ibsen . . . *The Wild Duck* is in all respects executed with his unique mastery'; and he concluded, unfashionably, by declaring that the play had 'a demonstrably healthy moral attitude'.

On 14 November Ibsen addressed a letter to Hans Schrøder, of the Christiania Theatre, which is full of sharp practical observations invaluable to any modern director of the play. Foreseeing the danger that whoever acted Hjalmar Ekdal might be tempted to play him as a figure of fun (a temptation which too few actors have resisted, just as too many have played Gregers as spiteful), Ibsen warned Schrøder:

Hjalmar must not be acted with any trace of parody. The actor must never for a moment show that he is conscious that there is anything funny in what he says. His voice has, as Relling observes, something endearing about it, and this quality must be clearly brought out. His sentimentality is honest, his melancholy, in its way, attractive; no hint of affectation. Between ourselves, I would suggest you cast your mind towards Kristofer Janson, who still contrives to give an effect of beauty whatever drivel he may be uttering. There is a pointer for whoever plays the part . . . Where can one find a Hedvig? I don't know. And Mrs Sørby?

She must be beautiful and witty, not vulgar ... Gregers is the most difficult part in the play, from the acting point of view. Sometimes I think Hammer would be best, sometimes Bjørn B[jørnson] ... I hope you will spare me Isachsen, as he always carries on like some strange actor instead of like an ordinary human being.[6] However, I suppose he might possibly make something out of Molvik's few lines. The two servants must not be cast too casually; Petersen might possibly be played by Bucher, and Jensen by Abelsted, if the latter is not required for one of the dinner guests. Yes, those guests! What about them? You can't just use ordinary extras; they'd ruin the whole act ... The play demands absolute naturalness and truthfulness both in the ensemble work and in the staging. The lighting, too, is important; it is different for each act, and is calculated to establish the peculiar atmosphere of that act. I just wanted to pass on these random reflections. As regards everything else, please do as you think best.

Wherein does the 'method' of *The Wild Duck* differ, as Ibsen told Hegel, from that which he had previously employed? At first sight there is no immediately obvious difference; it seems, like *A Doll's House, Ghosts* and *An Enemy of the People*, to be a realistic play about realistic people, and the method seems to be his old method of raking over apparently dead ashes and exposing the live embers beneath. The symbolism? But Ibsen had used symbolism at least as freely in *Brand*.

Nevertheless, I think there is little doubt that it was the symbolism in *The Wild Duck* to which Ibsen was referring when he spoke of a new method. In *Brand* the symbols are incidental to the play, or at any rate are not fully integrated into it. The Ice Church and the hawk are left deliberately imprecise; there is room for intelligent argument about their

6. Schrøder ignored Ibsen's plea regarding Isachsen and cast him as Relling, in which role he proved a disaster. 'I hear from reliable sources', wrote Ibsen to Schrøder on 30 December 1886, 'that by his lunatic conception and dreadful performance ... he ruined the whole effect of the play.'

meanings; perhaps, indeed, they are intended to mean different things to different people, like the symbols of Kafka. In *The Wild Duck*, however, there is a single and precise symbol, that of the bird itself; and, so far from being incidental to the play, it is the hub and heart of it. *Brand* is a play into which symbols have worked their way; *The Wild Duck* is a play dependent on, and held together by, a symbol; as though the wild duck were a magnet and the characters in the play so many iron filings held together by this centripetal force. This was not a method that Ibsen was to use invariably in his subsequent plays; *Rosmersholm*, for example, and *Hedda Gabler*, have more in common (as regards their symbolism) with *Ghosts* than with *The Wild Duck*. But we find him returning to it in his later plays: the towers and spires of *The Master Builder* and the crutch in *Little Eyolf* serve a similar structural purpose to the wild duck. They are images from which the characters cannot escape, any more than the iron filings can escape the magnet.

Ibsen probably borrowed the image of the wild duck from a poem by Welhaven called 'The Sea-Bird' which describes how a wild duck is wounded and dives down to die on the sea-bed; and Professor Francis Bull suggests that he may also have been influenced by Darwin's account in *The Origin of Species* of how wild ducks degenerate in captivity. Some astonishing theories have been advanced as to what the bird is intended to stand for. Surely Ibsen makes it abundantly clear that he intended it as a double symbol with two precise and obvious references. Firstly, it is, like Hedvig, a by-product of Haakon Werle's fondness for sport which has been rejected by him and is now cared for by the Ekdal family (at any rate in Hjalmar's eyes, though we never know, any more than Gina does, which of the two men is the father).[7] Secondly, with a more general application, it represents the refusal of most people, once they have been

7. Gina's answer to Hjalmar in Act Four ('I don't know ... I – couldn't tell') is open to several interpretations. I take it to mean that she was irregular in her periods, missed one soon after Werle had slept

wounded, to go on living and face reality. Both Hjalmar and
his father have sought to hide themselves in the deep blue sea
of illusion, and Gregers, like the 'damned clever dog' trained
by his father, hauls them back to the surface. The cynics,
Relling and Haakon Werle, watch this operation; so do the
two sensible, earthbound women, Gina and Mrs Sørby.
These women, Ibsen seems to imply, offer the only real
refuge: love. Mrs Sørby can save Haakon Werle, despite
Gregers's cynicism, just as she could have saved Relling, who
had also once loved her; Relling knows this, and it is hinted
that the loss of her is partly responsible for his having
turned into a drunkard. And Gina, if Gregers had not intervened, could have saved Hjalmar. Yet Ibsen leaves a question mark here: is love simply another illusion, like the
Ekdals' loft? And if so, then is not the illusion of the loft
justified, just as much as the illusion of love?

At the same time, while the wild duck has these two
specific significances within the play, it is possible that, consciously or unconsciously, it reflects Ibsen's impression of
himself when he wrote it: one who has forgotten what it
means to live wild, and has grown plump and tame and content with his basket, as unlike the author of *Brand* as the
duck is unlike the hawk of the earlier play, of which, likewise, the climax is a shot fired at (or supposedly at) a bird by
a girl of fourteen. How far, Ibsen must have asked himself –
and he was to ask the question again through Allmers in
Little Eyolf and Rubek in *When We Dead Awaken* – does
the artist, like the Ekdals, shut himself off from life? Is his
world so very different from their loft with its imitations of
reality? Which is the more cowardly refuge, the Ekdals' loft
or Brand's Ice Church?

Hjalmar seems to have had several models – Kristofer
Janson, the writer whom Ibsen had known in Rome, Edvard
Larsen, a photographer with whom Ibsen had lodged in ear-

---

with her, told him, he introduced her to Hjalmar, they slept together
at once or almost at once, and so the child could be either man's.

lier days, Magnus Bagge, a failed artist from whom he had taken drawing lessons around 1860 and who is said to have had a constant longing to lift himself above everyday prose (when he went to live in Germany he called himself von Bagge), and a sculptor in Rome, C. D. Magelssen, who was always talking of a great invention he was about to perfect which would revolutionize the craft of casting in bronze and also, in some strange way, the manufacture of torpedoes. Gregers Werle was at first (as we know from Ibsen's notes for the play) based on the novelist and playwright Alexander Kielland, whose radicalism Ibsen regarded as bogus, but he gradually developed into a kind of *reductio ad absurdum* of Dr Stockmann, a living illustration of the danger of a single-minded pursuit of truth if not tempered by common sense and an understanding of human limitations. More importantly, Hjalmar and Gregers both represent different aspects of Ibsen himself: on the one hand the evader of reality, on the other the impractical idealist who pesters mankind with his 'claims of the ideal' because he has a sick conscience and despises himself. How far, one wonders, did Ibsen identify himself with Gregers in that curious episode when the latter, finding that the stove smokes, throws water on it to put out the fire and only makes the stink worse? He had already portrayed these two conflicting aspects of himself in *Brand* and *Peer Gynt*, and the conflict between Gregers and Hjalmar is as though Brand and Peer Gynt had been brought face to face.

There is one other respect in which the method of *The Wild Duck* was, or seemed, new, and that was the way in which tragedy and comedy tread on each other's heels. This was one of the things about the play which so upset its contemporaries, though it delighted Bernard Shaw – 'to look on with horror and pity at a profound tragedy, shaking with laughter all the time at an irresistible comedy', as he wrote of the 1897 London production in the *Saturday Review*. Ibsen instinctively knew what Shakespeare and the Greeks knew, and what Brecht was to remind playgoers of, that if

you want to make a tragic event really hurt you must precede it with comedy, a Porter jesting as he leads the night
visitors to Duncan's death-chamber, a Grave-Digger who
jokes in Ophelia's grave, a Clown to carry the asp to Cleopatra. This was a lesson which had been forgotten by dramatists; and if Ibsen was referring to this when he said it would
be easier for him than for younger dramatists to attempt
this effect, critical reaction was to prove him right.

As a postscript to *The Wild Duck*, one may remark how,
as in almost every play he wrote, Ibsen anticipated one of the
main discoveries of modern psychology. 'Liberation', he had
noted in his preliminary jottings for the play, 'consists in
securing for individuals the right to free themselves, each
according to his particular need.' To free *themselves*; how
many of Ibsen's contemporaries who regarded themselves as
revolutionaries realized that? Ibsen understood that the
demand must come from within, and that truth, if it comes
from without, is often regarded as an attack on the defensive
system which the 'life-lie', as Relling called it, represents.

The good book sales of *The Wild Duck* saved 1884 from
being one of Ibsen's worst years financially, for he had made
barely £100 from performing rights and had had only one
earlier play reprinted. Of his total income of £688, the two
editions of *The Wild Duck* contributed £517. Nevertheless,
he asked Hegel (23 November) to buy him 'good, sound securities' to the face value of £222, and on 10 January in the
New Year gave his agent in Christiania, Nils Lund, instructions that the first £167 of the fees due to him from the
Bergen and Christiania theatres for *The Wild Duck*, 'plus
my pension and whatever else may come', should be held
and paid out in instalments to Sigurd in Stockholm.

PART FIVE

The Explorer of the Unconscious

23

Rosmersholm
1885–6

BERGEN proudly staged the world première of *The Wild Duck* on 9 January 1885, Christiania, Helsinki and Stockholm following suit within the month, and Copenhagen in February. The audiences were, for the most part, as bewildered as the critics had been. However unpleasant the messages of *A Doll's House*, *Ghosts* and *An Enemy of the People* may have been, at least they contained a 'hero' or 'heroine' with whom one could identify one's sympathy, but the characters of *The Wild Duck*, apart from the child Hedvig, seemed a thoroughly bad lot; and it was difficult to avoid the implication that they mirrored the audience. In Copenhagen the public expressed its disapproval audibly. 'Ibsen', commented Edvard Brandes, reviewing the production in *Politiken* on 23 February, 'is the finest dramatist writing in Scandinavia and . . . because he punches the Tartuffes of the world in their unctuous phizzes, people hissed him yesterday at the Royal Theatre.'

In Stockholm, alone, was the play well received, mainly because August Lindberg, who directed it there, understood the special problems that *The Wild Duck* posed. 'With your new play', he wrote to Ibsen before starting rehearsals, 'we stand on new and unbroken ground . . . These are quite new human beings, and what will it avail to use the common approach of actors – people who have lost touch with nature through spending their lives playing boulevard comedy? I realized this with *Ghosts*, and it is the same with *The Wild Duck*.' 'My mind reels,' he confided in a friend. 'Such unaccustomed problems for us actors! Never before have we been faced with the like.' He cast an unknown actress as Gina and an eighteen-year-old pupil from drama school as Hedvig. At this flouting of the tradition that the best parts went to the most established performers (in Copenhagen Hedvig had been played by Betty Hennings, the Royal Theatre's leading actress, who was over forty) three of the principal members of the Stockholm company held a press conference to protest.

Lindberg's production of *The Wild Duck* was a landmark in theatrical history, for it anticipated in almost every respect the naturalism which André Antoine was to introduce five years later at his Théâtre Libre in Paris. Lindberg's son tells how his father astonished audiences by making his actors move and talk as though unconscious of the footlights and the audience, not like actors but like human beings such as one might meet outside a theatre, people living in an ordinary room – a room, moreover, which had doors with *handles* that shut with a click instead of the usual canvas flaps, and which even contained a commode. Lindberg's commode became a symbol for this new kind of production, a forerunner of the modern kitchen sink. His own performance as Hjalmar antagonized the conservative critics, probably (reading between the lines of the complaints) because he did not shrink from the contradictions which are so important a part of the character; Gustaf af Geijerstam, praising his performance in *Aftonbladet*, wrote that Lindberg made Hjalmar 'a human being of whom one gradually sees new aspects, now comic, now pathetic, just as in life one gets to know a person intimately so that in the end one sees him rounded and whole'. He was evidently not afraid, as so many actors have been, of the moments of ridiculousness. Later in his career Lindberg was a famous Gregers; the two roles are closely interlocked, as even Othello and Iago are not, and there can have been few productions of the play when the actors playing them have not at some time felt a compulsive desire to change parts.

Germany had to wait three years before seeing the play (as with *An Enemy of the People*); but Ibsen was about to be introduced to a new and important public, for, as he informed Hegel on 11 February, an 'Italian biographer and translator, Alfred Mazza, has made an excellent translation of *A Doll's House*', and was about to try his hand at *The Wild Duck*. This was to have important results, for although he was never to take Italy by storm as he was to take Germany, England and (less permanently) France, he was to find there his greatest female interpreter. Further north, he added to Hegel, *A Doll's House* had been revived in Warsaw, 'with an actress who is having an extraordinary success in the role [Helena Modjeska]. But of payment to the author there is of course no question.'

On 24 March *Brand* was at last staged – in its entirety, moreover – at Ludvig Josephson's Nya Teater in Stockholm, nineteen years almost to the day after the play's publication. Josephson himself directed it, as he had directed the first production of *Peer Gynt*. 'It lasted for six and a half hours, until 12.30 a.m.,' recalled August Lindberg. 'Such ladies as survived to the end lay dozing on their escorts' shoulders, with their corsets and bodices unbuttoned.' Yet, 'although its length and difficulty preclude complete success on the stage', wrote *Dagens Nyheter* on 26 March, 'it proved always interesting and at certain moments highly effective' and, although demanding 'a closer attention on the part of the audience than most modern plays', elicited 'frequent and loud applause' from the full house. Ibsen wrote Josephson a grateful letter on 9 April, saying that the event 'has at last erased from my mind the impression of all those cold, uncomprehending eyes which you yourself remember from a certain other place in the high north', and expressing the hope that it would not be the last time that he and Josephson would work together 'since I still have a whole heap of lunacies in my head out of which I think one might make quite good plays'.

The day after the *Brand* première, *A Doll's House* received its first English performance in anything approaching the original text. It was not a grand occasion; the performers were an amateur group called the Scribblers, the place the School of Dramatic Art in Argyle Street, London, and it was in aid of the Society for the Prevention of Cruelty to Children. William Archer was there, and wrote about it the following week in the *Dramatic Review*:

It has been proved of old that amateurs rush in where artists fear to tread, but never was there a more audacious case in point than the late performance of *Et Dukkehjem*, at the School of Dramatic Art. Since I assisted with two or three other barbarians at a Chinese tragedy in San Francisco, I have not seen an audience so hopelessly bewildered as that which stoically sat out Miss Lord's translation of Ibsen's play. The actors themselves had a glimmering idea of the plot and situations, but even this they failed to convey to the spectators; as for the characterization, the tendency, the satire, had the play been in Chinese they could not have been more completely lost on performers and spectators alike. The whole affair reminded me of the memorable performance of the 1603 Quarto of *Hamlet* at the St George's Hall, with the stage arranged after the Elizabethan manner. Imagine the conception of Shakespeare which a spectator who had never heard of him would have received from this performance of *Hamlet*. As far, or further, from the truth is the conception of Henrik Ibsen conveyed by the Scribblers' travesty to the minds of those who witnessed it. Miss Lord's *Nora* stands in relation to *Et Dukkehjem* somewhat in the relation of the 1603 *Hamlet* to the perfect text, and the Helmer of Mr Addison was to Emil Poulsen's as Mr Poel's Hamlet to Mr Irving's; yet I could not but reflect that the best possible translation of Ibsen's drama, played by the best available English actors, would have been scarcely less bewildering to an average English audience ... Miss Lord's translation is clumsy, and though I believe it has attracted attention in one or two narrow circles (the performance at the School of Dramatic Art seems to prove as much), it has been little noticed by the press, and has certainly not reached the general public.

Despite the 'cold, uncomprehending eyes' of which Ibsen had complained to Josephson, he had begun to dwell with increasing earnestness on the possibility of returning to settle in Norway. Rome had begun to lose its magic; and on 25 April he wrote to Hegel that he felt doubtful whether they would return after their summer holiday. 'For several reasons', he explained, 'it would be convenient for me to spend another year in Germany, where I could take better care of a deal of literary business than I can from down here.' This sounds rather a thin excuse; if he had still been really happy in Rome, he could easily have conducted his correspondence with translators and theatre directors from down there. 'Besides', he continued more convincingly, 'it will bring me somewhat nearer home, and I have lately begun to think seriously of buying a little villa, or rather a cottage, in the neighbourhood of Christiania, by the fjord, where I could live isolated and exclusively occupied with my work. What I most miss here is the sight of the sea, and this longing increases each year. Besides, I have over the years assembled a not so small collection of works of art, mainly paintings, and all these are now in store in an attic in Munich, without our getting any joy from them.' The sea, in Ibsen's work, always stands for the dark, mysterious force within one over which one has no control, and at fifty-seven he was feeling the compulsion, like so many exiles, to spend his old age in the place where he had been born. It is common for writers to react against the place which first spiritually liberated them. The warmth and colour of Italian life and the Italian landscape, which had so excited him as an aesthetically starved man in his middle thirties, seem to have ceased to stimulate him as he approached sixty. He no longer enjoyed presiding over a Socratic symposium at a crowded *osteria*.

He had intended to holiday in the Tyrol or on Lake Constance; but instead, he went to Norway. After a short stop in Copenhagen, he reached Christiania on 6 June. But if he had hoped that his bitter memories would be speedily dispelled, he was to be sharply disillusioned. On 10 June he sat in the gallery of the Storthing to listen to a debate on what came to be known as the 'Kielland affair'. The immediate issue was whether a civil list pension like his own should be awarded to the novelist Alexander Kielland, but the debate turned into a general discussion of the right of freedom of thought in religious matters. Kielland was a professed free-thinker, as Ibsen had been when his application for a pension had been rejected over twenty years earlier; but now, for the first time, there was a liberal government in power headed by a champion of free thought, Johan Sverdrup, and the result would surely be different.

It was not. The government failed to take a decisive stand, the progressives were defeated and Kielland's application was rejected. Ibsen was outraged. The government seemed to him, more forcibly than ever before, to have betrayed its principles, and no longer to represent the true feeling of the left. Next day he took the train north to Trondhjem, and was seen off at the station by Bjørnson's son, Bjørn. 'Tell the youth of Norway from me', he said to him, loudly, so that all could hear, 'that I will stand with them as the corner-stone of the left. What may seem madness in the young will conquer in the end. Be sure of that.'

Three days after his arrival in Trondhjem, on 14 June, the local Workers' Association honoured him with a banner procession, and he used the occasion to deliver a speech demanding a new attitude from those in authority, an attitude which he summed up in that word so beloved of Dr Stockmann, and as unfashionable in Norway then as it is in most countries now: aristocracy.

There is still much to be done in this country before we can be said to have achieved full freedom. But our present democracy scarcely has the strength to accomplish that task. An element of aristocracy must enter into our political life, our government, our members of parliament and our press. I am of course not thinking of aristocracy of wealth, of learning, or even of ability or talent. I am thinking of aristocracy of character, of mind and of will. That alone can make us free.[1] And this aristocracy, which I

1. The question had evidently been on Ibsen's mind much during the past three years. Apart from *An Enemy of the People*, Ibsen had

hope may be granted to our people, will come to us from two
sources, the only two sections of society which have not yet been
corrupted by party pressure. It will come to us from our women
and from our working men. The reshaping of social conditions
which is now being undertaken in Europe is principally concerned with the future status of the workers and of women. That
is what I am hoping and waiting for, and what I shall work for
with all my might.

Ibsen and Suzannah remained a full month in Trondhjem,
where they were joined by Sigurd, on leave from Stockholm.
They then moved down the coast to the pretty little town of
Molde, where they stayed for two months at the newly-built
Hotel Alexandra. Molde was, he wrote Hegel on 11 July,
'one of the most beautiful places in the world for panorama.
There is a lovely fjord, bounded by an infinity of snow-
capped peaks, yet with a rich, almost Mediterranean vegetation. But I would not wish to stay here long; so there will be
nothing of my earlier notion of buying a property up here.'
A newspaper correspondent in the town reported that 'he
and his wife keep very quietly to themselves, associate with
no one and seldom speak to anyone. After meals they return
to their rooms.' He noted that Ibsen spent hours each day
standing on the jetty below the hotel staring down into the
water. 'He stands there most of the day.' When he did talk to
anyone he preferred, as at Berchtesgaden and Gossensass, to
chat with the common people rather than the bourgeoisie;
and several times he had himself rowed in a boat along the
fjord to the open sea.

A fortnight after his arrival, on 24 July, the town held a
reception for him; but he noticed that few people who were
not of left-wing sympathies attended, and when, the fol-

---

written in his preliminary notes for *The Wild Duck*, jotted down
during the winter of 1882–3: 'A new aristocracy will arise. It will not
be the aristocracy of birth or wealth, of talent or knowledge. The
aristocracy of the future will be the aristocracy of the mind and of the
will.' The thought may not seem particularly relevant to *The Wild
Duck*, but it was to be very relevant to *Rosmersholm*.

lowing month, civic receptions were given in honour of the Prince of Wales (26 August) and William Gladstone (27 August), who were independently touring the Norwegian west coast that summer, Ibsen was not invited. He would probably have found little in common with the Prince of Wales, though they could have conversed in German, but one would think that he might have got on well with Gladstone, who loved Norway and found its inhabitants 'a small people living happily in a spirit of democracy', a more charitable verdict than Ibsen would have delivered.

Ibsen's suspicion that he was being ostracized by the conservatives was deepened by a coolness that he discerned, or thought he discerned, in two old friends who were in Molde at the time, Ludvig Daae and Lorentz Dietrichson. He especially sensed that Dietrichson was being stand-offish towards him, he could only suppose in deference to the latter's fellow-conservatives in the town. Dietrichson denies this, saying that when he met Ibsen there on 12 July he found him 'unusually nervous, almost touchy. He had a feeling, which I am sure was exaggerated, of being hated and looked askance at in Norway.' He adds that he knew Ibsen was busy with a new work (which he wasn't), and had no wish to disturb him; also, that Ibsen's radical friends had untruthfully told Ibsen that Dietrichson had said harsh things of him. One's instinct is to blame Ibsen's hypersensitivity; but Gerhard Gran, a sober judge in most matters, thinks that Ibsen may have been right in his suspicions. The hatred between conservatives and liberals in Norway then was almost pathological. 'A left-winger', writes Gran, 'was ... a materialist, an anti-Christian and a moral anarchist.'

Still, if Ibsen felt slighted by his political adversaries in Molde, he found ample compensation in the company, from 11 to 15 August, of another old acquaintance from Rome, Count Carl Snoilsky. In his youth Snoilsky had been a fertile and gifted poet; but after he had married and become a civil servant his creative springs had dried up and for ten years he had found himself scarcely able to write a line. 'I have

wasted my life', he had noted sadly in 1874, 'and it is too late
to change things now.' But in 1879, at the age of thirty-eight,
he had left the Foreign Office, divorced his wife, married one
of her relatives, and gone abroad into voluntary exile. At
once he had found himself able to write again, and published one volume after another.

Three years after their divorce Snoilsky's first wife had
died of consumption, and many people had blamed him for
her death. But Ibsen, during the four days he spent with
Snoilsky at Molde, took a great liking both to him and to his
new wife; he thought her sensitivity and strength of character largely responsible for Snoilsky's regeneration as a
human being. Ibsen was to base the chief character of his
new play, John Rosmer, very recognizably on Snoilsky; and
Rebecca West in that play bears certain resemblances,
though she is not to be identified with her, to Snoilsky's
second wife.

On 4 September, the day before Ibsen left Molde, the local
Choral Society and Horn Group serenaded him outside his
hotel room. Ibsen replied with a brief speech, in which he
hinted that the new play he was planning would upset some
people since 'the things that he found it vitally necessary to
say would not please everyone', and asked that 'those elements of the community whom it disturbed should respect
his views, as he respected theirs'. He added that his stay in
Molde 'with its charming landscape and calm and peaceful
inhabitants' might possibly 'have some mollifying influence
on what he felt compelled to say'.

From Molde he sailed down the coast to Bergen. It was his
first visit since he had gone there as an alcoholic failure of
thirty-five to the Choral Festival twenty-two years earlier,
and his first new impression of the town might have been
designed by a malicious Providence to revive those melancholy memories. As he came on deck wearing formal dress
with decorations, he saw waiting on the quay four of his old
drinking companions – two carpenters, a broker, and a
sexton – who greeted him with cries of, 'Welcome, old

Henrik!' Ibsen hastened back to his cabin and did not emerge until assured that they had departed.

Later impressions, however, were more agreeable, and he spent a pleasant week there. His old theatre had arranged a special production of *Lady Inger of Østraat*, which had been such a failure at its première there in 1855, and had persuaded Laura Gundersen, the star of the Christiania Theatre, to return to the stage where she had made her début to play the lead. They wanted to make the première a special performance in Ibsen's honour, but for some reason, courteously but firmly, he refused. He astonished them, however, by agreeing to attend a rehearsal and, yet more amazingly (for his unwillingness to involve himself with any production was famous), made several suggestions regarding the placings and the speaking; he also gently remarked on the 'improvement' of one of his lines by the young director, Gunnar Heiberg, but allowed it to stand. He came, too, to the dress rehearsal; but when, at the première, the audience called for the author, they had to be told that he was not present. And when the artisans' guild wanted to honour him with yet another torchlight procession, he refused – partly, perhaps, to save having to prepare another of those speeches which he so disliked writing and delivering.

Among the acquaintances he renewed in Bergen was one which stirred deep memories. His old love, Rikke Holst, now Fru Henrikke Tresselt, came to see him at his hotel with a bouquet of wild flowers. 'I've been gazing at myself all day in the mirror to make sure I looked all right for you,' she told him. 'I didn't want you to find me too changed.' He asked if she had found any trace of her in his writing, and she said she could only think of Fru Strawman and her flock of children in *Love's Comedy* (for Rikke was now the mother of a large family). He asked, 'What have you been doing all these years?' and she said, 'While you have been writing all these plays that have made you famous I've just been bringing children into the world and mending old pairs of trousers.' He took both her hands and said, 'You'll never change,

Rikke – God bless you!' It was on this occasion that, as recorded earlier,[2] he wondered aloud that nothing had come of their relationship, she reminded him that he had run away, and he replied: 'Yes, yes. I never was a brave man face to face.'

Bergen, then, after that unfortunate first episode at the quay, had been a success – though he told a young journalist on the ship to Stavanger that he was sad to find his old theatre in debt, and to hear that the citizens of Bergen were willing to pay £4,000 for a statue of Holberg but not the £100 that were required to save the theatre from possible closure. Christiania, to which he now returned, was to revive his sense of being unwanted, and in a way that confirmed his darkest suspicions. At a meeting of the Students' Union on 26 September, Frits Thaulow[3] (son of that battling chemist on whom Ibsen had partly based Dr Stockmann) suggested that they should greet Ibsen with (of course) a torchlight procession. The conservatives in the union opposed the idea in a tepid kind of way, but not absolutely; the motion was carried, and Lorentz Dietrichson, as chairman of the union, went with another committee member to inform Ibsen. Ibsen, mindful of Dietrichson's treatment of him in Molde, rejected the proposal, explaining that he had just refused a similar one from the Workers' Association of the city (as he had done in Bergen), and that he disliked public appearances; but he asked Dietrichson to convey his thanks to the students for the idea. The result was to be a dismal and undignified public row from which none of the principals, including Ibsen, emerged with any credit.

While he was in Christiania he met August Lindberg who, after his productions of *Ghosts* and *The Wild Duck*, could claim to be his most distinguished living interpreter. Lindberg found Ibsen more forthcoming than at their previous

2. See pp. 130–31
3. Later a distinguished painter who befriended two notable outcasts in Strindberg (during the latter's 'Inferno' crisis) and Oscar Wilde.

meeting in Munich, but in a state of great hatred towards Christiania. 'His hair was quite white and standing on end. He said: "Yes, Lindberg, I would give much to see you play Oswald and Hjalmar Ekdal. But not, at any price, in this city." ' Lindberg asked him about the character of the devious Bishop Nicholas, which he was about to rehearse at Nya Teatern in Stockholm, but all Ibsen would say was: 'Well, you can see him any day here in Norway.' The Christiania Theatre might, one would have thought, have arranged a performance of one of his plays during the week he was there; but they did not.

On 29 September Ibsen sailed to Copenhagen, where there were no such problems. The Royal Theatre put on a special performance of *The Wild Duck*, which Ibsen attended, and Frederik Hegel gave a dinner for him at which Georg Brandes delivered the principal speech of welcome. One meeting must have touched Ibsen's conscience; Laura Kieler, now working as a journalist on *Morgenbladet*, came to interview him, and wrote a disappointingly unoriginal and unrevealing article on him which was reprinted in several Norwegian papers. They met, she recalled years later, 'like two strangers who had never known each other'. It was not to be their last encounter.

On leaving Scandinavia that autumn Ibsen had re-settled in Munich in a new apartment at Maximilianstrasse 32, a big corner-house with a bust of mad King Ludwig II as an eighteen-year-old, full of hope, on the stairs. 'A maid opens the door', reported a journalist from the Swedish paper *Aftonbladet*, 'and we enter a lobby where a great many felt hats and rough natural walking-sticks recall Dr Stockmann in *An Enemy of the People*. "Yes, Dr Ibsen is at home," says the maid, and one enters a simple living-room, a little stiff and cold, for the rooms are "furnished". Ibsen does not want a home. He wants to live as a foreigner in a foreign land.' The reporter noted of Ibsen himself that 'he has the inquiring, piercing look of a doctor'; his glance reminded the man of 'an old seaman I saw one night on a steamer off the north coast near Trondhjem, standing at the rudder, peering out into the night'.

Ibsen described his new surroundings rather differently. 'We are now living handsomely and spaciously in the smartest and most aristocratic street in Munich', he told Hegel on 26 October, 'and yet pay only half the rent we had to pay in Rome.' Three weeks later, on 15 November, he informed Gerda Brandes that he was 'now starting on a new dramatic work which I hope to have ready during the winter'. 'We live pleasantly and quietly; almost too quietly,' he wrote to Hegel on 4 December. 'We wish travelling Scandinavians would visit us a little more often. I have now almost completed my plans for my new play and shall begin to write it in a few days. It will be in four acts and interests me much.'

There was excellent news for the family that month. After only nine months in Stockholm, Sigurd had been appointed attaché to the legation in Washington, and had been awarded a stipend of £400, which he was to receive annually for three years. For the past year he had been working in Stockholm with no salary at all. 'It has been an expensive time for me,' wrote Ibsen to Hegel on 22 December, and it could hardly have come at a worse juncture. His income that year had consisted almost entirely of fees from performances of *The Wild Duck,* which had not run long anywhere, plus reprints of *Brand, The Vikings at Helgeland* and *Peer Gynt,* and a little from the Stockholm production of *Brand*: in all, £652. It had been his poorest year financially since 1881.

'I am much happier here than I was last year in Rome,' Ibsen wrote to Nils Lund on 16 January 1886. He fell back at once into his old Munich routine. After his frugal breakfast and his morning at his desk, he would spend the afternoons walking the city streets in his tail-coat and top hat, umbrella in hand, looking closely at the people and stopping wherever there was any small gathering. Each evening at the same precise hour he would enter the Café Maximilian, in the street where he lived, and seat himself at the second or third table on the right of the entrance, opposite the door and facing a large mirror in which he could see the rest of the room. He would order a cognac and seltzer or a glass of dark Munich beer, arm himself with a stack of newspapers (he especially liked to read the comic ones) and sit there, sometimes glancing at people above his newspaper, sometimes motionless as a marble figure, his lips pursed, his hand as though holding a pen, brooding. After an hour he would silently pay the waitress, take up his silk hat and his ever-present umbrella, and walk out with his short, quick steps.

M. G. Conrad, the editor of *Die Gesellschaft*, who made the above observations, also records a conversation from this period in which Ibsen referred to the necessity of knowing a character fully before starting to write about him or her. 'Before I write one word, I must know the character through and through, I must penetrate into the last wrinkle of his soul. I always proceed from the individual; the stage setting, the dramatic ensemble, all of that comes naturally and causes me no worry, as soon as I am certain of the individual in every aspect of his humanity. But I have to have his exterior in mind also, down to the last button, how he stands and walks, how he bears himself, what his voice sounds like. Then I do not let him go until his fate is fulfilled.' He added yet another warning against the tendency of critics to find symbols everywhere. 'The critics ... like to symbolize, because they have no respect for reality. And if one really gives them a symbol, then they reduce it to a triviality or they revile the author.' No doubt he was thinking of the incomprehension with which they had greeted the simple and clearly explained symbol of the wild duck.

On another occasion, Ibsen explained his method in more detail:

As a rule, I make three drafts of my plays, which differ greatly from each other – in characterization, not in plot. When I approach the first working-out of my material, it is as though I knew my characters from a railway journey; one has made a preliminary acquaintance, one has chattered about this and that. At the next draft I already see everything much more clearly, and I know the people roughly as one would after a month spent with them at a spa; I have discovered the fundamentals of their characters and their little peculiarities; but I may still be wrong about certain essentials. Finally, in the last draft, I have reached the limit of my knowledge; I know my characters from close and long acquaintance – they are my intimate friends, who will no longer disappoint me; as I see them now, I shall always see them.

He once remarked that he 'liked if possible to plan his day's work in the morning when he awoke, for then he felt his imagination to be at its liveliest; whereas his critical sense was at its least sharp then, in the half-dreaming hour of dawn. This did not fully awake till he was seated at his desk, when it often rejected all the ideas he had hit upon when lying in bed.' He also kept small guttapercha devils with red tongues on his desk. 'There must be troll in what I write,' he said, and in a tone midway between jest and earnest he spoke of his 'super-devil'. 'He only comes out last, when things are really difficult. Then I lock my door and bring him out. No other human eye has seen him, not even my wife ... He is a bear playing the violin and beating time with his feet.'[4]

Sigurd visited his parents in January en route to his new post in America; it was to be the last time they were to see him for three years. He wrote to them each week, with vivid descriptions of the New World, especially of people he thought might interest his father. Ibsen waited impatiently for these letters; Georg Brandes relates that he was present when one arrived, and that Ibsen's hand was so shaking with excitement that he could scarcely open the envelope. And when, in 1888, Sigurd was transferred to Vienna and came to see his parents at Munich on the way, Ibsen was waiting for him at the station an hour and a half before the train was due.

4. William Archer doubted the existence of these devils, as he never saw them in Ibsen's study. One imagines that when not actually working, Ibsen kept them in a drawer.

Henrik Jæger was preparing a biographical study of Ibsen, to commemorate the dramatist's sixtieth birthday in 1888, and Hegel, who was to publish it, wrote to Ibsen asking for information about photographs, paintings and busts of him, and about his own paintings. 'The oldest photograph', replied Ibsen on 25 February, 'was taken by the author Edvard Larsen [one of the originals of Hjalmar Ekdal] in either 1861 or 1862.' He named eight others, four busts ('the oldest are from 1867') and three paintings, none of which (not even the one by Kronberg, which he owned) he thought really good. 'My own drawings', he concluded, 'have hardly any artistic value. Should they be reproduced, it could only be as curiosities.'

In March he heard that yet another edition of *Peer Gynt* (the seventh) was required, although one had been printed only the previous year, and that *Love's Comedy* was to be staged by the Royal Theatre in Copenhagen. He had written to them on 20 February suggesting that they might reconsider this play, which they had twice previously rejected, in 1863 and 1874, and had also asked them to think again about *Ghosts*; but despite the success of the latter play on the stages of Sweden and Norway, they remained (like the Christiania Theatre) adamantly opposed to it. Ludvig Josephson staged *The Pretenders* at Nya Teatern in Stockholm, with August Lindberg as Bishop Nicholas; and on 19 April, Ibsen attended the German première of *Ghosts* at Augsburg, where the young poet Felix Philippi had persuaded August Grosse to present it. The police had banned a public performance, so the play was given in private before an invited audience. The cast was young and keen, and despite certain imperfections the evening was a success. The police ban naturally excited curiosity, and people unable to obtain tickets stormed the bookshops in search of copies.

By now Ibsen was working hard on his new play, to which he had given the provisional title of *The White Horses*. 'Ever since my return here', he wrote to Georg Brandes (10 November), 'I have been plagued by a new play which absolutely demanded to be written'; and to Carl Snoilsky (14 February) he mentioned that he had 'made some close studies for it during my trip to Norway during the summer'. As we have seen, he had hoped to complete it during the winter; but it would not come, and on 20 February he had to inform Edvard Fallesen, director of the Royal Theatre in Copenhagen, that 'it cannot be expected before the autumn'. He had made some brief notes and begun a draft, but had completed less than an act. The notes show that he was basing his two main characters recognizably on the Snoilskys:

WHITE HORSES

He, a refined, aristocratic character, who has switched to a liberal viewpoint and been ostracized by all his former friends and acquaintances. A widower; had been unhappily married to a half-mad melancholic who ended by drowning herself.

She, the governess of his two daughters, emancipated, hot-blooded, somewhat ruthless beneath a refined exterior. Is regarded by their acquaintances as the evil spirit of the house; an object of suspicion and gossip.

There were also, at this stage, to have been two daughters, one 'in danger of succumbing to inactivity and loneliness', the other 'sharply observant; rich passions beginning to dawn'; but Ibsen eventually removed them from the play and kept them for his next.

But the draft made painful progress, and on 25 May he scrapped it and began an entirely new one. This new draft (still under the title of *The White Horses*) progressed swiftly; he finished the first act by 1 June and the second by 8 June. On 10 June he began the third act; but five days later he scrapped the whole of his second draft and started a third one, re-naming the play *Rosmersholm* – perhaps feeling that *White Horses* was too similar a title to *Ghosts*, especially since Rebecca had been made to say in the second draft that freedom consisted in 'getting rid of one's white horses'. He completed this third draft in a day over seven weeks; Act One took him from 15–28 June, Act Two from 1–12 July, Act

Three from 15–24 July, and Act Four from 26 July to 4 August. Two days later he began his fair copy but, although the third draft is essentially the play as we know it, he made a number of small revisions and did not finish it until 27 September. 'It cannot', he told Hegel in a letter of 2 October, 'so far as I can surmise, offer grounds for attack from any quarter. I hope, though, that it may provoke a lively debate.'

Rosmersholm was published on 23 November 1886, in an edition of 8,000 copies. 'Under better conditions', Hegel had written to him on 7 October, 'I would have suggested a somewhat larger edition.' (*The Wild Duck* had, despite its mixed reviews, sold out its first edition of this size very rapidly, but there was a general slump in the book trade in 1886.) Even more than *The Wild Duck*, *Rosmersholm* baffled the critics, and, like *The Wild Duck*, won nothing like the acclaim that had greeted his earlier plays, from *Brand* to *A Doll's House*. Indeed, it got the worst notices of any of his mature plays except *Ghosts*. One of the few critics to admire it was Edvard Brandes, who thought that the final scene 'equals in tragic imagination the best that Ibsen has written', and that the only modern work with which it could be compared was *Crime and Punishment*. 'They are akin, Dostoyevsky and Ibsen', he concluded, 'and there is something about Rebecca West that reminds one of young Russian girls in their revolutionary struggles. *Rosmersholm* is a masterpiece.' 'I kneel before *Rosmersholm*', he wrote to Strindberg a few weeks later; and Strindberg himself, despite his increasing hostility towards Ibsen, wrote an appreciation of the play the following spring in an essay entitled 'Soul-Murder'. In this, he declared that *Rosmersholm* was 'unintelligible to the theatre public, mystical to the semi-educated, but crystal-clear to anyone with a knowledge of modern psychology' – one of the very few occasions on which he ever paid public tribute to Ibsen.[5] One can understand the attraction that *Rosmers-*

5. Though, with characteristic inconsistency, he seems to have reacted against the play by the summer. On 11 May he sent Edvard

holm held for Strindberg, for he, too, was deeply interested in 'magnetism' and hypnosis, the ability of one person to gain control over the mind of another. He had treated this theme himself in *The Father*, which he began only two months after *Rosmersholm* had appeared, and was to do so again the following year in *Creditors*; while the degenerating effect of an aristocratic heritage, Rosmer's tragedy, was to be the theme, also the following year, of *Miss Julie*.

The hostile press that *Rosmersholm* received was reflected in its sales, as had not been the case with *The Wild Duck*. Even more damagingly for Ibsen, the Royal Theatre in Copenhagen, which was treating him so generously in the matter of royalties, rejected the play. Nor, as with *Ghosts*, did the play seem more accessible when performed; for years, it was to succeed nowhere. Many even of Ibsen's admirers agreed that the play was hopelessly obscure and that the characters were abstractions rather than human beings.

This reaction is not surprising. If he had been breaking new ground in *The Wild Duck*, Ibsen was breaking much newer and more dangerous ground in *Rosmersholm*. To begin with, the play is about two lovers as potentially passionate as Romeo and Juliet or Antony and Cleopatra; but Rosmer and Rebecca, unlike Shakespeare's couples, are children of the nineteenth century; they are, much as they would like not to be, dominated by bourgeois moral values and, because of forces both outside and within them, they never touch each other until the moment when they clasp hands to walk out and drown themselves. Unless these banked passions are suggested (and how often has one not seen Rebecca played as an intellectual bluestocking and Rosmer as a sexless parson!), there seems no earthly reason

---

Brandes an article in which he asserted that Ibsen had written no true work of art since *The Pretenders*. Brandes thought the article reactionary and stupid and told Strindberg so; and it was never printed.

why they should commit suicide. The actors must be able, in Bernard Shaw's words, to 'sustain the deep black flood of feeling from the first moment to the last'. It is only Rebecca's enemy, Dr Kroll, who calls her an intellectual. Of course she had an intellect, but that is another thing. Ibsen, like George Eliot, knew well the predicament of the woman of intellect whose passions can find no outlet. Rebecca and Dorothea Brook of *Middlemarch* have a good deal in common.

Moreover, in this play Ibsen was, for the first time not merely in his work but in any play for over two centuries, overtly probing the uncharted waters of the unconscious mind. As already remarked, the problem of how one human being can gain control over the mind of another and persuade him or her to act, not against their will, but according to inclinations within them which they repress, was much in the air; yet although we know that it deeply interested Ibsen (his preliminary jottings for *Rosmersholm* contain references to 'the sixth sense' and 'magnetic influence'), it was not something of which the ordinary theatre-goer was aware, and although readers would have understood it in a novel, where the author can explain and clarify the actions of his characters, they were not sufficiently used to reading between the lines of plays to comprehend what was merely implied (and implied with marvellous subtlety) in the dialogue.

Of all Ibsen's plays, *Rosmersholm* is the most inexhaustible. To a modern reading public or audience, as to Freud (who wrote most penetratingly about the play thirty years later in his essay *Character-Types*), that is cause for admiration and fascination; but can we blame Ibsen's contemporaries for finding it impossibly obscure, when we remember that Freud's own *Interpretation of Dreams*, published fourteen years later, was to take eight years to sell its first edition of six hundred copies?

On the stage, *Rosmersholm* proved even more perplexing than on the page. The première, at Bergen on 17 January

1887, was coolly received, as was the Christiania production
on 12 April, which ran for only ten performances – a particular calamity for Ibsen who, in response to a suggestion
from Schrøder, had agreed to take ten per cent of the gross
instead of his usual flat fee. No more than six further performances of it were given in Christiania during the next
two years, and it was not revived there again before 1900. Its
first German production, at Augsburg on 6 April 1887, was a
disaster, as was the first English production in 1891. It failed
in both Gothenburg (March 1887) and Stockholm (April
1887). The Royal Theatre in Copenhagen, as we have seen,
rejected it, and it fell, as so often, to August Lindberg to get
to the heart of the play. He toured with it through the
Swedish provinces and Denmark with himself as Rosmer
and with an inadequate Rebecca; and in September 1887
he played in Christiania in the previously unsuccessful production by Bjørn Bjørnson. 'Act after act', Lindberg recalled,
'I felt the atmosphere tighten, both on the stage and in the
audience . . . The applause rolled up over the stage like waves
of heat. The last act is fever and ecstasy. To enter the
ecstasy, to feel it rise in one, without losing control over
oneself! To feel how Rosmer and Rebecca are gripped by
love – it was like being in a trance. It was like exchanging
souls. And at last, out from the closed air of that drawing-
room, out of human smallness, out to the mill-race.' After
the performance the Norwegian actress Laura Gundersen
told Lindberg that they had never understood the play
before.

Before presenting the original Christiania production of
Rosmersholm, Hans Schrøder, the head of the Christiania
Theatre, had written to Ibsen telling him of his plans for
casting. Replying on 2 January 1887, Ibsen delivered himself
of some pungent comments on Schrøder's taste and some
valuable observations on the play:

You think Fru Gundersen was born to play Rebecca. I don't
agree. Fru Gundersen's strength is for the big declamatory line,
and there are none of those in my play. How could she manage

these seemingly light but extremely pregnant dialogues? Dual personalities, complex characters, are not her forte. Then you want Gundersen to play Rosmer. Permit me to ask what the effect is likely to be when Rebecca tells how she had been gripped by 'a wild and sensual longing' for him? Or when Brendel calls him 'my boy', etc.? Or when Dr Kroll hectors and browbeats him? Is G's personality compatible with this and much else? For Rosmer you must choose the most delicate and sensitive personality that your theatre can lay its hands on ... That the role of Dr Kroll, that pedagogic autocrat, should be entrusted to Hr [Bjørn] Bjørnson is, I trust, a joke on which I need waste no further ink. Is it, though, conceivable that this monstrous idea is seriously being harboured? If the artistic direction of the theatre is so totally lacking in critical and self-critical ability, I can await the production only with the direst misgivings.

Schrøder yielded with a fair grace, and the cast was altered in accordance with Ibsen's wishes. A month later, on 5 February, Ibsen addressed to him some further advice about the characters, including meticulous details regarding their dress:

Dr Kroll is an authoritarian with a passion for domineering, as is so often the case with headmasters. He is of course of good family; Major Rosmer's son married his sister. The Doctor's manner is therefore that of a well-born government official. Despite a certain asperity which now and then manifests itself, his behaviour in general is friendly and agreeable. He can be amiable when he pleases, or when he is with people he likes. But it is to be noted that he only likes those people who share his opinions. The rest irritate him, and with them he easily becomes ruthless and reveals a tendency towards malice. His appearance is distinguished; he is handsomely dressed, in black. Coat almost down to his knees, but no lower. He wears a white cravat, large and old-fashioned, which goes twice round his neck, i.e. no tie. His dress explains why Ulrik Brendel at first takes him for Pastor Rosmer and then for a 'brother of the cloth'. In Act One Rosmer also wears a black coat, but grey trousers and a tie or cravat of the same colour. In Acts Three and Four, however, he is dressed entirely in black.

Rebecca's manner must on no account carry any hint of imperiousness or masculinity. She does not *force* Rosmer forward. She *lures* him. A controlled power, a quiet determination, are of the essence of her character.

During rehearsals for the Christiania production, Constance Bruun, the young actress who had been chosen to replace Laura Gundersen as Rebecca, was taken ill, and the part was given to another young actress, Sofie Reimers. She wrote to Ibsen asking his advice; he gave it briefly (25 March 1887), and it still serves as a general warning to any actor or actress attempting any Ibsen role. 'No declamation! No theatricalities! No grand mannerisms! Express every mood in a manner that will seem credible and natural. Never think of this or that actress whom you may have seen. Observe the life that is going on around you, and present a real and living human being.' No wonder Sarah Bernhardt and Henry Irving disliked the demands this awkward dramatist made.[6]

Rosmersholm marks Ibsen's final withdrawal as a playwright from the political field. A year after writing it he was to declare (in a speech at Gothenburg) that his political interests were waning and, with them, his eagerness for battle. He may have based the character of Rosmer principally on Snoilsky, but he put a good deal of himself into it too. Although he enjoyed writing and making speeches on controversial subjects, he disliked embroiling himself; and what he had seen of the results of party strife in Norway in 1886 determined him to withdraw still further from the battle. *Rosmersholm* is the last of his plays which introduces national or local politics as a decisive factor in shaping

6. Irving never acted in Ibsen, though attempts were made to persuade him to play Bishop Nicholas in *The Pretenders* and John Gabriel Borkman, and although Sarah Bernhardt tried herself out as Ellida in *The Lady from the Sea* at Sens in 1904 I can find no record that she played any other of his roles. When Christian Krohg asked Lugné-Poe in the nineties whether Sarah had ever played Ibsen, Lugné-Poe replied, 'She will not. She says contemptuously of him, Strindberg and everything new: *"C'est de la Norderie".'*

people's characters and destinies. In *The League of Youth*, *The Pillars of Society*, *Ghosts* and *An Enemy of the People*, such politics had played an important part; the actions of Stensgaard, Bernick, Manders and Peter Stockmann are, at critical moments, influenced by a fear of offending local political opinion. Gregers Werle in *The Wild Duck* is very much a political animal; and *A Doll's House*, though politics do not enter directly into it, struck at the heart of one of the most controversial issues of the day. But in the six plays which follow *Rosmersholm*, the battle is out of earshot. It is the trolls within, not the trolls without, that determine the destinies of Ellida and Hilde Wangel, Hedda Gabler, Halvard Solness, the Allmers, the Borkmans and Arnold Rubek. They are conscious of strange, sick passions which direct their lives; and *Rosmersholm* provides a link between Ibsen's old method and his new. Rosmer is the last of his characters to be caught up in and undermined by local politics; and Rebecca is the first of those passionate but inhibited lovers who dominate the dark plays of his final period.

His disillusionment with politics, arising from his experiences in Norway in 1885, was complete. In his speech in Trondhjem that year he had declared his belief that the present age was the end of an era and that a new age was dawning, a third kingdom in which 'current political and social conceptions will cease to exist'. As Professor Francis Bull has put it, in Trondhjem in 1885 he had a programme, in Stockholm in 1887 a dream vision; in 1885 he had identified himself with the age, in 1887 and afterwards he cherished only a vague hope for an unguessable future.

24

'All the Women Are in Love with Him'
1886–7

As the Scandinavian theatres perplexedly got down to rehearsing *Rosmersholm* during the last weeks of 1886, Duke
Georg of Saxe-Meiningen was preparing a production of
Ghosts. Ibsen had fallen sharply out of fashion in Germany
since the heady days of *The Pillars of Society* and *A Doll's
House*; indeed, apart from the private production of *Ghosts*
at Augsburg in April 1886 there does not seem to have been
a new production of any of his plays at a German theatre
since 1880, a gap of over five years. *Ghosts* was still forbidden
by the censors; *An Enemy of the People* had been translated
but not performed, and *The Wild Duck* had not even been
translated. But if the German establishment had written
Ibsen off, the young still believed in him. In November 1886
Otto Brahm, then thirty-one, published an enthusiastic
article about him in *Deutsche Rundschau*; and the Meiningen production of *Ghosts*, and that in Berlin which
followed, were to convert many people to Brahm's
judgement.

With Maria Berg as Mrs Alving and Alexander Barthel as
Oswald, the former production proved as great a triumph as
the same company's production of *The Pretenders* ten years
earlier. The duke, who had invited Ibsen to attend the
single performance, gave Ibsen another medal to add to his
collection: the Saxon-Ernestine Order of Commander, First
Class, with star. This medal was the occasion of a rare breach
of protocol by Ibsen. His fellow-guest at Meiningen, Paul
Lindau, tells that on receiving it Ibsen pinned it to his breast
next to the Knight Cross that he had previously received

from the duke. Lindau pointed out that it was incorrect to wear the two together, 'as though a colonel were to wear his lieutenant's pips'. But Ibsen replied that the Knight Cross was the first German medal he had been awarded. 'It has dear memories for me, and I don't care to be parted from it.'

Lindau, who seems not to have been the most tactful of men, also offended Ibsen by making some unappreciated joke about the character of Regina; when he apologized, Ibsen said, 'One doesn't joke about spiritual matters.' Another German guest, a journalist named Gotthelf Weisstein, noted that Ibsen 'looks older than his age, with his snow-white hair, and with his stiff silence suggests a small-town German professor, despite his many decorations'. He also remarked acidly that Ibsen said the simplest things with an impressive air, 'as though he wished to inscribe for ever on the tablets of our memories the fact of his having informed us: "Tomorrow I shall take the train to Munich." '

Lindau and Weisstein sound a tedious pair, and Ibsen was never at his best with people who bored him. One is reminded of a remark Georg Brandes once made when a journalist wrote that a conversation he had had with Ibsen had been empty. 'The fool, getting nothing out of a conversation with Ibsen! When we were together just for a few minutes it was a complete experience!¹'

On his return to Munich, Ibsen made up his accounts for 1886. At £668, his income was about the same as in the two

---

1. After Ibsen's death Brandes wrote: 'Rarely has he been described as he was in daily life. In his younger days he was animated, brilliant and observing, cordial and at the same time caustic, but never what one might call good-natured even when cordial. If alone with one or two friends he was spontaneous, communicative and frank, an excellent listener as well as a remarkable talker; but at social functions or among many people he was silent, easily embarrassed and slightly peevish. It did not take much to put him out of humour or to arouse his suspicion ... but how many examples have I not had of his cordiality, his thoughtfulness, his gentleness!' And William Archer wrote that he 'always found him not only courteous but genial and even communicative'.

previous years, rather better than in the mid-seventies but nothing like as good as the years of *The Pillars of Society* and *A Doll's House*. Performing rights had brought him no more than £160; only the advance of £350 on *Rosmersholm* and £150 from reprints of *Peer Gynt* and *Poems* had saved it from being a disaster. However, the interest on his shares for the year came to £170, he still, of course, had his pension of £111, and Sigurd was now financially independent – very fortunately, for 1887, thanks to the failure of *Rosmersholm* in the theatres of Europe, was to be Ibsen's worst year financially since 1872.

The Meiningen production of *Ghosts* was such a success that the duke tried to take it to Berlin, as he had done so triumphantly with his production of *The Pretenders* in the previous decade. But *Ghosts* was a different matter. The police censor had not allowed it to be publicly performed anywhere else in Germany and, duke or no duke, he was not now prepared to make an exception. However, the Berlin Dramatic Society gave a private performance of the play on 2 January 1887, and such was the interest aroused by this production that Fritz Wallner of the Berlin Residenztheater determined to follow suit, and managed to obtain permission to present *Ghosts* for a single charity matinée on 9 January. Ibsen travelled up from Munich to see it. 'I had scarcely settled down on my return from Meiningen,' he explained to Hegel on 5 January, 'and now I must be off again . . . I would rather have stayed at home; but after the many requests I have received I cannot well not accede to them, especially since *Ghosts* has become a burning literary and theatrical talking-point in Germany. In Berlin I am prepared for some opposition from the conservative press. But this, too, is, for me, an additional reason why I should be present.'

Charlotte Frohn played Mrs Alving, Emmanuel Reicher Manders, and Wallner himself Oswald. The result exceeded all expectations. Wallner recalled: 'I have never experienced anything like it. After the first fall of the curtain, silence reigned for several seconds; everyone was held spellbound by the powerful drama. But then a storm, a hurricane, broke forth, such as I had never witnessed in a theatre. The dramatist was acclaimed by all – no one expressed disapproval – and, willingly, drunk with victory, he appeared repeatedly on the stage, tears of joy running down his cheeks.'

The conservative critics, as Ibsen had anticipated, rejected the play; but it was an important occasion for those who were dissatisfied with the existing state of the German theatre. Otto Brahm praised 'the unconditional truth, the relentless, garish if you like, truth in the portrayal of human character ... human beings, actual, living men and women, fully and completely observed ... If the aim in the development of literature is to absorb more and more of nature into art, to wrest new poetic fields from life, as Faust obtained land from the sea, then no recent dramatist has gone forward more boldly and more magnificently than the author of *Ghosts*.' Another member of the audience was the twenty-five-year-old Gerhart Hauptmann, already on the way to becoming Ibsen's most distinguished disciple in Germany. Eugen Sierke, in an article in *Unser Zeit*, states that they could have sold fourteen thousand tickets for the performance, and Julius Hoffory records that the book sold out so completely in the city that five thousand fresh copies had to be ordered from Leipzig.

On 11 January there was a banquet for Ibsen at the Hotel Kaiserhof, with representatives from all walks of life seated at a horseshoe table. Otto Brahm made a speech praising Ibsen as 'a great artist who unites a rich and mature technical mastery with the fresh courage of an eternally youthful mind', adding that, just as Lessing had in his day led German literature away from the pattern of French drama by showing them the example of Shakespeare, so 'we too have to fight against the renewed preponderance of French drama and turn our eyes to this writer of German [*sic*] blood to aid and liberate us'. The Germans were already claiming

Ibsen as a German, as they had claimed Shakespeare.[2] At this banquet Ibsen asked Anton Anno, who had directed the production of *Ghosts*, why they had omitted Mrs Alving's line about the fabric of Manders's reasoning coming apart because it was machine-sewn. Anno explained that sewing-machines had by now reached such a state of refinement that sewing could not possibly come apart on its own. 'You can be sure', replied Ibsen, 'that Mrs Alving still had her old-fashioned sewing-machine up at Rosenvold.' When people expressed regret that the play was still banned from public performance, Ibsen said, 'I can wait. I can wait.'

The excitement aroused by these productions of *Ghosts* sharply revived German interest in Ibsen. He informed Hegel on 26 January that *An Enemy of the People* and *Rosmersholm* had both been booked for performance in Berlin that spring, and that two German translations of the latter play were appearing 'almost simultaneously'. *The Wild Duck*, too, was to be belatedly translated this year. 'My visit to Berlin, and everything connected with it,' he wrote to Julius Hoffory on 4 February, 'I regard as a great and genuine stroke of fortune for me. It has had an amazingly refreshing and rejuvenating effect on me, and will pretty surely leave its mark on my future writing.' And indeed, his next play was to approach optimism more closely than anything he had written for years.

Ibsen's new-found success in Germany must have compensated him for the failure of *Rosmersholm* in the Scandinavian theatres. He was particularly annoyed that the Norwegian critics took exception to the portrayal of Kroll and Mortensgaard as representatives of what was narrowest in the conservative and liberal points of view. Writing to Jonas Lie on 27 January of his intention to spend the summer in Denmark, he added: 'I shall not, in any event, go as far as

2. Sigurd Høst tells a story of a German officer who, when asked by the Belgian historian Henri Pirenne, then a prisoner of war, to name a single great German since 1870, answered without blinking: 'Ibsen.'

Norway. I find little attraction in the happenings, atmosphere, and general tone of things up there. It is in the highest degree painful to see with what a greedy zest they seize on every kind of petty target as if it were an object of the greatest significance.'

On 5 March the Ostend Theatre in Berlin presented the German première of *An Enemy of the People*. Despite an under-rehearsed opening performance, the production was greeted with a storm of approbation and, although the theatre was situated in an unfashionable part of the city, an hour's carriage ride from the centre, ran for two weeks at a stretch and even succeeded when revived during the hottest part of the summer. On 16 April, *Rosmersholm* was performed at Augsburg; but, as in Scandinavia, the play bewildered the public. It was evidently a lamentable performance. Ibsen attended the dress rehearsal, and Julius Elias, who was with him, noted his reaction:

He witnessed the performance with weeping and gnashing of teeth. Seated in the front of the stalls he winced in pain at every word uttered from the stage; with both hands clutching the plush of the orchestra rail, he groaned ceaselessly: 'Oh, God! Oh, God!' In the third act John Rosmer conceived the grotesque idea of appearing with elegant *piqué* spats over shining polished calfskin boots. When the man appeared, Ibsen reeled as though struck, and clasped my arm. 'Look, look at that!' The Rosmer he had created was wearing bright yellow spats. We were convinced that Ibsen would prohibit the whole performance at the last moment, with some vehement outburst, but then, suddenly, he straightened himself and, with a gesture as though to brush away a bad dream, said, 'I must forget my original conception. Then it isn't too bad.' And, with quiet resolve, he adopted this attitude. Once he had forgotten his original conception, he found everything satisfactory.

The following month, on 5 May, *Rosmersholm* was much better staged in Berlin, by Anton Anno at the Residenztheater, with Charlotte Frohn and Emmanuel Reicher, the team that had been responsible for the triumphant performance of *Ghosts*. The conservative critics greeted it with a fierce broadside. Karl Frenzel, Ibsen's old enemy, was still writing in *Deutsche Rundschau*, and predictably he liked the play no better than he had liked *The Pillars of Society* and *A Doll's House*. He complained that it was never genuine tragic guilt nor a powerful destiny that crushed an Ibsen hero, and that the sickness from which Ibsen and his characters suffered was not life, but Norway. If ever his heroes had had the opportunity to walk down the Unter den Linden, or even the Paris boulevards, they would have been cured of their whims. But if the main purpose of dramatic art was to excite a kind of 'moral sea-sickness', then Ibsen was indeed a master of that art.

Another critic, H. von Pilgrim, writing in the *Magazin für die Literatur des Auslandes*, asserted: 'Realism ... is a canker of the time, like the sentimental bias which called forth *Werther* a hundred years ago. At present no physician for the malady is at hand, but I do not for a moment doubt that he will come ... Such dramas as those of Henrik Ibsen demonstrate by their vogue how little vitality they contain. It has never been the concern of art to offer the repulsive; symmetry and calm, exalted beauty, are the criterion.'[3]

Yet *Rosmersholm*, like *Ghosts*, was appreciated by the young and restless in Germany, and if they were not represented among the professional theatre critics, they found outlets to express their admiration. Following up his November article, Otto Brahm published a seventy-page pamphlet on Ibsen that spring, in which he wrote:

Ibsen's dramas are a continued struggle against the lie, and a victory of the spirit of truth. Wherein is their dramatic strength to be found? In the plot? There are hundreds of plays with more significant plots. In the dialogue? More elegant, flowing and perspicacious dialogue is to be found. In their effectfulness? The common effects are avoided with almost puritanical rigour. The victorious strength of the plays lies solely in the idea, in the

3. This passage, like the quotations from Otto Brahm, is given in W. H. Eller's translation.

resolute prosecution of the idea, which is never deflected by bogus effects and ornaments, by empty phrases, by superfluous romance. The one idea which constructs the play is so great, so true and staggering that it carries us away, crushes us – and liberates us.

Although Anno's production of *Rosmersholm* had to contend with an unusually hot spring, it played for twenty-three consecutive performances and was withdrawn only because Charlotte Frohn was contracted to appear at another theatre.

Ibsen did no writing that spring or summer of 1887, and at the end of June he left with Suzannah for what turned out to be a three months' holiday in Denmark and Sweden (he ostentatiously avoided Norway). His longing for the sea had by now become almost obsessive. 'Both my wife and I', he wrote to Hegel on 12 June, 'look forward immensely to seeing the sea again,' and he added that they felt a strong inclination to settle permanently in the north – 'but it is perhaps best that we should have, at any rate for the present, a fixed point to which we can return outside the boundaries of our homeland.'

They had planned to stay in Frederikshavn, near the northern tip of Jutland, but after ten days he moved to the smaller resort of Sæby, farther down the coast. Here he had a visit from William Archer, who described their meeting in a letter dated 25–28 July:

It was a delightful drive – a perfect summer day, the corn ripe all round, the wild flowers brilliant, and the Cattegat dancing in the sunlight. All the way we could see Sæby Church straight ahead, and at last we rattled over a bridge, past a lovely old watermill, and into the quaint old main street of Sæby – one-storey houses, with great high gables, and all brightly painted or at the very least whitewashed. The moment we were over the bridge, I saw a short, broad figure ahead in an enormously long surtout and a tall hat made of silk looking far too small for his immense head. It was Ibsen, evidently on the lookout for me. I stopped the trap, we greeted each other with effusion, and then he insisted that I should remain in the trap and drive on to the Hotel Harmonien, where he was stopping, he following on foot . . .

We drove into the courtyard of Hotel Harmonien, and by the time I had settled with my fellow-traveller Ibsen had arrived. He took me up into an enormous, barely-furnished, uncarpeted room on the first floor, with four if not five windows, and two bedrooms opening off it at the back. This formed his apartment, and here we sat and talked for about an hour, until Fru Ibsen came in from a walk in Sæby forest . . . After about another hour we had dinner, then coffee and cigars . . .

Now for a few Ibseniana. I must say in the first place that the old man was really charming throughout – perfectly frank and friendly, without the least assumption of stiffness of any sort. If I only had the art of drawing people out I could have got any amount of ideas out of him. Unfortunately I haven't the art – on the contrary, I have a morbid shrinking from talking to people about their own works; so that our conversation was, on the whole, far too much devoted to mere small talk and (strange to say) politics, Norwegian, Danish and Irish. However, I shall jot down a few of the things that turned up in the course of our talk. He said that Fru Ibsen and he had first come to Frederikshavn, which he himself liked very much – he could knock about all day among the shipping, talking to the sailors and so forth; and besides he found the neighbourhood of the sea favourable to contemplation and constructive thought. Here at Sæby the sea wasn't so come-at-able, but Fru Ibsen didn't like Frederikshavn because of the absence of pleasant walks about it; so Sæby was a sort of compromise between him and her. Fru Ibsen afterwards added that the Norwegian steamers of Frederikshavn were a source of perpetual temptation to her. For the present Ibsen is not writing anything, and hasn't been all last winter, because his time has been greatly taken up with business connected with the production of his plays in Germany . . . Meanwhile the old man is resolving plans, and hopes to have '*noget galskab færdigt til næste aar*' [some tomfoolery ready for next year].

I tried to get at the genesis of a piece in his head, but the fear of seeming to cross-examine him prevented me from getting at anything very explicit. [However] it seems that the idea of a piece generally presents itself before the characters and incidents, though when I put this to him flatly he denied it. It seems to follow, however, from his saying that there is a certain stage in the incubation of a play when it might as easily turn into an essay as a drama; and he has to incarnate the ideas, as it were, in character and incident, before the actual work of creation can be said to have fairly commenced. Different plans and ideas, he admits, often flow together, and the play he ultimately produces is often very different from the intention with which he started. He writes and re-writes, scribbles and destroys an enormous amount before he makes the exquisite fair copy he sends to Copenhagen. As to symbolism, he says that life is full of it, and that therefore his plays are full of it, though critics insist on discovering all sorts of esoteric meanings in his work of which he is entirely innocent. He was particularly amused by a sapient person ... who had discovered that Manders in *Gjengangere* was a symbol for mankind in general, *l'homme moyen* (not especially *sensuel*), and therefore called *Manders* ...

In politics he came out very strong against the 'compact majority', but on this point his thinking is scarcely less crude than U.D.'s for example. This may seem a hard saying, but the fact is I am becoming more and more convinced that as a many-sided thinker, or rather a systematic thinker, Ibsen is nowhere. He is essentially a kindred spirit of Shaw – a paradoxist, a sort of Devil's Advocate, who goes about picking holes in every 'well-known fact' as J. would say; or, as Ibsen himself would put it, looking at the teeth of every 'normally built truth' and proclaiming it too old to pass any longer. And Ibsen is even worse than Shaw, who (in the main) knows himself for what he is and remembers that the exception proves the rule. To Ibsen, on the other hand, his paradoxes are apt to present themselves as the whole truth, and his general idea is that the exception destroys the rule. To say that the minority is always right, as Ibsen did in so many words, is at least as unphilosophical as to proclaim the infallibility of the majority. But this question of Majority *v.* Minority is really one which can only be treated thoroughly in a scientific, one might almost say in a mathematical essay; whereas the minority-paradox is the very thing for enforcement in dramatic form. The upshot of all this is that if Ibsen were not a great poet he would be a rather poor philosopher – but that is in fact what you can say of all the leading spirits of this century; for example, of Carlyle and Ruskin; George Eliot is the one exception that occurs to me at the moment. But then Ibsen is Ibsen, and I am the last to complain that he is *not* Herbert Spencer. Of course even as a thinker he is on a totally different plane from men like Tennyson and Browning, who only pretend to think and never get any forra'der.

Altogether my day at Sæby was an unforgettable experience. You'd better preserve this letter – it may be useful sometime ... A greater than Shelley is here; at least a greater than Shelley ever *was*, though it is hard to say what he might have been but for that white squall in the Gulf of Spezia. It gives one a strange sensation to sit at a man's table and eat and drink and talk with him on equal terms, and then to think every now and then: This is the man who wrote *Peer Gynt* and the fourth act of *Brand*, and *Et Dukkehjem* [*A Doll's House*] and *Gjengangere* [*Ghosts*]. Except Shakespeare ... I don't know that there is anyone in all literature whom I would care so much to know as Ibsen. Of course one would like to have seen Goethe or Thackeray or George Eliot, but they have not the enigmatic attraction of Ibsen ...

I was glad to find Ibsen and his wife warm in praise of [Bjørnson's] *Over Ævne* [*Beyond Mortal Power*], though there is a suggestion of *Brand* about it which a small-minded man, with any ungenerous sense of rivalry, might have turned to Bjørnson's disadvantage ...

'Jutland is a beautiful place to spend the summer in,' Ibsen wrote to Hegel on 13 August. 'The people are kind and likable; we have the open sea practically under our noses, and the weather is as perfect as one could wish.' As at Molde two years earlier, he spent hours each day gazing out to sea. A nineteen-year-old Danish girl named Engelke Wulff, who was also staying there, noticed on the shore 'a little broad-shouldered man with grey side-whiskers and spectacles. He stood staring out across the water, with his hand shading his eyes. He had a stick with him with which he supported himself while he took a book out and wrote something in it. From where I sat and watched him, I supposed him to be drawing the sea.' Ibsen saw her, too, as she sat doing her handiwork, and after a time got into conversation with her.

She told him of her longing to see the world, and of her love of the theatre, and he promised he would put her into his next play. One thinks immediately of Bolette; but, as we know, he had already conceived Bolette's character in his early plans for *Rosmersholm*, and when they met by chance in a street in Christiania some years later he called Engelke 'my Hilde'; so one must assume that some of Hilde's lines in *The Lady from the Sea*, if not her character, stemmed from those conversations on the shore at Sæby.

Another young lady from Sæby imprinted herself on Ibsen's memory, though he never met her, for the good reason that since 1883 she had been lying in the town churchyard. Her name was Adda Ravnkilde; she was a talented young writer who had killed herself at the age of twenty-one, leaving behind her several stories and a novel, which was later published with a foreword by George Brandes. One theme recurs throughout her writings: the unsuccessful efforts of a young girl to free herself of her obsession for a man she knows is not worthy of her. Ibsen read her writings, and visited her home and her grave.

Her story must have reminded him of an early and similar adventure which had occurred to his mother-in-law, Magdalene Thoresen. In her own words: 'While I was studying in Copenhagen I met a young man, a wild, strange, demented creature. We studied together, and I had to yield before his monstrous and demonic will. With him I could have found passion and fulfilment. I still believe that ... So I have lived my life oppressed by a feeling of want and longing.' She had fled to Norway to escape from this affair and had married a man nearly twice her age; he 'was my friend, my father and my brother, and I was his friend, his child.'

And at Molde, two years earlier, the local people had told him two strange legends about the sea, and the power it had over those who lived near it. One was of a Finn who, by means of the troll-power in his eyes, had induced a clergyman's wife to leave husband, children and home and go away with him. The other was of a seaman who left home

and stayed away for many years, so that his family believed
him dead; suddenly he returned, and found his wife married
to another man. These four tales, with their related themes
of the power of the sea and the demon lover, were to form
the starting-point of Ibsen's next play. 'People in Norway', he
said to a German friend the following year, while he was
writing *The Lady from the Sea*, 'are spiritually under the
domination of the sea. I do not believe other people can fully
understand this.'

At the end of August the Ibsens returned to Frederikshavn, where Henrik Jæger, busy preparing his biography
of Ibsen, visited them and stayed for three days. He took
detailed notes of their conversations, which remained unpublished until 1960:

Henrik Ibsen's life follows an extraordinarily regular pattern.
He rises at 7 in the summer, a little later in the winter; he dresses
slowly and carefully, spends an hour at his toilette, then eats a
light breakfast. At 9 he sits down at his desk, where he stays till
1. Then he takes a walk before dinner, which in Munich he eats
at 3. If anyone wishes to visit him he will be told that he is at
home at 2.30. In the afternoon he reads; he takes his evening
meal early, at 7. At 9 he drinks a glass of toddy and retires to
bed.[4] He eats with a hearty appetite and sleeps well. He spends
the winter planning his books, the summer in writing; the
summer is his best working time; almost all his books have been
written in the summer; of those which he has published since he
left Norway in 1864 only two, *The League of Youth* and *Emperor and Galilean*, have been written during the winter. When
he begins to write a book he eats and drinks no more than the
barest minimum; it inhibits him in his work; a small piece of
bread and half a cup of black coffee are all he takes before sitting
down to his desk. He smokes a little when working, otherwise not
at all.[5] He cannot understand how people who have to work can
use stimulants; the only thing he can imagine that might be
beneficial is a couple of drops of naphtha on a lump of sugar. In

4. It is interesting that Ibsen apparently omitted to mention to
Jæger the fact of his daily visit to the Café Maximilian.

5. This was untrue; several witnesses (William Archer for one) have
testified to his liking for a cigar during conversation.

this respect he is like the caterpillar which ceases to take nourishment when it has to spin its cocoon.

In general he is regular to the point of pedantry; his day is divided according to the clock. These three days I have been living in his immediate proximity, dwelt next door to him and eaten at his side, we have lived by the clock from morning to night to a degree I could never tolerate indefinitely. One small example: each day when we have risen from the dinner-table, he has walked over to the window and looked at the thermometer which hangs outside. To do so before sitting down to table, or to ask the servant what the outside temperature is, seems not to occur to him.

He needs good air in quantity; lofty, airy rooms are an absolute necessity to him, he told me yesterday when we were discussing where he might lease an apartment in Munich for the winter. He much praises the air up here in northern Jutland because it is so clean and fresh on account of the unceasing wind. It must be for this reason that he has so often spent his summers in the Gulf of Naples or at Gossensass in the Tyrol. To my question why he chooses to settle in so cold and harsh a climate as Munich he replied that the Munich climate suited his temperament excellently; he said he liked it greatly. Although it is already September here and has been very windy these past few days so that we have had to put double fasteners on the open windows, he has kept two windows open all the time, one in each bay, though his desk is set right next to one bay. Each morning and evening he takes a cold rub down.

Concerning Ibsen's method of work, Jæger noted that 'he likes to meditate what he is writing in the fresh air on long walks, and during the time he takes to dress. Works through the whole thing in his head before starting draft. Likes to stop with several lines ready in his head with which he can start the next day, which helps him to begin work. But if he gets stuck he stays put until he has got the thing moving again. Regards first draft as a means of getting to know his characters, outside and in, the way they talk, etc. Then the rewrite, and finally the fair copy.[6] Feels a great sense of

6. Extraordinarily for so meticulous a writer, he never (even after

relief as he approaches the end of a work, but as he does so new plans start popping up. He has to keep walking when working – he needs three or four rooms to move around in while he is working on his books.'

On politics:

He shares the views of the extreme left, but cannot join their party because it is too dishonest; people don't seek truth but only whether it is a 'respectable' person who has said something; if one of these respected gentlemen talks nonsense, nobody dares tell him so ... Ibsen this evening compared the people at home with tadpoles. Some time they will become fully developed frogs, but they still have black tails hanging down behind, and these black tails which they use to steer their course are obsolete ideas which they ought to have dropped long ago.

Ibsen spoke much to Jæger of his love of the sea. ' "There is something extraordinarily fascinating about the sea," he said. "When one stands and stares down into the water it is as though one sees that life that moves on earth, but in another form. Everything is connected; there are resemblances everywhere." ... He would have liked to have ... gone to the west coast of Jutland, where the full force of the North Sea tumbles in; but he gave up that idea because he said that here on the north-east Jutland coast he found the same thing on a slightly smaller scale.' He also told Jæger of his hatred of public speaking. 'The worse thing he knew was to address a large gathering, and he greatly admired people who can do it ... "I could never learn to speak publicly," he said, "however long and assiduously I might practise." '

In the second week of September Ibsen crossed the Sound to Sweden, and spent six days in Gothenburg. On his fourth day there, 12 September, he made a speech at a banquet given for him by a literary society, Gnistan, in which he sur-

---

his return to Norway in 1891) read proofs. 'I don't bother about proofs,' he once remarked, adding: 'I have never personally read any of my books ... When I have finished a new book I don't look at it again. I begin at once on something new.'

prised his listeners by saying that his political interests were waning and, with them, his eagerness for battle. He visited the distinguished Valands Club, founded the previous year, and attended a French opera – Massenet's *Don César de Bazan*. On 14 September he left for Stockholm by ship along the Göta Canal.

A handsome blonde lady of thirty-eight named Anne-Charlotte Leffler accompanied him on the SS *Pallas*. She was well-known as a dramatist and short story writer, and an outspoken champion of women's rights; three years earlier she had visited England, where she had met (among others) Oscar Wilde, whose mother had just written a book about Scandinavia, Jenny Lind, Karl Marx's daughter Eleanor, and Annie Besant. She had met Ibsen in Gothenburg and had got on excellently with him; the night before their departure, he told her, he had dreamed that he was going on a honeymoon with her, but realized in his dream that this was impossible 'for she is married and I am married'. Then, still in his dream, he said, 'Of course – it is a dramatic honeymoon'; and he added to her, 'Perhaps the future will show it to have been so' – which baffled Anne-Charlotte, who assumed it meant that they might co-operate on a play together, but knew he never wrote in collaboration with anyone else. He also spoke cryptically of *The Magic Flute* and the water test which the two characters undergo, and added that 'he thought we had done that, and wondered what it would lead to'. She was much intrigued by this unfamiliar preoccupation with dreams, and noted in her diary as they sailed along the canal:

Ibsen is very quiet, but what he says is always interesting. But he is a curiously lonely soul – he seems to read almost nothing – he has certainly read vastly less than I. He associates with almost no one, he just lives and dreams, or lives quietly and looks at life without living it himself. He doesn't work much, years go by when he writes nothing – he hasn't written a line since *Rosmersholm* ... Ibsen was very amiable to me and told me repeatedly that it was a great pleasure for him to travel with me. They are of course going to fête him tremendously in Stockholm. We must give a dinner for him too.

There was another interesting passenger on the *Pallas*; a young Swedish explorer and author named Sven Hedin, who had returned the previous autumn from an adventurous expedition into the heart of Persia. Ibsen invited Hedin to join them, and questioned him closely about Persia; Hedin showed him drawings he had made of Xerxes' palace at Persepolis and other memorabilia, and was surprised to find Ibsen particularly interested in the great ruins at Ctesiphon, which (he later realized) figures in *Emperor and Galilean*. Ibsen asked him the most minute details about this, including the materials of which it was constructed, and Hedin, in turn, questioned him about his trip to Egypt. Hedin, then twenty-two, was to become one of the greatest explorers and orientalists of his time; also; sadly, an enthusiastic Nazi and a personal friend of Hitler and Himmler. I met him in 1950, shortly before his death, and he expressed to me his amazement that historians were describing these men as cruel. 'I knew them both,' he said. 'They were gentle, humble men.' But, as with the Norwegian Nazi, Knut Hamsun, the follies of Hedin's age do not detract from the achievements of his saner years.

Ibsen stayed a week in Stockholm, where reception after reception was given in his honour. The Swedish novelist Gustaf af Geijerstam met him at several of these, and noted his dislike of large gatherings. 'I sensed that he was not in his element. He never once spoke so that his voice could be heard throughout the room, and it was noticeable that he only relaxed when he was in a corner talking *à deux*.' On 22 September Anne-Charlotte Leffler and her husband gave a small dinner for him. She wrote to a friend, Adam Hauch:

He is so inexplicably kind to me, kisses my hand and gives me the warmest assurances of his affection. Yet he is still a closed book to me. I don't understand him. Although I have been together with him quite a lot, and although I usually read people's characters quickly, I couldn't write a character sketch of him ... Yesterday I had a very interesting day with Ibsen. Gösta [her husband] gave a stag party. Sonja[7] and I were the only ladies, and it was a select gathering of interesting men, so that Ibsen became quite high-spirited and forthcoming. He isn't anyway nearly as wary and calculating as most people suppose, just a little shy and embarrassed, and needs to be in a special atmosphere to be able to express himself. But he answers quite happily whatever one asks him – how he works, who were his models, etc. ... Ibsen is no public speaker, but when he replied yesterday to Gösta's speech he said something very surprising. 'Of all my fatherlands,' he said, 'Sweden is the one where I have found most understanding ...' How angry they would be in Norway if they heard that! ... He can say terribly crushing, cutting things sometimes, and then a glint appears in those cold steel eyes, which fits well with something he often says, 'A writer must never be afraid of a little devilry.' He evidently loves devilry before all else. The Devil is his god, like Carducci's in his *Inno Satanico*.

Two days after Anne-Charlotte Leffler's dinner, a gala banquet of the kind Ibsen disliked most was given for him at the Grand Hotel. In his reply to the official speech of welcome, Ibsen surprised his listeners by describing himself as an 'optimist', declaring that he believed that the world was entering a new epoch in which old differences would be reconciled and humanity would find happiness. August Lindberg was there, but had difficulty in getting near Ibsen because of the press of grand ladies who surrounded him – so many head-plumes, Lindberg noted, as to make Ibsen look as though he were seated in the royal hearse. Lindberg determined, if possible, to give a party for Ibsen where he could meet the young, and especially the young of the theatre, the actors and actresses who had performed in his plays. He and his wife managed at last to get through to Ibsen and asked if

7. Sonja Kowalewski was Russian-born, and in 1884 became Professor of Mathematics in Stockholm. She wrote a play in collaboration with Anne-Charlotte Leffler, who after Sonja's death wrote a biography of her. Anne-Charlotte herself died shortly afterwards at the age of forty-three.

he would attend such an informal lunch gathering the next day; and to their delight, he smiled and accepted, 'as though he sensed that it was a plot by those who had not been able to get near him during the banquet'.

The next day was a Sunday, and they had some difficulty in fixing the food and wine in time; but they managed, and at two o'clock on the dot Ibsen appeared, wearing a top hat but, they were glad to note, no medals or even ribbons.

It was said that he always liked to sit on a small and uncomfortable chair; he always wanted to appear stiff and correct, and a comfortable chair easily causes a man to hunch himself unattractively. Nevertheless, he was put into a large, high-backed chair with arms, but at least hard, for it was of oak. He did not protest, and even took our one-year-old daughter on his knee. Beside him there stood a bottle of wine, and we saw to it that his glass was always full. 'I don't understand,' he said. 'I keep on drinking, and yet my glass grows no emptier.' He enjoyed himself; his old bohemian self emerged from the tightly buttoned coat and he sat and told us about his travels and how *A Doll's House* came to be written. In the end the ladies took hold of him and – chaired him. And he replied kissing each of them on the cheek.

Gustaf af Geijerstam, who was there adds:

I don't doubt that Ibsen, like other mortals, is capable of feeling pride at being respectfully acclaimed. But this is sure, that he enjoyed it twice as much when the tribute found expression in a style of unforced gaiety, when stiff formalities were banished and merriment reigned, when the great man was allowed to be simply a human being among other human beings. Pehr Staaff in his speech of welcome at this gathering hailed Ibsen as 'no pessimist, prepared to sign his name to a declaration of mankind's bankruptcy, but an optimist who believes in the ability of humanity ... to rise like the Phoenix renewed from its ashes ... I give you the health of Henrik Ibsen, optimist!'

It was very strange to see Henrik Ibsen when this tribute was paid to him by a group of young people at a private party. The great man suddenly became communicative, once or twice underlining the speaker's words by murmuring, 'Yes! Exactly!'

He had an appointment that evening at the theatre, to see *An Enemy of the People*, and they parted on the warmest terms. Geijerstam continues: 'But when I saw Henrik Ibsen later, he was seated in a box surrounded by notabilities, and his face wore something of that expression which commonly appears in his photographs.' He concluded:

It is perfectly true to say that Henrik Ibsen can be uncommunicative and off-putting, but it is equally true that no one can be more open-hearted than he, more freely and unforcedly friendly and kind, more susceptible to personal affection ... All that is needed to arouse this feeling is that he himself should feel unconstrained and know that he is understood by those with whom he is speaking. That is why Henrik Ibsen is in his heart an enemy to everything official, and why, when lionized by too many people, he can suddenly become enclosed and buttoned-up ... Amid all the cheering which echoes around him he searches for a sympathetic and understanding eye to meet his own.

Ibsen's visit to Stockholm had been a triumph. 'All the women are in love with him,' wrote Anne-Charlotte Leffler to her friend Adam Hauch, '... and one said on Saturday that she wasn't going to wash her hands for a week now that Ibsen had touched them ... I was delighted to find that, like almost all men of genius I have met, he fully and firmly believes in a socialistic future.' She had been one of Ibsen's companions in the theatre box. 'You can't imagine', she continued to Hauch, 'how much talk there has been in the press all week about Ibsen's box in the theatre. All the papers have had something to say about us lucky chosen ones, all the scandal sheets have been joking about the "bouquet of ladies" with whom he surrounded himself ... I really think it's ladies who get the most out of him. He's a ladies' man like all poets.'

On 26 September Ibsen returned to Denmark, and on 5 October he attended a dinner given for him by Hegel. In his address of thanks he said that this summer, in Denmark, he had discovered the sea; that the smooth and pleasant Danish sea, which one could come close to without feeling that mountains cut off the approach, had given his soul rest and peace, and that he was carrying away memories of the sea which would hold significance for his life and his writing.

What were the reasons for this sudden mellowing in Ibsen, as exemplified in his utterances in Gothenburg, Stockholm and Copenhagen? Partly, no doubt, the acclamation he had received in Meiningen and Berlin at the turn of the year; partly, perhaps, his discovery of the sea, though one would guess this to be a reflection rather than a cause of his change of mood. Possibly, too, as Francis Bull has suggested, those conversations with Henrik Jæger at Frederikshavn in September may have had a therapeutic effect. In the course of these conversations, Professor Bull observes, Ibsen had recalled many old memories, to help Jæger with the early chapters of his book. These memories included some which Ibsen had tried to forget; but now, when he dragged them out into the daylight, he found that they no longer had the power to frighten him. Consequently, Ibsen must have felt impelled to ask himself whether it did not lie within a man's power to drive away 'ghosts' or 'white horses' of whatever kind, provided he had the courage to look his past in the face and make his choice between the past and the present, a choice taken (to quote from the play he was about to write) 'in freedom and full responsibility'. In *Rosmersholm* a potentially happy relationship between two people is destroyed by the power of the past; in *The Lady from the Sea*, Wangel and Ellida overcome that power, and it may be that Ibsen's conversations with Jæger gave him a new confidence, if only a temporary one, in man's ability to escape from the terror of his own history.

Yet in certain matters he remained as inflexible as ever, and one was his relationship with his family, always excepting Hedvig. His brother, Ole Paus Ibsen, who seems to have inherited all his father's inability to hold down a job on land, asked Ibsen to support an application he was making for the humble post of lighthouse keeper; this being a state post, Ole, who started his letter 'Dear brother Henrik' and described his circumstances as 'very bad', begged Ibsen to use his personal influence with the Prime Minister. Ibsen's note to Sverdrup on the subject, dated 3 October 1887 from Copenhagen, is as frosty a reference as one brother can ever have written for another:

Your Excellency!

My only surviving brother, Ole Paus Ibsen, domiciled at Tjømø, is applying for a post as lighthouse keeper and asks me to put in a word on his behalf to Your Excellency. May I in this connection ask Your Excellency to be so good as to read the enclosed letters and testimonials. I myself have nothing further to add on the subject.

I remain Your Excellency's respectful and most obedient servant

Henrik Ibsen

Ole Paus Ibsen got the job and kept it for seventeen years before retiring for the remainder of his long life (he lived until 1917) to a home for retired seamen.

That month, *Ghosts* was publicly performed in both Berne and Basel, arousing, as it did everywhere, violently conflicting reactions. On the other side of the world the German actor Friedrich Mitterwurzer was touring the play, in English, through America under the title of *Phantoms, or The Sins of the Fathers*, and advertised on the posters as 'BANNED IN GERMANY'. Clemens Petersen saw it in Chicago and wrote to Bjørnson that it was excellently performed but that the theatre was 'disagreeably empty', adding the hope that 'Ibsen will write a new *Ghosts* or *Rosmersholm* or the like every year, for then I shall live to see this bubble burst.'

Ibsen returned to Munich in the second week of October, and in a letter he wrote on 15 November to a Swedish bookseller named Hans Österling there appears, for the first time in his letters, the name of that former admirer of his to whom his own name was gradually becoming anathema:

> During my visit to Stockholm in September you were so kind as to send me a copy of Strindberg's recently published play *The Father*, and I beg you to accept my sincerest thanks for this most valuable gift.
>
> One does not read a new work by a writer such as Strindberg during the restlessness and changing moods of travelling. I have therefore postponed the perusal and study of this work until now, when I have returned to the peace of my home.
>
> Strindberg's observations and experiences in the sphere of which *The Father* principally treats do not accord with my own. But this does not prevent me from recognizing and being gripped by the author's violent strength, in this as in his earlier works.
>
> *The Father* is soon to be performed in Copenhagen. If it is acted as it needs to be, with merciless realism, the effect will be shattering.

During the past twelve months, Strindberg's references in his correspondence to Ibsen had become less and less complimentary. In a play *The Marauders*, which he wrote in November 1886, he had appealed: 'Give us back joy, you who preach the joy of life! Give us the cheerful little spirit of compromise, and send the Old Men of the Dovre back to their caves!' On 10 December 1886, replying to his publisher's offer to send him the latest works of Ibsen and Alexander Kielland, he declared: 'Ibsen and Kielland have nothing to teach me, two ignorant women's writers.' Apart from Ibsen's championship, or supposed championship, of the feminist cause, Strindberg disliked him for his praise of aristocrats (though Strindberg himself was secretly attracted to them), and because he, Strindberg, always developed a resentment against anyone who had influenced him. When Edvard Brandes suggested that Strindberg might address himself directly to Edvard's brother Georg, Strindberg replied (3 January 1887): 'Why don't I write myself? Because I am afraid, afraid of him as of all fertilizing spirits, afraid as I was of Zola, Bjørnson, Ibsen, of becoming pregnant with other men's seed and bearing other men's offspring.' In *The Father* itself, which he wrote that January, there is a reference to *Ghosts* ('When I sat in the theatre the other evening and heard Mrs Alving orating over her dead husband, I thought to myself: "What a damned shame the fellow's dead and can't defend himself!"'), and on 22 January (his thirty-eighth birthday) he wrote to Edvard Brandes, with reference to his own play *The Marauders*: 'That I have portrayed a mean and dishonourable woman is not more unjust or unaesthetic than Ibsen's and his sisters'[8] scandalous attacks on men. Woman is, in general, by nature mean and instinctively dishonest, though we ruttish cocks have not been able to see it; so, I have portrayed a typical woman.'

In May, Strindberg sent Edvard Brandes an article in which he asserted that Ibsen had written no true work of art since *The Pretenders;* and on 3 June he wrote to August Lindberg, who was preparing to present *Rosmersholm* and other Ibsen plays at Dagmars Theatre in Copenhagen, that Ibsen was through: '... his *genre* is on the way out. You should read the Germans on *Rosmersholm*! Let him go his way, and us ours!' The fact that he himself had, however reluctantly, admired *Rosmersholm* did not prevent him from rejoicing in the Germans' denigration of it. Strindberg knew that all men are full of contradictions, and never bothered about them in himself.

Ibsen lost a good friend and counsellor that Christmas of 1887; on 27 December Frederik Hegel died at the age of seventy. Their relationship had never been close. But during the two decades of their acquaintance Ibsen had trusted him as he had trusted few people; Hegel had always been ready to advance Ibsen money when he needed it and, although only eleven years older, had been something of a father-figure to Ibsen, as a publisher should be to his authors. His son Jacob, who succeeded him, was a much lesser man – 'a

8. Ibsen's 'sisters' were the feminist writers such as Anne-Charlotte Leffler.

decent and well-meaning fellow', wrote Alexander Kielland
to his brother, 'but ... I wonder if he isn't really more
interested in horses than writers'. However, Jacob Hegel had
an unusually pretty wife, Julie, and continued his father's
tradition of hospitality at Skovgaard. Ibsen's relationship
with him remained cordial, and he continued to ask him, as
he had asked his father, for advice on investments.

It was not the best time for Ibsen to have lost his publisher, for 1887 had been financially a disastrous year. *Rosmersholm* had failed in the Scandinavian theatres, the flurry
of German productions of his plays at the beginning of the
year had brought him virtually no money, and he had had
no reprints. His experiment of taking ten per cent of the
gross for the Christiania production had lost him over
£100; his total earnings for the year came to no more than
£259.

'Ibsen's plays aren't earning him as much as before,' wrote
Edvard Brandes (who presumably had the information from
someone at Gyldendal) to Jonas Lie on 16 March 1888. 'What
will he cook up now? Let's hope he doesn't retreat; we'd be in
trouble then; we who dabble in the theatre would lose our
standard-bearer.' And indeed Ibsen might have been forgiven if he had made his next play a straight discussion
drama of the kind that had proved so popular, a successor to
The Pillars of Society and *A Doll's House*. It was typical of
his courage and integrity as a writer, however Peer Gynt-like
he may have been in his private life, that he followed his own
stern bent and wrote a play as difficult and psychologically
experimental as the one which had just proved so un-
popular.

25

The Lady from the Sea,
and the Breakthrough in England
1888–9

IBSEN's sixtieth birthday, on 20 March 1888, was marked by the publication of Henrik Jæger's biography of him, a sober and intelligent appraisal containing some carefully censored biographical matter provided by the subject himself. Among the many telegrams of good wishes was one signed by fifty-four members of the Storthing, one from the actors at the Christiania Theatre, and one from Bjørnson which included the sentence, 'Today the world comes to the recluse.' Many German writers and artists visited him personally to deliver their greetings. *Aftenposten* printed an anonymous front-page leader (by Professor Bredo Morgenstierne, who disliked and wrote hostile reviews of most of Ibsen's mature plays), paying tribute to 'our greatest living writer', stressing how Norwegian he was and declaring that no foreigners could ever more than partially appreciate him, words which must have rung somewhat hollowly in Ibsen's ears. As evidence of his international fame the newspaper proudly published extracts from his early poem 'Terje Vigen' in English, German and Polish translation; one would have thought they might have found something more recent. Yet, while the left-wing papers joined in saluting him, the leading Tory paper, *Morgenbladet,* said not a word.

Ibsen's gratitude for the liberals' acclaim of him was tempered by the evidence it gave that he was still the adopted champion of a party in which he no longer had any real confidence. 'One of the things that has pained me most in

my literary connection with my fatherland', he wrote to
Amandus Schibsted, the editor of *Aftenposten*, on 27 March,
'is the knowledge that, over a number of years, ever since
The League of Youth appeared, I have always been claimed
as the possession of one or other of the political parties. I,
who have never in my life concerned myself with politics, but
only social questions! And my presumed opponents refuse to
understand this. It is not praise or favour that I ask for, but
understanding. Understanding!'

Earlier that month *An Enemy of the People* had been
staged at Meiningen, 'where [noted William Archer] the
fourth act was naturally found to offer a superb opportunity
for the Meiningen methods of stage-management'. And
indeed one would like to have seen what Duke Georg made
of that crowd scene, on which so many productions of the
play fall down. Max Grübe played Dr Stockmann; but
Ibsen, a little surprisingly, did not attend. 'I hardly ever go
to the theatre here,' he wrote to the Danish playwright Jens
Christian Hostrup on 2 April, 'though I like to read a play
now and then of an evening, and since I have a strong power
of imagination for the dramatic ... the reading serves
almost for a performance.' No doubt it served much better
than most of the performances he saw. Productions of his
plays in Munich, however, he could hardly help attending,
and he was present when the Residenztheater presented *The
Wild Duck* on 4 March, a performance which elicited sixteen
curtain calls. There would probably have been more productions to mark his birthday had not the old Kaiser Wilhelm died a few days earlier; but there was scarcely a serious
newspaper or periodical which did not commemorate the occasion with a piece about him.

Irgens Hansen wrote a long article on 'Ibsen in Germany'
which *Dagbladet* in Christiania published in four instalments on 20, 22, 25 and 28 March. In 1880, Hansen recalls,
despite the success of *The Pretenders*, *The Vikings at Helgeland* and *The Pillars of Society*, and the discussion
aroused by *A Doll's House*, Ibsen was not on all men's lips in

Germany, and was in fact less well known than Bjørnson, thanks to the latter's stories and *A Bankrupt*. Nor had the banning of *Ghosts* helped; but now 'what admirers thought impossible in 1886 has become a reality. German actors have dared to perform the play, and German audiences have seen it.' So hotly are his plays debated (continues Hansen) that it has even been seriously suggested that 'four young Jews have written his entire works', and the recently published translation of *Emperor and Galilean* is to be seen in every bookshop window. Hansen quotes from numerous German newspaper and magazine articles about Ibsen published during the preceding twelve months, but expresses surprise that the German theatres stage his plays for so few performances at a time, for 'here is a writer who follows no one and sets sail for unknown shores'. The first of the four instalments includes a vivid picture of the dramatist in exile:

In the high rooms at Maximilianstrasse he has hung his beloved paintings. For the third year now one may of an afternoon see his figure, so familiar to the citizens of Munich, in his long Ulster and top hat, slowly walking the streets. Behind the spectacles the eyes smile oftener than the severe features would have one suspect; for it amuses him to walk among the crowd. He likes to stop where people throng before a window. He knows everything on his routes and notices every little new thing. For an hour to an hour and a half he walks thus in the city, never in the country – 'the country is uninteresting' – and soon after 6.30 one will see him at his regular table at the Café Maximilian. There he sits for half an hour, then returns home. Now and then he spends an evening at the Writers' Club when they have a meeting. Otherwise he is not seen.

Julius Hoffory, a Dane working as a professor in Berlin, wrote a perceptive appraisal of Ibsen's standing in Germany in the Copenhagen magazine *Tilskueren* this year. The critics, he reports, are divided into two factions, 'some hailing him as a new leader, others denouncing him as an evil messenger of darkness who strives only to destroy everything that one regards as sacred', contrasting his 'gloomy art' with the 'bright and beautiful world of Goethe' (a curious comparison, Hoffory comments, remembering that Goethe was the author of *Götz* and *Werther*). The debate cut across party lines; left-wing papers such as *Berliner Tageblatt* and *Volks-Zeitung* were among Ibsen's bitterest opponents, while others such as *Vossische Zeitung* and *Die Nation* championed him in lengthy articles. *Post* and *Deutsches Tageblatt* attacked him; but other right-wing papers such as *Fremdenblatt* and *Börsen-Zeitung* supported him. The government organ *Norddeutsche Allgemeine Zeitung* violently condemned him, while another government publication, *Deutsche Reichs-Anzeiger*, praised his 'great art and Titanic strength'. Hoffory concludes:

> It must not be forgotten that the attacks on Ibsen contributed just as much as the eulogies to impress the significance of his work on the German public. It can already be claimed without exaggeration that no living German writer is as well known, as widely read, and as earnestly discussed as Henrik Ibsen. In newspapers and books, in brochures and literary magazines, literary historians and essayists, philosophers, lawyers and doctors compete in the interpretation of his work. In the bookshop windows his latest plays are on show by the score, and if one enters, a carefully arranged collection of Ibsen's works is very often the first thing to meet one's eye. His plays are circulated in cheap editions which reach the widest circles and are read and prized by people who are seldom seen with a work of literature in their hand.

Evidence of the continued increase of Ibsen's reputation in Germany over the next few years appears in an article which Georg Brandes contributed to the same magazine two years later. Brandes declared Ibsen to be a more creative influence in German writing than any other living author, and thought the reason was that he demanded the unusual combination of socialism and individualism – not the individualism of selfishness but the individualism of self-fulfilment. As examples of young German dramatists who were disciples of Ibsen, Brandes cites Richard Voss, Hermann Bahr, Wolfgang Kirchbach (who had been born in London of German parents) and Gerhart Hauptmann who, although only twenty-seven when Brandes was writing, had already completed *Vor Sonnenaufgang, Das Friedensfest* and *Die Selicke auf Arno Holz und Johannes Schlef*. All these writers, explained Brandes, admired Ibsen as a realist. 'His name has become a banner, and a whole new generation is rallying to this banner in such magazines as *Freie Bühne, Modern Dichtung*, etc.' The fact that Ibsen never declared his principles or contributed a line himself to these magazines, concludes Brandes, impressed the Germans hugely; and he was very amiable to his young admirers such as Otto Brahm, Paul Schlenther and Hermann Bahr when he met them or they sent him their work.

A new play was due from Ibsen this year, especially after the poor returns of the previous year, and on 5 June he jotted down his first notes, nearly two and a half thousand words:

The sea's magnetic power. The longing for the sea. Human beings akin to the sea. Bound by the sea. Dependent on the sea. Must return to it. One species of fish is a vital link in the chain of evolution. Do rudiments of it still reside in the human mind? In the minds of certain people?

Images of the teeming life of the sea and of 'what is lost for ever'.

The sea operates a power over one's moods, it works like a will. The sea can hypnotize. Nature in general can ... She has come from the sea ... Because secretly engaged to the young, carefree ship's mate ... At heart, in her instincts – he is the one with whom she is living in marriage ...

Five days after he had made these notes Ibsen began to write Act One, provisionally entitling the play *The Mermaid*, and he completed his first draft in just over seven weeks. Act One is dated 10–16 June; Act Two, 21–28 June; Act Three, 2–7 July; Act Four, 12–22 July; and Act Five, 24–31 July. Early in August he began to revise it, and by 18 August he had corrected the first two acts to his satisfaction. Two days later he began to revise the third act, and on 31 August he started on the fourth. On 25 September he was able to send his fair copy to Jacob Hegel. 'The work was finished a little later than I had calculated,' he wrote to Hegel the following day, 'but I hope it is still in good time, provided the printing can begin at once. May I ask that the title page be printed last and the title kept secret – as, likewise, I trust that the printers will observe the maximum of discretion . . . I am confident that this play will arouse general interest. In many respects I have struck out in a new direction here.'

He was still as bitter as ever about Norway; despite the birthday tributes, his experiences of three summers previously continued to rankle. It would be totally impossible for me to settle for good in Norway,' he wrote to Georg Brandes on 30 October. 'There is nowhere where I would feel more homeless than up there. The old conception of a fatherland no longer suffices for anyone intellectually mature. We can no longer rest content with the political community in which we live.' Another of his current preoccupations, his disillusionment with the left, inevitably came in for treatment. 'The leaders of the left are wholly lacking in worldly experience and have consequently been cherishing the most unreasonable illusions. They imagined that a leader of the opposition would and could remain the same man after he had achieved power as he had been before' – a note of disenchantment which has been echoed by many a radical voter since.

Ibsen indulged in, for him, an unusual amount of correspondence that November, while awaiting the publication of *The Lady from the Sea* (as he had now re-entitled it). Henrik Jæger, his biographer, had written from Bergen passing on a suggestion from the theatre there that, instead of paying the usual lump sum, they should give him ten per cent of the gross takings; but this he refused, after his unfortunate experience with *Rosmersholm* in Christiania. 'Our impecunious theatres', he replied on 17 November, 'would be tempted to perform the plays as seldom as possible; whereas if they have paid the author his whole fee it will be in their own interest to get the money back from performances as quickly as possible. I must therefore stick to the old fixed fee system as the only practicable one as long as the present laws concerning literary copyright persist.' He may have sensed that none of his future plays would be popular successes as *The Pillars of Society* and *A Doll's House* had been.

On 20 November he thanked his old Holland friend Ludvig Daae for a long appreciation of Paul Botten Hansen which Daae had recently published in the Danish magazine *Vidar*. 'It gripped me with an extraordinary power to take myself back again so vividly into those times which exercised so decisive an influence upon my later development and from which I have never really freed myself – never been able or wanted to free myself.' (It is interesting that he did not reject the Christiania years of humiliation as he rejected Skien). He ended the letter by asking Daae to 'greet all the survivors' of the Holland circle 'from their, and your, affectionate old friend, Henrik Ibsen', a little surprisingly when one remembers how many of that circle had by now retreated into conservatism. This mellow note is repeated in a letter he wrote the following day to Bredo Morgenstierne thanking him (five months late) for his birthday tribute in *Aftenposten* and assuring him that 'when I return to Christiania – if that ever happens – I will visit the circle where I feel most at home'. And on 25 November, acknowledging to Magdalene Thoresen the repayment of a debt she said she owed him, he wrote that he could not recall having lent her the money and insisted that she take it back. 'Use the money on something that will bring you joy. You must in some way or other celebrate your freedom from debt, on which I congratulate you with all my heart. I know from my own experience what such a liberation means' – a reminder, were one needed, of how this particular subject obsessed him.

Jonas Lie visited Ibsen this month on his way to Paris, and, so Lie wrote to Georg Brandes on 26 November, they 'had as always an unusually pleasant evening. We've been

friends since youth, and although we were so different then
he often used to choose me to preach to about his dramatic
plans.' The next day we find Ibsen expressing an opinion on
one of the very few contemporary writers who shared his
own stature. Thanking Emmanuel Hansen, a translator who
lived in St Petersburg, for sending him a copy of Tolstoy's
play *The Power of Darkness* in Danish, he wrote: 'I have
read *The Power of Darkness* with much interest. I have no
doubt that, carefully and respectfully performed, it must
make a considerable effect on the stage. Nevertheless, it
seems to me that the author does not possess a complete
insight into dramatic technique. The play contains conversations rather than scenes, and the dialogue strikes me in
many places as epic rather than dramatic, the work in general as being less of a drama than a narrative in dialogue' – a
verdict with which most directors and actors would agree.
He added, however, that 'the great writer's genius lives and
is revealed there'.

This was, parenthetically, a more charitable judgement
than Tolstoy was to pass on Ibsen, for he found all of the
latter's plays (except, oddly enough, *Rosmersholm*) repellent.
'Have read *Love's Comedy*', he wrote in his diary on 19 November 1889. 'How bad! Clever German sophistry – terrible!'
V. L. Nemirovitch-Dantchenko lent him *An Enemy of the
People*, but he disliked that too, remarking: 'This Dr Stock-
mann is much too conceited.' On 20 August 1890 he noted;
'Have read Ibsen's *Wilde Ente* [*The Wild Duck*]. Not good.'
(As he called the play by its German title he had presumably
read it in that language; it was not translated into Russian
until 1892). The next day he noted: 'Have read Ibsen's
Rosmer [*sic*] . . . So far not bad.' But it seems doubtful if he
liked the rest of it, for on 14 September 1891 he wrote to
Ibsen's Russian translator, P. G. Hansen, that he loved
Bjørnson's writing and personality, 'but I cannot say the
same of Ibsen. I have read all [*sic*] his plays too, and his
poem *Brand*, which I was patient enough to read to the end.
Everything is contrived, false, and very clumsy, in the sense

that none of his characters is consistent and lived-through. His reputation in Europe merely proves the poverty of European creative writing.' In his essay *What is Art?*, written in 1898, Tolstoy made particular mockery of *Little Eyolf* and *The Master Builder;* but Ibsen was in good company, for Tolstoy poured equal scorn on Beethoven, Baudelaire, Wagner, Verlaine and Zola. In his diary of 28 October 1900, citing Ibsen as an example of 'the poetry and art of the cultural mob', Tolstoy linked his name disparagingly with those of Shakespeare and Dante, finding all three immoral and irreligious and, therefore, bad artists; and, dismissing Chekhov's *The Seagull* as 'utterly worthless', he added that it was written 'just as Ibsen writes his plays'. Chekhov's own attitude towards Ibsen was to be most oddly ambivalent.

On 28 November 1888 *The Lady from the Sea* was published in an edition of 10,000 copies, 2,000 more than *Rosmersholm* or *The Wild Duck*. Ibsen's conviction that the play would be 'completely understood outside Norway' proved sadly unfounded; it was not even understood inside Norway. The critics were as bewildered by it as they had been by *Rosmersholm*, and although it got a slightly better press on account of the happy, or seemingly happy ending, such tributes as it received were grudging. 'The play is not free from riddles and problems,' wrote an anonymous critic in *Morgenbladet*, regarding this as a defect, 'but wholesomeness emerges victorious ... It certainly moves in a cleaner air.' At the same time, he complained, Ellida's story 'is from first to last a story of sickness, a bizarre psychological case history, the development of which taxes the action of the play ... There is no real drama in this.' Knut Hamsun dismissed it as an 'insanity', and the historian J. E. Sars doubtless expressed many people's views when he declared: 'It seems to me a proof of how modern aesthetics have strayed that Henr. Ibsen has almost [*sic*] overtaken Bjørnson in public estimation. He is a purely negative spirit ... Surely this pessimistic problem writing must by now have reached its limit.' Tolstoy would have agreed with that, although it is ironical to reflect that he himself was never to receive the Nobel Prize for Literature, despite the fact that he lived for nine years after its inception, because the Swedish Academy regarded him as insufficiently idealistic.

The Swedish and Danish press were scarcely more favourable. Edvard Brandes welcomed the play enthusiastically in *Politiken*, but found himself almost alone. Strindberg declared that Ibsen 'ought now to be repudiated as moralistic and religious', though within the decade he was to become both himself, Erik Bøgh advised the Royal Theatre in Copenhagen to reject it, and in a Scandinavian newspaper on the other side of the world a forgotten enemy took up his pen to denounce it. Clemens Petersen gave it a bad review in the Chicago *Nordisk Folkeblad*.[1]

It was fortunate for Ibsen that Jacob Hegel did not consider printing a smaller impression of *The Lady from the Sea* following the failure of *Rosmersholm*, for otherwise 1888 had been an even worse year financially than 1887. Not only had there been no reprints of his earlier works; he had received no performance fees from Scandinavia at all, apart from £10 for two performances of *An Enemy of the People* in Stockholm. Luckily for him the German theatres were beginning to pay a little more; even so, his earnings for the year, excluding an advance of £475 for *The Lady from the Sea*, totalled only £130.

However, the interest on his investments brought him £180 to add to his pension of £111; and so economically did he live that on 11 December and 20 January he asked Hegel to buy him further securities to a total value of £780, which suggests that, with Sigurd now earning a sufficient salary, Ibsen and Suzannah were living on little more than his pension. The fear that he might find himself incapacitated by illness or a stroke (as eventually happened), or that he might lose his public (as now seemed not impossible), was always in his mind, and he was determined that he and his wife should

1. Petersen never gave up. As late as 1895 he was still protesting to Bjørnson that Ibsen 'is a critic, not a creative writer'.

never find themselves in the situation in which, half a century earlier, his father had left him.

At last there were signs of a belated breakthrough in England. In the closing weeks of 1888, thanks to William Archer's efforts, a publisher bearing the illustrious name of Walter Scott issued a volume, in a series called the Camelot Classics, containing Archer's translation of *The Pillars of Society*, a careful revision by him of Henrietta Frances Lord's version of *A Doll's House*, and a translation by Karl Marx's daughter Eleanor of (as she called it) *An Enemy of Society*. The volume was introduced by a twenty-nine-year-old ex-medical student named Havelock Ellis, then earning a living as editor of the Mermaid Series of Old Dramatists. Ellis expressed his envy of the Scandinavian countries for having a stage on which 'the burning issues of the day [may] be scenically resolved', and concluded by declaring that Ibsen's ideas 'are of the kind that penetrate men's minds slowly. Yet they penetrate surely, and are proclaimed at length in the market place.' Ellis's own first book, *The New Spirit*, which appeared just over a year later, was to contain a forty-three page section on Ibsen. It is a measure of the impact which Ibsen was about to make on the English scene that the little Camelot volume of his plays sold, during the next five years, no fewer than fourteen thousand copies, a quite unprecedented figure for a volume of plays by a living dramatist, and thereby established a new trend which, in due course, Shaw and Galsworthy were profitably to follow.

On New Year's Day, 1889, Edmund Gosse returned to the Ibsen scene after an absence of five years with a long article in the *Fortnightly Review* entitled 'Ibsen's Social Dramas', dealing with all the prose plays from *The Pillars of Society* to *The Lady from the Sea*. He welcomed the last-named play as possessing 'a glamour of romance, of mystery, of landscape beauty, which has not appeared in Ibsen's work to anything like the same extent since *Peer Gynt*'. And before the year was out Ibsen was to enjoy his first success on the London stage. All in all, 1889 was to prove an important year for him abroad.

The Lady from the Sea, however, failed on the stages of Europe as calamitously as *Rosmersholm* had done. It received its première on 12 February, simultaneously in Christiania and Weimar.[2] *Aftenposten*, reviewing the Christiania production, dismissed the play as 'one of Ibsen's feeblest', and although it managed twenty-one performances that season it was thought worthy of only two the following season. It was poorly received in Weimar and also in Copenhagen and Stockholm. Like *Rosmersholm*, *The Lady from the Sea* was to fail time and again when staged, with occasional (and memorable) exceptions, and for two reasons. Firstly, like *Rosmersholm*, it delved into depths of the human soul with which both audiences and actors were unfamiliar. Secondly, the part of Ellida needs a very special kind of actress. It is one of those roles, like Lear and Othello, Strindberg's Father and Miss Julie, which demand a particular quality of personality, and the most accomplished actress in the world, if she lacks this quality, cannot succeed. She may get excellent notices for her performance, but the play will fail. But with the right actress, the result is one of the rarest experiences that the theatre can offer, like a great Othello. The first to encompass the role was Eleonora Duse. James Agate, in a memorable passage, described her in the part:

This play is a godsend to a great artist whose forte is not so much doing as suffering that which Fate has done to her. With Duse, speech is silver and silence is golden . . . The long second act was a symphony for the voice, but to me the scene of greatest marvel was the third act. In this Duse scaled incredible heights. There was one moment when, drawn by every fibre of her being to the unknown irresistible of the Stranger and the sea, she blotted herself behind her husband and took comfort and courage

2. Four other German theatres applied for the right to stage the first production, but all declined after reading the play.

from his hand. Here terror and ecstasy sweep over her face with that curious effect which this actress alone knows – as though this were not present stress, but havoc remembered of past time. Her features have the placidity of long grief; so many storms have broken over them that nothing can disturb again this sea of calm distress. If there be in acting such a thing as pure passion divorced from the body yet expressed in terms of the body, it is here. Now and again in this strange play Duse would seem to pass beyond our ken, and where she has been there is only a fragrance and a sound in our ears like water flowing under the stars.

Greta Garbo would have been supremely suited to play Ellida; why did nobody think of making a film of it with her? Vanessa Redgrave interpreted the role memorably under Michael Elliott's direction in Manchester in 1978 and in London in 1979, one of the great Ibsen productions.

At the beginning of March there was an Ibsen week in Berlin, with *The Lady from the Sea* at the Schauspielhaus, *The Wild Duck* at the Residenztheater and *A Doll's House* at the Lessingtheater. Ibsen went up for the occasion, staying at the Hotel du Nord, and was feted as enthusiastically as he had been two years earlier. Various banquets were given for him, and he himself invited Otto Brahm, Paul Schlenther and Julius Hoffory to 'a splendid luncheon which lasted almost till evening ... It will be good to have some peace again,' he wrote to Suzannah on 5 March, after attending a charity matinée of *The Lady from the Sea* the previous day. 'I already feel quite tired.' But in a letter of thanks on 26 March to Hoffory, whose translation of *The Lady from the Sea* had rapidly gone into a third edition, he described his stay in Berlin as 'the most exciting time of my life. When I look back on it, the whole thing seems like a dream. It makes me almost afraid.' Before returning to Munich he spent a week in Weimar, where he found the production of *The Lady from the Sea* (he told Hoffory in the same letter) 'quite excellent. I could not wish, nor could scarcely imagine, the Stranger better interpreted – a tall, lean figure with a long face, black, staring eyes and a magnificent, deep, subdued voice.'

In Munich he found a new edition (the seventh) of *The Pretenders* awaiting him, with the news that an eleventh edition of *Brand* was in the press, and that he now had over £900 to his credit with Gyldendal, information which he described to Hegel (11 April) as 'a great and joyful surprise'. The idea of spending any of this windfall on luxuries did not occur to him, or if it did it was firmly rejected, for the next day he wrote Hegel that the whole amount was to be invested in gilt-edged securities, £400-worth of it in Russian railways.

The Pillars of Society was revived in April at the Deutsches Theater in Berlin, and the same month he heard from Snoilsky that two of his plays had, at last, been translated into French. The translator was not a Frenchman, any more than Hoffory in Berlin was a German or P. G. Hansen (his Russian translator) a Russian; he was a Lithuanian, Count Moritz Prozor. Married to a niece of Snoilsky, he had, when secretary at the Russian embassy in Stockholm in 1883, seen *Ghosts* performed there; the play had made a deep impression on him, and on moving to the Berne embassy in 1887 he had, with the aid of his wife, turned both *Ghosts* and *A Doll's House* into French. Now, in 1889, he had managed to get both translations published in Paris. (It is typical of the piratical conditions then governing copyright as far as a Norwegian was concerned that Ibsen should not have known even of the translations' existence until after they had appeared in print.) 'I have not yet seen it', he wrote to Snoilsky on 19 April, referring to the *Ghosts* translation, 'but even if I had read it I would be unable to pass any well-founded judgement, since my knowledge of the French language is very inadequate. I am all the happier that you find the translation very well done.' He added that two Frenchmen had been negotiating with his German translators to make versions of his plays from the German, a common practice in several countries up to recent times (one of the most frequently performed 'translators' of Ibsen in England during the forties and fifties worked from German texts which were often wildly inaccurate).

On 7 June 1889 Ibsen achieved his first real breakthrough on the English stage. Hitherto, he had been represented only by the single matinée of *The Pillars of Society* in 1880, the dreadful travesty *Breaking a Butterfly* in 1884 and the amateur performance of '*Nora*' in 1885. Now, however, a young Irish actor-manager named Charles Charrington produced *A Doll's House* in Archer's revised translation at the Novelty Theatre in Kingsway (later the Kingsway Theatre) with his wife, the twenty-five-year-old Janet Achurch, as Nora. Before her premature death in 1916 at the age of fifty-two Janet Achurch was to become one of the great actresses of her generation (in 1907 she was a memorable Mrs Alving), and this production established her reputation at the same time that it established Ibsen's. William Archer recorded the occasion in the columns of the *World*, of which he had, since 1884, been dramatic critic, starting at a salary of three guineas a week. At the age of thirty-three, he had already proved himself the best English dramatic critic since William Hazlitt:

The general public [wrote Archer on 19 June] has risen heroically to the occasion. It has come – nay, more, it has paid – to see *A Doll's House*, and that in larger numbers night by night ... So far from having drunk its fill of Ibsen in a single week, it is crying out for more, and the departure of Miss Achurch and Mr Charrington for Australia has with difficulty been postponed in answer to that demand. If these things had been prophesied six weeks ago, who would have believed them?

Years later, Archer recalled: 'It was this production which really made Ibsen known to the English-speaking peoples. In other words, it marked his second stride towards world-wide, as distinct from merely national renown – if we reckon as the first stride the success of *The Pillars of Society* in Germany

... The Ibsen controversy, indeed, did not break out in full virulence until 1891, when *Ghosts* and *Hedda Gabler* were produced in London; but from the date of the Novelty production onwards, Ibsen was generally recognized as a potent factor in the intellectual and artistic life of the day.'

Harley Granville Barker, in *The Coming of Ibsen,* noted: 'The play was talked of and written about – mainly abusively, it is true – as no play had been for years. The performances were extended from seven to twenty-four. The takings were apt to be between £35 and £45 a night. Charrington lost only £70. This was not bad for an epoch-making venture in the higher drama.'

The newspaper criticisms were, as Barker says, generally unfavourable. 'I never sat out a play more dreary or illogical as a whole, or in its details more feeble or commonplace,' complained the *Sporting and Dramatic News*. 'It is as though someone had dramatized the cooking of a Sunday dinner' (no bad subject for a play, one might think nowadays). Bernard Shaw praised it anonymously in the *Manchester Guardian* (8 June); so did R. K. Harvey in the *Theatre* (1 July): 'Those who have not read *A Doll's House* or seen it acted can have no conception with what a master hand the characters are drawn.' But the same issue contained a violent attack on the play by the editor, Clement Scott: 'The atmosphere is hideous ... it is all self, self, self! ... a congregation of men and women without one spark of nobility in their nature, men without conscience and women without affection, an unlovable, unlovely and detestable crew.' Scott had already written an anonymous attack in the radical organ *Truth* (13 June) on the people who supported this new cult, dismissing them as 'a scant audience of egotists and Positivists assembled to see Ibsen ... and to gloat over the Ibsen theory of woman's degradation and man's unnatural supremacy'. Among these despicable characters was W. B. Yeats, then twenty-four, who left an account of the occasion and the impression it made on a young writer in *The Trembling of the Veil*:

... somebody had given me a seat for the gallery. In the middle of the first act, while the heroine was asking for macaroons, a middle-aged washer-woman who sat in front of me stood up and said to the little boy at her side: 'Tommy, if you promise to go home straight we will go now'; and at the end of the play, as I wandered through the entrance hall, I heard an elderly critic murmur 'A series of conversations terminated by an accident.' I was divided in mind. I hated the play; what was it but Carolus Duran, Bastien-Lepage, Huxley and Tyndall all over again; I resented being invited to admire dialogue so close to modern educated speech that music and style were impossible. 'Art is art because it is not nature,' I kept repeating to myself, but how could I take the same side with critic and washer-woman? As time passed Ibsen became in my mind the chosen author of very clever young journalists who, condemned to their treadmill of abstraction, hated music and style; and yet neither I nor my generation could escape him because, though we and he had not the same friends, we had the same enemies.

Archer, in an essay entitled 'The Mausoleum of Ibsen' which he contributed to the *Fortnightly Review* in 1893, listed some of the comments of those 'enemies' on Charrington's production of *A Doll's House*:

By the new school of theorists the *genre ennuyeux* is assigned a place of distinction; for *A Doll's House* with its almost total lack of dramatic action is certainly not an enlivening spectacle – *The Times*

It would be a misfortune were such a morbid and unwholesome play to gain the favour of the public – *Standard*

Such a starting point has dramatic possibilities. A Sardou might conceivably turn it to excellent account on the stage ... It is simply as a mild picture of domestic life in Christiania that the piece has any interest at all. It is a little bit of genre painting, with here and there an effective touch – *Daily News*

Of no use – as far as England's stage is concerned – *Referee*

Unnatural, immoral and, in its concluding scene, essentially undramatic – *People*

Ibsen ... is too faddy and too obstinately unsympathetic to please English playgoers – *Sunday Times*

Strained deductions, lack of wholesome human nature, pretentious inconclusiveness ... cannot be allowed to pass without a word of protest against the dreary and sterilizing principle which it seeks to embody – *Observer*

The works of the Norwegian playwright are not suitable for dramatic representation – at any rate on the English stage – *St James's Gazette*

Among those who made the production possible was, of all people, Henry Irving, who remained until his death in 1906 an implacable opponent of Ibsen. Janet Achurch, relates Irving's grandson, 'had asked him for money to sustain her and her husband ... in a comedy, *Clever Alice* ... He had sent her £100, only to discover that she and Eleanor Marx-Aveling were conspiring to produce Ibsen. She asked him to come and see *A Doll's House*. He went. "If that's the sort of thing she wants to play she'd better play it somewhere else," was the only comment he made.'

Ibsen was delighted with the success of Charrington's production. 'The movement in London', he wrote to Archer on 26 June, enclosing a signed photograph for Janet Achurch, 'marks a shining epoch in my life, far surpassing anything I had ever dreamed of.' The interest in *A Doll's House* stimulated a brief revival of *The Pillars of Society* the following month for a single matinée at the Opera Comique in the Strand. R. K. Hervey, despite his editor's views on the playwright, again wrote enthusiastically in the *Theatre* ('It is impossible in a short article to do justice to this remarkable play'), and Austin Brereton in the *Stage* thought that 'the piece ... would in all probability succeed for a time in an evening bill, more particularly after the excitement and controversy the production of *A Doll's House* created'. An American actress named Elizabeth Robins made her first appearance in an Ibsen part, in the role of Martha; she was to do much to pioneer his work on the English stage during the coming decade.

The Charringtons took their production of *A Doll's House* to Australia that year; also to New Zealand and, in due course, to Egypt, India and America. It was well received everywhere except in Sydney, where 'an indignant and out-raged audience greeted Nora's exodus with howls and hisses'.

Ibsen had spent the previous summer in Munich, working on *The Lady from the Sea*, but this year he decided to take a holiday. 'In the beginning of next month,' he wrote to Nils Lund on 29 June, 'we shall be going to the Tyrol to spend the rest of the summer there. We shall probably choose Gossensass, where we have so often stayed before.' It was a fateful decision. That summer in Gossensass in 1889 was to throw Ibsen sharply out of the mood of mellow optimism which had found expression in *The Lady from the Sea*, and was to leave its mark on all his future work.

26

The Summer in Gossensass
1889

IT was Ibsen's first visit to Gossensass for five years, since he had spent the summer of 1884 alone there finishing *The Wild Duck*. Sigurd, now transferred from Washington to the embassy in Vienna, joined his parents there; they stayed, as before, at the Gröbner family hotel, and a sister of the proprietor remembered how Ibsen 'lived like a clock', just as in Munich. Each day he took a walk along the river Eisach, standing for a long while on the bridge and staring broodingly into the water. The locals, indeed, nicknamed him 'Der Wassermann', which might not unfairly be translated as Old Man River. Fräulein Gröbner recalled how *soigné* he was in his dress, even on his country walks, and, from his weekly bills, how simply and modestly he lived.

The little town had decided to celebrate his return by naming his old look-out on the hill the Ibsenplatz, and on 21 July the ceremony took place. There was a grand procession and Ibsen, despite the steep ascent, climbed at the head of it and received with friendliness and dignity the homage accorded him. A concert followed, and after the concert he met a young Viennese girl named Emilie Bardach. As she remembered seventeen years later, this happened at a crowded reception; but they first really got to know each other when he came on her seated alone on a bench, reading a book, in a valley named the Pflerschtal on the outskirts of the town. He seated himself beside her and, questioning her closely as was his wont, learned her age (eighteen), details of her home and family, and the fact that they lived so near each other in Gossensass that his windows looked into hers. A few days later she ran into him at a dull birthday party. 'It is a pity', she noted in her journal, 'that German gives him so much difficulty, as apart from that we understand each other so well.'

She fell ill, and a few days later Ibsen came to see her, climbing over the garden gate to do so. 'He remained with me a long while, and was both kind and sympathetic.' A little later: 'We talk a great deal together. His ardour ought to make me feel proud.' He asked her endless questions, and seemed particularly anxious to catch her in a lie. Then (her diary continues):

Ibsen has begun to talk to me quite seriously about myself. He stayed a long time with me on Saturday, and also again this evening. Our being so much together cannot but have some painful influence over me. He puts such strong feeling into what he says to me. His words often give me a sensation of terror and cold. He talks about the most serious things in life, and believes in me so much. He expects from me much, much, much more than I am afraid he will ever find. Never in his whole life, he says, has he felt so much joy in knowing anyone. He never admired anyone as he admires me. But all in him is truly good and noble! What a pity it is that I cannot remember all his words! He begs me so intensely to talk freely to him, to be absolutely frank with him, so that we may become fellow-workers together.

Next she writes:

Mamma has just gone out, so that I have the room to myself. At last I am free to put down the incredible things of these recent days. How poor and insufficient are words! Tears say these things better. Passion has come when it cannot lead to anything, when both of us are bound by so many ties. Eternal obstacles! Are they in my will? Or are they in the circumstances? ... How could I compare anything else that has happened to an outpouring like this? It could never go so far, and yet – !

She swings off to Baron A., the only lover who offered a standard of comparison.

But how much calmer *he* was, how inarticulate, beside this volcano, so terribly beautiful! Yesterday afternoon, we were alone together at last! Oh, the words! If only they could have stamped themselves on my heart more deeply and distinctly! All that has been offered me before was only the pretence at love. This is the true love, the ideal, he says, to which unknowingly he gave himself in his art. At last he is a true poet through pain and renunciation. And yet he is glad of having known me – the most beautiful! the wonderful! Too late! How small I seem to myself that I cannot spring to him!

Neither Suzannah nor Emilie's mother seem to have suspected what was afoot. But:

The obstacles! How they grow more numerous, the more I think of them! The difference of age – his wife! – his son! – all that there is to keep us apart! Did this have to happen! Could I have foreseen it? Could I have prevented it? When he talks to me as he does, I often feel that I must go far away from here – far away! – and yet I suffer at the thought of leaving him. I suffer most from his impatience, his restlessness. I begin to feel it now, even when we are in the salon, quite apart from each other . . .

It all came to me so suddenly! I noticed for the first time how he began to change his regular ways of life, but I didn't know what it meant. Of course I was flattered at his sympathy, and at being distinguished among the many who surround him, eager for a word . . .

An early snowstorm came, and the guests at Gossensass began to leave. Emilie realized they would soon have to part.

And I have nothing to give him, not even my picture, when he is giving me so much. But we both feel it is best outwardly to remain as strangers . . . His wife shows me much attention. Yesterday I had a long talk with his son . . .
I am reading *Love's Comedy*, but if anyone comes I am seen holding Beaconsfield's *Endymion* in my hands. Nearly everyone has gone. The days we have still to spend can now be counted. I don't think about the future. The present is too much. We had a long talk together in the morning, and after lunch he came again and sat with me. What am I to think? He says it is to be my life's aim to work with him. We are to write to each other; but what am I to write?

Ibsen confided his feelings to two ladies. One fainted; another described the scene to Emilie as 'beautiful and terrible as a thunderstorm. She wonders that I do not lose my head. She says that she herself would have been absolutely overcome. This consoles me. I do not seem so weak.'

Did something happen between Ibsen and Emilie on 19 September, and if so was it anything like what Hilde Wangel in *The Master Builder* describes as having happened on another 19 September?

HILDE . . . Was it just a little detail that I happened to be alone in the room when you came in?

SOLNESS. Were you?

HILDE. You didn't call me a little devil then.

SOLNESS. No, I don't suppose I did.

HILDE. You said I looked beautiful in my white dress. Like a little princess.

SOLNESS. So you did, Miss Wangel. And besides – I felt so happy and free that evening –

HILDE. And then you said that when I grew up, I would be your princess.

SOLNESS (*with a short laugh*). Well, well! Did I say that, too? . . .

HILDE. It sounded as though you were making fun of me.

SOLNESS. I'm sure I didn't mean that.

HILDE. I can well believe you didn't. Considering what you did next –

SOLNESS. And what on earth did I do next? . . .

HILDE. You took me in your arms and kissed me, Mr Solness.

SOLNESS (*gets up from his chair, his mouth open*). I did?

HILDE. Yes, you did. You took me in both your arms and bent me backwards and kissed me. Many, many times.

SOLNESS. Oh, but my dear, good Miss Wangel –

HILDE (*gets up*). You're not going to deny it?

SOLNESS. I certainly am! . . . All this that you've told me must have been something you've dreamed . . . No, there's more to it than that . . . I must have thought all this. I must have wanted it – wished it – desired it. So that – couldn't that be an explanation? . . .

HILDE. Perhaps you've also forgotten what day it was? . . .

SOLNESS. Hm – I've forgotten the actual day, I must confess . . .

HILDE. It was . . . the nineteenth of September.

Nearly forty years later, in 1927, Emilie told A. E. Zucker that Ibsen had never kissed her; perhaps with Ibsen, as with Solness, these things only happened in his mind. Next day, 20 September, he wrote in Emilie's album a line from *Faust*: '*Hohes, schmerzliches Glück – um das Unerreichbare zu ringen!* [Oh, high and painful joy – to struggle for the unattainable!]'

The following day, 21 September, another young girl, a German painter named Helene Raff, who was staying at Gossensass and had met Ibsen for the first time four days earlier, wrote in her diary: 'The B[ardach] completely crazy about Ibsen'; and the day after, she noted: 'Miss B. brokenhearted.'

On 27 September Emilie wrote in her diary:

Our last day at Gossensass. Then nothing but memory will remain. Two weeks ago, memory seemed to Ibsen so beautiful, and now –! He says that tomorrow he will stand on the ruins of his happiness. These last two months are more important in his life than anything that has gone before. I am unnatural in being so terribly quiet and normal? . . . Last evening, when Mamma went to talk to his wife, he came over and sat at our table. We were quite alone. He talked about his plans. I alone am in them – I, and I again. I feel quieter because he is quieter, though yesterday he was terrible.

That night, at 3 a.m., the express from Verona to Vienna passed through Gossensass and Emilie left on it. A few hours earlier she had confided to her diary:

He means to possess me. That is his absolute will. He intends to overcome all obstacles. I do what I can to keep him from feeling this, and yet I listen as he describes what is to lie before us – going from one country to another – I with him – enjoying his triumphs together . . . Our parting was easier than I had feared.

Emilie told Zucker in 1927 that Ibsen had, in Gossensass, 'spoken to her of the possibility of a divorce and of a subsequent union with her, in the course of which they were to travel widely and see the world'. Once back in Munich, however, Ibsen seemed to resign himself to the impossibility of going through with such a plan. Perhaps he feared the scandal; perhaps he felt a duty towards his sickly and ageing wife, who had stood so firmly behind him during the long years of failure; perhaps he reflected that the difference of forty-three years between their ages was too great; perhaps, away from Gossensass, he felt old. At any rate, his letters from Munich to Emilie in Vienna are no more than those of an affectionate old man to a charming schoolgirl (though we must bear in mind that he was writing in a foreign language that 'gives him ... much difficulty', that he was always an extremely inhibited letter-writer, and that he must have been very careful not to commit himself on paper):

> Munich, Maximilianstrasse 32
> 7 October 1889
>
> With my whole heart I thank you, my beloved Fräulein, for the dear and delightful letter which I received on the last day of my stay at Gossensass, and have read over and over again.
>
> There the last autumn week was a very sad one, or it was so to me. No more sunshine. Everything – gone. The few remaining guests could give me no compensation for the brief and beautiful end-of-summer life. I went to walk in the Pflerschtal. There there is a bench where two can commune together. But the bench was empty and I went by without sitting down. So, too, the big salon was waste and desolate ... Do you remember the big, deep bay-window on the right from the verandah? What a charming niche! The flowers and plants are still there, smelling so sweetly – but how empty! – how lonely! – how forsaken!
>
> We are back here at home – and you in Vienna. You write that you feel surer of yourself, more independent, happier. How glad I am of these words! I shall say no more.
>
> A new poem begins to dawn in me. I want to work on it this winter, transmuting into it the glowing inspiration of the summer. But the end may be disappointment. I feel it. It is my way. I told

you once that I only corresponded by telegraph. So take this letter as it is. You will know what it means. A thousand greetings from

Your devoted

H.I.

The 'poem' (the Norwegian word *digt* means, like the Greek *poema*, not merely something in verse but a 'thing of creation') may have been *Hedda Gabler*, which he was to write the following year, or it may have been *The Master Builder*, which he did not write until three years later but may have conceived at this stage and then deliberately put aside until he could consider it with more detachment. On receiving this letter, Emilie, the following day, noted in her diary:

A few words before I go to bed. I have good news. Today, at last, came Ibsen's long-expected letter. He wants me to read between the lines. But do not the lines themselves say enough? This evening I paid Grandmama a quite unpleasant visit. The weather is hot and stuffy and so is Papa's mood. In other days this would have depressed me; but now I have something to keep me up.

We do not know how she replied to Ibsen, for he did not preserve her letter. On 15 October, however, he writes again:

I receive your letter with a thousand thanks – and have read it, and read it again. Here I sit as usual at my desk, and would gladly work, but cannot do so.

My imagination is ragingly at work, but is always straying to where in working hours it should not. I cannot keep down the memories of the summer, neither do I want to. The things we have lived through I live again and again – and still again. To make of them a poem is for the time being impossible.

For the time being?

Shall I ever succeed in the future? And do I really wish that I could and would so succeed?

For the moment, at any rate, I cannot – or so I believe. That I feel – that I know.

And yet it must come. Decidedly it must come. But will it? Or can it?

Ah, dear Fräulein – but forgive me! – you wrote so charmingly in your last – no, no! God forbid! in your *previous* letter you wrote so charmingly 'I am not Fräulein for you.' – So, dear child – for that you surely are for me – tell me – do you remember that once we talked about Stupidity and Madness – or, more correctly, *I* talked about it – and you took up the role of teacher, and remarked, in your soft, musical voice, and with your far-away look, that there is always a difference between Stupidity and Madness . . : Well, then, I keep thinking over and over again: Was it a Stupidity or was it Madness that we should have come together? Or was it both Stupidity *and* Madness? Or was it neither?

I believe the last is the only supposition that would stand the test. It was a simple necessity of nature. It was equally our fate . . .

Your always devoted

H.I.

Of this letter, Emilie wrote in her diary:

I left it unopened until I had finished everything, and could read it quietly. But I was not quiet after reading it. Why does he not tell me of something to read which would feed my mind instead of writing in a way to inflame my already excited imagination? I shall answer very soberly.

Before he wrote to her again, he had started up a close acquaintance (it was never to be anything more with any of the young girls who henceforth successively seized and filled his imagination) with his other youthful admirer from Gossensass, Helene Raff. Determined to meet him again when he had no Emilie to dazzle him, Helene spent several days walking up and down Maximilianstrasse until at last, on 19 October, she was successful. The next morning she ran into him again at an art exhibition; and later that day, they saw each other again. Five days later, having meanwhile primed herself by reading Otto Brahm's pamphlet on him, she waylaid Ibsen in Maximilianstrasse, accompanied him to his apartment and spent an hour with him, which she found 'very interesting, but rather upsetting'. He spoke about hypnosis and the power of the will. 'He stressed that women's will in particular tends to remain undeveloped; we dream and wait for something unknown that will give our lives meaning. As a result of this, women's emotional lives are unhealthy, and they fall victims to disappointment.' The words precisely enshrine the theme of the play he was about to write, *Hedda Gabler*. When Helene left he saw her down to the courtyard, and there they kissed.

They do not seem to have met for a fortnight after this, and in the meantime, on 29 October, four days after that meeting with Helene, he wrote again to Emilie:

I have been meaning every day to write you a few words, but I wanted to enclose the photograph. This is still not ready, and my letter must go off without it . . .

How charmingly you write! Please keep sending me a few lines, whenever you have a half hour not good for anything else.

So you leave my letters unopened till you are alone and quite undisturbed! Dear child! I shall not try to thank you. That would be superfluous. You know what I mean.

Don't be uneasy because just now I cannot work. In the back of my mind I am working all the time. I am dreaming over something which, when it has ripened, will become a poem.

Someone is coming. Can write no further. Next time a longer letter.

Your truly devoted
H.I.

Emilie's diary:

I wrote to him on Monday, very late at night. Though I was tired, I did not want to put off doing so, because I had to thank him for the books I received on Sunday. The same evening I had read *Rosmersholm*, parts of which are very fine. I have had to make so many duty calls, but this and a great many other things I can stand better than I used to. They are only the outward things, my inner world is something very different. Oh, the terror and beauty of having him care about me as he never cared about anyone else! But when he is suffering he calls it high and painful joy!

Helene noted in her diary for 7 November: 'Painted in afternoon, then went in vain to Maximilianstr.' But the next day she was luckier, and was 'touched by his pleasure at my coming'. The day after that: 'Visited Frau Ibsen, he also present. Extraordinary situation!' Suzannah told her how at the time of their marriage Ibsen 'had an easel and wanted to paint; but I did not like that; I thought a dramatist should not divide himself.' Three days later: 'Met Ibsen in evening, he wants to visit me – I was much relieved. He accompanied me home; tender parting.' It pleased him when she told him she had been educated at home, not at school or in church (her father was a composer).[1] 'Well, then,' he declared, 'you are a little heathen!'; then, becoming serious, he said: 'That is the education of the future, without state, school or church,' and suddenly seized her hands as though in triumph and cried: 'Yes, yes, child, the future is ours!' And then: 'Only when one is free of the mass of inherited opinions which school and church hand down can one become outwardly and inwardly strong like you, who are like a child of the forest.'

Six days later, on 18 November, he visited her in her studio, bringing a copy of Jæger's biography with him. Helene asked him why he liked her and what he saw in her.

He replied: 'You are youth, child, youth personified – and I need that – for my work, my writing.' I was troubled that he used certain phrases which reminded me of what Fräulein Bardach had told me. I asked him not to speak to me as he had to her, to which he naïvely answered: 'Oh, that was in the country. In town one is more in earnest.'

Helene was clearly displacing Emilie as the object of his

1. Joachim Raff, well known in his time. Among other things he was the author of a popular tarantella.

affections, for two reasons: she was in Munich while Emilie was in Vienna and (it is a fair assumption) she was less emotionally demanding. He had (in Solness's phrase) offered Emilie a kingdom, and she (like Hilde) did not regard the offer as a joke. Helene, much cooler and harder-headed, seems to have wanted no more from Ibsen than he was giving her, admiration and flattering companionship. The day after this last meeting with Helene he wrote to Emilie in a noticeably cooler (though still affectionate) mood:

> At last I can send you the new picture. I hope you may find it a better likeness than the one you have already. A German sketch of my life will appear within a few days, and you will receive it at once. Read it when you have time. It will tell you my story to the end of last year.
>
> Heartfelt thanks for your dear letter; but what do you think of me for not having answered it earlier? And yet – you know it well – you are always in my thoughts, and will remain there. An active exchange of letters is on my side an impossibility. I have already said so. Take me as I am.
>
> I am greatly preoccupied with the preparations for my new play. Sit tight at my desk the whole day. Go out only towards evening. I dream and remember and write. To dream is fine; but the reality at times can still be finer.
>
> Your most devoted
H.I.

On the back of the phograph Ibsen had inscribed: *An die Maisonne eines Septemberlebens* – 'To the May sun of a September life.'

On 28 November Ibsen and Suzannah both visited Helene at her studio; the next day she went to them, and that same evening he wrote her a letter:

Dear Child!

How beautiful, how lovable of you to visit us yesterday. My wife is so deeply fond of you. And I – too. As you sat there in the dusk and spoke to us so sensibly, so understandingly, do you know what I thought and wished? No, you cannot. I wished: Ah, if only I had such a sweet and lovely daughter.

Come and visit us again very soon. But in the meantime keep working hard in your studio. You must not let yourself be distracted.

Blessings on your dear head.

Your devoted
H.I.

Helene was baffled at the way Ibsen was drawing Suzannah into their relationship. When, one evening a couple of weeks later, she hovered on Maximilianstrasse in the hope of seeing him, and was successful, 'he towed me off to his wife; I was confused and vexed'. Helene did not yet comprehend, any more than Emilie ever would, that, as she phrased it nearly forty years later: 'Ibsen's relations with young girls had in them nothing whatever of infidelity in the usual sense of the term, but arose solely from the needs of his imagination; as he himself said, he sought out youth because he needed it for his poetic production.'

Some fanciful theories have been advanced to explain Ibsen's unwillingness to attempt to develop any of his infatuations into a full sexual relationship, when his plays show him to have been (to borrow Emilie's metaphor) a volcanically passionate man. But there are many passionate men who are terrified by the reality of sex, even to the point of impotence when offered it, and Dr Edvard Bull's evidence about Ibsen's unwillingness to expose his sexual organ even during medical examination suggests that this may well have been Ibsen's tragedy. Neither Solness, Borkman nor Rubek, the three most obvious self-portraits among Ibsen's characters, suffered from this inhibition (or did Rubek? He never touched Irene, and his wife was unsatisfied). But John Rosmer and Alfred Allmers (in *Little Eyolf*) were both sexually shy; and so was the chief character of the play which he was now planning, 'tight at my desk', and which he might well have sub-titled: *Portrait of the Dramatist as a Young Woman.* 'The great tragedy of life,' he wrote in his notes for *Hedda Gabler*, 'is that so many people have nothing to do but yearn for happiness without ever being able to find it'; and 'It is a great delusion that one only loves one person.'

A psychiatrist's view of Ibsen may be noted here. On reading the first section of this biography a distinguished member of that profession, and a distinguished author in his field, Dr Anthony Storr, wrote to me:

Ibsen appears to have been what psychiatrists call an obsessional character. This type of person is generally meticulous about cleanliness, disturbed by disorder, punctilious, punctual and polite. He is often tied to routine – for example, may feel compelled to take his clothes off and put them on in a particular order. If he becomes neurotic, he may be plagued by irrational thoughts which he cannot banish; parsons fear that swear-words will interrupt their sermons, etc. Ritual cleanliness – compulsive hand-washing, for example – attains a symbolic significance. This kind of character is built upon a fear of letting instincts or emotional forces loose. Emotions must be controlled, for spontaneity is dangerous. Such people find it difficult to 'let go' physically or emotionally. They are often constipated and may also have difficulty in reaching orgasm. As Dr Charles Rycroft has put it in his book *Anxiety and Neurosis*: 'the obsessional defence leads to antagonism to emotion as such and feelings come to be regarded as intruders which disturb the orderliness of the world of which the obsessional has made himself master'. Creative people of this temperament may be led into creativity because they (a) want to create an imaginary world in which everything can be controlled, and (b) want to avoid the unpredictability and spontaneity of real relationships with real people.

A week after leaving Helene 'confused and vexed', on 6 December, Ibsen wrote in a warmer manner than of late to Emilie:

Two dear, dear letters have I had from you, and answered neither till now. What do you think of me? But I cannot find the quiet necessary to writing you anything orderly or straightforward. This evening I must go to the theatre to see *An Enemy of the People*. The mere thought of it is torture. Then, too, I must give up for the time being the hope of getting your photograph. But better so than to have an unfavourable picture. Besides, how vividly your dear, serene features remain with me in my memory! The same enigmatic princess stands behind them. But the enigma itself? One can dream of it, and write about it – and that I do. It is some little compensation for the unattainable – for the unfathomable reality.

In my imagination I always see you wearing the pearls you love so much. In this taste for pearls I see something deeper, something hidden. I often think of it. Sometimes I think I have found the interpretation – and then again not. Next time I shall try to answer some of your questions, but I myself have so many questions to ask you. I am always doing it – inwardly – inaudibly.

Your devoted
H.I.

In her diary, Emilie repeated his words: 'It is some little compensation for the unattainable – for the unfathomable reality.' She wrote to him and he replied, again warmly and affectionately, on 22 December:

How shall I thank you for your dear and delightful letter? I simply am not able to, at least not as I should like. The writing of letters is always hard for me. I think I have told you so already, and you will in any case have noticed it for yourself.

I read your letter over and over, for through it the voice of the summer awakens so clearly. I see – I experience again – the things we lived together. As a lovely creature of the summer, dear Princess, I have known you, as a being of the season of butterflies and wild flowers. How I should like to see you as you are in winter! I am always with you in spirit. I see you in the Ring Strasse, light, quick, poised like a bird, gracious in velvet and furs. In *soirées*, in society, I also see you, and especially at the theatre, leaning back, a tired look in your mysterious eyes. I should like, too, to see you at home, but here I don't succeed, as I haven't the data. You have told me so little of your home-life – hardly anything definite. As a matter of fact, dear Princess, in many important details we are strangers to each other . . .

More than anything I should like to see you on Christmas night at home, where I suppose you will be. As to what happens to you there, I have no clear idea. I only imagine – to myself.

And then I have a strange feeling that you and Christmas don't go well together. But who knows? Perhaps you do. In any case accept my heartfelt wishes and a thousand greetings.

Your ever devoted

H.I.

That same day, 22 December 1889, Emilie wrote to him from Vienna enclosing at last her photograph. It is one of the only two letters from her which have survived:

Sunday

Here is the photograph – very unlike the original – to wish you a happy Christmas. Are you satisfied with it? Do you think it a good one? I don't think any better picture of me can be expected, but I hope it may give you some small pleasure. Now I must confess that I have had this proof for a fortnight – I kept it back so long in order to send it to you as a Christmas greeting. It was hard to keep it a secret from you for so long, but I wanted to have some little thing to contribute to the lower holiday. Should I play no role at all in that? It's bad enough that I am not able to do more. In spite of my '*Nicht Rönnaug*' a few weeks ago I painted a trifle for you which would have been altogether pointless if it did not recall Gossensass. I used to buy little deer bells there, and since I so often met you on my way home from my study trip to the Strassberg ruins I perpetuated the picture on one of these bells. Then I waited for your son to come here as I would have liked to give it to him to take to you – but he didn't come and it seemed too small a thing to make a business of sending it. I will be silent for a while, then I will be able to tell you better about that. How much longer are you going to make me wait? This detailed letter which is to tell me so much – but no – don't think this is a reproach – I don't mean it like that. I will send a Christmas greeting to your wife – I must write a few words just to her.

Well, once more many tender wishes and regards.

Sincerely

Emilie

On Christmas Day Helene paid an afternoon visit to the Ibsens but saw only Suzannah and Sigurd – 'she very kind, the son very dull'. Four days later she went again to Maxi-

milianstrasse in the hope of seeing him, but 'in vain'. On
New Year's Eve: 'With Aunt again to Maximilianstr., where
we met Ibsen ... He promises I may paint him. To bed contented.' The previous day he had written to Emilie:

Your lovely and charming picture, so eloquently like you, has
given me a wholly indescribable joy. I thank you for it a thousand times, and straight from the heart. How you have brought
back, now in midwinter, those brief sunny summer days!

So, too, I thank you from the heart for your dear, dear letter.
From me you must expect no more than a few words. I lack the
time, and the necessary quiet and solitude, to write to you as I
should like ...

Shortly before Christmas Ibsen fell a victim to the
influenza epidemic which swept Europe that winter (this,
perhaps, was why Helene did not see him on her Christmas
visit to Maximilianstrasse). It was the first time he had been
ill for twenty-eight years; but with his iron constitution he
threw it off. Emilie, in Vienna, caught it too. 'How sorry I
am,' Ibsen wrote to her on 16 January, 'to learn that you, too,
have been ill. But what do you think? I had a strong pre-
sentiment that it was so. In my imagination I saw you lying
in bed, pale, feverish, but sweet and lovely as ever ... How
thankful I am that I have your charming picture!'

But he had made the decision to break off their correspondence. Her next letter to him has not survived; but on 6
February he wrote to her:

Long, very long, have I left your last, dear letter – read and
read again – without an answer. Take today my heartfelt thanks
for it, though given in very few words. Henceforth, till we see each
other face to face, you will hear little from me, and very seldom.
Believe me, it is better so. It is the only right thing. It is a matter
of conscience with me to end our correspondence, or at least to
limit it. You yourself should have as little to do with me as possible. With your young life you have other aims to follow, other
tasks to fulfil. And I – I have told you so already – can never be
content with a mere exchange of letters. For me it is only half the
thing; it is a false situation. Not to give myself wholly and unreservedly makes me unhappy. It is my nature. I cannot change it.

You are so delicately subtle, so instinctively penetrating, that you will easily see what I mean. When we are together again, I shall be able to explain it more fully. Till then, and always, you will be in my thoughts. You will be so even more when we no longer have to stop at this wearisome halfway house of correspondence.

A thousand greetings.

Your
H.I.

'Till we see each other face to face' – 'When we are together again' – such words must have excited Emilie's most passionate hopes. And yet he wished to break off their correspondence. She replied to his letter of 6 February the following day:

Please forgive me for writing again so soon. All these days I have been intending to write to you, for it is part of my nature to feel anxious about persons to whom I am deeply attached if I do not hear from them for a longish while. Possibly this is a petty characteristic, but it is impossible to control one's feelings. Nevertheless, I mean to control mine, and since I know how sensitive you are in this respect I came halfway to meet you. Yes, I knew very well that you are an unwilling letter-writer, and from time to time I even felt that you might find my letters a nuisance. All the same, your last letter has shaken me badly, and I have needed all my self-control to conceal my feelings. But I don't want this to prevent you from carrying out your intentions. I certainly do not wish you to write to me frequently, and since you wish it I shall also refrain. However, I cannot allow myself to prescribe the problems and the moods to which, as you say, I should surrender myself in my young life. What I have so often told you remains unaltered and I can never forget it. Unfortunately the fact remains that I cannot surrender myself completely, nor taste unalloyed enjoyment. Forgive me for drawing you into a conflict with fate. That is ungrateful of me, seeing that you have so often said to me that whatever happens we shall remain good friends, and that I must hold fast to that. And is it friendship not to know if the other is ill or well, happy or wretched? And then can I prevent the thought coming to me that *you* want to avoid seeing me again, and anyhow, if you do not write, how am I to know where we can find each other again? Well, I'll be very, very patient; I can wait, but I shall suffer very much if I don't get a line or a book from you from time to time, or some other proof that you think of me. I am not noble enough to dispense with such little proofs of your interest.

Ought I to be ashamed of my frankness? Will you think less of me for not wishing to give up what has made me so happy and more contented through all these months? I know you a little and that is why I understand so much that is in you, but I am sure that *your* conscience should never hinder you from continuing to write to me. By so doing you only show your kindness. I will try to understand all other reasons that may prevent you from writing and certainly I don't want you to act against your feelings. What a multitude of things there are to write about, but you do not wish me to write, even though I should not expect an answer.

Tonight I have an invitation to a ball – with friends; I never go out in public. When I am there I shall allow myself to think a little about you because I often find parties like these extremely uninspiring, unless I have something of my own to fall back on. Anyhow, I mean to go, if I can.

> With love,
> Emilie

Emilie made no entries in her diary for four days after receiving the news that Ibsen wished to break off their correspondence. Then she writes of balls, singing lessons, domestic duties. Then suddenly: 'What is my inner life after Ibsen's letter? I wrote at once and henceforth will be silent, silent.' Ten days later: 'Will he never write any more? I cannot think about it. Who could? And yet, not to do so is in his nature. In his very kindness there is often cruelty.'

On 30 December he wrote, again briefly, to thank her for a Christmas present:

I have duly received your dear letter, as well as the bell with the beautiful picture. I thank you for them, straight from the heart. My wife finds the picture very pretty. But I beg you, for the time being, not to write to me again. When conditions have changed, I will let you know. I shall soon send you my new play. Accept it in friendship – but in silence. How I should love to see you and talk with you again! A Happy New Year to you and to Madame your mother.

Your always devoted

H.I.

She did not write to him again, nor did the meeting to which they had both looked forward so eagerly ever take place. For seven years there was no contact between them. Then, for his seventieth birthday, she sent him a telegram of congratulation. His letter of reply was the last message that passed between them:

Christiania, 13 March 1898

Herzlich liebes Fräulein!

Accept my most deeply felt thanks for your message. The summer in Gossensass was the happiest, the most beautiful in my whole life.

I scarcely dare to think of it – and yet I must think of it always. Always!

Your truly devoted

H.I.

Only once, as far as is known, did Ibsen ever comment on his relationship with Emilie. The German literary historian Julius Elias (later to become one of Ibsen's executors) writes that in February 1891, less than two months after Ibsen had made the final break with Emilie, he and Ibsen were lunching together in Berlin:

An expansive mood came over Ibsen and, chuckling over his champagne glass, he said: 'Do you know, my next play [*The Master Builder*] is already hovering before me – in general outline, of course. One thing I can see clearly, though – an experience I once had myself – a female character. Very interesting – very interesting.' Then he related how he had met in the Tyrol (where she was staying with her mother) a Viennese girl of very remarkable character, who had at once made him her confidant. This gist of it was that she was not interested in the idea of marrying some decently brought-up young man; most likely she would never marry. What tempted, fascinated and delighted her was to lure other women's husbands away from them. She was a demonic little wrecker; she often seemed to him like a little bird of prey, who would gladly have included him among her victims. He had studied her very, very closely. But she had had no great success with him. 'She did not get hold of me, but I got hold of her – for my play. Then I fancy she consoled herself with someone else.'

This account by Ibsen of his relationship with Emilie is impossible to reconcile, either with Emilie's diary extracts and letters to him, or with his letters to her. It reveals him at his most cowardly; and it came especially ill from one who preached the importance of responsibility. The girl he described to Elias was not Emilie Bardach but the Hilde Wangel he was about to create in *The Master Builder*. But from the time Elias published this account (just after Georg Brandes had published Ibsen's letters to Emilie) people identified the unfortunate Emilie with Hilde, just as they had identified Bjørnson with Stensgaard and Laura Kieler with Nora.

The change which Ibsen's relationship with Emilie wrought on him was immediate and drastic. For years he had deliberately suppressed his own emotional life; but his encounter with Emilie had awoken him to the realization that, as Mr Graham Greene has somewhere remarked, fame is a powerful aphrodisiac. 'All the women are in love with him,' Anne-Charlotte Leffler had written during his visit to Stockholm in 1887; but it had happened too late for him to gain any joy from it. Throughout his plays he had preached that whatever a man turns his back on gets him in the end; and now the chickens were to come home to roost with a vengeance. In 1887 he had startled his audience in Stockholm by describing himself as an 'optimist', and *The Lady from the Sea*, written the following year, had reflected this optimism. 'It is in some respects', Edmund Gosse had written on its appearance, 'the reverse of *Rosmersholm*, the bitterness of restrained and balked individuality, which ends in death, being contrasted with the sweetness of emancipated and gratified individuality, which leads to health and peace.'

But none of his five subsequent plays could by any stretch of the imagination be described as comedies. The mood of *Hedda Gabler*, *The Master Builder*, *Little Eyolf*, *John Gabriel Borkman* and *When We Dead Awaken* is, like that of *Rosmersholm*, 'restrained and balked individuality', and I do not think there can be much doubt that this stems from the realization that for various reasons (fear of scandal, sense of duty towards Suzannah, consciousness of old age, perhaps the consciousness or fear of physical impotence), he, who had suppressed his longings for so long, now had the opportunities to fulfil them but was unable to do so. As a result of his meeting with Emilie Bardach, a new glory, but also a new darkness, entered into his work.

27

Portrait of the Dramatist as a Young Woman
1889-90

IBSEN's name had come before the readers and audiences of various countries a considerable amount that autumn. In September, August Lindberg, visiting Christiania with his company, gave a special performance of *Ghosts* for members of the city Workers' Association; the play had still not been performed in the capital in Norwegian. On the twenty-ninth of the month Otto Brahm and Paul Schlenther opened their Freie Bühne in Berlin (a private theatre modelled on Antoine's Théâtre Libre in Paris and likewise limited to members in order to escape the shackles of censorship) with a production of *Ghosts*. The cast included a promising young actress named Agnes Sorma as Regina. The Freie Bühne was to last only three seasons, but its effect on the German theatre was incalculable. On 25 October we find Ibsen writing to Moritz Prozor thanking him for his efforts in France, and on 3 November he addressed a similar letter to William Archer, thanking him especially for the 'handsome edition' (limited to 115 copies) of *A Doll's House* which Fisher Unwin had brought out, bound in vellum and illustrated with photographs of the Charrington-Achurch production. 'I have the book always on my table and it excites the lively admiration of everyone who sees it and who knows anything of the art of typography. I cannot deny that I am somewhat proud that a work of mine should have appeared in great England in such a dress.'

The previous day, 2 November, the *Academy* magazine had reported:

Ibsen's vogue seems to be spreading through all parts of the world. A Dutch translation of *The Wild Duck*, one of the least known[!] of Ibsen's plays, has been acted this week in Amsterdam and in the Hague. A Russian version of *The Pillars of Society* is appearing on the stage of one of the St Petersburg theatres. *A Doll's House*, *Ghosts* and *The Young Men's League* are all being played in different cities of Germany. An English version of *The Lady from the Sea* will be published next week by Mr Fisher Unwin [translated by Eleanor Marx-Aveling with an introduction by Gosse], and we hear of more than one translation of *Rosmersholm* as ready to appear. Finally, there is a rumour of a complete edition of Ibsen's works, to be published first in New York, under the joint supervision of Mr Archer and Mr Gosse.

A few days earlier there had occurred the first respectable production (in English, at any rate) of Ibsen in the United States. On 30 October, Beatrice Cameron presented *A Doll's House* in Boston, playing Nora herself, and toured with it with fair success through several other large cities. But Ibsen's progress in the New World was slow, and it was not until the middle nineties that he was to gain any kind of foothold in the American theatre (and then thanks principally to visiting actors from Europe such as the Charringtons, Gabrielle Réjane and Herbert Beerbohm Tree).

Sigurd, after his promising start in the diplomatic service, had run into difficulties; he was still prevented from advancing further by the fact of his not having taken the Norwegian law examinations, and his proud assertion of his Norwegianness was a constant source of irritation to his Swedish superiors. Although his Swedish was as good as his Norwegian, he wrote his reports from Vienna, which the ambassador had to sign, in Norwegian, and thus they appeared on the Foreign Minister's desk in Stockholm. He caused further vexation by stating that he did not wish to serve in the Swedish Foreign Office; and when it was made clear to him that unless he agreed to do so he would not receive promotion he announced that in such a case he would resign.

On 11 December Ibsen wrote to Emil Stang, who had succeeded Sverdrup as prime minister, asking him to intercede on Sigurd's behalf and reminding him that twenty-five years earlier he (Stang) had acted as intermediary in obtaining for Ibsen the travel stipend which had enabled him to go to Rome. But neither Sigurd nor the Swedes would yield, and that month he implemented his threat, to the considerable annoyance of his by now (in Norwegian eyes) embarrassingly pro-Swedish father. Sigurd's future wife Bergliot notes that this was probably the first time Ibsen and Sigurd had disagreed as adults.

Sigurd returned to Christiania and wrote a series of articles in *Dagbladet* attacking the conditions under which Norwegians serving in the diplomatic service were forced to work, and indicting his fellow-countrymen for their willingness to truckle to the senior partner in the union. Henceforth, he was to be as lone a wolf in the sphere of politics as his father was in the theatre.

Thanks mainly to the productions (albeit unsuccessful) in Christiania, Stockholm and Copenhagen of *The Lady from the Sea,* the reprints of *The Pretenders* and *Brand,* and a number of small German payments, 1889 had been a rather better year financially; Ibsen had earned £739.

In his letter of 19 November, Ibsen had told Emile that he was 'greatly preoccupied with the preparations for my new play. Sit tight at my desk the whole day'; but it is unsure whether he was yet working on *Hedda Gabler.* Some notes which would appear to date from that October or November seem to refer to an idea he later abandoned; of two women friends who make a suicide pact, which only one of them carries out. There is a mass of notes and jottings dating (presumably) from this autumn, winter, and spring, some in a notebook, others on odd sheets of paper, a jotting pad and even a visiting card; even the notebook entries may not necessarily have been written in chronological order, and we cannot be sure that he decided definitely on the theme of *Hedda Gabler* before the spring.

Meanwhile, having severed his connection with Emilie, he was seeing even more of Helene, who made avid notes of their conversations. He told her that he needed very little sleep ('four hours is enough for me') and defended his reticence. He warned her: 'You must never tell everything to people ... To keep things to oneself is the most valuable thing in life ... I don't write letters willingly or well, mostly in a shorthand style. I can only speak freely through the mouths of characters in a play.' And even plays 'are always better while still unwritten than when they have become reality. So one prefers the unwritten to the finished work.'

On another occasion he said: 'My plays make people uncomfortable because when they see them they have to think, and most people want to be effortlessly entertained, not to be told unpleasant truths ... People who are afraid of being alone with themselves, thinking about themselves, go to the theatre as they go to the beach or to parties – they go to be amused. But I find that people's eyes can be opened as well from the stage as from a pulpit. Especially as so many people no longer go to church.' He complained how badly his plays were usually acted, especially by 'actresses who declaim instead of speaking', but confessed that he did not interfere at rehearsals. On the subject of fame he said: 'I haven't written to become famous. But of course fame has served me in so far as it has created interest in my ideas and my writing.'

He inveighed vehemently against indolence, as people who need little sleep often do. Once, he told Helene, on a train journey from Rome to Gossensass, he had shared a compartment with a lady who had slept the whole way without once looking out through the window. Even the memory of her made him angry again. 'What a *lazy* woman! To sleep the whole way! How can anyone be so lazy?' On another occasion he remarked: 'Most people die without ever having lived. Luckily for them, they don't realize it.' He disappointed Helene by his almost (not complete, as John Paulsen supposed) lack of interest in music; he admitted to her that he had once 'positively wallowed' in Hans von Bülow's concerts – 'and that says a lot, for music usually only makes me nervous'.

He spoke to her of Suzannah; and those who have assumed that, because he loved the company of young girls and longed for what she had never been able to give him, his relationship with his wife was now dead should note his words. He admired (wrote Helene in her diary) Suzannah's 'intellectual quickness', and the way she maintained her own individuality. Despite her almost passionate belief in him, she would not hesitate to speak her own mind when her view differed from his. He praised her 'inner freedom and completeness of personality', a compliment, he added, which he could not pay to many people. Yet, while he respected strength of character, 'strength and subtlety must always go together. Brutal strength is something unbearable'.

We have seen how he admired, in Michelangelo, Bernini and the architect of Milan Cathedral, those artists who had the courage to depart from accepted standards of taste, to 'commit a madness', as he himself was never afraid to do; and this too, he discussed with Helene. He said he thought it was a longing that everyone possessed, though few yielded to it. As a schoolboy, he remembered, he had often yearned to hit his teacher over the nose with a ruler, without feeling any hatred for the man. 'This longing to commit a madness stays with us throughout our lives. Who has not, when standing with someone by an abyss or high up on a tower, had a sudden impulse to push the other over? And how is it that we hurt those we love although we know that remorse will follow?' (a thought that must have been much in his mind at that time). 'Our whole being', he added, 'is nothing but a fight against the dark forces within ourselves.' Those last eight words sum up the theme of *Rosmersholm* and *The Lady from the Sea*, and of the two plays he was to write next, *Hedda Gabler* and *The Master Builder*.

He told her of his dislike and distrust of abstract thought. 'Philosophical theories, unless put into practice, seem worthless to me.' On the subject of suffering, he remarked: 'It is not what we experience that matters, but how we understand it.' He spoke much of the importance of will-power. 'To me will is always the most important thing. Few people have strong wills. It always strikes me as comical when people tell me that something they wanted didn't work out. They have merely desired or longed for something, not willed it. He who really wills something attains his goal.' He had dramatized this theory in *Emperor and Galilean*. 'Self-realization', he declared, 'is man's highest task and greatest happiness.' One of the tragedies of women, he thought, was that their will-power tended to remain undeveloped. This was to be very much the theme of *Hedda Gabler*. 'What is healthy is the happiness one acquires through one's own will.'

On 19 March Helene took a small oil-painting she had done, apparently an imaginary portrait of Solveig in *Peer Gynt*, to Suzannah and asked her to give it to Ibsen on the following day (his birthday), as she herself would be away then. Suzannah thanked her but did not want to unwrap the present, saying: 'He must do that himself.' Helene feared the paper might stick to the paint, which was not yet quite dry, so Suzannah unwrapped it, liked the painting greatly, and said: 'I am quite sad to have seen it first – that pleasure should have been his.' She repeated this several times. When, on 31 March, Helene saw Ibsen and told him of Suzannah's remark, 'he seemed quite surprised, and said "Oh. She doesn't say such things to *me*." Then he was silent for a long time.'

His new play, *Hedda* (as he at first entitled it), was making the most painful progress. The character he was attempting to portray was of a complexity unprecedented even in Ibsen's work; it was a curious amalgam of himself and the young girl in Vienna to whom he had made such extravagant and unkept promises, and it involved the most searching and agonizing self-analysis.

On 29 May 1890 an Ibsen play was seen for the first time in France, when André Antoine staged *Ghosts* at the tiny Théâtre des Menus Plaisirs – 'a dark corner, deep hidden in a passage, and beyond this passage some ten feet of gallery', as George Moore described it – for two performances. Moore, who managed to get in ('Once the doors are opened, a thousand pounds would fail to procure you a seat. But M. Antoine is always anxious to oblige a *confrère*'), thought Mlle Barny excellent as Mrs Alving and Antoine himself 'wonderful' as Oswald, and declared the production to be the Théâtre Libre's greatest triumph since they had presented Tolstoy's *The Power of Darkness* two years previously, six years before it was allowed to be performed in Russia. Of the final scene of *Ghosts*, Moore wrote: 'Most assuredly nothing finer was ever written by man or god. Its blank simplicity strikes upon the brain, until the brain reels, even as poor Oswald's brain is reeling.' The young Aurélien Lugné-Poe, shortly to establish himself as Ibsen's most assiduous champion in France, wrote of the occasion that it was 'a thunderbolt in French theatrical history. It can never be described how stunned and shaken we were that day.' Antoine toured with his production around France, presenting it for over two hundred performances.

As if Ibsen had not enough guilt on his conscience concerning women that summer, Laura Kieler now dramatically re-entered his life. Two years earlier she had sent him a play she had written called *Men of Honour*. As he had shown in the case of her autobiographical novel, he could be severe on work he did not like, but of this play he had written to her (23 July 1888) that he had read it 'with *keen* interest, and I think that *all* our theatres should *hasten* to perform it'. Poor Laura's luck, however, continued as bad as ever. Dagmars Theatre in Copenhagen accepted it but went bankrupt before they could stage it, and although the Casino Theatre in Copenhagen put it on in 1890 and the Christiania Theatre in 1891, it failed on both occasions. It was keenly and eloquently defended by Bjørnson, and brought her a number of grateful letters from young people; but the pleasure this gave her was more than countered by a vicious article from the pen of (alas) Georg Brandes who, reviewing

J. B. Halvorsen's *Dictionary of Biography* (which contained a long section on Ibsen), went out of his way to assert that the original of Nora had committed her crime for reasons much less idealistic than those which had inspired Ibsen's heroine.[1] Laura wrote to Ibsen's friend in Stockholm, Fredrika Limnell, begging her to ask Ibsen to deny this and the other rumours that were circulating about her; and Fru Limnell wrote to Ibsen on 10 June, enclosing various press cuttings to show that Laura's complaints were justified.

Ibsen refused; and his reply to Fru Limnell of 1 July is difficult to defend.

I don't quite understand what Laura Kieler really has in mind in trying to drag *me* into these squabbles. A statement from me such as she proposes, to the effect that 'she is not Nora', would be both meaningless and absurd, since I have never suggested that she is. If untrue rumours have been spread in Copenhagen that something happened earlier in her life which bears a certain similarity to the business of the forged document in *A Doll's House*, then she herself or her husband, preferably both, are the only people able to kill these rumours by an open and emphatic denial. I cannot understand why Herr Kieler has not long since taken this course, which would immediately put an end to the gossip. I am genuinely sad that I cannot accede to your request to intervene. But I think that on considering the matter more closely . . . you will agree that I can best serve our mutual friend by remaining silent and not intervening.

Ibsen's attitude in this matter was as cowardly and hypocritical as his account to Julius Elias of his relationship with Emilie Bardach. Whether or not he had suggested that Laura was the original of Nora, she was, and many people knew it; and he could easily have written an open letter to a newspaper stating truthfully that her conduct had been deserving only of praise and flatly contradicting Brandes's assertion. Such an action would have established her as what she was, a figure no whit less heroic than Nora.

1. As late as 1917 Brandes was still asserting that Laura got the money 'not in order to save her husband's life but to beautify her home'.

Bjørnson would have done it; and was Ibsen so afraid of offending Brandes? But there was something of Pontius Pilate in him, as in Peer Gynt.

On 18 July there occurred in London an event that was ultimately to prove of great importance in the establishment of Ibsen's reputation. Bernard Shaw, then an unsuccessful novelist of thirty-four who had yet to complete his first play,[2] delivered a lecture on Ibsen to the Fabian Society at the St James's Restaurant. Since it was from this lecture (mainly devoted to *A Doll's House*) that *The Quintessence of Ibsenism* grew, it is worth recalling the particular terms of reference within which it was written. As Shaw states in his original preface to the *Quintessence*, the Fabian Society had arranged a series of lectures under the general heading of Socialism in Contemporary Literature. 'Sydney Olivier consented to "take Zola"; I consented to "take Ibsen" ... and ... purposely couched it in the most provocative terms.'

The Quintessence of Ibsenism, Shaw's first important book, was to perform a great service for Ibsen in drawing attention to his work; but it was one of the most misleading books about a great writer that can ever have been written. Had it been entitled *Ibsen Considered as a Socialist,* or *The Quintessence of Shavianism* (not that the word Shavianism had been coined then), one would have no quarrel with it.

As a result of Shaw's lecture, a correspondent of the London *Daily Chronicle* questioned Ibsen on 12 August concerning his views on socialism, and next day the *Chronicle* printed the following report:

In consequence of the continuous efforts of the Social Democrats to represent Henrik Ibsen as one of their party, and specially on account of the abuse of Ibsen's name by certain moral philosophers in England ever since *A Doll's House* was performed in London, I interviewed Ibsen, who since his return from Italy resides with his family [*sic*] permanently in Munich. Ibsen was

2. He had begun *Widowers' Houses* (at Archer's instigation) in 1884, but did not finish it until 1892.

very pleased to receive me, and glad to converse on the subject I had called to see him about. He declared that he had never at any time belonged to the Social Democratic Party. He never had studied the Social Democratic question, nor does he intend to join the Social Democratic Party at a future date. In fact, he declared he never was or ever would be a Social Democrat. He was surprised to find his name used as a means for the propagation of Social Democratic dogmas. If a mere accidental coincidence of certain tendencies or principles involved in his book *Nora* with regard to the matrimonial and woman question are [*sic*] identical with or cover certain planks of the Social Democratic platform, his *Nora* is not, he explained, an abstract hypothesis conceived to demonstrate certain party dogmas, but was taken from life. Nora existed; but he never intended to lay down a hard and fast rule that all women in a similar position to Nora should or must act like Nora.

This report grossly distorted what Ibsen had in fact said to the reporter. He had no intention of being used as a stick to beat the socialists in any country, and on 18 August, he addressed the following letter to H. L. Brækstad, the Norwegian bookseller who had first introduced his works to Edmund Gosse in Trondhjem seventeen years earlier, and who had for the past ten years been living in London, where he was Norwegian consul:

Dear Herr Brækstad,
Since an article from Berlin concerning me in the *Daily Chronicle* of 13 August strikes me as likely to be misinterpreted in several respects, as has already happened in Norwegian newspapers, I should like, for your sake and that of my other British friends, to correct some of the remarks attributed to me. I feel that what I said was not in all instances reported quite clearly or fully.
I did not say that I have never studied the question of Social Democracy. On the contrary, I have, as far as I was able and could spare the time, sought with keen curiosity to understand it. What I said was that I have never found time to study the great mass of literature on the subject dealing with the different socialist systems.

When the reporter quotes me as saying that I did not belong to the Social Democrat Party I would prefer that he had not omitted to mention what I added on the subject, namely, that I had never belonged and probably never would belong to any party.

In other words, it has become a necessity for me to operate as a complete independent.

The reporter's statement that I was astonished at seeing my name used as a means of spreading Social Democratic doctrines is likely to be especially misleading.

What I in fact expressed was my surprise that I, who had made it my principal task to portray human characters and human destinies, had, on certain issues – without having consciously or deliberately so intended – arrived at the same conclusion as that reached by the Social Democrat moral philosophers through scientific research.

This surprise – and, I may add, pleasure – I expressed as the result of the reporter telling me how someone, or some people, had given lectures in London which, according to his account, had been largely devoted to *A Doll's House* . . .

Your affectionate and bounden

Henrik Ibsen

This letter was published in the *Daily Chronicle* on 28 August, and must have given considerable satisfaction to all good socialists.

A few days after Ibsen had written the above, William Archer visited him, en route for Oberammergau. He described the meeting in a letter to his brother:

His fame in England is, as he says, 'a fairy tale' to him . . . He is obviously older, but looks very well and is quite alert and cheerful. He trotted me round a vast exhibition of modern pictures, where there is a portrait of himself by a Norwegian named Smith – a vivid enough but far from flattering one. He won't go into the room where it hangs, but waited round the corner. Just as I discovered it, an Englishman and his wife were standing before it. The man looked up his catalogue and said: 'Oh, that's Ibsen, the Norwegian poet,' to which the lady replied with the greatest interest 'Oh, is it? Well, now, that's just what I would have expected him to look like.' I was tempted to tell them that they need only step into the next room to see the original; but instead, I reported their conversation to the 'Old Man', who was amused . . .

You would see from Shaw's letter which I sent you that Ibsen was supposed to be infuriated at being classed as a Socialist by G.B.S. He explained to me, however, that his rage existed only in the imagination of the *Daily Chronicle* interviewer. What he really said was that he never had belonged, and probably never would belong, to any party whatsoever; but he expressed himself as pleasantly surprised that English Socialists, working on scientific lines, had arrived at conclusions similar to his. This the *Chronicle* interviewer . . . twisted into an expression of unpleasant surprise that anyone should have the audacity to make use of his name in Socialist propaganda. The Old Man was quite put out about this, for the thing had got into the German and Dutch papers too. While I was with him he received a letter from Wollmar, one of the Socialist leaders in the Reichstag, asking him what the devil he meant by this seemingly contemptuous disclaimer, not only of Socialism but of all sympathy with Socialism. Ibsen had already written a letter to Brækstad, intended for the English papers; and he forthwith sat down to write a German translation of this letter for Wollmar.

Fru Ibsen and he had an amusing little scene apropos of this incident. She said 'I warned you when that man came from Berlin that you would put your foot in it. You should have let me see him; women are much more cautious than men in what they say.' Whereupon the Old Man smiled grimly and said that wasn't generally supposed to be the strong point of the sex; adding that since the interviewer was going to lie about what he said, it didn't much matter whether he was cautious or not. Then Fru Ibsen suggested that he ought not to have seen him at all, and I closed the discussion by assuring her that in that case he would have made up the interview entirely from his own consciousness.

Archer found the rooms in Maximilianstrasse no more homely than the apartment in the Capo le Case: 'lofty and handsome, but still, to my thinking, unattractive'.

Ibsen's unwillingness to commit himself to any political party has often been criticized; but he was not the only man of progressive sympathies who has felt unable to identify himself with the left-wing party in his country. He once said to Laura Kieler: 'I sympathize with all my heart with the cause of the left, in both Norway and Denmark. I am a man of the left, in so far as the left fights against what is conservative. But if they do not also make the workers' cause their own, then the left has shirked its task; I am no longer one of them.'

The cause of the controversy in the *Daily Chronicle* himself almost met Ibsen that summer. Bernard Shaw was in Munich at the beginning of August, on a trip with Sidney Webb to see (like Archer) the Passion Play at Oberammergau; but 'my total ignorance of Norwegian' (he wrote to Archer on 17 August) 'prevented my calling on him during my stay ... to explain his plays to him'. The two could have conversed in German, and one wonders why Shaw did not make the effort; perhaps he felt he would make a dull impression on his hero in any language but his own. The two were never to meet.

Meanwhile, Ibsen had continued to make heavy weather of *Hedda*. On 29 June he had written to Carl Snoilsky that he would probably have to sacrifice his summer holiday, since 'I shan't leave Munich before I have completed the first draft, and there is little or no prospect that I shall get that far during July.' He did not even begin his first draft of Act Two until 13 August, and in the next three weeks he wrote only the opening stage directions (the scene was to take place in Hedda's garden) and three lines of dialogue (or if he wrote more, he destroyed it). There was obviously some deep technical or (more probably) psychological block. 'I am not likely to get out into the country this summer,' he wrote sadly to Nils Lund on 24 August. 'I sit here fully occupied with my new work, and anyway the weather this year is not inviting for a country holiday. It is cold and rainy, with occasional days of intolerable heat and closeness.' On 6 September he started a new draft of Act Two, and at last the play began to move. Nine days later, the act was ready; the third act took him only twelve days, and the fourth and final act a week.

On 16 November, after nearly six weeks of revision, he at last finished fair-copying *Hedda Gabler* (as he had re-entitled it, as though to underline the fact that, though officially Hedda Tesman, she was her father's child, a general's daughter who should have been born a boy). Two days later, late indeed for a Christmas book (and how badly he needed those Christmas sales), he posted the manuscript to Copenhagen. 'It leaves me with a strange feeling of emptiness,' he wrote to Moritz Prozor on 20 November. 'But I am glad to be done with it. Living incessantly with these imagined characters was beginning to make me more than a little nervous.' On 4 December he stressed in another letter to Moritz Prozor: 'I have not tried in this play to deal with so-called problems. My main object was to portray human beings, human moods, and human destinies, as conditioned by certain relevant social conditions and attitudes.' Though happy to be reckoned a socialist, he was tired of being branded a sociologist, a reputation which Bernard Shaw's lecture, and the controversy it had aroused, had considerably fostered.

The English publisher William Heinemann, impressed by the constant publicity that was now being accorded to Ibsen in England – apart from the *Doll's House* production, Shaw's lecture, and the appearance of Jæger's biography, the first four volumes of the collected edition under Archer's editorship had appeared that November – had offered Ibsen £150 for the rights of *Hedda Gabler*, provided the proof-sheets could be sent direct from Gyldendal to Edmund Gosse (who was to translate it) as they came off the press. Ibsen happily accepted this windfall, telling Gosse (29 November) that he felt 'much bounden to Mr Heinemann for so liberal an honorarium' and expressing his 'deep joy and satisfaction at seeing how my writings increasingly win an entry into the immense territory of the English-speaking peoples, in which a foreign author generally has such difficulty in establishing a foothold'. To secure his copyright Heinemann, then only twenty-seven and in his first year as a publisher, issued an edition of twelve copies of the play in Norwegian on 11 December, five days before the Gyldendal edition – a procedure he was to adopt with Ibsen's subsequent plays. On 16 December the Gyldendal edition appeared, in a printing of 10,000 copies.

Hedda Gabler received the worst press notices of any of Ibsen's mature plays, not excluding *Rosmersholm*. Bredo Morgenstierne, who had written a front-page tribute to Ibsen on his sixtieth birthday, regretted in *Aftenposten* that, after the 'cleaner air and brighter perspectives of *The Lady from the Sea*', Ibsen had now reverted to the unpleasant thematic matter of *Ghosts* and *Rosmersholm* – 'and the obscurity, the eccentric and abnormal psychology, the empty and desolate impression which that whole way of life leaves, is here stronger than ever ... With the best will in the world one has difficulty in following the master's thought. We do not understand Hedda Gabler, nor believe in her. She is not related to anyone we know.' Alfred Sinding-Larsen in *Morgenbladet* described Hedda as 'a horrid miscarriage of the imagination, a monster in female form to whom no parallel can be found in real life ... far from likely to cause any joy or much admiration'. Even some of Ibsen's warmest supporters were disappointed. Gerhard Gran wrote sadly in *Samtiden*: 'It is a law, or anyway has until now been a law, that drama, in its present state of technical development, can only present comparatively simple characters ... Everything that should make this curious being intelligible to us, her development, her secret thoughts, her half-sensed misgivings and all that vast region of the human mind which lies between the conscious and the unconscious – all this the dramatist can no more than indicate. For that reason, I think a novel about Hedda Gabler could be extremely interesting, while the play leaves us with a sense of emptiness and betrayal.' Gran's remarks explain why people who accepted Emma Bovary, Anna Karenina and Dorothea Brooke were baffled by Ellida Wangel, Rebecca West and Hedda Gabler. Neither actors nor audiences, nor even those who bought the play in book form, were able to read between the lines of dialogue as we can today.

Some of the critics were embarrassed that the first Norwegian author to gain widespread international recognition should give such a gloomy picture of their country's way of life and morals. Alfred Sinding-Larsen, in the *Morgenbladet* review quoted above, suspected him of pandering to contemporary European fashion. 'Ibsen is *fin-de-siècle*,' he declared. '... As long as his works were healthy they remained unnoticed [abroad]. But ... once his plays had the right tinge of darkness and comfortlessness, the right undertone of pessimism, Godlessness and despair, they were fitted to satisfy the contemporary craving for sensation and titillation ... The fact that Ibsen has become fashionable does not mean that the works with which he has achieved this will have any real permanence or significance ... Ibsen's modern drama is the drama of abnormality. His main characters have nothing human about them save the flesh in which they are clothed.'

Almost the only critics to appreciate what Ibsen was trying to do in *Hedda Gabler* were Henrik Jæger in Norway and Edvard Brandes in Denmark. Jæger, who had come a long way since he had stumped the country lecturing against *Ghosts*, wrote a late review of the play in *Dagbladet* on 4 February, and after lambasting the other critics for their treatment of the play, he declared: 'Bigness and pettiness are so blended in Hedda's character that she belongs neither to hell nor heaven but to earth. She is neither a monster nor a saint ... simply a tragic character who is destroyed by the unharmonious and irreconcilable contrasts in her own character ... Tragedy is not very popular in Norway just now. People do not want to see tragedies on the stage ... So naturally the play is "foul", "contemptible", and "immoral".' And Edvard Brandes, reviewing the Copenhagen première in *Politiken* on 26 February, wrote:

Ibsen's latest play is being debated round the world. There are today two or three writers who set people's minds in motion when a work leaves their desk – Tolstoy, Zola – but a novel does not nag at the mind and *demand* an answer like a play. Whether *Hedda Gabler* is in the top rank of Ibsen's works is difficult to decide. For people who are interested in things of the mind, Ibsen's plays are milestones in their development; people have *thought* differently in Scandinavia since *Ghosts* and *Rosmersholm* ... *The Lady from the Sea* did not have quite the same impact, and *Hedda Gabler* too will scarcely have a significance comparable to that of *Ghosts*. Many will rejoice that the supernatural element is absent from *Hedda Gabler*. No white horses ride here, no Stranger rides to Hedda Gabler by night.

Brandes found Hedda like the heroines of Russian novels – cold, scornful, ambitious to win men and oust other women, blasé, and eager for excitement. Though doubtful whether she would have killed herself, he found the play 'gripping and powerful', and concluded: 'One may read it again and again and find new things to marvel at.'

One suspects, too, that, as with *Ghosts* (and, for that matter, *Rosmersholm* and *The Lady from the Sea*), there were many young men and women whose views were inadequately represented by the main body of printed criticism. Carl Georgsson Fleetwood was probably speaking for many of his generation when he noted in his diary his amazement that anyone should be puzzled by the psychology of Hedda or think her unreal.

Herman Bang, one of Ibsen's most eloquent Danish admirers, also saw the point. 'Most of Ibsen's plays', he declared perceptively in a lecture delivered in Christiania on 14 November 1891, 'had been about egotistical men and selfless women; but here was a play about an egotistical *woman*, and whereas a man's egotism may at least often cause him to accomplish much, a woman's merely drives her into isolation and self-adoration. Hedda has no source of richness in herself and must constantly seek it in others, so that her life becomes a pursuit of sensation and experiment; and her hatred of bearing a child is the ultimate expression of her egotism, the sickness that brings death.'

Hedda Gabler is, today, perhaps the most universally admired of Ibsen's plays, the most frequently performed (in England, at any rate), and certainly one of the easiest for an average audience to appreciate. Why did it so baffle its contemporaries? Partly because, as stated, people who could comprehend a complex character in a novel, with the aid of narrative explanation and the character's reflections, were often helpless when faced with the same character expressed only through dialogue. And partly, too, because Ibsen was using a new technique, though it has since become so much a part of common practice in play-writing that it is difficult for us to realize that it can ever have been new. Several times in contemporary criticisms of *Hedda Gabler* one comes across the comment that here, for the first time, Ibsen has virtually dispensed with long speeches, that he has written the play almost entirely in short exchanges of two or three sentences per character, a kind of dramatic shorthand. 'No concession is made to the general public to help it to understand,' wrote Henrik Jæger in the review quoted above. 'No explanations by other characters, no self-characterization to excuse or defend herself, even a minimum of information about events that have gone before – Ibsen has scorned all this as the quackery of salesmanship. Nor is that all. He has so striven to make the dialogue natural and lifelike that everything is chiselled out in very short lines, usually no more than a few words, seldom more than one or two lines.' And Edmund Gosse, reviewing the play in the *Fortnightly Review* on 1 January 1891, remarked:

In the whole of the new play there is not one speech which would require thirty seconds for its enunciation. I will dare to say that I think in this instance Ibsen has gone perilously far in his desire for rapid and concise expression. The *sticomythia* of the Greek and French tragedians was lengthy in comparison with this unceasing display of hissing conversational fireworks, fragments of sentences without verbs, clauses that come to nothing, adverbial exclamations and cryptic interrogations. It would add, I cannot but think, to the lucidity of the play if some one character were permitted occasionally to express himself at moderate length, as Nora does in *A Doll's House*, and as Mrs Alving in *Ghosts* . . . On the stage, no doubt, this rigid broken utterance will give an extraordinary sense of reality.

But with actors and actresses looking less for reality than for big theatrical moments, it didn't.

Hedda has been rather glibly assumed by some critics to be a portrait of Emilie, on the grounds that both were beautiful and aristocratic and did not know what to do with their lives, and that Ibsen's description of Hedda (aristocratic face, fine complexion, veiled expression in the eyes, etc.) corresponds to early photographs of Emilie. The same characteristics could, however, be found in the photograph of almost any well-born young lady of the period (the description would apply equally to Queen Alexandra), and few women of Ibsen's time, let alone girls of eighteen, knew what to do with their lives. In any case, the idea of creating such a character had been at the back of Ibsen's mind long before he met Emilie, for his rough notes for *Rosmersholm* in 1886 contain a sketch of a girl, intended as Rosmer's elder daughter (though he finally decided not to include her in the play), who 'is in danger of succumbing to inactivity and loneliness. She has rich talents which are lying unused.'

On the other hand, Emilie must certainly have been at the back of his mind when he was writing *Hedda Gabler,* and it is possible that Hedda may be a portrait, conscious or unconscious, of what Ibsen felt Emilie might become in ten years if she did not marry the right man or find a fixed purpose in life. If so, it was a prophecy that came uncomfortably near the truth, for Emilie, though she lived to be eighty-three – she died on 1 November 1955 – accomplished nothing and never married.

But a Norwegian psychologist, Dr Arne Duve, has persuasively argued that Hedda is a self-portrait, and that she represents Ibsen's own repressed and crippled emotional life. Hedda longs to be like Løvborg, but lacks the courage; she is repelled by the reality of sex, as (can we doubt?) Ibsen was (what man not frightened of sex would be shy about exposing his sexual organ to his own doctor?); she prefers to experience it vicariously by encouraging Løvborg to describe his experiences to her. Two emotions are dominant in her, the fear of scandal and the fear of ridicule, and we know that Ibsen, though willing to trail his coat in print, was privately dominated by these emotions. But if Hedda is a self-portrait, it is almost certainly an unconscious one – not that that makes it any the less truthful; rather the reverse.

One contemporary who particularly hated *Hedda Gabler* was August Strindberg, now fast approaching his 'Inferno' crisis when he hovered on, if he did not indeed cross, the brink of madness. He was convinced that Ibsen had based Ejlert Løvborg on him (as, six years previously, he had believed himself to be the original of Hjalmar Ekdal in *The Wild Duck*). He had, he explained to Karl Nordström on 4 March 1891, revealed some secrets about his private life to friends, and:

Hedda Gabler is based on this! And it's obvious that Ibsen has just patched this together from gossip, not observed it at first-hand ... How can a man of talent be 'destroyed' because he gets drunk, whores, and fights with the police? It seems to me that Ibsen realizes that I shall inherit the crown when he's finished. (He hates me mortally and had the impertinence to refuse to contribute to Jacobsen's tombstone unless my name was struck off the list).[3] And now the decrepit old troll seems to hand me the revolver a second time! But his shit will rebound on him. For I shall survive him and many others, and the day *The Father* kills *Hedda Gabler* I shall stick that gun in the old troll's neck!

Strindberg repeated the accusation in another letter four days later, to the poet Ola Hansson, adding the charge that 'Hedda Gabler is a bastard of Laura in *The Father* and Tekla in *Creditors*'; and, querying whether Løvborg could have been destroyed by a night's drinking, he added irrelevantly, 'For my part, I have always felt refreshed by a good

3. The accusation about Ibsen and the tombstone was, of course, completely untrue.

debauch!' On 10 March, he wrote to Birger Mörner: 'Do you now see that my seed has fallen into Ibsen's brainpan – and fertilized! Now he carries my seed and is my uterus!'

The German publisher S. Fischer had bought the German rights of *Hedda Gabler* for the ungenerous sum of 300 marks, exactly one-tenth of what William Heinemann had paid. He also wanted to serialize the play in one of his magazines, but Ibsen refused him permission. 'If Herr Fischer really believes that my play will mean so much to his magazine,' he wrote to Julius Elias on 17 December, 'he need only print a much bigger edition of the book and advertise that he will give a free copy as a Christmas present to every subscriber.' He added that he had promised his German translator, Emma Klingenfeld, half of any fees he might get from German productions of the play, an extraordinarily generous arrangement, adding that 'on my table lies a mass of written requests from German theatre directors, including several from Berlin, begging for copies of the play so that they may stage it'.

Ibsen was having a little trouble with Fischer. 'A few days ago,' he wrote Elias the next day, 'he explained in a letter that he could not possibly have the book out before the New Year. Now he thinks he can have it ready by Monday. A few days ago he assured me that I need not worry about competition. Now he seems almost distraught at the thought of Fru *v.* Borch. But never mind.' Fischer printed an edition of 3,000 copies, Ibsen's return from which works out at about a halfpenny a copy.

Still, 1890 had been quite a good year financially, by Ibsen's standards. German fees totalled £188, not much, but something; and even England had provided £75 (Heinemann's fee for *Hedda Gabler* did not arrive until he published the English edition in January, and then only after two sharp letters from Ibsen asking why he had not fulfilled his contract). In all, the year had brought him £791. But Ibsen must, as he looked down his list of earnings for the year, have noted sombrely how little his earlier plays were bringing him. He had received nothing at all from Norway or Denmark, apart from Gyldendal's fee for *Hedda Gabler* – there had been no performances of his plays in either country, and no reprints. No wonder that, although he had £6,128 locked away in securities, he invested a further £833 during the next three months.

28

The End of an Exile
1891

1891 opened with a tremendous row between Ibsen's two British champions, Edmund Gosse and William Archer, in which Ibsen found himself an unwilling and embarrassed participant.

William Heinemann had offered Ibsen £150 for (as Ibsen supposed) first publication rights of *Hedda Gabler*. But Gosse did not send Ibsen the formal contract until 2 January, and it then became clear that Heinemann was demanding not merely the first, but the exclusive English rights, which would debar Archer from publishing his translation of the play in the collected edition which he was editing for Walter Scott. Archer, who had waived his rights in the matter to oblige Gosse, not unnaturally complained to Ibsen, and on 8 January Ibsen wrote to Gosse expressing the hope that Heinemann would withdraw his veto and regretting that 'through an excess of trust I may have helped to frustrate Mr Archer's intentions – something that his gentlemanly conduct towards me has in no way deserved, and which lay very far from my own intentions. The fee which Mr Archer has sent me from Walter Scott for *Hedda Gabler* I have of course returned. But the great collected edition will thus be incomplete, and that I deeply regret.'

This request was ignored. Gosse's translation of *Hedda Gabler* appeared on 20 January, and was the subject, three days later, of an uncharacteristically violent attack in the *Pall Mall Gazette* by Archer, normally the mildest of men. Archer described it as 'one of the very worst translations on record', which 'reproduces the terse and nervous original about as faithfully as a fourth form schoolboy, translating at sight, might be expected to reproduce a page of Tacitus'. Pointing out that 'some months ago I waived in Mr Gosse's favour a position of advantage which I held in regard to *Hedda Gabler* ... on the explicit understanding that the privilege I thus transferred to him could not and would not be used to impede Mr Walter Scott in completing his edition of Ibsen's Prose Dramas under my editorship,' Archer concluded: 'To find a parallel for Mr Gosse's conduct in this matter, I need go no further than the play itself. Yet the parallel is not exact. It was by chance, not through an act of courtesy, that Hedda became possessed of Løvborg's manuscript; and having become possessed of it, she did not deface, stultify, and publish it – and then claim copyright. She did a much less cruel thing – she burned it.'

Could any friendship survive such a betrayal on the one side, and such a public denunciation on the other? Amazingly, it did. Not only did Archer's translation of *Hedda* appear later that year, both independently and as Volume 5 of the Walter Scott Collected Edition; Gosse even included it, in preference to his own, in the Collected Ibsen which he himself was editing for Lowell's of New York. Indeed, as Archer's brother points out, 'the incident had the happy result of bringing Archer into relations with the firm [Heinemann] which was eventually to publish, under his editorship, the complete standard [English] edition of the poet's works'.[1]

So that unpleasant matter was settled; and the first six months of 1891 saw an unprecedented number of productions of Ibsen's plays, as the following list shows:

27 January	*A Doll's House* in London (single matinée)
31 January	World première of *Hedda Gabler* in Munich
6 February	*Hedda Gabler* in Helsinki
9 February	*A Doll's House* in Milan

1. Two years later, Gosse and Archer translated *The Master Builder* together!

10 February	*Hedda Gabler* in Berlin
19 February	*Hedda Gabler* in Stockholm
23 February	*Rosmersholm* in London
25 February	*Hedda Gabler* in Copenhagen
26 February	*Hedda Gabler* in Christiania
13 March	*Ghosts* in London
30 March	*Hedda Gabler* in Gothenburg
11 April	*The Pretenders* in Vienna
15 April	*An Enemy of the People* in Vienna
16 April	*The Wild Duck* in Vienna
20 April	*Hedda Gabler* in London
20 April	*A Doll's House* in Budapest
28 April	*The Wild Duck* in Paris
10 May	*The Pretenders* in Berlin
11 May	*The Lady from the Sea* in London
late May	*A Doll's House* in Paris (private performance)
2 June	*A Doll's House* in London (new production)

Before January was out, *A Doll's House* was published in
Italian, in a Rome theatrical magazine, *Carra di Tespi* (surprisingly, it did not appear in book form in Italy before
1895); and on 27 January it was performed in a new production in London, albeit only for a single performance. An
actress named Marie Fraser, who had played the part a few
months earlier in Edinburgh, acted Nora; Bernard Shaw
thought her 'desperately in earnest and desperately bad', but
the *Athenaeum* (31 January) observed: 'Whatever may be
the character of Ibsen's work ... that its influence is growing
day by day is one of the things that he who runs may read.'
Dagbladet in Christiania (2 February) offered the interesting
titbit that 'there is talk that the famous Mrs Langtry
intends to play Hedda Gabler at the earliest opportunity'.
Had this happened, Ibsen would doubtless have had the
gratifying experience of having one of his plays attended by
royalty, with one wonders what effect on the anti-Ibsen
movement in England; but sadly (or perhaps, from an artistic viewpoint, fortunately) Mrs Langtry found other fish to
fry.

On 31 January *Hedda Gabler* received its world première

at the Residenztheater in Munich; but it was not well done, and Ibsen, who was present, was much displeased at the declamatory manner of Marie Ramlo in the title role. The audience was as baffled as the critics had been when the play was published. Ibsen took a call, and bowed to those who clapped; but there was a good deal of hissing and whistling. When someone commiserated with him afterwards, Ibsen shrugged his shoulders and murmured: 'The public likes to laugh.'

On 9 February an Ibsen play was acted in Italy for the first time; Eleonora Duse, then thirty-one, acted Nora at the Teatro di Filodrammatici in Milan. Her translator, the novelist Luigi Capuana, Pirandello's mentor, had asked Moritz Prozor (from whose French version he had presumably made his own) for permission to change the last act so as to provide a happy ending; but a copyright agreement had recently been signed between Norway and Italy, which put Ibsen, at last, in a position to say No, and he did so. 'I can almost say', he wrote to Prozor on 23 January, 'that the whole play was written just for the sake of that final scene. And I think Herr Capuana is wrong in fearing that the Italian public would not be able to appreciate or understand my work if staged in its original form.' In Germany, he reminded Prozor, 'the play did not remain long in the repertory with the altered ending. But in its original form, it is still performed.'

The day after the Italian première of *A Doll's House*, *Hedda Gabler* was staged at the Lessingtheater in Berlin. Ibsen went up for the occasion, but although the performance was better than in Munich it was not really a success. Even the critics normally friendly towards him found the play illogical, and the liberal journalist Theodor Wolff wrote a parody in *Berliner Tageblatt*: 'Wie Röschen Müller in Schönheit starb.' A Swedish producer, Adolf Paul, who was present, noted how Ibsen 'took a curtain call after each act, his face copper-red, and returned without the slightest change of expression to his box'. The Danish novelist Henrik Pontoppidan, who was there too, thought that 'Ibsen cut a wretched figure. He looked like a troll that had been hauled up by the hair from the prompter's box.'

On 23 February *Rosmersholm* was staged for the first time in England, for two matinées at the Vaudeville Theatre in the Strand. Frank Benson, then a rising Shakespearean actor of thirty-one, played Rosmer, with Florence Farr as Rebecca; but it was evidently a far from satisfactory production. 'Archer was so disheartened by the rehearsals', wrote Bernard Shaw to Charles Charrington in Australia on 30 March, 'that I had the greatest difficulty in inducing him to come ... Rebecca ... got through by dint of brains and a certain fascination and dimly visible originality ... Benson ... forced his playing; but he did not distinctly fail except in the last act, which did not get for a moment on to the plane on which alone the catastrophe is credible.' At the second performance 'a sort of dim photograph of the play as it was meant to be was arrived at'. 'Being ill produced and on the whole poorly acted,' comments Charles Archer, '[it] gave the anti-Ibsenites a plausible excuse to say "Aha!".'[2] His brother William collected some specimens of press reaction:

A handful of disagreeable and somewhat enigmatical personages ... Ibsen is a local or provincial dramatist – *The Times*

2. The main reason why the Vaudeville was so often chosen for early Ibsen productions seems to have been that it was regarded as an 'unlucky' theatre, and so was cheap and easy to hire. 'Who does not know', asked the *Academy* on 23 March 1901, 'the forlorn and furtive enterprises undertaken at "unlucky" theatres, with afternoon sunlight coming in through the side windows, at which Ibsen's masterpieces have been exposed to the admiration of the few and the laughter of the many?' Sir Lewis Casson, who as a young man attended several of these occasions, told me when he was over ninety that both William Archer and Elizabeth Robins imparted to the proceedings an atmosphere of puritanism to which Archer's translations also contributed, and that he thought this one reason why the tradition of presenting Ibsen's plays as totally humourless has, until very recently, survived in England.

Impossible people do wild things for no apparent reason ...
Those portions of the play which are comprehensible are utterly
preposterous ... Ibsen is neither dramatist, poet, philosopher,
moralist, teacher, reformer – nothing but a compiler of rather disagreeable eccentricities – *Standard*

A singularly gloomy and ineffectual function was that undergone at the Vaudeville on Monday afternoon – *Observer*

The stuff that Ibsen strings together in the shape of plays must
nauseate any properly constituted person – *Mirror*

Ibsen's gruesome play ... His repulsive drama ... Greeted with
the silence of contempt when the curtain finally fell – *People*

The whole affair is provincial and quite contemptible – *Saturday Review*

To judge it seriously either as literature or as drama is impossible – *St James's Gazette*

These Ibsen creatures are 'neither men nor women, they are
ghouls', vile, unlovable, unnatural, morbid monsters, and it were
well indeed for society if all such went and drowned themselves
at once – *The Gentlewoman*

Rosmersholm is not very dramatic. It is hardly at all literary
... It is without beauty, without poetry, without sense of vista. It
is not even dextrously doctrinaire ... The farce is almost played
out – Mr F. Wedmore in *Academy*

There are certain dishes composed of such things as frogs and
snails, stews in which oil and garlic reek, and dreadful compounds
which we taste out of sheer curiosity, and which, if we expressed
our honest, candid opinion, we should pronounce to be nasty and
unpleasant ... *Rosmersholm* is beyond me – *Topical Times*

To descant upon such morbid, impracticable rubbish would be
an insult to the understanding of every reader, except an Ibsenite
... If Herr Ibsen were well smothered in mud with his two cre-

ations [*A Doll's House* and *Rosmersholm*] and with every copy of his plays, the world would be all the better for it – *Licensed Victuallers' Gazette*

'Alas, poor Ibsen!' commented Archer. 'It is well that he does not read English, else who knows but the disesteem of the *Licensed Victuallers' Gazette* might drive him into his mausoleum in good earnest!'

That last week in February was a bad one for Ibsen, or anyway for the theatres presenting his works. Two days after the *Rosmersholm* première in London, *Hedda Gabler* opened at the Royal Theatre in Copenhagen, and had the worst reception of any of his plays in Denmark. It was withdrawn after only five performances. In Bergen it managed only three; and when it was given in Christiania on 26 February the reception was again tepid. 'There was no real enthusiasm,' reported Henrik Jæger in *Dagbladet* the next morning. '... The applause weakened as the play progressed ... The whole thing takes place in an abstract realm in which the public is not accustomed to moving.' Nor, the previous week, had the play fared better in Stockholm. 'No dramatic talent can make a character as obscurely complex as Hedda Gabler really clear and dramatically consistent.' wrote Georg Göthe in *Ny Svensk Tidskrift*, and even Ibsen's champion J. A. Runström complained in *Ny Illustrerad Tidning* of the obscurity which 'surrounds the central character like a thick fog'.

While Ibsen's latest play was baffling the Scandinavians, the ones he had written a decade earlier continued to be belatedly discovered abroad; and on Friday, 13 March 1891, there occurred one of the most famous of all theatrical occasions, as controversial and epoch-making as the first nights of Victor Hugo's *Hernani* or Synge's *Playboy of the Western World*: the London première of *Ghosts*.

Inspired by the example of Antoine's Théâtre Libre in Paris and the Freie Bühne in Berlin, a twenty-nine-year-old Dutchman named Jacob T. Grein, working for a tea merchant in Mincing Lane at £180 a year, had resolved to found a similar venture in London, to stage plays from which the larger theatres shrank and which the censor would forbid. The era of the little theatres had begun, and it was from these that the new dramatists were to emerge; without the Moscow Arts there would have been no Chekhov as we know him, without the Dublin Abbey no Synge or O'Casey; in the following decade Strindberg was to found his own Intimate Theatre to perform his chamber plays. The next fifty years belonged not to the state- or city-subsidized theatres, still less to the commercial theatre, but to the little theatres, often possessing no locale of their own but performing in whatever halls or rooms they could afford to hire. They all lost money consistently and, except where saved by private patronage, ended by going bankrupt, as good theatres do.

The previous year Grein had produced Pinero and Henry Arthur Jones in his native Holland, and their plays had proved so successful that the Amsterdam Theatre sent him £50, to be used 'in the interest of art in England'. Thus, by a stroke of irony of which Ibsen would surely have approved, Jones, who had been chiefly responsible for the travesty *Breaking a Butterfly*, and was to be one of Ibsen's most vehement opponents in England, was also largely responsible for getting *Ghosts* on to the English stage. For it was principally with *Ghosts* in mind, since that play would obviously stand no chance with the Lord Chamberlain, that Grein added to his £50 another £30 which he had received for translating a play and founded, with Thomas Hardy, George Meredith and Henry James among its first members, the Independent Theatre Society, 'a modest organization [as Charles Archer described it] of most slender resources, intended to give the non-commercial drama, both native and foreign, a chance upon the stage, by means of occasional subscription performances in theatres hired for the purpose. Since no money was to be taken at the doors, the performances would be technically private.'

The Society, then, opened its first season, as the Freie Bühne had opened its, with a single performance of *Ghosts*, at the Royalty Theatre in Dean Street, Soho. Of the reception by the British press, William Archer noted: 'The shriek of execration with which this performance was received by the newspapers of the day has scarcely its counterpart in the history of criticism.' Three weeks after the performance, on 8 April 1891, he published in the *Pall Mall Gazette* an anthology of the choicest comments, worth quoting in full, for they show how Ibsen got under people's skin, whether they approved or disapproved of him:

'GHOSTS' AND GIBBERINGS

DESCRIPTIONS OF THE PLAY

An open drain; a loathsome sore unbandaged; a dirty act done publicly; a lazar-house with all its doors and windows open ... Candid foulness ... Offensive cynicism ... Ibsen's melancholy and malodorous world ... Absolutely loathsome and fetid ... Gross, almost putrid indecorum – *Daily Telegraph* (leading article). This mass of vulgarity, egotism, coarseness and absurdity – *Daily Telegraph* (criticism). Unutterably offensive ... Prosecution under Lord Campbell's Act ... Abominable piece ... Scandalous – *Standard*. Naked loathsomeness ... Most dismal and repulsive production – *Daily News*. Revoltingly suggestive and blasphemous ... Characters either contradictory in themselves, uninteresting or abhorrent – *Daily Chronicle*. A repulsive and degrading work – *Queen*. Morbid, unhealthy, unwholesome and disgusting story ... A piece to bring the stage into disrepute and dishonour with every right-thinking man and woman – *Lloyd's*. Merely dull dirt long drawn out – *Hawk*. Morbid horrors of the hideous tale ... Ponderous dullness of the didactic talk ... If any repetition of this outrage be attempted, the authorities will doubtless wake from their lethargy – *Sporting and Dramatic News*. Just a wicked nightmare – *The Gentlewoman*. Lugubrious diagnosis of sordid impropriety ... Characters are prigs, pedants, and profligates ... Morbid caricatures ... Maunderings of nook-shotten Norwegians ... It is no more of a play than the average Gaiety burlesque – *Black and White*. Most loathsome of all Ibsen's plays ... Garbage and offal – *Truth*. Ibsen's putrid play called *Ghosts* ... So loathsome an enterprise – *Academy*. As foul and filthy a concoction as has ever been allowed to disgrace the boards of an English theatre ... Dull and disgusting ... Nastiness and malodorousness laid on thick as with a trowel – *Era*. Noisome corruption – *Stage*.

DESCRIPTIONS OF IBSEN

An egotist and a bungler – *Daily Telegraph*. A crazy fanatic ... A crazy, cranky being ... Not only consistently dirty but deplorably dull – *Truth*. The Norwegian pessimist *in petto* [*sic*] – *Black and White*. Ugly, nasty, discordant and downright dull ... A gloomy sort of ghoul, bent on groping for horrors by night, and blinking like a stupid old owl when the warm sunlight of the best of life dances into his wrinkled eyes – *The Gentlewoman*. A teacher of the aestheticism of the Lock Hospital – *Saturday Review*.

DESCRIPTIONS OF IBSEN'S ADMIRERS

Lovers of prurience and dabblers in impropriety who are eager to gratify their illicit tastes under the pretence of art – *Evening Standard*. Ninety-seven per cent of the people who go to see *Ghosts* are nasty-minded people who find the discussion of nasty subjects to their taste in exact proportion to their nastiness – *Sporting and Dramatic News*. The sexless ... The unwomanly woman, the unsexed females, the whole army of unprepossessing cranks in petticoats ... Educated and muck-ferreting dogs ... Effeminate men and male women ... They all of them – men and women alike – know that they are doing not only a nasty but an illegal thing ... The Lord Chamberlain left them alone to wallow in *Ghosts* ... Outside a silly clique, there is not the slightest interest in the Scandinavian humbug or all his works ... A wave of human folly – *Truth*.[3]

One of the few English critics courageous enough to defend the play was A. B. Walkley. Writing in the *Star* (over the pseudonym of 'Spectator'), he asked:

Do these people really find nothing in *Ghosts* but a mere hospital-ward play? Is it really for them nothing but a painful study

3. The *Truth* article was by Clement Scott, who also wrote the *Daily Telegraph* review and leader.

of disease? Have they no eyes for what stares them in the face: the plain, simple fact that *Ghosts* is a great spiritual drama? Like nearly all other great masterpieces of the stage, it is a drama of revolt – the revolt of the 'joy of life' against the gloom of hidebound, conventional morality, the revolt of the natural man against the law-made, law-bound puppet, the revolt of the individual against the oppression of social prejudice ... This is the spiritual drama which I see in *Ghosts*.

The 1889 production of *A Doll's House* had established Ibsen as a force in the English theatre. The 1891 performance of *Ghosts* made his name a household word even among those Englishmen who never went to the theatre or opened a book. It elicited over five hundred printed articles. 'Behind the times indeed', noted a historian of the period, 'was the journal that omitted its daily column or so on Ibsen's iniquities. By the end of 1891 Ibsen was a name known to every reader of a London newspaper.' In the November issue of the *Fortnightly Review* William Archer wrote:

I can call to mind no other case in literary history of a dramatist attaining such sudden and widespread notoriety in a foreign country. His name is in every newspaper and magazine, his rankling phrases – call them catchwords if you will – are in every mouth. An allusion to Nora Helmer will be as commonly understood as an allusion to Jane Eyre. Hedda Gabler ... is now as well know as Becky Sharp ... This is the first time for half a century (to keep well within the mark) that a serious literary interest has also been primarily a theatrical interest.

The following January a London critic was to declare: 'To contest the influence of Ibsen upon this country would be needless ... It may be said of Ibsen's influence, as Napoleon said of the French Republic, that it is as obvious as the Sun in Heaven, and asks for no recognition.'
One wishes that the people who imagined Ibsen as a 'crazy fanatic' and a 'gloomy sort of ghoul' could have seen the target of their abuse on his walk in Munich, a deeply respectable citizen in top hat, umbrella and order ribbons.

That spring the Freie Bühne in Berlin planned a party. and a member who was a waxwork artist conceived the idea of making a model of Ibsen to serve as a kind of patron saint to the proceedings. The man wrote to Ibsen asking if he would lend one of his old suits to dress the model in; but clothes, like religion, were a sacrosanct subject as far as Ibsen was concerned. 'Be so good as to tell this gentleman', he informed Julius Elias, 'that I do not wear "old suits", nor do I wish a wax model of myself to be clothed in an "old suit". Obviously I cannot give him a new one, and I therefore suggest that he order one from my tailor, Herr Fries, of Maximilianstrasse, Munich.' Whether they solved the problem with a costume, or whether they dropped the idea, is not on record.

There was an Ibsen festival in Vienna that April, with productions (at different theatres) of *The Pretenders*, *An Enemy of the People* and *The Wild Duck*. Ibsen was invited to attend, and accepted; it was the first time he had been there since the Exhibition of 1873. The productions were, like those in London and Berlin earlier in the year, a mixture of success and failure. *The Pretenders* on 11 April went splendidly. Ibsen was called after each act, and at the banquet which followed at the Kaiserhof, where the guests were mostly young enthusiasts for the 'new naturalism' which Ibsen had long since left behind him, he was acclaimed in both verse and prose. He replied in two lengthy Germanic sentences, saying that when anything made him happy and moved him it 'became a poem', and that he thought that this occasion too would 'become a poem'. (There is no evidence that it ever did; the 'joy of life' appears in his last works only as something never achieved or, if achieved, lost.) Later that evening a radical Member of Parliament expressed his amazement that a fellow-radical should sit covered in medals. Ibsen replied: 'I like to wear these orders which I have received from my king when I am with younger friends who I anticipate may continue celebrating into the small hours. It reminds me that I need to keep within certain limits' – evidence, as Halvdan Koht remarked, of the division between Ibsen and the Ibsenites.

Radicals of every kind were claiming Ibsen as their champion. Some Viennese ladies, predictably, came to thank him for the pioneering he had done on behalf of their sex, and to name him an honorary member of the Society for Extended Female Education. It was in vain for him to protest that *A Doll's House* was not specifically about women's rights but about the rights of humanity in general, and he doubtless deemed it discourteous to point out that the play represented a phase in his work which he had now left behind him. A Freie Bühne was founded while he was in the city, on the model of the one in Berlin (another had been established in Munich), and they likewise elected him to honorary membership. *An Enemy of the People* went well on 15 April; but evidence that his more recent plays were less admired came the following evening when the newly-founded Deutsches Volkstheater opened its doors with a production of *The Wild Duck*, with Friedrich Mitterwurzer (who had toured *Ghosts* through the United States) as Hjalmar Ekdal. The play at first went well, and Ibsen was called after the second act; but thereafter it evoked increasing disapproval, expressed in whistles. At the final curtain his supporters countered with applause, and the hubbub of the rival factions did not cease until Ibsen, waving his hat at those who were applauding, left the theatre. Although the première had been sold out, so few people came afterwards that the production had to close after three performances. The director remarked that he had felt it a duty to open his theatre with an Ibsen play, but that it had cost him money.

On 18 April Ibsen's stay in Vienna was concluded with a final banquet at the Hotel Continental, given by the writers and journalists of the city. Many speeches were made, and the actor Max Devrient greeted him as the great liberator who had given mankind an 'inner freedom', banished ghosts, and had the courage to admit daylight into corners that had previously been kept in darkness. Ibsen, as before, replied briefly ('I am no speaker,' he declared), thanking the city both for the 'warm understanding' they had showed him, and also for the 'honourable opposition' which some had felt bound to express.

His return home, which he had hoped to make two days earlier, was further postponed, for he was persuaded to go on from Vienna to Budapest, where on 20 April the National Theatre gave a special performance of *A Doll's House* in his honour. Ibsen's reception here exceeded anything that he had yet experienced. When he took his call on the stage, and made a short speech of thanks in German, the cheering was such that, according to a newspaper report, he 'made huge eyes through his even huger spectacles'. The enthusiasm was not confined to the theatre, but followed him out into the street, where the students so mobbed him that he had to take refuge in a carriage. Two banquets were held for him. The first was official, with members of Parliament, distinguished scientists and men of letters, and the press; the second, much more to his taste, was given by the students, two of whom made speeches of welcome in Norwegian. In his reply, Ibsen recalled that as a young man (at Grimstad) he had written a poem in honour of the Magyar freedom fighters.

Ibsen's stay in Budapest was an unqualified triumph. The Hungarian press interviewed him on every possible subject, and German journalists who were present noted with amusement how passionately they questioned him and how little Ibsen answered. Strindberg, in the process of divorcing Siri von Essen, read of Ibsen's imperial progress with indignation. 'The "Lonely One",' he wrote to Ola Hansson on 12 May, 'has degenerated into a touring prima donna ... a self-styled aristocrat who greets the new aristocracy in the shape of women and artisans ... Farewell Ibsen, my youth's ideal!'

Ibsen returned to Munich in the last days of April. While he had been away, two highly controversial premières of his plays had taken place. On 20 April, the night that Ibsen was mobbed in Budapest, *Hedda Gabler* was performed at the

Vaudeville Theatre in London, thanks to the enthusiasm of two American actresses resident there, both ardent feminists, Elizabeth Robins and Marion Lea. Such unkind comments as had been passed on the play by the Scandinavian and German critics paled before the abuse poured forth by the English press:

It was like a visit to the Morgue ... There they all lay on their copper couches, fronting us, and waiting to be owned ... There they all were, false men, wicked women, deceitful friends, sensualists, egotists, piled up in a heap behind this screen of glass, which we were thankful for ... What a horrible story! What a hideous play! – Clement Scott in the *Daily Telegraph*

Hideous nightmare of pessimism ... the play is simply a bad escape of moral sewage-gas ... Hedda's soul is a-crawl with the foulest passions of humanity – *Pictorial World*

Tedious turmoil of knaves and fools – *People*

Mean and sordid philosophy ... Insidious nastiness of photographic studies of vice and morbidity – *Saturday Review*

Funereal clown [i.e. Ibsen] ... For sheer unadulterated stupidity, for inherent meanness and vulgarity, for pretentious triviality ... no Bostonian novel or London penny novelette has surpassed *Hedda Gabler* – Robert Buchanan in the *Illustrated London News*

For the Ibsen enthusiasts, however, it was a great occasion, for this was plainly an unusually perceptive and powerful production. William Archer, who never allowed his passion for the cause to blind his eyes to bad acting, wrote in *The World*: 'In rapidity and subtlety of intellect, I find it hard to think of a woman in the whole range of the drama who can rival Hedda Gabler; and Miss Robins makes us feel throughout that her own mind could work as rapidly as Hedda's. She played upon her victims with the crisp certainty of touch of the consummate virtuoso. Behind every speech we felt the swift intellectual process that gave it birth ... Miss Robins never forgot that Hedda is neither a hypocrite nor a fiend. I do not hesitate to call her performance in the last act the finest piece of modern tragedy within my recollection. Sarah Bernhardt could not have done it better; and it is long since Sarah attempted a scene so well worth doing.' Bernard Shaw, who saw the performance from the back of the pit 'in company with a large and intelligent contingent of Fabians', wrote to Elizabeth Robins that same evening: 'You may safely accept all the compliments you get about the play and the part. I never had a more tremendous sensation in a theatre than that which began when everybody saw that the pistol shot was coming at the end . . . You were sympathetically unsympathetic, which was the exact solution of the central difficulty of playing Hedda.' Thomas Hardy (who the previous Easter had noted in his diary that 'Ibsen's edifying is too obvious') went, and was sufficiently impressed to pay a second visit when it was revived in 1893. Oscar Wilde admired it too, 'I felt pity and terror,' he wrote to Lord Lytton, son of the novelist, 'as though the play had been Greek.'

The production made at least one important convert. Henry James had been trying for two years to appreciate 'the northern Henry', as he called him, and had failed. 'How provincial are all these Dear Norsefolk,' he had written to Edmund Gosse in 1890. 'They all affect me like intensely domestic fowl plucking behind a hedge – the big bristling hedge of Germany.' He saw the bad Marie Fraser production of *A Doll's House*, which did not help; *Rosmersholm* he found dreary, and *Ghosts* shocked him. By April 1891 he was still unconvinced. 'Must I think these things works of skill?' he asked Gosse, dismissing them as 'moral tales in dialogue – without the objectivity, the visibility of the drama'. But Elizabeth Robins's performance as Hedda won him over; six weeks later, after sitting through three performances, he wrote an essay on the play, which appeared that June in the *New Review*.

James's feelings towards Ibsen remained ambivalent. The

plays still seemed to him (as to Yeats) grey and parochial, even ugly; yet what contemporary writer had probed so deeply into the depths of the human, and especially the feminine mind, and how could one forget those awkward questions which he was forever asking? How unlike James's own settings were 'the ugly interior on which his curtain inexorably rises, and which, to be honest, I like for the queer associations it has taught us to respect; the hideous carpet and wall-paper and curtains (one may answer for them), the conspicuous stove, the lonely centre table, the "lamps with green shades", as in the sumptuous first act of *The Wild Duck*, the pervasive air of small interests and standards, the sign of limited local life!' And yet, James reflected, 'the oddest thing happens in connection with this effect – the oddest extension of sympathy or relaxation of prejudice. What happens is that we feel that whereas, if Ibsen were weak or stupid or vulgar, this parochial or suburban stamp would only be a stick to beat him with, it acts, as the case stands, and in the light of his singular masculinity, as a sort of sub-stitute – a little clumsy, if you like – for charm.' He went on to praise Ibsen's 'remarkable art, his admirable talent for producing an intensity of interest by means incorruptibly quiet, by that almost demure preservation of the appearance of the usual in which we see him juggle with difficulty and danger and which constitutes, as it were, his only coquetry. There are people who are indifferent to these mild prodigies; there are others for whom they will always remain the most charming privilege of art ... His recurrent ugliness of sur-face, as it were, is a sort of proof of his fidelity to the real, in a spare, strenuous, democratic community; just as the same peculiarity is one of the sources of his charmless fascination – a touching vision of strong forces struggling with a pov-erty, a bare provinciality, of life ... He deals with a homely and unaesthetic society, he harps on the string of conduct, and he actually talks of stockings and legs, in addition to other improprieties. He is not pleasant enough nor casual enough; he is too far from Piccadilly and our glorious standards.' In a shrewd and memorable phrase, he summed up Ibsen's peculiar magic as 'the operation of talent without glamour'. The plays which James himself was about to write owe an obvious debt to Ibsen (*The Other House* carries clear echoes of both *Hedda Gabler* and *Little Eyolf*); but the most important lessons which Ibsen had to teach him as a dramatist James sadly failed to learn.

Hedda Gabler, originally presented only for five matinées, did well enough at the Vaudeville for the manager of the theatre to transfer it to the evening bill, where it ran for five weeks and was taken off at the height of its success. Archer seems to have sent Ibsen a somewhat coloured account of the whole business, for Ibsen, sending him two signed photographs for Elizabeth Robins and Marion Lea ('I have, as you will see, written the inscription in Norwegian and beg you to be so kind as to append an English translation underneath'), expressed (29 April) his delight at Archer's information that *Hedda Gabler* 'has enjoyed a good and uncontested [!] reception on its performance in London'.

A week after the London première of Hedda Gabler, on 28 April, Paris had its first chance to see *The Wild Duck*, when André Antoine presented it at the Théâtre Libre, with himself as Hjalmar Ekdal – the first production of any Ibsen play in France apart from the same theatre's *Ghosts* eleven months earlier. It had a very mixed reception; some of the spectators showed their displeasure by quacking like the bird of the title, and it is indicative of how little the play was understood that Francisque Sarcey, writing in *Le Temps*, thought that Hedvig had shot herself out of grief because the wild duck was dead. '*La pièce est obscure*,' he concluded. '*Elle est incohérente; elle est insupportable*.' Yet again it excited a sizeable minority, especially among the young and the avant-garde. 'Ibsen's fame', wrote Georges Viollat in the *Revue Blanche*, 'increases daily. It already equals that of Tolstoy'; and Edmond de Goncourt, whose efforts at play-writing had brought him nothing but failure, complained in his diary that to be noticed in the French theatre one needed to be a Scandinavian. The unconverted included Romain Rolland, who wrote to Lugné-Poe that November: 'I am sorry that all his works are getting into France; what have they to do with us? He is a man; but he is not of our race; let him stay in his fjords, the barbarian!'

The flood of Ibsen productions continued. On 10 May *The Pretenders* was staged by Max Grübe at the Schauspielhaus in Berlin, and was a big success. The next evening Londoners had their first chance to see *The Lady from the Sea*, presented (for the usual five matinées) at Terry's Theatre in Eleanor Marx-Aveling's translation, and directed by her shady husband, Dr Edward Aveling (using the inappropriate pseudonym of Nelson). William Archer thought it 'an inadequate production', and Bernard Shaw, in a letter to Ellen Terry a year later, recalled how he 'went into an afternoon performance and found a poor ungifted, dowdy, charmless young woman [Rose Meller] struggling pathetically with Ibsen's *Lady from the Sea*. She was doing her best; and I thanked my stars that I was not a dramatic critic, and had not to go home and tell her that after all her study and toil she had done far more harm than good.' *The Times* dismissed the play with contempt: 'It offers no opportunity for powerful acting, while its general analysis of character is shallow and its dialogue commonplace ... Studies in morbid heredity are very well in a scientific treatise. On the stage, put forward as a public entertainment, they tend to perplex, irritate and repel, besides being useless for any practical purpose.'

Some time at the end of May *A Doll's House* had its first performance in France, privately at the salon of Madame Aubernon de Nerville, the part-original of Proust's Madame Verdurin.[4] '*Malheureusement*,' Ibsen wrote to her on 22 May (though the French wording was probably Sigurd's, since the letter is in his hand except for Ibsen's signature): '*il m'est impossible de quitter Munich, et je le regrette*

4. Unfortunately Proust was not at the performance. He did not join her circle until a few months later.

infiniment, car j'aurais été enchanté d'assister à la repré-sentation de Maison de Poupée.' A few days later the same play was revived for yet another single matinée in London, at the Criterion Theatre, with Rose Norreys as Nora.

As he was not writing a play this year, Ibsen decided to take a summer holiday. On 8 May he had written to Nils Lund that he was 'vaguely thinking of taking a trip north'. On 17 May, he told Julius Hoffory, who was threatening to descend on him in Munich, that he was 'considering going away for a longish time'. Suzannah was planning to revisit her relatives in Norway, but Ibsen seems to have been thinking only in terms of Denmark. 'It is still uncertain whether I myself shall come as far as Norway,' he wrote to Didrik Grønvold on 6 June. 'I am for the moment tired and sated with travelling, of which I have had so much this year, first in Berlin and then in Austria and Hungary. I should like best to settle for a while by the beautiful Sound, which I so love and where I can see hundreds of ships sail in and out.'

On 11 June he thanked Jacob Hegel for the news that an eighth edition of *Peer Gynt* and a sixth edition of *Love's Comedy* were in the press (a third edition of *Catiline* had appeared earlier in the year). At the end of the month *The Vikings at Helgeland* was revived in Munich at the Residenztheater, and Ibsen attended it. Early in July he left for the north, leaving his furniture, paintings and other possessions in the apartment at Maximilianstrasse. He would have been surprised, possibly incredulous, if anyone had suggested to him that he would never return to Germany again, and that he was to spend the remaining fifteen years of his life in Norway, broken only by two brief visits to Denmark and Sweden. His twenty-seven years of self-imposed exile were over.

PART SIX

The Top of a Cold Mountain

29

A Lion at Evening
1891

IBSEN returned to Christiania on 16 July. Reporters from the two left-wing dailies, *Dagbladet* and *Verdens Gang*, greeted him at the quayside as he disembarked from the SS *Melchior*, and *Dagbladet* welcomed him on behalf of 'all liberal-minded Norwegian men and women'. Embarrassingly, the right-wing papers welcomed him too, as a possible counterweight to Bjørnson. 'Our great and celebrated author', wrote *Aftenposten* on the day after his arrival, in language reminiscent of Dr Rørlund in the final act of *The Pillars of Society*, 'is now visiting his fatherland after several years absence. His stay will, again, be brief; but we must express the hope that it may be long enough for him to assure himself that his compatriots, too, are able to appreciate the fame he has acquired by his distinguished works, and the honour he has thereby helped to bestow upon his country. As our readers will be aware, we do not share Ibsen's view of life or of social conditions; but we are well able to perceive and admire the mighty poetic power which his country has fostered in him – and we would wish that Herr Ibsen could emancipate himself from the bitter feelings which have for so long caused him to prefer other countries to his fatherland. For, after all, it is from the spiritual soil of his homeland that Henrik Ibsen has drawn his best strength and, should he decide to settle permanently among his fellow-countrymen, his sharp pen and acute critical mind would soon find worthy subjects here, where vulgarity still dominates the intellectual scene, and where superficiality and dilettantism hold sway under Bjørnson's leadership.'

The words could scarcely have been more calculated to make Ibsen catch the next ship back to Germany.

He stayed in fact only a day or two in Christiania; the main purpose of his visit was to make the sea voyage up the west coast to the North Cape. He had never been farther north than Trondhjem, and by the time he returned his oft-expressed yearning for the open sea must have been amply satisfied. There are few more spectacular landscapes in the world than the west coast of Norway viewed from offshore, and one suspects that this voyage may considerably have influenced his subsequent decision to remain. Suzannah did not accompany him. Some commentators have adduced this as evidence that they had quarrelled, but a more likely reason is that her by now crippling gout and rheumatism would have made the journey, with its continual climbing and descending of narrow stairways, agony for her; and she had seen it before.

He returned to Christiania on 7 August, and spent the next ten days at the Grand Hotel. He had already decided to remain for some months; on 11 August, thanking August Lindberg for inviting him to attend a performance at Gothenburg 'on my projected return to Germany', he explained: 'I am not planning to go south just yet, but intend to spend the winter here.'

Georg Brandes was also staying at the Grand. After the suspicions and estrangements of recent years, they were now friends again, and on 15 August Brandes gave a dinner for him. Ibsen was at first reluctant to attend, agreed only on the understanding that it would be limited to a few friends, and was much disturbed when he discovered that a number of left-wing writers, artists and journalists had been invited. The resultant occasion was anything but happy. 'Yesterday', wrote Brandes to Alexander Kielland the next day, 'we had a small dinner of about twenty persons which I arranged for the Troll King, H.I., and which failed most comically when he found all the praise that was showered upon him insufficient, and behaved most coarsely and ill-temperedly.'

The painter Erik Werenskiold, who was present, has left a fuller account:

Well, the evening arrived, and we were around 30-40 [*sic*] people. I was fortunately placed so as to be able to see and hear everything. I had Fru Augusta Sinding to table; Ibsen, who liked young ladies, had Fru Kitty Kielland – not exactly beautiful nor young, but a well-known painter and hard-boiled bluestocking. He was clearly not much pleased. After a while Brandes rose and said: 'He who comes at the eleventh hour is just as good as he who comes at the seventh or ninth hour; but there is a difference, none the less; we of the North have come at the seventh hour; we understood Ibsen earlier than others.' Then Ibsen began to shake his heavy grey head. Brandes was somewhat taken aback and began a long explanation to show how we had understood him before the rest, but the more he explained the more Ibsen shook his head; and when we finally stood to drink Ibsen's health he merely half-rose from his chair and said: 'One could say much about that speech' – but did not enlarge further.

The atmosphere was oppressive. Then O. Thommessen [the editor of *Verdens Gang*], who had Constance Bruun to table, thanked Ibsen on behalf of the actors for all the great roles he had written for them. 'I have not written roles for actors and actresses,' snorted Ibsen. 'I have written to portray human beings, not to create roles.'

Then Kitty Kielland began to talk earnestly to Ibsen. She said she thought everything worthwhile in Norway had been accomplished by people from the west coast. 'You are from the west, are you not?' she asked. 'I am Norwegian', replied Ibsen, 'but I understand that you are from Stavanger [in the southwest].' A little later they were discussing *Hedda Gabler*. Kitty said she could not stand Mrs Elvsted – 'those women who sacrifice themselves for men'. 'I write to portray people,' said Ibsen, 'and I am completely indifferent to what fanatical bluestockings like or do not like.'

Whew! At last dinner was finished. But then Ibsen got hold of my wife, whom he knew well from Munich, took her under one arm and her sister under the other, and strolled up and down the room with them in the most sparkling humour.

Later that evening Thommessen mentioned to Ibsen that Brandes was going to apply for the professorship after Skavlan.

'Well,' said Ibsen, 'then he'd better not talk about Norwegian literature, because he doesn't know anything about it.' It became rumoured that Thommessen repeated this to Brandes later, when they were having a drink in the café. This may just have been gossip. But the next day Brandes returned to Copenhagen. What a party!

Ibsen disliked big gatherings. Johannes Steen, who became Prime Minister that year, invited him and Bjørnson to an official reception. 'So the animals are to be put on show,' commented Ibsen; but he accepted. There was a buffet supper, occupying several rooms. 'In one stood Bjørnson, the centre of a large circle of admiring guests; in another stood Ibsen, alone, holding his plate and facing a corner containing a tiled stove, presenting an unapproachable back to the company.' On the other hand, he enjoyed small, select parties, especially if he was given an attractive young lady to take to the table, and then he could talk charmingly and rewardingly. He disliked the custom of paying thank-you visits after a party, and would send a visiting-card on which he had written beneath his name: 'Active member of the Anti-Visit Society'.

On 17 August Ibsen and Suzannah leased (though they did not move in until October) an apartment at 7B (later 13B) Viktoria Terrasse, yet another corner-house, situated in the centre of Christiania, only a few minutes from the palace and the theatre. He saw two plays during the next couple of weeks. One was Strindberg's *The Father*, performed at the Tivoli Theatre by a Danish touring company under Hans Riber Hunderup, who had directed and played the lead in the original production of the play four years earlier at his Casino Theatre in Copenhagen. It was a tremendously hot evening, no less than 102° Fahrenheit, and the little theatre was almost empty (the night's takings were only 33 crowns). Ibsen – records one of the actors – sat by himself in a box almost on the stage, 'staring at us in lonely majesty'. After the interval following the final curtain, when there was to have been a French farce to round off the proceedings,

Ibsen and the other spectators had gone, and the theatre was completely empty; one old lady returned as the actors stood bewildered on the stage, but explained that she had only come to collect her programme; then she went home and so did the actors. Ibsen's opinion of the performance is, sadly, not on record.

On 28 August, he attended the Christiania Theatre, for the first time since 1874 when they had given *Love's Comedy* and *The League of Youth* for him on the occasion of his first return to Norway. Now they offered *Hedda Gabler*, and Ibsen sat in the place of honour, in the stage box. He was greeted with applause as soon as he was seen, after each act and, thunderously, after the final curtain.

By this time, Ibsen had decided to make Norway his base. 'We do not of course intend to stay here all the year round,' he told Hegel on 5 September, 'but to travel as hitherto. So it is just our starting-point which has altered. But we shall stay the winter and I have planned a big new dramatic work which I intend under all circumstances to complete up here. I have not for a long time felt in such good spirits as this summer. The voyage to the North Cape was quite glorious, and my wife has enjoyed the mountain air up at Valders. So my dream of spending a few months by my beloved Sound must be forgotten for this year; but henceforth it will be much easier for me to get down there.' He was not in fact to leave Norway for another six years.

On 14 September he was at the theatre again, for the hundredth performance of *The League of Youth* – a figure which none of his other plays had reached. He sat in the stalls, wearing his full panoply of medals, and again was greeted with tumultuous applause, which he acknowledged by rising from his seat and bowing; though, contrary to his custom in Germany, he refused to take a call from the stage. After the performance there was a banquet at the Tivoli Restaurant, at which a speech in Ibsen's honour was made by Schrøder, the man who still steadfastly refused to allow *Ghosts* to be staged at his theatre. Most of the guests that

evening were establishment figures; but three days later he
was equally fêted by his radical admirers. August Lindberg
and his Swedish company were playing in Christiania that
month, at the Tivoli Theatre, and Ibsen (possibly, one suspects, to needle Schrøder) expressed a desire to see their
production of *Ghosts*. It was some time since the play had
been in their repertory, but Lindberg managed to assemble
the original cast; and so at last Ibsen saw it as it had first been
staged in Europe. The audience, mainly young and left-
wing, acclaimed him as their champion. Nor did he only
attend their production of *Ghosts*. The company included a
young singer named Sigrid Arnoldson; every time she sang,
he came to the theatre, and when she left Christiania he was
at the railway station with flowers and a portrait of himself.

Yet while both political parties strove to make him their
own, there were still many of the extreme right who regarded him as a pariah, and these included some of his old
Holland friends. Christiania was by now full of people who
regarded themselves as the originals of various characters in
his plays; even the elderly Camilla Collett had improbably
claimed to be the inspiration of Ellida in *The Lady from the
Sea*. Professor L. L. Daae, who had been a friend of Ibsen's
for years, was convinced that he was the original of Dr Kroll,
the bigoted pedagogue of *Rosmersholm*, and cut Ibsen publicly in the street. More worrying was the number of people
who claimed him as a brother-in-arms; he cannot have been
pleased when the right-wing poet Kristofer Randers dedicated an aggressive volume to 'Henrik Ibsen, the poet of individualism, in deep gratitude for what he has taught me: to
write verse and despise the masses.'

Suzannah's gout was proving so troublesome that she had
gone south with Sigurd to take the cure at Salo on Lake
Garda, leaving Ibsen to make the arrangements for moving
into their new apartment. He was not, however, alone. He
had found a new companion to replace Emilie and Helene.
On his return from the North Cape in August he had re-

newed the acquaintance he had struck up in 1874 with Annette Andersen, the daughter of his old Bergen landlady,
Helene Sontum, and her daughter Hildur. Hildur, now
twenty-seven, had fulfilled the musical promise of her youth,
and was maturing into a distinguished concert pianist. A
close and warm friendship quickly developed between her
and Ibsen. When he first met her this year she had just returned from a holiday in the mountains, bronzed and fresh
– exactly like Hilde Wangel at the latter's first entrance in
the play which he was about to write.

In Suzannah's absence Hildur became his constant companion on walks and visits to art galleries and theatres. She
even got him to an occasional concert, and helped him with
the furnishing of his new apartment. The date 19 September
held some particular significance for Ibsen in connection
with their relationship, for he subsequently gave her a diamond ring with the date engraved on it, and referred to it in
other letters and dedicatory inscriptions. Was it the date of
their first meeting in 1874, or their first meeting this year, or
did something particular once happen between them on that
day? We do not know, just as we do not know whether anything happened on that same date two years earlier between
him and Emilie Bardach.

On 7 October they attended a lecture together at the
Brothers Hals's Concert Hall. It was a notable occasion. The
lecturer was a thirty-two-year-old working-class man named
Knut Hamsun, who the previous year had caused a sensation with his first novel, the grim autobiographical
Hunger. The advertised subjects of his three lectures, of
which this was the first, were Norwegian Literature, Psychological Literature, and The Literature of Fashion. It was
known, for he had already delivered them in other Norwegian towns, that they contained an attack on both Ibsen
and Bjørnson. Hamsun had boldly invited Ibsen to attend
and, to the general amazement, up he turned, and sat in seat
number one in the front row with Hildur beside him.

Hamsun pulled no punches. 'This evening', he began, 'I

shall be as aggressive, as destructive, as possible.' He attacked Ibsen, extraordinary as it now seems, for over-simplifying his characters and making them mere mouthpieces. For this, Hamsun largely blamed the literary form which Ibsen had chosen. 'A play', he declared, 'must always be easy for the gallery as well as the stalls to follow ... Molière's *Miser* is only miserly, Shakespeare's *Othello* only jealous, Iago only a scoundrel, and Rosmer in *Rosmersholm* only noble ... I suggest that any psychology which is sufficiently clear, that is to say sufficiently shallow, to be understood and enjoyed in the theatre, is to an indefensible degree a coarse and false psychology.'

Hamsun went on to deliver a particular attack on the character of Rosmer. 'There is no more strength in his noble body than could be contained in my fist. He crumples aristocratically at the first hint of opposition ... an exceedingly bourgeois conception of the meaning of aristocracy.' One reason for the inadequacy of Ibsen's psychology, he asserted, was 'the inherent stiffness and poverty of his emotional life'; and he attacked him for writing too much in 'fully-rounded, typical speeches instead of, at least occasionally, in fragments ... There has never yet lived a dramatist on this earth who has been a sensitive psychologist. Not as a dramatist. We have grown so accustomed to believe everything the Germans say about Ibsen that we read him pre-conditioned to find wisdom there, determined to find everything good ... If anything strikes us as odd, it is not the author's fault that we do not understand him.' Ibsen was too often wilfully obscure, as in *The Lady from the Sea* – 'a book for Germans. I read and read and ... cry in despair: "Damn you, man, talk clearly!" ... But if I have in any way suggested that Ibsen is a small writer, that he has not earned his fame, that he is not worth much ... then I have said something I did not intend, and I take it back, take it back most humbly. Ibsen's interest circles continuously around problems; that is his calling as a writer, and it is a sufficient calling ... Let Ibsen write about problems and questions, it enriches our literature and occupies our minds; we must naturally be interested in what a man like Ibsen thinks about this and that ... I say, too, that more than any other man Ibsen has raised our literature from being the literature of little Norway to the status of world literature, and that only a man of his mighty powers could have achieved this. But I say too, for it is a fact, that his writing is the literature of social questions, and that his personages are characters and types. I say this not in blame, but to state a fact.'

Hamsun's contempt for the drama as a literary form, and even his disparagement of Shakespeare as a psychologist, were, one must remember, widely shared by nineteenth-century men of letters; and his condemnation of Ibsen as a man who wrote mainly about social problems has been echoed by many critics since. Bernard Shaw's *Quintessence of Ibsenism*, expanded from his Fabian lecture and published a couple of months before Hamsun's Christiania lectures, widely encouraged this view. To most people then, as (alas) now, he was the author of *The Pillars of Society*, *A Doll's House*, *Ghosts* and *An Enemy of the People*. If it seems incredible now that the author of *Brand*, *Peer Gynt*, *The Lady from the Sea* and *Hedda Gabler* should still have been regarded primarily as a social commentator, we must remember that in these plays, too, he viewed man as a creature at the mercy of social as well as of inner psychological forces – as a thing, in other words, influenced by outward as well as by inward pressures. Today the outward pressures have changed, the inward pressures remain the same; and *A Doll's House*, *Ghosts* and the rest survive because we are still conscious of those inward pressures. It is odd that Hamsun, who the previous year had published an essay entitled 'From the unconscious life of the mind' in which he demanded that writers should investigate the dark and inexplicable powers that haunt and motivate us, should have failed to perceive the true significance of *Rosmersholm*, *The Lady from the Sea* and *Hedda Gabler*. Yet his indictment expressed the irritation of many people with Ibsen then; and his condemnation of him for making his characters speak too roundly, instead of in a broken and fragmentary style, would have been echoed by Strindberg, whose characters jump illogically (as Joyce's and Virginia Woolf's were to) from thought to thought, in a manner which many actors at first find disturbing, but which gradually imposes its own remorseless logic on them and their listeners.

Ibsen, we are told, 'sat quiet and serious, with unmoved countenance ... His strong blue eyes did not leave the speaker for a minute.' Two days later he said to Hildur: 'Well, tonight we must go to Herr Hamsun's second lecture.' 'You don't mean,' said she, 'that you want to listen to that impudent fellow again?' to which Ibsen replied 'Surely you realize we must go and learn how we are to write.' And they attended both that lecture and the third three evenings later. Ibsen is not likely to have bothered over-much about Hamsun's suggestion that he oversimplified his characters; but he must surely have found confirmation in the young man's words of the conviction he himself had already reached that a writer must explore the uncharted waters of the unconscious.

Hamsun's lectures held a further interest for Ibsen; they were revealing of something that increasingly intrigued him in his old age – the views of the young. Lugné-Poe, his youthful French champion, records (quoting an unnamed source) that Ibsen, during this first year after his return to Norway, showed an almost obsessive interest in the rising generation, and went out of his way to get to know the new artists and writers of Norway, as though afraid lest he might lose touch with the people who understood his plays most clearly. His interest in Strindberg, a portrait of whom he was about to buy and hang in his study, is further evidence of this; and his next play was to present a confrontation between his own generation and theirs.

On 21 October Ibsen moved into Viktoria Terrasse, and the following month he wrote Hegel asking for a further 2,000 crowns to cover furnishing expenses (he had requested

6,000 on 5 October). Suzannah was still in Italy; and he now initiated the ritual, which was to become so famous, of his daily walk across to the university, where he would check his watch (a 'frightful old Waterbury with no chain', curiously out of keeping with his smart clothes) by the university clock, and down Carl Johan gade to the Grand Hotel. This ritual has been described by many observers; Edvard Brandes noted that as he walked

he kept his eyes to himself, so that one felt unwilling to greet him even if one knew him, and he was certainly not insulted if you avoided forcing him into a brief acknowledgement of your presence ... At the hotel ... he had a kind of reading-room to himself which in the nineties lay separate from both hotel and restaurant. [The café which he was later to frequent had not yet been built.] But one could visit him there, more conveniently than at his home, if one had an errand to him or some topic of conversation that interested him. And it might happen that he became so interested that he would invite his visitor to take a glass with him. He always expressed his opinions in an individual and stylish form. The great master of dialogue chiselled and hammered out his words in short sentences, well considered, carefully shaped, and anyone who heard his slightly crackling voice and still retains the memory of it must regret not having noted at the time the sharp and forceful observations which emerged from those narrow lips.

Brandes adds the shrewd and probably correct surmise that the Grand Hotel somehow represented 'abroad' to him in the same way that the loft in *The Wild Duck* represented the forests of Højdal to Lieutenant Ekdal; and that had Ibsen been a poet instead of a dramatist no one would have been surprised at his unapproachability.

That November a ghost appeared from the past to prick his conscience. Laura Kieler arrived in Christiania, and wrote Ibsen a letter. One might have expected him to avoid a further meeting with that sad and emotional lady. But her letter must have touched him, for he replied at once:

Dear Laura Kieler!

I received your letter late yesterday evening. Today I am invited out and cannot meet you. But come tomorrow at 2.30, so that we can dine together and talk undisturbed about these things. Note the address: 7B. You will be most welcome.

Your affectionate
Henrik Ibsen

As an old woman, Laura remembered how they had talked for four hours. She told him her whole story. When she spoke of her hatred of illusion and her determination to look reality in the face, he replied, 'You and I are the same kind.' He was so moved he wept. She said he must, even at this late stage, tell Georg Brandes the truth, to which he replied: 'No, I can't. That's impossible.' She said he must think it over and she would return the next day for his answer. He said: 'Oh, Laura, Laura, I can't let you go – but you mustn't come tomorrow. No, no, I can't do it. I can't. It's impossible.' They never met or corresponded again. Did this really happen, or was it the confused and coloured fantasy of an old lady whose life had been a protracted tragedy? One suspects the latter; but Laura may not have been wrong in supposing that she had given something at least to the character of another cruelly treated model, the deranged Irene in *When We Dead Awaken*.

The same month, Herman Bang, the young Danish writer whom Ibsen had known in Munich, sent him tickets for two lectures he was to give in Christiania, one on Guy de Maupassant and one on *Hedda Gabler*. Ibsen came to both, on 10 and 11 November. At the first, on de Maupassant, Bang thought he had never seen so indifferent a listener. Ibsen 'sat staring incessantly into the bottom of his silk hat, as though into the depths of a well'. But when Bang spoke of the story, *Une Vie*, in which the heroine is locked in a room with a fly which she cannot catch, and from which she cannot escape, symbolizing the thought of death, Bang suddenly looked at Ibsen. Ibsen had raised his head and was staring at Bang. Such a look, Bang says, he had never seen except at the zoo, when a huge lion, before settling down to sleep at dusk, suddenly, with an indescribable emptiness of spirit, shot a glance from its half-closed eyes at the disappearing daylight. Such a glance Bang now saw in Ibsen's eyes, and the thought went through his mind: 'Yes, you should have guessed. He has lived and has achieved everything. Now he has only death awaiting him.'

The next evening Bang spoke of *Hedda Gabler*. The hall was full, largely (says Bang) because people wanted to see Ibsen listening to criticisms of himself. It was a perceptive lecture; Bang compared Hedda to the woman in Maupassant's *Notre coeur* who owned a triptych mirror and shut herself up inside it every day for several hours. Ibsen again kept his eyes fixed on the bottom of his hat, so that it was impossible to know whether the lecture was interesting him. The following day Bang met Ibsen in the street. After a sly reference to Hamsun, Ibsen said: 'But you were kind to me.' Then, giving him a sidelong glance, he added, 'At least you read the stage directions.' He made no reference to Maupassant and the fly.

On 17 December occurred the first attempt to stage Ibsen commercially in France. Albert Carré, the young director of the Théâtre Vaudeville, impressed by Ibsen's growing reputation in artistic circles, decided to try out *Hedda Gabler* as a matinée piece in the hope of transferring it to the evening bill should it prove a success. It did not. Marthe Brandes, a fashionable actress who was cast as Hedda, made no secret of the fact that she did not understand the play. 'People laughed,' records Lugné-Poe. 'There were smiles at this curious specimen of Scandinavian literature'; and he describes the production as 'a crushing failure'. Francisque Sarcey wrote in *Le Temps*: 'In spite of everything, I am glad this play has been performed. Perhaps after this effort we shall be left in peace. Ibsen is now dead in France.'

Despite the failure of *Hedda Gabler* on the stages of Scandinavia, 1891 had, thanks mainly to payments from German and Austrian theatres and various reprints, been a good year financially – Ibsen's best, indeed, since 1880. At the age of sixty-three, Ibsen had, for the second time in his career, earned (by a narrow margin) over a thousand pounds in one year. This was despite the fact that he had received no payments for Norwegian productions of any of his earlier plays (apart from a few performances of *Ghosts* at Bergen); which did not mean that none of them was staged. On the contrary, the 1890–91 season at the Christiania Theatre included revivals of *The League of Youth*, *A Doll's House*, *The Lady from the Sea*, *The Vikings at Helgeland* and *Hedda Gabler*. But as the theatre had paid him in each case a lump sum for the rights, these extra performances brought him nothing. He was as dependent as ever on book sales and German theatre royalties.

30

The Master Builder
1892

On one occasion when visiting the Andersens, Ibsen met
Hildur's cousin, a young doctor named Christian Sontum.
The two became good friends, and one of Dr Sontum's children, Bolette, who later settled in America, vividly recalled
(in English) her first impression of Ibsen during that winter
of 1891–2:

Ibsen came a great deal to our house, and I remember well the
first time we children were allowed to see him. We were at my
uncle's. My little brother and I were to play a duet sonata by
Beethoven for the famous guest. We were both very frightened. I
can still feel my fingers getting cold as they touched the keys.
When we rose I sent a timid, beseeching glance at the old man
standing in the doorway, in his long black frock coat with the
broad lapels, which he always wore with the pride of a dandy. He
came over to us at once and said: 'How wonderful! How wonderful!' so kindly that our dread for the great silent old man disappeared at once. To him the simplest accomplishment of a child
was always a wonder. No doubt it was our complete self-pos-
session that awed him. Ibsen's real knowledge of the music was
little better than our own.
He had no idea of how to treat children and addressed one by
the formal 'De' (You) instead of the familiar 'Du' (Thou) when I
was only eight years old. That winter he came often to our house
for dinner with a few other friends. He was always very prompt
... I remember once we children went to speak to him while he
was in the drawing-room. My mother was called out and my
father was still busy with his patients; no other guests arrived, so
we felt it our own duty to entertain our guest. My younger sister
promptly asked: 'Would you like to play dolls with us?' Ibsen

wrinkled his heavy white eyebrows, but in a moment was ready, looking as though he were going to do a serious job, but meant to do it well. She trotted out of the room and soon came back loaded with dolls, dolls of all sizes and in all conditions, dolls with heads and without. She placed them all in his lap, and told him all their names, giving him a maternal account of their rag and bisque tragedies.

One specimen, the doll Mette, who was perhaps worse-looking than any, had once been a great beauty in a wonderful red and white dress. Now she was headless and legless and of course my sister's pet. Mette had to have an honorary position on Ibsen's knee. My father opened the door just as the master of the Great Doll's House was taking all our dolls for a ride.

On 14 January *The Vikings at Helgeland* was performed at the Moscow Little Theatre – the first Ibsen play to be staged in Russia since *A Doll's House* eight years earlier. Several of his later plays had apparently offended the Tsar's censor, but they seem to have enjoyed a kind of underground circulation.

That February, Hildur went to Vienna to pursue her music studies. Possibly her parents felt that, platonic as her relationship with Ibsen was, they were seeing a little too much of each other. The tongues of Christiania had begun to gossip. He corresponded frequently with her while she was away, by both letter and telegram. Hildur, who lived to be ninety-two, kept these letters almost – not, alas, quite – until her death.

Ibsen had seen little if anything of Bjørnson since his return to Norway. Sigurd, however, had put himself very much in Bjørnson's good books by his polemics against the union with Sweden, and Bjørnson invited him to stay at Aulestad. He paid several visits there and, as Ibsen had forecast on his return from Schwaz seven years earlier, fell in love with Bjørnson's young daughter, Bergliot. They became engaged; Bergliot has left a pretty account of how it happened:

Much had been written and said of Sigurd, and we young ones

were greatly excited at the prospect of his visit. One night I dreamed we were engaged, and was foolish enough to tell my brothers and sisters. They so teased me about it that I did not dare to show myself when he arrived, but hid behind a curtain. I didn't see much of him the first few days; he spent most of the time talking with Father. They had long conversations up in his study. Sigurd was very serious, and I didn't altogether like him. But one day he was standing with Father on the upstairs verandah and I was standing on the one below. Then suddenly Sigurd smiled and looked down at me with his beautiful eyes, and from that day I loved him, as I have loved him ever since ...

We were very different. He was a true Ibsen, I a true Bjørnson, and a bigger contrast could not be imagined. Sigurd was by nature very melancholic; but how many times did I not succeed in making him laugh! When we got engaged he wanted to give me a ring, but I asked him instead to give me a concertina, as I did not much like ornaments. Sigurd could never forget this; it made him laugh even when he was old. But I got my concertina, and no girl ever received a more beautiful engagement gift. It was silver-plated, and sounded like a full orchestra. I still love to play it [she wrote in 1947] and then I remember the days at Aulestad when I used to play for him. The sun shone, the sky was blue, and I sat out in the fields with my concertina and sang, while Sigurd lay in the grass beside me and laughed till there were tears in his eyes.

The Bjørnsons were delighted, the Ibsens (according to Bergliot) less so. Certain 'so-called friends who were opposed to the engagement did their best to sustain Ibsen's distrust ... When Father and Mother came to Christiania they were not received with open arms as they had expected, and Father's enthusiasm and happiness changed. He became furious with Ibsen.' Bergliot adds that her father's extremes of mood must always have had an unsettling effect on Ibsen, and that Ibsen consequently avoided him on his return to Norway because 'he knew what emotional explosions Father could arouse in him'. On his return to Aulestad, Bjørnson wrote characteristically to his daughter:

Aulestad, 21 March 1892

Dear Bergliot,

You are much too young to understand all the *evil* Ibsen has done to me. It could all have been forgotten. But he came back to Norway without sending me a greeting ... He even disavowed the engagement. He did this repeatedly and to all kinds of people ... He wants nothing more to do with us. Very well! But then I shall be as free and shall say what I think about him and his writings and personality ...

Your father and friend, B.B.

Whom is one to believe? Bergliot says that Ibsen received her 'amiably but formally', and that the gossips of Christiania soon set to work, especially when Sigurd went off again to Italy with Suzannah, which they took to be the first sign that the engagement was short-lived. But they were wrong; and on 2 May Ibsen wrote affectionately in Bergliot's album: 'Always be yourself, as you are now. I know no better destiny I could wish you.'

By now Ibsen was working busily on his new play, although since his preliminary notes and first draft have disappeared we cannot, as with his other plays (except *An Enemy of the People*), trace its first beginnings. On 4 May he wrote to Jacob Hegel that it 'now occupies me completely and, as usual, takes all my time and all my thoughts. I should gladly like to spend the summer somewhere in Jutland. But alas, I dare not think of it; for I work best here in my own apartment and at my own desk. I have made my study up here very (to my mind) pleasant, comfortable, and good for work, and can sit here undisturbed. I couldn't do that in Munich, and often felt creatively inhibited down there. So this summer I shan't leave Christiania.'

Suzannah had by now returned from Italy. They saw a few friends; the Dietrichsons, with whom Ibsen had now patched things up, were invited to dine 'very plainly, at three', on 11 May; and he renewed one of his oldest friendships, with Christopher Due, his companion from Grimstad days, now a retired customs officer. The meeting was evidently a success, for we find a note from Ibsen on 9 May telling Due: 'I should be delighted if you could look in again; I am usually to be found here between 11 and 12 of a morning.' Yet even with so old a friend he retained an extreme formality. It was an ancient custom, but one scarcely observed among old friends, that the senior of any two walked on the right. Due records that one day

Ibsen was walking at his measured pace along Drammensveien when I happened to see him, caught up with him on his left side and greeted him. After a friendly response, a to me incomprehensible restlessness seemed to overcome him, and he shifted around me in a manner which I sought in vain to interpret, until I realized that he wanted to walk on my left. 'No,' I said, 'you cannot expect me to walk on the right of one who holds the Grand Cross of St Olaf.' 'Certainly', replied Ibsen. 'You are the elder.'

When Due remarked that Ibsen took his time over each play, since two years always elapsed before the next one appeared, Ibsen said: 'And yet I work hard each day.' 'But not just at your plays?' 'Yes, mostly on them. I spend at least five hours each day on creative work.' Due comments: 'Seeing Ibsen live this lonely life, I could not but think of him as a young man, when he was always so keen to have friends around him. Had life and humanity brought him so much disappointment that he had felt compelled to isolate himself and speak merely through his works?'

On 5 June, a hundred miles to the south, an event occurred of which Ibsen probably never heard, since it was not of sufficient interest to appear in any newspaper. An old blind pauper woman died, aged seventy-four: Else Sofie Jensdatter, who had borne him a son nearly half a century before. It may have been around now (the year is not recorded, and indeed the whole incident is based upon hearsay, though Professor Francis Bull, who is usually right in such matters, believes it to be true) that, for the first and last time, Ibsen met that son, Hans Jacob Henriksen, now a ne'er-do-well of forty-six. The story goes that Hans Jacob, penniless as always, knocked one day on the door of his father's apartment, revealed his identity and asked for financial help; to which Ibsen is said to have responded by handing him five crowns with the comment: 'This is what I gave your mother. It should be enough for you,' and shutting the door in his face. But there was so much malicious gossip about Ibsen in Christiana that there may be no truth in the story.

What is sure is that some of Ibsen's acquaintances, led by Christen Collin (later a professor at London University), hit on the idea of a fearful prank – to dress Hans Jacob, who in build and general appearance much resembled his father, in clothes such as Ibsen wore, and, having paid him a small sum to secure his willingness, to sit him in Ibsen's chair at the Grand to see what would happen when Ibsen himself walked through the door. But either they or Hans Jacob lost courage, and this macabre jest remained a thing of the imagination.

Ibsen kept in touch with his sister Hedvig, and grew fond of her daughter Anna. A touching little note to his niece has survived from this summer, begging her to look him up before leaving town and not to be afraid of disturbing him. Once he even attended a largish family party given in Christiania by one of his Paus half-uncles, and agreed, if only momentarily, to revisit Telemark. Among the guests at the party, relates Francis Bull (who had it from one of the Pauses present), was a gentleman named Løvenskiold who owned a large estate at Fossum, no distance from Venstøp, where Ibsen had spent so much of his childhood. Løvenskiold invited Ibsen to come and stay with him there, suggesting that it might amuse him to look over his old haunts. 'Ibsen', continues Bull, 'was clearly pleased at the invitation and said that he would gladly come. It is easy to imagine how as a child he must have gazed longingly at the great house which a bankrupt's son could never hope to enter, and that the invitation must at first have seemed like the fulfilment of a childhood dream. But later in the evening Ibsen came back to Løvenskiold, very depressed and in a totally different mood. He had thought over the matter, he said, and regretted that he felt bound to refuse the invitation to Fossum, for he realized that once he came there he would inevitably be forced to revisit the town of his birth and revive old memories and acquaintances which he preferred to keep at a distance.'

Bull also tells that at another party around this time Ibsen, on being presented to an attractive young lady, turned away in embarrassment on hearing her name. It transpired that her father, a lawyer, had been approached by Ibsen in 1862 for a loan. Ibsen had with him his manuscript of *Love's Comedy* as evidence that he would soon be in better financial conditions and be able to repay the money. 'The lawyer asked to read the play before deciding and, having done so, said that one passage offended him and that he would only lend the money on condition that Ibsen deleted it. Ibsen accepted the condition and took the money, but never forgot the humiliation and never repaid the loan, although the lawyer lived for several years after Ibsen's return to Christiania in 1891. They lived near each other, and when Ibsen saw him he would cross to the far pavement.'

Christian Sontum had by now become Ibsen's doctor. He was working that summer at a sanatorium at Grefsen, a short way outside Christiania, and Ibsen several times allowed himself the luxury of driving out to visit him. Little Bolette Sontum was there and remembered his visits:

Nothing could be a better advertisement of the tonic air of Grefsen than this fact, that Ibsen actually drove out to inhale it. His fear of driving was a by-word in Christiania. However, only one particular horse and driver were trusted. Certainly he had little to fear from their energies. As the funny little rig came creeping up the valley slowly and laboriously, like a very tired snail, it creaked and swayed with the roughness of the roads. Then the whole grotesque little outfit took up the motion – the old horse nodding from his ears to his tail, the fat lazy little coachman droning in his half-sleep, the reins lax in his podgy hands, his cap with its silver band tick-tocking like a pendulum. And behind on the soft, worn cushions sat Ibsen, conjuring up every accident possible to unrestrained speed ...

I used to run down to meet our old friend. 'Welcome to Grefsen!' I would call out, very cautious with my best muslin dress and my most ceremonial curtsey. '*Goddag, goddag*' [Good day, Good day]' he would call back, his whole face lighted up with smiles. Promptly, he would open the low door – 'You will drive the rest of the way, my little friend?' Then I would spring up to the back seat more respectfully than timidly. 'No, no, right here beside me,' Ibsen would urge, and I, trembling with happiness, quickly obeyed, murmuring, 'No, no, perhaps I had better not.' 'Grunt-grunt,' he would reply. Each time he came we had our little comedy.

The political strife between the conservatives and liberals reached a pitch of particular bitterness that summer in Norway. 'The party newspapers outbid each other in abuse and accusations,' Ibsen wrote to Jacob Hegel on 5 July. 'Speeches, processions and torchlight displays are held, and other demonstrations are being prepared. Today a big procession of the conservatives is to go to the palace to greet the king. The conservatives are in a decisive majority here in Christiania ... It interests me to observe all this at close quarters. But I don't involve myself in these conflicts personally; that would be against my nature. And this attitude of mine is respected up here. Since my return last year I am in the happy position of knowing, and daily experiencing, that I have both the right and the left behind me. I can therefore work with undisturbed peace of mind at my new play, and I do so daily. So I shall probably not leave town this summer. But the air here I find healthy and invigorating. I have not for a long time felt as well in myself as I do up here.'

All that summer of 1892 he was writing regularly to Hildur Andersen in Vienna, and she to him. Professor Francis Bull, who knew Hildur well, gathered from conversations with her that he discussed the progress of his play in detail in these letters. She promised to let Bull have them after her death; but most unfortunately for posterity, around the age of ninety in the late nineteen-fifties, she underwent a change of heart and burned them. Ibsen is usually assumed to have destroyed his notes and first draft during the spring or early summer; but since, according to the date on the manuscript, he did not begin his final draft until 9 August, it seems likely that he spent the summer writing a second draft and destroyed that too. *The Master Builder* was to be the most personal and revealing of all his plays, or at any rate the most consciously revealing, though *Hedda Gabler* possibly tells us more about him.

The final draft of the play went swiftly. Act One took him from 9 to 20 August, Act Two from 23 August to 6 September, and Act Three from 7 to 19 September – six weeks in all. On 4 October he told Hegel that he was busy on the fair copy and hoped to let him have it soon after the middle of the month. In fact, due to a brief illness, he did not post it off until the end of the month.

On 11 October Sigurd Ibsen and Bergliot Bjørnson got married at Aulestad. Bjørnson, still offended at Ibsen's supposed coolness towards him, issued a frostily-worded invitation:

Aulestad, 3 September 1892

Dear Friend,

The wedding is now arranged for 11 October, and it is an honour and pleasure for Karoline and me to invite you to attend.

You will reach Lillehammer in the evening and can stay the night there or carry on and arrive here between 9 and 9.30. In that case you would need to have a carriage waiting at the quayside (telegraph the Victoria Hotel to book one). If you are very busy you could return to Lillehammer the same day as the wedding (scarcely twelve miles) and be in Christiania the following day.

Questions will be asked if you don't come and for the sake of the young couple only good questions should be asked. More-over, since I (and probably Karoline) shan't attend the church ceremony, since we know it to be as much humbug for them as it is for us, you, who expressed the wish that it should take place, ought to be there, so that they won't be altogether parentless for the occasion, by which you set such store. For company on the journey I presume you will have Thoresen and my brother.

No one except close relatives will be there. We shall do our best to make things pleasant for you. I could of course meet you on the quayside at Lillehammer, but it would only be a bother for both of us. Apart from that we shall try to arrange everything for you as comfortably as possible. Karoline sends her best wishes to your wife, and I too beg you to convey my most respect-ful greetings and warmest thanks for our last visit to you.

Everyone here is well and happy.

Your friend,
Bjørnst. Bjørnson

A church ceremony would in fact have been far from humbug as far as Bergliot was concerned. 'I have always been a believer,' she comments, referring to the above letter. '. . . But it was useless to try to explain this to Father; he was so fanatical on this point that one dared not for the sake of one's life mention the subject of religion.' As things turned out, when the day for the wedding came Ibsen was ill and could not come, so to please Bjørnson Sigurd and Bergliot got married in his study. Suzannah, despite her gout, made the long journey with her brother, Judge Herman Thoresen. The predictions of the gossips who declared that for an Ibsen to marry a Bjørnson was asking for trouble were con-founded. It was a profoundly happy and successful mar-riage, though relations between the two fathers remained distant for some time. When the important occasion of Bjørnson's sixtieth birthday occurred on 6 December that year, Ibsen sent him the coldest of congratulatory telegrams. It comprised, in Norwegian, seven words: 'Henrik Ibsen sends good wishes for your birthday.'

On 6 December, six days before *The Master Builder* was published in Scandinavia, William Heinemann issued an

edition of twelve copies in Norwegian to safeguard his copyright; and the following morning, at 10 a.m., as a further
safeguard, the play was read in Norwegian at the Theatre
Royal, Haymarket. Edmund Gosse, who read Dr Herdal,
described this strange occasion:

> Yesterday we had a curious little excitement. The new Ibsen
> play had to be nominally performed here to save copyright, it not
> having yet been played or published even in its own country. So
> Heinemann rented the Haymarket Theatre, put a bill outside,
> and inside, with an audience of 4 persons, we read the play in
> Norwegian. I send you the bill (of which 12 copies only were
> printed); it marks my solitary appearance as an actor! It was odd
> to think that all this could go on in the very heart of London,
> where everybody thirsts for something new, and yet totally
> escape the newspapers. One journalist did discover the bill and
> wanted to make 'copy' of the affair, but was promptly nobbled.

Consul H. L. (misprinted on the bill as R. L.) Brækstad,
appropriately for the man who had introduced Gosse to
Ibsen's work, read Solness, and his wife, Kaja. Elizabeth
Robins and William Heinemann, who seem to have learned
some Norwegian between them, took Hilde and Knut
Brovik, and Amy Haldane was Mrs Solness.

Gyldendal published *The Master Builder* on 12 December
in Christiania and two days later in Copenhagen, in a printing of 10,000 copies. Although many of the critics were bewildered, it got, over-all, a better press in Scandinavia than
any other play Ibsen had written since *A Doll's House*. Both
the Brandes brothers praised it hugely. 'It is a masterpiece,'
wrote Edvard in *Politiken*. 'Only this man, already advanced
in years and belonging to a small nation, could write such a
play, in which supreme craftsmanship is allied to characteristic profundity ... A work of genius.' And Georg, in
Verdens Gang – the first review he had written of an Ibsen
play on publication since *Ghosts* eleven years previously –
thought it his best yet. 'The piece', he wrote, 'echoes in the
mind long after one has read it. And when one has read it,
one reads it again with increasing admiration. Technically

faultless, profound and precise in its symbolism ... Ibsen's new play is at the same time enthralling and liberating. Never has there existed a more perfect dramatic technique; never has dialogue been written like this.' Brandes's only regret, and it is a fair one, was that Ibsen had not made Solness more of an artist and established him more clearly as genuinely creative, a genius and not a mere tycoon. He concluded: 'Since Ibsen abandoned the matter and manner of his early plays, we have seen him acclaimed and attacked as a so-called "naturalist". Recently the so-called "symbolists" started a feud against "naturalism". That kind of catchword seldom means much, and all such are least applicable to Ibsen. For twenty years or more naturalism and symbolism have been harmonious partners in his work ... Although both as a man and as a writer he loves reality, he is poet and thinker enough constantly to underlay the reality he portrays with a deeper interpretation.'

Great arguments developed as to the meaning of the play, and some extraordinary theories were advanced. Solness was variously taken to represent Ibsen himself, Bjørnson, the conservative party, the liberal party, Man rebelling against God and, seriously, Bismarck (with Ragnar Brovik as the young Kaiser).[1]

Ibsen never ceased to be amazed at the meanings people tried to read into his plays. Ernst Motzfeldt records a conversation he had with him shortly after the publication of *The Master Builder*:

1. An anonymous critic in the London *Saturday Review* (4 March 1893, pp. 41–2) commented on these theories: 'We would undertake ourselves to get out of it a criticism on Mr Gladstone's Home Rule Bill, a system of phallic worship, a refutation of evolution and a diatribe against the Institution of British Architects ... The fact of course is that it is of the essence of a fantasy piece to admit of almost any number of interpretations. And it is of the essence of the intelligent reader of a fantasy-piece not to insist upon any.' But the reviewer summed up *The Master Builder* as 'an impossible play ... It will not stand examining.'

Ibsen said: 'It's extraordinary what profundities and symbols they ascribe to me. I have received letters which ask if the nine dolls [of Mrs Solness] signify the Nine Muses, and the dead twins Scandinavianism and my own happiness. They have even asked if the dolls are connected with something in some Epistle of St Paul which I don't even know, or something in the Book of Revelation. Can't people just read what I write? I only write about people. I don't write symbolically. Just about people's inner life as I know it – psychology, if you like ... I draw real, living people. Any considerable person will naturally be to some degree representative of the generality, of the thoughts and ideas of the age, so that the portrayal of such a person's inner life may seem symbolic. And I create such people. And with good reason. I have often walked with Hedda Gabler in the Munich arcades. And have undergone somewhat of the same experience myself.

'Solness and his wife are worthy people who don't suit each other and so aren't happy in their life together. They don't become what, being the people they are, they could and should have become – despite the fact that they aren't actually miserable, and despite their consideration for each other and a kind of tenderness and love. They keep each other down, cramp each other ... Their worst characteristics are brought out, and they brood perpetually, because each goes his own way mentally and doesn't share with the other. Contrast Hilde and Solness. They are not portrayed as extraordinary persons, it is just that they feel spiritually akin, strongly attracted to each other, feel that they belong together and that life together would be immeasurably richer than it would otherwise be, and also that they themselves would be better people (Hilde immediately makes him do for Brovik what he wasn't willing to do before – did his wife ever try to make him do that?) – and that their relationship would elevate instead of debasing them, and give their lives greater meaning. Then the collision comes – when one still has a zest for life, a need for happiness, and feels unable to live without joy in subdued resignation. And so they decide to build a castle in the air and to live together in spirit. This lifts him up higher than before, to do things he had not been able to do for a long time (symbolically). But he stakes his life on it – and is killed. But was it so mad if it cost him his life, if he did it for his own happiness and only then, for the first time, achieved it?'

During our conversation he said it was wrong to think of un-happy love as when two people who love each other don't get each other. 'No, unhappy love is when two people who love each other get married and feel they don't suit each other and cannot live happily together.'

Despite the generally favourable reviews it received on publication, *The Master Builder* at first failed almost every-where when staged. In Christiania it achieved only fifteen performances that season, and thirteen the next. In Copen-hagen, it managed no more than eleven. In retrospect, this is not surprising. More than any play Ibsen had yet writ-ten, it demanded the kind of acting between the lines of which very few actors then were capable; and, like *The Lady from the Sea*, *The Father* and *Othello*, it needs a very par-ticular kind of player in the leading role – an actor, as Yngvar Brun remarked when reviewing the Christiania production in *Morgenbladet*, 'as dazzlingly beautiful as love, as hideous as disease or egotism, as doubting and tormented as an evil conscience'. Another reason for its early failures on the stage was that in Scandinavia (then as now), and in Germany also, leading female roles tended to be awarded according to seniority rather than suitability. Edvard Brandes complained of the Copenhagen pro-duction that Betty Hennings was twenty years too old for Hilde.

Although today Hilde is usually played by actresses younger than Betty Hennings (then in her mid-forties), the age difference between her and Solness is still often under-emphasized. The Hilde too frequently looks thirty, the Solness a bare fifty or even less. For such a pair to become lovers strikes nobody as incongruous. Ibsen does not specify Solness's age – he merely called him 'ageing', probably to avoid too close an identification with himself – but he should surely be at least approaching sixty. Hilde is twenty-three; in other words, there should be not twenty, but nearly forty years between them; he should be old enough to be not merely her father but her grandfather. The theme of the play is an old man's fear of, and yearning for youth:

HILDE. What do you want from me?
SOLNESS. Your youth, Hilde.
HILDE. Youth, which you are so frightened of?
SOLNESS (*nods slowly*). And which, in my heart, I long for.

'Oh, high and painful joy – to struggle for the unattainable!' Ibsen had written in Emilie's album three years earlier in Gossensass. But if we see a handsome man of fifty wooing a girl of thirty, the point is lost. Even when Solness is played by an actor who is in fact sixty, one has too often seen him age himself down to forty-five.

Another fault too often committed by actors playing Solness is a tendency to push him up the social scale. Solness has fought his way up; his way of speaking is rough, not the language of one socially sure of himself. He is socially inferior not merely to his wife, but also to Hilde (whose language, by contrast, is immensely self-assured). Of course it is possible to argue that the son of 'pious, country people' (as Solness describes himself) need not be, or feel, socially inferior to the daughter of a country doctor; what is certain is that the play gains immeasurably if the social difference is there, between Solness and Hilde as well as between Solness and Aline. And he must be played sensually; one has seen Solnesses who behaved as though they would not have known what to do if Hilde had started to take her clothes off.

The character of Solness was the nearest thing to a deliberate self-portrait that Ibsen had yet attempted (though he was to follow it with two equally merciless likenesses in *John Gabriel Borkman* and *When We Dead Awaken*). He admitted in an address to the students of Christiania six years later that Solness was 'a man somewhat akin to me'; they shared an arrogance and ruthlessness, a readiness to sacrifice the happiness of those close to them in order to further their ambitions, and that longing for and fear of youth. The sensuality was Ibsen's, too, inhibited though he was about giving rein to it. Edvard Brandes noted that 'in his later years there lurked a strong sensuality in his bearing and speech'.[2]

Ibsen had, moreover, long regarded himself as a builder and his plays as works of architecture. In his youthful poem 'Building Plans' he had compared the artist to a master builder; and when the painter Erik Werenskiold, seeing him looking at some new buildings in Christiania, asked: 'You are interested in architecture?' Ibsen replied, 'Yes; it is, as you know, my own trade.' And Ibsen, like Solness, had always had a fear of looking down from a great height or into a chasm, and this had become worse as he had grown older.

It has been argued by several commentators that Solness's development as a builder corresponds precisely, if one reads between the lines, with Ibsen's career as a dramatist. 'The churches which Solness sets out by building', suggested William Archer, 'doubtless represent Ibsen's early romantic plays, the "homes for human beings" his social dramas, while the houses with high towers, merging into "castles in the air", stand for those spiritual dramas, with a wide outlook over the metaphysical environment of humanity, on which he was henceforth to be engaged.' The theory may at first seem fanciful, of the kind that Ibsen himself derided; but the more one ponders it, the more truthfully it rings, whether the analogy was conscious or not. And one interesting variant between his extant draft and the final version of the play reveals how closely he identified himself with Solness. In the second act, when Solness is telling Hilde how

2. Gunnar Heiberg describes how Ibsen looked at a girl he introduced to him. 'I presented her and Ibsen looked emotionally at her face and cast a quick, admiring glance at her figure. He said nothing but his lips trembled. "She's very pretty, isn't she?" I said. Suddenly a smile flickered across his mouth. "She is," he said quietly and unwillingly, and his smile grew so that it illuminated his whole face. "Yes, she is," he repeated in a clear voice, this time directly to the young lady, as though in thanks.' This took place in Christiania in the nineties.

success came to him, Ibsen originally made him conclude with the words: 'And now, at last, they have begun to talk of me abroad,' which was exactly Ibsen's situation when he began work on the play. But he deleted the sentence in revision, doubtless because he felt that it made the identification too obvious.

Ibsen's interest in hypnosis, and the power that one human being could gain over the mind of another, has already been noted; and he carried it further in *The Master Builder* even than in his three preceding plays, concentrating here especially on how unexpressed wishes could sometimes translate themselves into actions. But if Solness is to be identified with Ibsen, Hilde is not to be identified with Emilie, Helene or Hildur. Was it from the needs of the play that Ibsen made her a harpy, or was it, remembering Elias's account of his maliciously untruthful description of Emilie, from a sense of guilt towards her and frustration with himself? Whatever the reason, from the time that Ibsen's letters to Emilie and Elias's story were published, both within a few months of Ibsen's death, everyone identified Emilie with Hilde, and for the remaining forty-eight years of her long life she was regarded as a predatory little monster. The play brought her as little joy as *A Doll's House* had brought to Laura Kieler.[3]

Nor was Emilie the only person to whom *The Master Builder* caused distress. The grim relationship between Solness and his wife was generally assumed, at any rate in Norway, to be a picture of the Ibsens' own marriage. Things seem to have been getting difficult between Ibsen and Suzannah around this time (as we shall shortly see); and Magdalene Thoresen described their situation a couple of years

3. 'I didn't see myself', Emilie said, on seeing the play for the first time in 1908, 'but I saw him. There is something of me in Hilde; but in Solness, there is little that is not Ibsen.' Some commentators have suggested that Hildur Andersen was the original of Hilde. But he would hardly have modelled so unsympathetic a character on someone of whom he was so deeply fond, and he had originally created Hilde three years before he became interested in Hildur.

later in words which precisely reflect the Solness marriage. 'They live in grand style, all most elegant, but in a suburban silence; for they are two lonely people – each for himself – each wholly for himself.' The gossips of Christiania must have had a field day. And Francis Bull tells how a lady of his acquaintance who had known Ibsen in Munich was surprised, when Ibsen returned to Norway, to receive several invitations from him to dine out at restaurants. He seemed eager for her company and conversation until, suddenly, he stopped seeing her. She could not understand why until *The Master Builder* appeared. Then she recognized herself unmistakably in the character of Kaja Fosli, and realized that it was only as a model, not as a human being, that Ibsen was interested in her.

Shortly before Ibsen had left Munich two years earlier (on 22 April 1890, according to her diary), Helene Raff had mentioned to him the legend of the master builder who had built St Michael's Church there and had thrown himself down from the tower because he was afraid the roof would not hold. Ibsen remarked that he thought the legend must have originated in Scandinavia, since he had heard it there, and when Helene observed that every famous cathedral in Germany had the same legend he replied that this must be because people felt instinctively that a man could not build so high without paying the penalty for his hubris. Did he perhaps feel that his plays, taken as a whole, were now approaching the size and seeming permanence of a cathedral, or that in some way he was challenging God? Of the repeated imagery of spires, which make an old man feel dizzy and a young girl hear harps in the air, the significance scarcely needs underlining; and I do not think it is reading too much into the play to assume that when Hilde, at the age of thirteen, saw Solness standing dangerously at the top of the tower in Lysanger, she had her first sexual orgasm, and that she drives him to the top of another tower in order to repeat it. Of their first meeting alone, when she says he kissed her and he denies it, we never know whether he wanted it 20 much that she thought it had happened, or *she* wanted it so much that she thought it had happened, or whether it did in fact happen and either a sense of guilt or mere forgetfulness caused him to forget. There is a close analogy with the film, *Last Year in Marienbad*, in which a similar situation occurs; and in both instances, part of the fascination lies in the fact that neither the people involved, nor we, ever know the truth.

A few days after the publication of *The Master Builder*, on 16 December, there was a seemingly unimportant and almost unnoticed performance of an Ibsen play in Paris. The young Lugné-Poe presented *The Lady from the Sea* under the humble auspices of a theatre club which he had founded while still at school, Les Escholiers. He had lectured on the new dramatist of the north to his fellow-pupils, who included an awkward youth named Marcel Proust. The actors were all very young – Lugné-Poe himself played Dr Wangel – and it seems to have been a very bad production. Herman Bang, who saw it, declared that had Ibsen been present he would have 'wept blood or stared into his hat'.

The symbolist movement in poetry and art was then at its peak in Paris – Paul Fort had founded his Théâtre de l'Art, the first symbolist theatre, in 1890, with Maeterlinck as his idol – and it was as a symbolist, not as a realist, that the French welcomed Ibsen. They drew delighted parallels between his plays and those of Maeterlinck, whose work Ibsen detested (Lugné-Poe records that he even refused to read *Pelleas et Mélisande* to the end, and that when Bang told him how in Paris they played Maeterlinck behind a transparent veil, Ibsen exclaimed violently: 'Why? What does it mean? I don't understand that kind of thing!').[4] Moreover,

4. Maeterlinck, ironically, appreciated better than most of his contemporaries what Ibsen was trying to do, especially his use of sub-text ('dialogue du second degré'). *Le Trésor des humbles* (Paris, 1897, pp. 176–80) contains a penetrating section on *The Master Builder*: 'Hilde et Solness sont, je pense, les premiers héros qui se sentent vivre un instant dans l'atmosphére de l'âme, et cette vie essentielle qu'ils ont

they had borrowed the worst methods that the Germans had been applying to Ibsen. 'In the German theatre', wrote Francisque Sarcey, 'it has become a tradition ... when they play Ibsen, that they strive to make the audience forget that these are real people of flesh and blood whom they see treading the boards. They move but little, use almost no hand gestures and, when they do, make them broad, almost sacerdotal. Their whole recitation is characterized by a slow recitation, which seems to emanate from supernatural and symbolic lips.'

Lugné-Poe confirms that 'faced with the difficulty of doing [Ibsen's plays] they hit on this monotonous, religious intonation, which we in our turn yielded to and plagued others with', and adds that Ibsen, 'when he heard of my friendly relations with his German interpreters and directors, took pains to urge me above all to avoid them'. But this contact between Lugné-Poe and Ibsen did not happen until later, so that *The Lady from the Sea* was practically a model of how Ibsen ought not to be acted – and yet it was a success among everybody enamoured of symbolism. Avant-garde magazines such as *Mercure de France, l'Ermitage*, and *l'Académie Française* praised it glowingly, and its imagined obscurities were for months a talking-point in the cafés. And the occasion marked the beginning of an important partnership. Lugné-Poe was to do more for Ibsen than any other Frenchman, before or since; and within eighteen months, at the age of twenty-four, he was to be the first actor to succeed in the role of Master Builder Solness.

'A voice within me cries for you!' Ibsen wrote in the copy of *The Master Builder* which he sent to Helene Raff in Munich that New Year's Eve. He had not found any companion to replace Hildur Andersen. But he gave Hildur the

découverte en eux, par delà leur vie ordinaire, les épouvante ... Leurs propos ne ressemblent à rien de ce que nous avons entendu jusqu'ici, parce que le poète a tenté de mêler dans une même expression le dialogue intérieur et extérieur. Il règne dans ce drame somnambulique je ne sais quelles puissances nouvelles.'

manuscript of *The Master Builder*; also a copy of *Ghosts* inscribed with the lines from *Peer Gynt:*

> And the game can never be played again.
> Oh, here was my empire and my crown!

His earnings for 1892 had been as follows:

	crowns	£
6th edn of *Poems* (supplementary fee)	20	1
Unspecified German royalties from Felix Bloch	47	3
Unspecified royalties from Wien Burgtheater	540	30
Unspecified royalties from Munich Hoftheater	176	10
Fee for provincial tour of *Hedda Gabler* by the Royal Opera, Stockholm	150	8
4th edn of *Emperor and Galilean*	1,600	89
Unspecified royalties from Wien Burgtheater	265	15
Unspecified royalties from Felix Bloch	121	7
Unspecified royalties from Munich Hoftheater	83	5
Royalties for *The Wild Duck* from Royal Theatre, Copenhagen (14th–20th perfs.)	1,848	103
Unspecified royalties from Felix Bloch	1,058	59
Unspecified royalties from Munich Hoftheater	52	3
12th edn of *Brand*	1,360	76
Fee for illustrated edition of 'Terje Vigen'	250	14
Unspecified royalties from Felix Bloch	313	17
Fee from French publisher, Savine, for vols. 2 and 3 of Prozor's translations of the plays (250 francs)	180	10
Royalties from Munich Hoftheater	138	8
Fee for 1st edn of *The Master Builder*	8,550	475
Fee for German edn of *The Master Builder* (S. Fischer)	533	29
Fee from L. Dorsch and E. Zachrison for Swedish rights of *The Vikings at Helgeland*	50	3
Fee from Dorsch and Zachrison for Swedish rights of *The Master Builder* for one year	1,000	56
Fee from Wm. Petersen for Norwegian provincial rights of *The Master Builder* for one year	1,000	56
Royalties from Royal Theatre, Copenhagen, for 21st perf. of *The Wild Duck*	123	7
	19,457	1,084

31

'Dull, Mysterious, Unchaste'
1893

The Master Builder had two world premières simultaneously on 19 January 1893 – at the Lessingtheater in Berlin (with Emmanuel Reicher as Solness), and in the little north Norwegian town of Trondhjem, under the humble auspices of William Petersen's travelling company, which had acquired the provincial rights. One might have expected the play to appeal to German taste, but it failed disastrously; the Berlin production had to be removed from the repertory after three performances. A touring Swedish company staged it in both Åbo (in Finland) and Helsinki that month; but, as with *Hedda Gabler*, the first successful production of the play took place in London, again thanks to the American actress Elizabeth Robins.

England was beginning to atone for its long neglect of Ibsen. Thanks very largely to him, the theatre was again beginning to attract men of letters; the previous year had seen the dramatic debuts of Oscar Wilde, Bernard Shaw and J. M. Barrie (to say nothing of *Charley's Aunt*), and the literary world of London awaited Ibsen's new play with immense expectation. Elizabeth Robins recalled the pre-publication fever:

Months before *The Master Builder* reached these shores, the excitement that was set up by mere anticipation will never be credited in these times ... Impatience for the play to come was exacerbated by the darkness that shrouded it ... Neither the man who had committed himself to publishing it [William Heinemann] nor anybody else had even now the faintest idea what the play would be about. People lived on supposition, and were as hot over it as though they knew what they were contending for.

Among the enthusiasts who visited Miss Robins 'up those seventy-four steps' (as she described it) for news of the play were Henry James, Sidney Colvin, Sir Frederick Pollock, Mrs Humphry Ward, Rhoda Broughton, Bernard Shaw, Gertrude Bell the explorer, Herbert Beerbohm Tree, R. B. Haldane, Hubert Crackanthorpe, W. T. Stead, Arthur Symons and Oscar Wilde. The play arrived in instalments during November 1892, as each batch of proofs emerged from Gyldendal's presses – 'in small, in very small, violently agitating spurts – or, as one might say, in volts, projected across the North Sea in a series of electric shocks'.

But as the pattern of the plot emerged even the most ardent Ibsenites began to have qualms. 'More in the dark than ever,' wrote Miss Robins to Florence Bell on 12 November. 'Think the old man's stark mad.' A few days later she reported that Archer himself 'is a good deal puzzled; but he says the 1st Act is powerful and fascinating though he can't "see it" on the English stage. I am desolate.' As the second act came in 'W.A. seems less hopeful ... He writes: "The interest certainly hangs fire, etc etc." *I* fear the thing is hopeless!' Henry James also found the first instalments unpromising. 'I have kindly been favoured with the communication of most of it', he wrote to Florence Bell on 16 November, 'and am utterly bewildered and mystified ... It is all most strange, most curious, most vague, most horrid, most "middle-classy" in the peculiar ugly Ibsen sense – and alas most *un*promising for Miss Elizabeth or for any *woman*. What is already clear is that a *man* is the central figure ... and the man, alas, an elderly white-haired architect, or Baumeister, is, although a strange and interesting, a fearfully *charmless* creature.'

Miss Elizabeth tried several of the established theatres; but her enthusiasm for Ibsen was not shared by the managements. 'I was told *The Master Builder* was simply unintelligible. Oh, it was wild! It was irritatingly obscure. It was dull, it was mad, it would lose money.' She tried reading it to Herbert Beerbohm Tree, who 'was swept away by Solness, wants to play it'; but it transpired that before doing so he demanded 'amazing alterations' (including making all the characters English and Solness a sculptor), to which Heinemann and Archer refused to agree. Eventually Herbert Waring, who had acted Helmer to Janet Achurch's Nora in 1889, agreed to play Solness on Ibsen's terms, and on 20 February *The Master Builder* was presented, for the usual five matinées, at the Trafalgar Square Theatre in St Martin's Lane (now the Duke of York's).

Henry James tried to encourage intelligent appreciation of the play by an article in the *Pall Mall Gazette* three days before the première, in which he praised Ibsen's 'independence, his perversity, his intensity, his vividness, the hard compulsion of his strangely inscrutable art ... [and] his peculiar blessedness to actors ... No dramatist of our time has had more the secret, and has kept it better, of making their work interesting to them. The subtlety with which he puts them into relation to it eludes analysis, but operates none the less strongly as an incitement.' But this plug had little effect on the London dramatic critics, who greeted the play, like its predecessors, with a chorus of vituperation:

Dense mist enshrouds characters, words, actions, and motives ... One may compare it ... to the sensations of a man who witnesses a play written, rehearsed and acted by lunatics – *Daily Telegraph*

Platitudes and inanities ... The play is hopeless and indefensible – *Globe*

A feast of dull dialogue and acute dementia ... The most dreary and purposeless drivel we have ever heard in an English theatre ... A pointless, incoherent and absolutely silly piece – *Evening News*

Assuredly no one may fathom the mysteries of the play, so far

as it can be called a play ... It is not for a moment to be understood that we personally recommend anyone to go and see it –
Standard

Rigmarole of an Oracle Delphic in obscurity and Gamp-like in
garrulity ... Pulseless and purposeless play, which has idiocy
written on every lineament ... Three acts of gibberish – *Stage*

A distracting jumble of incoherent elements. There is no
story; the characters are impossible, and the motives a nightmare
of perverted finger-posts – *Saturday Review*

Sensuality ... irreverence ... unwholesome ... simply blasphemous – *Morning Post*

Dull, mysterious, unchaste – *Daily Graphic*[1]

On the day after the opening performance Henry James
wrote to Elizabeth Robins:

I have looked at the papers, and there is little edification in
them of course. They are stupid, angry and mean. The weaknesses of the play do indeed come out strongly in representation,
but it would have been only honest in them to acknowledge also
its *hold*, the odd baffling spell it works and remarkable spell
of the interpretation ... I thought Waring *extremely* good –
various and interesting, intelligent and coloured: BUT distinctly
not loud enough. You were – keep it up, *up*, UP.

However, when he revisited the theatre for a subsequent
performance James noted to his amazement that 'the house
... was *full*'. Intelligent opinion had decided to ignore the
critics. George Moore wrote to Elizabeth Robins: 'I thank
God I came a second time. It has grown upon me. I understand.' Indeed, he came a third time. Oscar Wilde attended

1. Her Majesty's Censor (a Mr Pigott) shared these opinions. 'I have
studied Ibsen's plays pretty carefully', he had declared in 1892, 'and
all the characters appear to me to be morally deranged. All the heroines are dissatisfied spinsters who look on marriage as a monopoly or
dissatisfied married women in a chronic state of rebellion ... and as
for the men, they are all rascals or imbeciles.'

the final performance and was greatly impressed; and Bernard Shaw wrote to Elizabeth Robins after the first matinée: 'There is no saying what the papers will come out with tomorrow morning; so I had better send you my certificate of the perfect success of the play as far as I am concerned. It held me and moved me from beginning to end.'

Unfortunately, very few of Ibsen's supporters ran a dramatic column. 'The New Critics are to the Old Critics', William Archer had written in the *Fortnightly Review* the preceding August, 'in number as one to ten, in opportunities for disseminating their views as one to ten thousand.' And even two of the most prominent of these New Critics, sad to relate, disliked *The Master Builder*. A. B. Walkley, who had praised *Hedda Gabler* as 'a masterpiece of piquant subtlety, delicate observation and tragic intensity', felt compelled to write coolly of *The Master Builder* in the *Fortnightly Review* that April, saying that he disliked symbolism on the stage; and Justin Huntly McCarthy, who had regarded both *A Doll's House* and *Hedda Gabler* as major plays, declared of *The Master Builder* in the *Gentlemen's Magazine*: 'A great man can blunder, and this great man has blundered.' Yet the play did well enough to be transferred on 6 March to the evening bill at the Vaudeville Theatre, where it continued until the end of the month. A fortnight after the London première, on 8 March, *The Master Builder* was staged simultaneously in Christiania and Copenhagen; and in both cities it failed.

In London, the Ibsen fever continued. From 29 May to 10 June *Rosmersholm*, *Hedda Gabler* and *The Master Builder* (together with Act Four of *Brand*) were presented in repertory at the Opera Comique in the Strand. Elizabeth Robins played Hedda and Hilde as before, and also Rebecca West, with Lewis Waller as Løvborg, Solness and Rosmer; William Archer wrote in the *World* that he thought her Rebecca West 'the largest, finest, most poetic thing [she] has yet done'. Thomas Hardy visited all three productions within a week, and was impressed; the doubts he had felt on reading Ibsen were, like Henry James's, dispelled when he saw the plays staged. His companion to *The Master Builder*, Florence Henniker, was 'so excited by the play as not to be able to sleep all night', and the final scene must curiously have reminded Hardy of his own first published novel, *Desperate Remedies* (1871), which begins with a master builder falling from one of his own towers. On 9 June Eleonora Duse opened a season of *A Doll's House* in Italian at the Lyric Theatre, and on 14 June Herbert Beerbohm Tree presented *An Enemy of the People* at the Theatre Royal, Haymarket, with himself as Dr Stockmann. Archer found the text 'monstrously mutilated' and noted that 'the first actor-manager performance of Ibsen, despite the excellent talents employed, was distinctly below the level of the so-called "scratch" performances to which we have become accustomed'; and Bernard Shaw thought that Tree's performance 'though humorous and entertaining in its way, was, as a character creation, the polar opposite of Ibsen's Stockmann'. But the play was a success, and Tree, who had originally presented it for seven performances only, made it a regular item in his repertory. Ibsen's reward from this expensive production came to approximately five guineas a performance; one wonders how many guineas Tree was getting.

In July William Archer published in the *Fortnightly Review* the article already cited, 'The Mausoleum of Ibsen', in which he surveyed Ibsen's progress in England since the breakthrough of 1889. Admitting that there had been a good deal of sane and competent criticism, and even some that had been extravagantly enthusiastic, Archer observed sadly that 'both in bulk and influence the favourable, or even the temperate criticism has been as nothing beside the angrily or scornfully hostile. All the great morning papers, the leading illustrated weeklies, the critical weeklies with one exception, and the theatrical trade papers, have been bitterly denunciatory.' And yet (he continued) the volume incorporating *The Pillars of Society*, *Ghosts* and *An Enemy of the*

People which Walter Scott had published in the Camelot Classics at a shilling had, in less than four years (to the end of 1892) sold 14,367 copies, plus 16,834 copies of the five-volume edition published by Scott in 1891-2 at 3s. 6d. Additionally, other publishers had issued single-volume editions of *A Doll's House, Rosmersholm, Ghosts, The Lady from the Sea, Hedda Gabler* and *The Master Builder.*

Thus, I think, we are well within the mark in estimating that 100,000 prose dramas by Ibsen have been bought by the English-speaking public in the course of the past four years. Is there a parallel in the history of publishing for such a result in the case of translated plays? ... The publishers to whom I proposed a collected edition of the Prose Dramas before Mr Walter Scott undertook it, dismissed the idea as visionary, roundly declaring that no modern plays could ever 'sell' in England ... For fifty years or more, the English public had lost the habit of reading plays ... yet the fact remains that 100,000 of his plays are at this moment in the hands of the reading public ...

Except in omnivorous Germany, have translated plays ever been known to take very deep root on a foreign stage? In adaptation there has for centuries been a brisk international trade ... but translations have been few and far between. In England least of all have we shown any appetite for them. Even of Molière we have made, for the stage, only crude and now almost forgotten adaptations. Since, then, Ibsen – translated, not adapted – has met with some acceptance in the English theatre. That fact is in itself practically unique. If he had indeed been 'impossible' on the English stage, he would have had as companions in impossibility Corneille, Racine, Molière, Marivaux, Lessing, Goethe, Schiller, Lope and Calderon; no such despicable fraternity. As a matter of fact, and in the face of the unexampled tempest of obloquy in the press, seven of his plays – not adapted, but faithfully translated – have been placed on the English stage. If our theatrical history presents any parallel to this, I shall be glad to hear of it. I certainly can think of none.

Archer goes on to point out that of the seven Ibsen plays so far produced in London (excluding *The Lady from the Sea*, of which he knew no details, and *Ghosts,* which did not

charge for its two performances), the receipts for *The Pillars
of Society* (one matinée) and *Rosmersholm* (in 1891, two
matinées) totalled £276. The three remaining plays – *A
Doll's House, Hedda Gabler* and *The Master Builder* – took
£4,600. *Hedda Gabler* made a profit, after paying all expenses, of £281 on its ten matinées. Yet he concluded with
the surprisingly pessimistic forecast that 'it is scarcely to be
expected ... that they [Ibsen's plays] should take deep and
permanent hold on the English stage,' and expressed the
hope that English successors to Ibsen would emerge and be
played instead. He would have been happy to know that,
a century later, around twenty professional productions a
year of those plays would regularly be mounted in the
English theatre, television, and radio.

The enemies of Ibsen, naturally, continued to fulminate.
In the prologue to his play *The Tempter*, written this year,
Henry Arthur Jones exhorted his audience to

> Shun the crude present with vain problems rife.
> Nor join the bleak Norwegian's barren quest
> For deathless beauty's self and holy zest
> Of rapturous martyrdom, in some base strife
> Of petty dullards, soused in native filth.[2]

On 11 July Sigurd and Bergliot had their first child, a boy.
Mercifully rejecting the suggestion of their landlord that he
should be called Bjørnstjerne (how could any child or man
have lived up to the name of Bjørnstjerne Ibsen?) they
christened him Tancred, a Norman name (wrote Bergliot)
so as to symbolize the union between the north and the

2. Two years later, in an essay entitled 'The Renascence of English
Drama', Jones declared: 'A strong, dirty man has written plays, and
now every feeble dirty person thinks himself a dramatist.' But in 1913,
in *Foundations of a National Drama*, Jones recanted, and spoke of
himself as one of 'those whom his shattering genius has at length
conquered', referring to him in the same volume as 'a great destroyer;
a great creator; a great poet; a great liberator ... There is no serious
modern dramatist who has not been directly or indirectly influenced
by him.'

south, between Scandinavia and the Mediterranean. Soon after he was born they moved to Christiania, and came to Ibsen to show him his first grandchild.

'I can still see Ibsen [recalled Bergliot] drifting with his short steps around his wife as she sat in the centre of the room with Tancred on her lap. Each time he passed he bent down and looked at him, childishly gentle and happy because it was a boy.' They had him baptized by Christopher Bruun, the part-original of Brand; he wore the robe in which his grandfather had been baptized, and Suzannah carried him to the font. Ibsen was very nervous lest any accident should befall the child, and as Suzannah approached the font he rose, crossed over to Bergliot, took her arm and whispered 'Do you think she'll drop him?' At the dinner afterwards in Viktoria Terrasse Ibsen made a speech thanking Bruun for everything he had meant to him, and Bruun replied with the eloquence which Ibsen had so admired in him in Rome.

For the first time, Bergliot was now seeing her parents-in-law regularly.

It was a new and strange world. The Ibsens' home was as quiet as Aulestad had been full of fun and life. Few people visited them ... There was one thing I could not understand at all. I came from the company of my own family, from Father, who believed in everything and everyone, the good that people told him and the bad; believed in people, both those who told the truth and those who lied; and then I came to the Ibsens, to Henrik Ibsen, who believed no one and nothing that anyone told him. I remember I would come up from town full of news which I enthusiastically recounted to them. Ibsen would sit and listen attentively, and when I had finished he would say 'Don't believe a word of it, it's all untrue.' I had to hide my disappointment; but what surprised me most was that he was nearly always right.

The strange thing about Ibsen was that he seemed so slow at grasping things. One always had to tell him a story twice. First he listened, the second time he always asked very searchingly for details which lay very far from my Bjørnson nature. But he would insist. He took note of every detail; one could literally see him absorbing them. When anything particularly interested him, he would raise one eyebrow like Sigurd, and one of his eyes seemed much bigger than the other. But soon after he would go into his room; he was always occupied with his work.

That summer Ibsen renewed a friendship, which had been allowed to lapse, with the only other Norwegian whose name was as internationally famous as his own. Edvard Grieg had recently returned from Germany in a state of poor health and extreme nervous exhaustion, and had gone to the sanatorium at Grefsen to recuperate. One Sunday in July Ibsen was visiting Christian Sontum and his family there, and Grieg walked over to join them. Bolette Sontum was present and, in her awkward English, recalled the occasion:

Ibsen sat brooding, solemn and relentless. But suddenly his face lighted up radiantly as Greig, light-hearted and buoyant as a sunbeam, tripped up the steps. The two masters clasped hands. They had not met for years, and there was a shot of questions and answers as between two boys, Ibsen's deep basso vibrating thunders to Grieg's piping Bergen soprano. Half-serious, half-jesting, they discussed the plan of Grieg's setting *The Vikings at Helgeland* to music ... After dinner at the Sanatorium we induced Ibsen, in behalf of the balmy summer afternoon, to walk with us to the 'Little Outlook', a particularly choice viewpoint on the Grefsen plateau, which commands an excellent perspective of Christiania miles below in the valley. Ibsen walked very slowly, his shoulders stooped, one hand against his back, the other clasping the gold head of his walnut stick. This stick was as personally associated with him as his big gold-rimmed spectacles. These he had twisted so that the left eye always seemed larger and more drooping than the right, and really exaggerated the severity of his piercing gaze. The stick itself was a necessary complement to the glasses, as his near-sightedness made him helpless one step beyond his immediate vision.

We walked very slowly on his account, especially when climbing the last steep round of the mountain. Finally, we came up breathless but rewarded with the inspiring view of the fjord. Ibsen sat down heavily on a rustic bench under one distinctly black fir, whose branches cut appealing grotesqwes against the blue sky.

Ibsen was to remember this place, and the view of the distant city with its factories, three years later when writing the final scene of *John Gabriel Borkman*. But he was to write another play before that, and on 18 September he informed Jacob Hegel that he had begun to plan it, and 'intend to complete it next summer'.

He seems to have kept largely to himself for the rest of that year; with Hildur still abroad, he paid fewer visits to the theatre and none to lectures or concerts. Among his infrequent visitors was Jonas Lie's youngest daughter Johanne, then at the start of her career as an actress. Ibsen, with her father, attended her début at the Christiania Theatre, and asked her to come and read to him at Viktoria Terrasse. When she arrived, Suzannah admitted her with the daunting welcome, 'Dr Ibsen is expecting you,' and showed her into his 'very small study'.

Ibsen wanted to chat. And I got the feeling that this great writer was no cold satirist but a man of strong and lasting passions. He was not taciturn nor coldly curt; indeed, there was something confidential about his manner of talking. Suddenly there would be a flash of lightning under those bushy eyebrows, and one felt that this man could see right through one. I rose to leave, certain that he had forgotten about the reading. 'No, now you must read for me.' ... I read him scenes [from *Love's Comedy*]. Dr Ibsen rose. 'You shall play that part.' And the amazing thing was that he actually wrote to Schrøder, the head of the theatre, and I did play Svanhild.

But she remembered how cold he could be to people he did not like, or who were over-familiar.

I see Dr Ibsen standing in a doorway at a big party at Dr Bœck's at Munkedammen, looking straight ahead as though in a dream. A gentleman claps him on the shoulder. 'Come on, Henrik, let's have a drink. Don't stand there brooding.' Ibsen did not reply, but a motion of the hand dismissed the speaker mercilessly, like a feather that one blows away ... He worked all the time, at home, on the street, in cafés ... He was not especially afraid of death – only, when he was working on a play he would fear he might be taken away before he had said what he had to say to the world. And he did not want to die abroad.

Once Johanne introduced another young girl to him as he was checking his watch by the university clock. 'Later that young girl often visited him at his home. She interested him.' Who this girl was we do not know, nor whether he used her in any of the three plays he had still to write. Like so many men who cannot fulfil themselves sexually for one reason or another (and I think there is little doubt that he could not, at any rate in old age), he needed a variety of attractive companions.

A Danish schoolboy, too, met Ibsen for the first time this year, and carried away an unusual impression. Jacob Hegel's son, named Frederik after his grandfather, was in the capital and had been told by his father to pay his respects. Aged thirteen, he arrived without warning.

I rang; and Fru Ibsen warily opened the front door. When I told her who I was, she let me in, and Ibsen, who had been lying on the sofa with a rug over him, unwrapped himself slowly and came to greet me . . . He began to talk and talk of Denmark. What Denmark had meant to him. He spoke warmly, not grandly but humbly, softly and with deep emotion. He took me out on to the balcony and looked over Oslo [sic] as he spoke, and became more and more moved. Remarkable to relate, this lonely man opened his heart completely to the youth from Denmark who he scarcely knew, and wept. He laid his head on my shoulder and wept . . . Fru Ibsen gave me an angry glance as I left. She sensed that something had happened.

No wonder she gave young Hegel a resentful look. Although he does not say so, and may not have realized it, Ibsen only behaved this way when he was drunk, and Suzannah must have wondered what story the boy would take back to his father in Copenhagen.

1893 was, as we have seen, an important year for Ibsen in England, and it was to prove equally so in France. That autumn Lugné-Poe founded, together with Edouard Vuillard and Camille Mauclair, a 'little theatre' on the lines of Antoine's Théâtre Libre and Paul Fort's short-lived Théâtre de l'Art (in which Lugné-Poe himself had played the Old Blind Man in Maeterlinck's *L'Intruse*). They called their new enterprise Le Théâtre de l'Oeuvre, and opened it on 6 October with *Rosmersholm*. Vuillard did the decor and designed the programme and posters; Lugné-Poe played Rosmer and Berthe Bady, Rebecca. The production was much better than that of *The Lady from the Sea* the previous year, for Ibsen, on hearing about the latter effort from Herman Bang, had asked Bang to advise Lugné-Poe on the way his plays ought to be done: realistically, as opposed to ritualistically, and above all quickly. Antoine had had the right naturalistic approach, but lacked any background of Scandinavian knowledge, and especially of Norwegian manners. Bang was able to provide this. The case was similar to that of Chekhov in England; he was never fully understood until Theodor Komisarjevsky, in the nineteen-twenties, was able to explain that what had been assumed to be eccentric and symbolic was far more effective if played with the simplest realism.

On 10 November the Théâtre de l'Oeuvre followed *Rosmersholm* with *An Enemy of the People*, as though to underline Ibsen's expressed hostility to overt symbolism in drama. Yet here again Ibsen showed his gift for reflecting topical issues anywhere and at any time, for the première occurred on a day when there were fierce anarchical demonstrations in the streets of Paris, and Dr Stockmann's hard words about the mob won an enthusiastic response from the young poets and artists who formed a large part of the audience and, odd as it may seem today, regarded themselves as an élite and dissociated themselves from the rioters outside.

The dress rehearsal itself turned into a riot. It was preceded by a lecture, ostensibly about the play, by Laurent Tailhade 'which [writes Archer] consisted not so much of an exposition of the play as of a violent attack upon all the "leading men" in French literature and politics. Beside it, Dr Stockmann's harangue in the fourth act seems moderate and almost mealy-mouthed.' Among the writers attacked were several who were present, including Sarcey; and Tailhade compared Dr Stockmann to the prophet Elijah. Archer continues: 'The audience listened, not without protest, to M. Tailhade's diatribe, until he thought fit to describe the recent Franco-Russian fêtes as an act of collective insanity. At this point a storm of indignation burst forth, which lasted without pause for a quarter of an hour, and was not allayed by an attempt at intervention on the part of M. Lugné-Poe. The lecture closed amid wild confusion, and altogether the preliminary scene in the auditorium was like a spirited rehearsal of the meeting at Captain Horster's.'

Thus Ibsen found himself simultaneously acclaimed as the opponent and the champion of anarchy. Clemenceau felt that the occasion recalled the brave days of 1830; the Théâtre de l'Oeuvre came to be regarded as a centre of anarchy, and was the subject of a debate in the French Parliament; and a young anarchist named Auguste Vaillant who had been arrested for an attempt to set off a dynamite explosion named among the writers who had inspired him Darwin, Herbert Spencer and Ibsen, three singularly law-abiding men. But the play received tepid reviews. Apart from Henri Bauer in *Echo de Paris*, the French critics found it ill-constructed (which it certainly is not).

One would like to be able to record the German productions of Ibsen that took place this year; but most of his royalties from that country were now coming through his agent, Felix Bloch, and are not separately itemized in his accounts, and the history of Ibsen on the German stage is lamentably ill-documented. W. H. Eller, in his book *Ibsen in Germany* (Boston, 1918), lists no new productions in 1892 and none in 1893 save the Berlin *Master Builder*; but although Ibsen's royalties from Bloch were down to £75 in 1893, compared with £85 in 1892 and £118 in 1891 (an outstanding year), one doubts whether those sums can refer only to repeats of old performances. Even if they do, the figures show that, contrary to some supposition, he was still being frequently performed there. A windfall of £200 from Heinemann for the English edition of *The Master Builder* brought his income for 1893 to £955, a fair figure for a year in which he had written no new play.

32

Little Eyolf
1894

LUGNÉ-POE'S enthusiasm for Ibsen continued unabated into 1894. On 3 April he directed and acted *The Master Builder* for his Théâtre de l'Oeuvre at the Bouffes du Nord. The production was received with derision. Gunnar Heiberg records that the audience shouted their own answers to Hilde's questions to Solness; the business about the crack in the chimney-pipe was greeted with roars of laughter; and whenever (as happens several times in the play) any character said, 'I don't understand this,' the audience echoed, 'Neither do we.' Yet again, the mockery of the first-night audience represented only one view. Heiberg, reporting on a revival of the production four years later, comments: 'The general public liked neither the play nor the performance, but the young, the supporters of Ibsen and l'Oeuvre, loved both. "God, what a play!" exclaimed one young man with long hair.' But despite Herman Bang's coaching, Heiberg still noted with regret the tendency of the French to intone Ibsen like a mass and surround his plays with a kind of mystique, even (indeed, especially) when having to express everyday sentiments; and he felt that Lugné-Poe acted Solness 'tastefully and intelligently, but without suggesting a living person'.[1]

Yet two more distinguished judges than Heiberg found both the production and Lugné-Poe's performance powerful

1. At the dress rehearsal of the 1898 production a disaster occurred in the final act when the dummy figure that was to drop from the flies (showing Solness's fall from his tower) burst and showered its contents over the front stalls.

and moving. When the company visited London the following year, Bernard Shaw wrote:

> Comparing the performance with what we have achieved in England, it must be admitted that neither Mr Waring nor Mr Waller were in a position to play Solness as M. Lugné-Poe played him. They would never have got another engagement in genteel comedy if they had worn those vulgar trousers, painted that red eruption on their faces, and given life to that portrait which, in every stroke, from its domineering energy, talent and covetousness, to its half-witted egoism and crazy philandering sentiment, is so amazingly true to life. Mr Waring and Mr Waller failed because they were under the spell of Ibsen's fame as a dramatic magician, and grasped at his poetic treatment of the man instead of at the man himself. M. Lugné-Poe succeeded because he recognized Solness as a person he had met a dozen times in ordinary life, and just reddened his nose and played him without preoccupation.

How much better Shaw wrote about Ibsen when reviewing productions of his plays than in the *Quintessence*! The other authority who set the seal of his approval on the production and performance was, as we shall see, Ibsen himself.

A fortnight after *The Master Builder* opening, on 20 April, Paris enjoyed another and more fashionable Ibsen première when Gabrielle Réjane played Nora at the Théâtre Vaudeville. Ibsen sent her a telegram thanking her for fulfilling his 'dearest dream, in creating Nora in Paris'. She enjoyed a great triumph in the role, thanks largely to Herman Bang, who advised on this production as he had on Lugné-Poe's. 'If I succeeded in overcoming the many difficulties in the part of Nora,' Réjane wrote to Lugné-Poe, 'I owe it to Herman Bang'; and she added that she had never met a director who exuded so strong a personality in the theatre. The production provided Ibsen with his first popular success in France, and even the critics who were usually hostile to him found something to praise. Sarcey himself declared *A Doll's House* to be the best constructed and most interesting foreign play yet performed in France, though he felt that it showed an obvious debt to Scribe and Sardou, and could not believe in Nora's abandonment of her husband and children. He summed it up as 'an enjoyable comedy, apart from its dénouement'. Nora's final action struck many observers as typifying the difference between Scandinavian and French manners. Edmond de Goncourt wrote in his diary that 'this naïvety, sophism and emotional perversion is characteristic of Scandinavian women', and Ernst Tissot thought it showed that Norwegian women read too much, with the result that 'a kind of intellectual hysteria forces itself into minds ill-equipped to think'.[2]

Numerous tributes reached Réjane from Norway; the artist Frits Thaulow sent her a painting, Jonas Lie a poem and Edvard Grieg a piece of music. The success of *A Doll's House* and the interest created by the l'Oeuvre productions opened the way for Strindberg in Paris. His *Creditors* was produced by the l'Oeuvre that June and *The Father* in December, the latter play being especially acclaimed. The consciousness of his debt to Ibsen annoyed Strindberg. '*Pourquoi servirai-je comme chien de chasse à Ibsen?*' he wrote to Lugné-Poe on 16 December 1894. '*J'ai été sa victime depuis dix ans,*' and he repeated his complaint that *Hedda Gabler* was a crib of *The Father*.

On 4 May London, for the first time, saw *The Wild Duck*, produced by J. T. Grein for his Independent Theatre Society at the Royalty in Soho, with Laurence Irving, the son of Henry Irving, as Relling. William Archer, who had been disappointed with the play on reading it, confessed himself 'utterly mistaken. The play now proved itself scenic in the highest degree ... Hardly ever before, as it seemed to me, had I seen so much of the very quintessence of life concentrated in the brief traffic of the stage.' Not all the critics

2. Goncourt's diary (6 May 1894) shows how wildly Ibsen's contemporaries speculated about his literary ancestry: 'Zola declares Ibsen to have sprung from French Romanticism, especially George Sand, while Léon Daudet says he sprang from the German Romantics.'

were enthusiastic; Clement Scott wrote that 'to call such an eccentricity as this a masterpiece, to classify it at all as dramatic literature, or to make a fuss about so feeble a production, is to insult dramatic literature and outrage common sense'.

The previous winter, steps had been taken in Christiania to found an Authors' Society, for the protection of literary rights. Ibsen readily agreed to join, signed the invitations to the inaugural meeting on 7 May, and attended himself; but it was the last time he did so. Three days before the meeting an article by a young writer named Gabriel Finne appeared in *Dagbladet* attacking the project on the grounds that such a society would inevitably be controlled by old men, and that the old hated everything that was young, fresh and alive. He specifically excepted Ibsen from this generalization; but at the supper following the meeting another young writer, Nils Kjær, jumped to his feet and delivered a violent denunciation of 'the old writers who have never been able to portray women but have always obstructed the ambitions of youth'. He did not name Ibsen but (despite the peculiar inapplicability of the words to him) aimed his speech at the table where the latter was sitting, and ended: 'We hate you! But your time is past! If you want to see the poet of Norway's future, here he sits!' So saying, he placed his hand on the shoulder of Gabriel Finne, who had fallen asleep with his head on the table. As Ibsen left, he said to Dietrichson: 'That was the most unpleasant occasion I have ever been present at. I shall never set foot in this society again.' Next day, Nils Kjær came to apologize to him, and received the immortal snub: 'Young man, the secret of drinking is never to drink less the day after.'

Meanwhile, his new play had been maturing in his mind, and on 15 June he wrote to Bergliot: 'Tomorrow I shall start writing the dialogue in earnest.' A week later he told Gerda Brandes that he was well under way, and by 10 July he had completed Act One. The next day he began Act Two, and a fortnight later, on 25 July, was able to inform Jacob Hegel:

'Yesterday I completed the second act of my new play, and have already today begun work on the third and last act. So I hope to have the final version finished in good time. This of course means that I cannot think of taking any summer holiday this year. But I don't need one. I am very content here, and happiest when I am working at my desk.' The third act he completed on 7 August, also in a fortnight. But he then revised the play so thoroughly that over two months elapsed before he was ready, on 13 October, to send *Little Eyolf* to the printers.

On 3 October, while Ibsen was fair-copying *Little Eyolf*, Aurélien Lugné-Poe and his company from the Théâtre de l'Oeuvre arrived in Christiania to give guest performances of *Rosmersholm* and *The Master Builder*. They were a very young group – 'ten players', recalled Lugné-Poe in his memoirs, 'whose total ages came to less than two hundred years.' He himself, one may repeat, was only twenty-four. Their first morning they went to the Grand Hotel to catch a glimpse of their author. At the stroke of twelve, Ibsen made his ritual entry.

We stood waiting for him, and recognized him immediately. As he walked through the hotel to the dining-room he reminded me of a doctor on the way to visit his patients . . . He paced with careful steps to seclude himself in a corner of the large restaurant. Berthe Bady . . . begged Hammer to present her to him . . . Ibsen was exactly as I had often heard described. He rose and adjusted his gold spectacles, then amiably and smilingly said a few words in a low voice and sat down again. Then he took out a small comb and smoothed his hair where it had been crimped by his hat. At first glance his appearance struck me as correct and somewhat diffident, his face luminous above a high white cravat . . . I would like to have had the extraordinary gaze of this man. Indeed, I have never been able to forget his eyes, which only the painter Edvard Munch once succeeded in reproducing. One eye, half-closed, seemed to reflect and ponder, while the other observed Bady sharply and with intense and surprising animation and warmth. The indeterminate colour of those eyes behind the spectacles seemed to shine with an unusual brilliance. His brow was unique, proclaiming intelligence, discipline and distinction, its breadth and proportions perfectly matched. Bady wept. At last she let Ibsen bury himself in his newspaper and disappear behind it. We had imagined Ibsen to be gruff and unapproachable, but after their conversation Bady told everyone, 'He is charming and his face is quite pink – and his eyes are so gentle and good – and how young his voice is!'

They were to play in the Carl Johan Theatre, 'a kind of large barn in the old Tivoli Gardens ... neither pleasant nor elegant'. Ibsen came to the first night of *Rosmersholm*. 'During the whole performance Ibsen remained motionless. He seemed to wish to restrain the audience from demonstrating in any way. Only at the end of every act did he applaud, without manifesting pleasure. After the final act he rose, bowed to us actors, then to the audience who were applauding him. That was all.'

At eleven the next morning Herman Bang took Lugné-Poe to visit Ibsen at Viktoria Terrasse.

He received us, as before, with that exceptional amiability which I have often remarked in him, like a doctor receiving a patient ... Dare I say without lack of respect that that morning Ibsen was '*dans le décor*'? ... Very *soigné*, his hair and beard shaggy yet combed in a curiously fastidious style, his glasses on his nose, just as I had seen him in the Grand Hotel. From time to time Bang came to my assistance. I felt so tall that the furniture, the knick-knacks, the paintings on the wall, even my host himself, all made me feel gauche and clumsy. I waited for Ibsen to indicate that I might sit. He, somewhat small compared with me, seemed visibly ill at ease. His eyes bored deeply into mine as though exploring me.

Bang explained that Lugné-Poe understood German, and Ibsen said he was grateful for the performance of *Rosmersholm* but was particularly looking forward to their interpretation of *The Master Builder*.

He was not surly as we had been led to expect, nor seemed distrustful, but almost immediately made that remark in German which I subsequently repeated in Paris and which helped me greatly the following evening [when acting *The Master Builder*]: 'French actors are more suited than many others to act my plays. People have not fully appreciated that a passionate writer needs to be acted with passion, and not otherwise.' ... As he saw us to the door he added something which I could not understand, but I heard two or three times the name Ulrik Brendel. When we left the Master after a reception that had been friendly and courteous, but nothing more, I expressed my amazement to Herman Bang that he had said nothing about the previous evening's performance of *Rosmersholm*. 'Well', said Bang, 'he was a little upset because in the last scene Brendel's entrance was lit by electricity. He doesn't want to have any stupid mysticism in his plays.'

Ibsen came to their opening performance of *The Master Builder* on 5 October and Herman Bang remembered his reaction:

By general agreement, this strange play had not succeeded in the Scandinavian theatres ... Ibsen took his place in his box. As usual he sat motionless throughout the first act ... Towards the end of the act it was as though something had been awakened in him. In the second act Ibsen rose to his feet and leaned against the wall of his box. His eyes followed every movement of the actors, and the Master's eyes dwelling on them seemed to increase their power and magic ... In the third act Ibsen leaned out over the balustrade of the box ... When I went to the Grand that night Ibsen came to greet me. Only once have I seen him moved, and that was on this occasion. He stretched out both his hands to me; they were ice-cold, as though his excitement had drawn all the warmth from them. 'This', he said, 'was the resurrection of my play.'

Ibsen used his influence to recommend that Lugné-Poe should be awarded a medal, which the latter received soon after his return to France and which proved useful in a way that neither Ibsen nor King Oscar can have foreseen. 'Shall I confess', Lugné-Poe writes, 'that that medal rescued many a performance? Every time we found ourselves short of money for a new production, off it went to the pawnbroker, and Ibsen never learned what a service he had done us.'

The Swedish actor-manager Albert Ranft was in Christiania at this time, anxious if possible to obtain Ibsen's forthcoming play before the bigger Stockholm theatres. He put up at the Grand Hotel and, having unpacked his bags, went down to the reading-room, and was about to enter when he was stopped by a waiter with the words: 'You can't go in there. The Doctor's there and mustn't be disturbed.' 'What doctor?' asked Ranft. 'Is someone ill?' 'No, it's Dr Ibsen. He's reading the newspapers.' Ranft bribed the waiter with a tip and went in. Ibsen gave him a look as though to say: 'Who's this who dares to enter while I am here?' But when he learned who Ranft was and why he had come, he treated him with kindness and courtesy. Ranft asked if he might read *Little Eyolf* before publication 'to see if we can play it, and if so, buy it'.

Ibsen said: 'So you want to read it first and buy it later?' He stared at me in such astonishment that I feared I had said the wrong thing. 'Well –.' 'I see, you want to read it first. Everyone else has wanted to buy it first and read it later. You shall have the play.' And he shook my hand and said, 'Won't you have a drink?'

But when, later, Ranft began to question him about the play, he found Ibsen accommodating but totally unhelpful. 'Can't this line be interpreted thus, and spoken thus?' asked Ranft. 'Oh, yes.' 'But how do you think it should be said?' 'Oh, my dear fellow,' replied Ibsen. 'You say it how you please, it's all the same to me.' Similar evidence of Ibsen's indifference to how actors spoke his lines is given by Helena Nyblom, quoting the great Danish actor Emil Poulsen. Poulsen told her that after Ibsen had attended a performance of *The Wild Duck* in Copenhagen the cast waited expectantly for his comments. 'But it seemed as though he no longer knew what he had meant by the play. He went around asking us actors, as though we should know better.'

At the beginning of December Suzannah, accompanied by Sigurd, went south again to escape the worst of the winter,

and on 11 December Ibsen wrote to her one of those touchingly Darby-and-Joan letters which they exchanged when
parted:

Dear Suzannah!
 I have received your telegrams, and now your letter. How happy
and relieved I am to learn that everything has so far gone so well!
I hope it will continue so! Here all is well. Frøken Blehr's[3]
cooking suits me excellently. And there is plenty of it, so that we
have ample left for supper should I want any. But I usually just
have herring then, with the most beautiful boiled potatoes which
Lina [their maid] prepares in the new machine. She does everything for me most attentively. Bergliot had dinner with me on
Sunday. Otherwise, no one has been here. The evenings are lonely,
of course; but then I sit and read at the dinner table. In the
morning I drink coffee, which I have brought to my bedroom at
eight o'clock sharp. Indeed, everything goes like clockwork, just
as if you were here. Every morning Augusta brings me a little
tray with crumbs for the birds. Lina is good to her and gives her
some of all the food that gets left over. My new play is being
published today, both here and in Berlin and London. I got the
fee from Heinemann yesterday, and am having Hegel invest
10,000 crowns for us. And later I hope a further 4,000 without
having to leave ourselves short. I am overwhelmed with correspondence, as you can imagine. But I answer it all in as few words
as I can – and so manage. Give Sigurd my warmest regards. I
shall soon see his new book [*Men and Powers*] to which I greatly
look forward. Greet also the Grønvolds, Frøken Klingenfeld,
and Frøken Raff – not to forget Clemence if she is still in
Munich, and thank both the last-named deeply for the beautiful
pictures! I wish you and Sigurd the happiest of times in our old
haunts! Write soon again.

> Your affectionate
> H.I.

William Heinemann having safeguarded his copyright by
a public reading at the Haymarket Theatre on 3 December,
Little Eyolf was, as Ibsen stated, published simultaneously
in Copenhagen, Christiania, London and Berlin on 11 De-

3. A lady who ran a domestic science school in the same street.

cember 1894 – though it almost missed being on sale in Christiania that day, for a fog prevented the steamer from Copenhagen containing the copies from arriving until the late afternoon, to the vexation of prospective purchasers who had been waiting in the bookshops since early morning.

Surprisingly, for it is one of Ibsen's subtlest and most elusive plays, it received an almost unanimously favourable (if somewhat bemused) reception from the Scandinavian press. 'A new triumph,' wrote the penitent Nils Kjær (who had so insulted Ibsen at the Authors' Society, but who was embarking on what was to be a distinguished career as a dramatic critic) in *Dagbladet*. Kristofer Randers, who had severely criticized several of Ibsen's recent plays, praised this one highly in *Aftenposten*: 'Has our old poet become young again? Does he wish to put our younger writers to shame, so youthful he is here, so fresh, immediate and powerful?'

Commercially, *Little Eyolf* was an immense success. The first edition of 10,000 copies sold out almost at once; a second edition of 2,000 appeared on 21 December, and a third of 1,250 on 20 January. A surprising proportion of these were sold outside Scandinavia. *Morgenbladet*'s Copenhagen correspondent reported on 15 December that, apart from the Scandinavian bookshops in America taking large quantities, 'there is scarcely anywhere in the world where people do not want to read Ibsen in the original and as quickly as possible. As soon as a new work by him is announced, orders begin to pour in to the publishers, not merely – indeed, perhaps least – from foreign booksellers, but from private individuals – in Germany, France, England, Russia, Rumania, Turkey, Greece, Italy ... And these orders, as their language proves, do not come merely from Scandinavians. It is no exaggeration to say that myriads of people in foreign countries all over the world have learned Norwegian in order to read Ibsen's works in the original tongue.'

Ibsen's fame in England was by now such that *Little Eyolf* was widely reviewed in the London press, though the reception was predictably mixed. The *Daily Chronicle* welcomed it, describing Ibsen as 'incomparably the most powerful influence in contemporary literature'; but the *Daily Graphic* thought the play exemplified his weaknesses as well as his strengths, and the *Daily News* found it wholly undramatic, the characters mere abstractions and the dialogue obscure and pointless.

Ibsen lost no time in informing Suzannah and Sigurd of the book's success. 'This has been a busy time for me, as you may imagine,' he wrote to them on 20 December. 'It has aroused a storm of enthusiasm, unanimous as never before. The first edition is sold out and a second is appearing tomorrow. Director Ranft has bought the Swedish theatre rights and paid 3,000 crowns for them. The Christiania Theatre ditto. My English fee has been paid. I am straightway investing *seventeen thousand* crowns, which yet leaves a good deal over for us. The play has been accepted by the Royal Theatre in Copenhagen. And the Burgtheater [in Vienna] and the Deutsches Theater [in Berlin]. And doubtless by many other German theatres I don't yet know about.'

Bergliot came to spend Christmas Eve with him. Christmas had always meant a lot to Ibsen; Fru Werenskiold, the wife of the artist Erik Werenskiold, once visited him in Munich shortly before Christmas and was surprised to find him occupied in cutting out paper decorations for the tree, which 'he did very skilfully', as in his childhood when old Mother Maren had sold his products at her stall in the market place in Skien.

Now [writes Bergliot] he no longer cut out paper decorations. Lina, the maid, had decorated the tree as Fru Ibsen liked it, just with candles and white cotton wool on the branches. We went in to the Christmas tree. Ibsen had a terror of fire, and was very worried about all the candles on the tree. Still, I had to light them, and a few moments later had to go out into the passage to fetch something. When I came back I saw to my astonishment Ibsen kneeling on the floor blowing the candles out, one after the other. The tree was on the floor and was not big. I can still see

Ibsen's profile, and how his nose disappeared each time he blew.

As we sat chatting afterwards, Ibsen told me he had discovered there were a lot of mice in the apartment. But he had his own way of keeping them at a distance. He said 'In the evening I take a glass of milk and some biscuits into my room. I put a little in a saucer for the mice and leave it in the next room, and then they don't come into mine.'

On 28 December Ibsen wrote to Suzannah:

Bergliot . . . has been up to me several times and has been very helpful with the Christmas things, which you prepared before you left; or rather, she did it all for me . . . I have bought you two pretty gifts, which are at present in the drawing-room. And a couple of landscapes from Lofoten . . . I have been invited out once or twice . . . Otherwise I sit at home in the evenings and read. Hegel has sent me several new books, and when I know where you are staying for the winter I will forward some to you. 29. 12. I was interrupted at this point yesterday, first by the designer and then by the producer. They are painting new décor for the play and rehearsals are in progress . . . I have received many flowers and cards . . . even from America. If only I were through with answering them all! The most welcome and useful present was from Bergliot. She gave me an enormous bath sponge, with which I wash and rub myself morning and evening; it suits me splendidly. Don't write your letters criss-cross. I have such difficulty with my eyes in deciphering it . . .

With the two editions of *Little Eyolf*, various sales of the performing rights, reprints of (at last) *Ghosts* and *The Pretenders* and a miscellany of small royalties and honoraria, 1894 had been a bumper year for Ibsen, though it would have seemed nearly disastrous to an author of comparable stature in England, France, Germany or America. He had earned over £1,300, more even than in his previous best year, 1880.

As with *The Master Builder*, proofs of *Little Eyolf* had been sent to London as they came off the Gyldendal presses, in order that the translation might proceed without delay.

Henry James persuaded William Heinemann to let him have an advance look at the English version, and on 22 November he wrote to Elizabeth Robins:

Heinemann has lent me the proofs of the 2 first acts of the Play – the ineffable Play – and I can't stay my hand from waving wildly to you! It is indeed immense – indeed and indeed. It is of a rare perfection – and if 3 keeps up the tremendous pitch of 1 and 2 it will distinctly stand at the tiptop of his achievement. It's a masterpiece and a marvel; and it *must* leap upon the stage ... The inherent difficulties are there, but they are not insurmountable. They are on the contrary manageable – they are a matter of tact and emphasis – of art and discretion. The thing will be a big *profane* (i.e., Ibsen and non-Ibsen *both*) success. The part – *the* part – is Asta – unless it be the Rat-hound in the Bag! What an old woman – and what a Young!

But three days later, in a letter of apology for having talked indiscreetly about the play 'in the despair of a dull dinner – or after-dinner', he wrote to Miss Robins:

I fear in truth, no harm can be done equal to the harm done to the play by its own most disappointing third act. It came to me last night – and has been, to me, a subject of depressed reflection. It seems to me a singular and almost inexplicable drop – dramatically, *representably* speaking ... The worst of it is that it goes back, as it were, on what precedes, and gives a meagreness to that too – makes it less interesting and less significant ... I don't see the meaning or effect of Borghejm – I don't see the value or final *function* of Asta ... I find the solution too simple, too immediate, too much a harking back, and too productive of the sense that there might have been a stronger one ... My idea that Asta was to become an active, *the* active agent, is of course blighted.

However, he admitted: 'Really uttered, *done*, in the gathered northern twilight, with the flag down and the lights coming out across the fjord, the scene might have a real solemnity of beauty – and perhaps that's all that's required!' But, he concluded: 'I fear Allmers will never be thought an actor-manager's part.'

James's objections to the third act of *Little Eyolf* have

been shared by many readers; yet, if properly understood and intelligently interpreted, this act is by no means meagre, nor the solution, as James supposed, simple. The great mistake is to imagine that Ibsen envisaged the ending as happy.[4] Surely it is obvious that devoting themselves to charity, sharing their 'gold and their green forests' with the poor, will not ultimately provide the answer and the peace which Alfred and Rita are seeking. They have reached rock-bottom; but unless they can prove that they have undergone a genuine change of heart, and are prepared to grapple with the realities of life, this will be no solution but merely another, more plausible but equally insidious 'life-lie'. They are only at the beginning of their long climb to salvation.

My own belief is that the third act of *Little Eyolf*, like the two that precede it, is among the greatest that Ibsen ever wrote, and that in it he achieved exactly what he set out to achieve, namely, to reveal the interior of what, in *Brand*, thirty years before, he had called 'the Ice Church' – the interior of a human soul in which love has died – so that, in Rita's words, all that is left to her and Alfred is to 'try to fill that emptiness with something. Something resembling love'. In Michael Elliott's delicate production of the play at the 1963 Edinburgh Festival, the two characters spoke the final lines of the play (after Alfred has hoisted the flag to the top of the mast), not facing, but half-turned away from each other, so that the effect was not of facile optimism, but of fear and uncertainty.

Yet James was right in one thing at least – the reluctance of actors of the 'actor-manager' type to play Alfred. Like John Rosmer, and Torvald Helmer in *A Doll's House*, Alfred Allmers is weaker than the woman with whom he is in love, and leading actors tend to be conscious of what is nowadays called their image (which means the kind of man their fans mistakenly imagine them to be). 'How', asked Bernard Shaw in his review of the first English production of

4. Witness his own remarks to Caroline Sontum, p. 767.

the play in 1896, 'could he recommend himself to spectators who saw in him everything they are ashamed of in themselves?'

Allmers is usually, in practice, either romanticized or (as with Rosmer) played as sexless; and a sexless or romanticized Allmers and a happy ending are burdens that no production of *Little Eyolf* can hope to survive. *A Doll's House*, *Ghosts* and *Hedda Gabler* are robust plays; they can be ill-cast, ill-directed, ill-acted, and yet make a goodish evening. *Little Eyolf*, like *The Lady from the Sea* and *When We Dead Awaken*, is fragile; if it is not done well, one would rather it had not been done at all; performed as it was written to be performed, it is a haunting and memorable experience. Nowhere else does Ibsen probe so mercilessly into the complexities of human minds and relationships; it is like a long, sustained and terrifying operation. On the occasion of the first English production William Archer wrote: 'I rank the play beside, if not above, the very greatest of Ibsen's works, and am only doubtful whether its soul-searching be not too terrible for human endurance in the theatre.'

33

John Gabriel Borkman
1895–6

SUZANNAH stayed abroad for nearly a year. It was the longest time they had been separated during their marriage. She spent the winter at Meran in the southern Tyrol, and he wrote to her regularly and at length, inquiring solicitously after her health, warning her against this or that possible excess and giving her dull little pieces of news and local or family gossip; his letters are more than ever those of a man to whom correspondence is an agony. He was 'overwhelmed' with preparations for the Christiania production of *Little Eyolf,* which in fact can have made little demand on him, and 'bombarded' with requests that he visit Berlin for the German première, 'which is of course an impossibility'. Suzannah's niece, Magdalena Falsen, meeting him on the street and suggesting that she visit him, received the reply that 'I was so occupied with business matters that I could not receive anyone'. Bergliot came to dine with him on Sundays; no one had filled the gap left by Hildur's absence.

The world première of *Little Eyolf* took place on 12 January at the Deutsches Theater in Berlin, with Emmanuel Reicher as Allmers and Agnes Sorma as Rita; it was a measure of the international fame which Ibsen now enjoyed that critics (or at least reporters) from all over the word attended. It was not a success, any more than *The Master Builder* had been in Germany, and, like the latter play, it does not seem to have been performed for several years in any other German town. Ibsen's social dramas were continually revived (his royalties from Bloch were considerably up this year), but his recent plays struck the Germans as less realistic and topical, and therefore less interesting.

In Christiania, by contrast, *Little Eyolf* proved such a success that it was performed thirty-six times that year, compared with eighteen performances for *Hedda Gabler* and fifteen for *The Master Builder* during their first seasons. Ibsen attended the première on 15 January, together with Christian and Caroline Sontum and young Bolette:

> Ibsen was very anxious about the reception. He kept saying to my mother, who sat next to him, 'Do let's get out before the curtain comes down.' It was always a torture to him to see his own plays ... *Little Eyolf* was received with great enthusiasm, and there were many curtain calls, but, persistently as they clapped, the audience could not persuade the author to take a bow. Finally, the stage manager promised to convey their congratulations personally to him.
>
> Ibsen, meanwhile, was driving to the Grand Hotel in a shabby little sleigh as fast as the plodding horse could carry him through the streets. It was snowing heavily ... When Ibsen reached the Grand, he was much overcome by the performance and exceedingly nervous. He begged my mother to order the supper for him, and seemed like a child asking for protection. The heavy food and some good wine soon raised his spirits. When my mother, still full of the play, said: 'Poor Rita, now she has to go to work with all those mischievous boys,' Ibsen replied: 'Do you really believe so? Don't you rather think it was more of a Sunday mood with her?' ... The only other remark I can recall him ever making on his own plays was in discussing *Love's Comedy* with my mother. 'But Svanhild should not have engaged herself to Guldstad,' she said. 'Console yourself, dear friend,' he replied. 'The next day she will have a rendezvous with Falk.'

Before the end of January, *Little Eyolf* was also staged in Bergen, Helsinki and Gothenburg; Milan and Vienna saw it in February. On 3 February he had another Russian première, when (of all plays) *The Feast at Solhaug* was performed in prose – only the third of his plays to be seen in that country.

At the beginning of February Sigurd returned to Norway leaving his mother at Meran. He had published a caustic article on Swedish liberalism in the December number of the magazine *Nyt Tidskrift*. Ibsen proudly wrote to Suzannah on 6 February that the piece 'has excited much attention, and not only in Norway; as have his articles on the consular question'. With equal pride he added: 'Can you guess how much I have already invested of the royalties that have come in? No less than 20,000 crowns [£1,111]! And I hope in the near future to be able to put by another 4,000 crowns, without our having to pinch in any way.' The winter in Norway, he told her, was the coldest for years; not merely shipping, but even railways were at a standstill; but 'the air is brilliantly clear and clean'. Sigurd looked in only occasionally; otherwise 'I sit by myself and read the newspapers, and am quite content'. He was economizing as much as ever as regards food. His lunch was being sent in; and for his evening meal 'I have hot soup and fish or meat left over from lunch, so that we hardly ever have to send out for anything.'

Georg Brandes sent him an essay he had written about the young Marianne von Willemer's infatuation with Goethe when the latter was sixty-six, and its stimulating effect on the poetry of Goethe's old age. He could scarcely have chosen a subject closer to Ibsen's heart. 'I cannot forbear', wrote Ibsen to him on 11 February, 'to send you especial thanks for your "Goethe and Marianne von Willemer". I didn't know anything about the episode you describe in it. I may have read about it years ago in Lewes's book, but if so I had forgotten it, because at that time the affair held no particular interest for me. But now things are somewhat different. When I think of the quality which characterizes Goethe's work during that period, I mean the sense of renewed youth, I ought to have guessed that he must have been graced with some such revelation, some such reassurance of beauty, as his meeting with Marianne von Willemer. Fate, Providence, Chance, can be genial and benevolent powers now and then.' Ibsen must have been comforted to know that other great writers had become emotionally involved with girls forty years their junior; and certainly his own last five plays, after his meeting with Emilie, have, like the aged writings of a young poet just then emerging into fame, W. B. Yeats, all the vigour and sharpness of youth.

His sixty-seventh birthday was looming, but any hope he might have had that it could be allowed to slip by peacefully in Suzannah's absence had been knocked on the head. He wrote to her on 12 March:

For the dreadful day, 20 March, Bergliot must manage as best she can, since you will have it so. And I shall receive everyone, even the spies, as politely as I can. I hope Falsen [his brother-in-law, a *generalkonsul* married to Suzannah's sister Dorothea] won't be able to come. Dorothea and Magdalena [her daughter] have influenza; so they won't be able to. Incidentally, I hear they have moved to Parkveien. Herman has twisted his foot and can't go out. Then I must tell you that a *third* edition of *Little Eyolf* is printing and will probably be out next week. The day after tomorrow the play will open in Copenhagen. Hegel has commissioned a big portrait of me from Eilif Peterssen, and I am now sitting to him. There is a very widespread epidemic of influenza in the city. But so far I haven't noticed any signs. On Sunday evening there was a fire upstairs in Fru Bjørn's boarding-house. They had overfilled a lamp, which of course exploded. The fire brigade arrived, and there was a great scene, with screaming on the stairs; but the fire was soon put out. At the exhibition I bought a fine painting by Chr. Krohg. It is actually a portrait of Strindberg; but Sigurd calls it 'The Revolution', and I call it 'Insanity Emergent'. Sigurd urged me to buy it, for the ridiculously cheap price of 500 crowns. Sigurd and his family are well. Bergliot has been so good as to give me some *gammelost* and pickled herring and a splendid joint of roast pork, which I enjoy in the evenings. I hope you are having a good time down there.

Ibsen hung the painting of Strindberg (a very large one) on the wall of his study; it helped him, he explained to astonished inquirers, to work with 'that madman staring down at me'. He especially liked the 'demonic eyes', and once remarked: 'He is my mortal enemy, and shall hang there and watch while I write.' August Lindberg, who knew Strindberg, relates how Ibsen once asked him if it was a good likeness and, 'in a whisper that he perhaps did not intend to be heard, muttered, "A remarkable man!" ' As with his visits to the Hamsun lectures, it seemed as if Ibsen wished to remind himself of the younger generation challenging and threatening him. Some writers are enervated by competition and hostility; Ibsen thrived on it. Bergliot recalls that once when Bjørnson was so ill that he was not expected to live, but recovered, Ibsen, on being gently taunted by Sigurd, declared with deep feeling: 'It would not have been easy to lose one's only rival.'

He was (he told Suzannah on 3 April) sitting each day to Eilif Peterssen; otherwise 'everything is as usual except that we have begun to cook meals here. Frøken Blehr's food got worse from day to day until it was practically uneatable. Lina, on the other hand, cooks quite excellently, just the kind of food she knows I like; a lot of fish, and excellent potatoes.' Ten days later he informed her proudly that he had invested 24,000 crowns' worth of royalties and hoped soon to be able to invest a further 6,000 [£1,667 altogether], and that his total investments now totalled 166,000 crowns [£9,222] 'which I venture to say is not bad'. Far from indulging in any luxuries, apart from the Strindberg painting, he boasted a few weeks later (2 July) that his household expenses over the past quarter have averaged 116 crowns [less than £6.50] a *month* – 'including laundry and everything'.

He did a lot of modelling that spring, for as soon as Peterssen had finished his portrait Erik Werenskiold moved in to paint another. 'This puts me somewhat behind in my work, I mean my correspondence,' he confessed to Suzannah on 27 April. 'But I find it an agreeable distraction, and a change, and it doesn't greatly inconvenience me since it all takes place in my study. After Werenskiold, Sinding is coming to model the statue for the new theatre.'

Both Erik Werenskiold and Stephan Sinding recorded their impressions of Ibsen. Werenskiold remembered him as an excellent model, who 'stood still as a pillar...stood happily for a couple of hours on end, he was so immensely strong. Even the last time I saw him, he was as round and firm as a rolling pin.' He found Ibsen 'extraordinarily winning, delightfully agreeable and full of jokes'. Before he started to paint, Ibsen liked to sit and chat, and 'was exceptionally curious, asking question after question; he was especially interested in women. Whenever I was able to tell him about some unusual woman he would sit there like a bird of prey and would not let me stop until I had told him everything I knew.' He remembered that Ibsen once used the phrase 'the terrain of the face', and rightly comments that 'it wasn't a phrase *anyone* would use'. Impressed by the size of Ibsen's forehead, he asked if anyone had ever measured his brain-pan; Ibsen replied that a German professor had, and had told him it was the largest he had ever come across. Werenskiold also recalled that every Saturday some little boys from a school in the street would come to Ibsen's apartment, and that he would give them each 25 øre (a penny). When his charlady complained that they dirtied his floors and would only spend the money on cakes, Ibsen replied, 'Why shouldn't they buy cakes?'

Stephan Sinding found Ibsen equally courteous and patient but (through no fault of his) a most awkward subject to model.

I worked and worked and couldn't get it right. I discarded one effort after another. While I was working on the sixth it occurred to me to ask Ibsen to take his spectacles off. He laid them aside and looked at me. I have never seen two eyes like those. One was large, I might almost say horrible – so it seemed to me – and deeply mystical; the other much smaller, rather pinched up, cold and clear and calmly probing. I stood speechless for a few seconds and stared at those eyes, and spoke the thought that flashed into my mind: 'I wouldn't like to have you as an enemy!' Then his eyes and his whole body seemed to blaze, and I thought instinctively of the troll in the fairy tale who pops out of his hole and roars: 'Who's chopping trees in *my* forest?'

Werenskiold made no fewer than six portraits of Ibsen during the first six months of that year, including one delightful one painted from memory entitled 'The Laughing Ibsen'. It is the only laughing painting or photograph of him in existence; Werenskiold notes at the foot of the portrait that it was a remark of Ibsen's own that put him into this good humour. Recalling a bad portrait that a Norwegian artist named Ole H. B. Olrik had painted of him in Rome in 1879, Ibsen said to Werenskiold: 'For a long time he had been painting nothing but saints, so I wasn't a very suitable subject for him.'

Peterssen, Werenskiold and Sinding were not the only artists to portray Ibsen that winter and spring. Edvard Munch had done the first of his lithographs of Ibsen just before the turn of the year, and Hans Heyerdahl and Christian Krohg painted him too. A contemporary Danish caricature by Alfred Schmidt shows Ibsen surrounded by Norwegian artists trying to capture his likeness.

Hildur Andersen had by now returned to Christiania, and Ibsen had been seeing a good deal of her. Their frequent appearances in public together had, naturally, Christiania being what it was, led to a good deal of gossip; the rumour had spread that Ibsen was considering divorcing Suzannah, and her stepmother, Magdalene Thoresen, thought fit to write to Suzannah and tell her of this. Suzannah, still in Meran, wrote to Ibsen asking him if there was any truth in the gossip, an action which is, perhaps, less surprising when one remembers that they had, for the first time in nearly forty years, been separated for six months. Ibsen replied on 7 May in a letter which one is surprised, though grateful, that she kept:

Dear Suzannah,

It hurt me deeply to read your last letter, dated 1 May. And I hope that, on closer reflection, you will regret having sent it. So your stepmother, that damned old sinner, has been at work again, trying to cause trouble by setting us against each other. But it's easy to guess who is behind that poor twisted woman. It is of course her good daughter, who is still wandering around the streets here and is doubtless angry with me because whenever I see her I slip into a side-street, which I have done once or twice. And now she is trying to take her revenge. And you can let yourself be fooled by that!

I don't understand your stepmother's hysterical utterances and sham profundities. I never have understood them. But when she writes this rubbish about my 'wanting freedom at any price' – then I can most solemnly and sacredly assure you that I have never seriously thought or intended any such thing and that I never shall think or intend it. What I may have blurted out in a temper when your moods and humours drove me to a temporary despair is something quite different to which no weight should be attached. But my earnest advice is that if you wish to retain the peace of mind necessary if you are to be cured, you should break off all correspondence with your mentally confused stepmother. It is possible that she means well. But that woman's intervention in any matter or situation has always proved disastrous. If you don't want to tell her this yourself, I will. But I must have your consent first. Enough of this for today.

And now I come to the next main point in your letter. You beg me to lease a new apartment. And of course, since you so positively demand it, I shall do this. But in your letter you reproach me for taking our present apartment without consulting you. (At that time you were in Valdres and in no frame of mind for me to consider asking your advice.) Now when you come home and find this new apartment leased and furnished, you must remember that I have acted in accordance with your expressed wishes and that on this occasion, too, I have been unable to consult your opinion. And the task of finding something that will suit you in every respect is one that I shall indeed not find easy. Remember how Sigurd and Bergliot had to search and search before they at last and at great expense found something suitable. Our difficulties will be even greater. You don't want to live on the ground floor because the floors will be cold, and you won't or can't live higher up because of the stairs. But, as I say, your demand will be met. A new apartment will be leased.

I neither can nor wish to write about other matters today. Nor have I anything to say as regards myself. Werenskiold is here every morning and paints for an hour, otherwise the household routine remains unchanged. I presume Sigurd and the newspapers keep you in touch with political events.

And let me soon receive a calm, and calming, letter from you. And above all, keep these damned witches out of your life! That is the best advice and the best wishes that I can send you. Warmest regards,

Your affectionate

H.I.

On 21 June he wrote again to Suzannah, by now in Monsummano, a spa near Pisa with a natural steam-bath in a grotto:

Well, I have now terminated our lease of Viktoria Terrasse and taken the first-floor apartment in a new house which the brothers Hoff are building on the corner of Arbins gade and Drammensveien. It was Sigurd and Bergliot who suggested this, and I think you will be happy with it. I have a big study with a door direct to the hall, so that people visiting me will not have to enter any other room in the apartment. You will have for your exclusive use a large corner room with a balcony and, next to it, an almost equally large drawing-room leading into the dining-room, which will hold 20–22 people and has an alcove for a sideboard, which I shall get. The dining-room leads straight into a large library and thence into your bedroom, which is much bigger than your one here. My bedroom is next to it on the balcony. You won't need to use the corridor except when you want to go to the bathroom. There is also of course a big, light kitchen, a pantry and a servery, and many built-in wall-cupboards. As I say I think you will be pleased.

It was to be the last of their many apartments, and both Ibsen and Suzannah were to die there.

William Archer, enclosing a couple of money drafts from

Beerbohm Tree that summer, seems to have suggested to
Ibsen that he should visit England to meet his many and
distinguished admirers there. What a gathering that would
have been! But Ibsen was as timid as ever of visiting a
country where he could not speak the language. 'More and
more do I feel it a painful deficiency', he replied on 27 June,
'that I did not in time learn to speak English. Now it is too
late! Had I mastered the language I would now come at once
to London. Or rather, I would have been there long ago. I
have been thinking over many things, recently, and now feel
sure that my Scottish ancestry has left deep marks in me.
But this is just an idea – possibly the wish is father to the
thought.' And indeed it must have been, for his only Scottish
ancestor had been seven generations earlier, in the seventeenth century. There seems to have been something of a
conspiracy to get him to England this year, for Georg
Brandes also wrote (on 16 December), but got the same
reply.

By now, Ibsen had become a kind of tourist attraction in
Christiania. Foreigners gathered at the Grand to see him
make his entry. Among them was the English poet Richard
le Gallienne:

The large café was crowded, but we found a good table on the
aisle, not far from the door. We had not long to wait, for punctually on the stroke of one, there, entering the doorway, was the
dour and bristling presence known to all the world in caricature –
caricatures which were no exaggerations but as in the case of
Swinburne, just the man himself. The great ruff of white whis-
ker, ferociously standing out all round his sallow, bilious face as
if dangerously charged with electricity, the immaculate silk hat,
the white tie, the frock-coated martinet's figure dressed from top
to toe in old-fashioned black broadcloth, at once funereal and
professional, the trousers concertinaed, apparently with dandaical
design, at the ankles, over his highly polished b⌐ots, the carefully
folded umbrella – all was there, apparitionally before me; a forbidding, disgruntled, tight-lipped presence, starchily dignified,
straight as a ramrod; there he was, as I hinted, with a touch of
grim dandyism about him, but with no touch of human kindness

about his parchment skin or fierce badger eyes. He might have been a Scotch elder entering the kirk.

As he entered and proceeded with precision tread to the table reserved in perpetuity for him, which no one else would have dreamed of occupying, a thing new and delightful – to me a mere Anglo-Saxon – suddenly happened. As one man, the whole café was on its feet in an attitude of salute, and a stranger standing near me who evidently spoke English and who recognized my nationality, said to me in a loud but reverent aside: 'That is our great poet, Henrik Ibsen.' All remained standing till he had taken his seat, as in the presence of a king, and I marvelled greatly at a people that thus did homage to their great men.[1]

A granddaughter of Queen Victoria, the lively young Princess Marie Louise, was intrigued to note that he carried a small mirror in the crown of his hat and used it like a woman when combing his hair. Foreigners did their best to obtain introductions; that summer he was visited by a Russian Count Galitzin, who (he wrote to Suzannah on 2 July) 'has been General in the Caucasus and has seen all the Russian borderlands touching India, Tibet and China, and the whole of the north coast of Siberia'. The Hungarian novelist Giula Pekar visited him too, as did his French translator Count Prozor and a Serbian Prince, Bojidar Karageorgevitch, 'whose father ruled until the present regime came into power'. On one occasion 'a group of forty to fifty tourists cheered me loudly outside the Grand Hotel, led by an Austrian Lieutenant-Field-Marshal'; indeed, he was (he complained) 'properly plagued' by tourists, one of whom, an American, gained entry to his apartment and, as Ibsen glared at him, slid round him into his study, seized a pencil from the desk and disappeared with it through the door. All this, except the last incident, he reported to Suzannah and Sigurd in his letters of that summer, urging Sigurd not to let Suzannah hurry home since 'I manage excellently alone'. Apart from two dinners, he told Suzannah (22 September), he had not been outside the city all summer.

1. Le Gallienne's daughter, Eva, became a distinguished interpreter of Ibsen on the American stage.

Lugné-Poe was in Christiania again, after his theatrical triumph of the previous autumn (which he had repeated in London that spring). He had staged *Little Eyolf* and *Brand* in Paris that summer, evoking the usual violently mixed reactions. On 10 August a dinner was given for him, which Ibsen attended – 'I cannot avoid going, little as I feel inclined to,' he grumbled to Suzannah the previous day. However, he seems to have enjoyed himself, for Lugné-Poe notes that he stayed until one in the morning, joined in a game of cards, and kept saying to him: 'I am so happy for your sake.'

On 15 October he moved with Bergliot's help into the new apartment at Arbins gade. Despite the pride with which he had written of it to Suzannah, it was to be as cheerless and unindividual as Viktoria Terrasse, or any of the furnished apartments they had inhabited abroad. 'Here he lodged for the eleven years that remained to him,' writes Gerhard Gran. 'I say "lodged" deliberately, for these rooms never acquired the character of a home. They seemed cold and unlived-in, as regards not merely ordinary comfort and intimacy, but every personal stamp or individuality of taste. The only room which possessed a little of this was his study.' A young child who lived in the flat below and occasionally visited Ibsen's kitchen for titbits from their maid Lina remembered it as drab and icy-cold; she also recalled the incessant sound above her head, when she was in her own room, of footsteps pacing back and forth, back and forth.[2] King Oscar gave Ibsen a key to a private section of the palace grounds known as the Queen's Park, so that he could walk there undisturbed.

August Lindberg, who had taken his productions of *Peer Gynt* and *Little Eyolf* to St Petersburg that March, was in Christiania in October preparing a production of *Brand*, and asked Ibsen if he could meet him to discuss it. Ibsen asked whom Lindberg had in mind to provide the music.

2. Told by Fru Signe Meyer, *née* Hansen, to Herr Gordon Hølmebakk, who told me.

'I'd thought of Grieg, naturally.'

'Why Grieg?'

'Well, he wrote the music for *Peer Gynt*.'

'Oh,' said Ibsen. 'You think that's good, do you?'

1895 had been an important year for Ibsen in America. Although there is no record of any native performances, apart from a *Little Eyolf* in Chicago in the spring, New Yorkers had had the opportunity to see three European productions: Janet Achurch in *A Doll's House*, Gabrielle Réjane in the same play, and Tree's *An Enemy of the People*. Of this last production, Lucy Monroe wrote in the magazine *Critic*: 'With a singular lack of faith in the discretion of the public, it was reserved for the close of the engagement and put on then, apparently more as an experiment than with any expectation of success. But the enthusiasm was of a kind not easily provoked in an American audience. The house was keenly appreciative throughout, and after the third act it fairly rose to the play, shouting and cheering.' By the following year, an American was to write: 'Ibsen has become so familiar to the American public that one need scarcely touch upon the incidents of his career.'

It had been another fair year financially: £1,239. New editions of *Brand*, *Little Eyolf*, *Love's Comedy* and *The League of Youth* had brought him £256, but this represented only about one fifth of his income. The rest came from performing rights. His German and Austrian royalties aggregated £503, his French royalties £164, his Danish royalties £190. His English royalties (from Tree's *Enemy of the People*) were only £17.50: and for Norwegian performing rights he received no more than £32, made up of £4 owed him from Bergen for the previous year and £28 for the touring rights of *Little Eyolf*.

Suzannah had returned home during the autumn, to settle for the first time in their new apartment; so he wrote no more letters to her, and few to anyone that have survived from 1896. Edvard Brandes visited him that winter and was amused to see how he 'enjoyed studying the harrowed and embittered face of his adversary' hanging on the study wall. The Strindberg portrait seemed to Brandes to provide the sole example of individuality in the furnishing of Arbins gade. When he remarked on it, Ibsen half-closed his eyes and said, 'I like to look at that face.'

Ibsen spent the first months of 1896 brooding on his new play, getting his 'little imps' in order. 'I am busy with preparations for a big new work,' he wrote to Georg Brandes on 24 April, 'and don't want to put it off for longer than I need. I could so easily have a tile fall on my head before I had "managed to write the last verse". And what then?' On 11 July he began his draft, and on 27 July was able to inform Jacob Hegel that it was 'progressing quickly and easily, despite the more than southerly warmth we are having up here this summer'. It went smoothly indeed, for by 26 August he had finished his draft. On 18 October he finished fair-copying his new play – he had spent eight full weeks polishing it – and two days later he posted it off to Hegel with the prophecy: 'I think we shall both have joy from it.'

In France, Lugné-Poe had presented *The Pillars of Society* that June; and on 12 November, greatly daring, he followed it with the French première of *Peer Gynt*. Bernard Shaw went over to Paris for the performance, and found it disappointing. 'The characteristic Northern hard-headed, hard-fisted humour, the Northern power of presenting the deepest truths in the most homely grotesques, was missed,' he wrote in the *Saturday Review*. 'M. Lugné-Poe, with all his realism, could no more help presenting the play sentimentally and sublimely than M. Lamoureux can help conducting the overture of *Tannhäuser* as if it were the "Marseillaise"; but the universality of Ibsen makes his plays come home to all nations; and Peer Gynt is as good a Frenchman as he is a Norwegian, just as Dr Stockmann is as intelligible in Bermondsey or Bournemouth as he is in his native town ... Peer Gynt will finally smash anti-Ibsenism in Europe, because Peer is everybody's hero. He has the same effect on the imagination that Hamlet, Faust and Mozart's Don Juan have had.' Yet the press (according to Bjørn Bjørnson, who was also there) was surprisingly good, and Shaw records that the play aroused such interest in Paris that Prozor's translation 'was sold out immediately after the performance'. The Old Man of the Mountains was played by a twenty-three-year-old actor who was the secretary of the Théâtre de l'Oeuvre – Alfred Jarry (appearing under the pseudonym of Hemgé), whose play *Ubu roi*, written for marionettes when Jarry was a schoolboy of fifteen, had been performed by the Oeuvre that year, with Bonnard, Vuillard and Toulouse-Lautrec among the designers of scenery and masks.

On 23 November *Little Eyolf* was staged in England for the first time, at the Avenue Theatre (later the Playhouse) behind Charing Cross station. The cast was the strongest that had yet been assembled in England for an Ibsen play. Not only were Janet Achurch and Elizabeth Robins paired together for the first time, as Rita and Asta; Allmers was played by Courtenay Thorpe, who had been a remarkable Oswald in New York in 1894, and a West End star, Stella Patrick Campbell, who had burst into fame as Pinero's Mrs Tanqueray in 1893, was secured for the part of the Rat-Wife. Bernard Shaw in the *Saturday Review* (28 November) commented:

The performance was, of course, a very remarkable one. When, in a cast of five, you have the three best yet discovered actresses of their generation, you naturally look for something extraordinary ... Miss Achurch was more than equal to the occasion. Her power seemed to grow with its own expenditure ... As Rita she produced almost every sound that a big human voice can, from a creak like the opening of a rusty canal lock to a melodious tenor note that the most robust Siegfried might have envied. She looked at one moment like a young, well-dressed, very pretty woman; at another she was like a desperate creature just fished dripping out of the river by the Thames Police. Yet another moment, and she was the incarnation of impetuous, ungovernable strength ... It is encouraging to see that the performances are to be continued next week, the five matinées – all crowded, by the way – having by no means exhausted the demand for places.

The production was such a success that it was transferred to the evening bill; but in the hope of ensuring a commercial success the new backers removed Janet Achurch from the part of Rita and replaced her with Mrs Patrick Campbell who (according to Shaw in the *Saturday Review*, 12 December) 'succeeded wonderfully in removing all unpleasantness from the play', and thereby ruined it. It was not to be the last time that an Ibsen production was to be spoiled by the replacement of the right player by a supposedly more magnetic star[3] (though in the next century Mrs Campbell was to be a memorable Hedda Gabler and Mrs Alving, with the young John Gielgud as Oswald).

Not all the critics, naturally, admired the play. The *Theatre* called it 'dull, wordy, unpleasant and prodigiously tiresome', and *The Times* wrote: 'Gloom, depression and a sense of the remoteness of the action from all living human interests overcome the spectator, whose abiding impression of the play is that of having seen in a dream the patients of a madhouse exercising in their yard.'

On 5 December *Emperor and Galilean* was staged for the first time, in a shortened form, at the Leipzig Stadttheater, and the same month *Love's Comedy* also received its German première, at the Belle-Alliance Theatre in Berlin – the first performance of that play outside Scandinavia. But neither was a great success.

On 15 December *John Gabriel Borkman* was published, in, thanks to the success of *Little Eyolf*, the unprecedently large edition of 12,000 copies. Even this proved insufficient; the demand was such that Hegel had to reprint another 3,000

3. Lugné-Poe tells that Ibsen hated to hear of any actor doing a play 'for his own sake', and that when told that Le Bargy was thinking of doing Oswald, Ibsen exploded: 'Of course, like that Italian actor who acts the whole play!' (He was referring to Ermete Zaccone.)

before publication. It was even better received than *Little Eyolf* – not surprisingly, the critics found it less obscure. 'Ibsen has never climbed so high as a dramatic master builder,' wrote Nils Vogt in *Morgenbladet*, and he thought the play 'fascinating and exciting'. Georg Brandes, in *Verdens Gang*, found it magnificently constructed 'as though built of iron on a foundation of granite. The play moves with the speed of youth, but the voice is that of age and wisdom, a stern wisdom' – and too, of 'a deep sympathy for human suffering which yet has not retracted a single one of its demands'. Naturally, there were dissidents, most of whom reacted against the play's apparent pessimism. But the ayes had it. *John Gabriel Borkman* was acclaimed as none of his plays had been since *A Doll's House*.

John Gabriel Borkman tells the story of a miner's son who becomes a financier and, for idealistic reasons, embezzles and is sent to prison. Released after eight years, he lives alone in an upstairs room of his house refusing to see his wife, visited only by an old clerk and waiting in the conviction that the people will demand that he emerge to save them. As a young man he had married not for love but to get his foot on the ladder; now his wife's twin sister, whom he had loved and rejected, comes to reproach him and to beg that she be given charge of his son, and that this son, Erhart, should take her name. Borkman agrees, but his wife, who overhears their conversation, refuses; as the two women argue, Erhart arrives to announce that he is leaving with a woman nearly twice his age. Borkman wanders out and dies on the mountainside.

The gossips of Christiania, naturally, took the loveless marriage of the Borkmans to be a picture of Ibsen's relationship with Suzannah, especially now that Hildur Andersen was back in town.[4] It is hardly that; yet, despite Ibsen's

4. As an example of the malicious rumours that circulated in Christiania about Ibsen and Suzannah, William Archer tells that 'my

demand that we should treat his plays as pure fiction, one may be forgiven for suggesting that *John Gabriel Borkman* does in fact represent a sad survey of the dramatist's bleak emotional life. The Ibsens were not precisely the Borkmans; the immense tie that bound Henrik and Suzannah together is absent from the marriage in the play; a kind of love, perhaps the most profound and lasting kind, existed between the Ibsens, but it was not, and never had been, romantic love, the kind that Ella Rentheim represents. Ibsen, like Borkman, had turned his back on romantic love for a woman who could enable him to achieve his ambitions, and Emilie Bardach, Helene Raff and Hildur Andersen were living symbols of what he had rejected. By choosing, and remorselessly pursuing, the career of an author he had sacrificed his chance of that other kind of happiness; and he may have felt that to some extent he had sacrificed Suzannah's chances too. The recent quarrel with Suzannah about his supposed intention to divorce her must have helped to make *John Gabriel Borkman* the guilt-ridden play it is. In a sense the play is about what Ibsen's marriage might have been like had he failed as a writer; in another sense, it is about emotional bankruptcy, the buried treasures of the heart that lie unmined; how a man may gain the whole world and lose his soul. Edvard Munch called *John Gabriel Borkman* 'the most powerful winter landscape in Scandinavian art'.

Formally, the last act of *Borkman* marks a return to the epic and poetic symbolism of *Brand* and *Peer Gynt*. As we have seen, Ibsen had deliberately suppressed the poet in him while writing the 'social' plays, from *The Pillars of Society* to

---

brother was one day going to call upon him in Christiania and remarked to a friend resident in the town that if Ibsen was not at home he hoped he might see Fru Ibsen. "Oh, no," said his friend. "You won't see her. She hasn't been able to live with him for years." My brother paid his call and the first person he saw on crossing the threshold was Fru Ibsen. The incident was typical.'

The Wild Duck; there are no moments of poetry in them, save perhaps Mrs Alving's speech about the ghosts that 'lie as thick as grains of sand'. But in every play he had written since *Rosmersholm,* with the solitary exception of *Hedda Gabler* (and was the laconic shorthand of that play the result of a desire not to let his hidden feelings break the surface?), there are times when we are aware of the buried river. A writer who delves into the dark unconscious, as Ibsen had done in these last plays, cannot wholly suppress the poet within him, far less the symbolist. But it is not, I think, until the final act of *John Gabriel Borkman* that we find the writer of realistic dialogue being edged aside by the symbolist and the poet:

BORKMAN (*stops by the precipice*). Come, Ella, and I shall show you.

ELLA. What will you show me, John?

BORKMAN (*points*). See how the country stretches out before us, open and free – far, far away.

ELLA. We used to sit on that seat, and stare into the distance.

BORKMAN. It was a country of dreams we gazed into.

ELLA. The country of our dreams, yes. Now it is covered with snow. And the old tree is dead.

BORKMAN (*not listening to her*). Can you see the smoke from the great steamers out on the fjord?

ELLA. No.

BORKMAN. I can. They come and go. They create a sense of fellowship throughout the world. They bring light and warmth to the hearts of men in many thousands of homes. That is what I dreamed of creating.

ELLA. But it remained a dream.

BORKMAN. Yes. It remained a dream. (*Listens*). Listen. Down there by the river the factories hum. My factories. Listen how they hum. The night shifts are working. They work both night and day. Listen, listen! The wheels whirl and the pistons thud, round and round, in and out. Can't you hear them, Ella?

ELLA. No.

BORKMAN. I hear them.

ELLA (*frightened*). No, John, you can't.

BORKMAN. Ah, but these are only the outworks surrounding my kingdom.

ELLA. What kingdom?

BORKMAN. My kingdom. The kingdom I was about to take possession of when I died.

ELLA. Oh, John, John.

BORKMAN. And there it lies, defenceless, masterless, abandoned to thieves and robbers. Ella! Do you see those mountains far away? Range beyond range, rising and rising? That is my infinite and inexhaustible kingdom.

ELLA. Ah, but it's a cold wind that blows from that kingdom, John.

BORKMAN. To me it is the breath of life. It is a greeting from the spirits that serve me. I feel them, those buried millions. I see those veins of iron ore, stretching their twisting, branching, enticing arms towards me. I've seen you all before, like shadows brought to life – that night when I stood in the vaults of the bank with the lantern in my hand. You wanted to be freed. And I tried to free you. But I failed. Your treasure sank back into the darkness. But let me whisper this to you now, in the stillness of the night. I love you where you lie like the dead, deep down in the dark. I love you, treasures that crave for life, with your bright retinue of power and glory. I love you, love you, love you.

That is the voice of the young Ibsen, the author of *Brand*. In his next play, the movement away from realism, or rather from the realism of prose towards the realism of poetry, was to be carried a stage further. In *When We Dead Awaken*, as in *Brand* and *Peer Gynt*, Ibsen seems to be writing for a theatre of the mind – though, like them, *When We Dead Awaken* works powerfully on the stage, given the right quality of imagination in the staging.

As though to underline the message of *John Gabriel Borkman*, that the quest for material success may lead to emotional bankruptcy, 1896 had proved, in terms of money, Ibsen's richest year yet, With £775 from the first two Gyldendal impressions of *John Gabriel Borkman*, £200 from the English edition, £272 from the German edition, £222 for

Swedish performing rights of the play, £195 from reprints of *A Doll's House* (4th edition), *The Pretenders* (9th edition) and *Peer Gynt* (10th edition), and £73 from German and Austrian performing rights, he had earned £1,944.

34

Irritations
1897

John Gabriel Borkman received two simultaneous
premières, on 10 January in Helsinki, when both the Finnish
and Swedish theatres staged it. On 16 January it was performed at Frankfurt-am-Main. The German censor had
ordered the excision of two passages which he found
offensive, Ella's line in Act Two about 'the sin for which
there is no forgiveness' (to murder love in a human being),
and Mrs Wilton's remark in Act Four about the advisability
of Erhart having another girl to fall back on if he should tire
of her, or she of him. Here, as in Helsinki, the play was a
success. Three days later it received its Norwegian première,
under bizarre circumstances. August Lindberg had secured
from Ibsen the rights to present it in the Norwegian provinces, and managed to stage it at the little town of Drammen, a
bare thirty miles from Christiania, six days before the Christiania Theatre was ready with its production. He enter-
prisingly ran special trains from the capital to Drammen
and so drew off a proportion of the Christiania Theatre's
public, which probably caused Ibsen no displeasure (as he
had received a fixed fee for both productions, it did not
matter to him which one people attended). The provincial
production got much the better reviews.

Lindberg had one or two meetings with Ibsen while preparing the production, to ask him about various points, 'but
he always answered briefly and evasively'. Lindberg thought
his attitude towards his plays was like what, as an apothecary, he must have felt towards his medicines; once he
had mixed them, there was an end to it. 'I had to console

myself with the thought that we actors were as air to him.'

One day Ibsen invited him to lunch at the Grand Hotel at noon.

I met him in the foyer and saw how he took out a small girl's comb and combed his hair meticulously, surveying himself in a small mirror in the crown of his hat. When we arrived at the table reserved for him there stood on it nothing but a carafe of schnapps and a bottle of light brown ale. The head waiter came, and was commanded to lay another place. Immediately there arrived another carafe of schnapps and a bottle of beer. Ibsen helped himself and bade me do likewise. Then he raised his schnapps glass and said; 'Skaal!' I repeated the word but did not drink. He continued; 'What I like about this schnapps is that it's a healthy drink and a native one. I don't order Hungarian wine in Bavaria or Bavarian lager in Hungary. One should do as the natives do, and since schnapps is the only wine this country produces one must enjoy it as such. Skaal!'

'But what about something to eat?' I asked squarely and without thinking.

'You want something to eat?'

'Well, I'm sorry,' I said. 'But didn't you invite me to lunch?'

'Are you hungry at this hour?'

'I must at least have a sandwich.'

He rang for the head waiter and ordered him to bring 'a sandwich for the director'.

Before the end of January, *John Gabriel Borkman* had also been staged in Stockholm, Berlin (where Hermann Nissen played the title role with a make-up suggesting both Ibsen and Bjørnson), and Copenhagen (where Emil Poulsen clearly identified the character with the author). The play proved a greater success in the theatres than any Ibsen had written since *A Doll's House*. No one could find this obscure, or politically or morally offensive – though Edvard Brandes, seated beside Ibsen at the Christiania dress rehearsal, noted his misery at the actors' failure to give the play life. In London Ellen Terry tried to interest Henry Irving in the role. He was ill, and she took advantage of his enforced immobility by reading him the first two acts; he read the third to her. 'What a play!' he commented, with an inflection that left no doubt of his opinion. To his note-book Irving confided: 'Threadworms and leeches are an interesting study; but they have no interest to me.'

If Irving found *Borkman* uninteresting, Henry James did not. In a London Letter to *Harper's Weekly* of New York, dated 15 January and published on 6 February, James declared:

The author who, at the age of seventy, a provincial of provincials, turns out *John Gabriel* is frankly for me so much one of the peculiar pleasures of the day, one of the current strong sensations that, erect as he seems still to stand, I deplore his extreme maturity and, thinking of what shall happen, look round in vain for any other possible source of the same kind of emotion. For Ibsen strikes me as an extraordinary curiosity, and every time he sounds his note the miracle, to my perception, is renewed. I call it a miracle because it is the result of so dry a view of life ... There is a positive odour of spiritual paraffin. The author nevertheless arrives at the dramatist's great goal – he arrives for all his meagreness at intensity. The meagreness which is after all but an unconscious, an admirable economy, never interferes with that; it plays straight into the hands of his rare mastery of form. The contrast between this form – so difficult to have reached, so civilized, so 'evolved' – and the bareness and bleakness of his little northern democracy is the source of half the hard frugal charm that he puts forth. In the cold fixed light of it the notes that we speak of as deficiencies take a sharp value in the picture. There is no small-talk, there are scarcely any manners. On the other hand there is so little vulgarity that this of itself has almost the effect of a deeper, a more lonely provincialism. The background at any rate is the sunset over the ice. Well in the very front of the scene lunges with extraordinary length of arm the Ego against the Ego, and rocks in a rigour of passion the soul against the soul – a spectacle, a movement, as definite as the relief of silhouettes in black paper or a train of Eskimo dogs on the snow. Down from that desolation the sturdy symbolist comes this time with a supreme example of his method. It is a high wonder and pleasure to welcome such splendid fruit from sap that might by now have shown something of the chill of age. Never has he juggled more

gallantly with difficulty and danger than in this really pro-
digious *John Gabriel*, in which a great span of tragedy is taken
between three or four persons – a trio of the grim and grizzled –
in the two or three hours of a winter's evening; in which the
whole thing throbs with an actability that fairly shakes us as we
read; and in which, as the very flower of his artistic triumph, he
has given us for the most beautiful and touching of his heroines
a sad old maid of sixty.

But when it was staged in London at the Strand Theatre
on 3 May, it was very inadequately done. 'Mr Vernon's Borkman was not ill acted,' commented Bernard Shaw, 'Only, as
it was not Ibsen's Borkman, but the very reverse and negation of him, the better Mr Vernon acted, the worse it was
for the play' – a statement which could be applied to many
subsequent Ibsen performances by this actor or that. Shaw
also denounced the poverty of the sets, which seem to have
been dire even for an experimental production. 'I beg the
New Century Theatre,'[1] he wrote, 'when the next Ibsen play
is ready for mounting, to apply to me for assistance. If I have
a ten pound note, they shall have it; if not, I can at least lend
them a couple of decent chairs.'

After the quiet of the previous year, when only *Little
Eyolf* of Ibsen's plays had been staged in London, the summer of 1897 saw a renewed flurry of activity. A week after the
Borkman opening, *A Doll's House* was revived for a series of
matinées at the Globe Theatre, with Janet Achurch in her
old part and Courtenay Thorpe (who was playing Hamlet in
the evenings) as Helmer. 'He plays Helmer with passion,'
wrote Bernard Shaw. 'It is the first time we have seen this
done; and the effect is overwhelming. We no longer study an
object-lesson in lord-of-creationism, appealing to our sociological interest only. We see a fellow-creature blindly

1. A private subscription society founded by Elizabeth Robins, William Archer, H. W. Massingham and Alfred Sutro, and patterned on
Grein's Independent Theatre Society, which was about to close after
six brave years.

wrecking his happiness and losing his "love-life", and are touched dramatically.'

On 17 May *The Wild Duck* followed at the same theatre (likewise for five matinées), and on 24 June *Ghosts* was revived at the Queen's Gate Hall for three performances, with Mrs Theodore Wright (who had played Mrs Alving in the first London production) and Courtenay Thorpe as Oswald, the role in which he had startled New York. The production coincided with Queen Victoria's Diamond Jubilee, which led Bernard Shaw to draw an irreverent comparison:

On the one hand, the Queen and the Archbishop of Canterbury; on the other, Mrs Alving and Pastor Manders. Stupendous contrast! . . . Suppose the Queen were to turn upon us in the midst of our jubilation and say, 'My Lords and Gentlemen! You have been good enough to describe at great length the changes made during the last sixty years in science, art, politics, dress, sport, locomotion, newspapers and everything else that men chatter about. But you have not a word to say about the change that comes home most closely to me? I mean the change in the number, the character and the intensity of the lies a woman must either believe or pretend to believe before she can graduate in polite society as a well-brought-up lady.' If Her Majesty could be persuaded to give a list of these lies, what a document it would be! . . . Depend upon it, seventy-eight years cannot be lived through without finding out things that queens do not mention in Adelphi melodramas. Granted that the Queen's consort was not a Chamberlain Alving . . . it is possible to have better luck than Mrs Alving without missing all her conclusions.[2]

In Norway, meanwhile, the spring of 1897 had brought a bitter personal disappointment to Ibsen. Three years previously Sigurd had proposed, in a series of articles, that a new chair of sociology be established at Christiania University. There was opposition to the scheme in the Storthing, which compromised by granting sufficient money for a series of lectures to be held during the autumn of 1896, leaving the

2. This passage has given rise to a curious myth among Ibsen commentators that Queen Victoria saw *Ghosts* performed.

question of the professorship open. (According to Sigurd's wife Bergliot, several of his colleagues in the Liberal Party disliked the idea of his becoming too important.) At all events, Sigurd delivered his lectures that autumn, with a panel of five professors present; the attendances were very large, and there was an atmosphere of great excitement. But on 29 April 1897 the panel published its verdict that: 'Dr Ibsen has not in his lectures succeeded in demonstrating such qualities that one could confidently at the present juncture entrust him with a university teaching post in sociology.'

Sigurd immediately left for Italy. 'Never since I left the diplomatic service,' he wrote to Bergliot, 'have I been as angry as I am this week ... It looks as though they have all conspired to make it impossible for me to live in Norway.' His father was, if possible, even more outraged. He had attended all Sigurd's lectures with immense pride; and when the university invited him to a banquet he replied curtly: 'I shall never enter those doors again.' Suzannah wrote to Bergliot from Monsummano: 'The truth is that Sigurd's talent, with his European viewpoint, does not suit their academic outlook. It is foreign and unpleasing to them, as his father's was, which they only accepted when the world acclaimed him. We owe nothing to Norway, and all the humbug and mean-mindedness we have experienced there makes me weep. They are trying to bar every road to Sigurd.'

Indignation was widespread in Christiania. 'It was clear to everyone', writes Bergliot, 'that Sigurd did not lack the qualifications. But they were afraid of his liberal views and of his consequent influence on the young.' The university tried to compromise by offering him a new series of lectures with a different panel of judges, but Sigurd refused. 'I dread the prospect of returning to Christiania,' he wrote to Bergliot from Monsummano on 17 July.

The affair caused Ibsen to think seriously again of finally abandoning Norway. 'Can you guess', he wrote to Georg Brandes on 3 June. 'what I am dreaming and planning, and

picturing to myself as so delightful? It is to settle by the
Sound, between Copenhagen and Elsinore, in a free, open
place, where I shall be able to see all the deep-sea ships
coming from afar and going afar. Here I can't do that. Here
every sound is locked (in both senses); every channel of
understanding is stopped. Oh, my dear Brandes, one does
not live for twenty-seven years out in the great, free, liberating world of culture for nothing. Here among the fjords is
my native land. But – but – but – where shall I find my
home? The sea is what draws me most. I live here alone and
plan some new dramatic work. But I can't yet see clearly
what shape it will take.' Twelve days later, thanking
Bjørnson for a note of condolence about Sigurd's treatment,
he wrote: 'If all roads are barred to Sigurd in Norway, I
do not see that I have anything more to do here. And I have
other places I can go to. I have lived long enough in Munich
to acquire Bavarian nationality, and I can be sure I would be
welcomed there. In Italy too. I must say, Norway is a difficult
country to have as a fatherland.'

Yet he stayed. Suzannah, no doubt, would have found
Munich or Italy more convenient for her gout cures. But
Ibsen, at sixty-nine, was reluctant to uproot himself. His
letters to Suzannah that summer are full of touching little
domestic details.

The hydrangea has begun to show its buds again as abundantly as last year. I have had to order a dozen new dress-shirts,
for the ones I had from Munich are now quite worn out. As
regards food, I have been eating very much to my taste: smoked
mutton, scrambled eggs, a lot of salmon done different ways,
spiced-beer soup, and other good, wholesome summer dishes. So
I am very content – and in my solitude I have begun to hatch and
germinate plans for a new play. I already sense the general
theme; but as yet I see only one of the characters clearly. Well,
the others will come too.

Thus on 13 June; and on 2 July:

Last week there was a great to-do here; my study was spring-cleaned from ceiling to floor. The paintings have been taken down for cleaning, and now glitter and shine so that it is a joy to see them. The curtains have been washed and the walls also. The floor was scoured and then lacquered, so that you would not recognize it. It took six days to dry, during which time the furniture had to stand in the yard and got a thorough going-over. I used the red room while this was happening. Now it is the turn of the blue room, the floor of which is likewise to be lacquered, as is that of the dining-room. I can eat in the library; it is lucky we have enough rooms, and Mina [the new maid] is very good; she has had the charlady to help her for a couple of days. I am now busy with correspondence about the German collected edition, which is to fill nine thick volumes. There are already masses of tourists here, and yesterday a flock of journalists arrived from the congress in Stockholm; most of them have left their cards or spoken with me here and at the hotel. I am really very content, and don't think I could be more so anywhere now that it is summer. And I have begun to think about a new play! To that purpose I have extended my walks, and start each day by strolling to Skillebæk and back, and then down into town; and find this very contenting. But the most important thing is how the steam cure is suiting you this year. The iodine tincture which you found painful in Labers you must of course throw away and get a new bottle down there. Let me know how everything is with Sigurd . . . I sent Bergliot a telegram on 16 June. That is her birthday, isn't it? . . . Well, I have rambled on; but I felt I had to write to you today. We have the most wonderful summer weather; it is lovely to breathe.

Lugné-Poe revisited Christiania later that summer. He had courageously followed his production of *Peer Gynt* with one of *Love's Comedy* on 23 June. Gunnar Heiberg attended the public dress rehearsal in Paris and, imperfect though the performance was, found the electricity and driving power of the young company stimulating; and 'a better, or anyway a more responsive public, no theatre, actor, or dramatist could wish for. They are artists, writers, joyful malcontents of every profession . . . They are young, these Frenchmen, as I have never seen young people in Norway or anywhere else . . . They shout with joy. They rejoice and cry Bravo and think life is full of meaning and beauty when such men as Ibsen are around.' At the premiere next evening, however, the play was less successful – not surprisingly, the general public found it small beer after the works of Ibsen's maturity.

Lugné-Poe brought to Christiania his young actress-wife Suzanne Desprès, who had replaced Berthe Bady as Hilde in his *Master Builder*, and had played Solveig in *Peer Gynt*. They met Ibsen at the Grand Hotel; Ibsen expressed the desire to hear some of her Solveig, so they got hold of Henrik Klausen, who had played Peer in the original production of 1876, and together they read all the great scenes between the two characters, Klausen in Norwegian, Suzanne in French. Ibsen also persuaded her to read some scenes from *The Master Builder*, and praised her warmly.

Ibsen's letters that autumn show him in a peppery mood; perhaps it was the change of the year, perhaps his loneliness was beginning to weigh on him. On 19 September he wrote a discourteously irritable note to the faithful Julius Elias forbidding him to include *St John's Night* in the German collected edition which Elias was preparing with Georg Brandes and Paul Schlenther (though for some reason he allowed them to use the much inferior *Warrior's Barrow*). He wrote so rudely, indeed, that a fortnight later he sent Elias an apology for 'my unseemly way of expressing myself'. Then the Christiania Theatre annoyed him by arranging a revival of *The Feast at Solhaug* without informing him, so that he first heard through a third party. When Schrøder penitently invited him to attend rehearsals and the première, he replied curtly (3 December): 'Dr Ibsen is grateful for the information but will not attend rehearsals and does not wish to have tickets for the performance.' And when Paul Clemenceau, brother of the statesman, raised his hat to him on Drammensveien and began: '*Cher maître! Permettez-moi de vous exprimer ma profonde admiration –* ' Ibsen replied: '*Je ne parle pas français,*' and walked on.

In a kindlier mood, he wrote (18 October) a charming little

note of congratulation to his doctor's wife, Caroline Sontum, on the birth of a new child; and when the young poet Sigbjørn Obstfelder, lately released from an asylum and shortly to die of consumption, sent him a volume of his poems, Ibsen thanked him (10 December) with the assurance that he had 'already begun to read the book which fascinates and interests me'.

Despite the absence of any reprints, except a small fourth edition of *An Enemy of the People*, Ibsen's income in 1897 amounted to £1,279. Over two-thirds of this came from Germany and Austria, where his performing rights totalled as much as £439, and where Fischer gave him a not very generous flat fee of £444 for the collected edition, from which that firm was to make immense sums over the next fifty years. From England he got only £18·30 for the Independent Theatre Society productions of *The Wild Duck* and *A Doll's House*, and £2·80 from the book sales of *Peer Gynt* in the translation by the Archer brothers. France did a little better by him with £40 for the publication of *John Gabriel Borkman* in the *Revue de Paris* and £11 in performing rights. The Russians had done *The Pillars of Society* on 24 September, but of course he got nothing for that; and from Norway he received nothing but £167 for the Christiania production of *Borkman* and £32 from Bergen. During the twelve months he had invested nearly £1,900 in securities, representing his entire earnings of the preceding year.

35

The Other Side of the Medal
1898

In normal circumstances, Ibsen would have spent the first
months of 1898 hatching his new play, so as to be ready to
write it in the summer and autumn. But this was the year of
his seventieth birthday, always an occasion of special celebration in Scandinavia, and in Ibsen's case it involved a
series of distractions not merely in Norway, but in Denmark
and Sweden too. Moreover, the proofs of the German collected edition had now begun to arrive, several thousand
pages of them. For the first time since *The Pillars of Society*
in 1877, there was to be a three-year gap between one play
and the next.

Jacob Hegel sent him the good news in January that he
was proposing to issue a cheap popular edition of the plays.
Ibsen was delighted; as he said in his reply of 16 January, it
would bring them 'into strata of society where the more expensive editions have difficulty in gaining entry'. He went on:
'Where do I intend to spend my birthday this year? Well, I
don't yet know. If the choice were mine alone I would escape
up to the mountains somewhere or other, where I could be
beautifully alone. But that time of year is unsuited to such a
recreation, so I suppose I shall stay where I am. But I hope
this won't exclude the possibility that I may later be able to
fulfil my favourite dream, which is to see again the Sound
and my Danish friends.'

As his birthday approached, the messages began to arrive.
Among the earliest was a telegram of congratulations from
Emilie Bardach, the first contact between the two for seven

years. His reply of 13 March has already been quoted.[1] On the day itself, telegrams, flowers and gifts of every kind poured in from all over the world. One of the first gifts to come was a handsome set of silver from his British admirers, comprising a loving-cup (a facsimile of one executed for King George II in 1730) and an original ladle and small cup of the same period, the three pieces being fitted into a case of polished oak. The contributors included Thomas Hardy, Henry James, Bernard Shaw, J. M. Barrie, William Archer, Edmund Gosse, Richard Garnett, A. C. Bradley, Gilbert Murray, A. W. Pinero, Elizabeth Robins, Herbert Beerbohm Tree, and the future Prime Minister, H. H. Asquith. Since none of these was able to make the journey, Karl Keilhau, the editor of *Norske Intelligenssedler*, presented the gift, together with a vellum address and a list of the subscribers' names. Keilhau reported to Gosse and Archer:

He was obviously very much moved. While we were standing in front of the oak case and admiring, visitors began to arrive – a deputation from the Storthing, headed by the leader of the House, deputations representing the University, the Christiania theatres, etc., etc. Ibsen then asked me to translate the address, and I took out of my pocket a translation of it, which I read to him and to the others. He then himself read out all the names of the subscribers from the flyleaf. Ibsen repeated again and again that it was a splendid present, and all the afternoon he was occupied in taking his hundreds of visitors, in parties, up to the case, showing them the objects and explaining their origin.[2]

Performances to celebrate Ibsen's birthday were given that evening in many countries: at two theatres in Christiania, two in Copenhagen, three in Stockholm, four in Vienna and six in Berlin. In London, surprisingly, there were none – indeed, there were no Ibsen productions there in 1898,

1. See p. 653.
2. The appeal was not launched publicly, but by private approach. Forty subscribers contributed £50 between them. Several of those not approached, including J. T. Grein, voiced their discontent, and Shaw, though among the subscribers, criticized in the *Saturday Review* of 26 March the way the thing had been done.

1899, or 1900. The Christiania Theatre gave *The Feast at Solhaug*, with selected scenes from *Peer Gynt*, and Centraltheatret did *Ghosts*. For the following evening a gala performance of *The Master Builder* was planned, and Bergliot records that when a deputation came from the theatre to ask Ibsen and Suzannah to honour them with their presence, Suzannah thanked them but asked that he and she should each sit in a separate box. 'Ibsen must sit alone,' she said. 'This is your evening, and I have nothing to do there.' And, despite his protests, so it was. Similarly (Bergliot recalled), when the students came to honour him with a torchlight procession:

> I can still see Ibsen walk over to her with his short steps, and hear him say, 'Won't you come with me to the window?' But she replied, 'No, you must stand there alone.' . . . She never bothered to borrow the reflected glory of his fame. She cared only about him, and that his work should succeed.

A *festskrift* had, naturally, been arranged, headed by a tribute from King Oscar, and containing contributions from, amongst others, Snoilsky (whose poem is one of the best things in the book) and two future Nobel Prize winners, Verner von Heidenstam and Selma Lagerlöf. Two unexpected names in the list are those of John Paulsen and Nils Kjær, who had both so insulted him; Kjær, since that unfortunate drunken outburst, seems to have undergone a remarkable change of heart. Old friends such as Georg Brandes and Jonas Lie reminisced affectionately, and August Lindberg and Emil Poulsen spoke for the acting profession. But what an opportunity was wasted by not inviting foreign admirers to contribute! Hardy, Henry James, Shaw, Hauptmann – other admirers such as Freud, Rilke, Pirandello and Joyce were scarcely if at all known, and Tolstoy[3]

3. The day before his birthday *Ørebladet* printed an interview in which Ibsen, after praising *Anna Karenina*, described Tolstoy as 'a great man when he isn't being crazy . . . Tolstoy . . . spends his life abusing me . . . But that is natural in view of his beliefs.'

would not have contributed, but Chekhov and Zola might have. Strindberg nearly did. In a letter to Gustaf af Geijerstam later that year asking him to send Ibsen a copy of *To Damascus*, he requested him to tell Ibsen that: 'Strindberg is ashamed that as a prominent Swedish author he did not join in the homage to the Master, from whom he learned much. But he was in a state of depression and did not think his homage could honour or gladden anyone.' Fearful lest this might be taken to imply a modification of his antagonism to Ibsen's general view of life, he assured Geijerstam that his homage would have been to 'the master of dramatic art, not the philosopher'.

On 23 March the city of Christiania gave an official banquet for Ibsen. In his reply, Ibsen, after a conventional paragraph of thanks, asked:

Were you perhaps expecting that I should speak about my books? That I could not do, for then I should have to bring in my whole life. And that alone would make a very thick book. And talking of that, I am indeed just now thinking of writing such a book – a book which will knit my life and my work together into an integral and explanatory whole. For I think I have now reached a sufficiently mature age to permit myself a short breathing-space – take a year's holiday; for such a book would be a holiday task compared with the nagging and exhausting work of dramatic composition. And I have not had a real holiday since I left Norway thirty-four years ago. I think I could do with one now. But, ladies and gentlemen, you must not therefore suppose that I intend to lay down my pen as a dramatist for good. No, I intend to take it up again and to cling tightly to it until the end. For I still have a few lunacies in my locker which I have not yet found the opportunity to express. Only when I have got them off my chest will it be time for me to stop. And how easy would it not be to stop then, in contrast to the time when I was still a beginner! What a silence and emptiness surrounded one then! One's fellow combatants were scattered, isolated and apart. It often seemed to me, after I had gone away, as though I had never been here. Nor my work, neither.

But now! Now the place where I stood is crowded. Young forces have arisen, confident of victory. They need no longer write for a tiny circle. *They* have a public to speak to, an entire people to whom to address their thoughts and feelings. Whether they meet with opposition or acceptance does not really matter. What destroys a writer is indifference and rejection. That is what I encountered.

I regret deeply that I have come into so little contact with many of those who are to continue my work in this country. Not because I would have wished to influence them, but so that I myself might achieve a deeper understanding. And I would especially have used this closer contact to dispel a misconception which has in many ways been a hindrance to me – I mean, the idea that unqualified happiness is a necessary consequence of the rare and saga-like fate which has befallen me, of winning fame in many foreign lands. I have, too, won friendship and understanding in those countries. That is the most important thing of all.

But true, inward happiness does not fall from heaven. It must be earned at a price which may often seem heavy. For the point is this, that he who has won a home in many foreign lands feels in his heart of hearts nowhere truly at home – scarcely even in the country of his birth.

But perhaps this may happen yet. And I should like to think of this evening as a starting-point.

The book he was considering writing – 'A Dramatist's Apology', he might have entitled it – had, as we have seen, been in his thoughts for years; only the opposition of his old publisher and counsellor Frederik Hegel had discouraged him from attempting it earlier. Yet he was fated never to write it; though in some ways, the theme was to be that of his next and final play.

Meanwhile, there were other capitals besides Christiania waiting to acclaim him, and on 29 March he left for Copenhagen to attend the celebrations which had been prepared there. It was the first time he had left Norway since his return eight years earlier. The editor of *Morgenbladet*, Nils Vogt, accompanied him on the journey, by train through south-west Sweden and across the Sound. Vogt later recalled that Ibsen was a little feeble on his feet, the first evidence we have that age was beginning to tell on him; the Swedish railways courteously arranged that food should be brought to his carriage at the various stops, to save him the trouble of getting out. When they reached Gothenburg Ibsen found a telegram awaiting him from Peter Hansen, who had been his companion on the trip to Egypt and was now head of the Royal Theatre in Copenhagen, telling him that he had been awarded his most impressive medal yet, the Grand Cross of the Danish Order of Dannebrog. Ibsen was hugely gratified. 'I can recall many Norwegians', he said proudly to Vogt, 'who are Knights or Commanders of Dannebrog, but none who has the Grand Cross' (a statement which was not quite accurate but which Vogt prudently refrained from correcting). As they approached Denmark on 31 March Ibsen sat long at the window staring silently out across the water. Suddenly he said: 'Do you know, when I come from Norway to the Sound I feel as though I were emerging from a tunnel into the sunshine.' Then, after a pause, he added: 'But please don't tell them that in Norway, at any rate until I am dead.'

Jacob Hegel and Peter Hansen met him on his arrival in Copenhagen, and took him to the Hotel Angleterre, where the royal suite had been placed at his disposal and the Norwegian flag was flying in his honour. As they entered the suite the first thing that met their eyes was a small box on the table. Ibsen opened it and there, resplendent, lay the Grand Cross. He gazed at it. 'How beautiful!' he exclaimed. 'This is indeed a great honour. No Scandinavian writer since Oehlenschläger has received so high a Danish decoration.' Suddenly his expression changed. 'But what is this?' he cried. 'This is no medal! It is papier-maché!' Hegel and Hansen were as amazed as he; on inquiry, however, they learned that it was the custom for the recipient of this great honour to buy the medal himself from the court jeweller, only a papier-maché copy being provided by the state.

Hegel gave a small lunch for Ibsen that day, the only other guests being Vogt and the Norwegian poet and novelist Alexander Kielland, who happened to be in town. In the evening, the Royal Theatre gave a gala performance of *The Wild Duck*. It was not the most inspired of choices, for Ibsen had already seen this production twice with the same cast, and Betty Hennings, the country's leading actress, was now, at forty-eight, more than ever too old for the role of Hedvig. But the theatre had omitted to do anything about arranging a new production of any of Ibsen's plays until it was too late. Still, the performance was royally attended, for not only were the King and Queen of Denmark there, but also their daughters, Princess Alexandra of Wales and the Dowager Empress of Russia, all in the royal box with Ibsen seated majestically alone in the box opposite.

The unfortunate Peter Hansen, already under fire for not having remembered to arrange a new production, was to have a bad evening. His troubles began immediately before the performance when, in his tactless way, he issued a military-sounding directive that the actors were to be ready to be presented to Ibsen after the final curtain. They were so offended at being thus commanded that they refused in a body. Hansen was desperate. Among other things, this refusal meant that Ibsen got no refreshment during the long interval, for Peter Nansen of Gyldendal (not to be confused with Hansen) records that when he mentioned the matter to Hansen the latter replied: 'I really have no time to think about refreshments,' and Ibsen had to go thirsty.

When the performance ended, at first all went well. The entire audience, including the crowned heads, rose and bowed to Ibsen in his box, applauding, while he bowed aristocratically back. He then waited for the company to be presented; but the company held to their refusal, and all Hansen could rustle up was a few of the younger actors who were sufficiently frightened of him to obey. With some presence of mind he presented them as 'my most promising actor', and 'my most promising dancer', and so partially saved the situation.

But Hansen's troubles were by no means over. The students of Copenhagen decided to greet Ibsen with a torchlight procession before he left the theatre. He stood on the theatre balcony acknowledging their applause; meanwhile, Hansen went on to the hotel, where he found Kielland waiting. As they chatted, there was a fearful noise outside, and Ibsen shot in 'like a cannonball from a gun, dazed, his coat torn, his top hat at the back of his head, and his medals dangling outside his overcoat', with a mob of students pushing and cheering him, so that 'it was a miracle that the helpless little old man survived unharmed'. Peter Hansen, however, seemed by now to have forgotten his famous guest. Not only had his company mutinied against him; that same evening one of his star actors, Karl Mantzius, had given notice because his wife had not been re-engaged. So Ibsen stood dishevelled and forgotten in a corner.

His fellow-Norwegian, Alexander Kielland, was furious. 'God Almighty, how typically Danish!' he cried. 'Typical bloody Danish! The Royal Theatre has the most famous author in Scandinavia as its guest and doesn't even hire a carriage to take him home! He ought to have been driven across the square in a bridal carriage with a white horse and the director of the theatre as postilion, and a proper dinner awaiting him. Instead of which the old man has to fight his way through a mob on foot and no one even bothers to ask whether he's hungry or thirsty!'

Nansen said to Hansen, 'Ibsen would like to have something to eat.'

The distraught Hansen turned to Ibsen. 'You want something to eat?'

'Yes, please.'

'Waiter! Bring a sandwich menu. Thank you. Now [to Ibsen] just tick off what you'd like. Steak, sausage, salmon, anything you like. Perhaps you'd like a drink too?'

'Yes, please.'

'A beer for Dr Ibsen. Do you want a schnapps too?'

Ibsen said yes. So he got three sandwiches, a schnapps and a glass of beer, and thus his first day in Copenhagen ended.

The next day, which was 1 April, began no more promisingly and ended even more disastrously. Nils Vogt and Peter Hansen, the latter no doubt anxious to redeem himself after his showing of the previous evening, had the pleasant idea of going out first thing to the court jeweller to buy Ibsen his expensive Grand Cross of Dannebrog. They bore this to Ibsen in his suite at the Angleterre but, as they entered, were much embarrassed to see one already lying in its box on the table. Ibsen, an inveterate early riser, had been to the jeweller before them. As the three stood there in confusion, the Minister of Culture was announced, and entered carrying a third Grand Cross as a personal gift from the king. The other two were silently removed and returned with apologies to the jeweller.

That evening a gala banquet was held for Ibsen at the Angleterre. Unusual difficulty had been experienced by the organizers in securing appropriate people to make the speeches of welcome. Georg Brandes was away. His brother Edvard was suggested but (says Nansen) he was 'as hated then as he was beloved later', and anyway was editor of the radical newspaper *Politiken,* so that for him to have made the principal speech would have offended the conservatives present. Eventually they chose the professor of philosophy, Kroman, with Peter Hansen following as the second speaker and Professor Sophus Schandorph as number three. So that was settled; but now the organizers learned that several of the invited guests considered the price of a ticket for the dinner (25 crowns, £1·35) excessive. (Nansen admits that it was 'a then unheard-of price'.) Among the objectors was Betty Hennings, whose husband had just become deeply religious. She declared it to be immoral to spend so much on a dinner, and could not be persuaded to attend.

The banquet was an almost total disaster. At two o'clock Professor Kroman, the principal speaker, sent word that he was too ill to come (Nansen suspected it was an attack of nerves). Five hours was not enough to find a substitute, and as Kroman had been going to make the formal speech, to be followed by Hansen in lighter vein, they had to compromise by persuading Hansen to introduce serious matter into a set comic speech of his which had been successful on previous occasions and which Ibsen had not heard. But Hansen found the time at his disposal insufficient to make the adaptation, so that his speech turned out an unhappy mixture of jokes and formality. Among other gaffes, he referred to Ibsen as 'one of our leading dramatists' and thanked him for the 'many full houses' he had brought the Royal Theatre.

A profound embarrassment settled on the company, and Ibsen, who had clearly prepared a speech on the assumption that it would be in response to the usual courteously formal welcome, made the briefest reply. 'Professor Hansen's speech has confounded me, and rendered inappropriate the reply I had intended to make ... I must therefore improvise, and ask your indulgence. Today is 1 April. This same day in 1864 I visited Copenhagen for the first time. That is now thirty-four years ago. Mark well the date and the year! I travelled south, through Germany and Austria, and crossed the Alps on 9 May.' He went on to describe his first sight of Italy, in words already quoted,[4] and concluded: 'This feeling of being released from darkness into light, of emerging from mists through a tunnel into the sunshine – this feeling I had again now, as I gazed along the Sound ... I felt that these two journeys had some hidden connection, and I therefore give you my most grateful thanks.'

As usual when Ibsen improvised, the result was almost certainly more interesting than what he had prepared. That crisis, then, seemed to have been bridged; but the troubles of the evening were by no means over. Professor Sophus Schandorph, who rose to speak next, proved to be so drunk that he had to support himself on the shoulders of his two neighbours, a count and a bishop. The guests, already embarrassed, began to titter and interrupt, at which Schandorph, clutching the bishop closer to him, thundered what can most

4. See p. 228.

faithfully be translated as: 'Shut your fucking mouths while I speak!'

He was allowed to finish, and a cantata, specially composed by Holger Drachmann, partially restored order, as did two tactful and appropriate speeches by younger guests, Professor Vilhelm Andersen and Dr Poul Levin. But now a new unrest developed as several of the guests began to complain about the food. The German proprietor of the hotel, one Heene, anxious to celebrate the occasion in style, had composed a gastronome's menu of real turtle soup, duckling, and out-of-season asparagus. The Danes, who had come expecting the enormous steak that was customarily served on such occasions, were now feeling hungry. 'If we'd charged twelve crowns and given them a piece of fish, a steak, cheese and an ice,' said Heene to Nansen, 'they'd have been happy. That's what they're used to.' Heene was so disillusioned by the whole business that he left the Angleterre shortly afterwards.

When the meal ended Ibsen rose and made his way to the door, escorted by the count and the bishop who had supported Schandorph. Suddenly an old painter named Thorvald Niss, in a flush of, among other things, enthusiasm, rushed from his place, embraced Ibsen, shook him backwards and forwards and cried: '*Du er kraft steile mig en gut! Tak for alt, gamle dreng!*' (something like: 'You're a right lad! Thanks for everything, old cock'). Ibsen stared in horror and murmured, 'Take this man away.'

As he sat drinking his coffee, Peter Nansen presented some young writers to him. He was courteous and affable to them until Nansen introduced a popular playwright of intellectual pretensions. 'I don't know, Dr Ibsen,' said Nansen, 'if you have heard of Sven Lange,' to which Ibsen in his silkiest tones replied: 'Of course I know of Sven Lange, the Scribe of Denmark.' Nansen tells that he did not dare to look at the unfortunate man (who had contributed a vapid article on 'Henrik Ibsen and the Young Europe' to the *festskrift*).

So, as they say in the sagas, that day ended.

The next morning, 2 April, Ibsen was received by King Christian to be formally handed his medal, and was presented to the Dowager Empress of Russia and the Princess of Wales. Ibsen's impression of the meeting is not on record but King Christian's, surprisingly, is. Not long afterwards the Speaker of the Storthing, Hegsbro, was received by the king and, on the latter's inquiring after his health, replied: 'Well, Your Majesty, one notices that one's getting old.' 'You should talk about growing old,' said the king. 'I'm several years older than you, and I don't notice any weakness. I felt rather proud some while ago. I had to receive the Norwegian writer, Henrik Ibsen. He was seventy, and I was ten years older. I thought: "It won't be easy to make conversation with such a genius. What is one to say to him?" But I must honestly confess I thought he seemed much older than me. He was really most timid and unhelpful. I had to keep nudging him along.'

By contrast, when, later that day, a young girl came to Ibsen's suite to offer him flowers and found herself speechless, Ibsen sat her down and put her at her ease with the greatest charm. After she had left, he said to Nansen: 'How pretty the young ladies of Copenhagen are!' Nansen adds that Ibsen would sometimes fantasize to young girls of what he would do if he were very rich – how he would buy the finest ship in the world, engage a gipsy orchestra and sail to some tropical island with a few good friends and 'the most beautiful young women in the world' – very much as Solness must have spoken to Hilde Wangel during their first encounter at Lysanger.

They kept him busy in Copenhagen, for he attended two receptions that same afternoon and evening, one given by the Women's Literary Guild and one by the Students' Union. At the latter, Valdemar Vedel (another contributor to the *festskrift.* on 'Ibsen and Denmark'), began his speech of welcome with the familiar second person singular ('*Mester, Du* — ') which Ibsen so detested. Accounts vary as to what happened next. According to some, Ibsen immedi-

ately rose and left the room. Peter Nansen simply says that
he left without replying to the speech; and Nils Vogt, who
accompanied him to the dinner as to everything else on this
trip, reports merely that he left early, and remarked to Vogt
on the way downstairs: 'Vedel's a good fellow, but I can't
remember having drunk *Du*'s with him.' Georg Brandes's
daughter Edith, who accompanied Ibsen to the dinner in a
carriage (and recalled that he was much annoyed on arrival
to find that he was not sitting next to her, as he had assumed, but to the much less youthful and attractive
suffragette Amalie Skram, to whom he did not address a
word all evening) writes that he said simply 'Thank you'
after the speeches of Vedel and Harald Høffding, made no
speech himself, but, although he had ordered a carriage for
10.30, did not leave till 11. What is sure is that as he left
(whenever it was) some wit recited Ibsen's own poem 'Gone',
substituting 'he' for 'she':

> He was but a guest
> And now he is gone.

which was greeted with laughter and cheers.

The next day, Sunday 3 April, the privately owned
Dagmars Theatre, now under solvent management, gave a
gala performance of *Brand*. It was a new production, the
company was young, and Nansen wondered with some trepidation how Ibsen would survive a performance lasting five
hours or more. But against all expectations, the evening
turned out to be the peak event of Ibsen's visit. Martinius
Nielsen, the head of the theatre, who was acting the title
role, had, with more foresight than Peter Hansen at the
Royal Theatre, supplied the royal box in which Ibsen sat
with an excellent cold collation, accompanied by 'champagne, beer, whisky, coffee, liqueurs and flowers'. Nansen
records: 'It was a *young* people's performance, and he liked it
far better than *The Wild Duck*.' He clapped loudly at the
fall of each curtain and showed no signs of tiredness.

It was the first time Ibsen had seen *Brand* played, and

another observer, P. A. Rosenberg, reports that 'he seemed moved and several times dried the tears from his cheeks during the fourth act. "Don't blubber! he muttered to himself.' He said to Nielsen's wife Oda, who sat next to him: 'This moves me. This is – my youth. I haven't thought about *Brand* for thirty years.' At the end he led the applause, which the audience then directed towards him. Although the performance lasted until midnight he did not return home, but stayed at a party which the actors improvised for him, and did not leave until 3 a.m. He was very lively and talked continuously. Of Nielsen's performance, he said: 'That is *my* Brand. That's how I saw him.' 'You haven't cut much,' he said to Rosenberg, and when told that they had in fact cut a third of the play he asked to see the prompt book and, as he leafed through it, seeing page after page deleted, murmured: 'I'll be damned. Yes, I suppose I've forgotten most of it.'

As they at last broke up, at three o'clock, Ibsen said: 'I must go home now. I must be at my desk at 7.' 'Not *this* morning?' exclaimed Rosenberg. 'Yes,' he replied. 'Come and see. I'll be there at 7.' 'But you won't have had enough sleep,' said Nielsen. 'Yes, I will,' said Ibsen. 'Under such circumstances I sleep more energetically. Thank you for tonight. It has been a good night.' As a favour he asked that his two companions at table, Fru Nielsen and Fru Rosenberg (who had played Agnes), should accompany him home in the carriage, declaring: 'Their husbands can manage without them for a few minutes.'

Yet (we are told) he did not sleep, but lay awake most of that night. As he lay there he may have remembered that thirty years before, just after *Brand* had brought him the recognition he had longed for, he had remarked to Georg Brandes (26 June 1869) that Brand 'could as well have been a sculptor or a politician as a priest'. The chief character in his new play was to be a sculptor, of the same uncompromising ruthlessness as Brand; and, like Brand, he was to die in an avalanche near the top of a mountain, his pride crushed, with a Latin blessing cried out to him as though from a forgiving deity at the moment of death.

The next day, luckily, was a rest day; and on 5 April, his last day in Copenhagen – the last that he was ever to spend there – Jacob Hegel gave a farewell dinner for him at his villa, Skovgaard. According to Vogt, Ibsen enjoyed himself, but the evening was spoilt by Sophus Schandorph, who had delivered the drunken speech at the Angleterre and now, in a fit of remorse and enthusiasm, attempted to kiss Ibsen on the cheek, causing him to leave early. However, on the way home with Vogt, in a carriage drawn by two white horses (like the ones in *Rosmersholm*, reflected Vogt, though he was tactful enough not to mention it), Ibsen thawed again. Speaking of a classical scholar of rigid conservative views, he said: 'He has no idea of what real classicism and humanism are. He has read some books in Latin and Greek which I, for good reason, have not. But I have lived myself into its spirit by studying its buildings and art, as you may possibly have gathered from *Emperor and Galilean*. X's aesthetic and intellectual horizon stops at Lübeck and Greiswald.'

On 6 April Ibsen left Copenhagen by train for a further round of celebrations in Stockholm. They installed him in the best suite at the Hotel Rydberg in Gustav Adolfs Torg and gave him a couple of days to recover his breath; then, on 9 April, he was received at the palace by King Oscar and given another medal to add to his collection, the Grand Cross of the Northern Star. The king, during the conversation, graciously employed the phrase 'we two kings', and spoke with some apprehension about Sigurd. The Norwegian government was considering setting up its own Foreign Office, something that Sigurd had urged ever since he had been a young attaché, and they had in mind to appoint him head. King Oscar expressed gloomy doubts. 'He doesn't want me as King of Norway,' he said to Ibsen. 'But let that pass. As long as that wife of his doesn't make him too much of a radical and an agitator!'

The combination of the leading pamphleteer against the

union and Bjørnson's daughter in joint charge of Norwegian affairs must have been an alarming prospect to that conservative monarch. Ibsen assured him that Bergliot's views were not as extreme as her father's. That evening, the king gave a banquet for Ibsen at the palace; among the guests was the explorer Sven Hedin, whom he had met on the Göta Canal eleven years previously, and whom he afterwards took back to his hotel and proudly showed his medals, carefully arranged on a table in little red and black boxes.

During the meal the king said to his guest of honour: 'But you shouldn't have written *Ghosts*, Ibsen. That's not a good play. Now, *Lady Inger of Østraat* – there's a good play.' Ibsen was embarrassed and remained silent. Queen Sophie tried to rescue him by speaking of other things; but after a long pause, Ibsen exclaimed: 'Your Majesty, I *had* to write *Ghosts!*'

Two days later, the Swedish Society of Authors gave a dinner for Ibsen at Hasselbacken Restaurant on Skansen. 'I'm not very curious about him,' wrote the poet Oscar Levertin to a friend that morning. 'Great men are best appreciated at a distance, and every utterance that the Sphinx has delivered during these past weeks of divine revelation seems to me about as empty as the usual wisdom of Sphinxes.' And the evening indeed was not a great success. Carl Snoilsky, who took the chair, had promised that there would be no speeches, but unfortunately Gustaf af Geijerstam improvised one, full of Ibsen quotations, and at the end of the evening Levertin, despite his lack of enthusiasm for Ibsen, made another. Ibsen replied (untruthfully) that he did not think he had ever belonged to any Society and that this was the first time he had attended one. 'I am pretty sure there is a Society in Christiania of the same name as this, but I am a member of that only for appearance's sake and for various reasons never partake in its meetings.' (He had still not forgotten how he had been insulted at the inaugural meeting.) He went on: 'A Society is not a thing for me. And in a way it might seem that a Society is least of all appropriate for authors, for they must go their own wild ways – yes, as wild as they wish, if they are to fulfil their life's calling.' (Loud applause.) However, he granted that such a Society might serve to protect writers 'which can often be very necessary', and concluded by expressing the hope that it might also encourage Scandinavians to read each other in the original language and not in translation – a hope which has hardly been fulfilled. To a foreigner, it is amazing how reluctant Scandinavians are to read each other in the original, despite the close similarity of Norwegian, Danish and Swedish.

After dinner, the Swedish writer and artist Albert Engström sang some Swedish country songs, which Ibsen, despite the view he had just expressed, was unable to understand; and (records a lady who was there) 'despite being primed with punch and other stimulants, he remained stiff and unapproachable. No amount of effort could provoke any Ibsenian profundities, far less any witty conversation. At last he turned to a lady seated near him and began: "Can you tell me – ?" The lady in question adopted an expression of deep concentration. "Can you tell me if I can go direct to Christiania by the night train, or if I have to change at Laxå?"'

Engström himself describes how Ibsen spent the second half of the evening surrounded by elderly authoresses, from whom he tried repeatedly to rescue him by saying; 'May I drink with you, Doctor?' for which Ibsen was grateful.

At last it grew late and the ladies departed, accompanied by some of the gentlemen. I had rescued Ibsen at least ten times during the evening. And now, when there were only a few young people left, he became a new man. He joked and toasted us continuously. It was just midnight when he declared that his age no longer allowed him to exceed a certain limit. So we gathered around him and he said a few words very simply, rather shyly; but I think that we who heard them will remember them and the mood of that moment. He clasped our hands in farewell. To me he said, 'Do you know how many brandies you've made me drink tonight, my dear Engström? I've lost count.'[5]

Next evening, 12 April, he attended a performance at Vasa Theatre of *The Pretenders*, with a distinguished cast: Emil Hillberg (the original Brand) as Bishop Nicholas, Tore Svennberg as Skule, and a new young star, Anders de Wahl, as Haakon. Harald Molander directed. Ibsen sat in a box with Gustaf af Geijerstam and, towards the end of his long life, de Wahl recalled:

I had received a flower arrangement in the form of a long, tall Viking ship, and the thought occurred to me that I ought to present these flowers to the author . . . I noted that the gentlemen had put this ship on the edge of their box so that they were invisible to us and the audience. During one of the intervals I was summoned to pay my respects . . . I was determined to have every sense alert so as to memorize every word the great man might utter, note every glance, engrave every nuance of the occasion on my memory and, at some future date, tell the world of this great meeting. Thus prepared, I entered the box on trembling legs. There he sat, the great man, beside my Viking ship, at a small table covered with glasses and bottles. 'What, what, what . . . what d'you want?' In a word, he was drunk. As I came closer he pointed at me and said, 'You're dolled up. Do you think Haakon was a dandy?'

On 13 April the city gave an official banquet for Ibsen at the Grand Hotel, and in reply to Snoilsky's speech of welcome Ibsen said that his life had been 'a long, long Passion Week' which, however, had now been 'transformed into a poem, a fairy tale . . . a midsummer night's dream'. Next day a deputation of students from Upsala brought him greetings; and in the evening the Royal Theatre gave *Lady Inger*

5. Strindberg was unfortunately in Paris, though one doubts whether he could have been persuaded to attend. On being asked during this visit by a Swedish journalist what he thought of Strindberg, Ibsen described him as 'a very great talent. I don't know him personally – our paths have never crossed – but I have read his work with *great* interest. Not least, his last book *Inferno* [written the previous year] has made a powerful impression on me.'

of Østraat, that play of which King Oscar approved and which he now graced with his presence. 15 April seems to have been a rest day, but on the 16th Ibsen, who so disliked the company of elderly bluestockings, found himself the guest at Skansen of the two women's societies of Stockholm: Nya Idun and the Fredrika Bremer Society. The officials of these two formidable bodies, indignant that the dinners arranged for Ibsen had been mainly male affairs, had managed to persuade him to stay an extra day in Stockholm to meet their members. When they put the idea to him 'Ibsen became nervous, waved his arms and exclaimed: "No, no I shall be like Carl XII, I shall be carried across the frontier a corpse!"' But a historian present reminded him that when Carl XII had crossed the frontier from Sweden to Norway, he had been very much alive (he had been killed on the other side of the border at Frederikshald in 1718); so Ibsen accepted.

Perhaps he hoped that he might have at least one reasonably youthful and attractive lady to table. But as usual on these occasions, he found himself flanked by dragons, in this instance the presidents of the two societies, Ellen Key and a Fru Anckarsvärd; nor did Ellen Key help matters by beginning her speech: '*Du . . .*,' as Valdemar Vedel had done in Copenhagen. She thanked him for his 'new religion, under which every human being will obey his or her own laws without being daunted by a sense of guilt, and self-fulfilment shall be deemed as justifiable and meaningful as self-sacrifice'.

To entertain their guest the ladies had arranged an exhibition of folk dancing, and here at least there were some young faces. One, twenty-six years old, especially attracted his attention. Her name was Rosa Fitinghoff, the daughter of a well-known popular author, Laura Fitinghoff (whose *The Children from Frostmoor Mountain* is still one of the most read children's books in Sweden). Ibsen spoke to Rosa several times during the evening, expressing particular admiration of her long and beautiful hair, and asked her to see him off at the station next day. She was to be the last of his dream girls, following in the footsteps of Emilie, Helene and Hildur.

Ibsen's rather pathetic longing for young girls was demonstrated several times during these days in Stockholm. Gurli Linder reports that he received several in his hotel room, gave them signed photographs of himself, said: 'You are just like my Hilde,' and kissed them; and that when a lady at one of the receptions told him that she had once been in the same town as he in Norway and had only with difficulty restrained herself from running up to him, seizing his hand and saying: 'Thank you!', he replied: 'Do you know what I would have done if you had? I would have hugged you to my breast and kissed you many times' – precisely as Hilde Wangel claimed Solness had done to her.

On 17 April he returned to Christiania. He had been away for over a fortnight of almost unbroken celebration, but his constitution seemed unimpaired. 'I am always well,' he had told an interviewer on 13 March. 'I have never been ill, not for a single day in my life. I have never consulted a doctor. I have never used a prescription. Despite the fact that I have often lived in feverish atmospheres and exposed myself to illnesses.' It was not quite true; he had been ill in 1861, 1889 and 1892; but even then he had probably not consulted a doctor, though the period of his immunity was almost past.

Eight days after his return he sent a photograph of himself to Rosa Fitinghoff, with an accompanying letter.

Dearest Miss Fitinghoff!

When I received your beautiful postcard yesterday it was as though you had entered my house yourself with a spring greeting to warm my heart. There was music and dance in what you wrote; and it was through dance and music that we met. That is the happy part of the story. The sad part is that we did not meet until my last evening. Parties are often like life; people do not meet until they have to say goodbye. But go on writing to me. Write of everything you wish to, and can – and make happy

Your affectionate
Henrik Ibsen

On 26 May he had another formidable body of ladies to face. The Norwegian Society for Women's Rights gave a banquet for him in Christiania. Suzannah, appropriately for one who had for so long been a champion of that cause, for once attended with him. In his reply to the toast Ibsen said something that must have disconcerted his hearers, and that every dramatic critic ought to learn by heart before reviewing any production of *A Doll's House*:

I have been more of a poet and less of a social philosopher than people generally tend to suppose. I thank you for your toast, but must disclaim the honour of having consciously worked for women's rights. I am not even quite sure what women's rights really are. To me it has been a question of human rights. And if you read my books carefully you will realize that. Of course it is incidentally desirable to solve the problem of women; but that has not been my whole object. My task has been the portrayal of human beings.

On 29 May he informed Julius Elias that, owing to the distractions occasioned by his birthday celebrations, it was doubtful if he would be able to finish his projected new play that year, adding 'I have never planned to complete my so-called "Memoirs" in the immediate future.' (He presumably regarded the childhood memories which Jæger had incorporated in his biography as the foundation.) On 26 June he wrote again to Rosa Fitinghoff thanking her for a profile photograph of herself 'so that now I can sit each day and look at you from the side without your knowing. And when I want to look into your eyes I take out the big group photograph. There you sit so still and thoughtful, as though you were dreaming and had no idea that anyone was looking at you ... Your letters can never be too long for me. But I must, alas, limit myself to telegraphic brevity. But do not think ill

of me for this. What I do not write I say to your photograph.'
On 8 July he wrote suggesting that she should visit him in
Christiania on her way back to Stockholm from her holiday
with her mother on the Swedish west coast. This visit did not
materialize, but she wrote to him twice from Lysekil and
continued the correspondence on her return to Stockholm.

Gustaf af Geijerstam visited him in Christiania that
August; so did William Archer, who was somewhat surprised to see 'holding a very prominent position in his study,
a bright corner-room looking out upon the palace park, a
huge gilt-edged and brass-clasped family Bible. "You keep
this close at hand?" I said, pointing at it. "Oh, yes," he replied. "I often read in it – for the sake of the language."'
(Bolette Sontum likewise records that she heard him assure
people, 'gazing fiercely at them', that he read it only for the
language. 'But we knew him to be a faithful reader of the
Bible, as the worn pages of his own huge copy testify.') On
Archer's expressing further surprise at seeing the portrait of
Strindberg, Ibsen replied: 'I think he looks so delightfully
mad.' The same month Ibsen received news from Hegel that
they had decided to increase the first printing of the popular
edition of his collected works to 15,000 – the more gratifying
since Bjørnson's works in the same series were being printed
in an edition of only 4,000.

In September he received his first letter for over a year
from Georg Brandes. Brandes had been gravely ill and,
quarrelsome as ever, had apparently rebuked Ibsen for not
writing. 'You know how much I owe you,' Ibsen replied on 30
September, 'recently as well as of old, and that I gratefully
acknowledge this. And if you doubt it, would a written assurance help? Good God, you know how easy it is to put
together a French-general-staff kind of letter. I can therefore
not feel that the crime of silence is sufficient to justify your
addressing a friend of many years standing as "Respected
Sir". I don't think it worthy of you to take this attitude because of a couple of unwritten letters – especially from someone whose main passion is certainly not correspondence,

even with his best and dearest friends.' Of Ibsen, Bjørnson and Brandes, which was the most difficult to remain friends with? Yet somehow, against the odds, the friendships survived.

On 3 October Ibsen sent a photograph of himself to his sister Hedvig with a tender little note: 'I think we two have been close to each other. And so it will continue.' In a similar mood he inscribed a copy of *Peer Gynt* that Christmas for a two-year-old boy, Odd Arstal:

To little Odd!
You shall have this book for Christmas. But you won't read it till you've grown into a big boy. And then, please remember the man who wrote this book.

H. Ibsen

Thanks to the 75,000 crowns (£4,167) for the popular edition of his works, Ibsen earned £4,912 in 1898, over three times as much as in any previous year. Without this windfall, however, his earnings would have fallen well below £1,000. It is ironical to note that for most of the birthday performances in Scandinavia he received nothing, thanks to the fixed fee system which gave a theatre rights to a play in perpetuity.

36

The Top of a Cold Mountain
1899

DURING the first weeks of 1899 Ibsen at last got down to work on his new play. On 13 February he wrote Hegel that he had 'now begun to grapple with it in earnest', and on 20 February he made his first notes. Two days later he began to write the dialogue, giving the play the provisional title of *The Day of Resurrection*. But spring came, and summer, and still he, who normally wrote so rapidly, had not finished the first act. No doubt the theme was partly to blame: this play was to be about an artist's final reckoning with himself. Perhaps, too, he found it difficult to adapt himself to the unusual task of writing in winter instead of, as had for so long been his habit, during the summer or autumn.

On 19 February an important event (though Ibsen would not have realized its significance, and received no money from it) occurred in Russia. The Moscow Arts Theatre staged their first Ibsen production – *Hedda Gabler*, with Konstantin Stanislavsky as Løvborg. They were to perform seven more of his plays during the next nine years: *An Enemy of the People, When We Dead Awaken, The Wild Duck, The Pillars of Society, Ghosts, Brand* and *Rosmersholm*. Surprisingly, only *An Enemy of the People* and *Brand* were complete successes. One would have expected plays such as *Ghosts* and *The Wild Duck* to have been perfectly suited to the Stanislavsky method, but the company seems to have found as much difficulty in comprehending their realism as other countries at first did with Chekhov. 'More's the pity I was not a Scandinavian,' mourned Stanislavsky, 'and never saw how Ibsen was played in Scandinavia. Those who have been there tell me that he is interpreted as simply, as true to life, as we play Chekhov.'

In March Ibsen wrote to Edvard Brandes, asking him to look after Hildur Andersen who was visiting Copenhagen to play in a concert. He was still seeing much of her, and corresponding with Rosa Fitinghoff. On 17 April he wrote to Rosa thanking her for sending him a little blue flower – ' "*die blaue Blume*", which signifies so much and is so seldom found. And thank you for thinking of me and of 11 April last year. I shall never forget that day. Be assured of that! Your letters live in a special little place in my desk and when I go to my work in the morning I always look into that little drawer and greet my Rosa.' His memory had slipped; it had been on 16 April that he had first met her; 11 April had been the date of the Society of Authors banquet in Stockholm.

On 15 June he attended the last performance of the Christiania Theatre, which was to close its doors after seventy-two years to make way for the National Theatre. The play was *The Pillars of Society*, with Lucie Wolf, who had worked under Ibsen as a young actress at Bergen, in her old role of Lona Hessel, which she had played in the original production twenty-one years before. As Øyvind Anker has written, it must have been a moving occasion for Ibsen; this was the theatre which had rejected his early work and had employed him at a starvation wage, and the demolition of which he had so long advocated. He had first written for it as a young rebel; now he sat himself among the pillars of society, loudly cheered from both the auditorium and the stage.

His play still eluded him; but July brought good news for the family. Sigurd was appointed head of the new Foreign Office; after eight years in the wilderness, he was to return to active politics. 'At last, at last!' he wrote to Bergliot, adding: 'My parents were transported with joy.' He was a tremendous success in his new post, far-sighted, able and popular; importantly, too, he and Bergliot established an admirable relationship with the suspicious old king. Sigurd would have made a great prime minister; but his cosmopolitan and independent outlook and lack of chauvinism were always, as hitherto, to make him an object of distrust in political circles, a kind of Norwegian Churchill.

Rosa at last visited Christiania that month, with her mother (inevitably) in tow. They met Ibsen at the Grand Hotel, where the three drank champagne on the verandah. Thirty years later she remembered how he had spoken of 'the emptiness of Christmas'. He invited them back to his home, and told her how he kept small pieces of paper, each bearing the name of a character in the play he was writing, on a string in front of his desk. When a character died, he pulled off that piece of paper and tore it up. 'One doesn't want too many bits of paper in front of one's nose,' he explained. She remembered his alternations of deep brooding and urchin merriment. 'Sometimes', he said, 'all these characters I have imagined weary me with their squabbles and griefs and lovings and hatings, and when I get really tired I pull out the drawer of my desk and look into this little box.' He showed it to her; it contained her letters. 'Then I sit and talk with you and after a little while I can carry on with the people I'm writing about.' He spoke of the play he was writing. 'If only my powers last! But they must, they must! This play will be the best and the biggest I have ever written.' On her departure, on 26 July, he gave her a photograph of his study with the inscription: 'In memory of a summer meeting in Christiania, 1899.'

Rosa's visit may have helped to thaw his inspiration, for on 31 July he finished the first act. On 2 August he began the second act, and finished it on 23 August; and on 25 August he started the third and final act, completing it on 21 September. By this time he had altered the title from *The Day of Resurrection* to *When the* [sic] *Dead Awaken*.

On 1 September the National Theatre was formally opened. Bjørnson's son, Bjørn, had been appointed director, and faced the ticklish problem of which dramatist should be performed on the first night. Clearly, it had to be a

Norwegian writer, and to have performed either Ibsen or Bjørnson would have mortally offended the other; and although Bjørnson had written half-length plays, Ibsen had not, so that there could be no question of sharing the evening between them. Ibsen reminded Bjørn that he was the senior of the two. Bjørn replied: 'There is a Norwegian dramatist who is senior to both of you,' and diplomatically solved the question by presenting an evening of extracts from Holberg. When the day came, statues of Ibsen and Bjørnson were unveiled in front of the theatre, Ibsen staring pensively at his feet, Bjørnson, as Ibsen uncharitably but accurately observed, looking as though he were competing in a spitting contest. At the performance, they sat in the centre of the dress circle in separate boxes, tactfully segregated by a vast garland of red and white roses. 'They were the objects of universal attention,' noted Edmund Gosse, who was there, 'and the King never seemed to have done smiling and bowing to the two most famous of his Norwegian subjects.' Bolette Sontum, who was also present, says that 'the whole house cheered as they entered. Bjørnson stood and bowed gracefully to each salute, while Ibsen sat rigid, looking straight at the curtain, nervously tapping his chair.'

Earlier that day Gosse had met Ibsen for the first time, twenty-seven years after having first introduced his name to the English reading public. Being the man of letters that he was, Gosse was a little shocked at seeing in his apartment 'no books at all, except the large Bible which lay always at his side' – referring presumably to Ibsen's own study; he cannot have seen the room they proudly called the library, which was full of books. Gosse mentioned Tolstoy, and Ibsen exclaimed: ' "Tolstoy! He is mad!" – with a screwing up of the features such as a child makes at the thought of a black draught.' Gosse adds that Ibsen had read of Tolstoy 'with contemptuous disapproval, only some of the polemical pamphlets' – another inaccurate observation, for we know that Ibsen admired *Anna Karenina*. He also remarked to Gosse that 'it was almost useless for actors nowadays to try to perform the comedies of Holberg, because there were no stage directions and the tradition was lost', an observation which doubtless sprang from his own frequent productions of the plays in earlier years.

Gosse noted 'the smallness of his extremities' in contrast to his burly figure and huge head of hair. 'His little hands were always folded away as he tripped upon his tiny feet ... His voice was uniform, slow and quiet. The bitter things he said seemed the bitterer for his gentle way of saying them ... His movements were slow and distrait.' Some time that day or the next, presumably at the theatre or at one of the receptions afterwards, Gosse witnessed 'his *sang-froid* under distressing circumstances. Ibsen was descending a polished staircase when his feet slipped and he fell swiftly, precipitately, downward. He must have injured himself severely, he might have been killed, if two young gentlemen had not darted forward below and caught him in their arms. Once more set the right way up, Ibsen softly thanked his saviours with much frugality of phrase – '*Tak, mine Herrer*' – tenderly touched an abraded surface of his top-hat and marched forth homeward, unperturbed.'

The following evening, 2 September, the National Theatre performed *An Enemy of the People*. Gosse describes the scene:

He occupied, alone, the manager's box. A poem in his honour, by Nils Collett Vogt, was recited by the leading actor, who retired, and then rushed down the empty stage, with his arms extended, shouting: 'Long live Henrik Ibsen!' The immense audience started to its feet and repeated the words over and over again with deafening fervour. The poet appeared to be almost overwhelmed with emotion and pleasure; at length, with a gesture which was quite pathetic, smiling through his tears, he seemed to beg his friends to spare him, and the plaudits slowly ceased. *An Enemy of the People* was then admirably performed. At the close of every act Ibsen was called to the front of his box, and when the performance was over, and the actors had been thanked, the audience turned to him again with a sort of affectionate ferocity. Ibsen was found to have stolen from his box, but he was waylaid and forcibly carried back to it. On his reappearance, the whole theatre rose in a roar of welcome, and it was with difficulty that the aged poet, now painfully exhausted from the strain of an evening of such prolonged excitement, could persuade the public to allow him to withdraw. At length he left the theatre, walking slowly, bowing and smiling, down a lane cleared for him, far into the street, through the dense crowd of his admirers. This astonishing night, September 2 1899, was the climax of Ibsen's career.

No wonder that the next day, refusing an invitation from J. B. Halvorsen, he wrote: 'The interruptions during these past few days of my normal routine have much affected my strength, and now I must catch up on almost a whole week's neglected work.' But in less than three weeks, on 21 September, he had finished his draft. He took a full two months revising it; but on 20 November he was able to telegraph Gyldendal that *When We Dead Awaken* was ready. On 19 December Heinemann published the now customary London edition of twelve copies in Norwegian to cover general copyright, and on 22 December the Gyldendal edition appeared. Hegel printed 12,000 copies, the same as he had for *John Gabriel Borkman*, and again he had to reprint a further 2,000 before publication.

The press reaction in Scandinavia was, predictably, respectful, despite the obvious problems that the play presented. Kristofer Randers, who had been critical of so many of the earlier plays, described it in *Aftenposten* as 'less a truthful and objective picture of life than a personal expression of his own needs and feelings – a confession from the heart, a desperate cry of doubt, an apotheosis of love. It is as though the ageing poet wishes to say: "Let everything in life fail, woman will not fail; let everything in life break, the power of love will hold." And never has he proclaimed this gospel more beautifully and powerfully than here.' Georg Brandes, in *Verdens Gang*, wrote: 'This work is born of no happy view of art, any more than Zola's *œuvre* ... With sad bitterness he dwells, as in *The Master Builder*, on what Art and Genius cost the artist and, especially, what they cost others ... It speaks as every artist, even the greatest, speaks in the moments of despair and bitterness.' And Edvard Brandes, in *Politiken*, declared: 'The deeper one digs into the play, the better one is able to appreciate its greatness.'

When We Dead Awaken tells of an aged sculptor, Arnold Rubek, who has achieved fame at the expense of personal happiness. His marriage with a much younger wife, Maja, is a failure. Returning to Norway after a long absence, he meets a former model, Irene, who had loved him but in whom he had only as an artist been interested. She is now deranged. She accuses him of destroying her life (as Ella had accused John Gabriel Borkman); together, painfully, they dredge up the past; then she asks him to climb with her to the top of the mountain on different levels of which the action of the play takes place. They climb together, and near the top meet Maja and a huntsman, Ulfhejm, with whom she has become enamoured. As a storm rises, Maja and Ulfhejm go down the mountain to safety, while Rubek and Irene continue towards the top where, like Brand, they are killed by an avalanche. In other words, Maja and Ulfhejm return to what they think is life but what Rubek and Irene regard as death, while Rubek and Irene climb upwards to what the others regard as death but they regard as life. As long as people remain imprisoned in flesh, Ibsen seems to say, they are dead; it is only when the body dies that the dead awaken.

It is a very short play, much the shortest Ibsen ever wrote; in performance, it lasts under two hours (unless one is foolish enough to have two intervals, of which more anon). The third and final act occupies only a quarter of an hour. This brevity is curious; and so is the language in which the play is written. In the last act of *John Gabriel Borkman*, Ibsen had moved into a heightened prose very near to poetry; in *When We Dead Awaken*, he uses this heightened prose a great deal more – for most, indeed, of the dialogues between Rubek and Irene. I well remember that when I translated this play I found myself continually feeling how much easier my task would have been if he had written it in poetry. There is a certain kind of abstract high-flown writing which in any prose sounds grandiose, even windy (when I translated *Brand* I tried at first to put it into prose, and found exactly this result). I cannot but feel that *When We Dead Awaken* would have been a much greater play if he had written it in poetry – as he nearly did. He told C. H. Herford, a Welshman who translated *Brand* into English, that he would probably write his last play in verse 'if only one knew which play would be the last'. To have done this with *When We Dead Awaken* would have been tantamount to an acceptance that he would never write any more. Yet the straining is clearly there.

The shortness of the last act is a mystery; not merely its shortness but its (to my mind) inadequacy. It is the only less-than-great final act that Ibsen wrote after *The Pillars of Society* (whatever objections may be raised against the endings of *The Lady from the Sea* and *Little Eyolf*, they both work wonderfully well if – to borrow Henry James's phrase – really *done*). There are, I think, two possible explanations. One is physical exhaustion; he was within a few weeks of his first stroke, and there are hints of weakness that summer and autumn – his remark to Rosa: 'If only my powers last! But they must, they must!'; his remaining seated at the theatre as the audience applauded, while Bjørnson stood; his fall down the steps; his words to Halvorsen about his strength being 'much affected'; Gosse's observation that his movements were 'slow and distrait'. He may have sensed that he had not an indefinite time left, and perhaps felt unequal to the immense strain of executing an appropriate final act, especially to so self-searching a play.

But it is also possible that he felt some strange compulsion to leave it as a fragment. Another sculptor, Henry Moore, once remarked:

There is a fact, and for me a strange fact, about the really great artists of the past; in some way their late works become simplified and fragmentary, become imperfect and unfinished. The artists stop caring about beauty and such things, and yet their works get greater.

This is one way to assess *When We Dead Awaken,* as a marvellous and flawed fragment, like those unfinished statues of Michelangelo's old age which Ibsen may have seen, and drawn inspiration from, on his way to Rome thirty-five years before. Many admirers of Ibsen dislike and even dismiss it; but on some it has always exercised a peculiar fascination. 'His magic is nowhere more potent,' wrote Bernard Shaw. 'It is shorter than usual. That is all.' And the young James Joyce proclaimed: 'On the whole, *When We Dead Awaken* may rank with the greatest of the author's work – if indeed it be not the greatest.'

It is not the greatest; but he is at his greatest in it, and in some ways it is a more moving memorial to him than if it had been a perfected whole. As Michael Elliott, who staged the play memorably at the 1968 Edinburgh Festival, has written: 'Like the last quartets of Beethoven, *When We Dead Awaken* has all the intensity of the master at the height of his powers ... It too is a quartet. At times it may seem impossible to rise to the music, but the score itself can only be regarded with wonder.'

It needs gigantic yet delicate acting: a Rubek who can suggest genius, an Irene who can suggest madness without alienating our sympathy. Rubek is sometimes played soft on the excuse that Irene accuses him of being 'soft and self-indulgent, and so ready to forgive all your own sins'. But it should come as a shock to us when she says that; he should seem a figure of granite, a Sibelius, a Hemingway. Like *Brand* and *The Master Builder* and *John Gabriel Borkman, When We Dead Awaken* has to be played big or it had better not be played at all. It is no place for gentlemanly or ladylike understatement; Rubek and Irene are the shadows of mighty archetypal creatures moving near the sun. And

the way to solve the briefness of that last act is to have no
interval between Acts Two and Three. The scene-change,
from one level of the mountain to another, can easily be
made during a brief blackout.

It is significant that *When We Dead Awaken* should have
so appealed to Joyce, for although Ibsen sub-titled it 'A Dramatic Epilogue', he took pains to make it clear that he intended it, not as his final work, but as a declaration that he
had now finished with the realistic type of drama through
which he had won international recognition, and was intending to break out into new and experimental fields. When, a
few days before the publication of the play, the Danish
newspaper *Politiken* assumed from the subtitle that 'with
this play the author will have said his last word, and will
thereby have written *finis* to his dramatic work', the correspondent of *Verdens Gang* asked Ibsen if this were true.
Ibsen replied:

No, that conclusion has been too hastily reached. The word
'Epilogue' was not meant by me to have any such implications.
Whether I write any more is another question, but all I meant by
'Epilogue' in this context was that the play forms an epilogue to
the series of plays which began with *A Doll's House* and which
now ends with *When We Dead Awaken* ... It completes the
cycle, and makes of it an entity, and now I am finished with it. If
I write anything more, it will be in quite another context;
perhaps, too, in another form.

On 5 March 1900 he wrote to Moritz Prozor: 'If it be
granted to me to retain the strength of body and spirit which
I still enjoy, I shall not be able to absent myself long from
the old battlefields. But if I return, I shall come forward with
new weapons, and with new equipment.'

I do not think there is much doubt that, by these remarks,
Ibsen meant that he was finished with orthodox realism and
was intending to move, as Strindberg had recently done,
back towards poetry and symbolism. In 1898 Strindberg had
sent Ibsen the first two parts of his highly symbolic drama,

To Damascus, and it is known that he read both volumes. One can only speculate on what Ibsen would have written if illness had not struck him down and rendered him helpless; but *When We Dead Awaken* gives us a hint, and one may speculate on its possible influence on Joyce, who was to make the same decision to abandon realism in favour of symbolism barely a dozen years later.

Ibsen had been planning to write an autobiographical book which would relate his life to his work. Did he perhaps, before starting *When We Dead Awaken,* decide to write that book in dramatic form? For the play certainly covers that ground; it is Ibsen's final account with himself. He had portrayed different facets of himself in most of his plays: the unsatisfactory husband preoccupied with his work (Tesman in *Hedda Gabler,* Allmers in *Little Eyolf*), the uncompromising idealist who brings unhappiness to those he loves most (Brand, Gregers Werle, Dr Stockmann), the egotistic artist (Ejnar in *Brand,* Hjalmar Ekdal, Lyngstrand in *The Lady from the Sea*), the ruthless old man who despises the world and neglects his wife (Solness, Borkman). But nowhere do we find so complete and merciless a self-portrait as the character of Arnold Rubek. The ageing artist, restless in his married life, restless in the homeland to which he has returned after a long sojourn abroad, restless in his art, shocked, like Brand, near the top of a mountain, into the realization that to reject love is to reject life; such is Ibsen's Portrait of the Dramatist as an Old Man, painted at the age of seventy-one.

When We Dead Awaken received its première at Stuttgart on 26 January 1900, and within the next few weeks was performed in Copenhagen, Helsinki, Christiania, Stockholm and Berlin. Despite the acclaim with which it had been received on publication, it failed everywhere (in Christiania it achieved only eleven performances that season), for the same reason that *The Master Builder* had failed; it was beyond the range of any of the actors who tackled it. 'The play is good enough, big enough,' wrote Edvard Brandes on the occasion of the Copenhagen première. 'The actors were too small.'

Ibsen's earnings for 1899 had been as follows:

	crowns	£
German royalties from Felix Bloch	1,664	92
Royalties from Wien Burgtheater	699	39
Royalties from Munich Hoftheater	570	32
Fee from S. Fischer for German edn of *When We Dead Awaken*	4,444	247
Fee from Gyldendal for 1st edn of *When We Dead Awaken*	9,360	520
Fee from Gyldendal for 2nd edn	1,560	87
14th edn of *Brand*	1,870	104
8th edn of *The Vikings at Helgeland*	520	29
9th edn of *The Pretenders*	1,200	67
Swedish performing rights of *When We Dead Awaken* (Albert Ranft)	3,000	167
Royalties from Royal Theatre, Copenhagen, for *The Lady from the Sea* (12th–14th perfs.) and *The Pillars of Society* (26th perf.)	1,460	81
Fee for *Rosmersholm* from Dagmars Theatre, Copenhagen	600	33
Unspecified fees from Bergen Theatre	260	14
Extra fee from Christiania Theatre following 50th perf. of *A Doll's House*	220	12
Fee from Olaus Olsen for 1 perf. of *Lady Inger of Østraat*	100	5
Fee for Danish provincial rights of *The Pretenders*	500	28
Fee for Danish provincial rights of *The League of Youth*	400	22
French royalties from Société des Auteurs	1,024	57
Unspecified fees from Mr Perrin and M. Prozor	279	15
	29,730	1,651

He invested more than this amount during the year in gilt-edged securities – 34,000 crowns (£1,890).

37

The Running Demon
1900–1906

O friend, if you should venture to that country,
Pass guardedly, be unseduced
By its too subtle promises of peace.
Its quiet is of a kind you should not seek . . .
This is a very ancient land indeed;
Aiaia formerly or Cythera
Or Celidon the hollow forest called;
This is the country Ulysses and Hermod
Entered afraid; by aging poets sought,
Where lives no love nor any kind of flower –
Only the running demon, thought.

Sidney Keyes, *Sour Land*

THE new century dawned, and Ibsen, though approaching seventy-two and at last showing signs of physical fallibility, seemed as intellectually vigorous as ever. Ernst Motzfeldt visited him on New Year's Day:

He was then already weakened by illness, but said that when he had taken a short rest and settled a few business matters, he would start on a new play. 'Then your last play, which you have described as an Epilogue, is not your final work?' I asked. 'No, it is only a phase which is now completed. Now I want to start on a new one.' When I asked him if he would not publish some guide to the meaning of this 'recently completed phase', about which there was so much speculation, Ibsen said, 'No. Just as I myself claim complete freedom as far as the public is concerned in my choice and treatment of material, so the public too must have complete freedom in interpreting my writings as they choose. I have no right to deny the public that freedom.' And I did not question him further.

That he had at last had cause to break his proud record of never having consulted a doctor is evidenced by a letter he addressed to Christian Sontum three days later:

Dear Dr Sontum,

I can no longer permit myself to parade in your files as an unreliable debtor from the last century. And since you take no steps to secure what is due to you, I must take the matter into my own hands, and presume to send you the enclosed trifle as compensation for your trouble and time. The rejuvenation you have caused I could not repay with its weight in gold. A Happy New Year to you and yours.

> Your most grateful friend
> Henrik Ibsen

On 15 January he wrote to Jonas Lie, who had likewise returned to live in Norway, that he was thinking of giving himself a holiday that summer, the first since his trip to the North Cape nine years previously, and that 'it would be delightful if we could chat about all things as we did in Berchtesgaden twenty years ago'. He was well able to afford it; on 6 February he asked August Larsen of Gyldendal to invest a further £1,778 in gilts, a sum which a decade earlier would have represented three years' normal earnings. Yet that same evening he did not attend the première of *When We Dead Awaken* at the National Theatre, and it is not easy to imagine what other cause but illness could have prevented him.

On 5 March he wrote to Moritz Prozor that he still enjoyed intellectual and physical strength; but within a few days his health had deteriorated badly. 'I have been very poorly since the day after the palace ball,' he confessed to Nils Vogt on 2 April, and on 30 April he had to tell August Larsen: 'I have been sick (though not bedridden) since the beginning of March, and my doctor has forbidden me the use of pen and ink. But now that is over, and I have leave to write short letters to my closest friends.' It seems likely that he had suffered his first stroke,[1] resulting in a partial para-

1. So thinks Francis Bull. Halvdan Koht dates Ibsen's first stroke as

lysis of his right side, and he was never to be a fully fit man again.

On 1 April the *Fortnightly Review* in London published a review of *When We Dead Awaken* by an eighteen-year-old Dublin student, the first example of the young man's work to appear in print outside school and university magazines. The student's name was James Augustus Joyce; his enthusiasm for Ibsen, which was to last throughout his life, had probably been fired by his fellow-Irishman Shaw's *Quintessence*, a book which Joyce is known to have read as a boy, though unlike Shaw Joyce admired Ibsen not for his sociological iconoclasm so much as for what, in *A Portrait of the Artist as a Young Man*, he called 'a spirit of wayward boyish beauty' that blew through him 'like a keen wind'. At first he read him only in translation, drinking him. as Yeats unkindly put it, through William Archer's hygienic bottle (though his opinion of *When We Dead Awaken* was based on a reading of the French translation). On 20 January Joyce had read an essay in the Physics Theatre of University College on 'Drama and Life', in which he had praised Ibsen for the way he put real life on the stage – life 'as we see it before our eyes, men and women as we meet them in the real world, not as we apprehend them in the world of faery ... *Ghosts*, the action of which passes in a common parlour, is of universal import – a deep-set branch on the tree Igdrasil, whose roots are struck in earth but through whose higher leafage the stars of heaven are glowing and astir.' He had concluded this essay by quoting Lona Hessel's line from *The Pillars of Society*: 'I will let in fresh air, Pastor.'

Joyce had written to the editor of the *Fortnightly*, a confirmed anti-Ibsenite Oxford don named W. L. Courtney, asking if he would consider a general article on Ibsen's work. Courtney had rejected this idea, but had suggested that Joyce review *When We Dead Awaken*. His letter reached

---

coming the following year, but a lesser illness would hardly have caused him to be forbidden to use a pen.

Joyce on the morning he was to read the essay in the Physics Theatre. For this article, Joyce received the then handsome sum of twelve guineas.

It is an extraordinary eulogy. 'It must be questioned', declared Joyce, 'whether any man has held so firm an empire over the thinking world in modern times. Not Rousseau; not Emerson; not Carlyle; not any of those giants of whom almost all have passed out of human ken ... His genius as an artist faces all, shirks nothing.' After a detailed appreciation of the play, Joyce expresses particular admiration of Ibsen's understanding of women, and perceptively observes: 'If one may say so of an eminently virile man, there is a curious admixture of the woman in his nature. His marvellous accuracy, his faint traces of femininity, his delicacy of swift touch, are perhaps attributable to this admixture. But that he knows women is an incontrovertible fact. He appears to have sounded them to almost unfathomable depths. Beside his portraits the psychological studies of Hardy and Turgenev, or the exhaustive elaborations of Meredith, seem no more than sciolism. With a deft stroke, in a phrase, in a word, he does what costs them chapters, and does it better.' He also shrewdly notes (and one must remember that this is a boy of eighteen writing): 'One cannot but observe in Ibsen's later work a tendency to get out of closed rooms. Since *Hedda Gabler* this tendency is most marked. The last act of *The Master Builder* and the last act of *John Gabriel Borkman* take place in the open air. But in this play the three acts are *al fresco* ... And this feature, which is so prominent, does not seem to me altogether without its significance.'[2] The article concludes:

2. The six plays from *The Pillars of Society* to *Rosmersholm* are all set entirely indoors. By contrast, four out of five acts of the 'optimistic' *Lady from the Sea* take place out of doors. Then followed the meeting with Emilie and the darkly pessimistic *Hedda Gabler*, again set totally indoors. But the last act of *The Master Builder*, the last two acts of *Little Eyolf*, the last act of *Borkman* and all of *When We Dead Awaken* are out of doors; surely, as Joyce observed, not without significance.

Henrik Ibsen is one of the world's great men before whom criticism can make but feeble show. Appreciation, hearkening, is the only true criticism. Further, that species of criticism which calls itself dramatic criticism is a needless adjunct to his plays. When the art of a dramatist is perfect the critic is superfluous. Life is not to be criticized, but to be faced and lived. Again, if any plays demand a stage they are the plays of Ibsen ... At some chance expression the mind is tortured with some question, and in a flash long reaches of life are opened up in vista ... In this play, Ibsen has given us very nearly the best of himself ... On the whole, *When We Dead Awaken* may rank with the greatest of the author's work – if, indeed, it be not the greatest. It is described as the last of the series which began with *A Doll's House* – a grand epilogue to its ten predecessors. Than these dramas, excellent alike in dramaturgic skill, characterization and supreme interest, the long roll of drama, ancient or modern, has few things better to show.

This article, over eight thousand words long, came to Ibsen's attention and, despite his faulty command of English, he took the trouble to send his new admirer a personal message of thanks via William Archer.

Christiania, 16 April 1900

Dear Mr William Archer,

I should long ago have thanked you for *Wehn* [sic] *We Dead Awaken*, but I have been ill for five weeks and my doctor has forbidden me to write during all that time.

The English edition looks handsome and in every way distinguished, and I have found it quite easy to read and understand most of it; though I am sure the book has been difficult to translate.

I have also read – or rather, spelt out – a review by Mr James Joyce in 'Fortnightly Review', which is very benevolent and for which I should greatly like to thank the author, if only I had sufficient knowledge of the language ...

Your ever affectionate and grateful

Henrik Ibsen

Archer relayed Ibsen's message to Joyce on 23 April. Five days later Joyce replied:

13, Richmond Avenue,
Fairview, Dublin
April 28, 1900

Dear Sir,

I wish to thank you for your kindness in writing to me. I am a young Irishman, eighteen years old, and the words of Ibsen I shall keep in my heart all my life.

Faithfully yours,
Jas A. Joyce

William Archer, Esq.
Southampton Row
London

Joyce's biographer, Richard Ellmann, comments: 'Before Ibsen's letter Joyce was an Irishman; after it he was a European.' A few months later, in one of the prose poems which he called 'Epiphanies', Joyce, describing a dream which he interpreted as being about Ibsen, wrote:

But here he is himself in a coat with tails and an old-fashioned high hat ... He walks along with tiny steps, jutting out the tails of his coat ... My goodness! how small he is! He must be very old and vain ... But then he's the greatest man on earth.

Within a year, Joyce was to write a passionate letter of admiration to Ibsen himself, an admiration he was never to lose. Both *Ulysses* and *Finnegans Wake* are full of references to and echoes of Ibsen.[3]

Dr Sontum was working at Sandefjord, a watering-place

3. For example, from *Finnegans Wake*: 'For peers and gints, quaysirs and galleyliers, fresk letties from the say and stale headygabblers, gaingangers and dudder wagoners, pullars off societies and pushers on rothmere's homes.' (Cf. J. S. Atherton, *The Books at the Wake*: *A Study of Some Literary Allusions in James Joyce's* Finnegans Wake [London, 1959], pp. 152–7 and 257–8). *Kejser og Galilæer, Gengangere*, and *Naar Vi Døde Vaagner* are the Norwegian titles of *Emperor and Galilean, Ghosts* and *When We Dead Awaken. Peer Gynt, The Lady from the Sea, Hedda Gabler, The Pillars of Society* and *Rosmersholm* are the other plays punned upon in this passage. Atherton lists over sixty such examples of puns on Ibsen's plays (or his name) in *Finnegans Wake*.

on the Christiania fjord, that summer, and Ibsen, anxious to be near him in case he should suffer another stroke, went there on 8 June. Suzannah, after several months back in Norway, was about to leave again for Italy, and on 13 June Ibsen wrote what was to be his last letter to her:

Dear Suzannah!

Thank you for your letter, which I have just received. Everything goes excellently. Sleep well. Appetite ravenous at every mealtime. I have massage daily, and it does me remarkable good. No trace of pain. I can already walk as far as I wish without my foot feeling tired.

This is the last time I shall write to you before you leave. I received Sigurd's letter yesterday.

The room must not be locked without Helga [their maid] having access to the key. This is because of the insurance. Be sure to remember this! Otherwise I shall not have an hour's peace down here.

Well, I wish you with all my heart a good and successful trip. I shall at least celebrate the red-letter days 18 and 26 June[4] quietly here. May you receive as much benefit from the grotto as I from the massage. My best wishes to Sigurd.

Your affectionate
H.I.

According to Bolette Sontum, he had had Sandefjord in mind when describing the setting for the first act of *When We Dead Awaken*. Ironically, he found himself attended, like Irene in that play, by a nun. Soon after his arrival, erysipelas developed in his right foot, and the attack was sufficiently critical for Suzannah to be summoned back from Italy. But he recovered rapidly. A beautiful old house, Hjertnes hovedgaard, was secured as a retreat for him where he could enjoy privacy, and he ate many of his meals with the Sontums. Bolette remembered:

While he was ill, we were allowed to pay him short visits. My youngest sister was only three years old, and a very popular little pet among the patients. She had heard so much about the Great

4. Their wedding anniversary and Suzannah's birthday.

Man, and was anxious to see him. One day when my mother went to take tea with Mrs Ibsen she brought little Ellen with her. While Mrs Ibsen and my mother were chatting, Ibsen was busy in his study with some letters, and as the little girl thought the teatime very long and tedious, she left them to hunt for the Great Man herself. Ibsen was just stepping out on the verandah with his nurse when little Ellen came peeping in the door. When she saw him she stopped short, opened her baby lips round and said: 'Oh, are you the Great Man?' Her little face showed how disappointed she was that any Great Man was not a Great Big One.

Ibsen was much amused and winked at the nurse. To make up for her disappointment he took her around to his study, and as he never knew how to treat children or what to give them, he offered her some claret. Shortly afterwards she came tripping in to her mother, her eyes shining from the wine. 'I have had such a good time with a little, kind man in there!' she said . . .

Since his illness my father had ordered a special shoe for him, flat and broad. He did not like these, as they were not nearly as neat as his own patent leathers, but he was partially consoled when my father told him he could have them tan.

Bolette wanted to photograph him, and as she was about to click the shutter Ellen came running down the street. Ibsen tried to catch her and asked why she was in such a hurry. 'It's dinnertime,' she replied. 'Papa says I must get there early today because the old doctor is coming.' As he paused a moment, his hand on her shoulder, Bolette snapped them together – one of the very few occasions when Ibsen was photographed off his guard.

He was as regular in his routine on the promenade at Hjertnes as on his walks down Carl Johan in Christiania. Bolette recalled:

When my sister said one day, 'The old doctor is my clock,' it so pleased Ibsen that he told my father that he thought his little daughter was extremely intelligent. The last day of our summer vacation he gave a special dinner for us, as my mother too was going to the city. He slyly gave us children champagne when our parents were not looking. In a little speech he thanked us for the pleasant summer and hoped we would study hard and please our teachers.

On 11 August he wrote to his niece, Anna Stousland:

My dear little Anna,

Thank you for your kind and dear letter. It warmed my heart to read it, and I wished I had you here with me. You may certainly continue to call me your 'Sun God'. All the fire of my youth still burns in me.

I am almost completely well again and take long walks on the roads.

Your 'Sun God'

But during the autumn his health began to fail again. Bolette writes:

I went to see him a couple of times and he looked pale and thin, but was still interested in everything ... One day when my father made his daily call at noon Ibsen handed him a parcel, saying that his brother-in-law had brought something for him, if my father would give it to me on my Confirmation Day. It was a beautiful brooch with a large amethyst in an exquisite setting.

It must have been this 19 September, nine years since their meeting, that he sent Hildur Andersen a bouquet of roses with a card:

Nine red roses for you, nine rose-red years for me. Take the roses as thanks for the years.

H.I.

He also sent her, probably this year or the next (it must have been after the appearance of *When We Dead Awaken* and before he became unable to write) a set of his collected works, twenty-four plays plus the *Poems*, bearing the dedication:

Hildur!

These twenty-five twins are all ours. Before I found you I wrote seeking, groping. I knew you were somewhere in the world, and once I had found you I wrote only of princesses in varying forms.

H.I.[5]

5. Neither the card nor the dedication exist; shortly before her death Hildur destroyed not merely Ibsen's letters to her but also sev-

On 4 November he sent Dr Sontum a photograph of himself with an inscribed message of thanks, and the children were amused to see that he had ruled pencil lines so as to be able to write straight – a sad sign of how shaky that iron hand had become. But three weeks later he felt well enough to allow himself to be interviewed, by Hans Tostrup for the newspaper *Ørebladet*. He declared that he was in excellent health save that 'perhaps my left leg is not quite as it should be; but that is a trifle ... I do most of my walking now on my home ground – the handsome pavements out here on Drammensveien.' He was, he said, mooting a new play and doing a bit of groundwork for it; but this year, being the one following that in which he had produced a work, he would regard as a rest year, as was his custom.

Tostrup asked Ibsen's opinion of Nietzsche, who had died in Weimar that August. Ibsen replied that he 'did not know so much about him', but that he was 'a rare talent who, because of his philosophy, could not be popular in our democratic age'. When Tostrup remarked that some people regarded Nietzsche as 'a spirit of darkness, a Satan', Ibsen cut in: 'No, he wasn't that.' And when asked about the Boer War, which had been in progress for just over a year, he surprised his interviewer, and no doubt many who read the interview, by saying that his sympathy for the Boers was somewhat divided. 'Remember that the Boers themselves took possession of the country illegally by driving out the original inhabitants. And they came only as a half-civilized people, not with the purpose of spreading civilization. And now a more civilized people, the British, come and force their way in. That is no worse than – indeed, it is not as bad as – what the Boers have done. The British are simply taking what the Boers themselves have stolen.'

These remarks naturally offended the Dutch, and a young journalist, Cornelius Karel Elout, editor of the Amsterdam

eral pages bearing dedicatory inscriptions. Her servant remembered these two items, however, and told Francis Bull.

Algemeen Handelsblad, attacked Ibsen's attitude in the Copenhagen newspaper *Politiken* on 7 December. Ibsen defended his viewpoint with dignity in an open letter to *Algemeen Handelsblad* on 9 December, saying: 'I owe a deep personal debt of gratitude to your country. But you cannot ask me to repay part of this debt by denying my convictions.' It was the last public appearance that he was to make in print.

Thanks mainly to performing rights, especially German and Danish, the first year of the new century had been a good one. German royalties and fees alone had amounted to nearly £800.

	crowns	£
Royalties for *An Enemy of the People* at		
National Theatre, Christiania	2,950	164
Unspecified royalties from Wein Burgtheater	535	30
Fee for *The Pillars of Society* at		
Mannheim Hoftheater	80	4
German royalties from Felix Bloch	13,479	749
Additional royalties from National Theatre,		
Christiania	3,106	172
French fees from Société des Auteurs	1,869	104
Fee from *Revue de Paris*	725	40
11th edn of *Peer Gynt*	1,815	101
8th edn of *Love's Comedy*	625	35
English edn of *When We Dead Awaken*		
(Heinemann)	2,160	120
Extra fee from Archer for book sales	24	1
Royalties from Royal Theatre, Copenhagen:		
The League of Youth (25th–31st perfs.)	1,299	72
The Lady from the Sea (15th–18th perfs.)	1,035	57
The Pretenders (20th–28th perfs.)	2,224	124
The League of Youth (32nd–35th perfs.)	451	25
The Lady from the Sea (19th–23rd perfs.)	489	27
Swedish rights of *The League of Youth* and		
The Pillars of Society (A. Ranft)	1,600	89
Unspecified rights from Danish director,		
Stephensen	300	17
	34,766	1,931

On 1 January 1901 he received 1,836 crowns from the National Theatre and 2,460 crowns from Felix Bloch. These are the last entries in his account book, apart from a note on 21 January that he had bought 5,000 crowns' worth of shares in the Sundsvall Cellulose Company, bringing his total investments to 338,310 crowns, or £18,795. Over half of this amount, 171,000 crowns, he had purchased in the past four years – 34,000 in 1897, 25,000 in 1898, 34,000 in 1899, 73,000 in 1900, and this last purchase of 5,000 in January 1901.

Ibsen's optimism about his health proved sadly false. He was very ill that winter, with repeated small apoplectic fits, and Bolette Sontum remembered how 'we were all very anxious every time the night telephone rang and my father was called out'. These fits paralysed his right arm and leg and the right side of his face, left his speech slurred and occasionally caused hallucinations. Henceforth his health showed little change. Occasionally there were small improvements. The newspapers prepared their obituaries; but his strength carried him through, and he even spoke confidently of writing a new play. It was, he told Christian Michelsen (later to become Prime Minister), to deal, like *John Gabriel Borkman*, with the conflict between love and the desire for power, a conflict finally to be resolved by a third driving passion, envy. But this he was never to begin.

One hopes he was well enough to appreciate a remarkable letter of tribute which arrived for his seventy-third birthday that March from his young Irish admirer, James Joyce. Joyce wrote it in Norwegian, which he had begun to teach himself so as to be able to read his idol in the original;[6] this letter has not survived, but luckily Joyce drafted it in English first, and the draft remains:

8, Royal Terrace,
Fairview, Dublin
March 1901

Honoured Sir,
    I write to give you greeting on your seventy-third birthday and

6. As did Thomas Mann and Stefan George.

to join my voice with those of your well-wishers in all lands. You may remember that shortly after the publication of your latest play, 'When We Dead Awaken', an appreciation of it appeared in one of the English reviews – The Fortnightly Review – over my name. I know that you have seen it because some short time afterwards Mr William Archer wrote to me and told me that in a letter he had from you some days before, you had written: 'I have read or rather spelt out a review in the "Fortnightly Review" by Mr James Joyce which is very benevolent and for which I should greatly like to thank the author if only I had sufficient knowledge of the language.' (My own knowledge of your language is not, as you see, great but I trust you will be able to decipher my meaning). I can hardly tell you how moved I was by your message. I am a young, a very young man, and perhaps the telling of such tricks of the nerves will make you smile. But I am sure if you go back along your own life to the time when you were an undergraduate at the University as I am, and if you think what it would have meant to you to have earned a word from one who held as high a place in your esteem as you hold in mine, you will understand my feeling. One thing only I regret, namely, that an immature and hasty article should have met your eye, rather than something better and worthier of your praise. There may not have been any wilful stupidity in it, but truly I can say no more. It may annoy you to have your work at the mercy of striplings, but I am sure you prefer even hot-headedness to nerveless and 'cultured' paradoxes.

What shall I say more? I have sounded your name defiantly through a college where it was either unknown or known faintly and darkly. I have claimed for you your rightful place in the history of the drama. I have shown what, as it seemed to me, was your highest excellence – your lofty impersonal power. Your minor claims – your satire, your technique and orchestral harmony – these, too, I advanced. Do not think me a hero-worshipper. I am not so. And when I spoke of you, in debating-societies, and so forth, I enforced attention by no futile ranting.

But we always keep the dearest things to ourselves. I did not tell *them* what bound me closest to you. I did not say how what I could discern dimly of your life was my pride to see, how your battles inspired me – not the obvious material battles but those that were fought and won behind your forehead — how your wilful resolution to wrest the secret from life gave me heart, and how in your absolute indifference to public canons of art, friends and shibboleths you walked in the light of your inward heroism. And this is what I write to you of now. Your work on earth draws to a close and you are near the silence. It is growing dark for you. Many write of such things, but they do not know. You have only opened the way – though you have gone as far as you could upon it – to the end of 'John Gabriel Borkman' and its spiritual truth – for your last play stands, I take it, apart. But I am sure that higher and holier enlightenment lies – onward.

As one of the young generation for whom you have spoken I give you greeting – not humbly, because I am obscure and you in the glare, not sadly because you are an old man and I a young man, not presumptuously, nor sentimentally – but joyfully, with hope and love, I give you greeting.

Faithfully yours,
James A. Joyce

Mr Henrik Ibsen
Arbiens Gade 2
Kristiania

A second stroke in the summer of 1901 left Ibsen virtually unable to walk; though occasionally he would obstinately struggle out for a few painful paces. An observer recalled one such occasion as he crossed Drammensveien on his way from Arbins gade to the Queen's Park twenty yards from his door.

A young man held him firmly under one arm while he struggled forward with short, dragging steps, his body heavily slouched, his head bowed, his eyes on the ground. His mouth, which had always looked like a line, had acquired an underlip.

That summer of 1901 Dr Christian Sontum himself became afflicted by an illness which in a few months was to prove fatal. He and his family had to return from Sandefjord to Christiania. Bolette records:

[Ibsen] called every day at our house to hear how the patient was. I usually went down to his carriage ... He was so kind and sympathetic to us all in our sorrow . . . He was so touching when one day he asked me if he might go in and see my father for the last time. 'I cannot walk, you know, but they can carry me.' My father was too ill to see anybody so Ibsen asked me to take his card in to him. On it was written in pencil and with a trembling hand the word '*Tak*' [Thanks] . . . After my father's death Ibsen called again and when I came down to his carriage he took my hand and his voice quivered as he said: 'How are you all? I am thinking about you all the time. I, too, have lost my best friend.'

Dr Sontum's successor as Ibsen's private physician was an eminent professor of medicine at the university, but his unpunctuality greatly annoyed Ibsen; and when, on one occasion, he arrived an hour late, Ibsen, sitting up in bed with a sweater up to his neck, ordered him from the house and swore he would never consult him again. He asked his friends if there was a good doctor in the capital who could be relied on to arrive in time, and was recommended Edvard Bull, a Bergenser aged fifty-six. An appointment was fixed for two o'clock and, as the hour of Dr Bull's appearance approached, Ibsen sat waiting with his watch in his hand. From five to two, Ibsen glanced cynically every minute at Dr Bull's recommender, who was sitting with him. As the clock struck two, Ibsen opened his mouth triumphantly, but before he could speak the doorbell rang. Edvard Bull remained Ibsen's doctor until the writer's death.

Ibsen took the air daily in his carriage, accompanied either by Dr Bull or by the masseur who now attended him, Arnt Dehli. He would make the coachman stop before the university clock, so that he could set his watch by it as he had been wont to do on his walks down Carl Johan to the Grand Hotel, and he was now as familiar a sight on his rides as he had been during those walks, a top hat on his head in summer, a round fur hat covering his ears in winter. The great muff of white hair that had surrounded his neck for the past few years was now shaven at the front of the chin. Once he decided that instead of riding he would take a walk.

By now he had a nurse permanently in attendance; she helped him down the stairs and no sooner had they reached the street than Ibsen commanded her to disappear. When she hesitated (Suzannah told Bergliot), 'Ibsen swung his stick at her so that she fled back into the house. And all the way down the street Ibsen kept turning to see if she was still there.' Bergliot had never heard Suzannah laugh so as when she told this story. 'She was always amused when Ibsen got angry. He always jutted out his underlip, showing his lower teeth. He hated being ill. He never addressed a barber who visited him each day, except once, when he suddenly hissed at him: "Ugly devil!" '

Exaggerated reports of his state of health were printed from time to time in most western countries, and in August the New York *Critic* published a long letter purporting to be from Georg Brandes which stated that Ibsen could not possibly live beyond the autumn. Brandes denied authorship, pointing out that so far from having been at Ibsen's side, as the letter claimed, he had not been in Christiania since 1893. But similar rumours continued to appear over the next five years.

That autumn the first Nobel Prize for Literature was awarded. The world speculated which living writer would be the first to receive this honour: Tolstoy, Ibsen, Zola, Chekhov, Hardy? But the Swedish Academy chose the French poet Sully-Prudhomme, the first of many curious decisions which that body was to make over the years. Incredible as it seems, none of the five great writers named above ever received it, though Ibsen was to live another five years, Chekhov three, Tolstoy nine, and Hardy twenty-seven. Nor did Strindberg, Gorki, Proust, Henry James, Joseph Conrad, H. G. Wells, or James Joyce. Bjørnson was to be awarded it in 1903, in Ibsen's lifetime; but Ibsen enjoyed one small piece of revenge. When Bjørnson went to Stockholm to receive the prize, he tried to enter the palace through a side door but found his way barred by a sentry. 'My good man,' Bjørnson informed him. 'I am Norway's greatest writer.' 'Oh,' said the sentry, making way. 'I beg your pardon, Herr Ibsen.'

On 10 September Ibsen's second grandchild was born. Sigurd and Bergliot named her Irene, after the heroine of *When We Dead Awaken*. Ibsen became very devoted to her, and called her 'my little princess', as he had called the young girls who had been the dream images of his old age, from Emilie Bardach to Rosa Fitinghoff. 'Little Irene is beautiful,' he once said to Suzannah. 'But my Irene was also beautiful.' He greatly missed Sigurd, who was able to make only infrequent visits from Stockholm. On one such visit (tells Bergliot) 'as soon as he caught sight of Sigurd, he raised both arms towards him and cried despairingly: "Oh, I have been so sick – so sick." He took Sigurd's hand between his and so they stood.'

Yet on 24 November he felt well enough to give another interview to Hans Tostrup of *Ørebladet*.

Dr Henrik Ibsen sits in his black morning coat with a pocket watch before him at the corner window of his apartment . . . He looks well, and his complexion is healthy. His eyes shine with the same sharpness as before. Only his hair has grown somewhat whiter than when we saw him last. We asked how he was and Ibsen replied, 'Thank you, better than I have been for a long while. But I cannot walk easily nowadays. To drag myself through the streets would cause me such difficulty that I have to drive. My head is all right. That is fine. But I get tired easily, and my doctor has forbidden me to work very much.' He spoke of his hope of completing a new play once he had regained his full health, and even of travelling abroad, though not in the immediate future, since 'I would then have to take a masseur and a servant with me, and it would be no fun to travel with such an army.'

He managed to accompany his interviewer through three large rooms to the front door.

On 8 December 1902 Bjørnson celebrated his seventieth birthday, and surprised Ibsen with a visit. Both Ibsen and Suzannah were much moved that he should have come on such a day, and Suzannah left them alone together in

Ibsen's study. On returning home, Bjørnson told his family
that Ibsen had said to him: 'When I think back – I can't
think ahead, I'm too ill for that – when I think back, my dear
Bjørnson, in spite of everything it's you who have been
closest to my heart all these years. And in that play, you
know – the one about the doctor at the baths –' 'The doctor
at the baths?' asked Bjørnson, puzzled. 'The one about
those microbes. You know.' 'No.' They both pondered. '*The
[sic] Enemy of the People*', said Ibsen eventually. 'I was
thinking of you when I wrote it. Partly. Of course, you're not
a bourgeois like him. But it's you all the same.' When
Bjørnson finally rose to leave, Ibsen suddenly gripped his
hand tightly and would not let it go. They remained thus for
a long time. At last Ibsen said: 'You are the dearest of all
men to me.' It was the last time they met.

About this time Georg Brandes saw him for the last time.
'His mind', he recalled, 'was as brilliant as ever. An extraordinary mildness pervaded his manner, supplanting his
former sternness. His charm had grown, while his distinction of manner was as great as ever. Yet the general impression was one of weakness.' And Brandes remembered
Oswald's terrible cry in *Ghosts*: 'Never to be able to work
again! To be dead, yet alive! Can you imagine anything
more horrible?'[7]

On 19 February 1903 he granted Hans Tostrup a last interview:

As we crossed Drammensveien yesterday morning we caught a
glimpse behind the corner window on Arbins gade of a handsome, white-bearded and white-haired old head, staring with a
friendly and gentle expression, half-dreaming, half-observing,
down the street towards the wintry trees of the palace park.

'Well, Henrik Ibsen looks brisk and well!' we thought, so we go
up and visit him. It is long since any word was heard from him
... We announced ourselves and were received.

7. Brandes adds that 'he no longer spoke with bitterness of Norway,
but merely complained about its slow development. Norwegian ideas
and theories seemed old-fashioned and out of date to him.'

'I don't usually receive anyone now. I don't feel really strong in the daytime, and conversations, much as I'd like them – no, no, do sit down.'

So we sat beside him in the corner window, inquired after his health, and the old poet was friendliness and kindness itself.

Unfortunately, the interview dealt only with the question of closer co-operation between the Scandinavian kingdoms, and Ibsen's views on the subject, that small nations could achieve more by co-operation than by squabbling – a useful reminder at a time when squabbling was the order of the day, but one would have liked to have learned his views on something less parochial as he moved, in Joyce's phrase, near the silence.

On 28 March Magdalene Thoresen died at the age of eighty-three; luckier than her stepson, she had retained her physical and mental vigour to the last. That spring Ibsen had another stroke. He tried to learn to write with his left hand, practising every day; he sadly remarked to Suzannah: 'Strange that I, who was once quite a dramatist, now have to learn to write the alphabet.' Yet on 17 August he let the sculptor Gustav Vigeland, who had made busts of him in 1901 and 1902, make sketches for a new one. These sketches show a sad change, the mouth slack, the expression almost vacant. Gunnar Heiberg, who was present on one of these occasions, says that Ibsen 'complained that there was a limit to how long he could sit in that cold room; his health would not stand it, and anyway he had not promised to give so many sittings. Vigeland gave him a look but said nothing. Ibsen glanced at the clock and said he was expecting someone.' Heiberg said he had to go; Ibsen accompanied him to the next room, where he stumbled and had to grasp a chair. 'I asked if he would like to lean on my arm. No, he replied, there was nothing wrong. His face was stern and splendid; he looked like a Jupiter betrayed.' As they got to the door Heiberg asked who was the visitor he was expecting, and Ibsen gave a little smile and replied: 'The tailor.' Heiberg remembered that Ibsen was bitter because he felt that the

National Theatre, under Bjørn Bjørnson's direction, was playing too much of Bjørnson's work and too little of his own.

On 14 February 1904 Ibsen wrote the last word we have from his hand: '*Tak*,' shakily pencilled on a card to Dr Bull, who told his son that it took Ibsen three days to write it. On 19 March he granted his last interview, to *Verdens Gang*:

Tomorrow the poet celebrates his seventy-sixth birthday. One of our colleagues who visited him yesterday reports that Dr Ibsen is comparatively well and has in general been in quite satisfactory health all winter.

'There is nothing much wrong with me just now,' said the poet. 'I just have to be careful, and Dr Bull says that March with its changeable weather could be dangerous for me. I find walking a little difficult, but as soon as the air becomes milder I shall try to take a stroll outside. I am allowed to enjoy myself in the Queen's Park, which gives me great pleasure.' Our colleague extended his best wishes to the poet for his birthday and asked if he was receiving any visitors. 'No,' he replied. 'It is so difficult to speak with so many people that I am not receiving anyone.'

Halvdan Koht, who had recently edited Ibsen's letters, visited him during the autumn of 1904.

He had difficulty with his speech and forgot his words, sometimes using the wrong ones, e.g. 'lexicon' instead of 'letters'. [Arnt Dehli was present at the meeting to interpret his meaning when the right words would not come.] One could see how it pained him. His eyes were dull and had lost their colour. But they could still sparkle. It happened twice during our conversation, once when I greeted him from old German friends of his whom I had recently seen, and again when I mentioned that I knew his sister, Hedvig Stousland of Skien. Both times his eyes suddenly went steel-blue and shot like a flash at me.

That same autumn Bolette Sontum saw him for the last time, before going to America to study at the Carnegie Library School in Pittsburgh:

He was very much changed, so thin and white and, oh, so

little. His shoulders, always so proudly erect, had shrunken pathetically, and his lion head had grown so small that it was only the intense fire of his eyes that quickened it. It seemed to pain him that he did not have the strength to keep up a conversation. Yet he recognized me, and smiled when I came in, and in a few minutes he regained his interest and asked about all my America plans. Mrs Ibsen had told him that I was sailing for New York and had come to say good-bye. We talked about the happy days at Grefsen and my father. Then he said: 'And now you are going to America. Are you going to write books?' 'Oh, no,' I laughingly answered. 'I am going to learn how to put them correctly on the shelves.' He said: 'Yes, their libraries are famous,' and then he sat thinking. 'It must be a great country with many chances,' he repeated slowly, twice. 'But it seems so far away. You must be careful with yourself. My son says, beware of the iced water and the hot bread.' Mrs Ibsen also asked me not to have too many of those American dishes. Chivalrous as always, despite his absolute frailty, Ibsen wanted to see me to the door, but asked me to excuse him, adding he was so tired. He kissed my hand and I left him. When I was out on the street. I looked up to his window where he was standing in his black frock coat, and I waved my last good-bye to 'the old Doctor'.

Hildur Andersen does not seem to have visited him during these years of sickness; presumably Suzannah, despite Ibsen's protestations of innocence, still took their relationship seriously. Nor, being unable to go out alone, did he visit her. One winter's day, driving in his carriage, he saw her on the pavement. Raising his hand, he called weakly: 'Bless you! Bless you!' It was the last time they saw each other.

Yet the old man lived on. One January night in 1905 he was heard to cry in his sleep: 'I'm writing! And it's going splendidly!' Dreams, too, brought him occasional comfort and joy. He, who had always been so taciturn and self-contained, was now pathetically grateful for someone to talk to him, provided it was someone he knew. Jens Wang, the artist, paid him several visits to show him his designs for new décor and costumes, and he especially enjoyed these occasions. He even allowed an American photographer to take two portraits of him, rigid-faced and clutching the arm of his chair. But his helplessness increased; that spring another visitor noticed that he sat with a piece of paper in his hand wishing to put it on the table but unable to do so. His guest did it for him and received a grateful glance. A frequent visitor at this time was Christopher Bruun, who half a century earlier had helped to inspire Ibsen with the character of Brand. One day he tentatively brought up the question of Ibsen's relationship with God. Ibsen went red in the face with anger and said: 'Leave that to me!'

Sigurd, meanwhile, had run into trouble over the question of dissolving the union with Sweden. His skilful diplomacy in Stockholm, where he had taken up residence in 1903, and especially the trust and friendship he had inspired in King Oscar, had achieved what a few years earlier had seemed impossible. The king (who, on Sigurd's first mentioning the question of dissolution soon after taking office, had replied: 'If anyone suggests that to me I shall shoot him with my own hand'), now seemed not totally to reject the idea, and several Swedish newspapers began actively to support it. Unfortunately, this produced a reaction, and a new and chauvinistic Swedish Prime Minister, E. C. Boström, enraged Norwegian opinion by closing down on the proposals for a separate consular service. The Norwegian government resigned and the new Prime Minister, Christian Michelsen, wanted Sigurd to remain in charge of foreign affairs, but Sigurd believed that the Treaty of Union should be dissolved legally by changing the constitution and not violently by a *coup d'état*, and refused. As a result, he was suspected by jealous circles in Norway of having played a double game, and felt compelled to resign. 'I am one of those', he commented to Bergliot, 'who work for eleven hours of the day and at the twelfth hour have to look on while others gather the fruits of my labour.'

At least this meant that for the last year of his life Ibsen had Sigurd constantly with him in Christiania. Bergliot relates that when Sigurd returned, Ibsen 'not only was no worse; he was up again, and followed Sigurd's account of the latest developments in Stockholm with great interest. Fru Ibsen listened silently while Ibsen asked question after question. The conversation continued through dinner. I can still see Ibsen as he sat there, his hands far apart gripping the table edge. He looked like some powerful judge. When Sigurd had finished Ibsen suddenly rose and said loudly and firmly: "Sigurd shall give up politics. He shall continue my life's work." ' Sigurd was beginning to write a philosophical work called *The Quintessence of Man*, which was to take him several years; and one day when he asked his father about one of his plays which had just been revived with great success, Ibsen waved his hands and said: 'Don't talk about my things, I'm only interested in what you write.'

That summer Sigurd arranged the outright sale of his father's Danish and Norwegian copyrights for a lump sum of 150,000 crowns (£8,333), of which 20,000 crowns were to be paid forthwith, 10,000 annually for the next eight years and 5,000 annually for the following ten. Sigurd signed the contract on his father's behalf on 3 June. It seems a terribly bad bargain from the point of view of Ibsen's grandchildren; but the news galvanized Bjørnson into demanding 200,000 crowns from Gyldendal for the outright purchase of his copyrights. 'Ibsen is a rich man and I a poor one,' he told Peter Nansen, who negotiated on behalf of Gyldendal, 'and who knows whether my work won't last longer than Ibsen's?' He got the sum he asked, spread over twenty years.

On 7 June Michelsen's government, by a *coup d'état*, dissolved the union with Sweden. Dr Edvard Bull told Ibsen that people now referred to a famous restaurant called The Queen as 'Fru Michelsen', and was able to report to his family that the joke had made Ibsen smile, something Dr Bull had seldom seen. His difficulty in speaking had, however, now worsened, though his other senses remained sharp. He liked to sit hour after hour at his corner window gazing out, and tourists would stand in the street below to catch a glimpse of him, just as (noted Peter Nansen) a few years earlier the old Kaiser Wilhelm had been exhibited like a mummy in a window of his palace in Berlin. His only pleasure was when Sigurd came; he would sit with his watch before him, waiting for the visit.

In 1906 Sigurd and Bergliot had their third child, another girl.

She was only a few weeks old when Sigurd and I took her up to the Ibsens. Ibsen was sitting in an armchair at the table in the library when we came in. I showed him the baby, and he looked at her for a long time. Then I asked him if we could call her Eleonora. He became very moved, so that he could only slowly reply: 'Yes.' Then he turned towards me and added: 'God bless you, Bergliot.' He was happy to see his family grow. When we had gone he said to Fru Ibsen: 'My Nora was also called Eleonora.'[8]

That was one of the last times Sigurd and I saw him up. Afterwards, Ibsen lay mostly in his bed. His wife was the only person whom he allowed to give him food; and when he was up he only wanted to eat in her bedroom, which lay next to his.

He lived in a permanent fear lest she should die before him. He said: 'If you die before me, I shall die five minutes later.' Towards the end he had difficulty in speaking and always called her '*Fruen*' [Ma'am]; it was easier to say, and he always heard the nurse call her that.

Once I was sitting with him – it was the last time. He lay holding my hand, and his eyes and face shone with kindness as he spoke many loving words to me. It is a beautiful memory. Sigurd was with his father every day. One evening his father said to him: 'Soon I shall go into the great darkness.'

That February another Eleonora came to Christiania. Duse was visiting Norway for the first time, largely in the hope of meeting the dramatist who had provided her with her greatest triumphs. On her arrival she sent a letter and flowers to Ibsen asking if she might call merely to say

8. Ibsen enjoyed stressing that 'Nora' in *A Doll's House* was the kind of affectionate abbreviation that one uses to a child, and that Helmer employed it as Nora's father had done, her real name being Eleonora.

'Thank you.' Suzannah, however, telephoned that Ibsen was too ill to receive anyone. Lugné-Poe, who was with Duse at the time, tells what followed:

I remember very well that morning when she had just received this sad message. I went in to her and found her swathed in the long white *palandrane* which she loved to wear. She sat fearful, annihilated, hollow-cheeked, her face tired and lined as though life was abandoning her. She asked me: 'What shall I do? Please, what shall I do?' . . . What could I do for her? I had hoped so much, for her sake . . . Next morning around noon Duse and I found ourselves outside Henrik Ibsen's house. She had bought Norwegian boots, for she wished to go there on foot. We walked round the left of the palace, and at the stroke of twelve we stood beneath the corner window, where, every day at this time, people could see Dr Ibsen in person, sometimes with a secretary or someone at his side. Duse stood there waiting in the cold and snow. Who, even thirty years later, would not be shaken by the memory of having been present at that sad and silent meeting? Eleonora Duse on the pavement, looking for the old poet's silhouette behind the big window.

His seventy-eighth birthday passed, and still death would not come to relieve him. Suzannah, herself in almost constant pain, sat by his side. 'I could not do without her greatness,' he told Bergliot; and the nurse told her that she heard him say to Suzannah: 'You have been my guiding star. You were the eagle that showed me the way to the summit.' Occasionally, little spurts of strength seemed partially to revive him. Once when Dr Bull asked the masseur how Ibsen was, Dehli replied: 'Not too bad. He's sworn a couple of times.'

From 16 May he was too weak to stand, and lay in a coma, occasionally muttering a word or two indistinctly and incoherently. At noon on 22 May he opened his eyes, pressed Dr Bull's hand and murmured: 'Thank God!' A little later, the nurse said to the others who were in the room that he seemed to be a little better. From the bed came the single word: *'Tvertimod!'* ('On the contrary!'). It was the last word

Ibsen ever spoke;[9] and it came appropriately from one who had devoted his life to the correction of lies.

He died at 2.30 p.m. on 23 May 1906. Bergliot was present:

> One morning our telephone rang and we were told we must come at once. We came in to Ibsen, who lay calm and beautiful with closed eyes. Fru Ibsen sat crying in the next room. We went in to her. It was so strange to see her cry. Most people distort their faces when they cry, but not she. Tear after tear simply streamed down her cheeks. I can still see her large, clear face as she sat and spoke of the one she loved and must now lose. The nurse came and asked us to go in to Ibsen, since she thought the end was near. We went quickly in, but Fru Ibsen, who had difficulty in walking, came slowly after. Death brings with it a sublime stillness, and in this stillness we heard her approach with very short steps. First the stick was heard, then her foot which she dragged after her. It seemed an eternity. I can still see her as she stood as though lost above his bed. Now it was finished.
>
> There was a majestic peace and greatness about Henrik Ibsen's departure from this world. We remained with him a long time and then went and sat down in the library. There she told us very emotionally that the previous night, before falling into a doze, his last words to her had been: 'My dear, dear wife, how good and kind you have been to me.'[10] This had made her happy. After a while she rose and said: 'Now I must go. Ibsen liked me to look after the house.' In this sad atmosphere we again heard her small steps and the sound of the stick growing weaker and weaker until at last they were gone.
>
> Before he was taken away from Arbins gade we gathered for the last time around his open coffin. His face was transfigured in death; all the tightness and severity that had marked it in life

9. Some deny this, but cf. Dr Edvard Bull's journal, quoted in Lis Jacobsen's 'Ibsens sidste ord', in *Ibsen-Årbok, 1957–1959*, p. 81. There is a legend that in his last moments Ibsen cried: 'No!', but this seems to be without reliable foundation.

10. But Dr Bull's journal states that he was in a coma from the afternoon of 22 May. Bergliot recorded her memories over forty years later, and may have misremembered Suzannah's exact wording; or she may have been right and Dr Bull wrong. It hardly seems to matter.

were smoothed away. It was as though for the first time I saw how beautiful he was; the mighty brow lay smoothly serene, and the chiselled features stood classically forth.

The Norwegian government granted him a state funeral, and this took place on 1 June at Trinity Church. Bolette Sontum, now back from America, was among the mourners:

For the last time he was dressed in his black frock coat with the broad lapels and laid out in state ... The day before the funeral people flocked to the church and thousands stood outside waiting for their turn to pay their last respects to him. In the choir the coffin stood loaded with flowers and around it the students of the university kept a guard of honour. The organ played softly and the crowd [estimated at 12,000] filed past the coffin. There was nothing in the white little Ibsen that awed them now. The task of the fiery judge was done.

Suzannah was forbidden by Dr Bull to attend the ceremony, and remained alone in the apartment at Arbins gade. Afterwards, Bergliot and Sigurd returned there. 'There seemed an enormous emptiness in all the rooms. I sat and watched Sigurd and his mother as they talked together. Now those three had become one.' A column was erected over Ibsen's grave bearing the simple and appropriate symbol of a hammer.

Epilogue

SUZANNAH lived on for eight years at Arbins gade; she died there on 3 April 1914. Only once during that time did she leave the apartment, when she had herself carried down the stairs and driven to see her husband's grave. Despite her condition, she would never let anyone else dust the paintings which Ibsen had brought so proudly back from Italy. Twice a month she would have steps brought in, send her maid out of the room and painfully climb up to wipe the dust off each picture. Dr Bull once suggested to her that her discomfort would be eased if he designed a special chair for her to sit in; and she thanked him, moved that anyone should think of her, who had always lived in the shadow of her husband. But the next time he came, and showed her the drawing, she asked what it would cost, and when he replied: 'About a hundred crowns,' she declared that having managed for so long without such a luxury, she could continue for the short time that was left to her. Dr Bull's son Francis once visited her with his mother and remembered that, before she rang the bell, his mother told him to take a deep breath so as to have fresh air in his lungs, since the atmosphere in the closed apartment was so suffocating. 'I remember that I was shocked at how unbeautiful Fru Ibsen was, and how lacking in any kind of feminine charm; but when she spoke of the old days, she became alive.'

A few days before she died she spoke to Bergliot about the early years of her marriage. 'With great difficulty she said: "When we were young, many so-called friends came to Ibsen, but I sent them away." After a long pause: "I had many unkind words for it, but I didn't care. He had to have peace for his work." After another long pause: "Ibsen had no steel in his character – but I gave it to him." Finally she said:

"I have never spent a day in bed in my life, and I don't want to die there. I want to die standing or sitting." ' She died in her armchair early one morning.

Sigurd never returned to politics. The year after his father's death he settled in Italy, but three years later, at Suzannah's request and with the greatest reluctance, came back to Norway. Despite his gifts, he remained unwanted there and could obtain no permanent post, even in journalism or teaching. His philosophical work, *The Quintessence of Man*, was translated into many languages and was especially successful in America; Eugene O'Neill, in his autobiographical play *Ah, Wilderness!*, made his hero name it as one of the influential progressive books of his youth. In 1913 he published an interesting play, *Robert Frank*, about the conflict between the proletariat and the Old World; it was translated into English, French and German, but was as viciously attacked in Norway as his father's early works had been. After Suzannah's death he resettled in Italy, and died in 1930. Bergliot lived on until 1953. Their son, Tancred, became a pioneer aviator and a distinguished film director; he lived until 1978, his sisters Eleonora and Irene until 1978 and 1985, and there are many great- and great-great-grandchildren.

Jonas Lie and Edvard Grieg died within a year of Ibsen, and Bjørnson in 1910, in a Paris hotel. Bergliot was at her father's deathbed, as she had been at Ibsen's, and noted that where Ibsen had said: 'Soon I shall enter the great darkness,' Bjørnson spoke of ascending into 'the great whiteness'. Strindberg died of cancer in 1912, aged sixty-three; George Brandes in 1927, aged eighty-five.

The young girls whom Ibsen loved in his last years all lived to a ripe age. Helene Raff achieved some success as a painter and novelist, and died in Munich in 1942 at the age of seventy-seven. Emilie Bardach survived until 1 November 1955. By good fortune she left Vienna for Switzerland before Hitler's invasion and settled in Berne; during the Second World War she was called before Hitler's Austrian representatives there and (being a Jewess) stood in danger of being returned to her native country, but (writes Mrs Reginald Orcutt, whose husband was instrumental in persuading the Swiss authorities to let her remain) 'she was too old and dotey to travel and obviously harmless ... She was sweet and kind up to the last.'[1] So she escaped the gas chambers. She died a spinster.

Hildur Andersen lived even longer; she died in December 1956 at the age of ninety-two. She, too, never married; nor did Rosa Fitinghoff, who died on 27 March 1949, aged seventy-six. Rosa wrote several novels and children's books of moderate quality, and a trivial autobiography, *Minnenas kavalkad*, which contains no reference to her friendship with Ibsen. Her Swedish publisher, Dr Ragnar Svanström of Norstedts, remembers her as 'a rather eccentric little old lady always accompanied by about ten poodles'. During the Second World War she turned up in Oslo at the offices of Cappelen and asked if they would be interested in publishing a book about poodles. On being asked: 'Would you not consider writing something about Ibsen?' she left without reply.

Ibsen's contribution to the theatre was threefold, and in each respect the drama owes more to him than to any other dramatist since Shakespeare. Firstly, he broke down the social barriers which had previously bounded it. He was the first man to show that high tragedy could be written about ordinary people and in ordinary everyday prose, and the importance of that seemingly simple achievement can hardly be exaggerated. Soon after his work had been introduced to England, W. L. Courtney, that Oxford don who edited the *Fortnightly Review* and also wrote dramatic and literary criticism for the *Daily Telegraph*, complained that Ibsen's plays were 'singularly mean, commonplace, parochial ... as if Apollo, who once entered the house of Admetus, were now told to take up his habitation in a back parlour in South

1. Letter to the author, 14 February 1969.

Hampstead. There may be tragedies in South Hampstead, although experience does not consistently testify to the fact; but, at all events from the historical and traditional standpoint, tragedy is more likely to concern itself with Glamis Castle, Melrose Abbey, Carisbrooke or even Carlton House Terrace.' In other words, as William Archer commented, Ibsen's characters were not what the Victorians called 'carriage people'. Before Ibsen, tragedy had (always excluding Büchner) concerned itself with kings and queens, princes and princesses or, at the lowest, Montagues and Capulets. Ibsen showed that high tragedy could and did take place at least as frequently in back parlours as in castles and palaces. He was, of course, not the first dramatist to attempt this, any more than the Wright brothers were the first people to build an aeroplane; they were the first to build one that got off the ground, and *Ghosts* is, after *Woyzeck* and *Danton's Death*, the first tragedy about back parlour people that gets off the ground.

His second great contribution was technical. He threw out the old artificialities of plot which are usually associated with the name of Scribe, but of which Shakespeare and Schiller were also guilty: mistaken identities, overheard conversations, intercepted letters, and the like. It was a slow and painful process to rid himself of these; something of the old machinery is still there as late as *A Doll's House*; but his last ten plays are free of it. As A. B. Walkley noted as early as 1891: 'Whatever we learn we learn at first-hand, from the characters themselves, not from a Dumasian commentator or *raisonneur*.' Equally important, he developed the art of prose dialogue to a degree of refinement which has never been surpassed; not merely the different ways people talk, and the different language they use under differing circumstances, but that double-density dialogue which is his peculiar legacy, the sub-text, the meaning behind the meaning. Through this he was able to create characters as complex as the most complex characters of Flaubert or Henry James, without the aid of explanatory narration or monologues. And this demanded, and opened the way for, a new kind of acting, analytical, penetrating, self-effacing and sensitive. There was no place in his plays for the old operatics.

What nowadays seem technical limitations, such as the over-exposition in the opening scenes, the excessive and sometimes repetitive planting of information needful to the audience, was dictated by the limitations of those audiences; as we have seen, when he tried in *Hedda Gabler* to reduce his exposition to a modern minimum, the reaction was almost total bewilderment. (Even Henry James on reading it was left 'muddled and mystified'.) It is no coincidence that this, the least popular of his mature plays in his own time, is the one most frequently performed today and for which fewest allowances have to be made.

But none of these technical contributions explains the continued life of Ibsen's plays on the stage today; and one regrets the (very natural) tendency of the compilers of programme notes to stress his importance as an innovator. Few things put an audience off a play as much as reading beforehand that its author was the first man to do this or that; it is like being asked to sit for three hours in the first armchair, or in the first house to have been equipped with central heating. Ibsen's enduring greatness as a dramatist is due not to his technical innovations, but to the depth and subtlety of his understanding of human character (especially feminine character), and, which is rarer, of human relationships.

None of the great novelists, Stendhal and Flaubert included, created more memorably observed women than Agnes, Nora, Helen Alving, Rebecca West, Ellida Wangel, Rita Allmers or Ella Rentheim. And he created a succession of male characters of a size and strength that represent a challenge to any actor equal to that of Hamlet or Lear – Brand, Peer Gynt, Oswald Alving, Thomas Stockmann, Halvard Solness, John Gabriel Borkman, Arnold Rubek – characters which defy shallow or 'clever' acting, but which, worthily interpreted, offer as rewarding experiences as it is possible to receive in a theatre. Yet so delicate was Ibsen's understanding of human relationships that a selfish actor can only partially succeed in these roles. Unless the relationships with the other characters are right, the performance fails. And it can never be sufficiently stressed that, as Ibsen himself insisted, his leading characters are almost without exception passionate characters, even when those passions are inhibited. They are never sexless (though how often has one not seen them played so!). It would be an exaggeration, perhaps, to say that Ibsen's plays are about sex, for they are about so much besides; but there is none of his plays, except *Brand* and *An Enemy of the People*, in which sex is not a major and decisive element.

Ibsen's uniqueness among dramatists as a contributor to the social debate has been noted, but one must underline an essential difference in this respect between him and his great contemporaries. A major writer's biography is only partly the story of his life; perhaps more importantly, it is the story of a series of explosions which he causes in places he has never seen and among people he has never met. With a poet, a novelist, or a philosopher, these explosions occur in myriads of individuals reading in their homes. But this was only partially true of Ibsen. Unlike Tolstoy or Zola, Mill, Nietzsche, Freud or even Marx, unlike, indeed, any writer before him, more like a preacher, a Savonarola or a Wesley, he wrought his effect most powerfully on crowds, gathered together not in a market place or a church or chapel, but in a theatre. It is a commonplace that a man may more easily be converted in a crowd than alone, and it is not the least of Ibsen's numerous contributions to the theatre that he turned it from a place of entertainment and occasional catharsis into a place from which men emerged compelled to rethink basic principles which they had never before seriously questioned. Euripides had done this, but no dramatist since – or anyway not on the same scale. Shakespeare never questioned the established tenets and beliefs of his time as Ibsen did. There were more social abuses in Shakespeare's England than in Ibsen's Norway, but Shakespeare never challenged one of them. Who ever walked out of a Shakespeare play, in his time or since, feeling compelled to re-think their basic concepts of life? Yet that was the effect of Ibsen's 'social' plays on his contemporaries, like reading Darwin or Marx or Freud. Nowadays we tend to regard his later plays, less appreciated in his time, as his greater. But because Ibsen's supreme quality was his understanding of the human mind and his ability to portray its depths and nuances (so that no actor or actress can ever honestly say that he or she has totally explored or filled that character), and because he did this as surely in the 'social' plays as in everything else he wrote, *A Doll's House* and *Ghosts* and *An Enemy of the People* remain as hypnotic today as when it was their messages rather than their psychology that buzzed like a caged fly in the minds of their audiences. As Desmond MacCarthy wrote: 'Ibsen's theatre is the theatre of the soul. Important as he was, and is, as a social reformer, it is that which makes him even more important as an artist. Society changes quickly, the mind hardly at all; it is that which makes his work permanent.'

Ibsen's two great successors in the realm of tragedy explored fields that he did not. Strindberg, like no writer before him, mapped that no-man's-land where reality and fantasy, sanity and insanity abut; and he wrote of sex with a frankness which Ibsen, being Ibsen, could not match, especially of sex divorced from love and riding hand-in-hand with contempt or hatred. The only other dramatist since Ibsen who is his peer in stature is Chekhov, and to argue whether he or Ibsen is the greater is like arguing whether Bach is superior to Beethoven. Chekhov's feelings about Ibsen were as mixed as Strindberg's. He read him, we must remember, in bad translation (by non-Russians), and Stanislavsky remembered only his frequent expressions of distaste for Ibsen's work. 'I recall A. Chekhov once being present at rehearsals of *The Wild Duck*. He looked bored. He did not like Ibsen. He said: "Look here, Ibsen does not know life. In life it does not happen like that." ' 'Just as much as Chekhov disliked

Ibsen's plays, he liked Hauptmann's.' 'At a rehearsal of
Hedda Gabler at the Moscow Arts, Chekhov said: "Look
here, Ibsen is not a playwright."' And in his autobiography
Stanislavsky summed up: 'Chekhov did not like Ibsen as a
dramatist, although he placed Ibsen's talents very high. He
thought him dry, cold, a man of reason.' But this may have
been due to the bad translations and the unrealistic way in
which Ibsen was played in Russia. Towards the end of his
life, however, Chekhov's attitude would appear to have
changed. On 30 October 1903, when planning to visit
Moscow, he wrote to Stanislavsky: 'I haven't yet seen *The
Lower Depths*, *The Pillars of Society*, or *Emperor and Galilean*. I very much want to see all three'; and a week later, on
7 November, he wrote to A. L. Vishensky: 'You know Ibsen
is my favourite writer.'[2] Pirandello had none of Chekhov's
doubts. 'After Shakespeare,' he declared, 'I unhesitatingly
place Ibsen first'; and O'Neill found him 'much nearer to me
than Shakespeare'.

A reaction against Ibsen's work inevitably set in, even
before his death. In 1902 Max Beerbohm, reviewing a production of *The Lady from the Sea*, noted with dismay that
Ibsen already seemed old-fashioned.

'Byron is dead' – can that message have fallen with a more
awful suddenness on our grandfathers than 'Ibsen is old-
fashioned' falls on us? . . . But Time is a cyclist. The things of the
day before yesterday are nearer to us than the things of yesterday, and nearer still are the things of the day before the day
before. Ellida and the rest, creatures of yesterday, will grow grad-

2. Martin Nag has argued persuasively that *The Wild Duck*, which
had been translated into Russian in 1892, four years before Chekhov
wrote *The Seagull*, may well have influenced the latter play, which
likewise has a dead (or about to be killed) bird as its central symbol.
But we must remember Ibsen's warning against confusing parallelisms
with influence. It is interesting to note that the Theatre Literary Committee of St Petersburg approved *The Seagull* for performance only
after much criticism, condemning, in the words of the report, 'its symbolism, or more correctly, its Ibsenism' as ineffective and unnecessary.

ually younger, and will doubtless be much admired at the close of the century.

Beerbohm was right as far as England is concerned. It has not been the same in all countries; in the Mediterranean lands (because they and their ways of acting are southern, or because they are Catholic?) he is not often played, and then usually in the wrong way for the wrong melodramatic reasons. To the French Ibsen is still, as Georg Brandes wrote in 1902, a Protestant who protests too much. In Germany he is, as he was until recently in England, still regarded primarily as a social commentator, and is in urgent need of re-assessment. But in England his reputation stands higher than ever, he is performed with annually increasing frequency, and it is difficult to imagine that other western countries will not soon follow suit, As a Swedish critic, Martin Lamm, has written, Ibsen is the Rome of modern drama. All roads ultimately lead from him and to him.

Ibsen was a poet who used prose as other poets have used the sonnet, as a medium which, by its strict confinement, intensifies and liberates. Let the last word on him be spoken by a poet. Four years after Ibsen's death, Rainer Maria Rilke addressed to him, in *The Notebook of Malte Laurids Brigge*, one of the most eloquent and penetrative tributes ever paid by one great writer to another:

Loneliest of men, withdrawn from all, how rapidly have they overtaken you by means of your fame! But lately they were fundamentally opposed to you, and now they treat you as their equal. And they carry your words about with them in the cages of their presumption, and exhibit them in the streets and excite them a little from their own safe distance: all those wild beasts of yours.

When I first read you, they broke loose on me and assailed me in my wilderness – your desperate words – desperate, as you yourself became in the end, you whose course is wrongly traced on every chart. Like a fissure it crosses the heavens, this hopeless hyperbola of your path, that only once curves towards us and draws off again in terror. What mattered it to you whether a woman stays or goes, whether one is seized with vertigo and another with madness, whether the dead live, and the living appear to be dead: what mattered it? It was all so natural to you; you passed through it, as one might cross a vestibule, and did not stop. But yonder, within, you remained stooped, where our destiny seethes and settles and changes colour, farther in than anyone has yet been. A door had sprung open before you, and now you were among the alembics in the firelight. Yonder where, mistrustful, you took no one with you, yonder you sat and discerned processes of change. And there, since your blood drove you to reveal and not to fashion or to speak, there you conceived the vast project of magnifying single-handed these minutiae, which you yourself first perceived only in test-tubes, so that they should be seen of thousands, immense, before all eyes. Then your theatre came into being. You could not wait until this almost spaceless life, condensed into fine drops by the weight of centuries, should be discovered by the other arts, and gradually made visible to the few who, little by little, come together in their understanding and finally demand to see the general confirmation of these extraordinary rumours in the semblance of the scene opened before them. For this you could not wait. You were there, and you had to determine and record the almost immeasurable; the rise of half a degree in a feeling; the angle of refraction, read off at close quarters, in a will depressed by an almost infinitesimal weight; the slight cloudiness in a drop of desire, and the well-nigh imperceptible change of colour in an atom of confidence. All these: for of just such processes life now consisted, our life, which had slipped into us and had drawn so deeply in that it was scarcely possible even to conjecture about it any more.

Given as you were to revelation, a timeless tragic poet, you had to translate this fine-spun activity at one stroke into the most convincing gestures, into the most present things. Then you set about that unexampled act of violence in your work, which sought ever more impatiently, ever more desperately, equivalents among things that are seen to the inward vision. There was a rabbit, a garret, a room where someone paced to and fro; there was the clatter of glass in a neighbouring apartment, a fire outside the windows; there was the sun. There was a church and a rock-strewn valley that was like a church. But that did not suffice; towers had ultimately to be brought in; and whole mountain ranges; and the avalanches that bury landscapes destroyed the stage, overladen with things tangible used for the sake of expressing the intangible. And now you could do no more. The two extremities that you had bent together, sprang apart; your mad strength escaped from the flexible shaft, and your work was as nothing.

Who should understand, otherwise, why in the end you would not leave the window, headstrong as you always were? You wanted to see the passers-by; for the thought had occurred to you that some day one might make something out of them, if one decided to begin.

January 1965–March 1970. London, Stockholm, Oslo.

Select Bibliography

AGERHOLM, EDVARD. 'Henrik Ibsen og Det Kongelige Teater', in *Gads Danske Magasin* (Copenhagen), 1910–11.

AMDAM, PER. 'Ibsen og Molde', in *Edda* (Oslo), 1952.

ANDERSEN, ANNETTE. 'Ibsen in America', in *Scandinavian Notes and Studies* (Menaska, Wis.), 1935–7.

ANDERSEN, HANS CHRISTIAN. *Brevveksling med Edvard og Henriette Collin*, ed. C. Behrend and H. Topsøe-Jensen, I–VI. Copenhagen, 1933–7.

Dagbøger og Breve, 1868–1875, ed. Jonas Collin. Copenhagen, 1906.

ANDERSON, RASMUS B. *My Life Story*. Madison, 1915.

ANKER, ØYVIND. *Christiania Theaters Repertoire, 1827–1899*. Oslo, 1956.

Henrik Ibsens brevveksling med Christiania Theater, 1878–1899. Oslo, 1965.

Kristiania Norske Theaters Repertoire, 1852–1863. Oslo, 1956.

ARCHER, CHARLES. *William Archer*. London, 1931.

ARCHER, WILLIAM. 'Ibsen as I Knew Him', in *Monthly Review* (London), June 1906.

Introductions to *The Collected Works of Henrik Ibsen*, revised and edited by William Archer, I–XII. London, 1906 ff.

'The Mausoleum of Ibsen', in *Fortnightly Review* (London), July 1893.

The Theatrical 'World' of 1893, 1894, 1895, 1896, *1897*. London, 1894 ff.

ARVESEN, O. *Oplevelser og erindringer*. Christiania, 1921.

BANG, HERMAN. *Teatret*. Copenhagen, 1892.

Ti Aar. Copenhagen, 1891.

BERGGRAV, EIVIND, and BULL, FRANCIS. *Ibsens sjelelige kriser*. Oslo, 1937.

BERGMAN, GÖSTA M. *Den moderna teaterns genombrott, 1890–1925*. Stockholm, 1966.

BERGSØE, VILHELM. *Henrik Ibsen på Ischia og 'Fra Piazza del Popolo.'* Copenhagen and Christiania, 1907.

BEYER, HARALD. *Søren Kierkegaard i Norge*. Christiania, 1924.

BJÖRKLUND-BEXELL, INGEBORG. 'Ibsen's *Vildanden*, en studie.' Unpublished thesis, 1962.

BJØRNSON, BJØRN. *Bare ungdom*. Oslo, 1934.

Fra barndommens dage. Christiania, 1922.

Hjemmet og vennerne. Oslo, 1932.

BJØRNSON, BJØRNSTJERNE. *Breve til Karoline, 1858–1907*, ed. Dagny Bjørnson-Sautreau. Oslo, 1957.

Brevveksling med danske, 1875–1910, ed. Øyvind Anker, Francis Bull and Torben Nielsen, I–III. Copenhagen and Oslo, 1953.

Brevveksling med svenske, 1858–1909, ed. Øyvind Anker, Francis Bull and Örjan Lindberger, I–III. Oslo, 1960–61.

Brytnings-aar (brev fra aarene 1871–1878), ed. Halvdan Koht, I, II. Christiania, 1921.

Gro-tid (brev fra aarene 1857–1870), ed. Halvdan Koht, I, II. Christiania, 1912.

Kamp-tid (brev fra aarene 1879–1884), ed. Halvdan Koht, I, II. Oslo, 1932.

BLANC, T. *Christiania Theaters historie, 1827–1877*. Christiania, 1899. *Norges første nationale scene*. Christiania, 1884.

BLYTT, PETER. *Minder fra den første norske scene i Bergen*. Bergen, 1894.

BOTTEN HANSEN, PAUL. 'Henrik Ibsen', in *Illustreret Nyhedsblad* (Christiania), 19 July 1863.

BRANDES, EDVARD. *Litterære Tendenser*. Copenhagen, 1968. *Om Teater*. Copenhagen, 1947.

and BRANDES, GEORG. *Brevveksling med nordiske Forfattere og Videnskabsmænd*, ed. Morten Borup, Francis Bull and John Landquist, I–VII. Copenhagen, 1939–42.

BRANDES, GEORG. *Henrik Ibsen*. Copenhagen, 1898. 'Henrik Ibsen i Frankrig', in *Norden* (Stockholm), 1902. 'Henrik Ibsen og hans Skole i Tyskland', in *Tilskueren* (Copenhagen), June 1890. 'Henrik Ibsen: Personal Reminiscences and Remarks about His Plays', in *Century Magazine* (New York), February 1917. *Levned*, I–III. Copenhagen, 1905–8.

BREDSDORFF, ELIAS. *Sir Edmund Gosse's Correspondence with Scandinavian Writers*. Copenhagen, 1960.

BULL, FRANCIS. *Essays i utvalg*. Oslo, 1964. 'Henrik Ibsen', in *Norsk litteratur-historie*, ed: Francis Bull, Fredrik Paasche, A. H. Winsnes, and P. Houm, IV. Oslo, 1960. 'Hildur Andersen og Henrik Ibsen', in *Edda* (Oslo), 1957. Introductions to *Catiline, The Warrior's Barrow, Norma, St John's Night, The Feast at Solhaug, Olaf Liljekrans, The Vikings at Helgeland, Love's Comedy, Peer Gynt, Ghosts, The Wild Duck, Rosmersholm* and *The Lady from the Sea* in *Henrik Ibsen, Samlede verker, hundreårsutgave*, q.v. *Nordisk kunstterliv i Rom*. Oslo, 1960. *Tradisjoner og minner*, 3rd edn, Oslo, 1963. *Vildanden, og andre essays*. Oslo, 1966.

BULL, MARIE. *Minder fra Bergens første nationale scene.* Bergen, 1905.

CHESNAIS, P. G. LA. Introductions to *Oeuvres complètes d'Henrik Ibsen, traduites par P. G. la Chesnais,* I–XVI, Paris, 1914–45.

COLLIN, CHRISTEN. *Bjørnstjerne Bjørnson, hans barndom og ungdom,* I, II. Christiania, 1902, 1907.

DAAE, LUDVIG. 'Paul Botten Hansen', in *Vidar* (Copenhagen), 1888.

DARDEL, FRITZ VON. *Dagboksanteckningar, 1873–1876.* Stockholm, 1916.
Dagboksanteckningar, 1881–1885. Stockholm, 1920.

DERRY, T. K. *A Short History of Norway.* London, 1957.

DIETRICHSON, LORENTZ. *Svundne tider,* I–IV. Christiania, 1894–1917.

DOWNS, BRIAN W. *Ibsen: the Intellectual Background.* Cambridge, 1946.

DUE, CHRISTOPHER. *Erindringer fra Henrik Ibsens ungdomsaar.* Copenhagen, 1909.

DUVE, ARNE. *Symbolikken i Henrik Ibsens skuespill.* Oslo, 1945.

EITREM, HANS. *Ibsen og Grimstad.* Oslo, 1940.

ELIAS, JULIAS. 'Ibsenminne af hans tyske oversætter', in *Samtiden* (Oslo), 1940.

ELLER, W. H. *Ibsen in Germany, 1870–1900.* Boston, 1918.

ELLMANN, RICHARD. *James Joyce.* London, 1959.

FENGER, HENNING. *Georg Brandes Læredr.* Copenhagen, 1955.
'Ibsen og Georg Brandes indtil 1872', in *Edda* (Oslo), 1964.

FLEETWOOD, CARL GEORGSSON. *Fran studiedr och diplomattjänst,* I, II. Stockholm, 1968.

FORESTER, THOMAS. *Norway in 1848 and 1849.* London, 1850.

FRANC, MIRIAM. *Ibsen in England.* Boston, 1919.

GEIJERSTAM, GUSTAAF. 'Två minnen om Henrik Ibsen', in *Ord och Bild* (Stockholm), 1898.

GEORGE, DAVID E. R. *Henrik Ibsen in Deutschland: Rezeption und Revision.* Göttingen, 1968.

GLØERSEN, KRISTIAN. 'Henrik Ibsen: minder fra mit samvær med ham i utlandet', in *Kringsjaa* (Christiania), 1906.

GOSSE, EDMUND. *Ibsen.* London, 1907.
Two Visits to Denmark, 1872, 1874. London, 1911.

GRAN, GERHARD. *Henrik Ibsen: liv og verker,* I, II. Christiania, 1918.
ed. *Henrik Ibsen: festskrift i anledning of hans 70de fødselsdag.* Bergen, Stockholm and Copenhagen, 1898.

GRANVILLE BARKER, HARLEY. 'The Coming of Ibsen', in *The Eighteen-Eighties,* ed. Walter de la Mare. Cambridge, 1930.

GREGERSEN, H. *Ibsen in Spain.* Cambridge, Mass., 1936.

GRIEG, HARALD. *En dansk forlegger og fire norske diktere.* Oslo, 1955.

GRØNVOLD, DIDRIK. *Diktere og musikere.* Oslo, 1945.

GRØNVOLD, MARCUS. *Fra Ulrikken til Alperne.* Oslo, 1925.

HALVORSEN, J. B. 'Henrik Ibsen', in *Norsk forfatter-lexicon, 1814–1880,* III. Christiania, 1892.

HAMMER, S. C. *Kristianias historie,* IV. Christiania, 1923.

HAMRE, KARL. *Clemens Petersen og hans forhold til norsk litteratur i aarene 1856–1869.* Oslo, 1945.

HAMSUN, KNUT. *Paa turné.* Oslo, 1960.

HEDIN, SVEN. *Stormän och kungar.* Stockholm, 1950.

HEIBERG, GUNNAR. *Ibsen og Bjørnson på scenen.* Christiania, 1918. *Salt og sukker.* Christiania, 1924.

HEIBERG, JOHAN LUDVIG. *Om Vaudeville og dens Betydning paa den danske Skueplads.* Copenhagen, 1826.

HEIBERG, JOHANNE LUISE. *Et Liv gjenoplevet i Erindringer,* III. Copenhagen, 1892.

HØST, SIGURD. *Ibsens diktning og Ibsen selv.* Oslo, 1927.

IBSEN, BERGLIOT. *De tre.* Oslo, 1948.

IBSEN, HENRIK. *Efterladte skrifter,* ed. Halvdan Koht and Julius Elias, I–III. Christiania and Copenhagen, 1909.

IBSEN HENRIK. *Samlede verker, hundreårsutgave* (The Centenary Edition), ed. Halvdan Koht, Francis Bull and Didrik Arup Seip, I–XXI Oslo, 1925–58.

JÆGER, HENRIK. *Henrik Ibsen: et livsbillede.* Christiania, 1888.

JAMES, HENRY. *The Scenic Art.* London, 1949.

JANSON, KRISTOFER. *Hvad jeg har oplevet.* Christiania, 1913.

JOHNSEN, P. ROSENKRANTZ. *Om og omkring Henrik Ibsen og Suzannah Ibsen.* Oslo, 1928.

JOSEPHSON, LUDVIG. *Ett och annat om Henrik Ibsen och Kristiania Theater.* Stockholm, 1898.

JUST, CARL. *Schrøder og Christiania Theater.* Oslo, 1948.

KIELER, LAURA. *Silhouetter.* Odense, 1887.

KINCK, B. M. 'Henrik Ibsen og Laura Kieler', in *Edda* (Oslo), 1935.

KING, BASIL. 'Ibsen and Emilie Bardach', in *Century Magazine* (New York), October and November 1917.

KNORRING, OSCAR VON. *Tva månader i Egypten.* Stockholm, 1873.

KNUDTZON, FREDERIK G. *Ungdomsdage.* Copenhagen, 1927.

KOHT, HALVDAN. *Henrik Ibsen: eit diktarliv,* rev. edn, I, II. Oslo, 1954.
  Introductions to *The Pretenders, Brand, The League of Youth, Emperor and Galilean, The Pillars of Society, A Doll's House, An Enemy of the People* and *Hedda Gabler,* in *Henrik Ibsen, Samlede verker, hundreårsutgave,* q.v.

KOMMANDANTVOLD, K. M. *Ibsen og Sverige.* Oslo, 1956.

KONOW, KARL. *Bjørnson og Lie.* Oslo, 1919.

LAMM, MARTIN. *Det moderna dramat.* Stockholm, 1948.

LEFFLER, ANNE-CHARLOTTE. *En självbiografi.* Stockholm, 1922.

LIE, ERIK. *Erindringer fra et dikterhjem.* Oslo, 1928.
Jonas Lie, oplevelser, fortalt af Erik Lie. Christiania and Copenhagen, 1908.

LINDBERG, PER. *August Lindberg.* Stockholm, 1943.

LINDER, GURLI. *Sällskapsliv i Stockholm under 1880- och 1890-talen.* Stockholm, 1918.

LINDER, STEN. *Ibsen, Strindberg och andra.* Stockholm, 1936.

LINDSTRÖM, GÖRAN. *Strindberg contra Ibsen,* in *Ibsen-Årbok, 1955–1956.* Skien, 1956.

LUGNÉ-POE, AURÉLIEN. *Ibsen.* Paris, 1936.

LUND, AUDHILD. *Henrik Ibsen og Christiania Norske Theater, 1857–1863.* Oslo, 1925.

McFARLANE, J. W., ed. *The Oxford Ibsen,* II. IV–VII. London, 1962–66.

MEYER, MICHAEL. Introductions to and Stage Histories of *Brand, The Lady from the Sea, The Master Builder, John Gabriel Borkman, When We Dead Awaken, The Pillars of Society, The Wild Duck, Hedda Gabler, Little Eyolf, Peer Gynt, The Pretenders, A Doll's House, Ghosts, An Enemy of the People, Rosmersholm,* translated by Michael Meyer. London, 1960–66.

MIDBØE, HANS. *Streiflys over Ibsen.* Oslo, 1960.

MOHR, OTTO LOUS. *Henrik Ibsen som maler.* Oslo, 1953.

MOSFJELD, OSKAR. *Henrik Ibsen og Skien.* Oslo, 1949.

NAG, MARTIN. *Ibsen i russisk åndsliv.* Oslo, 1967.

NEIIENDAM, ROBERT. *Gjennem mange Aar.* Copenhagen, 1933.
Mennesker bag Masker. Copenhagen, 1931.

NIELSEN, L. C. *Frederik V. Hegel: et Mindeskrift,* I, II. Copenhagen, 1909.

NIELSEN, YNGVAR. *En Kristianiensers erindringer fra 1850- og 1860-aarene.* Christiania and Copenhagen, 1910.

NYHOLM, KELA. 'Henrik Ibsen på den franske scene', in *Ibsen-Årbok, 1957–1959.* Skien, 1959.

OLLÉN, GUNNAR. *Ibsens dramatik.* Stockholm, 1955.

ORDING, FREDERIK. *Henrik Ibsens vennekreds: Det lærde Holland.* Oslo, 1927.

ØSTVEDT, EINAR. *Henrik Ibsen.* Oslo, 1968.
Henrik Ibsen og la bella Italia. Skien, 1965.

PAULI, GEORG. *Mina romerska år.* Stockholm, 1924.

PAULSEN, JOHN. *Erindringer. Siste samling.* Copenhagen, 1903.
Mine Erindringer. Copenhagen, 1900.
Nye Erindringer. Copenhagen, 1901.
Samliv med Ibsen, I, II. Copenhagen and Christiania, 1906, 1913.

PETTERSEN, HJALMAR. *Henrik Ibsen 1828–1928, bedømt af Samtid og Eftertid.* Oslo, 1928.

ROBINS, ELIZABETH. *Theatre and Friendship.* London, 1932.

RUDLER, RODERICK. 'Scenebilledkunsten i Norge for 100 år siden', in *Kunst og kultur* (Oslo), 1961.

SCHINDLER, PETER. *En Ungdom.* Copenhagen, 1942.

SCHNEIDER, J. A. *Fra det gamle Skien*, III. Skien, 1924.

SEIP, DIDRIK ARUP. 'Henrik Ibsen og K. Knudsen: Det sproglige gjennembrud hos Ibsen', in *Edda* (Christiania), 1914.

Introductions to *Poems, The Master Builder, Little Eyolf, John Gabriel Borkman* and *When We Dead Awaken*, in *Henrik Ibsen, Samlede verker, hundreårsutgave*, q.v.

SHAW, GEORGE BERNARD. *Collected Letters, 1874–1897*, ed. Dan H. Laurence. London, 1965.

Our Theatres in the Nineties, rev. edn, I–III. London, 1954.

The Quintessence of Ibsenism, 3rd edn, London, 1922.

SKAVLAN, EINAR. *Gunnar Heiberg.* Oslo, 1960.

SONTUM, BOLETTE. 'Personal Recollections of Henrik Ibsen', in *The Bookman*, XXXVII (New York), 1913.

SPRINCHORN, EVERT, ed. *Ibsen: Letters and Speeches.* New York, 1964.

STANISLAVSKY, KONSTANTIN. *My Life in Art*, translated by J. J. Robbins. London, 1924.

STEINER, GEORGE. *The Death of Tragedy.* London, 1961.

STRINDBERG, AUGUST. *August Strindbergs brev*, ed. Torsten Eklund, I–XI. Stockholm, 1948 ff.

'Konstakademiens utställning, 1877', in *Kulturhistoriske studier.* Stockholm, 1881.

'Den litterära reaktionen i Sverige sedan 1865', in *Tilskueren* (Copenhagen), May 1886.

TEDFORD, INGRID. *Ibsen Bibliography, 1928–1957.* Oslo, 1961.

THORESEN, MAGDALENE. *Breve, 1855–1901*, ed. J. Clausen and P. F. Rist. Copenhagen, 1919.

'Om Henrik Ibsen og hans hustru', in *Juleroser* (Copenhagen), 1901.

VISTED, KRISTOFER. 'Henrik Ibsen i karikaturen', in *Boken om bøger*, II. Oslo, 1927.

WIESENER, A. M. *Henrik Ibsen og det norske theater i Bergen, 1851–1857.* Bergen, 1928.

WOLF, LUCIE. *Mine livserindringer.* Christiania, 1898.

ZUCKER, A. E. *Ibsen, the Master Builder.* London, 1929.

NEWSPAPERS AND PERIODICALS

Aftenbladet	Christiania	*Bergenske Blade*
Aftenposten	Christiania	*Bergens-Posten*
Aftonbladet	Stockholm	*Bergens Tidende*

NEWSPAPERS AND PERIODICALS (cont.)

Christiania-Posten
Dagbladet   Christiania
Dagbladet   Copenhagen
Dagens Nyheder   Copenhagen
Dagens Nyheter   Stockholm
Dansk Maanedsskrift
  Copenhagen
Dølen   Christiania
Edda   Christiania
Fædrelandet   Copenhagen
Fortnightly Review   London
Illustreret Nyhedsblad
  Christiania
Illustreret Tidende   Copenhagen
Illustrated London News
Juleroser   Copenhagen
Kunst og kultur   Oslo
London Figaro
Morgenbladet   Christiania
Morgenbladet   Copenhagen
Nationen   Christiania

Nordisk Tidskrift   Stockholm
Ny Illustrerad Tidning
  Stockholm
Ny Illustreret Tidende
  Copenhagen
Nya Dagligt Allehanda
  Stockholm
Nyt Tidsskrift   Christiania
Ord och Bild   Stockholm
Pall Mall Gazette   London
Politiken   Copenhagen
Samtiden   Oslo
Saturday Review   London
Spectator   London
Sunday Times   London
Tilskueren   Copenhagen
The Times   London
Urd   Oslo
Verdens Gang   Christiania
Vikingen   Christiania

Index

GUSTAV MAHLER

Alma Mahler

'I lived his life. I had none of my own. He never noticed the surrender of my existence. He was utterly self-centred by nature, and yet he never thought of himself. His work was all in all.'

Both Alma's devotion to Mahler and her own forceful character shine through her recollections of the ten intense years they shared from 1901 to 1911. Her lively account of these last days of the Hapsburg Empire mixes domestic detail with anecdotes of such figures as Richard Strauss, Debussy, Freud and Schoenberg, personal moments with musical analysis, and paints a vivid picture of the years when Mahler brought the Vienna Opera to the highest pitch of perfection in its history. Alma was herself a gifted musician and helped her husband considerably with his work when he forbade her to continue with her own. Combined with a collection of Mahler's letters and photographs, her memories contribute much to our understanding of one of the greatest composers of this century.

Donald Mitchell is an eminent music scholar and the author of the definitive Mahler biography. This new edition of *Gustav Mahler: Memories and Letters* takes account of recent scholarship and incorporates previously unpublished material.

0 7474 0317 1
BIOGRAPHY

THE MEMOIRS OF HECTOR BERLIOZ

Ed David Cairns

Writing with unreserved candour and emotion, sparing no one's feelings – least of all his own – Hector Berlioz began, when he was forty four (in 1848) to set down a memoir of this musical and personal life. Twenty one years later, the work was completed. It is regarded to this day, as one of the greatest of all biographies.

David Cairns, renowned Berlioz scholar and author of the definitive biography, has further updated and revised his original translation of 1969.

'By some alchemy, the unmistakable voice of Berlioz himself, passionate, witty, enraged, high-spirited, sardonic, tormented and infinitely proud, speaks from these pages. An overwhelming sense of identity unites life, book and translation ... Of the composers of the nineteenth century only Berlioz was a genius in the use of words. His *Memoirs* are more than a great musician's vivid account of his life. They are a crucial document of their age, for they illuminate as little else the early romantic temperament and its relations with the outside world'

Observer

0 7474 0582 4
BIOGRAPHY

SOME SORT OF EPIC GRANDEUR
THE LIFE OF F. SCOTT FITZGERALD

Matthew J. Bruccoli

'Definitive'
Anthony Powell, *Daily Telegraph*

F. Scott Fitzgerald's career as a novelist and short story writer soared like a meteor with the publication in 1920 of *This Side of Paradise*. But twenty years later he was dead, having succumbed to debilitating illness and debts. His reputation had predeceased him: nobody was buying his books and it seemed that both the Jazz Age and its foremost chronicler belonged to a forgotten past.

However, it took less than ten years for him to be 'rediscovered'; his books were celebrated as works of great literary merit, and, to this day, they continue to sell and be studied by millions worldwide.

Matthew J. Bruccoli, the world's leading authority on Fitzgerald and author of more than a dozen books on aspects of his work and career, now provides the definitive biography of the man. It is a work that corrects many of the enduring myths, that contains more facts than any previous biography, and that has been universally acclaimed as a masterpiece.

'Impeccably researched ... both comprehensive and judicious ... Bruccoli brings Fitzgerald vividly alive'
Newsweek

'Indispensable'
TLS

0 7474 1152 2
BIOGRAPHY

SYLVIA PLATH

Linda W. Wagner-Martin

A cult poet and posthumous winner of the 1982 Pulitzer Prize, Sylvia Plath has always astonished readers with the power of her poems; and her autobiographical novel *The Bell Jar* has become a classic.

In this outstanding and controversial biography, written despite the wishes of Ted Hughes, Linda Wagner-Martin traces Plath's childhood in Massachusetts, her brilliant academic career, her aggressive ambition to excel both socially and in her writing and the deep anxiety that plagued her all her life and led to her first suicide attempt at the age of twenty. When she came to Cambridge on a fellowship and fell in love with and married Ted Hughes, Plath's future looked dazzling. But the strain of caring for two infants and balancing her roles as wife and writer preceded a painful breakdown in the marriage. Alone in London with her babies in the icy winter of her thirtieth year, after a period of unhappiness that fuelled some of her finest writing, she ended her life. Linda Wagner-Martin draws on unpublished letters and journals and over two hundred interviews to explore every aspect of Sylvia Plath's life and brings new understanding to her development as a writer.

'Ever since her death in 1963 Sylvia Plath has invited easy myth-making and been forced into the role of the doomed poet, the frustrated female and the proto-feminist. This new biography offers a welcome return to the facts. It also brings us closer to the creative process that enabled her to communicate extreme emotion with chilling clarity'
Frances Spalding, The Listener

'Enlists respect as much as sympathy for a writer who all her life was perched on the cliff of her own unhappiness'
Peter Ackroyd, The Times

0 7474 0624 3
BIOGRAPHY

Cardinal offers an exciting range of quality titles by both established and new authors. All of the books in this series are available from:
Sphere Books,
Cash Sales Department,
P.O. Box 11,
Falmouth,
Cornwall TR10 9EN.

Alternatively you may fax your order to the above address. Fax No. 0326 376423.

Payments can be made as follows: Cheque, postal order (payable to Macdonald & Co (Publishers) Ltd) or by credit cards, Visa/Access. Do not send cash or currency. UK customers and B.F.P.O.: please send a cheque or postal order (no currency) and allow £1.00 for postage and packing for the first book, plus 50p for the second book, plus 30p for each additional book up to a maximum charge of £3.00 (7 books plus).

Overseas customers including Ireland, please allow £2.00 for postage and packing for the first book, plus £1.00 for the second book, plus 50p for each additional book.

NAME (Block Letters) ....

ADDRESS...

....

☐ I enclose my remittance for _____

☐ I wish to pay by Access/Visa Card

Number ☐☐☐☐☐☐☐☐☐☐☐☐☐☐☐☐

Card Expiry Date ☐☐☐☐

606 111

caRDiNaL

3165   8/06   (19-6-06)